Game Programming Gems 5

LIMITED WARRANTY AND DISCLAIMER OF LIABILITY

THE CD-ROM THAT ACCOMPANIES THE BOOK MAY BE USED ON A SINGLE PC ONLY. THE LICENSE DOES NOT PERMIT THE USE ON A NETWORK (OF ANY KIND). YOU FURTHER AGREE THAT THIS LICENSE GRANTS PERMISSION TO USE THE PRODUCTS CONTAINED HEREIN, BUT DOES NOT GIVE YOU RIGHT OF OWNERSHIP TO ANY OF THE CONTENT OR PRODUCT CONTAINED ON THIS CD-ROM. USE OF THIRD-PARTY SOFTWARE CONTAINED ON THIS CD-ROM IS LIMITED TO AND SUBJECT TO LICENSING TERMS FOR THE RESPECTIVE PRODUCTS.

CHARLES RIVER MEDIA, INC. ("CRM") AND/OR ANYONE WHO HAS BEEN INVOLVED IN THE WRITING, CREATION, OR PRODUCTION OF THE ACCOMPANYING CODE ("THE SOFTWARE") OR THE THIRD-PARTY PRODUCTS CONTAINED ON THE CD-ROM OR TEXTUAL MATERIAL IN THE BOOK, CANNOT AND DO NOT WARRANT THE PERFORMANCE OR RESULTS THAT MAY BE OBTAINED BY USING THE SOFTWARE OR CONTENTS OF THE BOOK. THE AUTHOR AND PUBLISHER HAVE USED THEIR BEST EFFORTS TO ENSURE THE ACCURACY AND FUNCTIONALITY OF THE TEXTUAL MATERIAL AND PROGRAMS CONTAINED HEREIN. WE HOWEVER, MAKE NO WARRANTY OF ANY KIND, EXPRESS OR IMPLIED, REGARDING THE PERFORMANCE OF THESE PROGRAMS OR CONTENTS. THE SOFTWARE IS SOLD "AS IS" WITHOUT WARRANTY (EXCEPT FOR DEFECTIVE MATERIALS USED IN MANUFACTURING THE DISK OR DUE TO FAULTY WORKMANSHIP).

THE AUTHOR, THE PUBLISHER, DEVELOPERS OF THIRD-PARTY SOFTWARE, AND ANYONE INVOLVED IN THE PRODUCTION AND MANUFACTURING OF THIS WORK SHALL NOT BE LIABLE FOR DAMAGES OF ANY KIND ARISING OUT OF THE USE OF (OR THE INABILITY TO USE) THE PROGRAMS, SOURCE CODE, OR TEXTUAL MATERIAL CONTAINED IN THIS PUBLICATION. THIS INCLUDES, BUT IS NOT LIMITED TO, LOSS OF REVENUE OR PROFIT, OR OTHER INCIDENTAL OR CONSEQUENTIAL DAMAGES ARISING OUT OF THE USE OF THE PRODUCT.

THE SOLE REMEDY IN THE EVENT OF A CLAIM OF ANY KIND IS EXPRESSLY LIMITED TO REPLACEMENT OF THE BOOK AND/OR CD-ROM, AND ONLY AT THE DISCRETION OF CRM.

THE USE OF "IMPLIED WARRANTY" AND CERTAIN "EXCLUSIONS" VARIES FROM STATE TO STATE, AND MAY NOT APPLY TO THE PURCHASER OF THIS PRODUCT.

Game Programming Gems 5

Edited by
Kim Pallister

CHARLES RIVER MEDIA, INC.

Hingham, Massachusetts

Publisher: Jenifer Niles
Cover Design: The Printed Image
Cover Image: © Sammy Studios, Inc.

CHARLES RIVER MEDIA, INC.
10 Downer Avenue
Hingham, Massachusetts 02043
781-740-0400
781-740-8816 (FAX)
info@charlesriver.com
www.charlesriver.com

This book is printed on acid-free paper.

Kim Pallister. *Game Programming Gems 5*.
ISBN: 1-58450-352-1

Library of Congress Cataloging-in-Publication Data
Game programming gems 5 / Kim Pallister, editor.— 1st ed.
p. cm.
Includes bibliographical references and index.
ISBN 1-58450-352-1 (hardcover with cd-rom : alk. paper)
1. Computer games—Programming. 2. Computer graphics. I. Pallister, Kim.
QA76.76.C672G3645 2005
794.8'1526—dc22
2004026858

Printed in the United States of America
05 7 6 5 4 3 2 First Edition

CHARLES RIVER MEDIA titles are available for site license or bulk purchase by institutions, user groups, corporations, etc. For additional information, please contact the Special Sales Department at 781-740-0400.

Contents

Foreword

Mark DeLoura

madsax@satori.org

Welcome to the fifth volume of *Game Programming Gems*. By now you probably know what we're all about: assisting you with your game programming challenges by tapping the wisdom of as many industry experts as we can possibly fit into one book. Kim Pallister and his team of section editors have done an excellent job of unearthing these gems and polishing them up for your reading pleasure. We all hope that some of the nuggets you find in this book will help you on your next game programming project.

The job of writing game engines has sure not gotten simpler since the launch of the first book in our series. Nor have games and game teams been shrinking. It's not uncommon these days to hear of development taking 3–5 years, nor to hear of projects with 200-person teams. Can game development cycles keep increasing? Can these teams possibly grow any larger? Well, we certainly hope not, but it seems quite likely. However, we see *Game Programming Gems* as one of the many Forces of Good that are lining up on the opposite side of the equation; we seek to provide you with as much wisdom from the experts as possible, complete with code, so that you at least have a chance of speeding up the process of developing your engine.

Engine Development

Fortunately, there are also middleware companies that will happily help you with your engine development, but recently they've begun consolidating just as the rest of the industry has. A few have merged together to provide a more complete game engine as a single package. A few others have been bought out by developers or publishers so that they can take advantage of the technology internally, reducing your options. While some of these packages are still available for you to purchase, the prospect of using an engine owned by one of your competitors is not optimal—to say the least—and must be considered carefully.

But as the cost of building an engine increases, does it really make sense to build your engine from scratch with each new project? It used to, but now engine development is such a complex and costly task that many studios are actively developing strategies for increasing the life span of their code base. Most developers now at least stretch the life spans of their engines by incrementally optimizing them with each SKU created during the lifespan of a platform. Publishers are also beginning to see the wisdom of developing core technology, and some even encourage the studios they work with to collaborate on common technology and toolsets.

So at least, on the technology side, we as an industry have some strategies to reduce the development costs as we move forward onto new and more complex platforms.

Moving Forward

One of the things that frightens many people regarding the next generation of consoles and PCs is the sheer amount of art content that will need to be created to suitably take advantage of these platforms. By one studio's estimate, creating next-generation character models will take approximately seven times as long, largely due to the need for higher-polygon meshes and multiple texture layers. With gigantic art teams already stretching the budgets and timelines, how will you cope?

We're clearly not going to solve these issues here, but as game development on PCs and consoles continues to increase in complexity, as the cost for these titles continues to increase, and as the team sizes keep getting larger, the impact on our industry takes a wide variety of forms. One of the most noticeable effects is that you see fewer risks being taken in game design. Since the impact of an unsuccessful, expensive title can put some of the smaller publishers out of business, there are more copycat titles being created, with less focus on innovation and creativity. If we do see innovation, it's "in the small": simply evolutionary tweaks to genres as opposed to any radical new concepts. Of course, this makes complete sense financially, but the more we do this as an industry, the more we stand the risk of boring our players. There are many other forms of entertainment competing for their attention and dollars.

One of the alternatives for studios is to create the more risky games on smaller platforms, which are less expensive to produce for. With the coming of age of capable mobile gaming platforms in the form of handheld game devices, game-capable cell phones, and PDAs, companies will increasingly be able to try out their gameplay innovations in a less risky setting. And from those titles that are successful, some of the innovations will certainly find their way onto the "big budget" platforms.

Game Developer Education

The most hopeful sign for the growth of our industry is that these past few years have seen enormous demand for schools to teach game development courses; according to the International Game Developers Association (*http://www.igda.org*) there are currently over 280 schools now offering game-related classes. The result of this increase in formal game development education is an increase in capable young developers with interesting ideas. This new core of excited, educated students flowing into our industry will bring with it many new and creative concepts, if we're just willing to listen. Of course, convincing a publisher to listen and then place a multimillion-dollar bet on an untested game concept from a new hire fresh out of school is challenging, admittedly.

As a result we've recently begun to see a rapid increase in the number of independently developed games, game mods, and casual games from small, young development teams. These small teams are able to test out risky ideas, and whether the results are successful or not, they're great experience for all involved—and excellent material for a resume. Those projects that are successful are an interesting opportunity for forward-thinking publishers.

The growth in demand for formal game development education is the fuel that feeds the fires of innovation in the indie game scene. Many publishers are continuing to simply evolve game concepts and play it safe, but revolutionary concepts can come from the independent game developer community, if we support it.

For professional developers, this means it's more important than ever for you to get out there and share your expertise with students and hobbyists. There are also more opportunities than ever for you to do so. Who knows, perhaps by working with a small group of independent developers on a risky game design, you'll find your own game development projects enriched and more exciting as a result.

Preface

Kim Pallister, Intel Corporation

Kim.Pallister@Intel.com

Why am I the editor of this book?

This is a book about game development, and I am not a professional game developer. I have been on the "fringes" of the industry for the past dozen years, with Intel for the past seven years, and with a graphics hardware vendor before that. In an industry that has traditionally catered to a young market, and attracted a similar vein of people to its ranks, this places me part way between bushy-tailed neophyte and grizzled curmudgeon.

Those of curmudgeon age will remember that during the first few decades of this industry, we saw a transition from one-person-shop development to an era of teams, where people relied on one another's skills and efforts to realize their creative visions. During the past decade, and perhaps the few years that preceded it, we have transitioned to an age where groups of people rely on each other. Groups of programmers and artists and designers make up development teams. Teams within a company leverage one another's tools and assets, and companies rely on one another at the meta level.

Inter-company relations aren't new to the business; the developer-publisher relationship has existed for a long time. But the past decade has ushered in new structures, dependencies, and channels of communication. Developers now license technology from other companies, looking to middleware, hardware, and platform vendors for knowledge on how to exploit new technology. In return, these vendors seek information on how to direct their technology efforts. Entities like CMP Game Group (*Game Developer Magazine*, Game Developer Conference) and the International Game Developers Association foster dialogs about design, business practice, and quality of life issues. A growing number of academic institutions, along with publishers like Charles River Media (who brings us the *Gems* series), work to educate and inform the entire cluster. Looking at all these relationships, we see a circle of life—one that is inherent to all successful industries.

However slowly, the industry is moving from a state of begrudging cooperation to open, directed facilitation. We are sharing source code with middleware and hardware companies and funding research in academic circles while increasing dialog and publication. Each member of the circle has a vested interest in the success of the medium and of those who create it. That circle includes me, and *that's* why I'm editing this book.

Where Do We Go from Here?

The near future is clear enough. The market will continue to grow as new users come on line (in both senses of the term), existing users grow older and continue to play, and the production quality of games increases, which in turn attracts users who previously weren't avid gamers.

One of the most difficult and important inflection points facing our industry is the move to multithreaded platforms and software development. At the time of this writing, desktop PCs are exposing multithreading technology in processors, and true multicore processors are around the corner. Server-side components of online games are being developed on multiprocessor and distributed systems, and the next generation of consoles promises to bring multiprocessor platforms to consumer living rooms in short order.

The transition to true multithreaded game engines and platforms looks to be a formidable challenge. We'll need new tools, new techniques, and even new languages if we hope to make this transition while still evolving our games. We'll also need to focus on sound software engineering—principles *and* practices. Projects with budgets of seven or eight (or—dare we say it—nine) figures with significantly larger teams will require a new level of discipline and rigor.

During this transition, knowledge sharing (between individuals, between companies— at all levels) will be critical. I'd like to think that the *Game Programming Gems* series will play a small part in this journey.

Further down the Road

Looking beyond the immediate future, things get fuzzier, but exciting! At the time of this writing, Asia (particularly Korea and China) is seeing an explosion in popularity of massive multiplayer online games. Several hundred million new broadband households will appear over the next four years. Game-capable cell phones and portable devices will continue to proliferate and connect. Televisions and other consumer electronics devices will become increasingly interactive. And if it interacts, it games!

Many in our industry have been quick to draw comparisons between our games and Hollywood movies. Usually the comparisons are between the revenues that the respective industries generate or between the similarities in the production processes. Another parallel exists.

At the 1939 World's Fair, a new technology was introduced that promised to entertain people: the television. Critics were skeptical. A *New York Times* article stated "The problem with television is that people must sit and keep their eyes glued on a screen; the average American family hasn't the time for it." Laughable now, but no one at that time, *even proponents of the technology*, could have imagined the impact that this new entertainment medium would have.

During a GDC session a number of years ago, Chris Hecker forecasted that gaming would be "The defining entertainment medium of the twenty-first century," and I can't think of a better way to put it. We are only just beginning to grapple with the possibilities of interactive entertainment mediums. We may call that interactive entertainment "games" today, but already, we're stretching the definitions and boundaries of the term; we are still figuring out what it all means.

Now it's up to you to play a role in defining that medium. Hopefully we've given you some tools to help you do so. Put them to good use forging your contribution to the future.

Acknowledgments

I opened this preface questioning my position as the editor of this book. Let me close by saying that I *could not have done it* without the direct and indirect contributions of a lot of people. At the top of my list are series editor Mark DeLoura and series publisher Jenifer Niles. I'd like to thank both for giving me the opportunity and guiding me through the journey with sage "Book Editing Gems" learned through the production of *Game Programming Gems 1* through *4*.

While this work represents a lot of my time and effort, it would certainly not have been possible without the many authors of the individual gems and the seven section editors:

General Programming: William E. Damon III, ATI Research
Mathematics: Eric Lengyel, Terathon Entertainment
Artificial Intelligence: Robin Hunicke, Northwestern University
Physics: Michael Dickheiser, Red Storm Entertainment
Graphics: Jason Mitchell, ATI Research
Network and Multiplayer: Shekhar Dhupelia, Studio Gigante
Audio: Mark DeLoura, Sony Computer Entertainment

We really are privileged to work in an industry where knowledge-sharing is encouraged and practiced by so many.

On a similar note, Pete Baker and the rest of my management at Intel deserve thanks for letting me contribute to the greater good. When I was adamant that working on this text wouldn't impact my day job, they knew better and let me do it anyway.

The biggest gratitude of all is owed to my wife, Alisa, for helping me pursue my passions in editing this text. Doing so during the same year that we welcomed our set of twins into the world meant a great deal more work for her as well as for me. Finally, a note of thanks is due to my mother and father, for instilling in me an insatiable curiosity about, well, everything (and for buying the Commodore64, which seems like a pretty good investment in retrospect).

About the Cover Image

© Sammy Studios

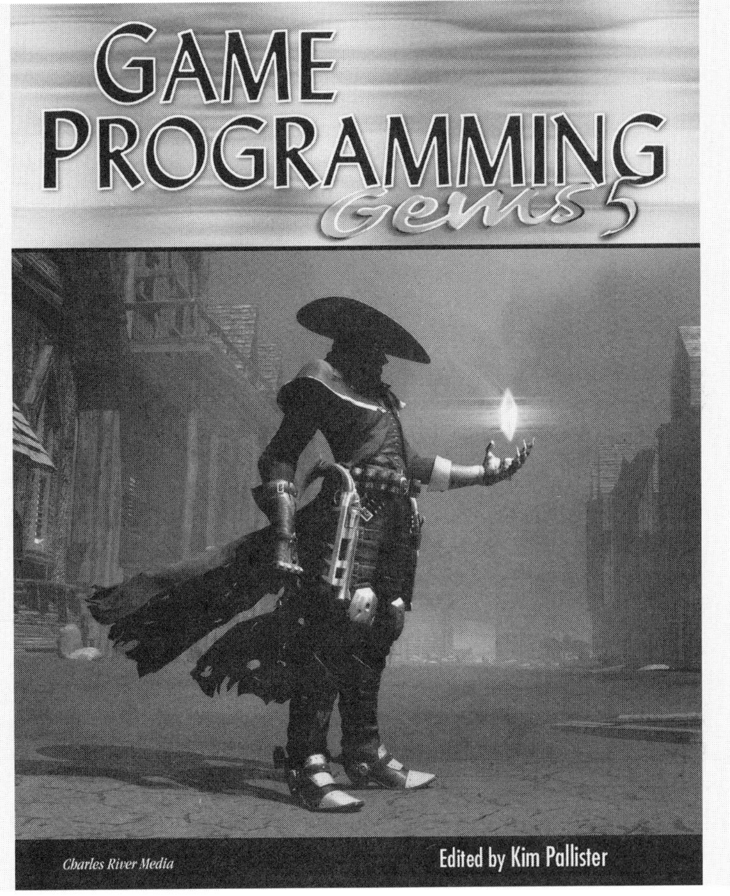

Half-vampire gunslinger, Jericho Cross, battles against the undead in the Old West in Sammy Studios' *Darkwatch* game, coming in 2005 for the Sony PlayStation® 2 and Microsoft® Xbox™ video game systems.

The environment and character were conceived in Sammy Studios' Carlsbad studio, with rendering and lighting by Los Angeles based Brain Zoo Studios. The image was art directed by Sammy Studios' Creative Visual Director, Farzad Varahramyan with additional artwork by Production Assistant, Dan Kit.

Contributor Bios

Contains bios for those contributors who submitted one.

Neeharika Adabala

nadabala@cs.ucf.edu

Neeharika Adabala obtained her doctorate for her work on modeling and rendering of gaseous volumes in which she introduced the concept of particle maps. She worked in Philips Research, MIRALab, University of Geneva, and the Media Convergence Lab, University of Central Florida. She has research publications in both the areas of dynamics simulation and realistic rendering. Her research interests include real-time rendering, physics based dynamics, illumination models, perceptual issues in rendering, scientific visualization, and smart graphics.

Barnabás Aszódi

ab011@freemail.hu

Barnabás Aszódi is a Ph.D. student at Budapest University of Technology and Economics. His areas of focus are computer graphics (e.g., real-time realistic shadow computation), creating animations, and games. He contributed to WSCG '04, CESCG '02, and other publications. He welcomes e-mail at the above address to provide him feedback or exchange ideas.

Tony Barrera

tony.barrera@spray.se

Tony Barrera is a certified autodidact math genius. He has published 25 papers in different subjects, of which 18 are scientific papers in computer graphics, numerical analysis, and mathemathics. Tony does research together with Ewert Bengtsson and Anders Hast.

Ewert Bengtsson

ewert@cb.uu.se

Ewert Bengtsson has been professor of computerized image analysis at Uppsala University since 1988. His main research interests are to develop methods and tools for biomedical applications of image analysis. This includes visualization and computer graphics aspects, since the visualization of 3D biomedical images is nontrivial. He has published about 120 international research papers. He received his Ph.D. from Uppsala University in 1974. He is a member of IEEE, SPIE, and IAPR.

James Boer

author@boarslair.com

James Boer has been an active participant in the game development industry since 1997, when he helped create the surprise hit *Deer Hunter*. He has also been a prolific writer, contributing to no less than seven game programming books (including his own book, *Game Audio Programming*) and several articles in trade magazines. James is currently employed as a programmer at Amaze Entertainment, where he is helping to develop new technologies for the Elemental Engine, Amaze's in-house cross-platform console engine.

John Bolton

johnjbolton@yahoo.com

John Bolton is a software engineer at Page 44 Studios in San Francisco. He is currently working on next year's lineup of Sony's hockey games for the PS2, PSP, and PS3. He has been programming games professionally since 1992 and has been lead programmer on several games including *I Have No Mouth and I Must Scream*, *Heroes of Might and Magic*, and *High Heat Baseball.*

Markus Breyer

thebreyers@comcast.net

Markus Breyer holds a master's degree in technical computer science, and has been in the game industry for eight years, working on numerous titles including *Star Wars Bounty Hunter*, *Gladius*, and *Return Fire*. Markus is now with Factor 5 developing technology for next generation platforms.

Martin Brownlow

mbrownlow@shiny.com

Martin started programming at age 10 on his friend's ZX81. After completing his education, Martin began his career at Virtuality, Ltd. (U.K.) writing VR arcade games. After three years, he moved to the U.S. to work for Shiny Entertainment. He has worked on several games for Shiny, including *MDK* and *Sacrifice*, and is currently knee deep in the *Matrix* video game.

Warrick Buchanan

warrick@chimeric.co.uk

Warrick Buchanan is development director at Chimeric Ltd, working on the Maxinima and ScreenSaverMax products. Among working for various game development companies over the years, he also did a stint in graphics card driver development for Imagination Technologies Ltd. He enjoys playing with toys that range from cutting-edge graphics cards to trampolines.

Jamie Cheng

jcheng@relic.com

Jamie Cheng is an AI programmer at Relic Entertainment. He recently developed the opponent AI in *Warhammer 40,000: Dawn of War*. He also serves as the core liaison between Relic and the GAMES group in the University of Alberta, working together to push the boundaries in commericial game AI. Away from work, Jamie enjoys collaborating with others to develop games that break away from the norm. Jamie received his BSc in computing science from Simon Fraser University.

Octavian Marius Chincisan

mariuss@rogers.com

Octavian graduated from the Technical University of Cluj-Romania in 1987 with a Master of Science in electrical engineering. One year later, he graduated with a post-university diploma in applied electronics and he finalized a project on building a Z80 based personal computer compatible with Sinclair Spectrum. From 1988 to 1994, he worked as a C++ programmer for a financial institution. He came to Canada in 1994 and worked for several companies as a C++ senior software programmer. In 2000, another challenge arose: game programming. Self-taught in this field, the results of his knowledge, passion, and work have been the creation of Getic 3D Editor and Getic SDK, currently under development. Currently, Octavian is working at Zalsoft Inc. as a software architect.

Ignacio Incera Cruz

ignacio@incera.net

Ignacio is a software engineer currently working on European Defense Area Projects in Madrid, Spain. Specifically, he works on real-time simulations, 3D terrain, geographic information systems (GIS), and missions planning and debriefing systems. He has a computer science degree and a master's degree in virtual reality, both from the University of Deusto. Also, he is currently getting a doctorate degree in computer science and artificial intelligence at the Technical University of Madrid. His research focuses on robotics, molecular computing, and artificial minds.

Szabolcs Czuczor

cs007@ural2.hszk.bme.hu, czsz@freemail.hu

Szabolcs Czuczor is a Ph.D. student at the Computer Graphics Group of the Department of Control Engineering and Information Technology at BUTE, Hungary. His research interests include multimedia, video and image processing, Web and game programming, and creating visual and sound effects for motion pictures. Szabolcs contributed to WSCG '04, CESCG '02, and other publications.

William E. Damon III

wdamon@ati.com

William is an engineer with ATI Research, Inc. His professional background at the time of this publishing includes five years of technical experience within the games industry, where he primarily focuses on software core technologies and platform performance. William holds a bachelor's degree with honors in computer science from Virginia Polytechnic Institute and State University.

Mark DeLoura

madsax@satori.org

Mark is the creator and series editor of the *Game Programming Gems* series of books. In his role as the manager of developer relations at Sony Computer Entertainment America, he gets the opportunity to share information, both technical and nontechnical, with game developers around the world. Mark is fascinated with the concept of creating shared, entertaining experiences that educate people and encourage them to communicate with each other. He has been pursuing ways to broaden the concept of what an "entertaining experience" is through a variety of roles, including former positions as editor-in-chief of *Game Developer* magazine and lead software engineer of Nintendo of America's Developer Support group.

Chuck DeSylva

Chuck.V.DeSylva@Intel.com

Chuck DeSylva is a senior software applications engineer in Intel's Software Solutions Group in Folsom, California. He currently manages a team of engineers working on optimization on some of the industry's leading software game and media titles. When not squeezing performance out of software, he enjoys practicing bass/guitar, playing first person shooters, and traveling the world.

Shekhar Dhupelia

sdhupelia@gmail.com

Shekhar Dhupelia's first foray into the games industry took the form of two years working with the SCE-RT group of Sony (SCEA) in San Diego, developing the online software and server infrastructure that powers *SOCOM: US Navy Seals*, *Frequency*, *Twisted Metal Black Online*, *NFL Gameday*, and many other Playstation 2 titles. He then moved onto Microsoft's *NBA Inside Drive 2004* XBox Live implementation, before spending some time at Midway Games, working on *NBA Ballers* for both PS2 and Xbox. Shekhar previously wrote for *Game Programming Gems 4*, and is also contributing to Charles River Media's *Secrets of the Game Business, Revised Edition*. He has spoken at the Game Developer's Conference (GDC) and the Penny Arcade Expo (PAX) on topics surrounding game design, and is now developing the Xbox Live gameplay for Studio Gigante and THQ's *WWE Wrestlemania XXI*.

Mike Dickheiser

mike.dickheiser@redstorm.com

Mike is a nine-year veteran of the games industry, and works as a software engineer for Red Storm Entertainment. His career has involved work on flight simulators, dynamic fluid modeling, collision systems, and vehicle physics models. Mike's current focus is development of vehicle AI control systems for the *Ghost Recon* product line. When not teaching helicopters how to hunt down and destroy tanks, infantry, and game designers, Mike enjoys computer games, sports, playing piano, and relaxing at home with his ever-supportive wife, Jaye.

Jean-François Dubé

jfdube@ubisoft.qc.ca

Jean-François (a.k.a. deks on Gamedev.net) has been working in the game industry for more than seven years. He's currently the technical lead programmer of an upcoming next generation console game at UbiSoft Montreal studio. Jean-François previously worked as the lead programmer of *Rainbow Six 3* on XBox and shipped several other games like *Batman Vengeance* on PS2 and *Speed Busters* on PC.

Patrick "Gizz" Duquette

gizmo@gizz-moo.com

Patrick, also known as Gizmo or "Gizz" for short, is like Pepsi: flat and still thinks that 15 degrees Celsius is the correct inside temperature to work, much to the general dismay of his fellow co-workers. While still working on his Seamless Server and many tools, he still longs for the day when he will find the time to finish his distributed raytracer.

Dominic Filion

dfiliong@videotron.ca

Dominic is senior 3D engine developer at Artificial Mind & Movement, performing research on 3D effects and physics simulations. Previously, he held the position of technical director at DC Studios, where he led the technology team to create the studio's in-house cross-platform 3D engine. He has worked on four commercial 3D engines before, acting as principal architect for two of the four. He also worked at Microids and Fun Key Studios. Feel free to drop him a note about the articles or just for a friendly chat. His Web site is found at *http://www.bingecoder.com*.

Mario Grimani

mgrimani@san.rr.com

Mario Grimani is an industry veteran who joined the gaming industry almost two decades ago. After publishing his first game in 1987, he poured all his development effort into the Amiga platform. The early demise of the Amiga platform marked his departure from the gaming industry, expecting never to come back. Since re-emerging in mid '90s, he has joined big name studios such as Ion Storm, Ensemble Studios, Verant Interactive, and Sony Online Entertainment. While at Ensemble Studios, he was a dedicated AI specialist in charge of improving the computer player competitiveness. He has developed a scripting system and a computer player AI for the *Age of*

Empires II: The Age of Kings and *Age of Empires II: The Conquerors*. During the early stages of *Age of Mythology* development, Mario served as AI lead in charge of AI architecture. After joining Verant Interactive, which later became Sony Online Entertainment, he took over as lead programmer on Sovereign and later worked on the *EverQuest II* team. Mario is now a partner in Xtreme Strategy Games, where he is using his technical expertise in bringing to market the next generation of games and gaming technologies.

Julien Hamaide

julien_hamaide@hotmail.com

Julien started programming text games on his Commodore64 at the age of 8. He wrote his first assembly program within the year. Years passed, but the passion remained. He has always been self-taught, reading all the books his parents were able to buy. He recently graduated as multitmedia electrical engineer at the Faculté Polytechnique de Mons in Belgium at the age of 21 (2003). He is now working on speech and image processing at TCTS/Multitel (*http://tcts.fpms.ac.be*; *http://www.multitel.be*). He is working very hard to get into the game industry. Open-eXtnd is his latest project (a free implementation of XTND), intented to be used in AI.

Sami Hamlaoui

disk_disaster@hotmail.com

Obsessed by AI, Sami was rather confused when he realized he'd written an article about audio. When not going off topic, he spends most of his time trying to make 500 bots look smart while keeping the frame rate in frames-per-second and not seconds-per-frame. Check out his Web site at *http://members.gamedev.net/sami/*, where content is occasionally added!

Matthew Harmon

matt@matthewharmon.com

Matthew Harmon has been developing games since college, working on Microsoft Flight Simulator for subLogic Corporation while earning his degree in film theory and criticism. Since then, he has served as lead programmer and director of development at Mission Studios Corp. and Velocity Development. Recently, he co-founded eV Interactive Corporation to continue developing games and use game technology in the military training and simulation arena. In his spare time, Matt chases his sons, Alex and Greg, around the house.

Anders Hast

aht@hig.se

Anders Hast has been a lecturer in computer science since 1996 and associate professor since 2004 at the University of Gävle. He received his Ph.D. from Uppsala University in 2004. Together with Barrera and Bengtsson, he has investigated fundamental algorithms in computer graphics and searched for new ways of solving the math behind the algorithms, which has led to about 20 research publications and book chapters.

Daniel F. Higgins

dan@stainlesssteelstudios.com

Dan Higgins is a proud member of Stainless Steel Studios, the Cambridge-based Historical RTS game company lead by Rick Goodman. Prior to working for Stainless, his background was not in games but writing both high-performance search engines for the History Channel, A&E (Arts & Entertainment), and Biography Channel. A passionate programmer for SSSI, Dan works in a broad range of areas including military AI, pathfinding, terrain analysis, optimization, animal AI, formations, and physics. Originally from Maryland, Dan and his family are "wicked" in love with Boston and feel like native New Englanders. He's a computer science graduate from Frostburg State University in Maryland, and most times when Dan is described in a conversation, the words "freak" and "spaz" seem to pop up with alarming frequency.

Charles E. Hughes

ceh@cs.ucf.edu

Charles E. Hughes is Professor and Graduate Coordinator in the School of Computer Science at the University of Central Florida. He holds a joint faculty appointment in the School of Film and Digital Media, and serves as Chief Scientist for the Media Convergence Laboratory, an interdisciplinary collaboration located within UCF's Institute for Simulation and Training. He has authored or co-authored over 100 refereed journal and proceedings articles, seven book chapters, and six books. His current research interests are in mixed reality and models of distributed computation.

Robin Hunicke

hunicke@cs.northwestern.edu

Robin Hunicke is finishing her Ph.D. in AI and Games at Northwestern University. In her copious free time, she strives to bridge the gap between academic study and industry application—working with the IGDA's Education Committee, teaching in the GDC Game Design and Tuning Workshop, and participating in events like the Experimental Gameplay Workshop and the Indie Game Jam. Her first love was M.U.L.E.

Hyun-jik Bae

imays@hitel.net

Hyun-jik Bae thanks God for letting him be enlightened, the Gospel, and the little talent afforded to him. He is a technical director at MowelSoft Co, which is currently developing *Blitz 1941*™, an MMO game with World War II as a setting. He has developed several 3D MMO games since 1997. The first game he authored is *SpeedGame* (not™) for MSX BASIC, which required the user to smash the space key rapidly, so it became the cause of the breakdown of computers in his elementary school.

Scott Jacobs

scott@escherichia.net

Scott Jacobs, educated to be a microbiologist, ditched that fancy college education to pay the rent by working in the games industry. Purported to be a networking programmer, he is often suckered into working in all sorts of other areas, like scripting engines, physics, and graphics. He has worked for Interactive Magic, Sinister Games (UbiSoft), and Red Storm Entertainment (UbiSoft). Currently he works for SimWars, where he yearns for them to put out *Super Puzzle America's Army II: Turbo.*

Wendy Jones

gamegirl@fasterkittycodecode.com

Wendy Jones is a game developer and industry evangelist. She's held roles ranging from industry journalist to game programmer to author. She is active in the IGDA of South Florida, participating as a board member of the local chapter. She currently keeps herself busy doing freelance software development for handheld devices as well as writing articles and books pertaining to game development.

Eric Lengyel

lengyel@terathon.com

Eric Lengyel is a senior programmer in the advanced technology group at Naughty Dog, Inc. He is the author of the bestselling book *Mathematics for 3D Game Programming and*

Computer Graphics, and he has written many articles for industry publications ranging from gamasutra.com to the *Game Programming Gems* series. Eric has been dedicated to 3D graphics research for over 10 years, during which time he has been the lead programmer for *Quest for Glory 5* and the chief architect of the *C4 Engine*.

Chris Lomont

Clomont@math.purdue.edu

Chris Lomont has been programming since the fifth grade, when he learned to make simple games on his new TI-55 programmable calculator. Progressing through all manner of computers, he got into PC programming in college, where he obtained a triple BS in physics, math, and computer science, writing a chess program as a senior project. A short time programming video games at Black Pearl (defunct) paid off his school loans, and he went to Purdue, obtaining a Ph.D. in math in 2003. As a grad student, he did consulting for many companies, mostly on graphics related development, although he has developed many types of applications professionally, including video games, financial modeling, robotics software, parsers and compilers, image processing tools, crypto, and more. He currently does quantum computing research at cybernet.com. Hobbies include piano, chess, sports, programming, puzzle design, and attempting to write books. His Web site is *www.math.purdue.edu/~clomont* and will hopefully move to *www.lomont.org* soon.

Michael Mandel

mmandel@gmail.com

Michael Mandel is a recent graduate of Carnegie Mellon University, where he earned his graduate and undergraduate degrees in computer science. His graduate work examined using simulation and data-driven approaches to character animation. He has various academic publications related to developing intelligent agents, and was a visiting scholar at CMU while finishing his thesis work. He has been professionally involved with the development of Xbox and PC game titles while at LucasArts and Microsoft. Currently, he is working as an engineer for Apple Computer, Inc.

Adam Martin

adam@grexengine.com

Adam Martin is the CEO of Grex Games, an MMOG middleware company. Much of Grex's products were based on Adam's own patents, although he now concentrates on strategy and business development. He has a degree in computer science from the

University of Cambridge, and has worked as a developer and producer on two published games. He has lectured at the MDC conference, and is often found on MUD-DEV. In 2004, he founded the Java Games Factory (*http://javagamesfactory.org*) to promote professional-quality java games development and help java games studios.

Maciej Matyka

maq@panoramix.ift.uni.wroc.pl

Maciej Matyka was born in Wrocław, Poland. He studies computational physics at the University of Wrocław (Theoretical Division of Physics and Astronomy Department), where he has a scholarship for his outstanding academic performance. For eight years, Maciej has been an active programmer in the Amiga and PC demo scene. His general interest lies in physically based modeling. Maciej is the author of physics simulation software, with awards for *Fluid* (second place in the Second Department Contest for Physics Software in 1999) and for *Waves* (first place in Third event in 2000). He is also the author of several publications in Polish journals, mostly related to physics simulations. At the University of Wrocław, he gave lectures for high school students, and he speaks about his physics software at department seminars. Maciej is the author of the book *Computer Simulations in Physics*, published in 2001 by Helion. He also wrote an article about soft body dynamics for the book *Graphics Programming Methods* by Jeff Lander, published in 2003 by Charles River Media.

Patrick Meehan

pmeehan@tenaciousgames.com

Patrick Meehan began his career at Nintendo Technology Development following his graduation from DigiPen in 1996. He has worked in the industry since as a developer for Interactive Imagination and Amaze Entertainment, among others. His experience includes most aspects of game and engine development on a variety of platforms. At the time of this publication, he is pursuing the bohemian life of a garage developer under Tenacious Games, a Seattle production company.

Nathan Mefford

nmefford@yahoo.com

Nathan Mefford is a software engineer at Firaxis, where his focus is on software architecture, optimization, and 3D graphics technology. He has enjoyed this opportunity to contribute to the *Game Programming Gems* series, which he has taken so much from, and he welcomes your correspondence and feedback.

Jason L. Mitchell

jasonlmitchell@comcast.net

Jason is the team lead of the 3D Application Research Group at ATI Research, where he develops and writes about novel 3D graphics techniques. Jason has written for the *Game Programming Gems* and *ShaderX* books, *Game Developer Magazine*, Gamasutra.com, and academic publications on graphics and image processing. He regularly presents at graphics and game development conferences around the world. Jason's publications and past talks can be found at *http://www.pixelmaven.com/jason/*.

Ian Parberry

ian@cs.unt.edu

Ian Parberry is a professor in the Department of Computer Science and Engineering at the University of North Texas, where he was an early pioneer of game programming education. He is the author of six books, three of them on game programming, and numerous papers in conferences and journals on a wide range of computing subjects from theoretical computer science to computer games.

Kim Pallister

Kim.Pallister@Intel.com

Kim Pallister is an engineering manager and technical evangelist with Intel's Software Solutions Group. His areas of focus are graphics and gaming technologies. Kim contributed to *Game Programming Gems 2* and *3*, as well as other publications. He welcomes email at the above address to provide him feedback or exchange ideas.

Borut Pfeifer

borut_p@yahoo.com

Borut graduated from Georgia Tech in 1998 with a B.S. in computer science. After working in various software development positions, he co-founded his own games studio, White Knuckle Games, in 2001. He currently works at Radical Entertainment as a game programmer on *Scarface*, and is the author of various articles on game development.

Frank Puig Placeres

fpuig2003@yahoo.com

Frank Puig is the Director of the Virtual Reality team at the University of Informatic Sciences, located in Cuba. He designed and implemented the CAOSS Engine and CAOSS Studios, which has been applied on several games titles like *Herlec* and *Knowledge Land*. He also has designed and produced several tools for game development that improve and simplify the treatment of motion capture data, advanced texture mapping, and animation blending, among others.

Steve Rabin

steve_rabin@hotmail.com

Steve Rabin has worked in the game industry for more than a decade and is currently at Nintendo of America. He has written AI for three published games and was a contributor to *Game Programming Gems 1*, *2*, *3*, and *4*. Steve served as the AI section editor of *Game Programming Gems 2* and was also the founder and chief editor of *Introduction to Game Development* and *AI Game Programming Wisdom 1* and *2*. He has spoken at the Game Developers Conference and is an instructor in the Game Development Certificate Program through the University of Washington Extension. Steve holds a degree in computer engineering from the University of Washington and is currently pursuing a master's degree in computer science.

Rishi Ramraj

thereisnocowlevel@hotmail.com

Rishi Ramraj is an undergrad at the University of Waterloo who has just finished his first year in systems design engineering. He spent the better part of his high school career learning and programming in C++, appearing occasionally at school to annoy his teachers. Rishi owes a great deal of his career to Jeff Molofee and the nehe.gamedev.net community. On his first work term he designed and built *VectorChrome*™, a 3D vector analysis suite for Bedrock Research Corp.™. He is currently employed at Alias® on his second work term. When he is not playing chess, designing code, or programming, he can be found studying. He has given up on any aspiration of getting to sleep and has instead written a program to do so, which is included in this book.

Michael Ramsey

miker@masterempire.com

Mike Ramsey is a lead programmer at 2015, Inc., where he has just completed work on *Men of Valor* for the Xbox and PC. He is currently developing technology for the next generation of consoles. Mike has also been the lead 3D client engineer on *Lost Continents* at VR1, wrote the 3D engine for *Mike Piazza's Strikezone*, *Master of the Empire*, and a slew of RPGs in the early 1990s. He has a B.S. in computer science from MSCD. Mike has contributed to both *Game Programming Gems* and the *AI Wisdom* series. In his spare time, Mike enjoys spoiling his daughter Gwynn.

Aurelio Reis

AurelioReis@gmail.com

Aurelio is currently a gameplay and technology programmer at Raven Software where he's worked on such titles as *Jedi Academy* and *Quake 4*. In his spare time, he likes researching new graphics algorithms, working on his own game engine, and coming up with interesting and exciting new gameplay ideas.

Bjarne Rene

bjarne.rene@circle-studio.com

Bjarne joined the industry in 1995 when he got a job at Bullfrog Productions. He was thrown in at the deep end, programming the computer opponent for the game *GeneWars*, before programming game logic and A.I. on *Theme Park World*. He then spent two years in his native Norway finishing his computer science degree at the University of Bergen, before moving back to the UK to rejoin the industry. He is currently at Circle Studio, where he is working on the object management system and the A.I.

Graham Rhodes

grhodes@nc.rr.com

Graham Rhodes is a principal scientist at the Southeast Division of Applied Research Associates, Inc. in Raleigh, North Carolina. He has nearly two decades of experience creating software for interactive and real-time 3D graphics, gaming, and physical simulation. Graham has been the lead software developer for a variety of game projects including: arcade-style games developed on Commodore VIC-20 and Atari 400 home computers as a teen; a series of sponsored educational mini-games for the *World*

Book Multimedia Encyclopedia; and first/third-person action games for commercial industrial safety training, built on a state-of-the-art 3D game engine. He is currently involved in developing software that provides physics-based solutions for military and homeland defense simulation and training. Graham previously contributed a chapter for *Game Programming Gems 2* and was the Physics section editor for *Game Programming Gems 4*. He is the moderator of the math and physics section of the *gamedev.net* game development Internet portal, has presented at the annual Game Developer's Conference (GDC), regularly attends GDC and the annual ACM/SIGGRAPH conference, and is a member of ACM/SIGGRAPH and the International Game Developers Association (IGDA).

Timothy E. Roden

roden@cs.unt.edu

Timothy is a lecturer and Ph.D. candidate in the Department of Computer Science and Engineering at the University of North Texas. At UNT, Timothy teaches courses in programming and computer graphics. Before joining UNT he worked as a graphics software developer in the simulation industry including six years with Evans & Sutherland. His primary research interest is procedural content creation for 3D graphics applications.

Thorsten Scheuermann

thorsten@ati.com

Thorsten is a software engineer in ATI's 3D Application Research Group where he works on graphics demos and novel rendering techniques as part of ATI's Demo Team. Prior to working at ATI, he was a member of the Effective Virtual Environments research group at the University of North Carolina at Chapel Hill, which gave him the opportunity to play with all sorts of expensive VR toys and to create sickness-inducing immersive games. Thorsten received a master's degree in computer science from UNC and previously studied at the University of Karlsruhe in Germany.

Shawn Shoemaker

shansolox@yahoo.com

Shawn Shoemaker is in his seventh year in the game industry, currently working as Assistant Lead Programmer for Stainless Steel Studios. His credits include physics, AI, combat, graphic effects, and random maps for *Empire Earth*, *Empires: Dawn of the Modern World*. At the moment, Shawn is hard at work on Stainless's next project, which is still under wraps. Shawn holds a bachelor's and master's degree in computer engineering from Virginia Tech. Before agreeing to sacrifice his summers for crunch, Shawn worked in hardware at Intel and in a CAVE virtual reality environment. While this is all well and good, Shawn is quick to point out that he never wanted to do this for a living. He always wanted to be a lumberjack.

Dr. Finnegan Southey

fdjsouthey@uwaterloo.ca

Dr. Finnegan Southey is part of the University of Alberta GAMES group and the Alberta Ingenuity Centre for Machine Learning. His Ph.D. is from the University of Waterloo, in the area of artificial intelligence. His research is focused on commercial games and includes planning, machine learning, and sampling methods for gameplay analysis. Aside from his work with Relic Entertainment, his research efforts have been used by industry partner Electronic Arts in the development of their FIFA 2005 title.

Shea Street

shea.street@tantrumgames.com

Shea Street got his start in multiplayer programming by developing online games for early dial-up service providers before the Internet became what it is today. He has been programming games for well over 15 years and is entirely self taught but holds a computer science degree from Full Sail in game design and development. Over those years, he has had a helping hand in creating countless games as well as providing private consulting to a number of companies for many of their project needs. Shea is currently the lead programmer and co-founder of Tantrum Games. Shea would like to thank everyone at Tantrum Games for all their hard work and dedication as well as for being very understanding and patient with him while he was writing for this book. He would also like to thank everyone in all the forums that took part in his discussions and lectures, as well as anyone who shared a late night cup of coffee with him. Last but not least, Shea would like to give thanks to all of his friends and family who helped support him through life, especially his father. If it wasn't for his father who helped him buy his first computer and got him interested in programming, none of this would have been possible.

Gábor Szijártó

szijarto.gabor@freemail.hu

Gábor is a Ph.D. student at Technical University of Budapest, Hungary. He started programming at age 10, and his master's thesis was on 3D face modeling. He specialized in shader programming and 3D graphics algorithms. Gábor's publications and programs can be found at *http://www.geocities.com/gabsprog*.

Andy Thomason

athomason@acm.org

Andy Thomason has recently completed the game *Galleon* with Toby Gard, designer of *Lara Croft*. Starting in the '70s with home-built Z80 hardware, he has worked with Psygnosis and Rage and is currently a freelance technology researcher and boat builder in Bristol, England. He maintains a Web site at *http://www.titibom.demon.co.uk/*.

Matthew Titelbaum

mtitelbaum@lith.com

Matthew Titelbaum is a senior software engineer at Monolith Productions, Inc., developing the AI systems for *The Matrix Online* MMORPG. After starting his career in the industry working on console titles at Crystal Dynamics, DreamWorks Interactive, and SCEA, he began his involvement with massively multiplayer games by joining Sony Online Entertainment. At SOE, he worked on *Sovereign* (an experimental MMO RTS title) and several *EverQuest* expansion packs; he is most proud of the contributions he made in overhauling and optimizing *EverQuest*'s pathfinding system. Matthew has a B.S. in computer science from Carnegie Mellon University.

Marco Tombesi

baggior@libero.it

Marco Tombesi is an Italian computer engineer, graduated from the University La Sapienza of Rome in 2002 with a first class degree. He has been a freelance game developer for years and now is actually considered a C++ and OpenGL master. He has published a successful article in *Game Programming Gems 2*, "3ds max Skin Exporter and Animation Toolkit." Currently he is working on a soccer game project.

Christopher Tremblay

chris@Barney.zapto.org

Christopher Tremblay lives in the San Fransisco bay area. He holds a B.S. in software engineering and is nearing a B.S. in mathematics. His work in the industry covers varied subjects including game AI, core networking, software rendering algorithms, and 3D geometry algorithms down to low-level and optimization. He currently works for

Motorola where he is building the next generation 2D/3D graphics rasterization engine for the next generation of cell phones. In his spare time, you may find him bruising himself with roller blades in the skate park, snowboarding, or yes, even with the radiation of his monitor while programming.

Bretton Wade

brettonw@microsoft.com, Bretton_Wade@acm.org

Bretton Wade is a 10-year veteran of the games and graphics industries, currently working as a manager in the Xbox system software team and as an instructor in the highly praised University of Washington Extension Game Development course. Previous game development roles include title lead for an independent studio contracted by Blizzard Entertainment, development lead on Microsoft's *Flight Simulator*, and individual contributor roles in a variety of titles published by Microsoft Game Studios. Bretton worked on VR authoring tools at SGI, and was a research engineer for Advanced Rendering Technology and Microsoft Research. He is a graduate of Virginia Tech and holds a master's degree from the Cornell University Program of Computer Graphics.

Niniane Wang

niniane@gmail.com

niniane Wang worked for Microsoft Games for five years, most recently as a dev lead on *Flight Simulator 2004*. Her work on weather graphics has been presented in SIGGRAPH, GDC, GDMag, and academic publications. She holds a bachelor's in CS from Caltech and a master's in CS from the University of Washington. Currently, she is a software engineer at Google.

Jon Watte

hplus-gpg5@mindcontrol.org

At 10 years of age, Jon started creating software and has never stopped. He helped deliver several large products, including the CodeWarrior development tools, the BeOS multimedia operating system, and the There virtual world. Jon currently works at Forterra Systems on a massively distributed simulation platform.

SECTION

1

GENERAL PROGRAMMING

Introduction

William E. Damon III

wdamon@ati.com

Content—the background art, settings, locations, characters, plots, stories, and actions that breathe life into the game experience—drives hit titles. For the production staff, this means constructing their product around a solid premise and employing outstanding, disciplined service organizations. The Information Technology department might spring to mind, but the organization addressed here is actually the software engineering team.

Software engineers solve problems. Sometimes problems in game programming are solved with a tremendous amount of programming effort, but a transition in thinking is occurring. Game programming is evolving into a disciplined practice of engineering general solutions for broader and more reusable application, whether it is adopting and adapting a middleware technology or creating something in-house. This evolution is allowing engineers more time to solve the real problems faced by their customers, the content creators, rather than reinventing old solutions. As a result, content creators are enabled to more rapidly iterate over implementations, tuning and tweaking details to achieve higher quality in the final product.

This is the common thread that runs through all the articles in this section. Whether discussing improved designs for low-level libraries built for other engineers on the project to use, general yet intelligent memory management techniques for the core of the systems (game, editor, or otherwise), remote debuggers, and/or visual and scriptable environments for designing user interfaces, all the articles in this section are aimed at providing reusable components in the production pipeline.

You'll see a broad range of topics in this section—and even various solutions for particularly large problems—to help guide you in building the best suite of tools for the title at hand. Absorb these articles, for as an engineer who solves problems, you never know when one will come in handy!

1.1

Context-Sensitive HUDs for Editors

Adam Martin, Grex Games

gpg@grexengine.com

Most games need custom graphical tools for content creation (level layout, AI behavior editing, etc.). Really good tools can greatly increase the efficiency of the content development team, often multiplying the amount of content created by a large ratio. For instance, one good level-editing tool can easily make a single level-designer become as productive as three equivalent designers working with inferior tools. However, excellent tools often turn out to be inordinately expensive, making it difficult to justify the risks of initial development, or the continued costs associated with maintenance.

This gem provides an approach to *heads-up editing* using some very simple techniques. It is designed to be extremely simple to maintain and should alleviate many of the costs and difficulties of in-house editor development. It unlocks end-user (designer) productivity boosts in earlier stages of the tool development process and reduces some of the project risks.

Problems

There are four sets of problems that apply to custom editors, each of which we will cover in detail to explain how and why the idea behind this gem works.

The first set of problems is due to the inherent complexity of a custom content editor. Custom editors always become complex (some would say *bloated*) sooner or later; if their work was simple, mainstream editors would have been sufficient in the first place, and the cost of making a custom editor could have been avoided altogether.

The other sets of problems are each associated with a particular role in the development team. For example, the ways in which content authors use the editor create problems unique to those people.

Editor and GUI Complexity

Taking a 3D modeler as an example, we usually have four views of the object being edited, each view represented in a dedicated viewport. Each viewport has to be independently controllable. Starting with basic camera control, the editor needs to provide all of the following separately in each viewport:

Display	Controls
Show the position of the look_at point	Zooming in and out (i.e., altering FOV)
Show the positions of the different viewport cameras in the other viewports, where visible	Panning in two dimensions
Render the "document" (3D model)	Rotation about three axes
Render world-landmarks (primary Cartesian axes, positive/negative axis directions, etc.)	Translation in three dimensions
Render the precise Cartesian coordinates of each salient item, at least the camera and the look_at point	Select each and every option to act upon EITHER the camera OR the look_at point OR both of them

So, for an "editor" that lets you do nothing more than move the cameras about (and without any fancy controls for doing so; just the basics!). We have five separate things that have to be displayed and five separate sets of controls to provide. These 10 items each requires unique algorithms, and although the algorithms themselves are simple to implement, they still need to be written. Already, we have enough separate algorithms (each of which we want to maintain, update, replace, and/or remove separately) that it would be nontrivial to maintain, and we haven't yet added essential features such as object selection and basic editing.

Typical game content editors consist of perhaps 50 unique display algorithms and 30 or more control algorithms, with continuous extension. This can be a nightmare to maintain, and most editors soon become so unwieldy (in terms of both code and architecture) that adding even the simplest of functionality incurs considerable cost. This is especially hard to justify when the end consumers (players) are often not even going to see the tool.

Users

The end users of content-editing tools are rarely the programmers. Although programmers do develop and use editors (including IDEs, of course) such tools are usually developed to make it easy for nontechnical people to create or customize content for the game. On large projects, the primary users are usually artists (creating 2D and 3D graphical content), writers (creating quests, subplots, game-logic widgets, etc.), and interpreted/proprietary-language programmers (e.g., developing AI scripts).

The main requirements for this set of users are:

- A powerful, feature-rich graphical user interface (GUI)
- Extendible, with the ability to add new features over time (an iterative process of end users' feedback to the tools' developer(s) resulting in new functionality)
- Reliable; most editing should be quick and easy for the end user, and the tool(s) must be stable

The first requirement in the previous list is perhaps obvious, but common platform utilities and APIs make it a surmountable task. The extendibility requirement, however, could prove to be a major challenge for the tool developers, because the tool is itself a custom solution. The need for editing that is both quick and easy is perhaps the most challenging requirement. How can the developers expose a long list of features (which will only grow longer over time) without making every command require some number of mouseclicks? To flatten the learning curve and make the end user more productive, we will assume that it is sufficient to give the end user some metacontrols allowing for GUI customization. That way, the end users can choose to lay out the interface in a fashion familiar to them.

Unfortunately, editor bugs are some of the most harmful on the project. A level-editor bug might, for instance, silently corrupt the save file. This has no long-term effect on the game itself, since it only damages some content that was "in development," and as such, the temptation is to give such bugs low priority in the general project (although, clearly, high priority in the content author's bug list). However, the users lose a huge amount of time to wasted effort working around such problems, especially since most damage cannot be retroactively fixed (when the data is lost, it's lost). Consequently, content authors must assume the bug could happen at any moment and preemptively guard against it on every edit, even if it only happens on average once every 100 edits. An unreliable editor can easily burn up most or all the efficiency gains it was destined to otherwise provide (had the tool been reliable). Worse, developers do not always appreciate that a "rare" bug slows the users down all the time, not just when it occurs.

Developers

Generally, tools such as editors do not directly increase a game's review scores or sales volume.

Editors, to put it bluntly, do not (in general) themselves make money.

Most games are developed with that in mind, and content-authoring tools tend to come in quite low on the priority list. Also, we know that developers rarely write editors for themselves; usually such tools are created to enable a wider range of people to contribute to the game (i.e., all the nonprogrammers, or programmers who know AI languages but not C++, etc.). The net effect is that the developer is usually developing something they do not expect to use, will likely not have to maintain, and that is arguably taking them away from spending time on their core tasks.

New features are added sporadically, and the developer is probably spending a lot of time on core code in the meantime, meaning that the editor source can often be prone to *bit rot* (i.e., each time they come to add the next feature, so much time has passed that even the original authors have forgotten how it works).

Some teams have highly skilled personnel dedicated to tools development, thus reducing the impact of these issues. Even so, these people will often have a variety of other tools to support, upgrade, and maintain, and to a lesser extent suffer the same problems.

So, for the developer of an editor, the main requirements for a tool like a level editor are:

- Minimal time investment. That is, spend as little time as possible developing the editor.
- Maintainability. Code must be very easy to understand after not looking at it for a long time.
- Extendibility. Adding new features must be very rapid and never require a refactoring of the existing code.

Producers and Project Managers

Producers look at a project in terms of critical paths, advantage/cost and advantage/risk ratios, etc. Custom editing tools look extremely good in terms of advantage/cost, because they simultaneously reduce the costs of content development and usually also enable the content authors to produce more complex content that they could not otherwise have managed.

However, custom editing tools are often useless (or worse than useless, for instance, if they only write to a file format that is no longer supported by the main game engine) until almost all the development on the tool has been completed. If a producer knows they may have to cancel or scale back tool development in the future to meet a deadline that will otherwise slip, it's a huge risk to spend time on such a front-loaded activity.

Worse, in practical terms, editor development work often starts simultaneously with the main team starting on the game project. Post-mortem articles by game producers frequently cite the damage done by the content authors: either waiting months for an editor to be ready or else using early versions only to have to delete everything and start again when later revisions of the editor turned out to be non-backward-compatible. The usual conclusion is to "try using more middleware next time," but the practical reality is that middleware can only provide the highest common factor functionality, if costs are to be kept low. However, most of the value is in having a tool that is fully customized to the game at hand (map formats, engine architectures, proprietary coding schemes, etc.), thereby achieving the biggest possible gains in productivity.

Solutions

Having covered the problems in depth, it's high time we discussed solutions. There are several areas we'll cover, starting with heads-up-displays, or HUDs.

HUDs

Most games developers are familiar with heads-up displays (HUDs) and frequently use them in the same kind of situation they were originally invented for: fast-paced games where the player can't risk bringing up a menu and looking away from the main viewport but requires instant access to certain key information at all times (e.g., current health, current ammo remaining, etc.).

The main benefits of HUDs for games and editors are:

- Instant access to critical data. Show the most critical pieces of data culled from a larger data set.
- Convenience. Merge data with the main viewport, enabling the user to see the data without looking away from the main viewport.
- Clarity of visualization. Arranged so that the areas of screen that they are overwriting are relatively unimportant information (e.g., targeting cursors appear as brackets *surrounding* a target, rather than on top of the target, creating blind spots over small uninteresting areas of sky or background rather than over the target itself).

These benefits are useful in a complex editor. However, they do not seem to do much to solve the problems highlighted in the earlier sections.

Context-Sensitive HUDs

We extend the concept of a single monolithic HUD to that of a context-sensitive HUD. A context-sensitive HUD is one that responds in real time to user actions, with a large amount of built-in intelligence. For example, a context-sensitive HUD for a first-person shooter (FPS) might normally display ammo, health, and frag-count; however, if the player is somehow poisoned, so that health is dropping continuously, it might replace everything with a simple thermometer reading of the player's health because all the other information becomes relatively unimportant.

In an editor, the position of the mouse cursor at any given time is the best indication of what the user is doing or thinking about; therefore, a context-sensitive HUD will typically be most sensitive to changes in cursor position. For example, the tool-tip pop ups in a standard Windows application are an example of a context-sensitive HUD, albeit a very simple one, which vanishes completely when the cursor is no longer floating over any button.

Microsoft in particular has spearheaded the use of context-sensitive HUDs in applications, showing great usability improvements, although so far they have barely scratched the surface of what is possible. For instance, whenever the mouse cursor is moved over any of the borders of a cell in Word, it changes to a resize cursor, and the function of the mouseclick is temporarily changed to match this (only the cursor change is a HUD change, but more on that later).

Heads-Up Editing

In the Word example mentioned earlier not only does the cursor change, but the entire function of the mouse does, too. A context-sensitive HUD merely provides rich and intelligent changes in what is being displayed; heads-up editing combines this with automatic switching of the current tool or mode of the editor.

A fully heads-up aware and capable editor is a step forward for users for the following reasons:

- Automation. Eliminates the need for manually changing tools all the time (the cursor changes automatically according to context, simultaneously switching tools as appropriate).
- User-interface simplification. Most of the little icons on toolbars can be removed, since the user no longer needs to select them manually.
- Learning curve reduction and productivity increase. Learning how to use the editor takes much less time because it automatically presents the user with the correct tool, saving the user from having to hunt for it in a menu, toolbar, or elsewhere.

But it gets better: heads-up editing can be implemented with a very simple architecture that makes maintenance and extendibility much easier for the developers, staving off bit rot almost indefinitely. The proposed architecture forces all new features to be added as fully encapsulated modules, preserving existing code and making components easy to replace in the future.

Implementation

The implementation of the solutions covered thus far is broken down in a number of areas: acetates, renderers, and tools. We'll also discuss details in sharing code between components.

Acetates

To the user, we present a conceptual model of acetates on an overhead projector (OHP) as seen in most conference and lecture rooms. Each acetate is merely a transparent sheet of plastic, which the lecturer can insert, remove, or edit independently of the others. Each acetate contains one or more diagrams or text, and the grouping is arranged to keep the number of acetates as small as possible (easier to manage) while allowing however fine a granularity the lecturer needs to rapidly change diagrams. Often the contents of a particular acetate make no sense on their own (for instance a set of disembodied arrows), but when placed in the context of the other acetates, they suddenly become meaningful.

With real acetates, it is easy to reorder them, to twist or translate individual layers, to hide and reveal sections, etc. This particular approach has proven very powerful, because it gives the user (the lecturer) the ability to instantly change the information being displayed in many ways: the user can very rapidly add or remove content and easily simplify or add more detail.

Our software approach is to build a system of layers, where each layer is akin to an acetate. Like acetates, each layer is transparent and overlays the main data (viewport); i.e., each layer is a HUD. However, unlike acetates, our layered HUDs have much richer control options, mainly because we have much more power with a computer GUI. Furthermore, each layer has one or more control modes (a.k.a. tools) associated with it; for instance, "translate selection" and "rotate selection." This turns each layer into an encapsulated context-sensitive HUD with associated editing modes.

Renderers

The main editor viewport is just like a traditional editor. It shows the current document being edited, where the document may be a textual document, a 3D model, or any arbitrary rendered data. The document is the set of data on the screen that is saved or loaded as opposed to being part of the GUI/editor. The main viewport displays nothing else; everything else will be handled by HUDs (and this can provide a convenient means for the user to see exactly what will be saved, without mistaking a HUD-applied tint on a texture as part of the model plus texture that will be saved. All they need to do is turn off all HUDs and they will then have a "What You See Is What You Save."

Where the document itself is particularly complicated, you may even render only part of the document in the core renderer and do the rest in HUDs. For instance, some 3D model formats save the vertex data, the texture data, the bones, and the animation all in one file. You can get an editor up and running quickly by implementing only the vertex reading and rendering in the core renderer, and later adding a separate HUD/layer for each more advanced element, without needing to alter your existing code. If there are any bugs in the texture renderer, for example, the user can always simply disable that layer and carry on viewing the vertex renderer as if they were using an early version of the editor.

Each HUD renders itself transparently on top of the editor viewport. As with acetates, some careful planning is required to divide up the desired visual features (selection highlighting, etc.) into HUDs, although generally it is better to have more HUDs rather than fewer.

The user has a simple tool for choosing which layer they are editing in, and wizard actions may programmatically select a queue of layers, transferring the user automatically from one to the next in order to complete the editing task.

This may sound familiar to the layers of modern paint programs: individual independent layers, with user actions constrained to only those they explicitly choose at any given moment. This interface should be immediately familiar to most artists. The main difference is that we are using acetates for the actual GUI, whereas paint programs typically use layers for isolation of content (make changes only in one layer) and for composition of content (e.g., blending to a background is very hard to undo once done, so compositing temporarily via layers makes things much easier; it acts like an instant preview without permanently committing the author to the current composition).

Tools

Each tool is either allotted a unique acetate of its own or shares one belonging to a display element (and zero or more other tools). If you are unsure, it is safest just to have one tool per acetate.

Shared Code and Extending the Context

Dividing the code up into one or more classes per HUD presents some problems with duplication of code. This is a natural side effect of attempting to make the HUDs as independent of each other as possible. However, code duplication could easily undermine the ease of maintenance, and so we definitely want to avoid it if possible.

Most of the code that typically gets duplicated is common display code, not tool code, such as x, y, and z coordinates of a point. It is duplicated because in any particular editor, the different tools tend to display or affect exactly the same information, although in different ways. This is fortunate, because it means we can safely encapsulate that code in a single HUD renderer, introducing only a very narrow dependency of each tool on that one single renderer (i.e., they are not dependent upon each other in any way).

A better long-term solution is to completely avoid the dependency by making *rendering X* a fundamental feature of the renderer (where X is some information that will be set at different times in different ways by different tools). We do this by supplementing our definition of *context*, which was originally just cursor position, to also include the current value of X. We also need to supply at least one HUD that queries that aspect of the context and renders it. One of the advantages of doing it this way is that you can have multiple different HUDs rendering that context at once in different ways (different formatting, different details, etc.) and leave it to the user to decide which they want to see (using the show/hide HUDs controls).

For example, if you have multiple tools that need to pop up the (x, y, z) coordinates of a point or for a vector, the context can be supplemented with a field *current point*, which the tools will fill whenever appropriate, and then assume that one of the HUDs will render it for them.

Source Code

There are two main elements to the source implementation, regardless of the windowing system you are using: a HUD manager and the individual HUDs themselves (all of which are of the same type).

The HUD manager is a Model in MVC (Model, View, Controller) terminology: it has data-structures containing references to all the current HUDs and has methods for adding or removing HUDs programmatically. It also keeps track of the state of the GUI (e.g., managing the HUD stack, described in the "User Controls" section).

All HUDs are implementations of a template/interface that provides callbacks for things like triggering rendering to a suitable surface (i.e., painting the HUD to a back buffer) and for feeding in GUI events (e.g., mouseclicks).

By encapsulating all the logic for a particular HUD into one class, we make it easy for the developer to add/remove HUDs from the editor and to alter existing ones without having to edit more than one source file at a time. Obviously, a particularly complex tool may itself consist of many classes, but the logic to activate that tool and render the interactive HUD parts is all in one place.

ON THE CD

The implementation given on the CD-ROM is simplistic, but should be easy to extend as you desire. The HUD manager is net.tmachine.gpg.hud.HUDManager. The interface/ADT for HUDs is net.tmachine.gpg.hud.HUD and the base abstract class (contains some common methods) is net.tmachine.gpg.hud.BaseHUD. A demo application is in net.tmachine.gpg.hud.HudDemo (which is run automatically if you try to run heads-up-editor.jar).

User Controls

There are three aspects to the users' interaction with the heads-up editing system:

- Interactive, heads-up selection of which tool to use
- Activation and de-activation of individual HUDs (and their tools)
- Peeking at the internal state of the heads-up editing system

Tool Selection

One HUD is a proxy for a set of other HUDs and tools. This HUD will have many context-sensitive rendering features, including an activation symbol for each and every HUD for which it is proxying. For instance, if it proxies for a translate object, a rotate object, and a stretch object, it will have icons that appear for each within suitable activation areas (e.g., the translate icon is activated while the cursor is inside the bounds of an object, rotate is activated when the outside object is within 10 pixels of a corner, and stretch is activated when the outside object is outside 10 pixels of a corner but inside 10 pixels of any edge).

LMB on an activation area delegates to the other HUD + tool mapped to that area, placing the current HUD + tool on a stack. When the delegated tool is finished, it can automatically pop the activating HUD + tool. This allows arbitrary nesting of proxying HUDs, which is good for extremely complex editing situations but also allows one HUD/tool to be invoked from several different contexts, without needing to be context aware, or having to be re-implemented with almost identical code once for each different context.

HUD Activation

To manage the different HUDs, we simply copy the standard layer palette from high-end paint programs. This is a well-established form of GUI—with which many users will already be familiar—that shows all the layers in order as a list, with controls to show/hide any particular layer and allow the layers to be dragged and dropped to reorder them in the list.

With our HUDs, reordering can be useful since it controls which HUDs are over-painting which other HUDS; with this feature, the user can usually resolve any paint conflicts on screen, keeping the underlying code simple. Otherwise, the individual HUDs would need to interact with each other so that they could avoid overlapping so as to negotiate use of screen space; e.g., to reserve particular screen regions for painting in.

The show/hide feature is used just as in a paint program: hiding a HUD simply turns off its painting code. This may be done to reduce clutter on the screen, to increase rendering performance, or simply because the user doesn't need a particular HUD during the current session. Since HUDs are persistent and identical across editing sessions (unlike layers in a paint program, which are ephemeral and tied only to the current document), a helpful feature in particularly complex heads-up editors is the ability for the user to quickly save and restore particular patterns of hidden HUDs. A particularly neat way of doing this is to create a tab along the top of the dialog for each saved preset of hidden HUDs, with the user providing a name for each preset when creating them. This allows extremely fast switching between different editing modes, in keeping with the aim of the user being able to do most of his work with minimal navigation of dialogs, menus, toolbars, etc.

Internal State

This serves two nonobvious purposes. Since the internal state of the system can arbitrarily mask out tools that would otherwise be available, it's often important for users to understand what they've selected mid-selection (e.g., if they make a mistake and select the wrong element they typically won't know what they clicked on, only what they intended to click on), and this acts as a navigation map. Secondly, it makes debugging much easier, since users can easily quote the situation they got into, rather than the developer having to guess or examine log files. This is especially helpful in that it empowers users to avoid particular situations that are subject to outstanding bugs; if they know that a certain part of the "map" causes crashes, it's easier to avoid ending up there.

Conclusion

This gem has shown how a simple editor design can give more power to the users and simultaneously make life easier for the developers. This is a virtuous circle that reduces stress all around: developers spend less time getting tangled up in unmaintainable code, and users spend less time waiting for seemingly simple (yet deceptively complex) features to be added.

Organizing your editor around HUDs keeps it very flexible in terms of features: adding a new feature is rarely difficult, thanks to the independence of individual HUDs. At the same time, the editor is effortlessly able to simultaneously run alternative implementations of the same control: both run at once, and the user turns them on/off in real time as desired. This allows you to experiment more easily with unusual features or new ideas for the editor, at a low development cost.

However, it doesn't go much beyond the basics of what can be achieved with heads-up editing (HUE). There are many ways this gem could be extended to provide far greater support for HUE, although most of these require considerable extra programming and are not to be attempted lightly. The core support presented in this gem is cheap to develop and maintain, while providing most of the benefits.

ON THE CD

Errata and updates for the source on the CD-ROM will be available from [Martin04]. The supplied code is minimal, but a library free for both commercial and personal use is being built on top of it, and later versions and improvements will be available free on that site.

References

[Eclipse04] Eclipse. Available online at *http://eclipse.org*. 2004.

[Martin04] Martin, Adam, et al. Java Games Factory, "Libraries and Code Snippets." *http://grexengine.com/people/adam/gpg5/* and *http://grexengine.com/sections/externalgames/*.

[Popa99] Popa, Adrian. "Re: How Does a Heads-Up Display (HUD) Work on the Aircraft?" *http://www.madsci.org/posts/archives/jul99/931328936.Eg.r.html.*

1.2

Parsing Text Data in Games

Aurelio Reis

AurelioReis@gmail.com

Most games require a vast amount of text data to be read and interpreted. From scripting languages to shaders, the text must most often be taken from a standardized format and converted to binary data structures the program can use natively. In this gem, we examine the creation and usage of a tokenizer: the module responsible for converting textual data into discrete units, ready for interpretation and consolidation into valid game information.

Before We Start

For clarification, a *token* is sometimes referred to as a *lexeme*, and the *tokenizer* the *lexical analyzer* (a word analyzer). We will use the terms *token* and *tokenizer* for this gem. Many free tokenizers are on the Internet, and you should check them out, particularly one of the more popular tokenizers, Lex (with Yacc) [Lex & Yacc], which is open source and can function as a valuable learning tool. Tokenizer and parser theory is an enormous field, and this gem will not attempt to cover every last facet. Instead, the purpose of this gem is to serve as an introduction and explanation on the usefulness of a tokenizer in game production, and how to approach implementing and using one in a practical manner. For more information on the history and theory behind tokenizers and parsers, there is a "References" section at the end of this gem.

So What Is a Token, Anyway?

A token is basically an indivisible grouping of characters used to represent individual basic symbols. Basically, it is a grouping of characters that form a special "word." As an example, examine the small C++ program segment in Listing 1:

Listing 1.2.1 A Simple C++ Code Segment

```
if ( i == 0 )
{
    return false;
}
```

If you were to break Listing 1.2.1 down into tokens, you would have a list such as that in Listing 1.2.2.

Listing 1.2.2 A List of Discovered Tokens Generated from the Code Segment in Listing 1.2.1

```
if          <string>
(           <left parenthesis>
i           <string>
==          <string>
0           <number>
)           <right parenthesis>
{           <left brace>
return             <string>
false              <string>
;           <semi-colon>
}           <right brace>
```

As you can see, the tokens are classified into specific types. A tokenizer would blindly read that segment as ASCII data and perform the classification process. We will get into what we do with these tokens later, but for now just realize that we define the basic types, then form a list of discovered tokens based on the data set (the text).

Making a Tokenizer

A tokenizer essentially works as a *finite state machine* (FSM), which generally functions by performing a specific action or event based on the current global state. To parallel with the world of games, an FSM might be used to guide an AI agent around a virtual world. Its current state for instance might be "wander," in which case it might randomly walk through a node grid (or similar navigation scheme).

An *input event* such as seeing an enemy may trigger a state change to "search and destroy" in which the agent hunts and attacks the enemy until it loses or kills it, at which time the state may change again. In this instance, virtual visual and auditory input functions as the *input events*. In a tokenizer, however, *input events* take the form of special characters. Let's examine one of the simplest situations; the comment. In C++, a comment may exist in two forms; a line comment specified with two forward slashes (`//`), or a block comment, specified by a forward slash and star to begin (`/*`) and star and forward slash to end (`*/`). The tokenizer walks through every character in the data set until it finds a forward slash (`/`). When it finds one, it skips ahead a character to see if this is actually a comment. If it is, we have a state change to "In comment."

The tokenizer then continues, skipping all new characters until either the end of the line or the end block statement.

The tokenizer itself can be as complex as you wish to make it. If simple text data is all you require, you can forgo token types entirely. All you would need to define are your delimiters. A delimiter specifies how you want your data set broken up into tokens much the same way punctuation does for the English language. The most common delimiter we use in written language is (of course) the space ( ). If you were to use the space as the delimiter for tokenizing this sentence, each word would become a new token. Notice however that a comma and period were also used. If you wanted to skip these characters while using them to define your token boundaries, you would also specify them as delimiters. The most common delimiters you might use are space ( ), comma (`,`), newline (`\n`), line break (`\r`), and tab (`\t`). You might also want to use the semicolon (`;`), but in some instances, it is better to reserve this as a special token type.

If you require more robust checking of token types, you need to represent them with something more concrete than just a string token. This may be more desirable, as doing so may allow for more straightforward parsing of tokens (more on this in a bit). Using C++ methodology, you can derive a new token type inherited from a base token. When a new token is to be created, it is matched with the token type most closely matching its characteristics. General rules can also be created to allow for string grouping. For instance, a string token might begin with a quote, contain multiple characters including would-be delimiters, then end with another quote (e.g., "This is a single token"). Expressions (1 + 2 * 3) can also be defined in this manner, but most people choose to define these after tokens have been created in the parsing stage.

As an example, examine Listings 1.2.1 and 1.2.2 again. Just from looking at the token types, you can see a basic structure to the tokens' placement. As you will see in a moment, when parsing a segment like this, it is far easier to expect data types than check for specific text at every token. For instance, a basic rule might be this: when an `if` string token is encountered, we expect an open parenthesis, a number of inside values representing an expression, and a close parenthesis, followed by more tokens. Instead of checking explicit names, we can merely ask for specific tokens by type. A mere convenience, but this certainly helps in code readability and usage. Also, it guarantees proper syntax when parsing the data. With proper error checking, tokenizing and parsing data is made much easier for the end user, which is why it is usually one of the most important aspects of a good parser.

How It Works

ON THE CD

On the accompanying CD-ROM you can find a simple tokenizer with a test app. To tokenize a string, the tokenizer follows a few simple steps. First, the file containing our text data is read into a buffer or mapped to a view (if you are using file mapping). We then call our tokenize function on this buffer, which goes through every character and categorizes it based on the current state (with the initial state being `TKS_INWHITE`; i.e., reading whitespace). The state changes many times during the entire process.

When a valid character is reached, the state turns to `TKS_INTEXT`, which means we are now reading actual characters. When a delimiter is reached, a token is created, categorized into a type, and added to the token list. On the other hand, if a quote is encountered, our state suddenly changes to `TKS_INQUOTES`, which means we are now reading in a text group. As soon as another quote is encountered, the text group ends and is finalized as a string token. The same process happens for single- and multiline comments.

The main function to examine is `TokenizeString()`. This is where the characters are sequentially iterated over, and states change based on character conditions. The token classification is done through the function `ClassifyToken()` (Listing 1.2.3), which basically determines whether it matches the characteristics of a float, a special character (from the special character table), or a string. This function is actually a prime candidate for being recursive, but this has been skipped for illustrative purposes. As you can see, it identifies whether a string can be converted to a digit, and if so, whether it is negative. `isdigit()` is used to determine whether the string is a number, but by comparison, it would be just as easy to scan the string for a period (denoting a fractional number). `IsSpecialCharacter()` merely checks the first character of the string to see if it is a one-character special token like an open brace, bracket, or quote. If you were to add a semicolon as a token type, for instance, this would be the place to check for it. When a token is ready to be made, the classified token is created with the `AllocToken()` function. If the tokenization ends prematurely, the `FinalizeToken()` function is called, which makes sure no token is left behind. After we have a token list, it is time to parse through it, but what exactly are we parsing? First we must create some kind of text format. Let's quickly examine something called the *BN Form*, shown in Listing 1.2.3.

Listing 1.2.3 Implementation of `ClassifyToken()` (Comments Removed for Clarity)

```
    TOKENTYPE CTokenizer::ClassifyToken( const char *strText,
unsigned long ulFlags )
    {
    TOKENTYPE TokenType;
    if ( !( ulFlags & TKFLAG_STRINGSONLY ) && ( isdigit( strText[ 0 ]
) ||
    ( strlen( strText ) >= 2 && ( strText[ 0 ] == '-' && isdigit(
strText[ 1 ] ) ) ) ) )
        {
    return TKT_FLOAT;
        }
    else if ( TokenType = IsSpecialCharacter( strText[ 0 ] ) )
        {
    return TokenType;
        }
    else
        {
    return TKT_STRING;
        }
    }
```

Making Your Own Format

At this point we actually need to have something to tokenize. In the included test app and code, you will find a very simple example. Basically, I started the foundations for a format we will call the *character file* (we'll keep the extension .txt though so you don't have to register any new file types to read it). The character file will explain the characteristics of a character in your game, non-player or player. For instance, imagine a role-playing game where you must first create your character or start from a precreated set of template characters. After your character is created, he needs to be saved. The character file is the file we would save the character to (or in the case of precreated characters, load from). The format is actually quite simple (perhaps too simple), but to explain it, we must understand the concept of the *Backus-Naur Form* (BNF; also referred to as Backus-Naur Notation). Basically, BNF is just an explanation of how grammar syntax should be applied. An excellent example directly related to everyday writing is available at [CS310] and an explanation of the symbols used at [Estier]. BNF is based around unbreakable rules that define how strings may be used together. My favorite example is the BNF for a date, shown in Listing 1.2.4.

Listing 1.2.4 The Backus-Naur Form (BNF) for a Calendar Date

```
<date>        ::= <month> '/' <day> '/' <year>
<month>       ::=     0 .. 12
<day>         ::=     1 .. 31
<year>        ::= 1900 .. 3000
```

As you can probably intuit, a BNF defines symbols and shows us what values a symbol may be assigned. Using the previously defined grammar, and ignoring the fact that some months don't have 31 days in them (plus leap years), we could easily construct a date—say, 12/25/04—and validate it using these defined rules. Translating to English, the BNF says "A date is a month, followed by a slash, followed by the day, another slash, and then the year. A month is a value between 0 and 12. A day is a value between 1 and 31. A valid year (to us) is between 1900 and 3000."

It's usually easy enough to go the other way around. Describe your "language" and then translate to BNF. If you would like a more detailed explanation, see [Garshol03]. One last thing to note is that a lot of people don't follow a strict BNF interpretation. If you want to separate the symbols with a +, for instance to signify and "in addition," the BNF would have been just as valid (although something like that may be valid when using multiple string symbols next to each other as shown in a moment). Find a system that works best for you but is not so esoteric that others will be unable to interpret your instructions. Ambiguity (opening up the possibility for too many possibilities to occur within your grammar without an idea of which one is actually correct) is also something to avoid. BNFs act more as a guide to help rationalize and think through key design decisions. As a fun exercise, see if you can make a BNF for the C++ segment in Listing 1.2.1.

Now that you have an understanding of what a BNF is, take a quick look at our example character file, Character.txt. A rule set for the grammar in our character file format may be defined as shown in Listing 1.2.5.

Listing 1.2.5 A Rule Set for the Grammar of Our Character File Format

```
    <CharacterFile>     ::=    'Character' + '{' <TextBody> '}'
    <TextBody>          ::=    <CharacterStat> <Value>
    <CharacterStat>     ::=    'Name' | 'Strength' | 'Dexterity |
Constitution | Intelligence | Wisdom | “Charisma | HitPoints
    <Value>             ::=    <Float> | <Bool> | <String>
    <Float>             ::=    0 .. 9+ + . + 0 .. 9+
    <Bool>              ::=    TRUE | FALSE
    <String>            ::=    a .. z+ | A .. Z+
```

As you may have already guessed, a few ambiguities have been introduced here on purpose. For starters, a `CharacterStat` right now can be one of three things: float, bool, or string. Using the supplied grammar, a name technically can be assigned `TRUE` or 3.14. This is obviously a fallacy. To remedy this, see Listing 1.2.6.

Listing 1.2.6 A Disambiguated Rule Set for the Grammar of Our Character File

```
    <CharacterFile>     ::=    Character + { <TextBody> }
    <TextBody>          ::=    <CharacterStat>
    <CharacterStat>     ::=    ( <FloatStat> <Float> )  |
( <BooltStat> <Bool> ) | ( <StringStat> <String> )
    <FloatStat>         ::=    Strength | Dexterity | Constitution |
Intelligence | Wisdom | “Charisma | HitPoints
    <BooltStat>         ::=    IsPlayer
     <StringStat>       ::=    Name
    <Float>             ::=    0 .. 9+ + . + 0 .. 9+
    <Bool>              ::=    TRUE | FALSE
    <String>            ::=    a .. z+ | A .. Z+
```

As you can see, the ambiguity has been completely resolved by specifying explicitly that a `FloatStat` may only take a float, `BoolStat` only a bool, and `StringStat` only a string. A few liberties were taken with the BNF by adding the + after the number and letter definitions, since it would be somewhat silly to define exactly what a number is every time you write up a new BNF. Putting the + there basically states that there may be an unlimited number of these values specified here. If you cross-reference this BNF with our character text file, you will see that we meet all the requirements. As a matter of fact, it helps to write out the format as you want it to look even before creating a BNF. As mentioned earlier, a BNF is an excellent way to poke holes in a format that may look good at first but may later have disastrous loopholes (don't laugh; it's been done).

Parsing Your Token List

Now that we have a defined format, written a file with valid input, and converted the text to discrete tokens, it is finally time to interpret these tokens and convert them to valid binary data structures. The process of doing this is often calling *parsing* since that collection of data is analyzed and processed individually. In our case, we process it so the computer can understand it. Parsing data can be a very involved and in-depth subject with many things that can go wrong. Some people prefer to parse recursively (i.e., Recursive Descent Parsing [RecursiveDescent]), analyzing the data at different levels and returning results as a whole. In our case, we will simply step through each token linearly, following our grammar rules.

The most important part of parsing data is to remember that error checking is essential. This cannot be stressed enough. If you do not ensure your data has been parsed correctly, disaster will surely follow. You may choose to use exception handling to take care of the situations where things break the format. It's simple enough to throw an exception when a rule has been broken. If you reference the code, you will see that we first check for the `Character` and `{` statements to ensure we are starting a new character entry. After this, we enter a loop that either terminates at a `} or assigns a value to our CharaterStats`. If we run out of tokens or an error occurs (using a `BoolStat` for a `FloatStat`, for instance), the loop terminates and kills further processing, exiting the program with an error.

ON THE CD

While not very exciting, the example application provided on the accompanying CD-ROM can easily be extended. For starters, imagine attaching script behaviors to a character with full expression checking and move/attitude commands. In addition to the basic character loading, the code has been extended to read in a weapon as well, but other items are easily added such as armor or shields. Also included is a neat trick you can use that takes a `CharacterStat` and matches it directly to its class data member using byte offsets into the Character class object (`CCharacter`). Using this technique, new class members are easily checked by the parser through the `CCustomField` array (more specifics are in the code). This trick also comes in handy for network variable synchronization or save/load functionality. There are lots of exciting ways to expand the app; have fun trying it.

Conclusion

In this gem, we delved into the basics of implementing a versatile tokenizer, which we use to break down text data into valid tokens, which in turn may be parsed into valid game data. Using this knowledge, we created a very simple text format for storing a game's virtual character along with some stats. The accompanying code is commented quite thoroughly so you should step through it in a debugger for a firmer understanding of how the code flows. Then, put this knowledge to work in your own game!

References

[Aho, Sethi, Ullman85] *Compilers: Principles, Techniques and Tools.*
[CS310] *http://marvin.ibest.uidaho.edu/~heckendo/CS310/grammar.html.*
[Eli] *http://eli-project.sourceforge.net/elionline4.4/lex_toc.html.*
[Estier] *http://cui.unige.ch/db-research/Enseignement/analyseinfo/AboutBNF.html.*
[Garshol03] *http://www.garshol.priv.no/download/text/bnf.html.*
[Lex&Yacc] *http://dinosaur.compilertools.net/.*
[Punctuation] *http://www.wordiq.com/definition/Space_(punctuation).*
[RecursiveDescent] *http://encyclopedia.thefreedictionary.com/Recursive%20descent%20parser.*

1.3

Component Based Object Management

Bjarne Rene, Circle Studio ltd

bjarne.rene@circle-studio.com

Traditional object management models often rely on inheritance hierarchies to share functionality between different types of objects. As games grow ever more complex, this approach leads to a design that is hard to change and where functionality is forced up the inheritance hierarchy if it is needed in several branches.

A good solution to this is to build objects from components, where each component is responsible for the data and behavior of one specific task. An object-management model based on this concept provides greater flexibility to create new objects and to modify existing behavior.

The first part of this gem outlines the differences between a traditional object-management system and a component-based system, and the main benefits gained from using the latter. The second part of the gem focuses on creating a component-based system from scratch. We conclude with a strong foundation for production-ready implementation.

Out with the Old, In with the New

In a traditional object-management system, objects derive from the same abstract base class. For the purpose of this discussion, we consider such a system where all classes derive from the class `CObject`. The next step is to decide which classes derive from `CObject`. More often than not, the classes that derive directly from `CObject` are also abstract and represent a split in the tree between classes that have some functionality and classes that do not. Typical examples of such splits would be renderable/nonrenderable and animating/non-animating. Figure 1.3.1 shows a simple inheritance tree.

At first glance, this looks quite good, and the seduction of such a system is that it often does look very good on paper, at least for a little while. One thing we know about making games is that requirements change as development progresses. This model is not one that accommodates change to a satisfactory degree. Let us look at a few examples to illustrate.

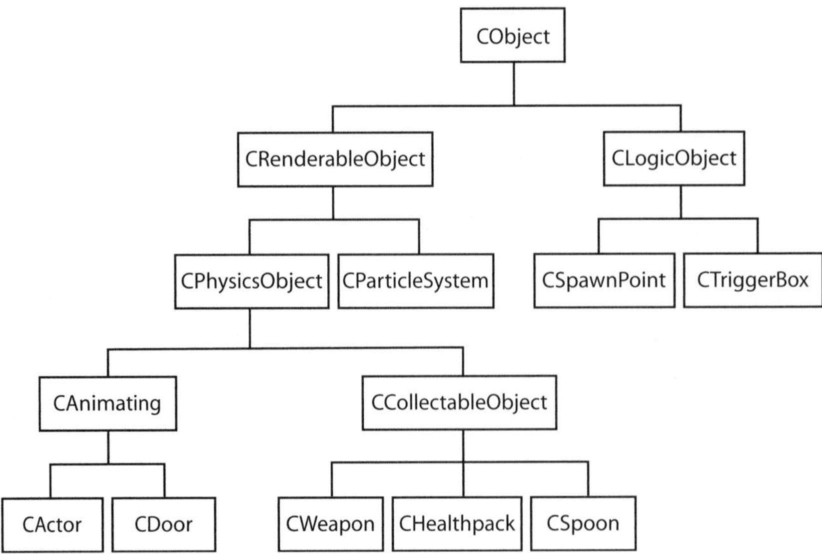

FIGURE 1.3.1 *Traditional inheritance tree.*

What do we do if it is decided that weapons need to be able to animate? As it stands, `CWeapon` and `CAnimatingObject` are in two different branches of the tree. A solution to this problem is to make `CWeapon` inherit from `CAnimatingObject`. But wait! A weapon is a collectable object, so we also have to make `CCollectableObject` inherit from `CAnimatingObject`. The result can be seen in Figure 1.3.2.

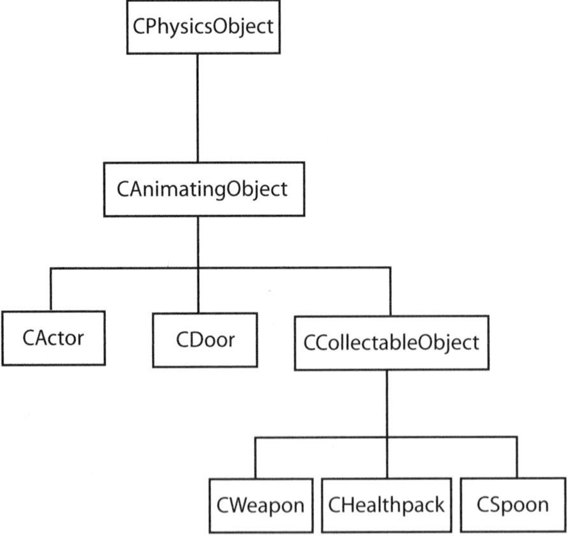

FIGURE 1.3.2 *Some of the classes have been moved to allow* `CWeapon` *objects to animate.*

This solves our problem (for now) but also introduces new problems. Now, all collectable objects have become animating objects because one of the classes that derived from `CCollectableObject` needed animation. That is quite a lot of baggage for a lot of objects to carry around. It also means that our poor health pack and any other collectable objects have to implement any pure virtual methods from `CAnimatingObject` just to be valid objects, even if those methods do not make sense for those objects.

Now let us consider what happens if we want to allow objects to take damage. We should only need a couple of methods to be able to do that, so we decide to add those methods to an existing class. Our design calls for objects deriving from the `CActor` class to take damage (these are not shown here but would typically include at least `CPlayer` and `CEnemy/CAICharacter`), so we go ahead and add the methods to `CActor`. This seems like a sensible choice.

As time goes on, it is decided that doors are supposed to be able to take damage and be destroyed as well. To give them the ability to do so, the damage methods are moved up to `CAnimatingObject`, as that is the first common ancestor of `CActor` and `CDoor`. It seems like a reasonable decision, and it gives us what we want. Another reasonable decision might be to move the damage methods up to `CRenderableObject` if a non-animating object needs the ability to take damage. The effect of a lot of these "reasonable" decisions is that our tree becomes increasingly top-heavy. A class high up the tree also ends up with a lot of methods that are not there because of what the class does but because of where it is in the tree. Such classes lose their cohesion as they try to be all things to all objects.

Components

We have seen that we run into quite a few problems if we rely on all objects being part of a big inheritance tree. What we would really like instead is a system where we can combine existing functionality into new objects and add new functionality to existing objects without having to refactor a lot of code and reshuffle the inheritance tree every time we want to do so.

A Simple Object

A good solution is to create an object from component parts. A component is a class that contains all the data members and methods used for a particular task. An object is in turn built up by compositing several components together. Figure 1.3.3 shows a spoon object and the components from which it is made.

The `Entity` component allows us to place the object in the world. The `Render` component allows us to associate a model with the object and render it according to the settings of that component. The `Collectable` component allows us to pick up the object and keep it in our inventory.

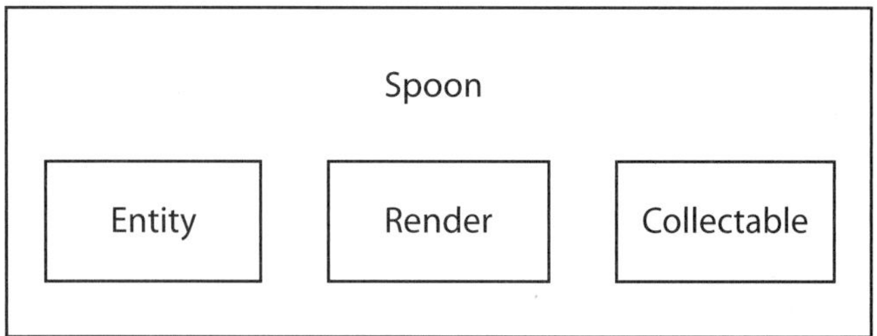

FIGURE 1.3.3 *A simple object built from components.*

Interfaces

All components derive from a base component interface. We will imaginatively call it `IComponent`. This interface contains a few methods that all components need to implement. It is mainly of use to the object manager (discussed in the next section) for being able to deal with all components through pointers to this base class.

We would prefer to concern ourselves only with the public interface that each component exposes. To make any sense, each component needs to derive from an interface that promises a bit of functionality. Let us use the `Render` component as an example.

Figure 1.3.4 shows the inheritance tree that leads to `CCmpRenderer`. At the top we have `IComponent`. Then we have `ICmpRenderer`. Finally we have `CCmpRenderer` that implements any functionality that the interfaces above it have promised.

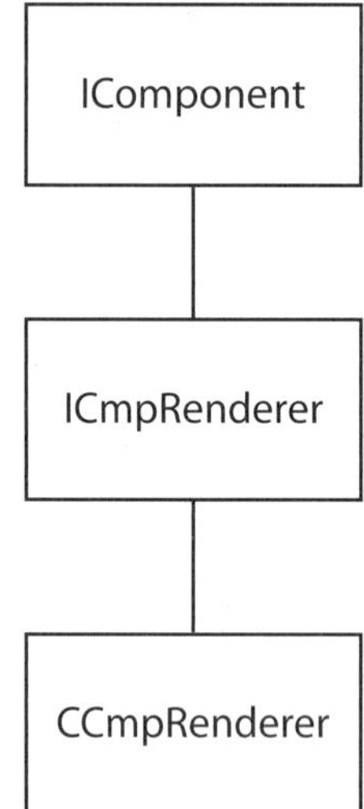

FIGURE 1.3.4 *The* `CCmpRenderer` *inheritance tree.*

This looks an awful lot like we are doing a lot of the things we just said are wrong with the traditional systems. Everything derives from one base class and we are using inheritance all over the place. How is this different? It is different because now all our inheritance chains lead to classes that perform a closely related set of tasks. In other words, the classes have tight internal cohesion.

Keeping Track

We need to organize all these components somehow. For that purpose, we have the object manager. It is really an interface to a database that the rest of our code is not allowed to see very much of. The database does not have to be (and is unlikely to be) of the Oracle or SQL kind; it just needs to keep track of all our components and make the access methods exposed in the object manager as efficient as possible. The object manager allows us to create, query, and destroy components, among other things. We will have a closer look at the object manager and one possible implementation of the database in the "Implementation" section.

There Is No Spoon

Let us go back to our spoon object example (illustrated in Figure 1.3.4). We have all these components, but what has happened to our object in all this? There is none! It may be tempting to keep a `CObject` class around for comfort, but we are not going to. There is nothing that requires us to retain a `CObject` class; if we did, how would we decide what was allowed to live in the `CObject` class and what would have to live in components? If we make everything live in components, that is one less choice to make when we are designing our system. All that remains of the object is an object ID. This can be anything as long as it uniquely represents an object and is convenient to pass around. Some kind of handle based on an `int` should do just fine. Of course, it is still convenient to talk about objects, because that is what they appear to be to the rest of the world. Any talk about objects from here on really means the collection of components that form an object when combined.

We Need to Talk

The components that form our spoon object all perform their own well-defined tasks, but it would be naïve to think that they can accomplish this without communicating with each other. The `Render` component needs to ask the `Entity` component about the world position of the object when rendering, and the `Collectable` component will probably have to tell the `Render` component to switch off rendering when the object is picked up.

There are two ways that components can communicate. In the case that we know of a particular interface that we would like to ask or tell something, we can ask the object manager for a pointer to the particular interface and then call methods on the particular component through that interface pointer. This would be a good solution to the `Render` component asking the `Entity` component for the object's world position. Any of the code in the game that has access to the object manager can query for an interface belonging to a particular object. All that is needed is the object ID.

The second means of communication between components comes in the form of messages. This is useful for the situation where a component has something to say, but does not quite know to whom to say it. A message can be sent to an object or to all objects. In the case of the `Collectable` component telling the object it belongs to that it is picked up and wants to be hidden, it would post a message to all the components in the object to say that it would like to be hidden. Each component type will tell the object manager at initialization time which messages it is interested in receiving.

Extending Our Object

So what to do if we want to be able to bend the spoon? At the moment, our spoon object is rigid and does not bend easily. The solution is simple enough: we add an animation component to the object.

Now, we have not really talked about how objects are defined. That bit seemed easy in the traditional system: the object was defined by where it was in the inheritance tree and by the methods it exposed to the rest of the world. We could still make a class for each object type and use aggregation so that each object class is built up from a bunch of has-a relationships rather than the is-a relationships of old. This brings us one step closer to what we want, but it still means that objects are set up in code, and that means we need to compile every time we change the structure of an object.

What we would really like to have is the whole process of creating objects be completely data driven. That way, designers can play around with existing objects and even create new object types without any programmer input. The system has everything that is needed to make this happen. We simply need to derive file formats for specifying components and objects and provide the designers with the tools they will need.

Creating the System

ON THE CD

Now that we have a reasonable idea of what we want, we can go ahead and create the system. The companion CD-ROM has all the code for a component-based object-management system, including a few different components and messages to get started using it. It is not a complete system, and there is not really any way that it can be considering that all games are different, but it should be easy enough to extend the system to make it work for a wide range of games.

The Component Interface

The first class that we are going to have a look at is the component interface. This is the class from which all other component interfaces and components derive. It looks like this:

```
class IComponent
{
public:
    IComponent();
    virtual ~IComponent() = 0;
    virtual bool    Init(CParameterNode &) = 0;
    virtual void    Deinit(void) = 0;
    virtual EMessageResult HandleMessage(const CMessage &);
    virtual EComponentTypeId GetComponentTypeId(void) = 0;

    CObjectId        GetObjectId(void) const;
    ICmpEntity       *GetEntity() const;
private:
    void             SetObjectId(CObjectId oId);
    CObjectId        mObjectId;

    friend CObjectManager;
};
```

So now we know what it looks like, but what does it do? Let us have a look at each of the declarations in turn. First we have the constructor and destructor. They do not really do much other than the virtual destructor signaling that this class is meant to be derived from and not instantiated. After that, it gets a bit more interesting. The next two declarations:

```
virtual bool Init(CParameterNode &) = 0;
```

and

```
virtual void Deinit(void) = 0;
```

are called on each component at initialization and de-initialization time, respectively. The one parameter to the `Init()` method is a reference to a `CParameterNode` object. `CParameterNode` is a node in a tree of component data. Think of it as a node in the XML datafile that lets us read data from it and its children without having to do all the parsing that reading XML would normally entail. The `Init()` method of each component then asks for the data it wants from this parameter node and initializes the component appropriately. The `Deinit()` method is responsible for cleaning up after the component, making sure to free any memory and release any handles that the component owns.

The next declaration:

```
virtual EMessageResult HandleMessage(const CMessage &);
```

is not declared pure virtual. Component classes do not have to override it if they do not want to. Its return value is of the enumerated type `EMessageResult` that looks like this:

```
enum EMessageResult
{
    MR_FALSE,
    MR_TRUE,
    MR_IGNORED,
    MR_ERROR
};
```

where `MR_FALSE`, `MR_TRUE`, and `MR_ERROR` all indicate that the message was handled. `MR_IGNORED` means that no attempt was made at handling the message. The implementation of `HandleMessage()` in `IComponent` simply returns `MR_IGNORED` without taking any further action.

The next declaration:

```
virtual EComponentTypeId GetComponentTypeId(void) = 0;
```

returns a value of the enumerated type `EComponentTypeId`. There is a one-to-one relation between the entries in the enum and instantiable component classes.

Then we have:

```
CObjectId       GetObjectId(void) const;
CObjectId       mObjectId;
```

`GetObjectId()` is a nonvirtual member function, and we added the member variable `mObjectId`. In a perfect world, we would not have this member variable, and `GetObjectId()` would be pure virtual to make the `IComponent` class a proper interface. In the real world, however, it makes a lot of sense to have `mObjectId` as a member variable of the `IComponent` class and to give the object manager access to change it through the two remaining declarations in the private section:

```
void            SetObjectId(CObjectId oId);
friend CObjectManager;
```

If we did not allow this, every component class would have to contain the same code to set up the object ID, and we would be introducing plenty of scope for error.

Finally we have the public method:

```
ICmpEntity      *GetEntity() const;
```

This is another situation where being practical is of greater importance than making it look pretty. In our system, we have decided that all objects have to contain a component that implements the `ICmpEntity` interface, so we add `GetEntity()` here to facilitate the lookup of this component from any other component that belongs to the same object. The `ICmpEntity` class can be seen on the companion CD-ROM.

ON THE CD

The Object Manager

The heart of the system is the object manager. The `CObjectManager` class is a bit too large for us to go through it method by method here, so we are going to focus on the core features. Refer to the code on the companion CD-ROM for the `CObjectManager` declaration and implementation.

The most important feature of the object manager is the database. It is implemented as a separate `struct` to hide the implementation details from users. We are going to have a little peek at it here though. Here it is:

```
struct SObjectManagerDB
{
    // Static component type data
    SComponentTypeInfo
       mComponentTypeInfo[NUM_COMPONENT_TYPE_IDS];
    std::set<EComponentTypeId>
       mInterfaceTypeToComponentTypes[NUM_INTERFACE_TYPE_IDS];
    // Dynamic component data
    std::map<CObjectId, IComponent*>
       mComponentTypeToComponentMap[NUM_COMPONENT_TYPE_IDS];
    // Message data
    std::set<EComponentTypeId>
       mMessageTypeToComponentTypes[NUM_MESSAGE_TYPE_IDS];
};
```

All the members of `SObjectManagerDB` are plain old arrays of more complex data types. They can all be thought of as two-dimensional arrays where one dimension is known at compile time because we know the number of component, interface, and message types.

The first two data members of this `struct` are set up at system initialization time and will not change while the game is running. Each component type calls `CObjectManager::RegisterComponentType()`, which sets up the data in these two arrays. `SComponentTypeInfo` contains data that we need to create components. It looks like this:

```
struct ComponentTypeInfo
{
    ComponentCreationMethod      mCreationMethod;
    ComponentDestructionMethod   mDestructionMethod;
    CHash                        mTypeHash;
};
```

The creation and destruction method members are function pointer typedefs:

```
typedef IComponent* (*ComponentCreationMethod)(void);
typedef bool (*ComponentDestructionMethod)(IComponent *);
```

We are going to create functions with these signatures as static member functions of each component class. They are responsible for creating and destroying components, respectively. The object manager only deals with pointers to components, which leaves effective management of component memory as an exercise for the reader. For the system implemented here, standard new and delete work just fine. The variable `mTypeHash` is used to look up the component type ID based on the hashed name string for the component.

For each interface type, we maintain a set of component types that implement it. That information is stored in the array `mInterfaceTypeToComponentTypes[]`. This is used in the `QueryInterface()` method of the object manager. To simplify things, we only allow one implementation of any interface in each object so that `QueryInterface()` either returns `NULL` if no components in the object implement that interface, or a pointer to the only component in the object that does so.

During the course of the game, we will be using the `mComponentTypeToComponentMap` array a lot. Each element of this array is a map that maps `IComponent` pointers to the object IDs of the objects to which they belong. When a component is created, its object ID and address (in the form of an `IComponent` pointer) gets added to the map at the array index determined by its component type. The `QueryInterface()` method will ultimately have to look at `mComponentTypeToComponentMap` to see if it can match an interface via `mInterfaceTypeToComponentTypes` to a component pointer. Look at the code on the companion CD-ROM for details of this method.

ON THE CD

The last member of `SObjectManagerDB` is `mMessageTypeToComponentTypes`. This keeps track of which component types subscribe to which message types. Message subscriptions tend to be set up at initialization time, although there is nothing stopping subscriptions or unsubscriptions while the game is running.

A Sample Component

If our game involves dealing and taking damage, we are quite likely to need a health component. The requirements are quite simple:

- Keep track of the current health of the object.
- Allow querying of the current health.
- Update the current health value when the message `MT_TAKE_HIT` is received.
- Send the message `MT_HEALTH_DEPLETED` when the health reaches zero.

The Interface Class

First we create the interface `ICmpHealth`. It looks like this:

```
class ICmpHealth : public IComponent
{
public:
    virtual int32 GetHealth()=0;
protected:
    static void RegisterInterface(EComponentTypeId);
};
```

The method declaration `GetHealth()` is the reason we create this interface in the first place. The implementation of the next method looks like this:

```
void ICmpHealth::RegisterInterface(EComponentTypeId compId)
{
   GetObjectManager().RegisterInterfaceWithComponent(
                                    IID_HEALTH,
                                    compId);
}
```

This method needs to be called from the `Init()` method of any component that implements this interface. The `RegisterInterfaceWithComponent()` function call tells the object manager that the component of type `compId` implements `IID_HEALTH`. `GetObjectManager()` as a global function.

The Component Class

We call our component class `CCmpHealth`, and it looks like this:

```
class CCmpHealth : public ICmpHealth
{
public:
    // Static methods
    static void         RegisterComponentType(void);
    static IComponent*  CreateMe();
    static bool         DestroyMe(IComponent *);

    // Virtual IComponent methods
    virtual bool              Init(CParameterNode &);
    virtual void              Deinit(void);
    virtual EMessageResult    HandleMessage(const CMessage &);
    virtual EComponentTypeId GetComponentTypeId(void)
                                 { return CID_HEALTH; }

    // ICmpHealth methods
    virtual int32 GetHealth()    { return mHealth; }
private:
    int mHealth;
};
```

First, we look at the implementation of the static methods:

```
void CCmpHealth::RegisterComponentType()
{
    ICmpHealth::RegisterInterface(CID_HEALTH);
    GetObjectManager().RegisterComponentType(
                                   CID_HEALTH,
                                   CCmpHealth::CreateMe,
                                   CCmpHealth::DestroyMe,
                                   CHash("Health"));
    GetObjectManager().SubscribeToMessageType(
                                   CID_HEALTH,
                                   MT_TAKE_DAMAGE);
}
```

This is arguably the most interesting of the three. It begins by registering itself as an implementer of the ICmpHealth interface. Then it calls RegisterComponentType() in the object manager to tell it about the CreateMe() and Dest'royMe() methods, and also what name (in the form of a hash value) it would like to be known under. The last thing it does is to register the component as a recipient of the MT_TAKE_DAMAGE message.

The next two methods take care of creating and destroying the component. We simply use standard new and delete to do so.

```
IComponent *CCmpHealth::CreateMe()
{
    return new CCmpHealth;
}

bool CCmpHealth::DestroyMe(IComponent* pComponent)
{
    delete pComponent;
    return true;
}
```

This is an area that would benefit from a little more work on a tailor-made memory-management system, as we will be doing a lot of creating and destroying components. Different component types could even use different allocation schemes as long as the create and destroy methods match for each type.

Now we move on to the methods defined in IComponent. The method:

```
bool CCmpHealth::Init(CParameterNode &compNode)
{
    mHealth = compNode.GetInt("Health");
    if (CParameterNode::GetLastResult() != EPR_OK)
        return false;

    return true;
}
```

reads the data that the component needs. compNode is the component level parameter node. The call to GetInt("Health") asks for the int value of the child node with name health. To simplify things, there is only one child layer of nodes under compNode. If the request for data fails, the CParameterNode class flags an error. That is checked for by calling GetLastResult().

The next method:

```
void CCmpHealth::Deinit(void)
{
}
```

does absolutely nothing. Our only data member is an int value, so there is not much to clean up. If the component had any memory allocated, we would have to free it here.

Let us look at the message-handling method:

```
EMessageResult CCmpHealth::HandleMessage(
                const CMessage &Message)
{
    int newHealth;
    switch(Message.mType)
    {
    case MT_TAKE_DAMAGE:
        newHealth = mHealth -
                reinterpret_cast<int>(Message.mpData);
        if(newHealth <= 0 && mHealth > 0)
        {
            GetObjectManager().PostMessage(
                GetObjectId(), MT_HEALTH_DEPLETED);
        }
        mHealth = newHealth;
        return MR_TRUE;
    }

    return MR_ERROR;
}
```

When we receive the `MT_TAKE_DAMAGE` message, we know that its data field is of type `int` and represents how much damage we have taken. If the health went from positive to negative, our health is depleted and we need to tell the other components that make up this object about that. We do this by calling the `PostMessage()` method in the object manager. We have to specify the recipient object, and for that, we will use the `GetObjectId()` method that we have inherited from `IComponent`. If we would like all objects to hear about a message, we would call `BroadcastMessage()`. Then we set the new health value and return `MR_TRUE` to indicate that all went well. If we did not recognize the message we received, that is an error. We use `MR_IGNORED` for messages to which we know we have subscribed but decide to ignore.

The last two functions are so straightforward that we have defined them inline with the declaration.

Conclusion

We have seen that static inheritance hierarchies do not stand up to the challenges of a modern game. This article has presented a strong alternative in the form of a component-based system. This system is flexible enough to cope with frequent changes of requirements. The game designers get the power to create and modify objects without programmer intervention. This leads to quicker turnaround time for testing a design change, which leads to more design iterations, which tends to lead to better games.

The programmers no longer have to spend their time refactoring the system every time the design changes but rather move the game forward by implementing the functionality called for in the design.

1.4

Using Templates for Reflection in C++

Dominic Filion, Artificial Mind & Movement

dfilion@hotmail.com

The C++ language has evolved quite a bit since its humble evolution from the original C language. It has grown from a language that was purposely devised to provide "readable assembler code" (C) to a programming language with a wide arsenal of tools supporting structured, procedural, object-oriented, and/or generic programming, depending on which style suits you best (or best fits your problem domain). The latest variant on the C++ language, C#, adds on many features of its own—garbage collection, just-in-time compiling, and many other things—but one feature is most worthy of note: reflection.

Reflection is the ability for a program to inspect (and sometimes modify) its own high-level structure at runtime. Compiling the program generally strips the assembled code of any easily externally observable structure; in reflective programming languages, this structural information is kept as *metadata*. An enormous effort has been put in by such notable companies as Microsoft into building reflective infrastructures, from COM to .NET.

Now, all this highbrow stuff about code that is *self aware* is all very nice for Star Trek fans out there, but how does it help us in the real world, and more to the point, how does it make your four-legged furry zombie giant better than the other guy's four-legged furry zombie giant?

There are many uses for reflection. One common use is to bind external interpreted script code to actual C++ engine code. As an example, you may write a class `CbigAssWhoopingWeapon`. You may expose this class to a script language so that a script engine could easily and automatically discover the class's type and structural information, such as properties and methods and automatically route script calls to `CBigAssWhoopingWeapon`'s methods and accessors.

Other examples of uses would be to automatically serialize (load/save) objects in your game as XML data or to provide basic network persistence of class objects. We will go more into applications of reflection after implementation details have been discussed.

As this gem will make ample use of advanced features of templates, it is assumed that the reader is quite familiar with templates in general. More obscure details on how the templates are used will be explained as we go along.

Requirements

Our goal is to build a user-friendly reflection system that can be used in C++. We would like this system to be:

Efficient: Making games today often means making console games. We want this reflection system to be lightweight so it runs on the limited memory footprint available on console machines.

Cross platform: Again, this comes with the territory when making console games. So, we cannot use compiler-specific knowledge, such as decoding PDB files. Besides, nobody would be too keen at the prospect of bundling debug information with a shipping game.

Transparent: Programmers should not need to change the way they normally code to be able to use the reflection feature. It should be the reflection system's burden to tie itself into the user programmer's code, not the reverse.

Without effect on compilation: The system should not adversely affect compile performance or make the compiling process more complicated. This precludes the possibility of making a separate C++ parser that would read the C++ code to discover types at compile time; such processes are generally slow and error-prone.

Flexible: Programmers should have exact control over which parts of their class interface they would like to expose to the outside world. Often you may want to expose a limited functionality from a class, not the whole class.

Robust: The system should be type-safe and catch any common errors (such as trying to set a value of a certain type to a property of the wrong type in a script). This should be the first hint that templates will be used in the system.

The functionality of the reflection system can be broken down into three main parts:

Registration: This deals with letting the programmer tell us which data members he would like to expose to the external world.

Introspection: This allows the programmer to inspect what property and method names are supported by the class and of what type.

Manipulation: This allows the world to call the programmer's code from an external interface (which could be a script, a GUI, a file, etc.).

Reflection normally entails exposing code elements such as data members and class functions. Because we will cover a lot of ground in this gem, we will focus on the implementation of reflection to expose data member accessors; implementation of function methods will be left as an exercise for the reader. The technique exposed here is easily extended to support exposure of class functions as well.

Properties are the central element in our reflection system. For the sake of definitions, a property is simply a data attribute whose access is controlled by read and write accessors. Often the accessors simply return or set a protected or private variable; other times they will compute a result or change an internal state. We will start by building the system around properties from the lower layers up, adding complexity as the need arises.

Part I: Runtime Type Information

At the most basic level, no reflection system can work without some notion of *runtime type information* (RTTI), or determining an object's type dynamically at runtime. While the C++ runtime's innate RTTI could be used for this purpose, using our own RTTI system will simplify the implementation of the property system, help for extensibility, and will ensure the system is optimal. While it may look like we are making a rather large detour before getting to our main topic, the implementation of our custom RTTI system will become very handy later on. We will build upon the knowledge gathered here to implement the reflection support in the second part of this gem. We will be using templates for our RTTI system as well, so this will prepare us for the template work ahead for the reflection system itself.

To be able to find the type of an object at runtime, that object must implement a virtual function overridden at each level in the class hierarchy that returns information about the type of the object. Our type information structure will contain:

- The name of the class
- A unique class ID identifying the class
- A pointer to the ancestor's RTTI information
- A function callback to a factory function

The class name will be the undecorated name of the class stored in a string. @T:The class ID is a unique user-provided 32-bit number that will be provided for effectiveness in terms of comparing class types, and in terms of serializing class type information to a file or over a network protocol.

The pointer to the ancestor RTTI is self explanatory.

The function callback will point to a factory function that will create a new instance of an object of this class type. This can be quite useful when we want to create an instance of an unknown type at runtime while only having its class ID.

The RTTI structure information should look something like this:

```
typedef DWORD         ClassID;
typedef CBaseObject* (*ClassFactoryFunc)( ClassID );

const DWORD CLASSNAME_LENGTH = 32;
```

```
class CRTTI
{
public:
    CRTTI( ClassID CLID, const char* szClassName,
           CRTTI* pBaseClassRTTI, ClassFactoryFunc pFactory );

private:
    ClassID          m_CLID;
    char             m_szClassName[CLASSNAME_LENGTH];
    CRTTI*           m_pBaseRTTI;
    ClassFactoryFunc m_pObjectFactory;
};
```

Public data accessors (`Get`, `Set`) would normally be added to this class but are not shown here for clarity. Each class in the application will contain a static instance of its RTTI structure and will implement a virtual function returning a pointer to this static RTTI structure. Note that the RTTI structure is only stored once per class, not once per class instance.

Using Templates for RTTI

The RTTI system could be implemented using macros, but a more elegant technique involves using templates to implement the RTTI.

Rather than using macros to effectively *paste in* the RTTI code in each application class, we can derive *all* of our application classes from a templatized `CSupportsRTTI` class that will implement the RTTI functionality.

If all our engine classes inherit from `CSupportsRTTI`, how can they ultimately derive from their true ancestor? Would this require us to write variants of `CSupportsRTTI` that derive from every possible ancestor? It does not, because it is entirely legal to write the template in this way:

```
template < class BaseClass >
class CSupportsRTTI: public BaseClass
{
};
```

Notice how the *ancestor* of the templatized class is actually a template parameter itself. Thus, when deriving one of our application classes from `CSupportsRTTI` we can also specify `CSupportsRTTI`'s ancestor, like this:

```
class CMyClass : public CSupportsRTTI<CMyBaseClass>
{
};
```

By deriving all application classes from `CSupportsRTTI`, we have our RTTI functionality sandwiched conveniently between each class and its ancestor. What we are effectively doing is *injecting* our RTTI code between each class and its ancestor, giving a hierarchy like the one in Figure 1.4.1.

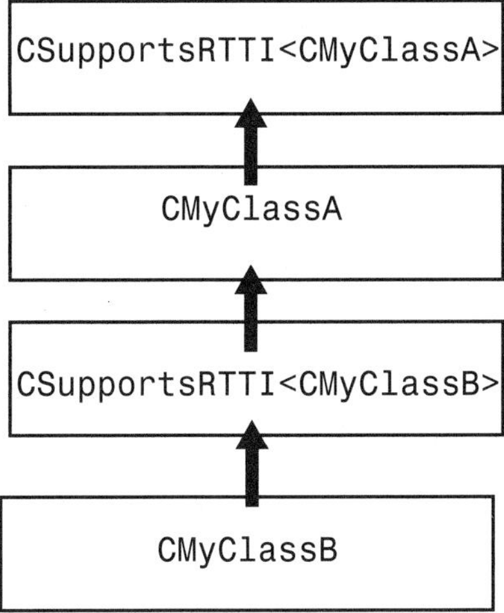

FIGURE 1.4.1 *The RTTI hierarchy.*

We can thus review the rest of our RTTI functionality.

```
#include <typeinfo.h>

template <class T, class BaseClass, ClassID CLID>
    class CSupportsRTTI: public BaseClass
{
public :
    const static ClassID ClassCLID = CLID;

    CSupportsRTTI();

    static T*       Create();
    static void     RegisterReflection();
    static inline   CRTTI* GetClassRTTI() { return &ms_RTTI; }
    virtual         CRTTI* GetRTTI()      { return &ms_RTTI; }

protected :
    static CRTTI ms_RTTI;
};

template <class T, class BaseClass, ClassID CLID>
CRTTI CSupportsRTTI<T, BaseClass, CLID>::ms_RTTI
    ( CLID, typeid(T).name(), BaseClass::GetClassRTTI(),
    (ClassFactoryFunc)T::Create, NULL );

template <class T, class BaseClass, ClassID CLID>
inline CSupportsRTTI<T, BaseClass, CLID>::CSupportsRTTI()
{
}
```

```
template <class T, class BaseClass, ClassID CLID>
T* CSupportsRTTI<T, BaseClass, CLID>::Create()
{
    return new T();
}

template <class T, class BaseClass, ClassID CLID>
void CSupportsRTTI<T, BaseClass, CLID>::RegisterReflection()
{
}
```

The RTTI info structure is put in as a static member in the template. Each template instance (we have one unique template instance per class type in our application) will spawn its own instance of the static member, which is exactly what we want. `GetRTTI()` is the virtual function that will return the correct RTTI information depending on the type of polymorphic objects.

`GetClassRTTI()` is a function that can be used to query the RTTI information of a specific class, as in `CClassType::GetClassRTTI()`. Note that static member functions *hide* static member functions in ancestor classes, which again is exactly what we need here. `CClassType::GetClassRTTI()` will hide `CBaseClassType::GetClassRTTI()`.

The `Create()` function is our class factory function. Its simple implementation allocates a new instance of the instantiated template type. `T::Create()` will resolve to `CSupportsRTTI<T, BaseClass, CLID>::Create()`, which is `T`'s base class.

The lines that declare the static RTTI structure merit our attention. Here, the RTTI structure is statically constructed, and all relevant RTTI constructor parameters are passed in to the RTTI structure:

- `CLID` is the 32-bit unique class identifier. This is a template parameter.
- `Typeid(T).name()` is the class's name string. It may appear that we are cheating here: are we not using the C++ runtime type info system to build our own system on top of it, which pretty much defeats the purpose of writing our own? Not really: `typeid(T)` here will be resolved by the compiler at *compile time*, so we are not really using the C++ dynamic RTTI structure. In fact, you will find that the code works even with the C++ runtime type info system turned off. In effect, this snippet of code will simply cause the compiler to create and fill the `type_info` structure for `T` and return the associated string, which does not require any runtime polymorphic checks.
- `BaseClass::GetClassRTTI()` is the base class's RTTI structure. `BaseClass` is a template parameter.
- `CSupportsRTTI<T, BaseClass, CLID>::Create()` provides the pointer to our factory class function, which was automatically instantiated by the template. It's useful to create instances of classes when only knowing the class ID or class name as a string.

When the static variable is initialized at application startup, all RTTI structures can be added to a global RTTI manager. Care must be taken to avoid dependencies between each static variable's constructor: the compiler cannot guarantee a specific order of initialization for static variables, and having a static variable *A* referencing a static variable *B* in its constructor can wreak havoc. Fortunately, there is no need for such dependencies in our static variable's constructor parameters, thus the order of initialization is irrelevant to the RTTI system.

Making an application class support our custom RTTI system is now very simple:

```
    class CMyObject  : public CSupportsRTTI< CMyObject, CBaseObject,
0x2e160f7a>          // 0x2e160f7a is a user-provided random unique ID
    {
    };
```

The RTTI system is thus complete.

To be able to create instances of classes by their class ID at runtime, we simply need to add some code in the RTTI structure's constructor so that all the RTTI structures are registered into a globally managed list or map. This map could then be searched by the *RTTI manager* who could find the RTTI structure associated with a class ID and call the factory function associated with the structure.

Other Comments about RTTI

The RTTI system described previously could be tweaked on several aspects:

- The class ID is not truly essential. The RTTI structures are unique static instances for each class type in the application, thus you could use pointers to the RTTI structures themselves as an ID of sorts for comparison and assignment purposes. Class IDs will be required only if you intend to save the IDs to a file or pass them over the network.
- The class factory function is optional if all you need is to query polymorphic class types at runtime.
- Using `typeid(T).name()` syntax to retrieve the class name is not obligatory if it causes problems with your compiler, but the syntax to bind the RTTI to the application classes will certainly not be as elegant. The class name string can be passed as a template parameter. However, it is not allowed to use *unnamed* objects as parameters to a template, so doing this:

```
template <const char* szString> class CMyTemplate
{
};

class CMyClass  : public CMyTemplate<"Hello">
```

will not be allowed, as the string `"Hello"` is an unnamed string variable. You will be forced to make the string a constant with a specified name, like this:

```
char szHello[] = "Hello";
class CMyClass : public CMyTemplate<szHello>
```

This will work fine but is somewhat messier.

Having built our own RTTI system, we can now reap the rewards throughout the reflective property system. Putting reflection into our software means extending the runtime type-information system so it includes metadata about supported properties, and eventually, methods. Our RTTI structure will be extended to include a list of property objects. We can now describe what these property objects will be.

Part II: Property Objects

A *property object* is a typed, named object that acts as a gateway to an internal data representation. Properties are a very abstract concept that will draw on many definitions and concepts that we will go through as we go along. We will build the property object as a layered hierarchy of three classes:

As an abstract property: The base property class will be untyped and not associated with any specific class type. This base class could be used for someone querying for a property, knowing its name but not caring about type or any specifics.

As a typed property: Building on top of the base property class will be a templatized typed version of the property object to be used when type-aware queries to properties are made.

As a class member property: The last layer in the property object is another templatized class where the property is actually bound as a member to a specific class type. We will see later why this is needed and how it fits in the overall picture.

We will examine the abstract property layer first:

```
enum ePropertyType
{
    eptBOOL,
    eptDWORD,
    eptINT,
    eptFLOAT,
    eptSTRING,
    eptCOLOR,
    eptENUM,
    eptPTR,
    eptMAX_PROPERTY_TYPES
};

class CAbstractProperty
{
public:
    virtual ePropertyType GetType() const = 0;

protected:
    const char*           m_szName;
};
```

The abstract property layer simply contains the property's name. It also contains an abstract virtual function for describing the property's type; we will see how we can describe property types later on in the article. This abstract property layer is very lightweight.

```
template <class T> class CTypedProperty: public CAbstractProperty
{
public:
    virtual ePropertyType GetType() const;

    virtual T    GetValue( CBaseObject* pObject ) = 0;
    virtual void SetValue( CBaseObject* pObject, T Value ) = 0;
};
```

It is at the next level of the property object that type-correctness is implemented. This is a templatized class, with the type of the data type this property represents as a template parameter. This layer contains abstract templatized functions for getting the value and setting the value of the property. This layer is very abstract as well, and contains little in the way of implementation. Again, we will see later how this class can implement the `GetType()` function.

Notice that the property expects the owner of the property (the object on which we are trying to access the property) to be passed in as parameter to the `GetValue()` and `SetValue()` functions. Our property class is not bound to any specific class *instance*; it binds access to a specific data member on a class *type*. All instances of a class will share the same property object. For this to work, all classes in our application must ultimately derive from a common class such as `CBaseObject`. `CBaseObject` could be empty; a common ancestor is just needed for consistency.

```
    template <class OwnerType, class T> class CProperty : public
CTypedProperty<T>
    {
    public:
        typedef T    (OwnerType::*GetterType)();
        typedef void (OwnerType::*SetterType)( T Value );

        virtual T    GetValue( CBaseObject* pObject );
        virtual void SetValue( CBaseObject* pObject, T Value );

    protected:
        GetterType   m_Getter;
        SetterType   m_Setter;
    };
```

At the level of the class member layer, we finally have enough information (type and class type) to perform an actual implementation of the property class.

The property will guard its data member and access it through standard getter and setter accessors. It would be possible for the property to have a pointer directly to the data member it is guarding, but that would mean exposing private details about classes. Using standard accessors will keep the data private to the system and be more compliant to object-oriented development rules. The accessors will be expected to have a standardized form, namely `T Get()` for getters and `void Set( T Value )` for setters.

With that in mind, the templatized property can define typedefs (as was shown in the previous code) for the accessor function callbacks it will use to access its associated data. Pointers to the function pointers are stored in the property object itself.

Getting or setting a value via the property will call relevant function callbacks.

```
template <class T>
T CProperty <OwnerType, T>::GetValue( CBaseObject* pOwner )
{
    return pOwner->*m_Getter();
}

template <class T>
void CProperty<T>::SetValue(CBaseObject * pOwner, T Value )
{
    if ( !m_Setter)
    {
        assert( false ) // Cannot write to a read-only property
        return;
    }
    pOwner->*m_Setter( Value );
}
```

You can see here that the `->*` C++ pointer-to-member operator is used. This is necessary as we are calling a function that is a member of a class object.

The property structure now has everything necessary to wrap the data type and access it through standard getters and setters. The property structure can be used and embedded in objects themselves.

Storing Properties

Properties are associated with a particular class type. It will be natural to extend our class's RTTI information to include a list of its properties. A global properties manager will also be needed to manage the overall allocation and deletion of properties.

This gem's implementation puts the properties in a C++ Standard Template Library (STL) list, organized as illustrated in Figure 1.4.2.

The global property system manager will manage a global list of properties that will contain all property objects. Properties are registered and added to the list sequentially, i.e., all properties that belong to the same class type will be contiguous in the list. Each class's RTTI structure also contains a list of its associated property objects.

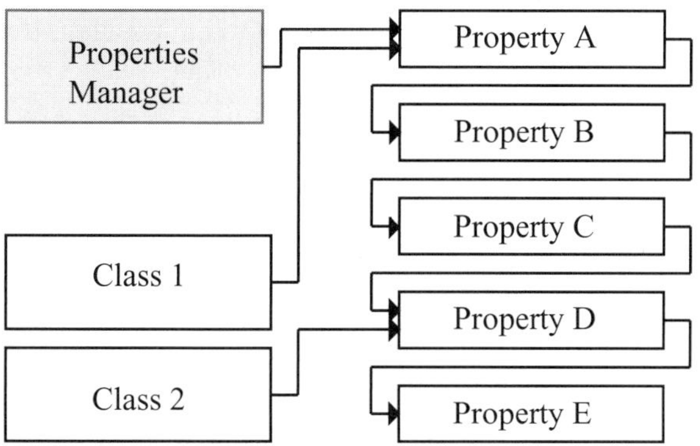

FIGURE 1.4.2 *Property storage organization.*

Property Types

A *property* is a typed construct. It must allow its type to be queried and compared with other property types. A simple way to do this is to declare an enumeration specifying every property type we plan to support: integers, floating-point values, bytes, words, double words, strings, colors, enumerations, vectors, and pointers to objects. It would be simple enough to have users of the reflection feature specify the type of a property as a parameter to the registration function; however, this can be done more elegantly by allowing the type of the property to be specified as a template parameter. Thus, instead of using syntax like this:

```
RegisterProperty( “MyProperty”, eptINT );
RegisterProperty( “MyProperty2”, eptPTR );
```

Syntax like the following could be used, which is more natural and less error-prone:

```
RegisterProperty<int>( “MyProperty” );
RegisterProperty<CMyClass*>( “MyProperty2” );
```

To achieve this, template types must somehow be associated by the compiler with the corresponding type enumeration value. We can do this by defining a `CPropertyType` template class containing a static data member. A static data member in a template will be instantiated once for every specification of the template. Thus `CMyTemplate<CMyObject>::ms_MyStaticDataMember` will refer to a different static data member than `CMyTemplate<CMyOtherObject>::ms_MyStaticDataMember`. We can use this fact to cause the compiler to automatically generate a static data member for every unique type that we plan to use with properties (remember, not for every type *reference* but for every unique *type*). In this way, we can associate a unique static data member with all types referred in code used by properties.

Using template specialization, we can associate our types with the correct enumeration type. Here are the results in code:

```
template <class T> class CPropertyType
{
public:
    static ePropertyType ms_TypeID;
};

template<class T> ePropertyType CPropertyType<T>::ms_TypeID =
                  eptUNKNOWN;
template<> ePropertyType CPropertyType<bool>::ms_TypeID  = eptBOOL;
template<> ePropertyType CPropertyType<DWORD>::ms_TypeID = eptDWORD;
template<> ePropertyType CPropertyType<int>::ms_TypeID   = eptINT;
template<> ePropertyType CPropertyType<float>::ms_TypeID = eptFLOAT;
template<> ePropertyType CPropertyType<char*>::ms_TypeID = eptSTRING;
```

Specializations of the templates are specified for all known types; types that have no specialization will get the enumeration member eUNKNOWN assigned to them as in the default template implementation code. Pointer properties are special cases and are handled through a separate property registration call (see the code on the accompanying CD-ROM).

ON THE CD

We can use this to have the property code associate a unique, repeatable number when it is given a property's type through a template parameter.

Property Registration Hook

Each object will include a description of the properties it contains, along with name, type, and access information. What is needed is a mechanism to initially describe the properties of each class and store them into a list.

Because we want users of the reflection feature to have control over which data members are to become reflective, properties will be registered manually by the programmer of the class who uses the properties. Those properties must be registered very early in the application's runtime so that they are usable as soon as possible.

We saw earlier how our RTTI information is initialized by the RTTI system through the use of instancing static variables. With static variables being initialized very early at startup of the application, this is the ideal time window to initialize class properties as well. What we need is a simple *hook* where each unique class type can register its specific properties.

A `RegisterReflection()` static function call can be added to our `CSupportsRTTI` templatized class. The RTTI system has been modified so that `T::RegisterReflection()` is passed in as a function pointer to the RTTI class's constructor. As it is being constructed, the RTTI class will call the function pointer, providing the hook that was mentioned earlier and giving a chance to the class designer to register its properties for that class type.

The default implementation of `CSupportsRTTI<T>::RegisterReflection()` is empty. The class designer can override this behavior by implementing `RegisterReflection()` in a class that derives from `CSupportsRTTI`. A static function will hide another static function with the same name in a derived base class. Thus, if `CMyClass::RegisterReflection()` exists, the following code in `CSupportsRTTI<CMyClass>` will pass `CMyClass::RegisterReflection()`; if `CMyClass::RegisterReflection()` does not exist, the compiler will resolve it to `CSupportsRTTI<CMyClass>::RegisterReflection()`:

```
template <class T, class BaseClass, ClassID CLID>
        CRTTI CRTTIClass<T, BaseClass, CLID>::ms_RTTI
    ( CLID, typeid(T).name(), BaseClass::GetClassRTTI(),
    (ClassFactoryFunc)T::Create,
    (RegisterReflectionFunc)T::RegisterReflection() );
```

If `CMyClass::RegisterReflection() is not defined, CSupportsRTTI<CMyClass>::RegisterReflection()` will be called, which is an empty implementation and is correct for RTTI classes that do not have any reflective data members.

Registering Properties

We have defined a way for programmers to run code that is associated with each class type at runtime, and now we can see how property descriptors that initialize the properties and bind them to classes can be declared.

Users of reflection will need to specify what the properties are in the `RegisterReflection()` call. Each property registered will need to specify:

- Name
- Type
- Getter accessor callback
- Setter accessor callback

Before calling the hook, a unique static variable is set by the RTTI system to keep track of the current class for which we are registering properties.

Users of the reflection system then write code in the hook to make calls to the static `RegisterProperty()` call, passing in the parameters enumerated previously:

```
void CMonster::RegisterReflection()
{
    RegisterProperty<int>( "Health", GetHealth, SetHealth );
    RegisterProperty<char*>( "Name", GetName, SetName );
}
```

The parameters of the property are put into a new property object and linked into the RTTI structure and the properties global list.

After this operation, each class's RTTI structure contains a list of its property objects. Great care was put throughout the reflection system code to ensure that the system was as transparent as possible to users of the reflection feature. Now it is time to see some real applications.

Applications for Scripts

Finally, it is time to see how all the effort put into this abstract system can be used for actual game production. The applications are diverse and can be very powerful. Our properties provide an effortless way for programmers to expose a particular data member to the outside world. The programmers do not need to change the internals of their classes and simply need to write short hooks for each class type that will tell the system what properties are available for a specific class.

The most common use of reflection use in games would be as a glue interface for scripts. Scripts often need to make calls to the core engine to affect gameplay mechanics. Reflection provides an ideal transport for such cross-boundaries communication. A script could use a line of code such as:

```
Player.Health = Player.Health – Monster.AttackDamage;
```

Global scope script calls could be wrapped into separate classes and registered as properties like this:

```
void CPlayer::RegisterReflection()
{
    // Assume CPlayer contains accessor functions GetHealth() and
    // SetHealth() for accessing health data.
    RegisterProperty<int>( "Health", GetHealth, SetHealth );
};

void CMonster::RegisterReflection()
{
    // Assume CMonster contains accessor functions
    // GetAttackDamage()
    // and SetAttackDamage() for accessing health data.
    RegisterProperty<int>( "AttackDamage", GetAttackDamage,
                                           SetAttackDamage );
}

void CGlobalScript::RegisterReflection()
{
    // Assume CGlobalScript contains accessor functions GetPlayer ()
    // and GetMonster () for accessing script sub objects.
    // Read-only property
    RegisterProperty<CPlayer*>( "Player", GetPlayer(), NULL );
    // Read-only property
    RegisterProperty<CMonster*>( "Monster", GetMonster(), NULL );
}
```

A scripting engine could use reflection to look up what objects are exposed by the global scope script class. It would thus find there is a property named `Player`; accessing this property would return a `CPlayer` object. This object can in turn be queried to see if it supports a property named `Health`, at which point the script engine could use reflection to directly retrieve the value of the player's health. The script could do the same to look up the value of the monster's attack damage and compute the result. The reflection system would call `SetHealth()` on the player object automatically to set the new value. Each property contains its type ID so the script engine can also use the reflection system to aid in type checking the script.

Applications for Tweakers

ON THE CD

Property information exposed by objects can be very useful to automatically expose tweakable data for editor applications. This is the example that is showcased on the companion CD-ROM.

In this scenario, a programmer writes a certain class, say, `CPlayerStats`, which exposes certain properties. An editor application can then use this property information to build a generic *property page* GUI interface for this object that will display a GUI control for each property type.

This can greatly help in making a game more data-driven. A typical scenario may be that an AI programmer has created a certain game class for controlling some AI. After some experimentation, the AI programmer may realize that certain aspects of the AI's variables are somewhat arbitrary and that they would be better left to a designer for tweaking. The AI programmer can easily make aspects of his code tweakable by exposing some of his accessors as properties. A "tweaker" application or editor can scan for these properties and provide a dynamic interface to the designer. This makes the whole process of data-driven design very fluid and tightly integrated.

Other Applications

Here are some more examples for applications of properties:

Implicit serialization: Properties could be used to automatically load and save certain objects of a game in a generic, open format. XML lends itself very well as a file format for saving property data.

Simple network persistence: Simple network persistence for game objects could be achieved through a system that uses properties to discover what data types need to be synchronized across the network.

Logging: Accesses to properties could be logged to aid in debugging scripts.

Conclusion

This gem outlines in detail a generic system that allows code to expose some if its structure at runtime, more specifically, named data members. Using templates, the system was made robust, cross-platform, type-safe, and transparent to the user.

We have only scratched the surface when it comes to the possible applications that reflection can be used for. Also, although it was not discussed here, reflection can also include the exposure of class functions. Templates can be used in the case of class functions as well, using template type parameters for type-correctness and binding to the code.

References

[BIL00] Bilas, Scott. "A Generic Function-Binding Interface." In *Game Programming Gems*, 56–67. Charles River Media.

[CAF01] Cafrelli, Charles. "A Property Class for Generic C++ Member Access." In *Game Programming Gems 2*, 46–50. Charles River Media.

[JEN01] Jensen, Lasse Staff. "A Generic Tweaker." In *Game Programming Gems 2*, 118–126. Charles River Media.

[OLS00] Olsen, John. "Stats: Real-Time Statistics and In-Game Debugging." In *Game Programming Gems*, 115–119. Charles River Media.

[POU02] Pouratian, Allen. "Platform-Independent, Function-Binding Code Generator." In *Game Programming Gems 3*, 38–42. Charles River Media.

[STR97] Stroustrup, Bjarne. "Templates." In *The C++ Programming Language, Third Edition*, 327–354. Addison Wesley, 2000.

[WAK01] Wakeling, Scott. "Dynamic Type Information." In *Game Programming Gems 2*, 38–45. Charles River Media.

1.5

Sphere Trees for Speedy BSPs

Dominic Filion, Artificial Mind & Movement
dfilion@hotmail.com

Binary Space Partition trees, or BSPs, have been the bread and butter of 3D programmers for years. While they are not as popular as they once were, BSPs are still used in many crucial areas within 3D engines, such as visibility preprocessing, collision detection, and polygon sorting. Few algorithms have been so successful at solving so many diverse problems.

As hardware capabilities and gamers' expectations evolve and the demand for higher polygon counts increases, however, BSPs show one of their weaknesses: long preprocessing time. Building a BSP is a process that is of the $O(n \log^2(n))$ order, and with next-generation video cards now pushing millions of polygons every frame, having an $O(n \log^2(n))$ preprocess algorithm passing on each polygon is simply not an option. Even for smaller data sets, BSPs are often the single thing preventing an engine's tools chain from going from "can preview levels in 20 seconds" to "can preview levels instantly," a noticeable improvement that will keep your level designers working at top speeds.

This gem describes an algorithm to effectively reduce BSP construction from an $O(n \log^2(n))$ process to an $O(n \log(n))$ process. The technique involves using a coarser but faster partitioning space (sphere trees) to optimize the BSPs' preprocessing step.

BSPs

BSPs will be reviewed very briefly here for completeness. However, for the most part, it will be assumed that the reader is familiar with both algorithms. For a more thorough review of BSPs, see [Ranta03].

A BSP is a partition of 3D space using infinite planes to split a space into recursive halves. This space partition can then be used to discover relationships among the polygons in a space; most commonly, if a polygon A lies in front or behind a polygon B.

A polygon soup is fed into the BSP construction algorithm. During BSP construction, one of the polygons is chosen as the *splitter*. The plane of the splitter polygon is computed, and other polygons are categorized as being either in front of or behind the splitter polygon plane. If a polygon straddles the plane, it is normally cut in two by the splitting plane, and the two halves are categorized as in front of or behind the plane separately. The two halves of the space are then separate spaces, and they are recursively partitioned by choosing splitter polygons in each half and again computing which polygons in the halves are in front of or behind the splitter polygon. The algorithm continues recursively until all polygons have been used as splitter polygons. At that point, the 3D space will have been divided into a hierarchy of binary spaces that form convex regions.

Building BSPs

To fully understand how the BSP construction process can be optimized so as to remove one order of complexity, it will be helpful to review the BSP construction process.

A good BSP tree must score highly with respect to two main criteria:

Minimum splits: A strict BSP must not have any polygons that overlap into neighbor BSP leaves. Thus, polygons organized in a BSP must be split so that each polygon can be categorized in one, and only one, BSP leaf. Split polygons add overhead to the BSP in terms of memory storage and complexity of the tree. A good BSP tree must then avoid this overhead by choosing split planes that will minimize the number of polygon splits.

Balance: Balance means having a roughly equal number of polygons on the front and back children of each BSP node. Having a good balance ensures that the BSP will, on average, be traversed with a uniform amount of steps. An unbalanced tree is unreliable, as some of the branches may be tens or hundreds of times longer than the shorter branches, thus making access times unreliable.

BSPs could also have other criteria depending on the situation, or may disregard some of the criteria listed previously, but this does not change the core of the algorithm optimizations presented here.

For the purposes of this gem, let's assume the two criteria mentioned earlier are the criteria for BSP fitness and that we are building a strict BSP, i.e., a BSP where each polygon is categorized into one, and only one, BSP leaf. We will assume that the polygon planes are used as BSP splitters and that the BSP is deemed complete when every polygon's plane has been used as a splitter in the BSP. As a review, a BSP is constructed as follows.

First, the BSP will recursively split the space into binary halves n times, where n is the number of polygons in the polygon soup; this is the first n in the $n \log^2(n)$ order of complexity and forms our outer loop. An outer loop will always be needed to put all polygons in the BSP so we cannot optimize out this loop.

Each split of the BSP must scan through all polygons in the current BSP half to find the best plane candidates that will cause the least number of splits and provide the best balance for the tree. Each polygon A scanned must be compared against all other polygons in the current BSP space to determine how many splits that polygon *A*'s plane would cause against polygons. Since we are splitting in halves recursively, each iteration of these two embedded inner loops need only scan half as many polygons as the last iteration (in the ideal case), and this is where the two $\log(n)$ powers from $n \log^2(n)$ come from. We will be optimizing out one of the $\log(n)$ powers from the algorithm's order of complexity.

Finally, once the best splitting plane candidate has been selected, all polygons in the BSP space must be categorized into the respective front and back child BSP nodes and clipped by the BSP as necessary. Technically, this would make the order of complexity of the algorithm $n (\log^2(n) + \log(n))$, but this does not include the second (added in) $\log(n)$ term in the original algorithm complexity estimate for simplicity, and because according to standard algorithm analytic rules, a quadratic function dominates the complexity order over linear terms. Still, we will be optimizing out this second (added in) $\log(n)$ term from the algorithm.

The Optimization: First Steps

We are removing the second $\log(n)$ loop, the one where a certain polygon's plane is tested against all other polygons to verify how many splits are caused and how balanced the tree would be if that plane was used to split the BSP in two.

The first idea that may come to mind is using the age-old trick of testing bounding spheres instead of actual objects (in this case, polygons) to get a rough idea of that polygon's location with respect to the plane. In the majority of cases, the polygon's bounding sphere will lie strictly on one side of the plane, and this will avoid the need to test each polygon's vertex individually.

Pushing the idea a little bit further is where it really starts to pay off though: using sphere trees to divide and conquer. A sphere tree is simply a hierarchical tree of spheres where each sphere in a tree node encloses all other spheres in the tree nodes below it. Thus, using this idea, a single bounding sphere test could be used to determine the location of tens or hundreds of polygons at a time.

Building the Sphere Tree

What we are effectively doing here is using a coarse and loose space partitioning algorithm (sphere trees) to optimize another refined and accurate space partitioning algorithm (the BSP tree itself). Sphere trees are ideal for this, as they can be built very quickly—orders of magnitude faster than the BSP tree. We wouldn't want the tree we are using to optimize our main algorithm to actually take longer to build than the time we are trying to save through the optimization.

So how do we go about building this sphere tree? We want a quick and dirty way of partitioning the polygon soup, and optimality of the sphere tree is not truly essential. One simple way to build a good sphere tree without much complexity goes as follows.

First, calculate a bounding sphere enclosing all the polygons in the polygon soup. This will be the bounding sphere for the sphere tree root node. The sphere does not have to be an optimal fit; simply calculate the bounding box for all polygon vertices, use the center of that box as the center of the bounding sphere, and adjust the radius of the bounding sphere accordingly.

Next, compute an axial plane on the *x* axis that coincides with the bounding sphere's center. Divide the polygons into two groups: those on the front of the plane and those on the back of the plane. There is no need to split hairs here (or polygons for that matter): if a polygon straddles the polygon, simply compute the number of vertices on each side of the plane and categorize the polygon as being on the side of the plane where it has more vertices. If it has just as many vertices in front of the plane as behind it, just categorize it as being in front of the plane by default. The important thing here is not accuracy but having a repeatable heuristic that will unambiguously categorize the polygon as either part of group *A* (in front of axial plane) or group *B* (behind axial plane).

Once the polygons are categorized, calculate the bounding spheres of each subgroup, create two child nodes in the sphere tree, attach them to the parent, and assign the enclosed polygons to the nodes. Continue the process recursively, this time using an axial plane on the *y* axis (then the *z*, and then back to *x*). Cycling through the axes allows a roughly even distribution through all dimensions. Recursively build the tree until the area covered by the sphere leaf is as small as the smallest polygon's bounding sphere, or when there is only one polygon in the leaf.

It is also important to store the number of polygons that each sphere tree node and all its children contain. The sphere tree root node will have a polygon count equal to the total number of polygons in the scene, and sphere tree leaves will only count polygons attached to the leaf itself. Sphere tree branches will count all polygons contained in the leaves that can be reached from that branch.

This process will produce a sphere tree that loosely groups polygons that are close to each other into clumps bounded by the spheres. See Figure 1.5.1 for an overview of the sphere tree structure.

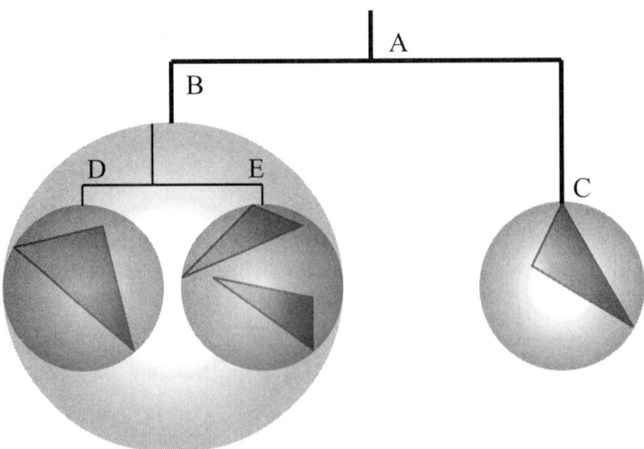

FIGURE 1.5.1 *Overview of the sphere tree.*

Optimizing the BSP

We are now ready to use the sphere tree to speed up the BSP building process.

Each polygon is tested as a splitter candidate. To determine if it is a good splitter candidate, it is tested against all other polygons in this BSP branch to determine the number of polygon splits and the tree balance. Using the sphere tree, we can now test each splitter candidate against the spheres instead of individual polygons.

The test against the sphere tree begins at the root node, which bounds all polygons. For each sphere tree node, the node's bounding sphere is tested against the splitter candidate's facet plane. If the bounding sphere lies entirely on the front or on the back of the splitter plane, it is known that no polygon splits occur with any of the polygons contained within that sphere tree branch. The tree balance can also be computed by looking up the number of polygons contained in that tree branch.

If the sphere overlaps the plane, the polygons contained within the sphere tree node may or may not overlap the plane as well. In this case, the sphere tree children must be tested recursively against the plane until sphere nodes lying entirely on one side or the other of the plane are reached.

If no such sphere can be reached—i.e., a sphere leaf is reached that still overlaps the plane—the individual polygons within that sphere leaf must be tested against the plane. This is actually the only case where individual polygons are tested.

In the majority of cases, all polygons in the space will be identified as in front of, behind, or straddling the plane after traversing only a few nodes of the sphere trees. This is where the bulk of the log(n) order is removed. Figure 1.5.2 shows how a BSP tree plane is compared with sphere tree nodes. See Listing 1.5.1 for an overview of the code that performs the BSP tests.

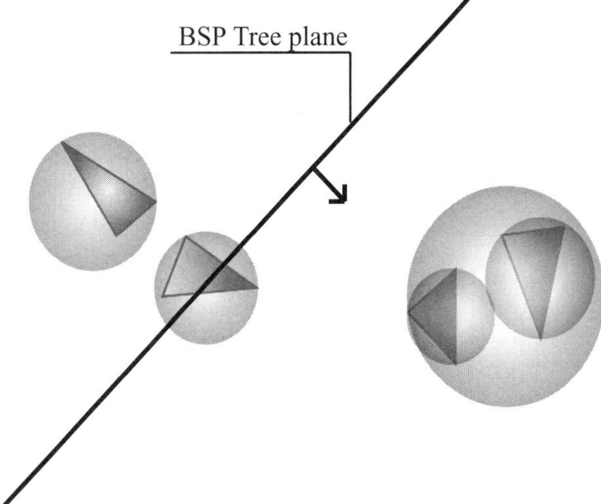

FIGURE 1.5.2 *BSP using the sphere tree for plane testing.*

Listing 1.5.1 Testing a Polygon Candidate

```
void CBSPTreeBuilder::TestSplitCandidate(
     CSphereTreeNode* pSphereTreeNode, bool& bTerminateEarly )
{
    // Test sphere tree node with plane
    float fDistance = m_pCurCandidate->m_Plane.GetDistance(
       pSphereTreeNode->m_Bounds.m_vPosition );
    if ( fDistance < -pSphereTreeNode->m_Bounds.m_fRadius )
    {
        // Sphere tree node completely in back
        m_dwBackCount += pSphereTreeNode->m_dwPolyCount;
    }
    else if ( fDistance > pSphereTreeNode->m_Bounds.m_fRadius )
    {
        // Sphere tree node completely in front
        m_dwFrontCount += pSphereTreeNode->m_dwPolyCount;
    }
    else
    {
        // Sphere tree node possibly straddles the plane
        if ( pSphereTreeNode->m_pPolygons )
        {
            // This is a sphere tree leaf, so we have to test the
            // polygon individually
            CPolygon* pCurPoly =
                (CPolygon*)pSphereTreeNode->m_pPolygons;
            while ( pCurPoly )
            {
                // Check for splits with the current candidate
                if ( pCurPoly != m_pCurCandidate )
                {
                    switch ( pCurPoly->GetSide(
                             m_pCurCandidate->m_Plane ) )
                    {
                    case CPolygon::epsFRONT :
                        m_dwFrontCount++;
                        break;
                    case CPolygon::epsBACK :
                        m_dwBackCount++;
                        break;
                    case CPolygon::epsBOTH :
                        // Ya, this one causes a split
                        m_dwSplits++;
                        if ( m_dwSplits > m_dwBestSplit )
                        {
                            bTerminateEarly = true;
                            break;
                            // Too many splits – This candidates a
                            // loser, discard it early, seeya
                        }
                        break;
                    }
                }
```

```
                    pCurPoly = pCurPoly->m_pNext;
                }
            }
            else
            {
                // Sphere tree node, so test both children
                if ( pSphereTreeNode->m_pChildren[0] &&
                     pSphereTreeNode->m_pChildren[0]->m_dwPolyCount >
                     0 )
                {
                    TestSplitCandidate( pSphereTreeNode->
                    m_pChildren[0],
                                        bTerminateEarly );
                }
                if ( !bTerminateEarly && pSphereTreeNode->
                     m_pChildren[1] &&
                     pSphereTreeNode->m_pChildren[1]->m_dwPolyCount >
                     0 )
                {
                    TestSplitCandidate( pSphereTreeNode->
                    m_pChildren[1],
                                        bTerminateEarly );
                }
            }
        }
    }
```

Cutting Down Trees

There is still an important piece missing to the algorithm for it to actually work, however. As the BSP is split recursively, polygons are categorized into separate half spaces. When choosing the next splitter candidate one level below in the BSP hierarchy, that splitter candidate must only be compared with the polygons that are contained within its own half space. It must not be compared with the polygon soup as a whole.

The sphere tree contains all the polygons. Using the same sphere tree for each BSP split would not only not produce the correct or best splitter, but it would also report an inaccurate balance of the tree for that half space. To solve this problem, as we cut the space into successive halves, we must also split the sphere tree into two separate parts.

The sphere tree has a `Split()` function that will remove all sphere tree nodes that are behind the plane from the sphere tree and put them in a separate *back sphere tree* that will be returned by the function.

The splitting algorithm compares each sphere node with the splitting plane, as was done for the polygon candidate tests. If the sphere node lies completely in front of the plane, nothing is done; the sphere node is part of the *front tree* that is the current tree. If the sphere node lies completely on the back of the plane, that sphere node must be *relinked* to be the back tree. Relinking the node implicitly relinks all the sphere node's children as well, thus adding a whole new branch to the back tree. If the sphere overlaps the plane, further processing will depend on whether the sphere node is actually a leaf.

If it is a sphere leaf, the polygons are compared individually against the splitting plane. Each polygon will be individually relinked to the front sphere node or the back tree node. If the polygon straddles the plane, this is where it will be clipped, and each clipped subpolygon will be linked to its appropriate sphere node. Notice that actual polygon clipping occurs as part of the sphere tree-splitting process, not directly as part of the BSP build process. As far as the BSP builder is concerned, it is splitting sphere trees not polygons.

If it is not a sphere leaf, a recursive split occurs. Splitting the node causes a recursive split of the children. The `Split()` call is called with each sphere node's child as a parameter. A *back node* version of the parent is created. Node child *A* will then create a back node version *A* of itself that will attach to the back node parent, and node child *B* will create a back node version *B* of itself that will also attach to the back node parent. See Figure 1.5.3 for an illustration.

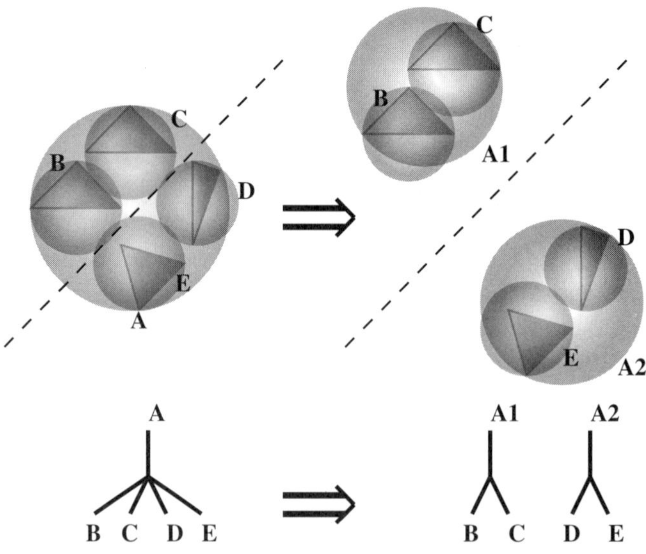

FIGURE 1.5.3 *Recursive split condition.*

Extra care must also be taken to update the polygon counts in the front and back sphere trees respectively, especially after a sphere tree split operation.

BSP to the Metal: O(*n*) and Beyond

The technique described earlier produces a well-optimized, well-behaved BSP. Sacrificing some of the runtime optimality could further speed up the algorithm. It is arguable that statistically a fairly good BSP splitter will be found by only looking at a subset of all available polygon candidates, say 5% or 10% of all available candidates. The resulting BSP may not be as efficient, but it could be produced in approximately $O(n\ \log(n)*0.1)$, making it relatively close to the <Eqn015.eps> theoretical limit. While suboptimal, the BSP produced by only evaluating a subset of polygon splitter candidates would still be much more efficient than randomly choosing splitters. A suboptimal BSP could be good enough for previewing levels or even when there is no need to have a completely optimal BSP.

Conclusion

Using the previously described algorithms can bring BSP building to an almost interactive process. This can make the difference between making last-minute level changes that take 10 to 20 minutes for each small change and level changes that take seconds; a speed up that will be especially valuable when time is short.

References

[FAQ99] "BSP Tree FAQ." Available online at *http://www.gamedev.net/reference/articles/article657.asp*. August 22, 1999.

[Ranta03] "BSP Trees: Theory and Implementation." Available online at *http://www.devmaster.net/articles/bsp-trees/*. November 9, 2003.

[RatCliff01] RatCliff, John W. "Sphere Trees for Fast Visibility Culling, Ray Tracing, and Range Searching." *Game Programming Gems 2*, 384–387. Charles River Media.

1.6

Improved Frustum Culling

Frank Puig Placeres

fpuig2003@yahoo.com

A typical game scene generally consists of many objects, which if not managed appropriately may hinder rendering performance. Libraries such as OpenGL and DirectX do some geometry management by clipping polygons that are partially off-screen and early rejecting those that are completely out of view from further processing. To perform the clip, however, each vertex in a polygon must go through the library pipeline, be transformed to screen coordinates, and be checked with the active viewport. When the polygon count is low, this process does the job, but when rendering many objects consisting of many hundreds (or thousands) of polygons, the high cost of transmitting and processing all the vertices quickly overloads the system. A higher-level per-object culling algorithm must be implemented to effectively manage rendering a typical scene. This gem describes a clever improvement to an already well-known scene-management technique: view frustum culling.

Frustum Culling

Frustum Culling works by defining a volume that wraps the space that is currently visible from a given point of view. As shown in Figure 1.6.1, that view volume is built by constructing a pyramid with the apex at the eye's position and the four triangular faces aligned with the screen borders. Two parallel planes, the near- and far- clipping planes, slice this pyramid; nothing closer than the screen or farther than some predefined distance will be included in the view volume. The resulting volume is known in mathematics as a *frustum*, and the objects that are completely outside of this volume have no chance to be seen by the camera and may be rejected on a per-object level.

Once the frustum is built, objects can be tested against it for visibility. Each object in the scene may be completely enclosed by a bounding primitive, such as a sphere, cube, cylinder, or cone, which is used to test against the frustum rather than using the object itself. This avoids the overhead of duplicating the work already in the rendering pipeline and allows a higher-level of efficiency than per-polygon culling. If

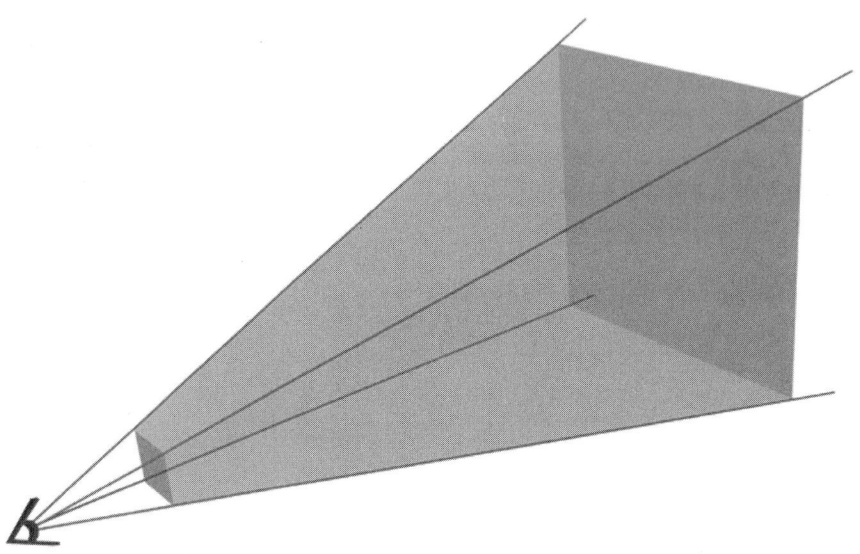

FIGURE 1.6.1 *The geometrical object that bounds the visible section of the world is called a frustum.*

the simple bounding primitive falls completely outside the frustum, the entire object (or objects) it contains may be rejected. The key is to use shapes that can be quickly tested against the frustum, so the most commonly used primitives are spheres and axis-aligned bounding boxes.

The Traditional Six Planes Approach

The most common representation of the frustum itself is six simple planes, which are extracted from the matrix composed of a concatenation of the model view and projection matrices, as shown in Figure 1.6.2. Each plane divides the space into two halves; the intersection of all the planes shapes a volume that defines what the camera sees.

Working with the six planes approach has some disadvantages, the first of which is processing expense. Determining whether a point falls inside the frustum means evaluating an equation for each plane. Only if the result is positive for every plane evaluation may the point in question be determined to fall within the frustum. A second drawback to this approach is that it is not so easy to extract the frustum's position and orientation, making operations such as an update quite difficult. This drawback is the reason why almost all implementations recreate the frustum every time the camera updates, which imposes a bit of overhead in the form of unnecessary floating-point operations (including divides and square roots!) as the six planes shaping the frustum are reconstructed [Morley00].

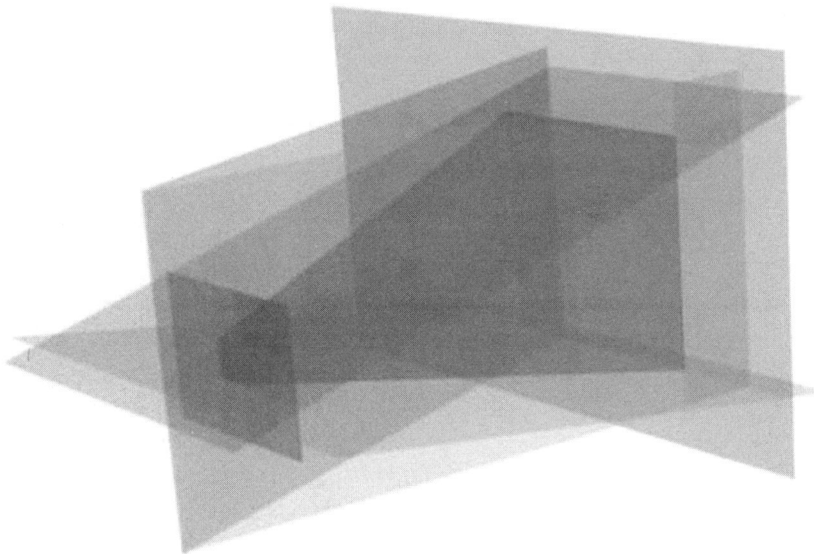

FIGURE 1.6.2 *The six planes that define a frustum.*

The Radar Approach

This algorithm was first designed for a two-dimensional radar system. The only intended purpose was to show the objects covered by a radar wave by leaving out those objects that were not covered. The approach proved to be very fast if some bounding primitives were inside the view, and the method was quickly extended to work in three dimensions. Now, the algorithm has been used for frustum culling with incredible results.

To describe how the radar approach works in a friendly way, let's first go back and introduce the two-dimensional algorithm and then extend it to the three-dimensional world.

When working on a system with two dimensions, a frustum becomes a triangle, and as a frustum is a symmetric object, the triangle is known to be isosceles as is shown in Figure 1.6.3. The segment that starts in the apex and is perpendicular to the base is called in mathematics the triangle height. The handy part of the height is that as the frustum is symmetric; it splits the isosceles triangle into two equal halves. Coincidentally, the height happens to be directionally parallel to the camera's forward vector.

Using the radar approach, a frustum is defined to be as intuitive as the camera, so frustum construction is almost free. The two-dimensional radar only needs to know the *field-of-view angle* (FOV), the *forward vector*, and the *right vector*. Conveniently enough, these are the same three parameters that the camera uses, so they can be extracted directly from the camera. The radar implementation does not, however, use the FOV

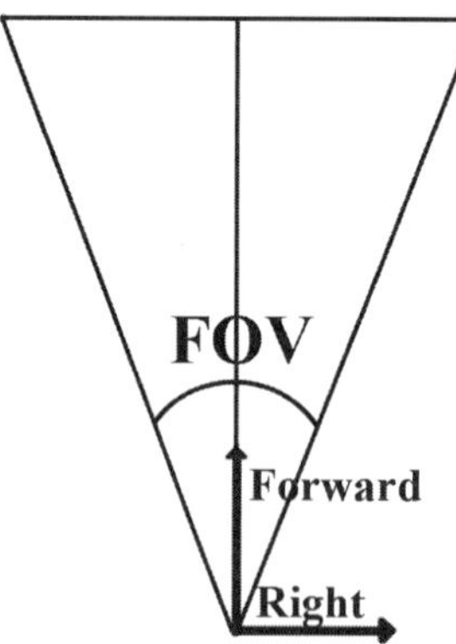

FIGURE 1.6.3 *A two dimensional frustum is represented as an isosceles triangle where the height matches the forward vector.*

directly but the tangent of that angle; so that is the only thing that must be computed when building the frustum. Even that, though, can be cached and only computed when the camera changes the FOV (which, in most games, only occurs when a zoom is performed, changing the perspective). While that angle remains unchanged, the frustum is built by copying the forward and right vectors directly from the camera. This is far cheaper than performing all the calculations required to build a frustum using the six planes approach.

And now, let's go to the really interesting part: knowing if something is inside the frustum.

Is a Point Inside a Frustum?

First, let's see what we need for knowing if a given point is inside the frustum; check Figure 1.6.4. To know if the point P is in the frustum, the radar approach projects OP to the forward and right vectors. The point P is known to be in the frustum if the forward projection F is between the far and near values and the right projection R is between *rLimit* and *–rLimit*; otherwise, it is meant to be completely out.

As described earlier, the first thing that must be done is to compute the projections F and R. To project one vector into another, a dot product is performed and the resulting scalar is multiplied by either of the two vectors to obtain the projection in the desired axis. Figure 1.6.5 illustrates. There are two vectors $\mathbf{V}_1$ and $\mathbf{V}_2$, and the dot product of them returns a scalar *s*.

$$s = \mathbf{V}_1 dot \mathbf{V}_2 = \mathbf{V}_1 \bullet \mathbf{V}_2 = \mathbf{V}_2.x \cdot \mathbf{V}_1.x + \mathbf{V}_2.y \cdot \mathbf{V}_1.y$$

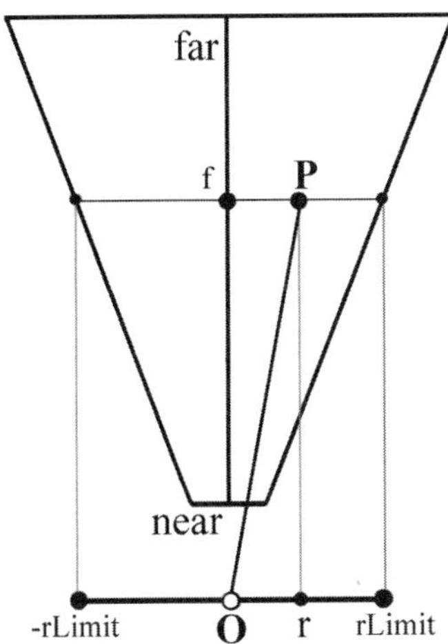

FIGURE 1.6.4 *Classifying a point against a frustum.*

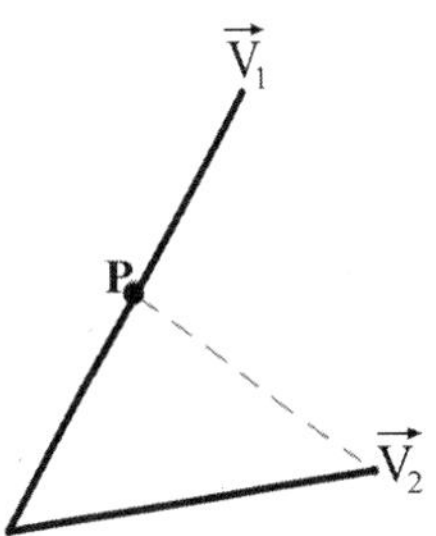

FIGURE 1.6.5 *Projection of one vector into another.*

The projection of $\mathbf{V}_1$ in $\mathbf{V}_2$ is $\mathbf{V}_2$* s with the condition that $\mathbf{V}_2$ be of length 1.

Using the previous equation and considering that the forward and right vectors are unitary, it is possible to compute the values **F** and **R** by performing:

$$f = \mathbf{Forward} \bullet \mathbf{OP} \qquad \text{And} \qquad r = \mathbf{Right} \bullet \mathbf{OP}$$

If the condition ($near \leq f \leq far$) is not true, the point is out of the frustum. Check the first part of the code:

```
bool cFrustum::IsPointIn( const cVector2f& Point )
{
        cVector2f OP = Point - EyePosition;
        float f = OP * ForwardVector;           // OP dot ForwardVector
        if (f < NearZ || FarZ < f) return false;
        float r = OP * RightVector;             // OP dot RightVector
        float rLimit = rFactor * f;
        if (r < -rLimit || rLimit < r) return false;

        // Up to here the point is known to be in the frustum
        return true;
}
```

Computing *rLimit* is trickier and involves the FOV tangent. The FOV tangent, called the *rFactor*, was discussed previously and is computed as follows (see Figure 1.6.6).

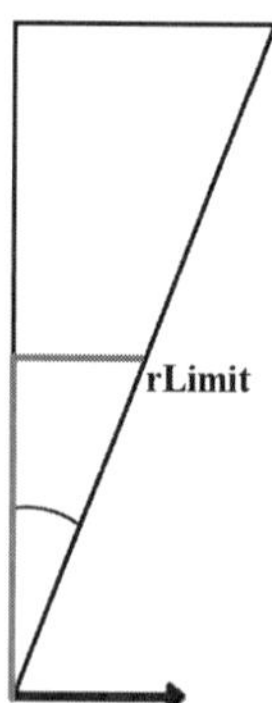

FIGURE 1.6.6 *Quantities needed to find rFactor.*

$$rFactor = \tan\left(\frac{\text{FOV}}{2}\right) = \frac{\text{opposite side}}{\text{adjacent side}} = \frac{rLimit}{f}$$

$$rFactor = \frac{rLimit}{f}$$

$$rLimit = rFactor \cdot f$$

The point is outside of the frustum if the condition ($-rLimit \leq r \leq rLimit$) evaluates to not true. Otherwise, the point is known to be in the frustum.

That sums up all that must be done to determine whether a point is inside a two-dimensional frustum.

Translating this to three dimensions is as easy as introducing another factor, the *uFactor*, which is the *rFactor* multiplied by the *ViewAspect* used when defining the perspective matrix so the frustum matches the viewport. Also, a new vector must be taken into account: the *Up* vector. The *Up* vector may be directly extracted from the camera exactly as the forward and right vectors. Using the point *P*, the *Up* vector, and the *uFactor*, a projection *U* and a *uLimit* value may be calculated. If that projection is not between the positive and negative values of *uLimit*, the point is outside of the frustum.

Combining this with the previous two-dimensional example, the position of a point with respect to a frustum in three dimensions can be known. The remarkable aspect is that it takes less than half the math necessary for the six planes approach, which is a great savings considering that there will be a lot of testing against the frustum each frame.

The point math was the easy part; however, there are just a few times when it is necessary to know whether a single point falls within a frustum. Most of the time, more complex geometries are evaluated. The good news is that almost all bounding objects used to test against a frustum in today's games follow the same point-to-frustum algorithm. Therefore, one must clearly understand the point-to-frustum algorithm in order to understand its application to more complex geometries. For this reason, it is recommended that you go back through this section if bits of it were unclear.

Spheres, Where Are You?

One of the faster and more commonly used bounding objects in today's games is a sphere. A *sphere* is defined as a center point and a radius. Spheres are quite easy to create and are almost as fast as the point-to-frustum algorithm since it is just a variation of it. Knowing the position of the sphere against the frustum can no longer be an inside or outside issue, though, because that test can also return if the bounding sphere is not completely inside or completely outside but intersecting the frustum planes, which allows some clever optimizations that are going to be covered later. For the purposes of this gem, however, we will only be covering the method that returns if a bounding sphere is *Visible* or *Completely Outside* of the frustum. Please refer to [Puig03] for more advanced methods.

Consider the definition of a sphere: a center point and a radius. With that in mind, you can think of testing a point against a frustum like checking a bounding sphere with radius zero against a frustum. Now all we do is extend that to include a nonzero radius. See Figure 1.6.7.

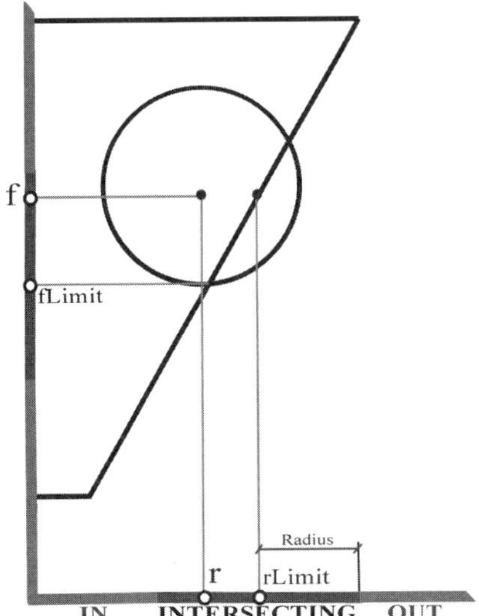

FIGURE 1.6.7 *If the projection lies in the Out area, the sphere is reported as Completely Out; otherwise, it is reported Visible because it has to lie on the In or the Intersecting area.*

The algorithm first checks if the sphere is in the frustum and returns true or false accordingly. This works much like the point code, but this time the limits are radius units farther.

```
char cFrustum::ClassifySphere(const cVector3f& Center, const float
Radius)
{
        cVector3f OP = Center - EyePosition;
        float f = OP * ForwardVector;          // OP dot ForwardVector
        if (f < NearZ-Radius || FarZ+Radius < f) return false;

// Unoptimized but more understandable
        float r = OP * RightVector;
        float rLimit = rFactor * f;
        if (r < -rLimit-Radius || rLimit+Radius < r) return false;

// Optimized ( a substraction is removed )
        float u = OP * UpVector;
        float uLimit = uFactor * f + Radius;
        if (u < -uLimit || uLimit < u) return false;

      return true;
}
```

As you can see, the test in the *r* axis is completely expanded here for illustration. This can be optimized, and in fact, the code in the accompanying CD-ROM rewrites that segment. Notice that the condition in the `if` statement (*–rLimit – Radius*) is the same as –(*–rLimit + Radius*), which is the second condition of the check. With this refactored math, the add operation is only performed once when computing *rLimit*, and used in its negative and positive.

ON THE CD

If the conditional checks fail, the bounding sphere is reported to be completely outside of the frustum. At first glance, the code to retrieve the position of a sphere according to a frustum can look a bit confusing, but once it has been carefully stepped through, it becomes quite basic, not to mention incredibly fast when compared to the six plane approach.

Bounding spheres may be fast but often grossly inaccurate, leaving large empty spaces around the object in question. For this reason, the frustum has to provide some functionality to determine the position of complex geometries like boxes, cylinders, etc., but as this gem is just an introduction to the radar approach, discussion of those methods is omitted. Nonetheless, the source code for these routines is provided on the accompanying CD-ROM, which includes methods for testing against axis-aligned bounding boxes and oriented boxes. Those two primitives in particular see comparatively big optimizations using the radar approach and behave as reliably in situations where the six planes version fails by returning visible when the object is completely outside of the frustum.

ON THE CD

Other Uses

Finding the eight vertices of the frustum was a huge task on the six planes approach due to the involvement of computing the intersection of three planes eight times which indeed is an expensive operation. However, this is very simple using the radar approach. Take a look at Figure 1.6.8.

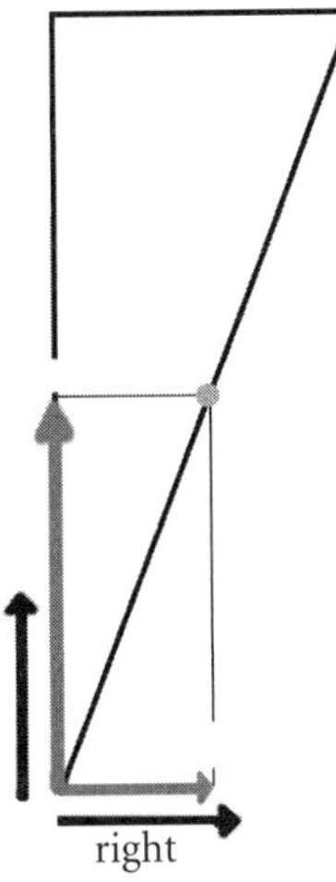

FIGURE 1.6.8 *Computing the point A by adding NVector and RVector.*

The position of point *A* can be computed by adding the two vectors marked in Figure 1.6.8. Computing the *nVector* is just a matter of multiplying the unit forward vector by the "near" value. Finding the **R** vector is a little trickier; it is just the right vector times a factor that comes from the following evaluation:

$$rFactor = \tan\left(\frac{\text{FOV}}{2}\right) = \frac{\text{opposite side}}{\text{adjacent side}} = \frac{factor}{near}$$

$$rFactor = \frac{factor}{near}$$

$$factor = rFactor \cdot near$$

Therefore, the **R** vector is defined as $rVector = \mathbf{Right} \cdot rFactor \cdot near$. Adding it to the near vector gives point *A*, and the same can be applied to get all eight points. Check the provided source for a full implementation.

Knowing the position of the eight points helps to do many handy things like drawing the camera frustum, surrounding the visible section of the world with an AABB or a bounding sphere, among others.

Further Improvement

The previous approach on its own is extremely fast, but there are some tips that can help to increase efficiency and speed. Let's check some of them in the order of the more to less obvious.

Earlier, you learned methods for checking against a frustum using the radar approach that only returns two values: *completely outside* or *visible*. The test against the frustum, however, can be extended to determine whether the geometry is completely inside, completely outside, or intersecting the frustum planes. This can be accomplished without too much trouble, and without a big speed sacrifice, allowing for the optimizations in the following section.

Hierarchical Scene Organization

Think of a big scene populated with many objects. Testing each object against the frustum and rendering the ones that are visible is actually faster than sending all the objects to the graphics hardware and letting it reject the nonvisible polygons at a per-vertex level. While that is the case, it is far from optimal taking into account that every object has to be checked. Using a scene hierarchy reduces the huge amount of tests required to reject all objects that are outside of the frustum by grouping objects and surrounding them with concatenated bounding geometries. If a bounding geometry is found completely outside of the view frustum, for example, all the objects that it contains (all the objects contained within the bounding geometries that compose the convex bounding geometry used in the test) are also completely outside of view. The same applies for the branch that reports to be completely inside of view, which is traversed but not checked again, since all the children of the bounding geometry are going to be completely inside by definition.

Several space partition algorithms allow hierarchical traversal of the scene with a frustum, rejecting nonvisible branches. The most widely used and simplest are octrees, BSP trees, KD-trees (short for "k-dimensional trees"), and ABT. Each algorithm keeps the scene organized in a hierarchical tree, but each has subtle differences or properties that make it more suitable on some scenes. Which one you select will be dependent on the application being implemented.

Plane Masking

Having the scene hierarchically organized allows rejecting groups of objects and by that allows rejecting groups of objects, making it unnecessary to test every single object against the frustum. However, if a parent object is known to be potentially visible (that is, it is not completely outside of the frustum) then all its children have to be tested against the frustum. That works fine and is pretty fast but, in some situations, can be optimized a bit.

When testing an object against the frustum—suppose a sphere for simplicity—there are three checks to perform: the *near-far* test, the *right* test, and the *up* test. If for example, the *right* test returns that the object is completely within view, that test does not have to be performed on the object's children because each one will also return completely inside (see Figure 1.6.9). Only tests that return *intersecting* must be checked again. As a result, some operations can be avoided when checking against the frustum, thereby gaining some extra performance.

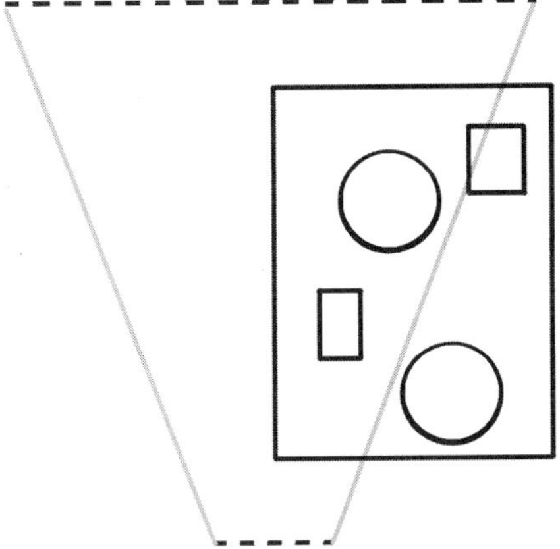

FIGURE 1.6.9 *The dot lines in the frustum represent the near-far test returning Completely_In for the object and all its children.*

The plane masking can be archived by storing a byte in the bounding object that links a bit to each of the three tests. So, if the binary code is 101, the first and third tests are performed but not the second one. This works pretty fast because it only involves clearing bits and checking them later rather than relying on more complicated operations.

Plane Coherency

In most applications, especially games, the camera moves smoothly, producing just small changes in the frustum configuration. Therefore it is very likely that if one of the three frustum tests fails, it fails also in the next frame. Consequently, in the next frame, the frustum must start checking by the test that previously failed. That will allow the frustum to potentially reject objects with just one test when the object doesn't change too much in the frustum (see Figure 1.6.10).

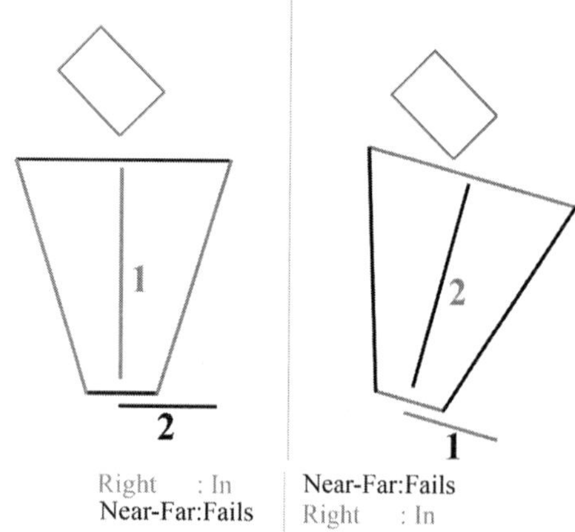

FIGURE 1.6.10 *Rearranging the test order with knowledge of the previous frame information potentially allows rejecting the object in the first test.*

The plane coherency can be implemented in many ways. The simplest is to store a byte in the bounding object that keeps the test that fails in the previous frame. When the frustum checks the object, it starts with the test that the byte points to, and if it succeeds, it continues with the other two as usual.

Checking Whether the Object Is Inside the AABB That Surrounds the Frustum

Determining intersection against an axis-align bounding box is almost always reduced to six comparisons, two for each axis. No expensive operations have to be performed, thus, it is incredibly fast compared to the usual frustum test. In the "Other Uses" section, a method to determine the AABB that surrounds the frustum was shown. That method is very proficient, and best of all, it only has to be called once per frame if the frustum changes.

If an object is known to be outside of the AABB that surrounds the frustum, it has to be also outside of the frustum (see Figure 1.6.11). Testing the object against the AABB is fast and allows rejecting the object just by doing simple comparisons. However, if the object is not completely outside, the usual test against the frustum is performed.

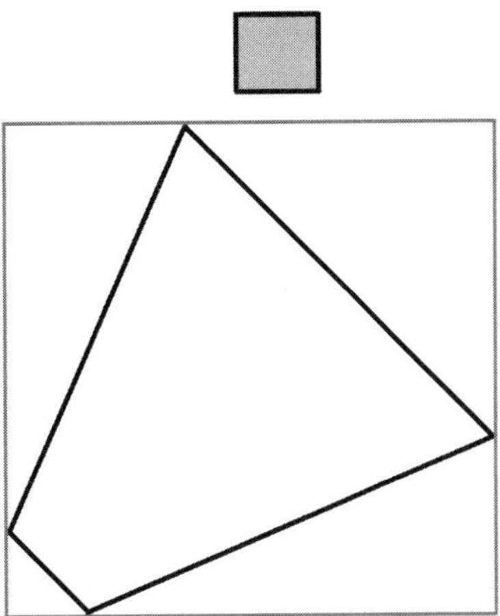

FIGURE 1.6.11 *If the object is known to be completely out of the AABB that surround the frustum, it can be said without further checking that it's completely out of the frustum, too.*

Conclusion

Frustum culling is one of the most widely used culling techniques and allows rejecting large amounts of primitives at the per-object level without much processing cost. In the majority of today's applications and games in which culling is implemented, it is done so using the six planes approach with excellent results. However, as is shown in this gem there is another fast alternative: the radar approach algorithm, which is more memory friendly, allows faster object-in-frustum tests, and is more intuitive. Best of all, it is possible to build the frustum almost for free.

References

[Jelinek&Sykora01] Jelínek, Josef and Daniel Sykora. "Efficient Frustum Culling." Available online at *http://www.cg.tuwien.ac.at/studentwork/CESCG/CESCG-2002/DSykoraJJelinek/.*

[Morley00] Morley, Mark. "Frustum Culling in OpenGL." Available online at *http:// http://www.markmorley.com/opengl/frustumculling.html.* December, 2000.

[Puig04] Puig, Frank. "A Fast Frustum Class." Available online at *http://fpuig.cjb.net/.*

1.7

Generic Pager

Ignacio Incera Cruz
ignacio@incera.net

We frequently find a situation in which at any given time we need to unload unnecessary information from our system in order to load new information. This simple task carries with it complicated management baggage to track the information that should be kept and that which may be excluded at any instant. The situation becomes even more complicated if there is more than one user that requires access to the same information at the same time. The process around this management of currently loaded data is commonly known as "paging."

Traditionally, solving this problem means designing complicated systems that are not always as efficient as we hope; they are also usually very limited because they are specifically designed to solve a particular instance of the paging problem. This gem introduces a more general, less complicated, and more efficient solution to the paging problem, called the *generic pager* (GP). By meeting all these criteria, the GP allows the system designer to completely forget about the challenges posed by creating a custom-brewed solution, allotting more of his valuable time for designing and implementing other critical parts of the title.

For you skeptics out there, I'd like to highlight the flexibility and efficiency of the GP presented in this gem by referring you to two major projects from completely unrelated domains.

- GP has been successfully integrated in an autonomous robots system where the resources of the robots are limited, and efficient management of the information needed at any given time is necessary.
- GP has been used in a navigation and visualization 3D terrain system.

The Old Paging Solution: Check Everything

The most widespread (though not necessarily the best) solution consists of the following steps:

1. Define the information to load/unload.
2. Define the size of each block of information.
3. Divide the search space into blocks.
4. Define the necessary structures to manage all the blocks.
5. Every time it is needed, check the information to load/unload, walking along *all* the blocks of the search space.

As you may have noticed, this solution is highly inefficient. It spends too much time in the division of the search space and consumes many resources, which is necessary in maintaining such complex structures with so much information for each block. Checking everything is excessively costly, too, and this solution is limited to loading/unloading the type of information defined by the design. If another type of information is required, it may be necessary to redesign the entire paging system! Finally, all these problems increase exponentially as soon as the search space grows, so let's go ahead and take the time to do it well the first time around.

The GP Paging Solution: Only Check What You Need

GP solves all the aforementioned problems in a really easy way through simple and intuitive interfaces. The main features of GP include the following:

- Almost complete transparency for the designer and user
- Search-space size independence
- No preprocessing, space divisions, or complex structures
- Memory only contains indispensable data
- Multiuser transparency (for the designer and the user)
- Information agnostic

The following sections will progressively describe the design of GP and some details of the implementation. It is worth noting that this implementation is not unique; GP can be implemented as desired, using most high-level programming languages and paradigms.

The Index Is the Key

In GP, as well as in other traditional paging systems, it is necessary to define the size of each block of information that will be loaded/unloaded. We will also define a mechanism to locate each block in the search space, along with a unique identifier per block.

We begin with a class called `Gpindex` that manages this information, thereby fulfilling three functions simultaneously:

- Define the size of the paging block.
- Locate the block in the search space.
- Uniquely identify the block.

GPindex contains two attributes: position and size. Each contains *n* elements where *n* represents the dimensions of the block. Usually the blocks are two-dimensional such as memory, images, or digital terrain models. In these cases, the position of the GPindex contains *x* and *y* (2D coordinates) while the size contains height and width. However, we are not locked into 1D or 2D blocks; note that we can add as many elements to each attribute as dimensions the block has.

The attribute position defines, locates, and identifies each block. Since each block determines a portion of the search space, its position is unique. Consequently and conveniently, the position of the block defines its location *and* unique identification.

GPindex provides another function that is extremely practical: it allows us to navigate through the blocks without creating any structures, without a previous division, and without loading anything into memory. It implements three methods:

```
GetIndex (position p);
    // Gets the GPindex that contains the position p.
GetNext(int n)
// Gets the next n-th GPindex in any dimension.
GetPrevious(int n)
// Gets the previous n-th GPindex in any dimension.
```

For example:

```
GPindex GetIndex (int x, int y);
    // Returns the GPindex that contains the position x, y
GPindex GetNextX(int n);
    // Returns the next n-th GPindex in X
GPindex GetPreviousX(int n);
    // Returns the previous n-th GPindex in X
GPindex GetNextY(int n);
    // Returns the next n-th GPindex in Y
GPindex GetPreviousY(int n);
    // Returns the previous n-th GPindex in Y
```

As shown in Figure 1.7.1, there is an index defined with position (100, 100) and size (50, 50).

This is so versatile for the reason that, as soon as the index is defined, we can consider that all the search space is divided, although it is not really divided (saving time and memory) as shown in Figure 1.7.2.

We can now navigate freely, moving over 50 × 50 (size) blocks creating just an index as Figure 1.7.3 illustrates.

ON THE CD

A very interesting characteristic is that the position and the size can reference any type of data. The example on the CD-ROM is implemented with integers, but you can use any data type or data structure, provided you take into account the following two criteria:

- Implement appropriately the methods GetIndex(), GetNext(), and GetPrevious() for every dimension of the block.

- The data type must contain, at least, the following operators:

```
operator <
operator ==
operator <=
```

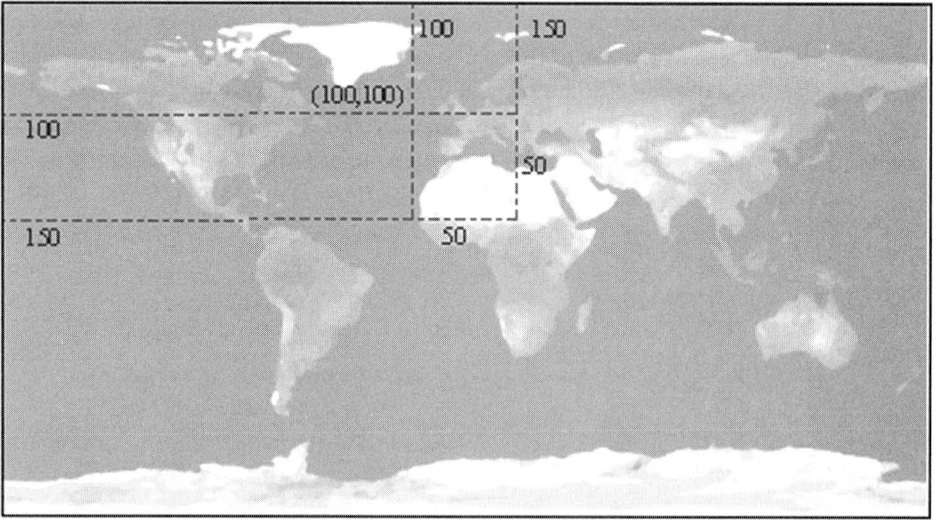

FIGURE 1.7.1 `GPindex` *at position (100, 100) with size (50, 50). Global Map used in the images in this article courtesy of Earth Observatory: The Blue Marble Web site (eobglossary.gsfc.nasa.gov).*

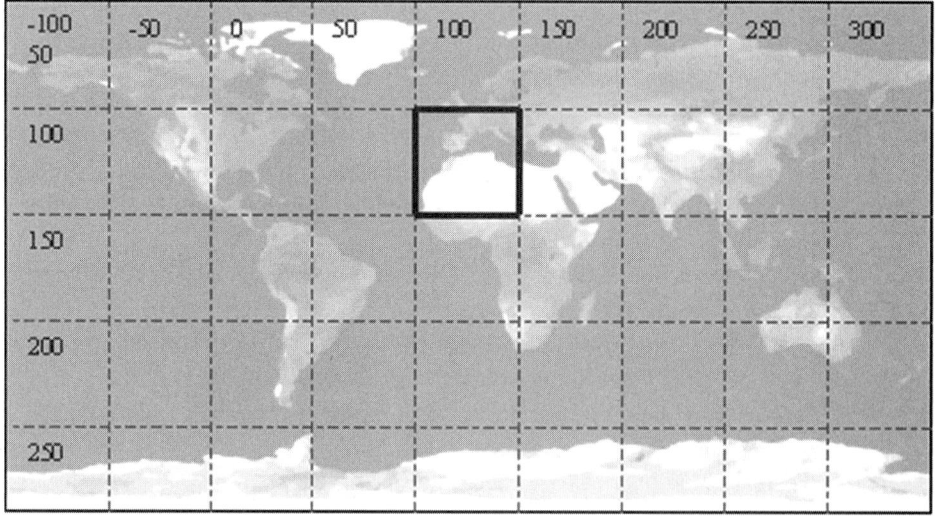

FIGURE 1.7.2 *Implicit division of search space.*

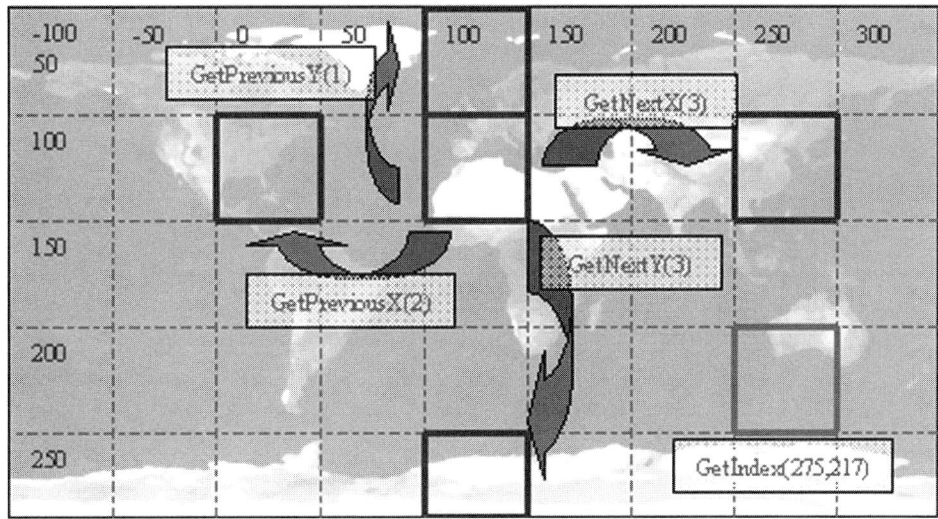

FIGURE 1.7.3 *Navigation through the search space.*

Nevertheless, integer use is common in most cases (or at least a type that converts easily into integers), so the CD-ROM implementation should suffice.

It is not a problem that an index can surpass the search space, nor is it a problem that there are potentially empty blocks. The solution for this is to check the limits and free space when the block must be loaded, as we will see in the next section. (See Figure 1.7.4.)

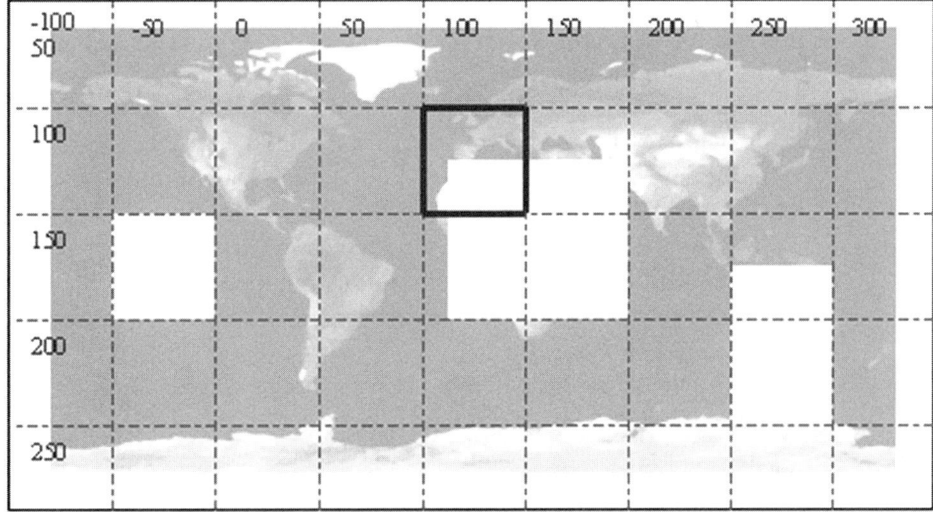

FIGURE 1.7.4 *Out of limits and free space.*

To review, the definition of the index in our system is almost ready to page:

```
GPindex
(
    Position,  //x, y, ..., n-dimensions
    Size       //width, height, ..., n-dimensions
)
```

The Tile: The Block of the World

Now that we know how to divide the search space and locate and identify a specific block, let us define the block itself. GP holds a simple class called `GPtile` that basically contains the `GPindex` that defines its position and size. This means that the *tile* is the block of the search space and is determined by the *index*. In the example of the terrain paging, every tile corresponds to a portion of terrain, with a position and size defined by the index of the tile.

Once the tile is defined by assigning the index, all that remains is to load/unload the data.

```
virtual void Load()
virtual void Unload()
```

The GP user simply has to design a class that carries out the next requirements:

1. Derive from `GPtile`
2. Implement the methods `Load()` and `Unload()`

In the implementation of these methods, the user can utilize the information contained in the index of the tile and the class derived from `GPtile` in order to load/unload the information.

Following the previous example, an index was defined with the position (100, 100) and the size (50, 50). Now we have the location and size of the block of the search space, but it was not necessary to know what the block was or what kind of information it contained. In our example, the information to manage is terrain portions. At this point, we define a class derived from `GPtile`. See Figure 1.7.5.

In the `Load` method, we load the information situated in the position (100, 100) and size (50, 50) as shown in Figure 1.7.6.

It is important to know that a `GPindex` can reference any data type, meaning the `GPtile` can load/unload any kind of information (see Figure 1.7.7.). The information contained by a `GPtile` can be a fragment of a 50×50 image, a height map, a portion of a digital terrain model, etc.

Every `GPtile` contains a very useful attribute, `State`. There are four different states for a tile:

`LOAD`: The `GPtile` is loaded.
`LOADING`: The `GPtile` is already loading but it is not completely loaded yet.
`UNLOADED`: The `GPtile` is unloaded.
`UNLOADING`: The `GPtile` is already unloading but is not completely unloaded yet.

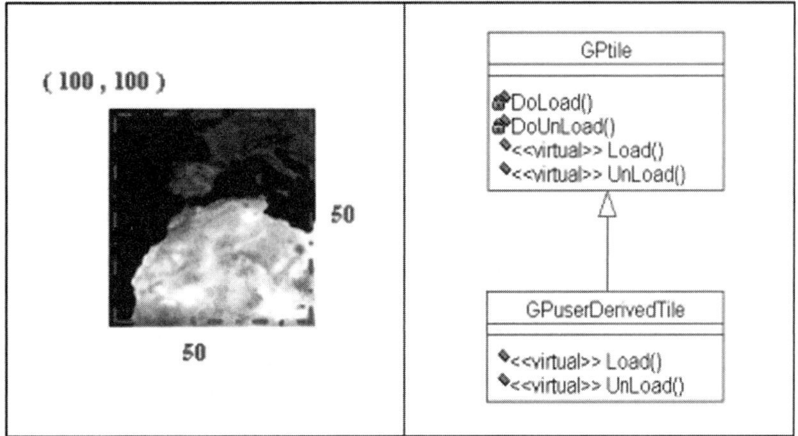

FIGURE 1.7.5 `GPtile` *definition.*

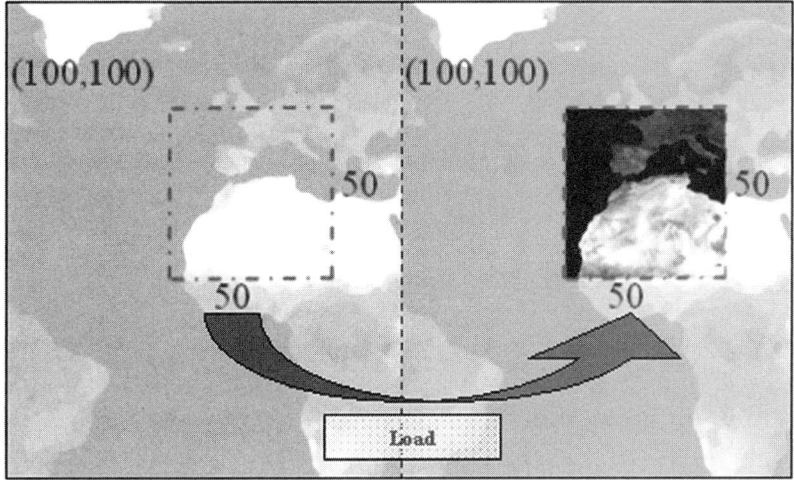

FIGURE 1.7.6 `GPtile Load`.

The class `GPtile` manages these states in a transparent way for the GP user (see Figure 1.7.8). The user will only need to implement the methods `Load()` and `Unload()`.

In some situations it will be necessary to load information of different types and origin, but conceptually in the same tile. In the example, the index (100, 100) (50, 50) can reference a terrain portion located in coordinate (100, 100) and size (50, 50) and, at the same time, it can reference to a fragment of an image with the same coordinates and size that is going to be used as the texture in that portion of terrain, as shown in Figure 1.7.9.

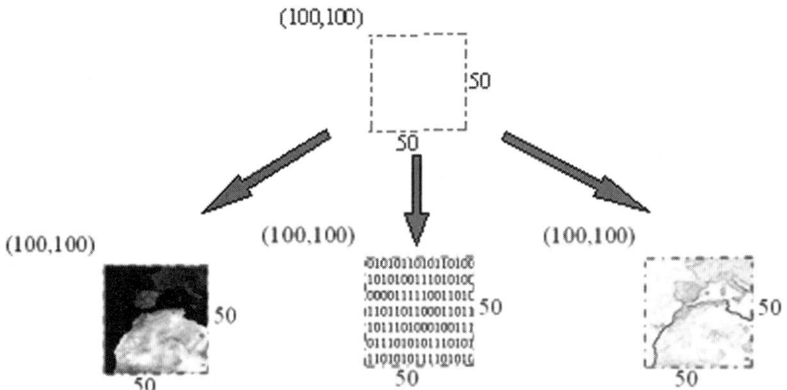

FIGURE 1.7.7 *Different types of information in the same* `GPindex`.

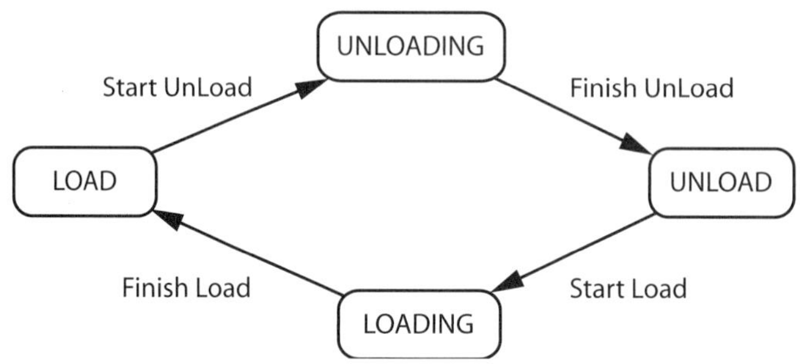

FIGURE 1.7.8 *States diagram.*

To manage this, the GP provides two alternatives:

Global Conception: The methods `Load()` and `Unload()` load and unload all the necessary information, respectively. The concept of *tile* includes all the information, no matter its type, that is located by the index. In the example, we load and unload both the portion of terrain *and* the fragment of texture, as shown in Figure 1.7.9.

Specific Conception: This uses simultaneously different instances of GP, each to page kind of information but updating simultaneously the navigation system (window, which is examined in following next sections).

To review, now we just need two steps to get the GP paging system:

1. Define the `GPindex`.
2. Implement the `Load / Unload` methods of the `GPtile`.

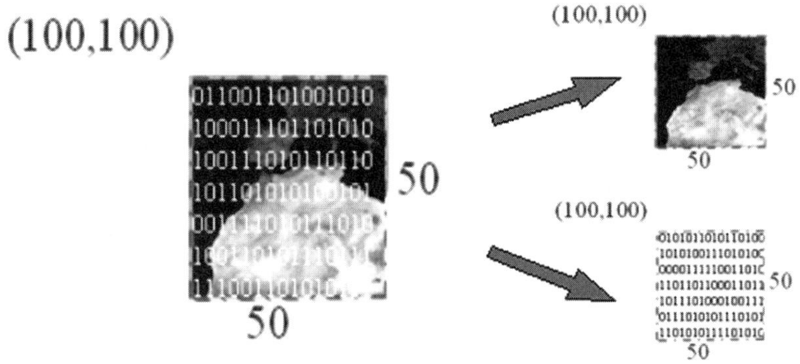

FIGURE 1.7.9 *Different information simultaneously in the same* `GPtile`.

The World: The Search Space

After discussing the index and the tile, we need to cover another very important concept that we referred to in several places earlier but did not fully explain: the search space. The search space, in the GP context, is the world where the paging blocks (`GPtiles`) exist and are located through the indices.

GP models this world through a class `GPworld`. This class contains all the created `GPtiles` that are in use. When a `GPtile` is needed, the `GPworld` creates it; when it is not necessary anymore, its information is unloaded and the `GPworld` destroys it automatically. This process optimizes the memory use and maintains in memory only strictly what is necessary.

When GP needs a `GPtile`, it makes a request to the `GPworld` through the method `GetTile()`, passing as parameter the `GPindex` of the sought after `GPtile`. At this moment, the `GPworld` will check if it contains the `GPtile`. If the `GPworld` contains it, this will return it, and if not, this will build it through its method `BuildTile`. When GP wants to load/unload a `GPtile` it does it through the `GPworld` with its methods `LoadTile()` and `UnloadTile()`. The GP user will just design a class derived from `GPworld` and implement the virtual method `BuildTile()`.

In the `BuildTile()` method, it is only necessary to build an object of the class derived from `GPtile`. The use of the parameter is not really necessary. The GP system will automatically assign to the created `GPtile` its corresponding `GPindex`. The user will only need to take into account the construction of the derived class, which can be a really easy task, as the following snippet shows, or as complicated as the system where GP is being integrated requires.

```
Tile* BuildTile(const Index& index)
{
return (new GPuserDerivedTile())
}
```

There is also another method that can be implemented by the class derived from the world class.

```
virtual bool IsValidIndex(const GPRindex& index);
```

This method returns true by default; its purpose is to let us know if a specific `GPindex` is valid inside this `GPworld`. This method is automatically used by GP. When GP wants to create a `GPtile` for a given `GPindex`, it checks if this `GPindex` is valid, and if the index is valid, the `GPworld` will create the `GPtile` through its method `BuildTile()` (explained earlier), as shown in Figure 1.7.10. If the index is not valid, the `GPworld` will not create anything, and the `GetTile()` method will return false. This validation of a `GPindex` falling inside the `GPworld` along with the check against errors works towards avoiding a subsequent wrong loading or other implications.

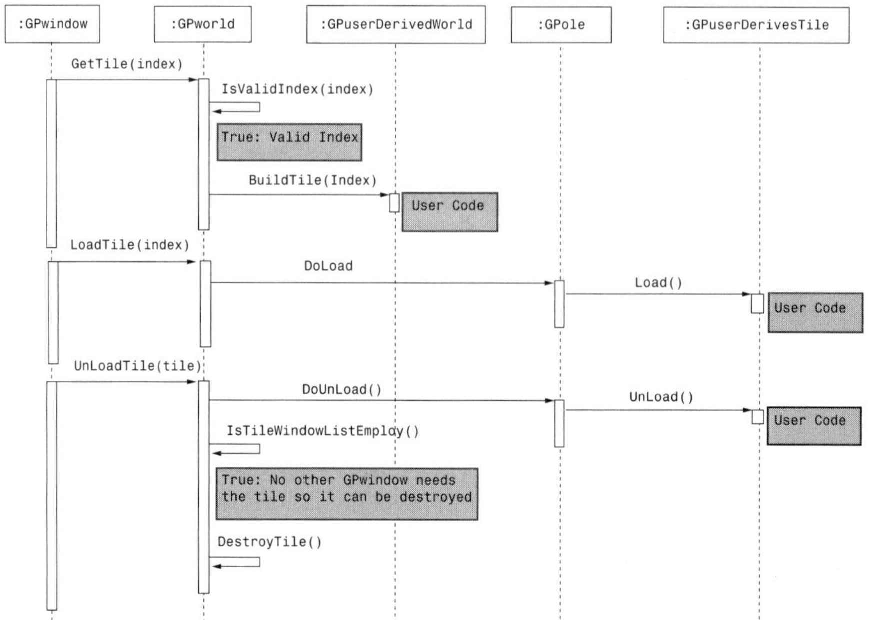

FIGURE 1.7.10 *Sequence diagram.*

A world can include `GPtiles` that contain all the necessary information although they are different types of information (global conception) or, on the other hand, many different `GPworlds` can exist in GP, one for each data type, that is, one for each instance of GP (specific conception).

GP is almost formed, and we are only at three easy steps:

1. Define a `GPindex`.
2. Implement methods `Load` / `Unload` of `GPtile`.
3. Implement the method `BuildTile` of `GPworld`.

The Window: Navigating in the World

Once we have our world (`GPworld`) and we can get any block of it (`GPtile`) just through its position (`GPindex`), we only need to know which blocks we want to load and unload. For this purpose, GP provides the `GPwindow`. With this, we can navigate around the `GPworld` using the `GPindexes` of the `GPtiles` without needing to know the information contained within them (see Figure 1.7.11).

The `GPwindow` has three main attributes:

`CenterIndex:` `GPindex` of the `GPtile` located in the center of the `GPwindow`
`Radius:` Indicates the number of `GPtiles` around the center `GPtile`
`GPtilesList:` Contains all the `GPtiles` of the `GPwindow`

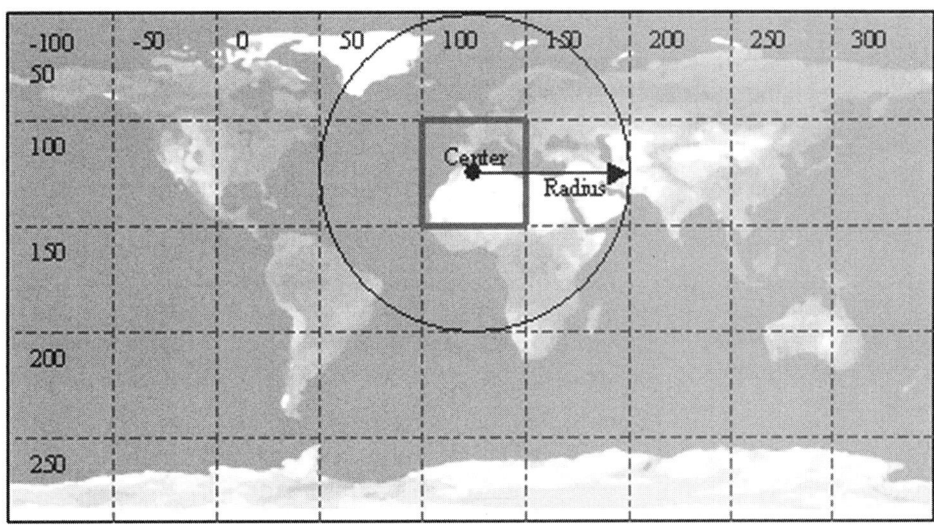

FIGURE 1.7.11 *The* `GPwindow`.

The initialization of the `GPwindow` is really easy:

1. Provide it with a reference to its `GPworld`.
2. Give the `GPwindow` a `GPindex`, which will position it.
3. Give it a `Radius`.

After this, GP automatically fills out the `GPtilesList`, taking the `GPindex` given as the center, using the methods `GetNextIndex()` and `GetPreviousIndex()` of that `GPindex`, and telling the `GPworld` to load the entire list, as shown in Figure 1.7.12.

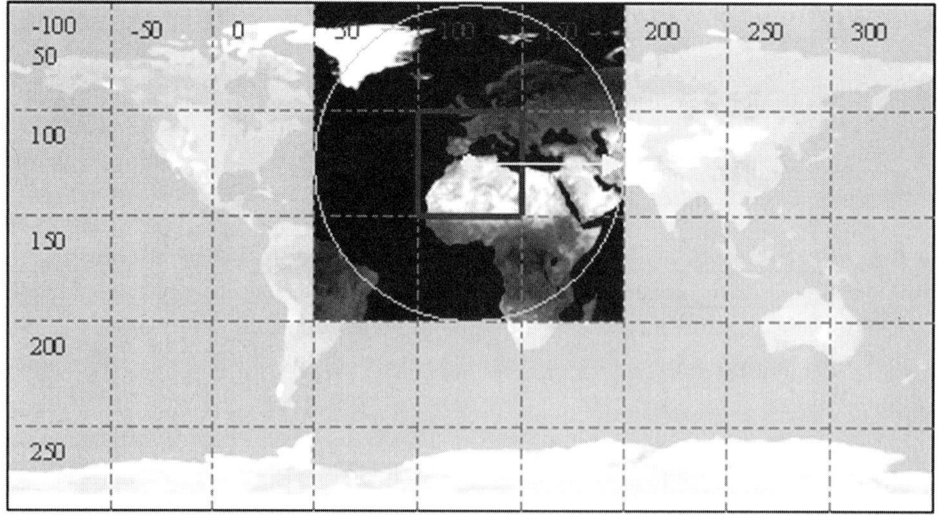

FIGURE 1.7.12 *Loaded* `GPwindow`.

To navigate, we simply give positions to the `GPwindow` through its update method, `Update()`. Every time this method is called, it will check if the new position is inside the center `GPtile`, meaning it is contained in the center `GPindex`. If the new position is inside the center `GPtile`, the `GPwindow` will not update itself; if not, we will take as a new center the `GPindex` that contains the new position, and the `GPwindow` will be updated with its new center and radius.

In the update process, the tiles list is modified, adding the new `GPtiles` that are inside the `GPwindow` and removing the `GPtiles that are not inside. The GPwindow` tells the `GPworld` to load the new ones and to unload the `GPtiles` deleted from its list. This process is automatic, transparent to the user, and completely independent of the type of information contained in the tiles, as shown in Figure 1.7.13.

If the radius is modified, the update process is the same, but note that in this case, the center remains invariable.

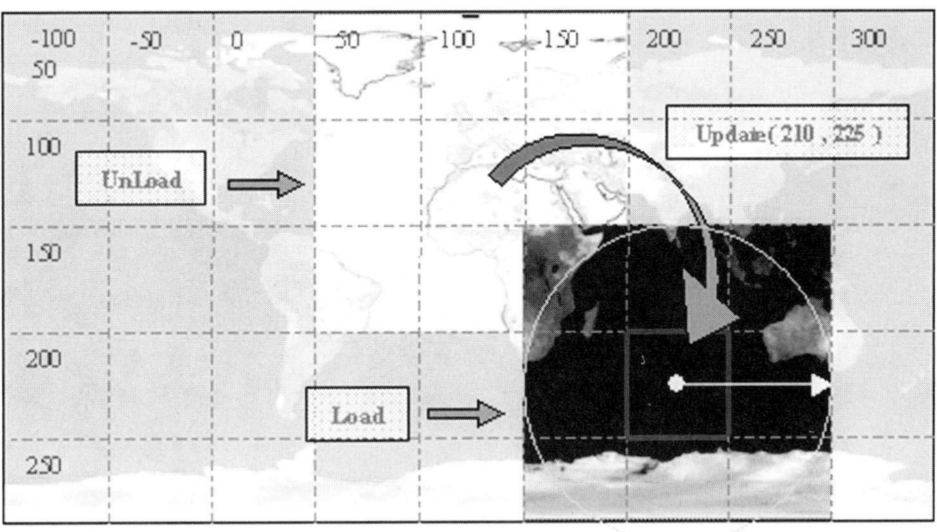

FIGURE 1.7.13 `GPwindow` *update process.*

Finally we are ready to use GP. Here are all the steps:

1. Define a `GPindex`.
2. Implement the methods `Load()` and `Unload()` of the `GPtile`.
3. Implement the method `BuildTile` of the `GPworld`.
4. Initialize the `GPwindow` by assigning:
   - The `GPworld`
   - A `Center`
   - A `Radius`
5. Update the position of the `GPwindow`.

Multiple Windows, Multiple Users

GP is multiuser in a natural and transparent way. The right term is *multiwindow*, because each user can have several `GPwindows`, and there can be several users at the same time (see Figure 1.7.14). GP takes each `GPwindow` as a different user. When a `GPwindow` calls to the `GPworld` for loading or unloading a `GPtile`, this realizes some easy checks:

`GPtile::Load()`: If the `GPtile` is already loaded, the world does nothing.

`GPtile::Load()`: The `GPtile` is unloaded only if there are not other `GPwindows` that need it. After unloading the tile, the world destroys the tile.

This entire process is transparent to the user, who only has to take care of updating the locally owned `GPwindow` (or `GPwindows`) when necessary.

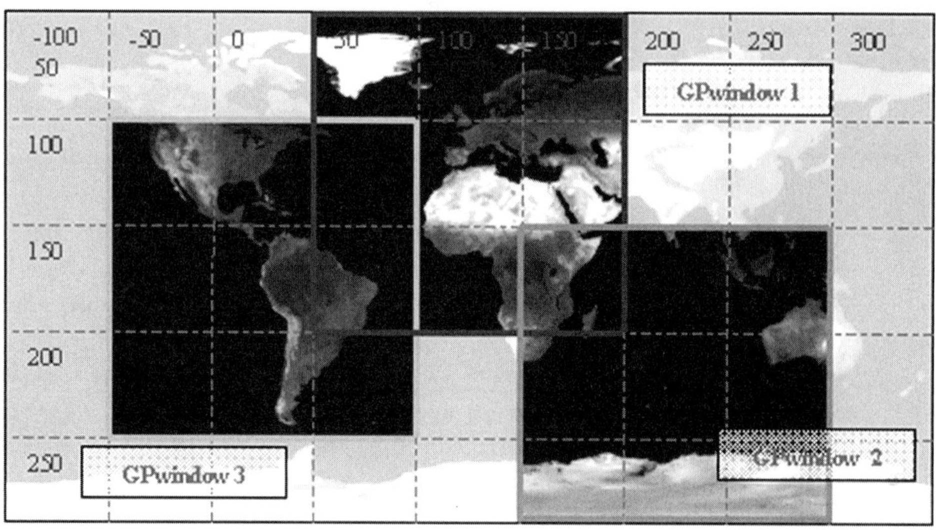

FIGURE 1.7.14 *Multiple windows, multiple users.*

Optimizing: Multithreaded Paging

An optimization of GP is to avoid the `GPworld` realizing the calls to the methods `Load()` and `Unload()` of the `GPtiles` immediately. The world will realize these tasks in a separate thread so as to avoid any interference of the load/unload processes with the rest of the system, and thus increase performance.

To do this, the world has a list of `GPtiles`. When a `GPwindow` calls to the `GPworld` for loading (or unloading) a `GPtile`, the `GPworld` adds this `GPtile` to the list and marks it as loadable (or unloadable). In the main loop of the load/unload thread, each element of the list is removed and processed.

Conclusion

This gem described a complete, multiuser general paging system (GP), capable of managing any type of information in an easy and efficient way, optimizing the resources of the system. The scope of GP is global, so it may be integrated into any other system that requires management of the loading and unloading of information.

The design of the GP follows some of the design suggestions of [Lakos96] and [Alexandrescu01]. The implementation of GP uses some of the suggestions of [Meyers96].

References

[Alexandrescu01] Alexandrescu, Andrei. *Modern C++ Design*. Addison Wesley, 2001.
[Lakos96] Lakos, John. *Large-Scale C++ Software Design*. Addison Wesley, 1996.
[Meyers96] Meyers, Scott. *More Effective C++*. Addison Wesley, 1996.

1.8

Large-Scale Stack-Based State Machines

James Boer

author@boarslair.com

In this gem, we examine a unique synthesis of traditional state objects with a stack-based management and queuing system. These combine into what might be called stack-based state machines. This mechanism is remarkably superior to traditional state machines, especially when dealing with traditionally messy logic flow, such as in deeply nested user interface screens. Stacked state machines also make it simple to handle other thorny state-related issues, such as how to implement a global state such as a game pause state without writing special-case code everywhere, or building intrinsic knowledge into the state about where it should return to when it is finished executing.

An advanced state-manager system is also demonstrated, adding functionality such as queued state commands, delayed state transitions, and centralized state timing functionality. States are, as expected, represented as hierarchical C++ objects and are designed to automatically handle details such as knowledge of previous and next states when entering and exiting, as well as stacking events (pushing and popping of states on top of other states). This system is an extremely effective way of managing large-scale state systems, such as the concept of a global application state (or game state) within a program.

Traditional State Machine Code and Associated Problems

One of the most fundamental tasks of any game is representing an internal "state" that represents the visual and logical elements that are currently presented to the user. Generally, games divide into two distinct sections of states: frontend user interface states and in-game states. For example, each user interface screen in the front end should likely be considered a unique state, since each screen has unique functionality as well as unique transitions to other states. Dialog boxes and other major screen elements with which the user must interact might also be considered unique states, although these have specific issues that will be addressed later.

Likewise, a game may have one to any number of unique global states within the actual gameplay. For example, a traditional first-person shooter (FPS) might allow the player to interface with a computer in the game. At this point, the game enters a different state: the rendering path changes, and the interface to the game is different. In essence, it is as though a completely different minigame is playing instead of the primary control mechanism. Figure 1.8.1 demonstrates how a standard state machine diagram might represent typical states such as these.

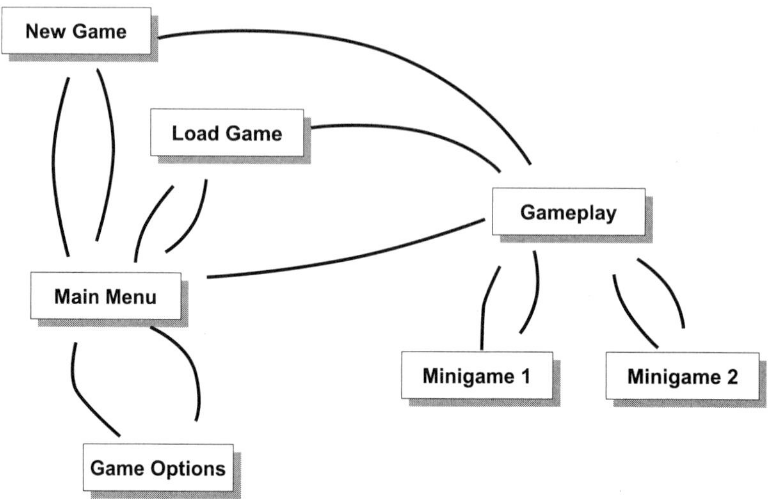

FIGURE 1.8.1 *A typical game-state diagram.*

It's fairly easy to create a simple state machine in C or C++ code. All you need is an enum variable and a switch statement, as demonstrated in Listing 1.8.1.

Listing 1.8.1 A Simple State Machine

```
enum GameState
{
    STATE_OPENING_TITLE,
    STATE_MAIN_MENU,
    STATE_RUN_GAME
};

GameState m_State;

//...
```

```
switch(m_State)
{
    STATE_OPENING_TITLE:
    // Do opening title code
    break;

    STATE_MAIN_MENU:
    // Do opening main menu code
    break;

    STATE_RUN_GAME:
    // Do main game code
    break;
};
```

Unfortunately, the real world is not quite so simplistic. A number of thorny issues often quickly arise. For instance, what happens if you need notification on the first update when switching states? A quick solution is simple enough: just add a counter that tracks updates and resets whenever the state changes. What about when leaving a state? Well, you could add separate sets of switch statements for entering, exiting, and updating states. How about if you need to change to a state at some specified time in the future? Again, you could add a timer with a delay element. What if you want to be able to queue up a number of state changes in sequence? By now, your simple C-style state machine is growing into a bit of a mess, with a number of variables, switch statements, and functions all lumped together. Although this C-style state machine may be highly functional at this point, readability, usability, and maintenance all become serious issues. Even worse, where exactly does one store data specific to any of these states? Since all you have are functions, it becomes much messier to actually create and use data specific to the lifetime of any particular state. To top it all off, this state machine is only usable for a single set of states; the code is not re-usable except to the extent of cut and paste.

Now, how about dealing with some even more fundamental problems? How exactly would you represent a state such as "pause game"? The behavior is unlike other states in that you probably expect it to return to whatever previous state existed before you paused the game. Likewise, many menu systems operate in a hierarchical fashion, with layers added upon layers. Using a traditional state machine to transition between these different user interface screens (such as when a confirmation dialog pops up over a user interface screen) is certainly possible, but may be less than optimal. Scott Meyers, a well-known C++ authority and writer makes the point if you find yourself writing code in the form of "if an object is of type TI, then do something, but if it's of type T2, do something else," you should stop because that isn't how it's done in C++ [Meyers98].

The intent of this article is not to extol the virtues of C++, but rather to demonstrate why object-oriented solutions are often vastly superior to their functional equivalents. As such, we will demonstrate how an object-oriented solution to the game state problem can vastly simplify your programming efforts and keep your code much cleaner.

The C++ Approach to Game States

While most programmers are quite used to the concept of designing classes based on physical entities (i.e., a `Weapon` or `Player` class), C++ classes can also be highly effective when modeling more abstract concepts, such as states [Gamma94]. If we standardize the meanings of specific functions, we can achieve a straightforward approach to modeling a single state with a class. Listing 1.8.2 demonstrates how this might look.

Listing 1.8.2 Modeling a Single State with a Class

```
class SomeState
{
public:
    void OnEnter();
    void Update();
    void OnExit();
};
```

Each function represents a specific event in the handling of this particular state. When the game requires this particular state to be activated, the class's `OnEnter()` function is called. This gives the state a chance to initialize, allocate, or activate anything necessary for this state to operate. On each update tick (update or render cycle) of the game, the class's `Update()` function is called to process any events that may need handling. Depending on your particular engine's design, you may or may not need a separate function call for doing any rendering work. Finally, when the state exits, meaning another state is about to become active, the `OnExit()` function is called to allow the state to clean up after itself.

This gives a nice home to any initialization, updating, and cleanup functionality required to represent this game state. However, almost as important is the fact that we now have a logical place to store any persistent data on which this functionality must operate. For instance, if this state represented a user interface screen, the class could contain all the various user interface elements that the screen must display and manage.

The State Interface Class

To ensure each state's compliance with this interface, and to be able to operate on different states through a common system, we can use a base state that acts as a standardized interface for all other states derived from it. Additionally, let's assume that we will add some functionality to the system: the names of states will be passed to the state object via these functions. Listing 1.8.3 shows what this class looks like.

Listing 1.8.3 State Interface Class

```
class IBaseState
{
public:
    virtual ~IBaseState() {}

    virtual void OnEnter(const char* szPrevious) = 0;
    virtual void Update() = 0;
    virtual void OnExit(const char* szNext) = 0;

    virtual void OnSuspend(const char* szNext) = 0;
    virtual void OnResume(const char* szPrevious) = 0;
};
```

You can see that when switching states, any state object will have easy access to the previous or next state, which can be useful when dealing with transition-specific code. You may have noticed the `OnSuspend()` and `OnResume()` functions and wondered what those are for. The next section will explain their significance. In fact, part of their functionality is designed to actually reduce the necessity of transition-specific code, which tends to complicate state machine design and maintenance.

Stacking States—Why Three Dimensions Work Better Than Two

In a typical game, it is not uncommon to have many different modes of gameplay represented by different state objects. As an example, a typical role-playing game may have a dozen different game states depending on whether the player is walking around outside, in a town, purchasing goods from a store, in combat, or playing a mini-game. At any point in the game, you would like the user to be able to bring up the same options screen then return to where the game left off. It may be desirable to leave the game rendering in the background, but in a paused state. Exiting completely out of the game state and coming back in is problematic in this case.

Another form of this problem comes up quite often in user interface screens. Often, it is desirable for a screen to continue rendering while a dialog box is drawn in front of it. There is no clean way of dealing with this in a traditional state machine, because we really do not want to completely exit the current state in order to enter a new one. Rather, we want to be able to suspend (or pause) one state while another supercedes its functionality, but then return to the original state and resume (or unpause) its behavior.

These types of issues can easily be solved with the concept of a state stack: *the ability to push and pop states on top of other concurrently running states.* This is what the `OnSuspend()` and `OnResume()` functions are for. When a state is pushed on top of another state, the original state's `OnSuspend()` function is called. However, the `Update()` function is still called each frame. Figure 1.8.2 shows how a state machine can work in three dimensions instead of in two through a stack mechanism.

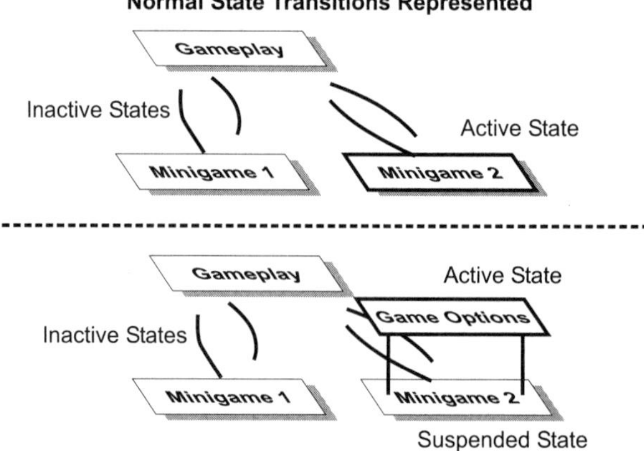

FIGURE 1.8.2 *Adding a third dimension to a typical game-state diagram.*

This gives the state two options. The first is, it may wish to pause itself when another state is pushed on top of it. This is a simple matter of setting an `m_bPaused` flag when `OnSuspend()` is called and clearing it when `OnResume()` is cleared. A simple check in the update loop could then prevent code from executing when another state overrides this state. Alternatively, the state object may wish to continue updating in the background, effectively allowing two states to execute in parallel. You may even wish to build this sort of functionality into the base class for consistent operation of all classes. For the sake of simplicity, we leave these options out of the base class interface (for this gem).

A State-Object Management System

You may note that we are emphasizing game states as opposed to other types of states that occur within a game, such as various states within a single AI entity or states of a UI widget. This is because an object-oriented state machine works best for more complex state systems, such as those representing the state of an entire game. The reason is two-fold. First, each state must be represented by an entire class; typically one derived from a base class (or implemented using templates) for reasons of polymorphism. This is a considerable amount of work to invest in a single state, and only pays off if the state itself is somewhat complex in nature. Second, these states must all be managed by an external system to be used effectively. Let's examine what such a state-management system would have to consist of. Listing 1.8.4 shows the interface to the `StateManager` class found on the accompanying CD-ROM .

ON THE CD

Listing 1.8.4 Interface to the `StateManager` Class

```
class StateManager
{
public:
    StateManager();
    ~StateManager();

    void Init();
    void Term();

    // Register a state object and associate it
    // with a string identifier
    bool RegisterState(const char* szStateName,
        IBaseState* pState);

    // Checks if the current state will change
    // on the next update cycle
    bool IsStateChangePending() const;

    // Returns the current state
    const char* GetState() const;

    // Get the state object based on the string ID
    IBaseState* GetStateClass(const char* szState);

    // Get the state object on top of the current
    // state stack
    IBaseState* GetCurrentStateClass();

    // Returns the size of the state stack
    int GetStateStackSize() const;

    // Passing bFlush = true will override any previous
    // state changing commands that may be pending.
    // Otherwise, state commands will queue and be
    // executed in the order of the calls made.

    // Changes the current state on the next
    // update cycle.
    void ChangeState(const char* szState,
        float fDelay = 0.0f, bool bFlush = false);

    // Pushes a new state on top of the existing
    // one on the next update cycle.
    void PushState(const char* szState,
        float fDelay = 0.0f, bool bFlush = false);

    // Pops off the current state or states to reveal
    // a stored state underneath.  You may not pop off
    // the last state
    void PopState(int iStatesToPop = 1,
        float fDelay = 0.0f, bool bFlush = false);
```

```
        // Pops all but the last state.
        void PopAllStates(float fDelay = 0.0f,
            bool bFlush = false);
        //—————————

        // Updates the state machine internal mechanism.
        // This function is called once by the main update
        // loop and should not be called by anyone else.
        void Update(float dt);
    };
```

****Insert CD Icon Here****

ON THE CD

In the interest in saving space, we're not showing the internal workings of the class (private data or function contents), but you can browse the source code on the accompanying CD-ROM in the files StateManager.h and StateManager.cpp.

As is apparent by the interface, our state manager associates states with simple string identifiers. We chose string identifiers for two reasons. First, strings are handy when printing the state for debugging purposes. Second, there is no reason to use enumerated identifiers for reasons of efficiency. We assume that state switching will occur relatively infrequently, especially if we use this system exclusively for tracking game states. Additionally, the use of strings to represent states is much easier to integrate with scripting systems.

The state manager easily and automatically handles problems such as queued and/or delayed states, in addition to allowing states to be pushed and popped on each other. This mechanism ensures a robust and uniform mechanism for handling all state-based transitions and situations. Additional functionality required by your game or engine may easily be added as needed, and other projects will be able to take advantage of these improvements if this system is utilized as a library (or engine) level component instead of a game-only component.

One of the benefits of standardizing on a uniform game-state transition and definition mechanism is that various library elements can represent entire game states rather than simple functional components. For instance, a library widget that represents an on-screen keyboard (a necessary component of many console games) can not only contain the widget element, but also the complete state code necessary to set up and handle all events that occur in this sort of complex screen. As games become more complex, developers need to think about ways of efficiently reusing larger and more complex components in order to reduce development time and avoid having to reinvent the same technology for every new title.

Conclusion

The simple concept of objects as states is certainly nothing new, even when combined with the technique of state stacking and implementing via a centralized state-management system. Unfortunately, all too often in the game programming field, these types of fundamental building blocks are eschewed in favor of an "evolutionary" design, meaning no thought is given to these systems before coding begins. This can, in the worse case, lead to nightmarishly twisted and complex code paths as your game evolves.

In truth, the detailed inner workings of the state manager are less important than the concept of how to organize large-scale states in your project. Whatever methodology or code you decide to use for managing these sorts of state-related problems—as long as your systems are able to overcome fundamental problems related to programming states in large-scale, complex software systems such as games—you will have a much easier time avoiding buggy, unmaintainable code in the long run.

References

[Gamma94] Gamma, et al. *Design Patterns: Elements of Reusable Object-Oriented Software*, 305–313. Addison Wesley, 1994.

[Meyers98] Meyers, Scott. *Effective C++*, Second Edition, 176–177. Addison Wesley, 1998.

1.9

CSG Construction Using BSP Trees

Octavian Marius Chincisan

mariuss@rogers.com

Constructive Solid Geometry (CSG) is a method that combines fundamental shapes, such as boxes, spheres, cylinders, and cones, to build more complex shapes, which may then be used throughout a game engine for a variety of applications. These fundamental shapes are generally referred to as *primitives*, and the operations that combine these primitives together in CSG construction are known as *Union* (+), *Intersection* (&), and *Subtraction* (_).

In this gem, we will see that CSG and Binary Space Partitioning (BSP) algorithms are actually quite simple and rely on no more than the partitioning and splitting of polygons against planes (and a little careful housekeeping). Additionally, we will step through the application of Boolean operations—such as those previously listed—between primitives, and even take the concept to the extreme to combine sets of complex results.

CSG Boolean Operations

Although classic CSG is not the subject of this gem, a brief explanation of all the fundamental Boolean operations is provided here for completeness.

The fundamental CSG operations between two solids are illustrated in Figure 1.9.1; where (b) is *Union*, (c) *Intersection*, and (d) and (e) *Subtraction*. To better illustrate the algorithms, the solids taken in the samples are reduced to simple 2D segments, where each line segment represents a face. All solid faces are facing outward; therefore, the contents of X and Y are considered *solid*. Exterior (outer) spaces are considered empty.

Union

The *Union* between two or more solids is realized by discarding geometry that ends up in solid space. In Figure 1.9.2, we have to discard faces C"C, CE, and EC'. A little later in this gem, all *segments* are referred to as *faces*, and all laying planes faces as *planes*. To perform a Union operation, all the faces of solid X have to be clipped by solid Y, and all solid Y faces clipped by solid X. The remaining geometry after the clip builds the final resulting solid is shown in Figure 1.9.3.

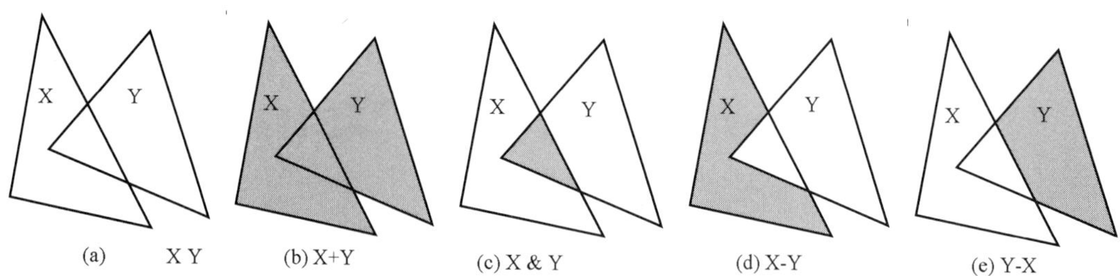

FIGURE 1.9.1 *Boolean CSG operations between X and Y.*

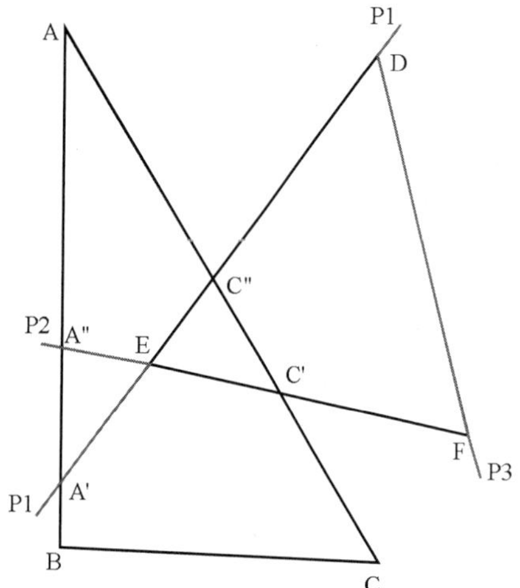

FIGURE 1.9.2 *Clipping ABC against DEF.*

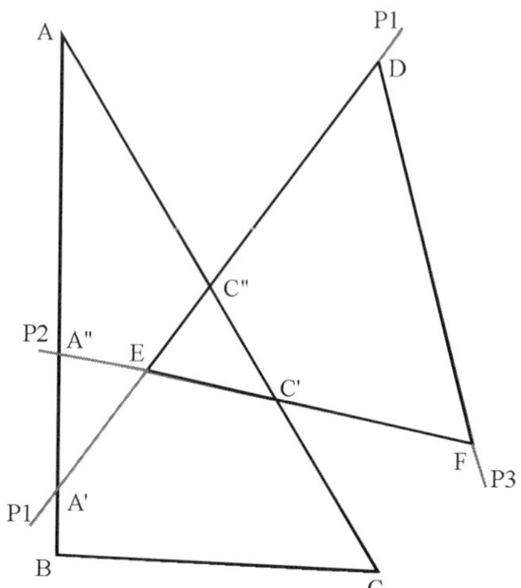

FIGURE 1.9.3 *X clipped by Y.*

We take one by one solid X faces (AB, BC, and CA) and clip them against solid Y planes (P1, P2, and P3) (see Figure 1.9.2). Clipping means we classify all of X's faces against all of Y's faces laying planes. The following function shows a *split-face-by-plane* function that is used in the clipping process. The function returns –1 if the face is completely in back of the plane, 1 if it is in front, and 0 if the plane splits the face. The `frontFace` and `backFace` variables carry out returned new faces. Further on, the clipping process drops off one of the two face fragments.

```
int Face::Split(Plane& plane, Face& frontFace,
                Face& backFace)
{
```

```
    Vertex vertex1 = m_points.first();
    Vertex vertex2 = m_points.back();
    float  fB;
    float  fA              = plane.DistTo(vertex2._xyz);

    for_each(vertex in m_poins)
    {
            vertex1 = *vertex;
            fB      = plane.DistTo(vertex1._xyz);
            if(fB > EPSILON)
            {
                    if(fA < -EPSILON)
                    {
                            float   t = -fA /(fB - fA);
                            Vertex midvertex = vertex1 +
                                              (vertex2-
                                               vertex1)*t;
                            frontFace << midvertex;
                            backFace << midvertex;
                    }
                    frontFace<<vertex1;
            }
            else if(fB < -EPSILON)
            {
                    if(fA > EPSILON)
                    {
                            float t = -fA /(fB - fA);
                            Vertex midvertex = vertex1 +
                                              (vertex2-
                                               vertex1)*t;
                            frontFace<<midvertex;
                            backFace <<midvertex;
                    }
                    backFace <<vertex1;
            }
            else
            {
                    frontFace << vertex1;
                    backFace << vertex1;
            }
            vertex2 = vertex1;
            fA    = fB;
    }
    if(m_points.size()==frontFace.size())
          return 1;
    else if m_points.size()==backFace.size()
          return -1;
    return 0;
}
```

During the clipping process, some of X's faces are split in two by Y's planes. If a face ends up behind one of P1, P2, or P3, it continues to be clipped until it has been clipped by all planes P1, P2, and P3. If that face survives, ending up being behind all

Y's planes, the face is dropped. The other faces, or fragment faces, are added to the final resulting solid.

We start by clipping faces AB, BC, and CA against planes P1, P2, and P3. AB is split by P1 in AA" and A"B. AA" is in front of P1, and therefore is no longer clipped forward by P2 and P3 and is added to the final brush before splitting on A' by P2. AB is added to the final brush result. A"B ends up behind P1, and is clipped by P2 and P3. Clipped by P2, A"B ends up in front (both ends are in front), and therefore face A"B is added to the final brush (and is no longer clipped by P3).

Next, face BC ends up behind P1 (both segment ends are behind P1). Because BC is in back, we send this face on to be clipped by P2, and BC ends up in front of P2 so it, too, is added to the final result solid (see Figure 1.9.3). One more face to go.

Face CA, clipped by P1, yields AC' and C'C. AC is in front of P1, and so is added to the final solid (see Figure 1.9.3). C'C is clipped forward by P2; as we can see in Figure 1.9.2, C'C is split by P2 in two faces, C'C" and C"C. C"C is the face fragment in front of P2 and is added to the final solid (see Figure 1.9.3). C'C", however, is clipped by the last Y plane, P3. C'C" is totally behind P3. Consequently, C'C" is dropped and not added to the final solid.

At this point, we have solved half of the problem. The next step is to clip the Y faces against the X planes (see Figure 1.9.4). We take the original faces (AB, BC, and CA) and their laying planes and clip faces DE, DF, and FD against them. We follow the same algorithm as before. Any face that ends up in back is clipped (Figure 1.9.5). If a face is clipped by all of P1, P2, and P3, that face is not added to the final solid (see Figure 1.9.4).

We start with face DE. DE is totally in back of P1 and is clipped by P2. DE is split by P2 in two faces. DD' is in front while D'E is in back of P2. DD' is added to the final result while D'E is clipped forward. D'E ends up in back of P3, and so is not added to the final solid. Following the same logic with EF, EE' ends up being dropped, and EF is added.

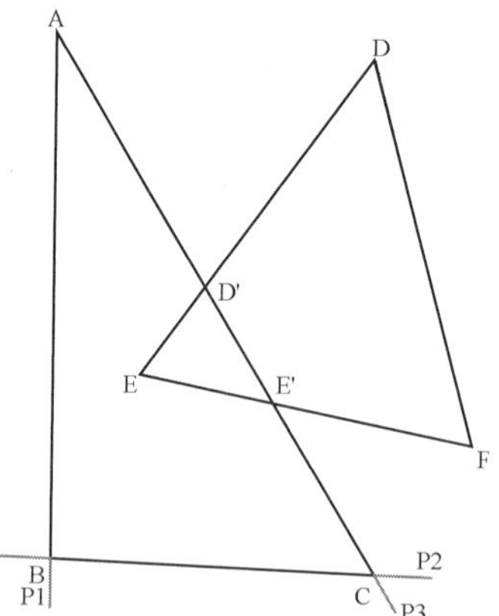

FIGURE 1.9.4 *Clipping DEF by P1, P2, and P3.*

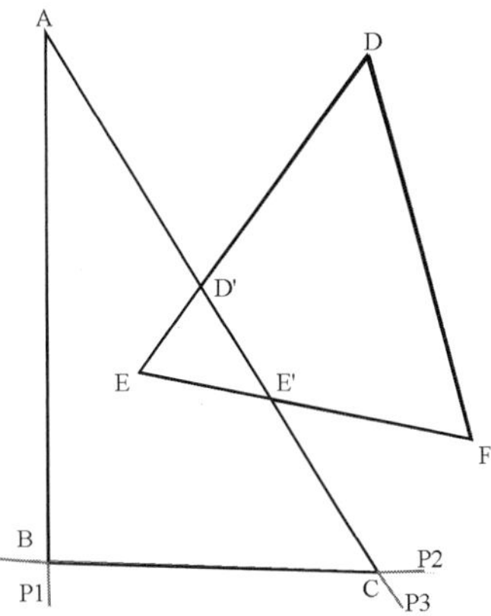

FIGURE 1.9.5 *Y clipped by X.*

All the faces that have been added to the final solid realize the union between ABC and DEF, as Figure 1.9.6 illustrates. Don't worry about the resulting solid looking a little bit sliced. AB is in fact AA' plus A'B (refer to Figure 1.9.7). When we analyze the BSP approach of CSG we are going to handle the unnecessary cuts due to the CSG operations.

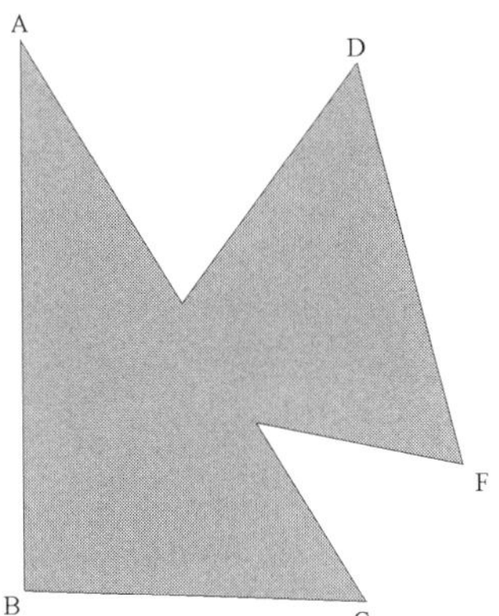

FIGURE 1.9.6 *The final result of the Union operation.*

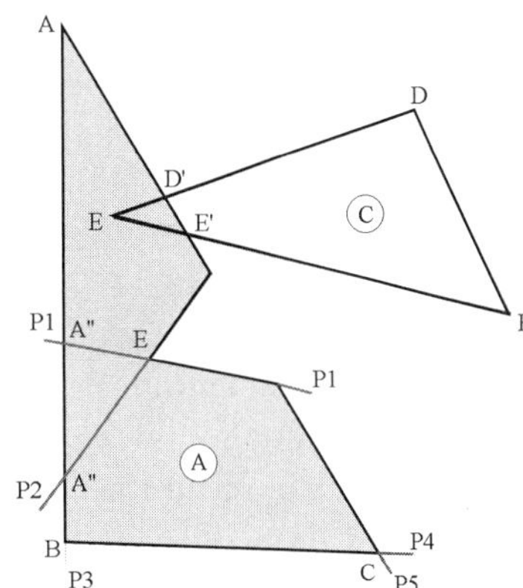

FIGURE 1.9.7 *Multiple CSGs.*

Don't be surprised, but at this point we have already managed to cover 90% of classic CSG construction. *Intersection* and *Subtraction* are no more than variations of *Union*.

Intersection

Intersection (Figure 1.9.1(c)) is performed by inverting the both solids, performing a Union on them, and inverting them back to achieve the final result. Inverting solids means reversing all faces' planes (plane normal and plane constant). By inverting the solids, they become empty and their surroundings become solid. Classic Union will eliminate any geometry ending up in solid AB, BC, AC', and CC" (see Figure 1.9.2) and DD', EE', and DF (see Figure 1.9.4).

Subtraction

Subtraction (Figure 1.9.1(d) and 1.9.1(e)) is performed as follows: we subtract B from A by inverting A, performing classic Union with B, and then reverting to get the final result. On the other hand, if we want to subtract A from B, we invert B, union reverse B with A, then revert back for the final result. The following table shows the mapping of operations to their symbolic equivalents:

Operation	Symbol
Union	+
Intersection	&
Subtraction	–
Reversed solid	!

Using these operators, *Intersection* and *Subtraction* may be defined as follows:

$$A \,\&\, B = !(!A + !B)$$
$$A - B = !(!A + B)$$

and

$$B - A = !(A + !B)$$

Why BSP?

BSP comes into the picture when one of the solids participating in the Boolean CSG operation is no longer convex. In Figure 1.9.7, we may want to subtract C from A. As we can see in the illustration, A is no longer a convex solid. If a solid has at least one of its faces' planes splitting itself, it is called *concave*. In Figure 1.9.7, the P2 and P1 planes are splitting A itself, therefore A is concave. Let's see how the classic CSG we covered in the earlier section fails to union A with C. We can assume we have already clipped all A faces and are now working on B faces. We clip face EF against P2, P3, P4, and P5 planes. Right away we can determine that EE' will be dropped because it is inside A. EE is behind P3 and is therefore clipped forward, ending up being behind P4, behind P2, but on front of P1. Being in front of at least one of P2, P3, P4, and P5, EE is added to the final solid. Allowing EE' to be part of the final result is wrong, however, because it is inside A. What do we do?

The solution is to split the concave solid into small convex regions and perform CSG operations between these regions. It is widely known that a BSP leafy tree solves this problem. Leafy BSP, or *Beam Tree*, helps us to partition any solid into small, convex regions.

The BSP

All you need for a good BSP is a good splitting polygon function and good housekeeping. For housekeeping, we threw in a node structure that caries a splitting plane and two references to front and back nodes, and a leaf structure that caries the BSP polygons. See Figure 1.9.8.

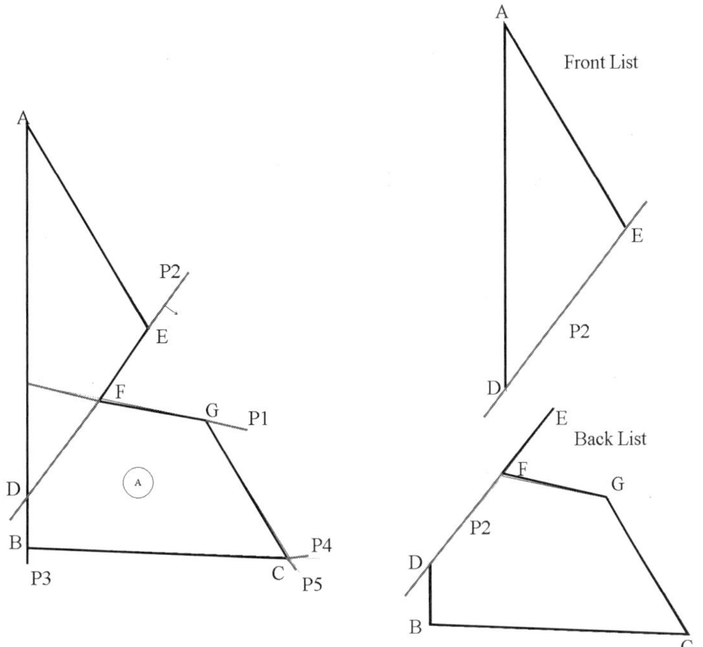

FIGURE 1.9.8 *Splitting A by plane P2.*

The implementation provided on the accompanying CD-ROM has the full Leafy BSP implementation. Here we will summarize the basic steps for building a BSP out of solid A, as illustrated in Figure 1.9.8.

1. We pick a random face to be root splitter. Let's say EF laying on P2.
2. We flag the face that its laying plane has chosen as being the splitter.

3. We split the solid by this splitter plane.
4. All faces or fragment faces ending up in front of the splitter are added on the *front* list. If a face is coplanar with the splitting plane, that face is partitioned by the plane's orientation as follows: if the normal of the face has the same orientation as the splitting plane, it is added to the *front*, otherwise, on the *back*.
5. All faces, or fragment faces, ending up in back are added to the *back* list.
6. We reference the *front* and *back* lists to the original splitter as front and back nodes.
7. We repeat the process for *back* and *front* lists starting at Step 1 but we always choose a nonflagged face for the next splitter as follows:
   - For the *front* list, we stop the recursive process when all polygons have been used as splitters or when front polygon's size is 1, and we create a terminal leaf node where we add all polygons from the *front* list.
   - On the *back* list, we continue the recursive process until no polygons are left in the list. At this stage, we create a terminal leaf node and flag it solid.

The BSP built by this algorithm has internal nodes with only splitter planes and pointers to front and back nodes. Figure 1.9.9 shows the final BSP tree for the solid A.

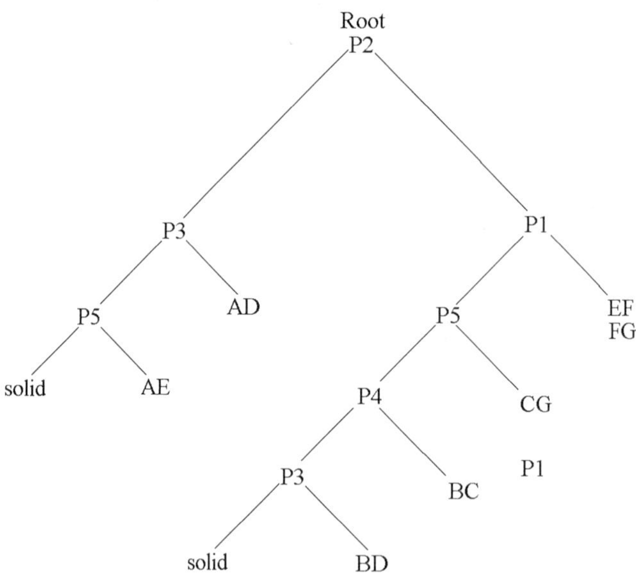

FIGURE 1.9.9 *Final BSP for solid A.*

Putting It All Together

Finally, we have the elements necessary to complete our CSG algorithm. Using the BSP, we no longer clip solid polygons against other solid polygons. Instead, we clip the polygons against the other solid BSP and vice versa. The CSG pipeline between X and Y looks like this:

1. Make X BSP.
2. Clip Y against X BSP and retain appropriate polygons.
3. Make Y BSP.
4. Clip X against Y BSP and retain appropriate polygons.

Clipping a solid with a BSP tree consists of partitioning all solid polygons with all partition nodes (the BSP tree's splitting planes). The clipping process starts at the root and continues down to the leaves. The following sample exemplifies the recursive process:

```
void Bsp::Recurs_Clip(int node,
                      list<Polygon>& polys2Clip,
                      list<Polygon>& finalList)
{
    BspNode       node = GetNode(node);
    if(node->IsLeaf())
    {
        if(node->IsSolid())
        {
            if(m_csgUnion)
            {
                return;
            }
            finalList << polys2Clip;
        }
        else
        {
            if(!m_csgUnion)
            {
                return;
            }
            finalList << polys2Clip;
        }
        return;
    }

    for_each(pSpPoly in polys2Clip)
    {
        Where_Is rp1 = pSpPoly.Classify(
        node->GetPlane());
        switch (rp1)
        {
        case ON_PLANE:
            if(SameFacing(pSpPoly,node.GetPlane()))
```

```
                {
                    backPolys.push_back(pSpPoly);
                }
                else
                {
                    if(m_csgUnion == FALSE)
                        frontPolys.push_back(pSpPoly);
                    else
                        backPolys.push_back(pSpPoly);
                }
                break;
            case ON_FRONT:
                frontPolys.push_back(pSpPoly);
                break;
            case ON_BACK:
                backPolys.push_back(pSpPoly);
                break;
            case ON_SPLIT:
                {
                    Polygon fp, bp;
                    pSpPoly.Split(node->GetPlane(),fp,bp);
                    frontPolys.push_back(fp);
                    backPolys.push_back(bp);
                }
                break;
            }
        }
        if(backPolys.size())
            Recurs_Clip(node->BackNodeIndex(),
                        backPolys, finalList);
        if(frontPolys.size())
            Recurs_Clip(node->FrontNodeIndex(),
                        frontPolys, finalList);
}
```

The polygons are partitioned into *front* and *back* lists at the root node. If we particularize our explanation, we end up dropping polygons DE, EF, and FD (see Figure 1.9.7) from the BSP root node (see Figure 1.9.9). All the polygons that make up C are clipped by the root node. Some of them end up being split, some not. All polygons ending up in front are added to a *front* list, all those ending up in back, to a *back* list. For the standard algorithm, all coplanar polygons with the splitting node planes are pushed onto the *back* list. There may be variations of how we process these, which depends on the current CSG operation. You can see this algorithm at work in the accompanying source to this gem. The *front* and *back* lists are forward clipped by P3 and P1, respectively. The process is repeated until the remaining polygons have reached the leaf level. When a list reaches the leaf depth, we decide which polygons we drop and which we retain to build the final CSG solid. If we refer back to Figure 1.9.1, here are the particular conditions for all enumerated CSG operations:

CSG Operation	Description
Union	Drop all lists that end with a solid leaf
Subtraction	Apply the formula !(!*A* + *B*) or !(!*BA* + *AB*), or slightly change the clipping algorithm without reversing front and back too many times (see the example source)
Intersection	Apply !(!*A* + !*B*), or simply drop all lists ending with an empty leaf

Conclusion

The CSG algorithm exposed in this gem covers two solids at a time, but it can be recursively adapted to perform complex CSG Boolean operations between multiple solids, as the accompanying example implementation demonstrates. The performance of the algorithm can be improved by eliminating unnecessarily splits, i.e., building the BSP tree out of polygons that are coming into contact with the other solid. This requires maintaining a bounding box for each face and testing the faces prior to CSG construction against the other solid's bounding box. The polygons untouched by the other solid's bounding box are simply copied into the final result. A second approach for reducing the splits is to track how many times a polygon has been split along with a reference of the polygon in each of its fragments. Finally, if all fragments having the same original polygon as a reference have survived safely, we replace the fragments with the original polygon. Now, go fire up the sample code, and enjoy the beauty of CSG!

Reference

[Rottensteiner] Rottensteiner, Franz. "Constructive Solid Geometry." Available online at *http://www.ipf.tuwien.ac.at/fr/buildings/diss/node38.html.*

1.10

Building Lua into Games

Matthew Harmon, eV Interactive Corporation

matt@ev-interactive.com

In the past decade, computer and console games have become less hardcoded and more data driven. The benefits have been numerous, from easier development to a whole subculture of user-extended products. In fact, when examined from a technical standpoint, many games now resemble a virtual machine or operating system more than a single special-purpose application.

The most powerful constituent of the movement toward data-driven design is undoubtedly the use of embedded languages. Simple data-driven design focuses on the externalization of hard game data: maps data, entity parameters, if/then triggers, and other arguments to the game engine. By using an embedded, or "scripting," language, games can also externalize logic. This has opened entire new worlds of end-user customization as well as produced sweeping changes in the way games, and game systems, are developed.

Unfortunately, creating an embedded language from scratch can be a significant undertaking. Even with a wide variety of tools available to assist in this endeavor, ending up with a complete, robust, and flexible system can consume many man-hours. Luckily, today there are several ready-made solutions that can be quickly integrated into a project. Languages such as Python, Ruby, and Lua are proven, reliable, and in heavy use. Other solutions exist, and some are even tailored specifically toward games, but those do not yet share the popularity of these general purpose languages.

This gem is designed to show how quickly and easily an existing embedded language can be added to a game system. The language of choice for this gem is a package that is being rapidly embraced by the game development community: Lua.

An Overview of Lua

Lua is a simple yet robust language with many features that make it attractive to game developers. It is already being used in many professional games, and many more are integrating it. By paying a visit to the Lua "uses" site (*www.lua.org/uses.html*), you can immediately see how the language has made inroads into the game industry. It's quite possible that game developers will look back at the 2000s as the "decade of Lua."

The following are some features that make Lua particularly suited to game development:

ON THE CD

- Lua is lightweight. A full Win32 library includes only a couple hundred KB of code. In fact, the entire demo executable on the CD-ROM is only 145 KB!
- Lua can run text scripts, or pretranslated byte-code files. Developers can expose some scripts, hide others, and even omit Lua's lexer, parser, and code generator. By doing this, some have reduced Lua's footprint to under 25 KB!
- Lua is a complete and surprisingly powerful programming language.
- Lua is suitable for "semiprogrammers." It is dynamically typed and includes automatic memory management and garbage collection.
- Lua is proven and reliable, with a very active user community.
- And, most of all, Lua is easy to embed and interface with C.

A Quick Program

The structure of a Lua program is quite straightforward. While a complete description of the language is beyond the scope of this gem, it is safe to say that most C programmers will quickly pick up the basics of Lua. Following is a snippet of Lua code to help familiarize ourselves:

```
– define a function ("–" signals a comment)
function EruptSequence()
    Camera.SetMode(CAMMODE_ORBIT);
    Camera.SetOrbitRate(PIOVER2);
    ent = Entity.Find("Volcano");
    Camera.SetTargetEntity(ent);
    end

– Run the erupt sequence every 20 minutes
while (1) do
    Script.WaitSeconds(20 * 60);
    EruptSequence();
    end
```

This code shows some simple Lua syntax. The bulk of the code actually involves calling functions from our game engine that we have registered with Lua.

Dynamic Typing

Lua is a dynamically typed language. You do not declare variables or even define their types; you simply start using them. For example, in Lua it is perfectly valid to say:

```
b = 24.5;
b = "Wait! Now b is a string.  How wild!";
```

Automatic Memory Management

Lua manages memory automatically. When a value is no longer referenced, it is made available for garbage collection. Thus, there is no need to specifically free any memory. Keep in mind, though, that holding references to unneeded objects will prevent them from being cleaned up.

The Lua State

There are a few Lua terms that warrant quick definitions, and the first is the Lua *state*. Essentially, a Lua state is a single operating environment for the Lua interpreter including the stack, execution state, global variables, and so forth. The Lua state is the object with which we interface when embedding the language into a game. Most architectures will need only one Lua state.

Lua Chunks

A *chunk* is a sequence of statements that are translated, and optionally executed, by Lua. Chunks can be thought of as programs, or fragments of programs, that are loaded into the Lua environment and made available for use. Chunks usually come from files in the form of scripts but can also come from static text strings within another chunk, or even directly from a command console. In the latter case, a chunk can be a single statement typed in by the user.

Interfacing Lua with C

From a game programmer's point of view, one of the most attractive aspects of Lua is how simply it interfaces with C. Before examining how to actually embed Lua and feed it with scripts, we will explore how to make C functions available to the interpreter.

Communication between the two languages is provided via a stack, which serves both as an insulation layer as well as a translation mechanism. Because Lua is dynamically typed, a single stack entry can represent data of any Lua type, so translation routines are provided to get the data into a format usable by C.

Calling C Code from Lua

The first task most programmers want to accomplish is to expose some functionality of their game engine to Lua and make it available for script-based control. This is done by registering simple "glue" routines with Lua. Say we want a Lua script to be able to control where our in-game camera is looking. We want the Lua script to look something like this:

```
– Point the camera at the volcano
Camera.SetTargetPos(100.0, 40.0, 230.0);
```

We first write a C-language "glue" routine to get the parameters from the Lua script to the C side, and then call our engine's camera function with those values. Glue routines take this form:

```
static int LuaSetTargetPos(lua_State* luaState)
{
    float  x;
    float  y;
    float  z;

    x = (float)lua_tonumber(luaState, 1);
    y = (float)lua_tonumber(luaState, 2);
    z = (float)lua_tonumber(luaState, 3);

    CameraSetTargetPos(x, y, z);
    return(0);
}
```

When Lua calls a C function, it pushes the arguments found in the script, in order, onto the communication stack. It then calls the registered glue routine for the given function, passing it a pointer to the `lua_state` in which the script is running. Remember, the Lua state is simply an object that represents the entire state of the Lua interpreter, including all data, the communication stack, and any functions you have registered with Lua.

The sample glue routine then attempts to pull three values from the communication stack, namely the camera's coordinates (*x*, *y*, *z*). Values are read from the stack using the `lua_toxxx()` calls, which convert the Lua values at the given stack offset to C types as requested. Note that we can arbitrarily address any stack position, and our first parameter starts at index 1, not 0. Next, we call our engine's camera code to make it all happen. Finally, the routine returns 0, which signifies that we have not pushed anything back on the communication stack as a return value to our Lua script.

Because Lua is dynamically typed, we must somehow know the types of parameters we are expecting and convert them appropriately. In the previous example, we need three floating-point values to represent the camera's position. Lua represents all numeric quantities as doubles, so while `lua_tonumber()` will convert the dynamic Lua value to a `double`, we still need to cast it down to a `float`. Lua includes many facilities for manipulating the communication stack, including the ability to check if a stack entry is of a given type. This allows the glue routine to present detailed errors to the user when incorrect or insufficient parameters are found.

Returning Values Back to Lua

Now suppose we need to let our Lua script query the player's current score. In Lua, we may want to do something like this:

```
– End the level after the player has scored 9 points
if Game.GetPlayerScore() > 9 then
    TriggerEndOfLevel();
    end;
```

Returning the player's score to the Lua script is accomplished by creating a glue routine that pushes a number value onto the communication stack as in:

```
static int LuaGetPlayerScore(lua_State* luaState)
{
    lua_pushnumber(luaState, game->playerScore);
    return(1);
}
```

In this case, our glue routine takes no parameters from the communication stack but does push one value onto the stack and alerts Lua by returning 1. In fact, Lua functions can have multiple return values, and it is perfectly legal for a C glue routine to return multiple values on the communication stack.

Registering the Glue Routines

Now that we know how to create glue routines, we need to register them with Lua to make them available to our scripts. The easiest way to register a set of functions is to use Lua's library management calls. These calls are provided to simplify the process of registering a group of related functions with the language.

First, we create a null-terminated array of function pointers and the symbolic names by which Lua scripts will recognize them.

```
// camera library glue routines and function names
static const luaL_reg cameraLib[] =
{
    {"SetMode",          LuaSetMode         },
    {"GetMode",          LuaGetMode         },
    {"SetTargetPos",     LuaSetTargetPos    },
    {"SetTargetEnt",     LuaSetTargetEnt    },
    {"SetOrbitRadius",   LuaSetOrbitRadius},
    {"SetOrbitRate",     LuaSetOrbitRate    },
    {"SetFov",           LuaSetFov          },
    {"SetWobble",        LuaSetWobble       },
    {"SetZoomPos",       LuaSetZoomPos      },
    {"SetPivot",         LuaSetPivot        },
    {"EnableShake",      LuaEnableShake     },
    {NULL, NULL }
};
```

Next, we call a handy Lua utility function that registers each function in the array with Lua.

```
luaL_openlib(luaState, "Camera", cameraLib, 0);
```

The first parameter is the Lua state with which we are working. The second parameter is the name we are giving to this library, and the third parameter is our array of function pointers and names. After this call, our functions will be available to Lua scripts, and their names will be prefixed with the library name. Thus, the C glue routine `LuaSetOrbitRate()` can now be called from a Lua script as `Camera.SetOrbitRate()`.

That's all there is to it. With just a handful of code, functionality of a game's engine can be quickly and easily exposed to Lua. There are many more sophisticated ways to link Lua and C, but they are beyond the scope of this introductory overview. Lua is not limited to integration with C either. Tools such as Luabind can also be used to help create relationships between Lua and C++ classes.

Embedding Lua into a Game

Now that we understand how to create a linkage between a game engine and Lua, we explore how Lua is embedded into a game.

Creating and Destroying States

To use Lua in a game, we must first create a Lua state and then load and execute chunks of Lua code. A Lua state is created as follows:

```
lua_State* luaState = lua_open();
```

When we are ready to shut down our game, we close the state:

```
lua_close(luaState)
```

This frees up all memory used by the interpreter and triggers any remaining garbage collection on code that has been loaded into the state.

Loading and Executing Code

Once Lua is initialized and we have registered our new functions as shown previously, it is time to start loading and executing Lua code. Lua provides support for feeding the interpreter with data from any arbitrary source. For this example, we will use some of Lua's helper routines that take input from files and strings. Executing a script from disk can be done with:

```
lua_dofile(luaState, "LuaScriptFile.lua");
```

This will compile and execute the script, if any execution point exists. If a file consists of nothing but function definitions, all the functions will be defined and added to the Lua state, but no actual code will be executed.

Likewise, the Lua code in a text string can be executed with:

```
lua_dostring(luaState, "a=14; b=7;");
```

As you can now surmise, creating an interactive command console with Lua requires only a few simple lines of code.

A very interesting feature of Lua's script loading is that any of these routines can take either text scripts or pretranslated binary Lua code. The Lua distribution ships with a pretranslator called luac that can compile scripts into a binary form. When this is done, applications can choose to omit the lexer and parser components of Lua, making the code overhead even smaller. This also gives developers the option of leaving some scripts available for modification in their original text form but others compiled, and thus hidden from prying eyes.

Code can also be loaded and translated without executing it, as follows:

```
luaL_loadfile(luaState, "LuaScriptFile.lua");
```

Calling Lua Functions from C

As shown earlier, it is often useful to load a script into Lua but not actually execute any code until a later time. A good example of this is the scripting of logic for game entities. Each class of entity may load a Lua script on startup that defines its in-game behavior. There may be separate Lua routines for setup, movement, and rendering. A simple entity's Lua code may look like this:

```
– functions for fictional "walker" entity

function WalkerSetup(walker)
    – our poor walker only lives for 1 minute
    timer = 60.0;
    end;

function WalkerMove(walker, elapsedSec)
    timer = timer – elapsedSec;
    if (timer > 0.0) then
        Walker.DoAI(walker, elapsedSec);
        Walker.UpdateControls(walker);
        Walker.DoPhysics(walker, elapsedSec);
        Walker.UpdateAccelAndPos(walker, elapsedSec);
        end;
    else
        Walker.Destroy(walker);
        end;
    end;

function WalkerRender(walker)
    visible = Walker.GetVisibility(walker)
    if (visible == 1) then
        matrix = Walker.GetMatrix(walker);
        Game.SetModelMatrix(matrix);
        Game.RenderModel(Walker.GetModel(walker));
        end;
    end;
```

When the entity class is initialized, it can use `luaL_loadfile()` to read and compile the script. Then, the entity's C code can call the Lua script routines as needed during the game loop. Calling a specific Lua function from C involves pushing the function, as well as all parameters, onto the communication stack and then calling `lua_call()`. An example of calling the walker's `Move()` routine is as follows:

```
– call this entity's Move script
lua_getglobal(luaState, "WalkerMove");
lua_pushlightuserdata(luaState, this);
lua_pushnumber(luaState, elapsedSec);
lua_call(luaState, 2, 0);
```

The first call pushes onto the stack a global value whose name is `"WalkerMove"`. That value happens to be a function in the script we loaded when the walker class was initialized.

The next call pushes our C++ entity's `this` pointer onto the communication stack for use by Lua. Really, Lua isn't going to use this value since it doesn't understand our C++ object at all. Instead, it will just pass this value right back to the C glue functions so they know which object pointer to use. To push our `this` pointer, we made a call to `lua_pushlightuserdata()`. "Light user data" is a special Lua data type that can be used when C code needs to give Lua data that it does not inherently understand. Most of the time, as in this example, light user data is used to hold pointers to C/C++ objects and structures.

Next, we simply call `lua_pushnumber()` to push the elapsed seconds since the last frame. Now that the function and all the parameters are correctly on the stack, we can execute the Lua code by calling

```
lua_call(luaState, 2, 0);
```

The second parameter (2) tells Lua how many arguments have been pushed on the stack, and the third parameter (0) tells how many return values we expect back. Lua will execute the entire function and, upon returning, the communication stack will contain any return values we expected.

Now we can call C functions from Lua and Lua functions from C. We're well on our way to making our game Lua enabled . . . or are we?

Real-Time Considerations

Notice that when we load and execute a chunk with `lua_dofile()`, or we call a function in a Lua script with `lua_call()`, the call does not return until the requested Lua script is done processing. This may be fine for some applications and architectures, but in many games this will not suffice. We need to be able to schedule events over time.

A Time Based Example

Say, for example, we want to use Lua to script the movement of a camera when a volcano erupts. We could call a `MoveCamera()` function in our Lua script every frame, and that Lua function would internally update timers and call out to different subfunctions as the timers trigger new camera states. This is messy, however, and we prefer a simple linear script that looks something like this:

```
– script to trigger volcano eruption
– every 20 minutes throughout the entire game

function EruptSequence()
    – start shaking the camera gently for 10 seconds
    Camera.SetShakeMag(0.002);
    Script.WaitSeconds(10);

    – suspend player control
    Game.SuspendPlayer();
    – set the camera to slowly orbit the volcano
    entTarget = Entity.FindByName("Volcano");
    Camera.SetMode(CMX_ORBIT);
    Camera.SetTargetEnt(entTarget);
    Camera.SetOrbitRadius(500.0);
    Camera.SetOrbitRate(0.003);
    – and jack up the shaking!
    Camera.SetShakeMag(0.01);
    Script.WaitSeconds(5);

    – ok, after 5 seconds ease up on the shake
    Camera.SetBankShakeMag(0.002);
    – and put the camera back in the player's eyes
    entPlayer = Entity.FindByName("Player");
    Camera.SetTargetEnt(entPlayer);
    Camera.SetMode(CMX_FIRSTPERSON);
    Game.ResumePlayer();
    Script.WaitSeconds(10);

    – after 10 seconds, turn shake off all together
    Camera.SetShakeMag(0.0);
    end

– This is the first executable code in the script;
– an implied main(), if you will
– Run the erupt sequence every 20 minutes
while (1) do
    Script.WaitSeconds(20 * 60);
    EruptSequence();
    end
```

This code first defines a function that handles our camera sequence. Then, the script calls that function repeatedly every 20 minutes. We schedule the various events using a new routine we registered called `Script.WaitSeconds()`, which simply delays for the given time.

This works great in theory, but if executing Lua code doesn't return until the code is complete, how can we ever expect to run our actual game loop? The answer lies in our implementation of the `Script.WaitSeconds()` function, and a Lua feature called coroutines.

Coroutine Support

Simply put, Lua's coroutine support provides a way for a Lua script to halt execution mid-stream and yield control back to the C program that called it. This is a form of cooperative multitasking, where it is up to the code itself, not the operating system, to suspend execution and transfer control back to the caller. This is known as yielding and can be done from either a Lua script, via `yield`, or from the C API via `lua_yield()`.

As you can imagine, our C implementation of `Script.WaitSeconds()` includes a call to `lua_yield()`, which returns control back to the game so we can render frames while the script is suspended. When our script management system has determined that enough time has passed, we call `lua_resume()` to continue processing where that script left off. To a game developer, coroutine support is one of the more attractive and important features of the Lua package.

Multiple Scripts

While it may be possible to get good results from using a single Lua script, it is far more practical to have many scripts running concurrently, waking up to perform actions as needed, or being called directly from C code on demand. Lua supports the concurrent execution of multiple scripts through a threading system.

Unfortunately, Lua's use of the term "thread" is somewhat confusing to beginners: that particular term carries with it an implication of preemptive multitasking, which is not the case in Lua. A Lua thread can be thought of as a child state of the main `lua_State` and can run its own script. A new state, or thread, is created with:

```
lua_State* newState = lua_newthread(mainLuaState);
```

Each new state shares all the global function and variables of the original `lua_State` but gets its own stack and execution state. Also, each new state can be independently yielded, allowing the system to manage many scripts, all potentially yielding for different reasons.

Thus, a common architecture for embedding Lua into games is to develop a script manager that creates a new child state for every script the system is running. The manager tracks why each script is yielded and resumes it as needed.

A Script Management Framework

Using what we know about states and coroutines, we can construct a basic script-management system to handle the details of creating and running multiple Lua scripts. The manager's most important job is to encapsulate the work of tracking and waking up any scripts that have yielded. We will allow scripts to yield for a given duration, for a number of frames, or until a given time. Additional conditions can be added easily.

This sample framework is implemented via two classes: a LUAMANAGER and a LUASCRIPT. While some details have been omitted from the text for brevity, a complete and functional skeleton is available on the CD-ROM.

ON THE CD

The Manager Class

The manager initializes Lua by calling lua_open() to create a lua_State. It maintains a linked list of running LUASCRIPT objects by providing a CreateScript() facility as the only way script objects can be created. The manager also includes an Update() function, which is called once every time through the game loop and calls down to each script object's respective Update(). This is where yielded scripts are checked for resumption.

A simplified skeleton for the manager object looks like this:

```
class LUAMANAGER
{
public:
                LUAMANAGER     (void);
                ~LUAMANAGER    (void);
    LUASCRIPT*  CreateScript   (void);
    void        DestroyScript  (LUASCRIPT*  s);
    void        Update         (float elapsedSec);

private:

    lua_State*  masterState;
    LUASCRIPT*  head;
};
```

The manager also registers a library of common script-management glue routines with the Lua interpreter, including those that allow a script to yield based on time or elapsed frames. From Lua, these routines look as follows:

```
Script.WaitSec(seconds);
Script.WaitFrame(frames);
Script.WaitTime(timestamp);
```

These routines are described in more detail in the following section.

The Script Object

A script object represents a single child lua_State derived from the masterState created by the manager. Each script object can run a Lua program as a (Lua) thread, yielding and resuming as needed. The script object maintains some additional data that lets us know why a script has yielded and when to reactivate it. The following code shows a simple skeleton of a LUASCRIPT object:

```
typedef enum
{
    YM_NONE,        // not yielded
    YM_FRAME,       // waiting for x frames to elapse
    YM_TIME,        // waiting for x seconds to elapse
} YIELDMODE;

class LUASCRIPT
{
public:
    void            RunFile   (char*    fileName);
    int             RunString (char*    buffer);
    LUASCRIPT*      Update    (UDWORD   elapsedSec);

private:
    lua_State*      childState;
    LUAMANAGER*     manager;
    LUASCRIPT*      next;
    YIELDMODE       yieldMode;
    int             waitFrame;
    float           waitTime;

                    LUASCRIPT  (void);
                    ~LUASCRIPT (void);
};
```

The `LUASCRIPT` script class gives us mechanisms to actually execute Lua code. `RunFile()` and `RunString()` feed the Lua interpreter from the given source. The script will execute until it is finished, or it yields.

As expected, the class creates and maintains a pointer to the new `lua_State` that it manages. However, as we will soon see, it is also important for Lua to know which C object owns a particular `lua_State`. To do this, we will store some data in a Lua construct called a table. A full explanation of tables is a bit beyond the scope of this gem, but think of them as arrays that can be indexed with any value.

To associate the address of our `LUASCRIPT` object with the `lua_State` that it created, we add an entry to a global table in the `masterState`. We use the `lua_State` pointer itself as the index, because we know it will be unique. We can then later retrieve the `LUASCRIPT` object pointer by using the address of the `lua_State` that is passed into our glue routines. This can be done when the child state is created:

```
// create a new state (thread) from the master
childState = lua_newthread(mgr->masterState);

// save a pointer to this script object in the global
// table using the new state's pointer as a key
lua_pushlightuserdata(mgr->masterState, childState);
lua_pushlightuserdata(mgr->masterState, this );
lua_settable(mgr->masterState, LUA_GLOBALSINDEX );
```

This sounds complex, but it is very much like storing the address of a window handling object in the `GWL_USERDATA` of a dialog box. This way, when a glue routine is called, it can determine the `LUASCRIPT` object that issued the call.

Yielding Routines

One of the keys to the script-management system is allowing Lua threads to yield for different reasons and resume when needed. To do this, we implement a few new functions and register them with Lua. For example, we'd certainly like to yield a script for a given amount of time with a call such as:

```
Script.WaitSeconds(seconds);
```

Following is the glue routine that implements this call:

```
static int LuaWaitSeconds(lua_State* l)
{
    LUASCRIPT*  s;

    // get a pointer to the C++ object associated
    // with this script
    lua_pushlightuserdata(l, l);
    lua_gettable(l, LUA_GLOBALSINDEX);
    s = (LUASCRIPT*)lua_touserdata(l, -1);

    // save our sleep time and wait state
    s->waitTime       = lua_tonumber(1);
    s->state          = YM_TIME;

    // tell Lua to return, yielding this thread
    return(lua_yield(l, 0));
}
```

When the glue routine is called from a Lua script, we don't know which C++ `LUASCRIPT` object is managing it. So, we must first retrieve a pointer to our object from the global Lua table where we previously stored it. Then, the number of seconds to yield are retrieved from the stack and saved. We also tell the object what type of wait we are performing. Finally, we call `lua_yield()` to suspend the script and return to C.

Now, it is simply a matter of checking the timer during the script's `Update()` routine. If enough time has elapsed, the script is resumed by calling `lua_resume()`.

By following this model, scripts can be made to resume based on time, elapsed frames, or even when a flag is raised. With some clever management, actions performed by one script can even trigger the resumption of other scripts. A complete working example of this simple manager can be found on the CD-ROM.

ON THE CD

Conclusion

This gem has shown that with very little work, developers can quickly embed the Lua language into their game. With a little more management, a game can easily take advantage of many of Lua's useful features, including running multiple scripts, yielding script execution, and resuming it again as needed.

To get a script up and running quickly, this article has glossed over many details of Lua that should be explored by any developer seriously considering embedding the language into their game. In particular, the concept of Lua tables and a more in-depth understanding of the communication stack are valuable to understand more completely. A visit to *www.lua.org* is the best starting place for anyone working with the language.

Lua has found its way into quite a few games to date, and readers are encouraged to give the language a try. If you are contemplating embedding a language into your game but have not yet begun the task, take a few hours and integrate Lua. They may be some of the most rewarding hours you spend on your project. You may even find yourself looking at your game code with a whole new perspective, thinking over and over: "How can I give more control of my game to Lua?"

References

[Ierusalimschy03] Roberto Ierusalimschy. *Programming in Lua*. Published by Lua.org, December 2003. *www.lua.org.luabind.sourceforge.net*

1.11

Improving Freelists with Policy Based Design

Nathan Mefford

nmefford@yahoo.com

Games are expected to be more and more dynamic every day, and our strategies for dealing with memory must keep up with that demand. Unfortunately, dynamic-memory allocation has downsides that limit our ability to treat memory as a truly dynamic resource. In *Game Programming Gems 4,* we were introduced to the concept of the *freelist* [Glinker04], a special-purpose allocator that solves the problems of dynamic-memory allocation by restricting itself to allocating objects of a single type.

In fact, freelists are such a powerful tool for improving allocation performance in games that they are appropriate to use in almost every project. Yet even with such a basic concept, design and implementation are filled with questions that have no clear answer. Should the list be allowed to grow? How should the chunks of memory be allocated? How should chunks and free blocks be tracked internally? Should objects be constructed and destroyed only once or with every allocation? Should chunks that are completely unused be returned to the memory manager? To accommodate different requirements, some projects end up with multiple freelist implementations. Other freelists wind up with complicated interfaces in an effort to achieve flexibility, making them harder for clients to understand and use.

Policy-based design allows the users of a library to provide the answers to such design questions, yielding classes that are flexible and highly reusable without sacrificing speed or introducing interface complexity. In this gem, a policy-based freelist is presented that can easily be configured with different behaviors suitable for different requirements and allocation patterns. In addition, we develop a default parameterization that improves upon the implementation in [Glinker04] by closely mimicking the behavior of operators new and delete, removing the need for applications to initialize nontrivial classes and reducing the per-allocation overhead to zero.

Overview of Freelists

A thorough discussion of the issues associated with dynamic memory management in games appears in the prequel to this gem [Glinker04]. Besides being slow, we are shown that allocation and release of memory from a general-purpose memory manager can cause poor locality of reference and—even worse—memory fragmentation. Additionally, most memory managers add some invisible bookkeeping overhead to each allocation. It may not sound like much, but even just 16 bytes of overhead per allocation can quickly add up to a megabyte or more of wasted memory with even a modest number of allocations.

A solution to these problems is then provided in the form of a freelist: a class made suitable for runtime allocations by restricting itself to allocating and freeing objects of a single type and, hence, size. You might question the usefulness of a memory allocator that is only capable of allocating objects of a single type, but it turns out there are many situations in a typical game where freelist allocation might be appropriate. Objects allocated by inherently dynamic effects like particles and decals are perfect candidates for freelist allocation. Freelists can provide a natural mechanism for recycling objects like vehicles and pedestrians in a sprawling world where it is impractical to allocate every instance of these objects up front. Nodes in common data structures such as linked lists and trees can also effectively use a freelist allocation strategy. In fact, the default allocator of the popular standard template library (STL) implementation *STLPort* [STLPort04] is a custom freelist allocator. Many modern design patterns result in a large number of small classes working together to accomplish a complex task. For example, applying the strategy, state, or decorator pattern [GoF95] sometimes results in many small objects being allocated that may be best managed by a freelist. In short, any type that needs to be allocated and freed frequently at runtime, and whose memory can be recycled many times, may benefit from allocation out of a specialized freelist.

While providing a freelist implementation, the previous gem rigidly hardcoded a series of design decisions resulting in a relatively inflexible library. For example, it has an immutable capacity and uses an additional list to track free memory blocks. Another example is the decision to store fully allocated objects in the list, avoiding calls to constructors and destructors on each allocation. This may lead to increased performance but at the expense of less-intuitive allocation behavior that requires the application to perform per-allocation initialization and cleanup. For many situations, these choices are entirely appropriate, and the freelist previously presented may be used as is. Unfortunately, the tradeoffs in that specific implementation ultimately limit its applicability across a wide range of requirements and allocation patterns. Some situations may call for a freelist that can grow and/or shrink its capacity, other situations may benefit from behavior that closely mimics operators new and delete, and still others may not be able to afford the additional memory overhead imposed by a separate list for tracking free blocks.

Instead of forcing a particular set of tradeoffs onto the user, we entertain the possibility of designing a single freelist implementation that permits its users to select the appropriate tradeoffs for their situation. Of course, this flexibility and reusability must come without compromising ease of use, safety, or performance.

Policies to the Rescue

There is a design mechanism in C++ that offers the promise of enabling safe, efficient, and highly customizable behavior: policies. What exactly is a policy in the context of C++ design? At a fundamental level, a *policy* simply defines an interface, which may include member functions, member variables, and type definitions. Any class that implements this interface is referred to as a *policy class*. A given policy can have an unlimited number of policy class implementations. Policies and policy classes by themselves are useless. Their power is realized only when other classes are designed to exploit a given policy. Classes that use policies and policy classes are called *hosts* or *host classes*.

With these basic definitions outlined, how do policies, policy classes, and hosts actually fit together, and what benefits do they give us? Game programmers are pragmatic people by nature, so I think we've reached the point where a few lines of code will help illustrate policies better than another paragraph of definitions and theory.

```
template <class APolicy>
class AHost : public APolicy
{
    ...
    void DoSomething()
    {
        ...
        APolicy::Foo();
        ...
    }
};
...
// Later on in client code
AHost< MyPolicy > hostInstance;
hostInstance.DoSomething();
```

It may not look like much is going on here at first glance, but if we look closely, we will see that there is actually a surprising amount of power, flexibility, and elegance contained in those few lines of code. In this simple example, `Ahost` is our host class, which has been designed around a policy named `APolicy`. Whenever an `AHost` is instantiated, a policy class that implements the `APolicy` interface needs to be provided as a template parameter, giving our host class access to a concrete policy implementation. When a call to `AHost::DoSomething()` is made, `AHost` defers some of its implementation to the policy class by calling `APolicy::Foo()`, allowing an aspect of `AHost`'s behavior to be configured by users instead of being hardcoded by `AHost`'s author. This open-ended ability to configure the behavior of a host class is at the heart of policy-based class design.

It gets even better. In the previous example, notice that the host class publicly derives from the policy class, which conveniently accomplishes the task of binding the host class to a specific policy class as well as aggregating any structure defined by the policy class. Because we have chosen to make the policy class a public base class of the host, the policy class can extend the interface of the host with public functions of its own. Complex policy classes can expose an enriched interface specifically tailored to their features and idiosyncrasies without requiring modification of the host class or complicating the base interface with functions and arguments used only by some implementations. If a user later switches to a policy with a more minimal interface, the compiler will catch any calls not supported by the new policy class, effectively enforcing design constraints.

This method of implementing policies also leverages incomplete instantiation. In C++, if a template function is never called, it will never be instantiated, and the compiler will never even look at it, except perhaps for syntax checking. In our example, this means that `AHost` can be configured with policies that do not even declare or define `Foo()`, perhaps because `Foo()` would be nonsensical for certain concrete policy classes. If `AHost::DoSomething()` is later called and `Foo()` is unimplemented, the compiler will immediately report the error, strictly and automatically enforcing both the policy design and the policy class's restriction. With this ability, host classes can take advantage of a potentially rich policy interface while still working with truly minimal policy classes, albeit with reduced functionality. Combined with the ability for policy classes to expose additional functionality, we have a truly powerful mechanism for customizing the functionality of our host class.

Using templates to bind the policy class to the host has a few other notable benefits. One of the biggest is that, because the binding is done statically, the compiler is capable of generating very optimal code, comparable to a handcrafted equivalent. Also, unlike classic interfaces, which consist of virtual functions, policy interfaces are more loosely defined. Policy classes need only conform to the interface syntactically, as opposed to overriding an exact virtual function signature. In our previous example, policy classes implementing `APolicy` are free to define `Foo()` as static, virtual, or neither. Finally, this method scales easily to more than one policy simply by adding additional template parameters and deriving our host class from each additional policy class. In fact, the real power of policy-based design is only realized with multiple policies, providing for a combinatorial explosion of behaviors with only a linear amount of additional code.

Now that we understand the mechanics of policies, how do we actually apply them to solve real design problems? A good way to start is to identify the high-level design decisions involved in crafting your class. Anything that can be reasonably implemented multiple ways or that involves making a tradeoff should be extracted from the class and delegated to a policy. Taken to an extreme, a host class may delegate all its meaningful design decisions to policies, in which case the host becomes a simple shell whose sole purpose is to assemble a combination of policy classes to perform the necessary tasks.

When decomposing a class into policies, it is imperative to strive towards policies that are orthogonal to each other. Orthogonal policies are policies that can be safely varied independently from one another. Non-orthogonal policies lead to complications in both the host and policy classes, which results in a class that is less type-safe and harder to use. An easy way to spot nonorthogonal policy decomposition is when two policies need to communicate with each other, or worse, when some combinations of policies result in an invalid host.

Unfortunately, this section has really only been able to scratch the surface of policy-based design. For much more information on both the theory and practice of using policies to enhance your C++ classes, I encourage you to read [Alexandrescu01] and [Vandervoorde03].

Decomposing the Freelist

Policies sound like a pretty promising candidate for achieving our goal of developing a reusable freelist that does not compromise ease of use or performance. Before we jump into creating a policy-based freelist, however, let's quickly review how freelists operate at a high level. The freelists that we are interested in pretty much all start out by allocating a relatively large chunk of memory capable of satisfying a large number of individual allocations. This large chunk of memory is then split up into memory blocks, which are cached for future retrieval. When an object-allocation request is received, a block of memory is popped from the list of available blocks, initialized for use as the given type, and returned to the application. If no free blocks exist in the list, a new large chunk of memory may optionally be allocated to repopulate the list of free blocks. Finally, when the application returns an object to the freelist, it is converted back into a simple memory block and placed back in the list of free blocks ready to be quickly recycled for a future allocation. With this high-level overview in hand, we can now begin to identify behaviors that should be split out into policies.

A good first step would be to separate out the growth behavior of our freelist. Some freelists may simply pre-allocate a single chunk of memory and not allow any future growth. Other situations may call for a constant number of blocks to be allocated each time the freelist is empty. The growth policy will give users the ability to configure this behavior, giving them relatively fine grain control over the number of free blocks a freelist will allocate and when. It will also provide a convenient hook for any custom behavior when our freelist has run out of free blocks.

It also makes sense to avoid hardcoding the method used to allocate and free the large contiguous chunks of memory that are later split into individual blocks. Some freelists might call `malloc()` to get an uninitialized chunk of memory from the heap, while others may allocate a fully initialized block of objects with `operator new()`. Deferring this to a policy will also enable our freelist to take advantage of custom memory managers without requiring a change to the actual freelist class.

Another responsibility that should be deferred to a policy is the manner in which free blocks are converted into objects of a specified type and back to blocks again. A freelist will be most natural to use if it fully constructs and destroys objects each time they are allocated and freed, respectively; however, this may be too costly in some situations. Customizing this behavior allows users to choose between various levels of performance and safety. More generally, this policy gives us a good place to perform any initialization and cleanup of an object just before and after an application uses it.

Finally, we need a policy that is responsible for storing the list of memory blocks that are currently available for allocation. There are a variety of methods for tracking blocks of memory, each with its own set of functionality, performance, and memory tradeoffs. This policy is slightly different from the others, because it is responsible for defining the structure of the freelist as well as aspects of its behavior. This ability to parameterize structure is one of the most powerful features of policies and is something that cannot be done with simple virtual functions.

It appears that we have now identified four policies that our freelist will use: growth, allocation, creation, and storage. Unfortunately, upon close scrutiny, the allocation, creation, and storage policies are not truly orthogonal to each other. Certain methods of storing free blocks may interfere with valid ways to create and allocate blocks. Some strategies for storing objects require a specific creation policy for some types of objects. Other nasty implied dependencies between these three policies also exist. Since a clean policy-based design is heavily dependent upon finding an orthogonal set of policies, we must solve this problem before moving forward.

The simplest solution is to combine the responsibilities of those three policies into a single policy that we will refer to as the allocation policy from here on out. Making this choice results in some tradeoffs. On the one hand, this new policy will have a more complex interface, which will make it more involved to author new policy classes. On the other hand, this new policy will enable more powerful and complex policy class implementations since it will control more aspects of our freelist. The fact that combining these policies enables implementations that would not have otherwise been possible is a good sign that they were never orthogonal to begin with. In the end, there is little choice but to consolidate them to avoid all the pitfalls associated with non-orthogonal policies.

So we will proceed with a freelist design involving two policies. One will be the growth policy, responsible for choosing how many blocks to allocate and what to do when our list is empty. The other is the allocation policy, which will define how our freelist allocates chunks of memory, partitions them into blocks, and converts blocks to and from objects.

Implementing the Freelist: Is That It?

With the policies and their roles identified, actually coding the freelist class becomes surprisingly straightforward. Applying what we learned earlier, the declaration of our freelist class writes itself.

```
template< typename T, class GrowthPolicy,
    class AllocationPolicy >
class FreeList : public GrowthPolicy,
    public AllocationPolicy
{
...
};
```

Let's start simple and look at our class constructor first. It needs to ask the growth policy for a number of blocks to pre-allocate and give the allocation policy a chance to prepare this many blocks for allocation. Omitting template parameters for clarity, this is how that looks in code:

```
FreeList::FreeList()
{
    unsigned int numToPrealloc =
        GrowthPolicy::GetNumberToPreallocate();
    if (numToPrealloc > 0)
        AllocationPolicy::Grow(numToPrealloc);
}
```

At its most basic level, the only responsibilities of a freelist are to perform fast allocation and release of objects of type `T`, so our freelist only needs two public member functions, `Allocate()` and `Free()`. Here is how `Freelist` implements them.

```
T* FreeList::Allocate()
{
    void* pBlock = AllocationPolicy::Pop();
    if( !pBlock )
    {
        unsigned int numAlloced =
            AllocationPolicy::GetNumAllocated();
        unsigned int growSize =
            GrowthPolicy::GetNumberToGrow(numAlloced);

        if( growSize > 0 )
        {
            AllocationPolicy::Grow(growSize);
            pBlock = AllocationPolicy::Pop();
        }
    }

      if( pBlock )
        return AllocationPolicy::Create( pBlock );
    else
        return 0;
}
```

```
FreeList::Free( T* pObject )
{
    if( !pObject )
        return;
    AllocationPolicy::Destroy( pObject );
    AllocationPolicy::Push( pObject );
}
```

`FreeList::Allocate()` requests a block of memory from the allocation policy. If that request cannot be satisfied, it queries the growth policy to determine how many new memory blocks should be reserved, if any, and the allocation policy is told to add that number of free memory blocks to its list. If the allocation still cannot be handled, `NULL` is returned; otherwise, the allocation policy is given a chance to make sure that the memory block being returned is a properly initialized object of type `T`. `FreeList::Free()` simply asks the allocation policy to convert the object back into a memory block, and then returns this memory block back to the allocation policy, ready to be quickly recycled in the future.

Notice that in all these functions, our `FreeList` host class is doing very little actual work of its own and is serving mostly as a framework to coordinate the behavior of its policies. This is typical of a policy-based design.

Earlier, it was stated that there were only two public member functions, which for all intents and purposes is mostly true. There are, however, additional overloaded template member functions that take a number of arguments of arbitrary type and pass them along to `AllocationPolicy::Create()`. As we will see later, these functions are used to make our freelist more natural and safer to use. There is also a template constructor that passes its single template argument to `GrowthPolicy`'s constructor. This can be used to conveniently configure a growth policy class at runtime. Thanks to the power of incomplete instantiation, the compiler will only bother to compile these functions if they are used, allowing policy classes and users to blissfully ignore them until they are actually needed.

That truly is all the code that is necessary to define our freelist and the policy interfaces it depends on. Once our policies were identified, implementing the freelist became straightforward and mechanical.

Choosing the Best Policy

Now that our freelist has been defined and our policy interfaces have been solidified, all that remains is providing some concrete policy classes.

Let's take a look at the relatively simple growth policy first. Its interface consists of only two functions: `GetNumberToPreallocate()` and `GetNumberToGrow()`. An example of a simple yet effective class implementing this policy might look like this:

```
struct ConstantGrowth
{
    ConstantGrowth( int pre = 16, int grow = 16 )
        : preAllocate( pre ), numToGrow( grow )
    {}
protected:
    int GetNumberToPreallocate() const
    {
        return preAllocate;
    }
    int GetNumberToAllocate( int unused ) const
    {
        return numToGrow;
    }
private:
    int preAllocate, numToGrow;
};
```

This class is ready for immediate use by `FreeList`. That is how easy it can be to create new policy classes, giving completely new and customized functionality to your host class. No arcane language tricks or special C++ prowess is required.

The interface for the allocation policy is slightly more complicated. It consists of interface functions to push and pop memory blocks capable of holding a certain type of object, functions to convert a memory block to and from that type, and a function to grow the capacity of the list. One such policy class that implements this interface is `PlacementNewEmbeddedLink`. Let's take a look how this class works starting with its class declaration and the data members.

```
template< typename T > class PlacementNewEmbeddedLink
{
public:
    ...
private:
    struct FreeBlock
    {
        FreeBlock* pNext;
    };
    FreeBlock* pFreeBlocks;
    std::vector< void* > chunks;
};
```

This particular allocation policy allocates chunks of contiguous memory and partitions them into blocks just large enough to hold an object of type `T`. The first four bytes of each memory block are then used to point to the next available block, and each block is pushed onto the head of a singly linked list. The `Grow()` function shows this in action.

```
void PlacementNewEmbeddedLink::Grow( int numBlocks )
{
    void* pChunk = malloc( numBlocks * sizeof(T) );
    chunks.push_back( pChunk );
    for( int ix = 0; ix < numBlocks; ++ix )
        Push( (char*)pChunk + ix * sizeof(T) );
}
```

The Push() and Pop() functions are responsible for maintaining these simple links as well as adding and removing blocks at the head of the list. Their implementation is as simple as you would expect.

```
void PlacementNewEmbeddedLink::Push( void* pBlock )
{
    FreeBlock* pNewHead = (FreeBlock*)pBlock;
    pNewHead->pNext = pFreeBlocks;
    pFreeBlocks = pNewHead;
}

void* PlacementNewEmbeddedLink::Pop()
{
    if( !pFreeBlocks ) return 0;
    void* pNewBlock = pFreeBlocks;
    pFreeBlocks = pFreeBlocks->pNext;
    return pNewBlock;
}
```

The major benefit of using the beginning of each block of memory to point to the next block of memory is that there is no per-block memory overhead. This can amount to hundreds of kilobytes of savings when compared to the overhead involved with many general-purpose memory managers. The obvious downside is that any data that may have been in that memory to begin with is overwritten by the pointer; including possibly a virtual function table. This policy's Create() and Destroy() functions solve the problem very elegantly while ensuring that our raw memory is converted into a full-fledged object.

```
static T* PlacementNewEmbeddedLink::Create( void* pBlock )
{
    return new( pBlock ) T;
}

static void PlacementNewEmbeddedLink::Destroy( T* pObject )
{
    pObject->~T();
}
```

Create() uses the placement new operator, which instructs the compiler to create a fully constructed object of type T at a given memory address. Since it makes no assumptions about the contents of the memory, the problem of overwriting potentially important data with our free block link is implicitly addressed.

Far more importantly, it makes freelists configured with this policy safer and easier to use. Because placement new invokes the object's constructor, this policy's create function naturally mimics the way objects are constructed when they are created by a call to `operator new()`. As an added bonus, defining templated overloads of `Create()` that pass arbitrary parameters to our class constructor becomes relatively trivial, allowing any public constructor to be called. Of course, the natural complement to initialization in a constructor is cleanup by a destructor, and that is exactly what happens in the `Destroy()` function.

Examining the result of configuring `FreeList` with this policy shows that we have met all our goals with flying colors. Allocating and freeing objects is certainly fast, consisting of only a few pointer operations plus a call to a constructor or destructor. It also has zero memory overhead per allocation. Most importantly though, using constructors and destructors to automate initialization and cleanup makes using our freelist a very safe and natural replacement for calls to `operator new()` and `operator delete()`.

Possibilities

If this were the end of the story, all the effort to split our freelist into policies would have been a waste. It would be great if the previously mentioned policies solved all our problems all the time, but unfortunately they do not. To illustrate just how versatile our policy-based design has made our freelist class, the following sections provide four separate allocation policies with varying behaviors and associated tradeoffs.

PlacementNewEmbeddedLink

This is the allocation policy described earlier. Its combination of performance, zero per-block memory overhead, type safety, and ease of use makes it a versatile choice. Due to all these positive factors, this is the allocation policy with which `FreeList` is configured by default. It is not without limitations, however. For one, freelists configured with this policy never return memory back to the global heap and do not share their free blocks in any way. Depending on your allocation patterns, a large amount of memory may end up just sitting in freelists as free blocks, unavailable for any other purposes. Also, in extremely performance critical areas, `PlacementNewEmbeddedLink` may not be appropriate for classes with expensive constructors and destructors. Because of its ease of use, however, this is the default allocation policy.

ConstructOnceStack

This allocation policy exactly matches the design and behavior of the freelist in [Glinker04]. The full set of that implementation's benefits and tradeoffs described in the beginning of this gem are encoded in `ConstructOnceStack`. The ability of our freelist to easily and perfectly emulate such a different implementation is a testament to the power of policies. This policy even exposes the additional function provided by the previous gem's freelist, `FreeAll()`, making the imitation complete.

CompactableChunkPolicy

A slightly more unusual allocation policy class is `CompactableChunkPolicy`. This policy behaves similarly to `PlacementNewEmbeddedLink` but with a twist. In this policy, each chunk maintains a count of how many free blocks are being used from that particular chunk. If two chunks have no blocks in use by the application, this policy will actually return the larger of the two free chunks to the heap. The tradeoff comes in the form of a significantly more expensive free operation. This policy might be beneficial in a situation where objects are allocated and freed in relatively infrequent bursts, or when many freelists will be instantiated, but many of them are empty at any given time.

SharedChunkPolicy

ON THE CD

Finally, the most exotic allocation policy class on the accompanying CD-ROM is `SharedChunkPolicy`. Internally, all instances of this policy class share a static set of freelists. This means that two separate freelists managing objects of similar size and configured with this policy will share memory blocks. If an application uses a large number of freelists that aren't always near peak usage, this can significantly reduce the amount of memory just sitting in freelists waiting for later use. The main tradeoff this policy makes is that objects allocated from a single freelist can no longer be counted on to be located near each other in memory, degrading locality of reference. There is also the potential for a small amount of per-object overhead depending on how this policy is configured. Some general-purpose memory managers actually operate this way internally, and this is almost exactly how the default allocator in `STLPort` works.

ON THE CD

All the allocation policies on the accompanying CD-ROM expose two additional member functions, `GetNumBlocksInUse()` and `GetPeakBlocksInUse()`, which can be used during development to tune your growth policy for optimal memory usage. Several growth policies are also provided, including one that will double in size, one that will grow linearly up to a fixed maximum capacity, and one that will ensure that each contiguous block fits tightly into a page of memory.

Of course, if none of these policy classes meet your particular requirements, changing behaviors is as easy as writing another policy class, and it can be done without changing one line of code in `FreeList`. That's the true beauty of a policy-based design.

Conclusion

The goal of this gem was to develop a freelist class that would be fast, easy to use, and flexible enough to be used in as many circumstances as possible without compromise. To meet these goals, we developed a freelist with a simple, consistent interface but open-ended behavior. In the end, we did not end up with a single freelist, but a highly configurable freelist framework. Not one but four different implementations are provided, each providing subtly different tradeoffs. Even if you are unhappy with all four of these implementations, it doesn't matter, because you can easily provide one that suits your particular needs without changing one line of the provided code, and most importantly, without altering the interface or core design.

Policy-based design was the key to achieving our goal. Even if you never use this freelist class, by reading this far, hopefully you've seen the power that can be wielded with policies. When it comes to developing flexible and configurable classes or even complete class libraries, this technique is simply unrivaled. It is a tool that every developer who strives for robust, reusable code should add to his toolbox.

References

[Alexandrescu01] Alexandrescu, Andrei. *Modern C++ Design*. Addison Wesley, 2001.

[GoF95] Gamma, Erich, et al. *Design Patterns*. Addison Wesley, 1995.

[Glinker04] Glinker, Paul. "Fight Memory Fragmentation with Templated Freelists." In *Game Programming Gems 4*. Charles River Media, 2004.

[STLPort04] STLPort Web page. Available online at *www.stlport.org*. September 20, 2004.

[Vandevoorde03] Vandevoorde, David, and Nicolai M. Josuttis. *C++ Templates: The Complete Guide*. Addison Wesley, 2003.

1.12

A Real-Time Remote Debug Message Logger

Patrick Duquette, Microïds Canada Inc.

gizmo@gizz-moo.com

For some years now, we have seen a rise in the interest for in-game, on-screen debugging panels. Although they are great and they normally do the job, they have the uncanny ability to clutter your game screen. Whenever we want to see more than the current frames-per-second (fps) stat counter, we end up losing a big chunk of the screen space. Consoles games are the worst, as their screen resolution is not very high to begin with, and to see something, we have to use a big font. It's hard to fit a lot of information on a 640×480 screen and still see something behind all this text.

There's also the trusted `OutputDebugString()`. But due to its single output pane and scrolling list type of display, real-time logging of frequently changing values is a nightmare. On one particular project, we used the output window on a regular basis for debug information. While it is true that the information was there, you cannot expect to easily find anything. This simply does not meet my vision of a productive debugging session.

For this gem, we will skip over the topic of log files as we try to focus on a real-time monitoring solution.

The Need for a Standardized Debug Log

With game projects now requiring 20 to 30 full-time programmers, it's important to have a standard way to manage and manipulate in-game debug information. If the data is present but in an unreadable format, it is almost useless. The same holds true for nonpractical data logging procedures. If we have too many steps to do before enabling data logging, chances are people will not use it.

Debug data should be presented in a concise, and more importantly, in a quantifiable manner. Having unrelated numbers scroll before us would not only give us a headache, but if we are not the person who created the logging function, we might as well not see the debug log, as the numbers will likely mean little to us.

Organize your debug data in related sections or pages. Having lots of unrelated data in a single page, as in the output window when using `OutputDebugString`, forces us to paddle through a lot of unnecessary lines. It takes time and might make us skip over the line we were looking for.

Debug pages should not be hardcoded, either. Although it might be tempting to hardcode the debug pages, we should restrain from this practice. There is no way we will foresee every debug data category while designing our debug logger, and as such, we should make provisions for dynamic page creation. Of course, some pages will most certainly appear in all our projects, but by letting the end user have the possibility to specify each page's properties, we aim to provide a convenient solution on top of a practical one.

Data Presentation: Do You See What I See?

Data presentation is one of the most important things. Making sure that the end user, be it a programmer, an artist, or a technical producer, interprets the results as we intended, is of utmost importance. Scrolling loggers are fine if we need to have a precise log of a value over time, but a graph might be better if we only need to see the variations over time. For variables where we only need the current values, a single line with the value being modified as needed is probably better than showing the last 500 values.

In a perfect world, the logged application should never experience any slowdown due to the logging process. That, of course, is impossible (since we do have to gather the information and send it), but we should aim for the smallest CPU and memory footprint possible. Asynchronous functions for sending the data should be used whenever possible. If the debug logger is not present, we also should not process the debug information gathering; this will give us the possibility to pause our logger if the need arises.

The logging solution should also support the same features on all the platforms on which the logged game is executed. Having a standard way to log the debug information, no matter which platform the game is running on, will alleviate the debug reviewer of having to learn different interfaces.

The Proposed Solution

The solution we will look into here is quite simple; a client/server where the debug console acts as the client and a cross-platform game module is the server. We could make the game module act as the client instead, but that would force us to tell the game module where and when it should connect. Having the game module act as the server enables us to connect to it from any station, at any time during the course of game execution.

How will the data be represented? We already know that the data should be divided into categories to help quickly find what we are looking for. But inside those categories, how are individual data segments displayed? Depending on the type and the needed visual representation, we have many possibilities:

Scroll: The standard representation where values are appended one after the other
Current value only: Only shows the most recent value
Graph: A quick visual representation of the evolution of the variable values over time

The Scrolling Representation

The values are shown via a standard `ListBox`, each entry mapping to a line. New values are added at the end of the list. No provision for sorting items is made, as this would slow down the insertion process.

To speed up the insertion process, we will preallocate a number of rows via the InitStorage `ListBox`. A context menu is present to help us manage the `ListBox` content:

Clear list: Clear the `ListBox` of all entries.
Copy: Copy on the clipboard the selected lines.
Copy all: Copy on the clipboard the whole `ListBox` content.
Save: Save the list content to a file.

Current Value

This representation is the simplest. It is done via a read-only `EditBox`. Having an `EditBox` instead of a static control will let us select the text for copy/paste operation using the standard `EditBox` context menu.

Graph/Datagram

`Graphs` are probably the representation that will give you the fastest clear view of what's going on in your game. When plotting data as received, though, one thing we have to watch for is the data going out of range. Two possible solutions to get around this caveat: give the user the possibility to change the range values and/or have the `Graph` invoke an adjustment when the data is out of range for an extended period. It is convenient to have both since manually overriding the `Graph` range will let the user see the previous value as he sees fit.

Many different `Graph` types can be incorporated in our logger, and a system to expand the graph library should be put in place early on. For an example of some `Graph` types, see Figure 1.12.1. The sample code has only one `Graph` type available, but improvements will be made available through the author's Web site [Gizz04].

While the debug data is categorized and kept together, it's important to let the debug logger show different data types on one page. The best data representation for one type of debug information might be different from others in the same category.

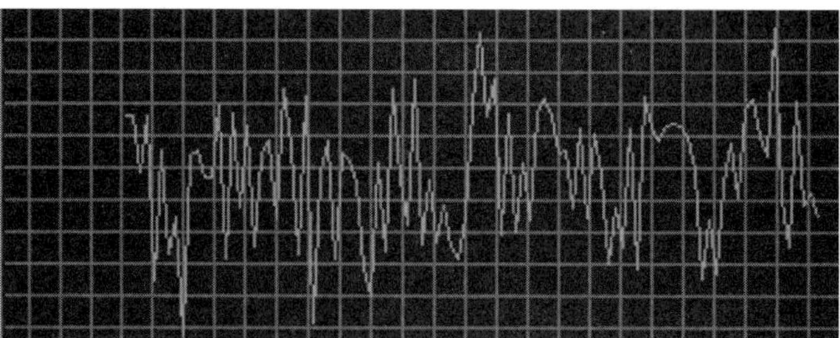

FIGURE 1.12.1 *Example of a graph from a logger.*

Putting It All Together

A `TabControl` inside a dialog-based window manages the displayed information. The `TabPages` are created dynamically from information sent by the debugged game.

For an example of a `TabControl` and `TabPages`, see figure 1.12.2.

MyListPage | MyValuePage

Name	Value
1st variable	123
2nd variable	weds
3rd variable	125.12

FIGURE 1.12.2 *Example of TabControl and TabPages.*

After starting the debug logger, we will try to connect to the logged game we want to log. Once connected, the logged game will send the `TabPages` name that it wants to register with the logger. These names will have an index associated, and only the index will be sent in further communication. Then it will send the list of the names it wants to have logged along with the type of representation that should be used and specific data if needed (such as a range, for `Graphs`).

Once it is connected and initialized, the logger will then start to receive the data. Each data packet contains the `TabPage` index, the `ValueName` index, and the actual data. A quick lookup tells us exactly which part of a specific page to update. The data representation class takes care of displaying the data as intended.

The Game Log Module

The `LogModule` is implemented inside a singleton. This gives us safe access to a globally available object. When the `LogModule` is created, it initializes the platform-specific network library.

`TabPages` and logged variables registration are done via one static function, which is called during the `LogModule` init phase. Enums are used for the `TabPages` and variables index. A macro is used to convert the enum member in the variable name used in the debug logger.

While the `LogModule` is considered as a server, in the code sample, it only accepts one connection at a time. No provision was made to let multiple loggers register for the `LogModule` debug info. Until the current connection is closed, the `LogModule` stops accepting incoming connections.

Because we specifically aim for a CPU-light logging system, the communication part is handled via asynchronous network function. This and network initialization are the two code sections that are platform specific.

Logging

The `log` function is a variable argument function to give the programmer using the debug logging system an easy-to-use system. It takes out the burden of having to format the debug info before giving it to the `log` function. That way, we still have the ability to send strings to the logger as when we were using `OutputDebugString`, only with more flexibility.

The entire debug log `LogModule` code is wrapped with an `#ifdef` barrier in order to take it out easily when we want to exclude the log information. The call to the `log` function is done via a defined macro. This will remove the need for further `#ifdef` wrappers in the game code as they will be defined to nothing when the logging system is not to be included in the build.

Possible Improvements or Extensions

The following is a list of possibilities for improving or extending the debug message logger:

- Scrolling representation should have the possibility to limit the number of lines that will be kept. Even a global variable that could be overridden in each list if the user wants, would be a step in the right direction.
- Let the user switch representation type for given debug information.
- Let the user modify the range of the `Graph`.
- Have the `Graph` modify its range when it detects that the data is out of bounds for a certain amount of time.
- Give the possibility to log to a file every received bit of information or by page. Every page should have a different file.
- Allow more than one debug logger to register with the `LogModule`.

Conclusion

In this gem, we presented a simple, extensible, yet efficient way to display our debug information while not cluttering the game screen. While not always high on the priority list, a good debug message logger/viewer can often save the day in crunch time where features are too often bugs in disguise.

Reference

[Gizz04] My Web site, *http://www.gizz-moo.com*.

1.13

A Transparent Class Saving and Loading Trick

Patrick Meehan

gems@tenaciousgames.com

A well-known method for minimizing load time is to pack structured data into a contiguous block for immediate use upon loading [Olsen00]. One limitation is that pointers (including virtual function table pointers) are not preserved, which makes it difficult to save and restore complex data structures or classes that include virtual functions.

The first part of this gem presents a simple way to preserve user-defined pointers and a trick for safely restoring virtual function table pointers. This means that game data may be freely described using classes, virtual functions, and pointers with no need to implement tedious per-class methods to serialize or restore them.

The rest of this gem tackles the design and implementation of a sample API. The implementation provides transparent class saving and loading functionality with few limitations placed on the end user. Details of the implementation are discussed in hopes that the reader will improve and extend it.

The Trick

The trick turns out to be a straightforward use of pointer arithmetic and the placement new operator.

Saving and Restoring User-Defined Pointers

If we don't want to deal with relative offsets at runtime, we can simply resolve them at load time by building a table of pointer remaps and storing it at the end of the file. Each entry contains the offset to the pointer that needs to be remapped and the offset to whatever the pointer remaps to. Both offsets are relative to the base of the file, so we can just add the address of the file's destination to resolve them.

Saving and Restoring Virtual Function Table Pointers

When you declare a virtual function in your class, the compiler adds a virtual function table pointer to the class's memory footprint. When the class is constructed, the pointer is filled with the address of whatever virtual function table is appropriate. Unfortunately, the virtual function table pointer is only valid during the session in which it was created. If you store a class with a virtual function table pointer in a file, the pointer will probably be garbage when you load the file back in during the next session.

So, to phrase the problem: how can we safely restore a class's virtual function table pointer when that class was constructed in a previous session?

The solution lies in the placement new operator. The placement new operator constructs an object "in place" using memory specified by the user. Unlike `operator new`, the placement new operator does not allocate any memory.

```
char rawMem [ sizeof ( Foo )]; // Raw memory to hold a Foo.
Foo* foo = new ( rawMem ) Foo (); // Construct a Foo in place.
```

If you want the class's destructor to be called, you will have to do so manually.

```
foo->Foo::~Foo(); // Explicitly call the destructor.
```

Calling placement new for constructing an object over memory already occupied by an object of the same type will ensure that its virtual function table pointer is valid. If we leave the constructors empty, we can restore objects saved during a previous session. The constructors are left empty to avoid reinitialization upon loading. An alternative is to create a separate constructor specifically for placement new restoration.

Implementing the FreezeMgr

ON THE CD

In this section, we move away from background information and actually go through the design of the implementation provided on the accompanying CD-ROM. It is assumed that you are a systems or engine programmer interested in a solution for use by other members of your team. The user to which this article refers is a game or tools programmer who will use (but probably not alter) the implementation.

It is hoped that you will read through this explanation and experiment with the sample, and go on to either write your own or modify this implementation to suit your needs. The sample under discussion is a limited version of an implementation, with some features combined and some glossed over to stay focused.

Usage Model

We want the end user to be able to create game data in whatever order pleases him. This includes classes, structs, and arrays of both compound and simple types. We also want the user's pointers to be automatically restored upon loading.

We need a way to keep track of data created by the user and to provide an interface for saving and restoring it. To do this, we'll use a singleton class called the `FreezeMgr`. The metaphor is that whatever data the user creates is frozen whole, in its natural state, ready to be thawed and used again later with no additional preparation.

For this reason, the key operations of the FreezeMgr are Freeze() and Thaw(). Since the FreezeMgr has to keep track of user-created data, its interface will also include methods for allocation and deletion.

As for the singleton design pattern used, we'll implement the singleton interface for this sample in the most basic way; see [Bilas00] for a more sophisticated approach.

From the end user's perspective, the process will be:

- Use the FreezeMgr to create game data.
- Initialize the data in whatever manner is appropriate.
- Command the FreezeMgr to pack all relevant data into a file and save it for optimal reloading.

Tracking User Allocated Memory

Whenever the user asks the FreezeMgr to create something, the FreezeMgr will allocate a memory block and store an internal record of it. This record includes the block's size and address. We'll provide the following method for allocating memory:

```
template < typename TYPE >
TYPE* FreezeMgr::AllocTyped ( u32 elements );
```

AllocTyped() is a template method that will use both malloc() and the placement new operator to create a user-specified type (or array of types) and call the appropriate constructor(s). We use malloc() instead of new because we want to control exactly when the class is constructed, independent of when its memory is allocated.

The record used to track memory allocations is called a MemBlock. MemBlocks are stored by the FreezeMgr in a map of addresses onto MemBlocks. The MemBlock contains a method that will check to see if a given address falls in its range. The method is:

```
bool MemBlock::ContainsAddress ( void* addr ) const;
```

In turn, the FreezeMgr contains a method that, given an arbitrary address, will return the MemBlock that contains the address, should such a MemBlock exist:

```
MemBlock* FreezeMgr::FindContainingMemBlock ( void* addr ) const;
```

Tracking User Declared Pointers

User declared pointers are tracked with the help of a template class called FreezePtr. Its template parameter is the pointer type. The only data member is the pointer itself.

Upon construction, FreezePtr will attempt to register itself with the FreezeMgr. If the FreezePtr falls within a MemBlock, a record of it will be stored in that MemBlock. Otherwise, the FreezePtr is ignored.

Determining whether a FreezePtr falls within a MemBlock is just a matter of calling FreezeMgr::FindContainingMemBlock().

Building a File

At this stage, we can accomplish two of our goals:

- We'll pack the user's data into a contiguous block of memory that can be loaded in one shot.
- We'll crawl through that memory at load time and patch all the pointers so that the user will not have to mess with relative offsets.

It follows that classes and structs will work right out of the box, as long as they do not include virtual functions (we'll cover virtual function tables in the next section).

Before we pack a file for the user, we have to think about how the user will want to access the data once it's loaded back into memory. Users will probably want to access their data through some class or struct that they themselves define. They will want to treat the file as though it has some root type through which they have access to the data. For example, if the file represents a game level, its type might be a `GameLevel` class created by the user, which contains pointers (`FreezePtrs`, of course) to things like spawn points, collision geometry, node graphs, etc.

The decision to ask the user to specify a root type suggests the method by which files are actually packed. The user will call `FreezeMgr::Freeze()` with a class of the root type as its parameter. The `FreezeMgr` will find the `MemBlock` that contains the class and pack it into the file. It will then recursively iterate through any other `MemBlocks` associated with the root type by walking along the `FreezePtrs` known to each `MemBlock`.

As we "flood fill" the network of `MemBlocks` connected by `FreezePtrs`, we do several things:

- Add each `MemBlock` encountered to a list of blocks to be included in the freeze
- Compute the block's location in the contiguous packed block
- Compute each `FreezePtr`'s value as an offset into the contiguous block
- Add each `FreezePtr` to a list of pointers to be included in the freeze

During the process, we assume that each `FreezePtr` points into valid memory tracked by `MemBlocks` or to `NULL`. In other words, if the pointer is not `NULL`, a call to `FreezeMgr::FindContainingMemBlock()` should always return a valid `MemBlock`.

Once the list of `MemBlocks` has been built, we scan through it and pack each block into the file. We then write out the table of pointers. Each entry in the table contains the offset of the pointer and the offset of the contents of the pointer.

The process for thawing a file, as intended, is simple and fast.

To load a file, we allocate a chunk of memory large enough to hold the contiguous block before pulling it in with a single read. Patching the pointers is then accomplished by scanning through the pointer remap table and performing pointer arithmetic.

Note that pointers are not sensitive about the order in which they are remapped, so sort the remap table (prior to output) in whatever order will most improve performance.

Restoring Virtual Function Table Pointers

As discussed earlier, we can use placement new to restore virtual function table pointers. For this reason, the `FreezeMgr` is also a factory class that can look at an instance of a class and restore it using placement new. You may use a discrete factory class; for the sake of our discussion we'll package that functionality into the `FreezeMgr`.

For this implementation to work, any class that contains virtual functions must inherit an abstract base class that will identify it. The class has only one data member, a 32-bit type identification number. We'll call the base class `Freezable`, though this is a bit of a misnomer, because it is used to qualify only a subset of what can actually be frozen.

A `Freezable` may be allocated whole or may be embedded in another class. Like the `FreezePtr`, `Freezables` are tracked by the `MemBlocks` that contain them.

To construct `Freezables` upon loading, the `FreezeMgr` keeps an internal table of abstract creator classes. Each type of `Freezable` must have its own concrete creator class. The abstract creator is called `AbstractCreator`. A template class called `ConcreteCreator<>` is provided to save users the trouble of having to write a creator for each `Freezable`. The method used to register a user-defined class is also a template:

```
template <typename TYPE>
void FreezeMgr::RegisterFreezableType(void);
```

This function declares a static `ConcreteCreator<TYPE>` and assigns it to the next sequentially available `AbstractCreator` table entry. The index of the table entry then becomes the 32-bit identification number for that class. We could use a map to convert user-defined identifiers into table entries, but it is more efficient to directly index into the table as we inspect the type of each `Freezable` at load time. The trade-off is that for the data created by the `FreezeMgr` to remain valid from session to session, the order in which types are registered must be respected as new types are added.

To make sure the right 32-bit type identifier is mapped to a given instance of a `Freezable`, we ask the user to overload a pure virtual method in `Freezable`:

```
char const* Freezable::GetClassName(void) const;
```

To figure out the identifier for a given class, the `FreezeMgr` keeps a map of class names onto identifiers. Any `Freezable` may determine its identifier by calling `GetClassName()` and using that name to see if the class has been assigned an identifier.

There are more robust and useful ways to deal with runtime type information [Wakeling01] that should be explored to replace the way it's been done here.

Since the `Freezable`'s constructor will be called during the thaw, the user must take care not to reinitialize its members. For example, if a `Freezable` initializes its members to `NULL` at construction, the members will be reinitialized to `NULL` during the thaw.

We could work around the problem of reinitialization by providing an alternative constructor that only gets called by placement new during the thaw. The problem is that there is no way to extend this to the `Freezable`'s members unless the user implements an alternative constructor for each member and sets up explicit calls to it down the constructor chain. That is a lot of hassle for what will probably amount to a bunch of empty constructors. A more pragmatic approach is to expose the problem from the start (so the user will be aware of it) and ask the user to check for reinitialization by calling `FreezeMgr::IsThawing()`.

To review the limitations placed on the end user:

- The user must derive all classes containing virtual functions from `Freezable`.
- The user must overload `GetClassName()`.
- The user must declare all `Freezable` types before using the `FreezeMgr`.
- The user must not change the order in which `Freezable` types are declared.
- The user should either do nothing in the `Freezable`'s constructor or its member class constructors, or should check to see if a thaw is in progress and only perform initialization if there is not.

To manage and freeze the user's classes:

- Track the `Freezables` as they are created.
- After all the `MemBlocks` and `FreezePtrs` have remapped, remap the `Freezables`.
- Write out the `FreezePtr` remap table.
- Write out a table of `Freezables`. This table just contains the relative offset of each `Freezable`.

To thaw from a file:

- Read in the contiguous data block.
- Patch all the pointers.
- Find each `Freezable` in memory and determine its 32-bit type number.
- Use the type number to index the table of `AbstractCreators`.
- Pass the `Freezable` to the `AbstractCreator::Construct()`.

A Few More Features

The `FreezeMgr` is still not quite ready for prime time. More features are necessary for it to be useful.

Serialized Data

There remain cases where we want to approach parts of our data as serialized streams. To support this, we add two virtual methods to `Freezable`:

```
virtual void Freezable::SerializeIn ( FILE* file );
virtual void Freezable::SerializeOut ( FILE* file );
```

The user may add serialized data to a Freezable class by overloading these methods. As would be expected, `SerializeOut()` is called during the freeze, and `SerializeIn()` is called during the thaw. In both cases, the user is given direct control over the file. The `FreezeMgr` remembers how many bytes (if any) are written by `SerializeOut()`, so `SerializeIn()` must read the same number of bytes.

Loading in Edit Mode

Up to this point we've assumed that the user will create and modify game data in one session and will load it in read-only mode for use in another session.

Implementing an edit or read-write mode option is a matter of rebuilding the `FreezeMgr`'s internal tables, including the memory block table and the pointer remapping table upon load. Once this is done, the user is free to augment or modify the data and then refreeze it.

This extension to `FreezeMgr` may dovetail with existing schemes for allowing players to save their games at any time [Brownlow02].

File References

You may give users the option of initializing `FreezePtrs` in such a way that they will resolve into files when loaded:

```
mFoo.PointAtFile ( "bar.bin" ); // mFoo is a FreezePtr
```

When the file containing `mFoo` is loaded, the resource manager will automatically load in "bar.bin" and point `mFoo` at it. To package this in a standalone sample implementation would either require ties to a resource manager [Boer00] or a callback interface, both of which are outside the scope of this gem. Nonetheless, it is a useful feature and you should consider implementing it.

Using the Sample Implementation

You can use the provided sample as is, but you should try reworking it to suit your own needs. It was composed for this gem as a standalone version of the utility used by the author. It is offered as is. There is no warranty for commercial use and no plans to support it, so it is recommended that you familiarize yourself with it, understand its flaws, and create exciting new flaws of your own. The `FreezeMgr` can become a key part of your project, so please accept this disclaimer and give your own implementation the careful attention it deserves.

For a variety of design reasons, the mechanism that calls the destructors of thawed classes is not included. This will be an issue if you use the serialized data feature, as you will probably be allocating memory. For this reason, you will have to decide how you want to handle freeing the memory allocated by serialized classes.

The FreezePtr Template Class

The `FreezePtr` automatically registers itself with the `FreezeMgr` upon construction. Just include it in your data and use it like a regular pointer. In a struct or class, declare:

```
FreezePtr<Foo> mFooPtr; // A pointer of type Foo
```

You should only point the `FreezePtr` at memory allocated using the `FreezeMgr`, or the `FreezeMgr` will `assert()` when you freeze your data.

The Freezable Class

If a class contains any virtual functions, it must inherit the abstract base class `Freezable`. Its interface is:

`virtual char const* GetClassName(void):` A pure virtual. You must overload this to return a constant to identify the class.

`virtual void SerializeIn(FILE* file):` Called at the end of the thaw, after the pointers and virtual function tables have been restored.

`virtual void SerializeOut(FILE* file):` Called at the end of the freeze. Overload this method to output data in whatever format you wish.

Because the class's constructor must be called upon loading to restore the virtual function table pointer, make sure you do not do anything in the constructor unless you call `FreezeMgr::IsThawing()` to determine whether a thaw is in progress.

You will need to call `FreezeMgr::RegisterType()` to map the type name onto a 32-bit identifier prior to freezing or thawing.

The FreezeMgr Singleton

The `FreezeMgr` singleton controls file creation, loading, and saving. It also provides memory allocation and class creation methods to create data that may be frozen. The `FreezeMgr` regards data it did not create with disdain and will `assert()` if you try to freeze it. It will also `assert()` if you point a `FreezePtr` at unmanaged data.

The interface is:

`template<typename TYPE>TYPE* AllocTyped(int total=1):` Allocate and return a class or array of type `TYPE`. To create an array, just pass in its size.

`void Flush(void):` Releases memory allocated by the `FreezeMgr` and purges the internal lists.

`void Free(void):` Delete memory allocated by the `FreezeMgr`. This includes files that have been loaded via `Thaw()`.

`void Freeze(char const* filename, void* addr):` Walks the graph of data to be frozen starting at the address provided and writes out a file. The address provided must be an address returned by `AllocTyped<>()`.

`static FreezeMgr* Get(void):` Returns the `FreezeMgr` singleton.

`bool IsThawing(void):` Returns true if a thaw is in progress. This is relevant to `Freezable` constructors that wish to avoid reinitialization.

`template<typename TYPE>void RegisterType(u32 typeID):` Register a class derived from `Freezable` with the `FreezeMgr`.

`template<typename TYPE>TYPE* ThawTyped(char const* filename, bool edit=false):` Load a file created by `Freeze()` and restore it for use.

If you are creating classes that derive from `Freezable`, you will have to register them with the `FreezeMgr` in your initialization code and before any calls to `FreezeMgr` are made. Remember that the `FreezeMgr` assigns type identifiers based on the order of registration, so the order must stay the same. If that is too limiting, it is easy to change at the cost of a slight performance hit.

It's possible to `void` pointers in `Freeze()` and `Thaw()`. This is dangerous, but removes the requirement to use `Freezables`. The hope is that the user will not abuse this feature. If you do not share this optimism, then again, this is easy to change.

Conclusion

This particular utility represents a large expanse of extremely uninteresting code that basically does a lot of behind-the-scenes bookkeeping. That said, we've laid the foundation for a turnkey API that can be used to manage a lot of the mess and hassle associated with writing and maintaining game files.

The sample implementation is heavily commented, so you should dive in and extend it to include the ideas of the many excellent authors whose work makes up the body of *Game Programming Gems*.

References

[Bilas00] Bilas, Scott, "An Automatic Singleton Utility." *Game Programming Gems*. Charles River Media, Inc., 2000.

[Boer00] Boer, James. "Resource and Memory Management." *Game Programming Gems*. Charles River Media, Inc., 2000.

[Brownlow02] Brownlow, Martin. "Save Me Now!" *Game Programming Gems 3*. Charles River Media, Inc., 2002.

[Olsen00] Olsen, John. "Fast Data Load Trick." *Game Programming Gems*. Charles River Media, Inc., 2000.

[Wakelin01] Wakeling, Scott. "Dynamic Type Information." *Game Programming Gems 2*. Charles River Media, Inc., 2001.

1.14

An Effective Cache-Oblivious Implementation of the ABT Tree

Sébastien Schertenleib, Swiss Federal Institute of Technology (EPFL), Virtual Reality Lab (VRlab)

Sebastien.Schertenleib@epfl.ch

Today, computer architectures describe multiple levels of memory becoming successively slower and larger. Those levels include registers, level-1 cache, level-2 cache, main memory, and disk. The access time increases from one cycle for registers to around 10, 100, and 100,000 cycles for cache, main memory, and disk, respectively (see Figure 1.14.1). According to the current and future CPUs and memory evolutions [Moore65], [Hennessy03], the penalty for algorithms that do not take benefit of this hierarchical memory representation will increase through many caches misses. For addressing this problem, cache-oblivious algorithms were introduce by [Frigo99]. The idea was to optimize the I/O model's scheme without specific knowledge about the memory block size. They describe that basic problems can be solved using optimal algorithms being cache-oblivious [Frigo99]. First attempts were dedicated to matrix and FFT transformation. Later, [Bender00] gives additional proposals for B-tree and search tree representation. Cache-oblivious algorithms differ from cache-aware algorithms, as they adapt themselves to any architecture.

Computer Memory Architecture

Most algorithms ignore memory architecture. Those driven by small data structures like binary trees suffer huge penalties in accessing their data. Each memory layer works in a similar fashion and is composed of cache blocks. Current architectures use cache lines of approximately 32–64 bytes. Notable improvement can be achieved by accessing data within the same cache line [Patterson97], [Hennessy03]. A cache line's lifetime depends on hardware-specific heuristics [Smith87]. Decisions are made on a

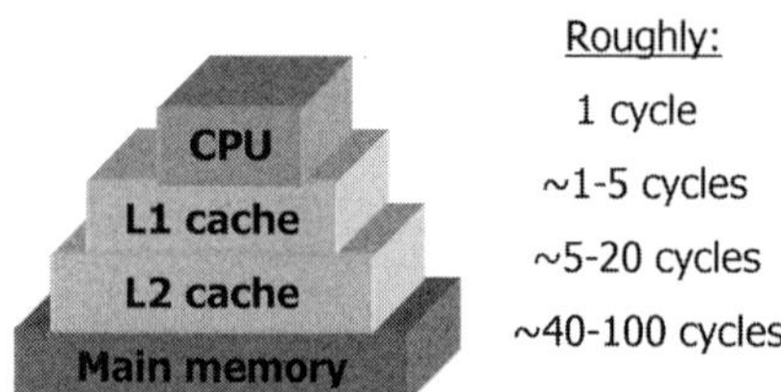

FIGURE 1.14.1 *Memory multilevel hierarchy.*

replacement and associative policy within the cache. Sometimes, cache misses are unavoidable [Hill02] such as in the following cases:

Compulsory: A cache miss cannot be avoided; this occurs when some data is accessed for the first time.
Capacity: The data fit in the cache in previous steps, but due to the renewal policy of the cache, the data was removed from this cache level.
Conflict: Cache trashing due to data mapping to the same cache lines.

Data Structure and Cache Coherence

Spatial alignments have an impact on the cache usage. Notably, data structures making intensive use of pointers are not good candidates. Pointers or data that will likely be accessed together should as well be stored together for optimizing memory access [Ericson03], [Ding04]. In some circumstances, they may not fulfill the object-oriented programming methodology.

Van Emde Boas Layout

The van Emde Boas layout [van Emde Boas77] (see Figure 1.14.2) is the standard way of laying out a balanced tree in memory so that a root-leaf path can be traversed efficiently in the cache-obliviously model using $O(4 * \log_B(n))$ $B = NbElement/Cache Line$ memory transfers [Agarwal03].

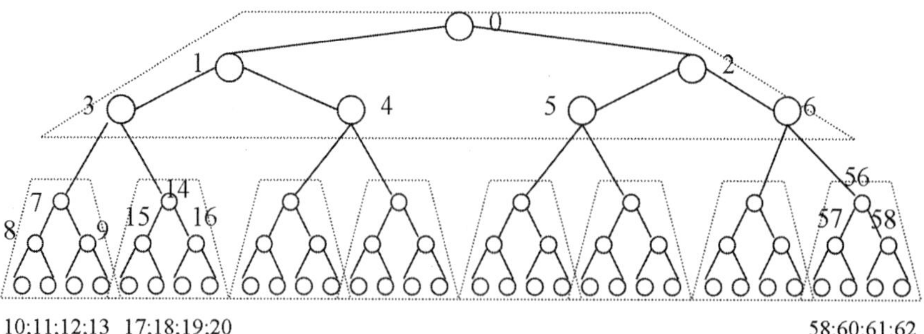

FIGURE 1.14.2 *Van Emde Boas's tree representation. In this example, each subtree is composed of seven nodes.*

ABT Tree

ABT trees are very similar to KD trees [Szécsi03]. At each step, two children may be created based on an axis-aligned splitter. One difference with KD trees is that the algorithm will minimize the resulting children's AABBs and store all the geometry exclusively in the leaves. Thus, each node becomes a totally enclosed region in space where the internal nodes are used for rejecting the traversal of nonvisible parts of the environment.

ABT Tree Creation

The creation of such a tree begins with the root node containing a reference to the whole scene AABB. The recursive building method subdivides the local current AABB into two parts along an axis-aligned splitter. Then, each face is assigned to one child depending on their median (see Figure 1.14.3).

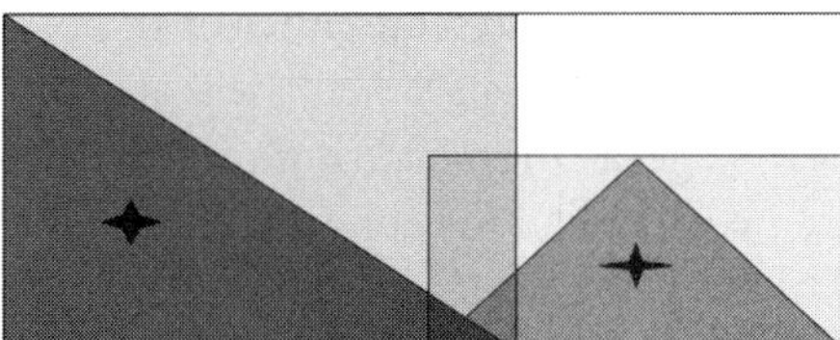

FIGURE 1.14.3 *Axis aligned bounding box readjustment.*

Once the distribution of all faces has occurred, each child recomputes its own AABB containing unique faces on this level. The ending criterion depends on the specific 3D environments and hardware envisaged. The splitting policy will try to minimize the following attributes:

- Space localization, as in Equation 1.14.1:

$$f_1(n) = Min(Area(boxLeft) + Area(boxRight)) \tag{1.14.1}$$

- Tree balancing, as in Equations 1.14.2 and 1.14.3:

$$f_2(n) = Min\left[\Delta\left(Area(boxLeft) - Area(boxRight)\right)\right] \tag{1.14.2}$$

$$f_3(n) = Min\left[\Delta\left(\sum(ExtendedArea) - \sum(Area)\right)\right] \leq \varepsilon \tag{1.14.3}$$

- Epsilon should stay below 5–10% before a noticeable performance penalty. In most cases, 90% of the faces will be contained in this 5% extended AABB

Scene complexity, as in Equations 1.14.4 and 1.14.5:

$$f_4(n) = Min\left[\Delta\left(\sum faces(boxLeft) - \sum faces(boxRight)\right)\right] \quad (1.14.4)$$

$$f_5(n) = Min\left[\Delta\left(\int ressources(boxLeft)dt - \int ressources(boxRight)dt\right)\right] \quad (1.14.5)$$

The final equation becomes that shown in Equation 1.14.6:

$$f(n) = w_1 * f_1(n) + w_2 * f_2(n) + w_3 * f_3(n) + w_4 * f_4(n) + w_5 * f_5(n) \quad (1.14.6)$$

The weights will change during the traversal with regard to the engine bottlenecks and scene organization (scenegraph, special effects, etc.). The methodology will also differ for the preprocessing stage and during runtime.

At runtime, typically each point of view will do a full or partial traversal during the different rendering phases (culling, shadow, collision detection, etc.). Thankfully, ABT-tree traversals are really simple and fast to compute. Starting from the last local root, the recursive function tests if either of the two children is in the frustum and if so, continues the tree traversal. When a leaf is reached, all geometry contained can be sent to the next stage in the rendering pipeline. Since each face is unique, no additional tests are needed (like for collision detection). We can also keep a small vertex buffer by leaf and local materials. For reducing the number of vertex buffers used, we can benefit from the neighbor child's location. Therefore, a single vertex buffer could be shared within their limits (generally 65K of 16-bit indices) among leaves. This provides a more efficient branching when neighbors need to be proceeding altogether, improving the rendering performance [Wloka03].

ABT-trees can also be tuned dynamically by simply reordering each moving AABB among their subtrees. One downside with dynamic trees is that they tend to degenerate with time.

Efficiency

All binary trees, notably BSP and KD trees, suffer from depth level. Even with ABT trees' abilities, it remains a significant issue. Assuming that the tree implementation is using pointers instead of implicit pointers, we can consider that every time the tree needs to follow a pointer, a CPU cache misses will occur. Relative to the depth level, the number of caches misses will increase accordingly up to a limit where they become more expensive than testing intersections. However, cache-oblivious trees reduce cache misses relative to the cache line size. The traversal then becomes less sensitive to memory access rather than CPU performance.

Complexity

ABT trees, like all binary trees, have an $O(\log n)$ search time [Sedgewick90]. By using the van Boas cache-oblivious layout representation, the search time can be majored to $O(4 * \log_B(n))$ where $B = CoupleNodesByCacheLines$ [Brodal03] (see Figure 1.14.4).

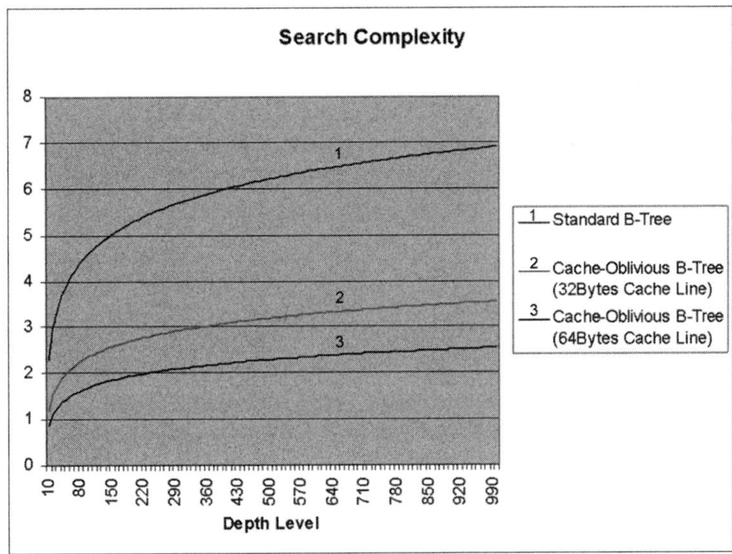

FIGURE 1.14.4 *Searching time order.*

Each node needs to store its local AABB and a pointer (or index) to its two children. Using a naïve implementation, the memory consumption becomes relatively important:

- AABB described by six floating-point values: 6 * 4 bytes
- Pointers to its two children: 2 * 4 bytes (32-bit CPU) or 2 * 8 bytes (64-bit CPU)

Total memory requirement per node is therefore 32 bytes (32-bit CPU) or 40 bytes (64-bit CPU).

However, [Gomez01] has shown that we only need to keep the relative extents for each child, which can be truncated to an 8-bit integer value. This conservative estimate will have a relative error of 1/255, or approximately 0.4%, which is covered by the average 5–10% AABB overlapping.

Exploiting Redundancy

[Gomez01] has described practical ways for reducing the memory footprint. At each subdivision, 6 extents from the 12 defining the children's AABB come directly from the parent, as all faces will be propagated to the leaves. For saving a few bytes by node, we store them by couple. Thus, instead of keeping the absolute AABB locally, each couple of nodes will keep the proportion to their direct parent's AABB.

Consequently, six bytes are needed to represent the children relative ratio. An additional byte specified through different flags will use this relative position from the two children and reuse the parent value. During runtime traversal, the recursive method will recompute the local AABB on the fly. Finally, since the last byte has unused two bits at this stage, we specify whether the left or right children are nodes or leaves (see Figure 1.14.5). For keeping a cache-oblivious data structure, we store them in eight bytes, leaving seven bits unused for the tree itself. For instance, they allow specifying whether the following subtree was loaded, which may be useful for streaming worlds.

63	62	61	60	59	58	57	56	55 48	47-40	39-32	31-24	23-16	15-8	7-1	0
LX	LY	LZ	RX	RY	RZ	LL	RL	LX Ratio	LY Ratio	LZ Ratio	RX Ratio	RY Ratio	RZ Ratio		L?

Since computer cache-line architecture is always a power of two, we aligned our data structure to be 64 bits or 8 bytes.

- L? specify if it's a node or a leaf.
- Ratio Lx,y,z: relative ratio based on the lowest part of the specific axis to enforce that the truncated AABB will be equal to or bigger than the absolute one. The ratio is split into 255 elements.
- Ratio Rx,y,z as above but using the higher part.
- Flags: Bit 63-58 specifies which child extend belongs to his parent (1 Left child, 0 Right Child). Bit 57-56 indicates if the left and right children are leaves elements (1 Leaf, 0 Node).

FIGURE 1.14.5 *ABT tree's node data representation (couple).*

Finally, as the subtree will always be a power of two minus one, and as the cache line size is always a power of two, we have eight bytes available for linking this subtree to the next subtree. As the hierarchy tends to use implicit pointers, four bytes are used to provide the index to the first child available. Parts of the four additional bytes specify which end node is connected to a child's subtree. Depending on the cache line size, some bits may remain unused (see Figure 1.14.6).

The build routine is done so that all subtrees coming from the last subtree are direct neighbors (see Figure 1.14.7).

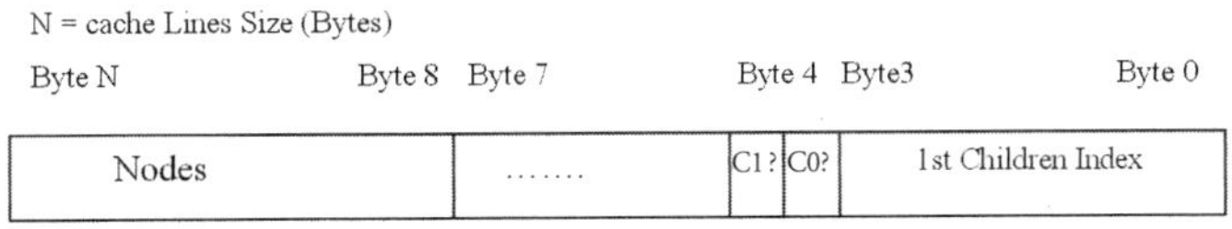

N = cache Lines Size (Bytes)

Byte N	Byte 8 Byte 7	Byte 4	Byte3 Byte 0
Nodes	....	C1 ? C0?	1st Children Index

- Bytes 0-3: Index to the first next child sub tree. All sub trees are direct neighbors.
- Bytes 4-7: Cx?: Flag specifying if the end-node i is connected to a sub tree.
- Byte 8-N: Each group of 8 bytes represents a couple of nodes or a leaf.

FIGURE 1.14.6 *Cache line organization.*

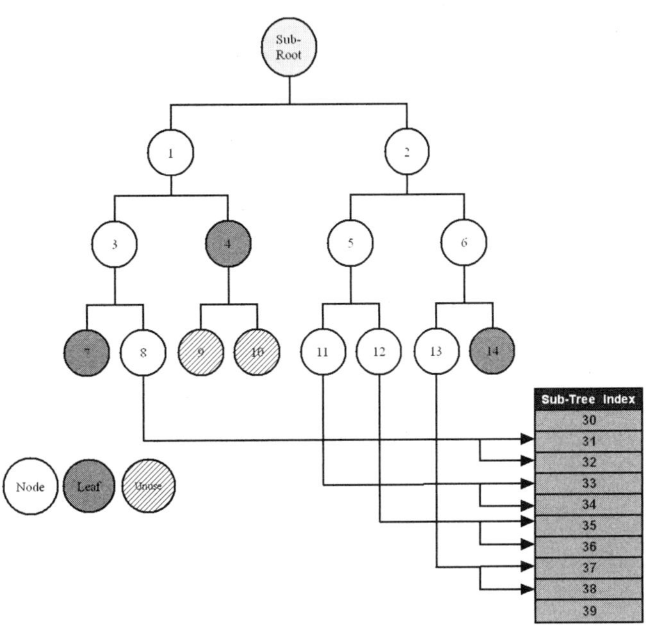

FIGURE 1.14.7 *Subtree organization with linking to following subtrees.*

Now consider a leaf, whose composition is made of eight bytes. One bit is used to specify its condition. Then again, it may depend on the number of nodes the system may use. On 32-bit systems, 31 bits are generally enough; leaving four bytes that can be used for additional information (mainly for dynamic management of resources; see Figure 1.14.8). However, 64-bit programs may want to use more nodes and therefore take more than 31 bits.

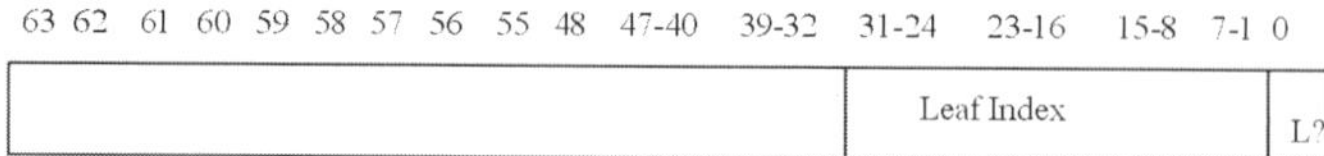

- L? Specify if it's a node or a leaf.
- In this configuration, 31 bits are used for referencing the leaf, the last 4 bytes aren't used for the tree itself, but can store extra information (like for streaming worlds).

FIGURE 1.14.8 *ABT tree's leaf data representation.*

Performance

For analyzing the performance of this approach, three different implementations were used (see Figure 1.14.9):

Intuitive: 6 * 4 bytes for storing the AABB and 8 bytes for the children's pointers (32-bit CPU), or 64 bytes for a couple.

Using redundancy: 8 bytes for the AABB, 8 bytes for children's pointers, or 48 bytes per couple.

Cache-Oblivious (64 byte cache lines): 8 bytes per couple + 8/7 extra bytes needed for implicit pointers, giving an average of 9.14 bytes. The global memory requirement depends on the tree balancing (see Figure 1.14.7).

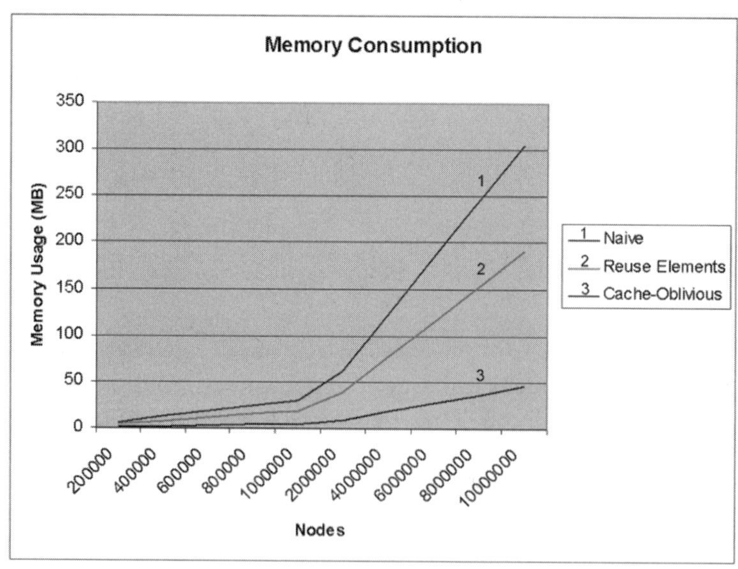

FIGURE 1.14.9 *Memory usage across implementation. The memory consumption for the cache-oblivious depends on the tree's balancing.*

With regard to the eight-bit integer value for representing the children's extents, the overhead to convert them back was measured. Experiments made on 16 K randomly distributed leaves have shown an overhead of about 7%, which is clearly compensated by the better cache-friendly design.

Validation Phase

Validations were made through several tools. [VTune04] was used for observing memory access and discovering nonrelated bottlenecks. Using [PAPI04] allows us to monitor hardware counters as well. They can keep track of cache misses, TLB misses, and similar events. However, specific measurements have required the creation of a dedicated profiler. Through the several implementations from RAM-based to cache-oblivious ones, statistics were collected for improving and understanding the cache-oblivious implementation.

Conclusion

Even if this gem was focused on culling algorithms, ABT trees are also useful for many others elements including AI or 3D sound management. This allows sharing the representation of the world using multiple views [Bar-Zeev03].

Current hardware evolutions require studying the cost of accessing data through the different layers of memory. CPU speeds will continue to improve greatly, but the memory evolution cannot follow. Computers will become more and more dependent on memory access rather than on pure raw performance.

Real-time simulation using large data sets will become limited by the memory bottleneck, reducing the impact of CPU evolutions. Finally, the adaptive nature of cache-oblivious algorithms provides a better alternative over cache-aware algorithms, while offering near to similar performance.

Reference

[Agarwal03] Agarwal, Arge and Bryan Danner. "Cache-Oblivious Data Structures for Orthogonal Ranger Searching." *ACM Proceedings of the 19th Annual Symposium on Conceptual Geometry.* 2003.

[Bar-Zeev03] Bar-Zeev. "Scenegraphs: Past, Present and Future." Available online at *http://www.realityprime.com/scenegraph.php.* 2003.

[Bender00] Bender, Demaine and Farach-Colton. "Cache-oblivious B-trees." In *Proc. 41st Ann. Symp. on Foundations of Computer Science,* 399–409. IEEE Computer Society Press, 2000.

[Brodal03] Brodal. "Cache Oblivious Searching and Sorting." Seminar, IT University of Copenhagen. Copenhagen, Denmark. 2003.

[Ding04] Ding, C. "Data Layout Optimizations, Computer Organization." Lecture, Rochester, NY, 2004.

[Ericson03] Ericson, Christer. "Memory Optimization." CDC 2003, Santa Monica. Sony Computer Entertainment, 2003.

[Frigo99] Frigo, Leiserson and Ramachandran Prokop. "Cache-Oblivious Algorithms." In *Proc. 40th Annual Symposium on Foundations of Computer Science* (FOCS), 285–297. 1999.

[Gomez01] Gomez, Loura. *Compressed Axis-Aligned Bounding Box Trees.* Charles River Media, 2001.

[Hennessy03] Hennessy, Patterson. *Computer Architecture: A Quantitative Approach.* Morgan Kaufmann Publishers Inc., 2003.

[Hill02] Hill, Lipasti. *Cache Performance.* University of Wisconsin-Madison, 2002.

[Moore65] Moore. "Cramming more components onto integrated circuits." In *Electronic Magazine* 38, 114–117. 1965.

[PAPI04] PAPI. "Performance application programming interface." Available online at *http://icl.cs.utk.edu/projects/papi*. 2004.

[Patterson97] Patterson, Hennessy. *Computer Organization and Design Second Edition: The Hardware/Software Interface.* Morgan Kaufmann, 1997.

[Sedgewick90] Sedgewick. *Algorithms in C.* Addison Wesley, 1990.

[Smith87] Smith. "Line (block) size choice for CPU cache memories." In *IEEE Transactions on Computers,* 1987.

[Szécsi03] Szécsi. "An Effective Implementation of the K-D Tree." In *Graphics Programming Methods,* Charles River Media, 2003.

[van Emde Boas77] van Emde Boas. "Preserving order in a forest in less than logarithmic time and linear space." *Inf. Process. Lett.,* 6:80–82. 1977.

[VTune04] *VTune.* Intel Corp, 2004.

[Wloka03] Wloka. "Batch, Batch, Batch: What Does It Really Mean?" *GDC, 2003.*

1.15

Visual Design of State Machines

Scott Jacobs

scott@escherichia.net

Not all the code that goes into a game needs to be written by programmers. Many activities that a game must accomplish may be better expressed using a specialized description that is converted during development into data and code. This process, known as code generation, potentially works very well for systems that can be implemented with state machines. For a more complete discussion of code generation, see [Herrington03]. Code generation requires expressing the requirements of the intended system completely and unambiguously prior to the generation process. Describing a state machine with this level of detail—the topic of this gem—can be accomplished visually using flow charts.

Why Code Generation?

Incorporating some level of automatic code generation into your development process has several benefits. For example, you could write (and debug) once the code that converts state machine descriptions into data and code has run, and you can reuse that converter throughout your project. This is also possible for the state machine itself that actually uses the generated data and code. Once written, debugged, and tested, those components may be used and reused to power UI screens, complex particle effects, in-game cinematic sequences, and even game logic. Building this level of runtime data and code generation into the system along with the ability to execute it on the fly provides enormous flexibility and freedom to content creators. The generation of a state machine from a specialized visual state machine description offers a number of advantages over the standard and all too common practice of having a designer write a description of a system in text as a specification for a programmer to implement.

Perhaps the biggest advantage of such a system is the most obvious one. The state machine description is expressed visually, and the final result is generated directly from the visual design, providing on-the-fly synchronicity between design and functionality.

A change in the design results directly and immediately in a change in runtime operation of the state machine. Another advantage is that special-purpose data creation and visualization tools can ease layout of the state machines.

An obvious first choice for data creation and editing would be a flow chart diagramming tool. As opposed to a textual description of a system's operation, a designer or programmer can take a look at a flow chart describing the entire system and spot logic flaws or design problems visually before any coding time is spent implementing the problematic system. Working within the constraints of a visual tool also enforces that the system is consistent and viable. Instead of a programmer running back to design to find out whether or not the player can fire his weapon while jumping, designers can make this decision at design time by either linking the weapon firing state from the jumping state or not. Rapid reconfigurations of logic flow can take place, and a number of different approaches towards runtime actions can be performed, without any manual code modification.

Making It Possible

To make visual design of state machines viable, a number of game engine parameters and methods will need to be predefined and presented to the state machine designer. These are parameters and methods that will also need to be exposed to the state machine engine from inside the game engine. They may be as simple as a global set of Booleans describing the current state of input from the player, or they could be a more complex scripting system exposing timers, event generation, game object management, and more.

A number of small, easily testable, possibly unrelated variables, methods, and modules can be linked together with a state machine to create the intended in-game activity. An example would be a simple state machine that modeled the actions of a pistol. A programmer could implement a number of discrete activities necessary for incorporating a gun in a game like providing hooks to play sounds, generate particle effects, and damage game objects. Then, a state machine can be laid out with a visual design tool, and a number of gameplay actions can be experimented with and iterated over, as will be discussed later in this article.

Applying General Tools

A number of different tools could be used to diagram the state machine flow. Perhaps a custom tool written to take advantage of your specific application would be the best solution, but a good starting point for your first experiments with visual state machine design and code generation is an existing flow chart editor. One such editor is UMLPad [Bignami04]. This GPL-licensed application runs on a number of platforms and works reasonably well as a simple state machine editor. Basic flow charts are easily composed with this tool, and the text-based file format is very easy to understand and parse, making the conversion of flow chart definitions into state machines that can run in your game engine a straightforward exercise.

Generic state machine engines that read visually designed state machine descriptions could be written in a variety of languages, but here we will use one written in Lua [Lua04]. In its tenth year, Lua is in ever-increasing use within the game development community [Burns04] and seems a natural fit for implementing our state machine engine.

Exposing game engine variables and methods via Lua to state machine designers is quite straightforward, and a number of readily available resources describe approaches for doing so. The process can often be made even more efficient with the help of a tool like tolua++ [Manzur04], which automatically generates the code that exposes C/C++ types to Lua. For help with Lua, you should check out the short but very comprehensive Lua manual [Ierusalimschy03a] and the book *Programming In Lua* by Roberto Ierusalimschy, available both in hardcopy and online [Ierusalimschy03b].

Lua is a dynamic scripting language where functions are first-class objects. This gives a lot of flexibility, as the flow chart to state machine conversion process can result in a mixture of data and machine-generated code. States can contain lists of methods that are run to determine if the machine should be advanced to a new state. Using a feature of Lua called *meta tables*, simple generic state machine management code can be written that operates the same for all instances of state machines in the game. Because all state machines share the same meta table, they all present the same interface, making the game engine's use of the state machines consistent. The uniqueness of each state machine is contained entirely in the (visually designed) data.

State Management

The state machine engine described here is concise but powerful. It seems even simpler if you keep in mind the fact that the data structures, methods, and relationships described here are all generated automatically by the conversion script based on the UMLPad file. Each state is implemented as a Lua table, and the state machine engine keeps track of which table is the current state. The table may contain any number of standard methods that the engine looks for and runs at appropriate times.

Among these methods, which need not exist for any given state, are methods run when a state is entered or exited. The current state is also given an opportunity to update itself when the state machine engine is updated. Each state table contains a list of links to the other states that are possible to enter from the current state, and each link may have an advancement conditional method that is run to determine whether the state machine engine should follow that link. Absence of a conditional means the engine will always follow the link. Following a link makes the linked state become the current state.

During each state machine's update cycle the current state's links' advancement conditionals are sequentially evaluated. If none of the conditions for advancement are met, the state machine remains at the current state. An advancement conditional is associated with a given link in the visual state machine design tool and can be as simple as a single Boolean (is input button X currently pressed?) or may be a more complicated function. (Has timer X expired or is the amount of ammunition left in the inventory sufficient to allow reloading?) Each state has its own table of state-specific data that is available to all the enter, exit, and update methods as well as each link advancement conditional method. This state-specific data area is a convenient place to put timers or counters.

State machines are created by asking a state machine factory for an instance of a named state machine. The state machine factory loads the file that was generated from the visual state machine datafile, installs the state machine engine meta table, and returns the object to the caller. Once the caller has this table, it can begin to update the state machine. The user of the state machine factory can be another Lua script, game engine C/C++ code, or any other code for which a Lua interface exists. Once the state machine starts, the user of the state machine should run Update()at an appropriate periodic rate. If the state machine completes, Update()returns the Lua value nil, which evaluates to false in conditional statements.

Putting It All Together

For a concrete example of this technique, let's design a state machine to operate a simple gun. The gun should be able to fire bullets, run out of ammunition, be reloaded from ammunition stored in an inventory, and perform a dry fire when there is no more ammunition left. To see the visual design, you can use UMLPad and open the file Gun1.uss from the accompanying CD-ROM; a snapshot of the state machine design is illustrated in Figure 1.15.1.

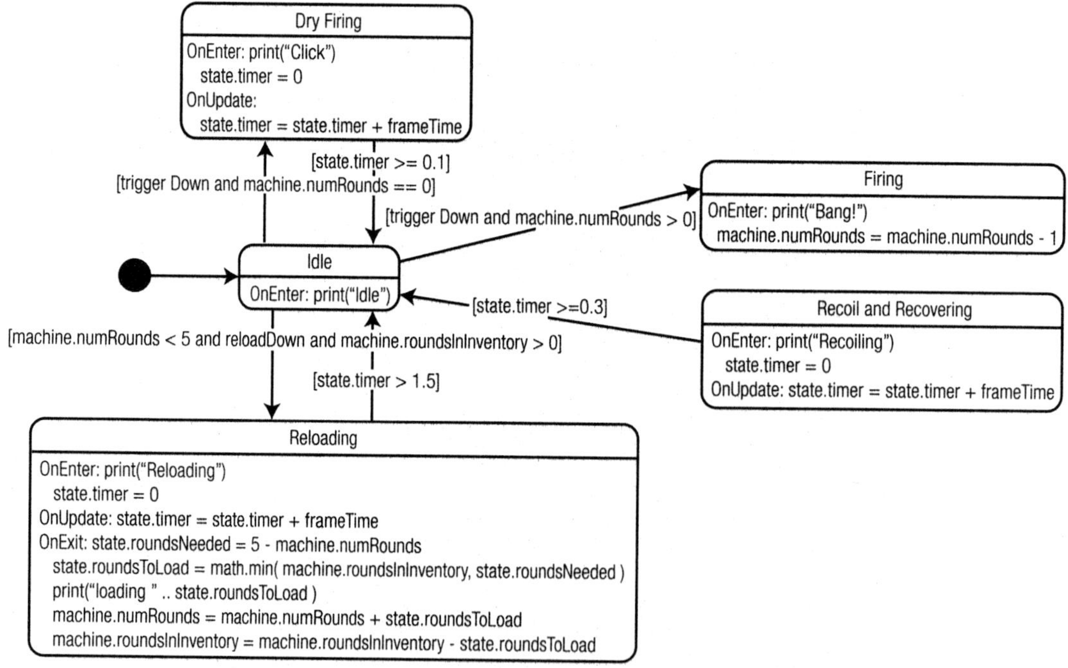

FIGURE 1.15.1 *A simple state machine describing the actions a pistol may perform.*

This state machine has a beginning (the large black dot) and no end. When begun, the state machine will progress immediately to the Idle state. Because we have repurposed a general state machine editor, we must be careful to follow a few conventions when filling in the data for each state. In the Activities and Description field, the code generation script will look for the special strings OnEnter:, OnExit:, and OnUpdate:. All text after each string will become the methods the state machine engine runs at the appropriate time. The methods will be supplied a single argument: state, which is a state-specific table that can be used to store data. If you incorporate this gem into your production pipeline, you may wish to alter UMLPad to include separate fields for each method. In the Idle state, only one method is defined: OnEnter. Every time the state machine engine progresses the state machine into the Idle state, the OnEnter method is run. In this example, the OnEnter method prints Idle to the screen.

From inspection, we can see that there are three ways for the state machine to leave the Idle state. The conditions required for advancement are detailed on each link. Every state machine update cycle, those conditions are evaluated in turn and if/when one is met, the state machine engine makes the linked state the current state, first running the OnExit method of the old current state, if it exists, then the OnEnter method of the new current state, if it exists.

In this case, pretend that triggerDown has become true because the game engine set this variable in response to the player pressing a fire button. The Firing state becomes the current state. In a real implementation, Firing's OnEnter method would probably call methods to play a gunshot sound and create an instance of a bullet in the game world. On the next update cycle, the state machine finds only one link out of the Firing state, and since there is no conditional, the link is immediately followed.

In the Recoil and Recovering state, there is also only one link out (back to the Idle state), but it cannot be followed until the timer has reached a certain threshold. Each update cycle, the state machine engine runs Recoil and Recovering's OnUpdate method, which increases the timer by the amount in frameTime, a variable set by the game engine. The rest of the state operates similarly.

A Showcase of Data Driven Design

Running the conversion script ussToState.lua on Gun1.uss results in a file Gun.lua that the state machine factory in StateMachineFactory.lua can use to provide gun state machines to requesting code. The script testGun.lua does just that, requesting a Gun state machine from StateMachineFactory, then simulating the role of a game engine by providing variables like frameTime, triggerDown, and reloadDown. The script testGun.lua runs the gun through the Idle, Fire, Recover, and Reload states until all the ammunition is spent, then the gun falls into an endless loop of idling and dry firing.

Now comes the beauty of this gem: reconfiguration of the existing state machine to meet new design requirements. Perhaps the design department would like to do some gameplay experiments with a weapon that automatically reloads when it is out of ammunition and the trigger is released. To facilitate this, a second link from the

Idle state to the Reload state with the conditional of not triggerDown and numRounds == 0 is created, and the state machine now has the desired behavior. Figure 1.15.2 shows Gun2.uss with the new link from Idle to Reload.

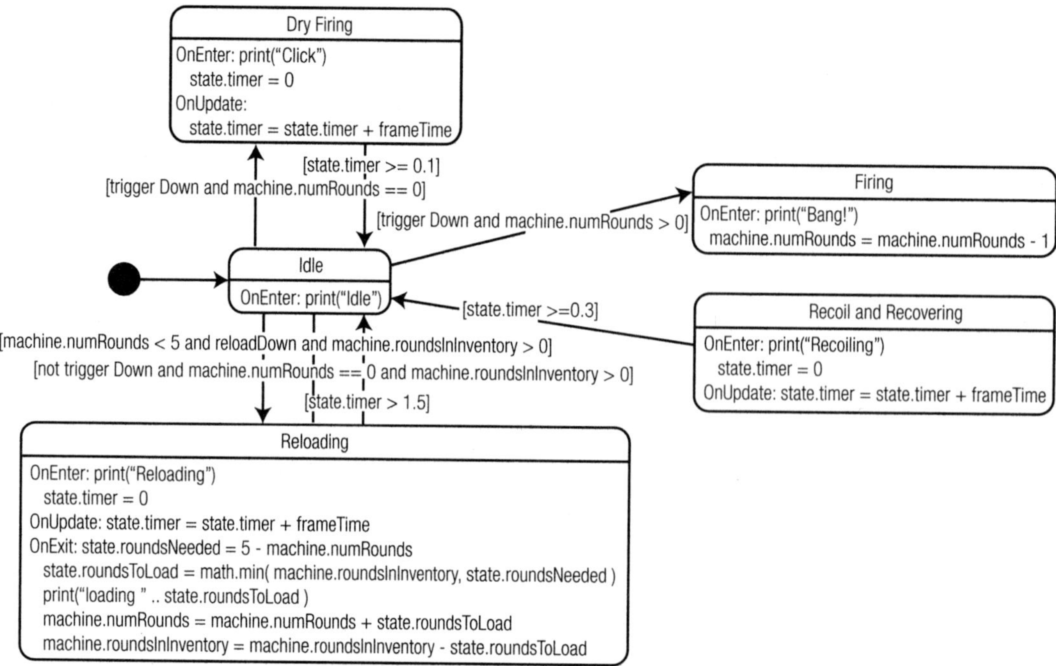

FIGURE 1.15.2 *A second link has been created from the "Idle" to the "Reload" state, which is followed when the gun is out of ammunition.*

Compare running the Gun.lua generated from Gun1.uss and Gun2.uss through testGun.lua with reloadDown hardcoded to false to see the effect of the new behavior. The gun will reload when out of ammunition, even though reloadDown is never true. Now pretend there is a new requirement from design. The gun needs to have a 4% chance of jamming, which requires three seconds to clear. Change the Idle state to calculate a chance of jamming during each OnUpdate cycle. When the trigger is down and there are rounds to fire, if the chance to jam is less than 0.04, the state machine makes the jammed state the new state. The jammed state's timer must be increased to three seconds before Idle becomes the current state again. We have just created two new game object behaviors with a few mouseclicks and a tiny amount of typing!

Conclusion

Hopefully, the potential to use something besides a text editor to create in-game actions and behaviors has intrigued you. The tools and languages presented in this gem, while a good basis for beginning your experimentation with state machine code generation, are not as important as being inspired by the concept that the core structure of systems like state machines can be abstracted, written, and debugged once, then enabled by data and code provided from tools that sport a number of benefits including self documentation of systems, rapid behavior modification, enforcement of system constraints, and no specific language knowledge requirements for system designers.

References

[Bignami04] Bignami, Luigi. UMLPad. Available online at *http://web.tiscali.it/ggb-home/umlpad/umlpad.htm.*

[Burns04] Burns, Jon and David Eichorn. "GDC 2004—Lua in the Gaming Industry Roundtable Report." Available online at *http://lua-users.org/lists/lua-l/2004-04/msg00164.html.*

[Herrington03] Herrington, Jack. *Code Generation in Action*. Manning Publications, 2003.

[Ierusalimschy03a] Ierusalimschy, Roberto., L. H. de Figueiredo, and W. Celes. "Lua 5.0 Reference Manual." Technical Report MCC-14/03, PUC-Rio, 2003. Available online at *http://www.lua.org/manual/5.0/.*

[Ierusalimschy03b] Ierusalimschy, Roberto. *Programming in Lua*. Lua.org, 2003. Also available online at *http://www.inf.puc-rio.br/~roberto/book/.*

[Lua04] Lua. Available online at *http://www.lua.org/.*

[Manzur04] Manzur, Ariel. tolua++. Available online at *http://www.codenix.com/~tolua/.*

1.16

A Generic Component Library

Warrick Buchanan

warrick@argonaut.com

With the increasing size and complexity of computer games, it becomes more critical that we embrace techniques that allow a more structured design methodology. The concept of viewing a software system as using a series of reusable components is not new, but it is still a practice that is not always applied where it should be within our industry.

This gem presents a configurable C++ template library that is designed to ease the process of developing reusable software components with support for features such as factories, interfaces, interface versioning, type identification policies, and reference counting.

First, we will introduce a number of elemental concepts that the library relies upon that are useful and usable separately in their own right. From these, we will build the foundation for the component system and demonstrate its use.

Type Identification System

The library is reliant upon a means of identifying the type of a class at runtime. As there are many preferences to how one can implement a type identification system, it is presented as a configurable parameter to the library. It is a simple user-defined class that must be implemented at least in the form of:

```
struct TypeID
{
    template<class Type> TypeID(const Type* type);
    TypeID();

    int operator==(const TypeID& typeID) const;
    bool operator<(const TypeID& typeID) const;

    static TypeID FromName(const char* const name);
};
```

This allows the relevant TypeID object to be created from a pointer to a class and from a string name of the class by means of a static member function. It also allows two TypeID objects to be tested for equality and provides an ordering method that is useful for when this class is used with STL container classes.

The type identification parameter is used as a template parameter to all the classes provided in the library so they are not tied to any specific type identification system. A sample implementation that uses the C++ type_info support as found in Microsoft Visual C++ 7 can be found in the supplied header file RTTITypeID.hpp.

Factories

A method of creating our components in a manner that insulates the client code from the actual component details is to use a Factory pattern [Gamma95]. If we temporarily view our components under the more generic moniker of an *object* it will allow us to design a Factory class that is useful in a more general sense.

The first requirement we wish the Factory object to fulfill is that, given the type of the object we wish to create, it will create an instance of the object:

```
template<class TypeID, class Base>
struct Factory
{
    Base* Create(const TypeID& typeID);
};
```

The first issue we see from this fragment of pseudocode is that we must decide what type of object is returned by the factory's creation method. For this implementation, we have all objects derived from a common base type, and that is what is returned from the creation method, as this keeps the actual concrete class of the object that is to be created further hidden from the client code.

The second issue is that of how we communicate to the factory which object it is we wish to create. We simply pass an instance of our type identification object that identifies the object we wish to create to the creation method.

As we wish to make our library as generic as possible, we also template our factory class on a type identification class parameter discussed previously and the actual base class that is returned from the creation method. This eliminates an unneeded reliance upon the rest of the component library.

Such a "sushi: pick and choose the pieces you wish" mentality to library design is crucial for users to achieve the most out of any library. It makes the difference between a generic library that has a long and productive lifespan and a library that is more an inflexible framework that continually needs refactoring.

We can now add overloaded versions of the creation method to allow C++ syntactic sugar that will make the use of the factory class even easier:

```
template<class TypeID, class Base>
struct Factory
{
    Base* Create(const char* const name);
    Base* Create(const TypeID& typeID);
    template<class Type> Base* Create();
};
```

This allows the following creation patterns:

Pattern 1:

```
Factory factory;
TypeID typeID;
Base* base = factory.Create(typeID);
```

Pattern 2:

```
class MyObject;
// ...
Factory factory;
Base* base = factory.Create<MyObject>();
```

Pattern 3:

```
Factory factory;
Base* base = factory.Create("MyObjectName");
```

Pattern 4:

```
class MyObject;
// ...
MyObject* myObject = 0;
Factory factory;
Base* base = factory.Create(myObject);
```

The first three creation patterns tend to be the most useful; and patterns 1 and 3 are paramount when the object to be created is not known at compile time, which is essential functionality for data-driven applications.

At this point, you may be wondering how the factories know how to create the objects we ask for. They must be told how to do so, and if we ask for an object the factories do not know how to create, they shall return NULL from their creation methods. We extend the factories class definition like so:

```
template<class TypeID, class Base>
struct Factory
{
    Base* Create(const char* const name);
    Base* Create(const TypeID& typeID);
    template<class Type> Base* Create();
```

```
    template<class Type> void RemoveSupport();
    template<class Type> void Support();
};
```

We now have two methods with which we can add support dynamically to our factory for any object type we wish (note that we are making the assumption that all classes have a default constructor). Given an implementation of an object we wish to create that is derived from the appropriate base class, that we will call `MyObject`, we can add support to a factory for it as follows:

```
class MyObject : public Base
{
   MyObject();
//...
};

Factory factory;
factory.Support<MyObject>();
```

Our factory object will now be able to create instances of the supported class. The ability to dynamically add and remove support of specific object types can be extremely useful and is not always available in other factory system designs.

The actual specifics of how the factory object is able to do this so simply will not be described here but is provided in the accompanying source code. A brief description is that the factory keeps a map of templated constructor objects for each supported object type with each constructor object knowing how to create the specific object type.

The Factory Singleton and Child Factories

It can be helpful to apply the singleton design pattern to factories for a myriad of reasons, the most significant of which is simplicity. We can easily provide this by adding the following static method to our `Factory` class:

```
struct Factory
{
    //...

    static Factory& Singleton()
    {
        static Factory factory;
        return factory;
    }
};
```

Employing the singleton design pattern allows us to access a single instance of our factory object from almost anywhere simply by referring to the factory object as `Factory::Singleton()`. Not only is this a helpful convenience but also safer. Further, we can add support for *child factories*, meaning we can connect factories in a hierarchal fashion to affect object creation in one simple way. If a factory does not know how to create the object we requested, we recursively descend its children until we find a child factory that does know how to create the object. For this support, we extend the factory class as follows:

```
struct Factory
{
    void RemoveChild(Factory* factory);
    void AddChild(Factory* factory);
};
```

Through these two new methods, our factory class can now maintain a list of pointers to child class objects (constructors). In this implementation, there is no support for cases where a child factory is destroyed elsewhere but is still referenced by another factory object. The system could be extended to cope with such circumstances by adding reference counting functionality (or some similar safety net) to the factory classes.

DLL Factories

For the Microsoft Windows operating system, we can enhance our factories even further to support the concept of dynamically loadable factories using Dynamic Link Libraries (DLLs). We achieve this by creating a class, `DLLFactory`, derived from `Factory`, that wraps the loading of the DLLs and binding to the factories exposed through them. The DLLs only have to export a function to return a pointer to the factory object to be exposed. Remember multiple factories can be exposed from a DLL by the use of child factories.

The implementation can be found in the supplied source code in the file, DLLFactory.hpp, and an example of its use in the supplied example workspace. Note that care must be taken if the factory DLL is to be unloaded. Objects created using the DLL may still be around, which will result in access violations. Objects created through a DLL factory must also be released by that DLL, so the base class from which all factory creatable objects are derived should provide a method of self-deletion. An implementation of this typically follows the form:

```
struct Base
{
    void DeleteThis()
    {
        delete this;
    }
};
```

More complicated and robust functionality in such circumstances could be added by requiring the factory objects to track and play a more active part in the lifetime of the objects they create, but that is beyond the scope of this gem.

Components

Now that we have the basic building blocks of our library in place, we can concentrate on the actual implementation details of the components themselves. Conceptually, a component should be a unit of code whose implementation details are hidden from the client code. Communication between the component and the client code should be abstracted through the use of interfaces. From this, we have two key concepts: the component and its interfaces.

The lifetime of the component must be managed in some way. Our factory class will provide creation facilities, but we can use a reference counting system to keep track of our components and provide the details of their destruction. The class provides reference-counting functionality as follows:

```
struct ReferenceCount
{
    //...

    void Reference();
    void Release();
};
```

The full implementation of `ReferenceCount` can be found in ReferenceCount.hpp. The methods provided allow the increase and decrease of an object's reference count, respectively. When the reference count of the object becomes zero, the object will automatically delete itself. From this we can configure a specific `Component` class implementation by deriving from the `ReferenceCount` class and a base `Component` class provided by the library (This is shown in the file ExampleConfiguration.hpp). Additionally, we can define a `Clone()` method in our `Component` class implementation in the form of:

```
virtual Component* Clone() { return 0; }
```

This allows a transparent way for client code to duplicate the component, and is optional for the component to implement. This still does not allow us to get much use from our components, as we can only create and destroy them. We need to add support for interfaces onto the components to make them usable.

Component Interfaces

The standard way of achieving this is to use what is known as a `QueryInterface()` method. We call this method with an identifier for the interface we wish to obtain, and we either get back a pointer to the requested interface or NULL:

```
struct Component
{
    template<class Type> Type* QueryForInterface();
    //...
};
```

We could use our type identification system to specify the interface we are after, but we shall arrange things so that we can use yet another class if need be. Our component class will actually have two template parameters: the type identification system to use and the interface identification system to use.

```
template<class TypeID, class InterfaceID >
struct Component
{
        //...
};
```

The `InterfaceID` class parameter is very similar to the defined type identification class; it should have the form:

```
struct InterfaceID
{
    template<class Type> InterfaceID(const Type* type);
    InterfaceID();

    int operator==(const InterfaceID& interfaceID) const;
    bool operator<(InterfaceID const& interfaceID) const;
};
```

In fact, it is so similar that we can still use our type identification system in its place if we wish. The reason to allow the possibility of an interface identification system that can be different from the type identification system used is that doing so allows us to add support for a feature called *interface versioning.*

Interface Versioning

Interface versioning in the library is supplied as an optional feature and was designed to overcome the problem of minor interface changes occurring during code development. In an ideal world, we would define an interface once and it would never change. If we wished to extend or change the interface, we would keep the old interface and add a new one to provide the new functionality.

This is all well and good if you are talking about official code releases meant for public consumption, but typically in practice, the frequency that the interfaces will be changed during internal development is quite high. It is simply impractical to create new interfaces that often. The catastrophic effect of this is that units of code that are compiled separately end up with definitions of interfaces that they believe are the same but in fact are not. If these units of code try to communicate with each other through these interfaces, the effect is often terminal.

A solution to this dilemma is to simply assign each interface a version number. When an interface is queried for on a component, part of the interface identification includes this version number. The version numbers must match for the query to be successful. It is much simpler for a programmer to increment a simple version number if he changes the interface than the alternative. It should also be possible to set up an auto-incrementing version number scheme when the code for interfaces is checked in or changed to further guard against such interface incompatibilities.

To add a version number to an interface, we simply derive it from the following template class with the version number as its parameter:

```
template<unsigned Number>
struct Version
{
    #ifdef _DEBUG
        enum { VersionNumber = -(int)Number };
    #else
        enum { VersionNumber = (int)Number };
    #endif
};
```

So an example versioned interface would be:

```
struct MyInterface : Version<2>
{
    //...
};
```

If the code is compiled in debug mode, we assign all interfaces negative version numbers. This is useful because we do not wish debug components to be used or mixed with release components (and have their use flagged as errors) in certain cases. In the case where we are allowed to freely mix debug and release code, only the absolute value of the interface version will be taken for interface identification comparisons. This behavior is optional and could be controlled by a compile time setting.

We can be even more flexible by allowing version numbers to be optionally specified. If they are not specified, version numbers default to zero or some other value, so they are called *relaxed versioning*. The provided file InterfaceID.hpp includes three interface identification classes that allow you to choose between strict versioning, relaxed versioning, or no versioning. For example, to select strict versioning you would declare your interface identification class as:

```
typedef  InterfaceID_WithStrictVersion <TypeID> MyInterfaceID;
```

Note that the class still requires an underlying type identification system with which to function, the one provided in RTTITypeID.hpp being ample for most purposes. The `InterfaceID` class provides its versioning functionality with C++ trickery that is evident in the code provided.

Defining Components and Their Interfaces

All that background information and setup code still does not tell us how we can implement a component and its interfaces. To best illustrate the implementation and binding of components and interfaces, a direct example follows.

```
// Define an interface
struct Movable
{
    virtual void GetPosition(float& x, float& y) = 0;
    virtual void SetPosition(float x, float y) = 0;
};


// The components implementation
struct Player : Component, Movable
{
    float x, y;

    Player ()
    {
        ExposeInterface<Movable>(this);
    }

    void GetPosition(float& x, float& y)
    {
        x = this->x;
        y = this->y;
    }

    void SetPosition(float x, float y)
    {
        this->x = x;
        this->y = y;
    }
};
```

The key is the templated `ExposeInterface()` method (inherited from the component class) that takes a pointer to the interface to expose. The base component class keeps a map of interface identifications to actual interface pointers that are used in the look-up when an interface is queried for.

One nice feature of this system is that interfaces do not have to be implemented by inheritance; they can also use object composition that can be preferable in many cases. For example, the previous component could have alternatively been implemented as:

```
// Define an interface
struct Movable
{
    virtual void GetPosition(float& x, float& y) = 0;
    virtual void SetPosition(float x, float y) = 0;
};


// Define an interface implementation
struct MovableHelper : Movable
{
    float x, y;
```

```
        void GetPosition(float& x, float& y)
        {
            x = this->x;
            y = this->y;
        }

        void SetPosition(float x, float y)
        {
            this->x = x;
            this->y = y;
        }
    };


    // The components implementation
    struct Player : Component
    {
        MovableHelper movableHelper;

        Player ()
        {
            ExposeInterface<Movable>(&movableHelper);
        }
    };
```

Using Components

Actually, a factory object may even create the previously defined component; we simply expose it to the factory class singleton in one line:

```
Factory::Singleton().Support<Player>();
```

Then, to use the component we would typically write the following:

```
Component* component = Factory::Singleton().Create<Player>();

if(component)
{
      Movable* movable = component->QueryForInterface<Movable>();

      if(movable)
          movable->SetPosition(3.2f, 4.0f);

      component->Release();
}
```

One thing to note is that unlike some component systems, such as Microsoft's COM (Component Object Model), management of the component lifetime is not done through the component's interface. This separation allows greater flexibility in component implementations because an interface is not tied to a component by inheritance.

Configuring the Library

Generally, users of the component library provided with this gem will use `typedefs` for particular configurations due to the complexity of the syntax associated with the template library classes. Even in the example code, some of the template parameters have been omitted for reasons of clarity. In the sample code provided on the CD-ROM, `typedef` configurations are given in the header file ExampleConfiguration.hpp.

Conclusion

A generic library that facilitates the structuring of code into reusable software component has been presented. It can easily form the basis of an off-the-shelf plug-in framework for many applications, and it has a syntax that is quite elegant compared to that of many other designs of such systems.

Many thanks to Achim Stremplat for the idea of interface versioning and Alan McDonald for various suggestions.

Reference

[Gamma95] Gamma, Erich, Richard Helm, Ralph Johnson, and John Vlissides. *Design Patterns*. Addison-Wesley Professional, 1995.

1.17

Choose Your Path—A Menu System

Wendy Jones

wendy2032@yahoo.com

The question of how to implement the menu system of a game is usually answered haphazardly near the end of the project, causing the implementation to be generally sloppy. Developers are typically more excited about the more challenging and seemingly more pressing issues, but menus hold a special importance to the overall perception and quality of the game. The game menus are the first thing the player sees upon sitting down to play the game, and if the players' first experience is with an interface that is hard to navigate, their perception of the game—along with its fun factor—will instantly diminish.

This gem focuses on the design and construction of a flexible and scalable generic menu system.

Why Do You Need a Menu System?

Most menus are added in a hurry with very little concern for good design or code reuse. When the next project comes around, the menus are once again started from scratch and tossed in. Menus can be a pain to work on, but racers want car selections and shooters need weapon choices, so menus are definitely necessary. When it comes to menu systems, you might as well start off with a good design to make your life easier.

Designing a menu system that will scale with an evolving project as well as be reused is not too difficult. Menus need only to perform a few basic tasks:

- Display a series of options
- Allow the user to easily select options using a given input method
- Move on to the next menu in the sequence based on the selection made

Taking these tasks into account, it is easy to see how they can translate into pieces of a menu system. Let's take a moment to break these tasks out into their abstract components and outline what each one's purpose is and what it does.

Let's start with the *menu component*. The menu component can be thought of as a single screen of options. For instance, the first menu in a game will normally present the user with a few high-level options such as Play, Setup, or Number of Players. This series of options would constitute a single menu component in your game. Each successive menu in your game would then be another menu component.

The next component is *user controls*. You may be familiar with common controls typically found in any windowing environment, i.e., buttons, listboxes, sliders, etc. These controls give the user a simple and consistent way of interacting with the system. Each menu component aggregates a series of controls to collect input from a user.

The final component is a *menu manager*. The menu manager is the primary controller of the menuing system. It creates the menus when necessary, collects information from the menus, and keeps track of the user's path through the system. The simplicity and elegance of the menu manager allows the designer of the user interface to create complex menu paths while allowing the programmer a minimal, one-time investment in development time. The general menu manager tracks the user's path through menu navigation, loading and presenting only the necessary menu components.

The Menu System Objects

Now that we have outlined the three major components and their associated tasks, we can start laying out the implementation details, such as what classes we need.

The menuing system consists of three main classes, each based on a menu task: the `menuScreen` class, `menuControl` class, and the `menuManager` class.

The `menuScreen` Class

The `menuScreen` class is the basis for all the menus that will be displayed. This abstract class includes a set of pure virtual methods providing a common interface to which all menus must adhere. By enforcing that all menus adhere to this interface, the menu system does not need to know the details of how each menu works. This allows new menus to be created quickly and plugged into the menu system easily. To take advantage of this feature, all menus in the system must inherit from the `menuScreen` class.

The `menuScreen` class contains three virtual methods that must be implemented by each concrete menu component class: `init()`, `update()`, and `render()`.

The `init()` function provides a single place to load the images for a menu as well as set up any controls needed. The `init()` function is called before the menu is displayed.

The `update()` function handles user input and updates the states of any onscreen items. `Update()` is called once per frame, right before the menu is drawn. Finally, the `render()` function performs the actual drawing of the menu to the screen. Within the `render()` function, you can modify the order in which menu items are drawn.

The `menuScreen` class also includes the `loadBackground()` method as well as a pointer to a background image. Since all menus will normally contain a background graphic, this function was placed in the menuScreen class for easy access. The background image stored in the parent class can be drawn during the call to the render function. Listing 1.17.1 shows the description of the menuScreen class.

Listing 1.17.1 Description of the menuScreen Class

```
class menuScreen
{
public:
    // menuReturn code
    // The update method will return one of these codes to inform
    // the menuManager of its status.
    // NONE - no action, continue showing current menu
    // NEXT - current menu should end and go to the next menu
    // PREV - current menu ends, display the previous menu
    // POPUP - the menu is requesting a popup menu be displayed
    // END  - This is the last menu and the menus are done
    static enum menuReturn { NONE=0, NEXT, PREV, POPUP, END };

    menuScreen(void);
    virtual ~menuScreen(void);

    // load all the resources needed for this menu
    virtual bool init(void) = 0;

    // called each frame to update the menu
    virtual int update(BYTE keys[]) = 0;

    // called each frame to draw the current menu
    virtual void render(void) = 0;

    // returns a string that represents the name
    // of the next menu
    std::string& getNextMenu(void);

protected:
    // loads the background image
    bool loadBackground(std::string imageName);

    // all menus have a background image associated with them
    resourceImage *bkgrdImg;

    // the name of the next menu
    std::string nextMenu;
};
```

Adding User Controls

User controls needed to gather input from the user are created with the menuControl class. MenuControl is implemented as an abstract class; all controls used in concrete menu classes will inherit their base functionality from this class.

The menuControl class contains information that is common to most types of user controls, such as control location, control type, and the current state. MenuControl also offers a render() function, again allowing the system to treat all controls similarly. Additionally, the menuControl class contains methods for altering the visibility, giving you complete control over whether a certain menu object will be displayed. Listing 1.17.2 contains the description of the menuControl class.

Listing 1.17.2 Description of the menuControl Class

```
class menuControl
{
public:
    static enum controlType {
        NONE   = -1,
        BUTTON = 0,
        STATIC,
        SLIDER,
        LIST
    };

    static enum controlState { ACTIVE=0, DISABLED };
    static enum controlView { VISIBLE=0, HIDDEN };

    menuControl(void);
    virtual ~menuControl(void);

    virtual void render(void) = 0;

    void setControlXY(int X, int Y) { locX = X; locY = Y; }
    int getType(void) { return type; }

    void activateControl(void) { state = controlState::ACTIVE; }
    void disableControl(void)  { state = controlState::DISABLED; }
    bool getControlState(void) { return state; }

    void showControl(void)    { view = controlState::VISIBLE; }
    void hideControl(void)    { view = controlState::HIDDEN; }
    bool getControlView(void) { return view; }

protected:
    // properties of a control
    int type;           // the type of control
    int locX;           // the X location
    int locY;           // the Y location

    bool state;         // whether the control is active
    bool view;          // whether the control is visible
};
```

Controlling It All: The `menuManager` Class

The `menuManager` class is the real workhorse of the menuing system, as its description hinted earlier. Implemented as a singleton, the `menuManager` ensures that only one instance is ever created, providing a single control center for creating and rendering menus as well as tracking the user's path through the system. The `menuManager` consists of two main pieces, the manager itself and the menu factory.

The Manager

Depending on the game, the amount of menus can become unwieldy very quickly; the menu manager keeps this in check. The manager accomplishes this by keeping a list of all the menus the user has already visited. The last menu in this list is seen as the current menu. When updating or rendering a menu, the manager simply accesses the last object in the list and passes on the command.

The list of menus, known as the menu trail, is how the menu manager tracks which menus the user has visited. At times, there may be multiple pathways that lead to a single menu, making it difficult to return the user to the correct previous screen. The menu trail solves this problem. If the user wants to backtrack through the menus, the manager need only traverse the menu trail in reverse.

We have only discussed how the menu manager uses the menus in the trail so far; in the next section, we will cover how the menus are created.

Listing 1.17.3 shows the `menuManager` class.

Listing 1.17.3 The `menuManager` Class

```
class menuManager
{
public:
    // singleton to ensure only one instance of the
    // menu system
    static menuManager& getInstance()
    {
        if (pInstance == NULL) pInstance = new menuManager();
            return *pInstance;
    };

    // initialize the menu system
    bool init(void);

    // close and release the menu system
    void shutdown(void);

    // passes down update messages to the menus
    int update(BYTE keys[]);

    // draws the menus
    void render(void);
```

```
private:
    static menuManager *pInstance;

    menuManager(void);
    ~menuManager(void);

    menuScreen *popupMenu;

    // flag to keep track of whether a popup window
    // is active
    bool popupActive;

    // the menu trail keeps track of the menus that the
    // user has gone through. This gives the system the
    // ability to track back the path the user took through
    // the system
    std::vector<menuScreen*> menuTrail;

    // menu factory implementation
    #define REGISTERMENU(a) registerMenu(#a, &CreateObject<a>);

    std::map<std::string, menuCreateFunc> menuList;

    // function that registers a menu with the factory
    void registerMenu(std::string menuName,
                      menuCreateFunc menuFunc);

    // creates a new menu
    menuScreen* createMenu(std::string menuName);

    // removes a menu from the system
    void destroyMenu(menuScreen* menu);
};
```

The Menu Factory

The job of the menu factory is the on-demand creation of menus. When a new menu is needed, the factory receives a request to create it. The factory then creates the menu and sends a menu pointer back to the caller. The manager then uses this pointer to interact with the new menu.

The factory also provides the benefit of limiting the amount of menus created to just the ones the user visits. In most cases, only a portion of the total menus are ever shown during a single session. For instance, if someone wants to just jump in and play, they most likely will not visit the options or credits screen beforehand. The menu factory keeps these menus from being instantiated, saving time and memory.

The menu factory is implemented using a set of function pointers and a Standard Template Library (STL) map. The map stores a pointer to the constructor for each menu and allows the menu manager access to these when required by simply using the menu name (string) as the look-up key. When a new menu is about to be created, the manager sends to the factory the name of the menu it wants. The factory looks this name up in the map and uses this to create the new menu. A pointer to the new (requested) menu is then sent back to the manager for use. Figure 1.17.1 shows this process.

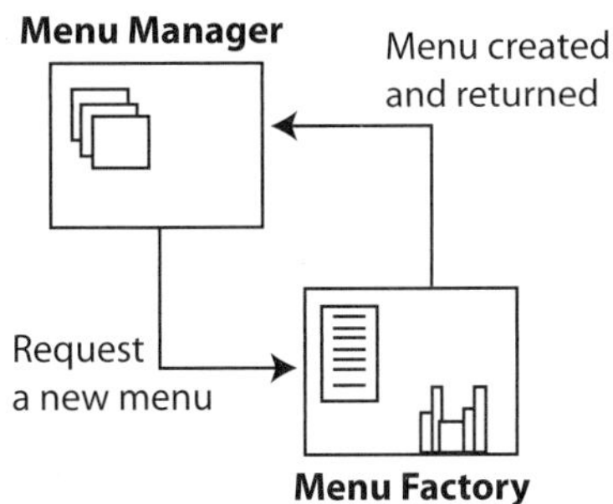

FIGURE 1.17.1 *How a menu factory creates a menu.*

In most menuing systems, the creation of menus is handled by using a switch statement. The constructors for each menu are hidden behind a label that the switch uses to figure out which menu needs to be created. For systems with only a few menus, this is all that is needed, but when the number of menus starts growing, this method quickly becomes problematic to maintain. By using a factory, the amount of code necessary to add a new menu to the system can be kept to a minimum.

Listing 1.17.4 shows the factory implementation.

Listing 1.17.4 The Factory Implementation

```
typedef menuScreen *(*menuCreateFunc)();
typedef std::map<std::string, menuCreateFunc>::iterator Iterator;

template<typename ClassType>
menuScreen *CreateObject()
{
   return new ClassType;
}

void menuManager::registerMenu(std::string menuName,
                               menuCreateFunc menuFunc)
{
    menuList[menuName] = menuFunc;
}

menuScreen* menuManager::createMenu(std::string menuName)
{
    // find the menu being requested in the list
    // of registered menus
    Iterator iter = menuList.find(menuName);

    // if the menu is not in the list, return null
    if (iter == menuList.end())
        return NULL;
```

```
        // second is the value, first would be the key
        // this should generate the constructor
        return ((*iter).second)();
    }

    void menuManager::destroyMenu(menuScreen* menu)
    {
        if (menu)
        {
            delete menu;
            menu = NULL;
        }
    }
```

Extendibility

The classes that make up the system discussed for this gem were designed to be cross-platform compatible with minimal changes. Since the requirements for each game are different, the menuing system presented here will provide you with a good base to expand on. Here is a short list of a few suggestions to extend the feature set of the system.

Scripting support: Each menu can be described in an external file that can be loaded at runtime. The placement of controls and even their behavior can be scripted, giving you a completely dynamic way to create menus.

Additional user controls: New controls can be added easily and plugged into the system allowing for menus to behave in any manner necessary.

Multiple input devices: Currently, the system supports only keyboard input, but this can be easily changed to include a gamepad or mouse device.

Conclusion

ON THE CD

You can find a sample implementation of this menu system on the accompanying CD-ROM. The sample project provided uses Microsoft Windows GDI calls for its graphics to keep things simple, though the system may easily be adapted for OpenGL, DirectX, or any other rendering API. As you can see, building a powerful menu system does not have to be overly complicated, and by keeping to and enforcing a simple yet extendible design, the system can grow to fit the needs of your game without too much—if any—additional overhead.

Reference

[Gamma95] Gamma, Erich, et al. *Design Patterns.* Addison Wesley, 1995.

SECTION

2

MATHEMATICS

Introduction

Eric Lengyel, Naughty Dog Inc.

lengyel@terathon.com

Most modern video games take place within some kind of simulated virtual environment. They usually attempt to make that environment appear and behave like the real world, at least to the degree that the computer hardware allows at an acceptable frame rate. Displaying a realistic representation of a 3D environment and simulating dynamic systems that follow the laws of physics requires that programmers understand the mathematics used to model what we experience in the world around us.

Mathematics as a whole is an unending series of generalizations—many are known, and many more await discovery. Two seemingly different mathematical notions applied in separate manners at one level can often be unified at some higher level of thinking and regarded as two cases of a single generalized concept. Our first gem, by Chris Lomont, discusses the branch of mathematics known as geometric algebra and presents the multivector generalization of commonly used operations such as rotations and cross products.

During the course of game development, it is often desirable for some set of data points to be smoothly interpolated. Examples of such data are a set of camera positions, animation keyframes, and even the vertices of a low-resolution mesh. A commonly used tool for performing smooth interpolation is splines, usually the cubic variety. This section continues with two gems that pertain to splines. The first, by Tony Barrera, Anders Hast, and Ewert Bengtsson, discusses a technique for minimizing the curvature of Hermite curves while maintaining smooth interpolation. The second is a gem by James Van Verth that discusses applications of splines to animation control.

Although game engines aim to simulate realistic environments as best they can, the result is inescapably an approximation at many different levels. In the realm of computation, precision and speed are opposing forces that need to be balanced in the way that best suits the application. Our next two gems offer approximation techniques whose goal is achieving the best possible speed while sacrificing as little precision as possible. Andy Thomason first describes approximations for quaternion interpolation, and Christopher Tremblay next discusses the minimax approximation technique.

We wrap up the mathematics section with a projection matrix modification trick written by Eric Lengyel. The mathematics behind the perspective projection matrix and the properties of homogeneous clip space are sometimes unintuitive, but a deeper understanding of their nature can lead to many useful adjustments. The technique described in the final gem distorts the view frustum so that the near plane is replaced by an arbitrary clipping plane and shows how to minimize the effect on depth buffer precision.

2.1

Using Geometric Algebra for Computer Graphics

Chris Lomont

Clomont@math.purdue.edu

Geometric Algebra (GA) is a compact way of representing many geometric ideas useful for computer graphics, which allows one to perform calculations in a more unified manner, simplifying equation derivation and algorithm design.

Introduction

GA provides a single language that unifies many areas of computer geometry and has applications to physics, computer vision, differential geometry, and other areas. The power of GA for computer graphics lies in the concise way it handles seemingly unrelated structures such as linear algebra, rotations in any dimension (including quaternions), intersections of subspaces, Plückerspace, dot and cross products, and even calculus and surface representations. For example, GA has a single formula giving the intersection of any subspace with another: line with line, line with plane, plane with plane, etc. Most derivations of intersection formulas need special cases and do not scale easily to higher dimensions. These are just a few areas where GA simplifies notation and thinking about geometric problems. Before continuing, the reader may wish to read the examples at the end of this gem to gain a better understanding of the benefits of GA.

Recall how long it took to master linear algebra, then quaternions (admit it—they are still weird!), thus don't assume GA will make sense and be useful after a single 10-minute reading. Although GA also seems weird at first pass, like quaternions, it becomes a powerful way to do geometric calculation, and the effort spent mastering it will be repaid with interest by simplifying future geometric calculations. Next, we'll capture the "flavor" of GA with an example capturing the essential ideas.

The Motivating Example

To illustrate GA, we consider a simple example starting with the two-dimensional vector space represented by the usual x–y plane. Treating the points (x_1, y_1) and (x_2, y_2) shown in Figure 2.1.1 *only* as points does not give much computational power, but if we think of them as vectors (each point defines an arrow from the origin to the point), we can add vectors in the usual way. This gives more structure to the plane and some added tools for solving problems. Next, we can create a way to "multiply" the points (or vectors) in a manner that behaves nicely with our addition. Of the many possible ways to do this, we will choose to think of each point as a complex number, that is, we treat (x_1, y_1) as $x_1 + iy_1$. Using $i_2 = -1$, we can multiply via $(x_1 + iy_1)(x_2 + iy_2) = (x_1x_2 - y_1y_2) + i(x_1y_2 + x_2y_1)$, which is another point (or vector). This is a very powerful way to think of points and vectors, because this "multiplication" of vectors is invertible, that is, we can divide by a point (i.e., a vector, or a complex number), allowing a richer framework in which to perform computations. This choice of multiplication is intuitive (after some study) since addition and multiplication of points acts very much like the usual operations on real numbers.

Note that the map $(x_1, y_1) \rightarrow x + iy$ sends the usual basis $\{\mathbf{e}_1 = (1,0), \mathbf{e}_2 = (0,1)\}$ to the complex numbers 1 and i. So we can think of a basis for the space we have constructed as 1 (the scalar part) and i (the complex part). Thus, another basis for the x-y plane is $\{1,i\}$.

A illustrative and powerful idea using this representation is that we can rotate a point (or entire drawing) by multiplication. Multiplying the point (x_1, y_1) by the point $\exp(i\theta) = \cos\theta + i\sin\theta = (\cos\theta, \sin\theta)$ will rotate (x_1, y_1) by an angle θ. Multiplication of vectors now has geometric meaning: multiplying by a general point becomes a rotation followed by a stretching. Figure 2.1.1 yields Equation 2.1.1,

$$\begin{aligned}(x_1, y_1)(x_2, y_2) &= \left(r_1 e^{i\theta_1}\right)\left(r_2 e^{i\theta_2}\right) \\ &= r_1 r_2 e^{i(\theta_1+\theta_2)},\end{aligned} \tag{2.1.1}$$

which represents the point (x_1, y_1) rotated by the angle from the x-axis to (x_2, y_2) and then stretched by the length r_2 of the vector to (x_2, y_2). We have made algebra out of 2-space, which means we can multiply any two elements of the 2-space and get another 2-space element.

Now we extend these ideas to any dimension.

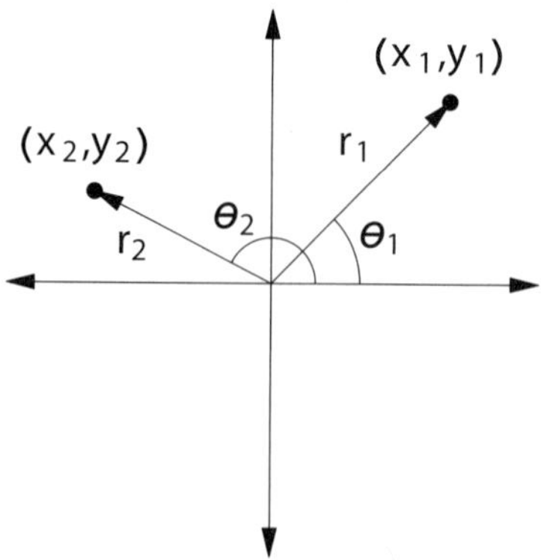

FIGURE 2.1.1 *The complex plane defines "multiplication" of vectors in real 2D space.*

Geometric Algebra

We fix some notation to clarify the presentation: Greek letters like α, β, γ, and δ will denote real numbers. Standard vectors will be bold lowercase letters like **a**, **b**, **c**. Later, we will use capital bold letters like **A**, **B**, **M**, **R** for *multivectors*, which are general elements of the geometric algebra, in the same manner vectors are general elements of a vector space.

The Algebra

Given an n-dimensional vector space V^n, we construct a new vector space CV (C for Clifford from mathematics), the geometric algebra of V, as follows. We usually think of V as a collection of vectors, which are just one-dimensional oriented magnitudes. The geometric algebra will extend this to handle tracking all two-dimensional oriented areas, all three-dimensional oriented volumes, etc. We start by defining what the objects of CV are, beginning with the *outer product*.

The Outer Product

For any two vectors **a** and **b** in V, we create a *bivector*, written $\mathbf{a} \wedge \mathbf{b}$. This represents the plane spanned by **a** and **b**, the orientation of the plane, and also encodes the magnitude of the area of the parallelogram with sides defined by **a** and **b**. See Figure 2.1.2(c) for a rough idea. A bivector is also called a 2-blade or a 2-vector. The operator $\wedge$ is called the *outer product* (also known as the wedge product or exterior product) and satisfies the properties outlined in Equation 2.1.2 for any scalars α, β, γ, and vectors **a**, **b**, **c**:

$$
\begin{aligned}
\lambda \wedge \mathbf{a} = \mathbf{a} \wedge \lambda &= \lambda \mathbf{a} && \text{vector and scalar commute} \\
\mathbf{a} \wedge \mathbf{b} &= -\mathbf{b} \wedge \mathbf{a} && \text{anticommutative on vectors} \\
(\lambda \mathbf{a}) \wedge \mathbf{b} &= \lambda(\mathbf{a} \wedge \mathbf{b}) && \text{associative with scalars} \\
\lambda(\mathbf{a} \wedge \mathbf{b}) &= (\mathbf{a} \wedge \mathbf{b})\lambda && \text{commutative with scalars} \\
(\alpha \mathbf{a} + \beta \mathbf{b}) \wedge \mathbf{c} &= \alpha \mathbf{a} \wedge \mathbf{c} + \beta \mathbf{b} \wedge \mathbf{c} && \text{bilinearity} \\
\mathbf{a} \wedge (\alpha \mathbf{b} + \beta \mathbf{c}) &= \alpha \mathbf{a} \wedge \mathbf{b} + \beta \mathbf{a} \wedge \mathbf{c} && \text{(linear in both factors)}
\end{aligned}
\tag{2.1.2}
$$

We extend the outer product in the same manner to products of three or more vectors. One important rule we find is that for any vector **a**, anticommutativity gives $\mathbf{a} \wedge \mathbf{a} = -\mathbf{a} \wedge \mathbf{a}$. Since the only quantity that equals its negative is zero, we must have $\mathbf{a} \wedge \mathbf{a} = 0$, a real number.

The geometric intuition for the outer product is illustrated in Figure 2.1.2. A vector **a** is a directed one-dimensional object. It has magnitude and direction. We extend this to scalars by treating α as a zero-dimensional point with magnitude α. A bivector

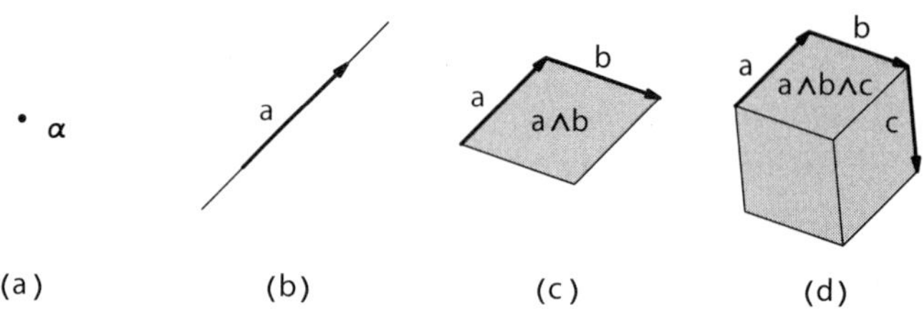

FIGURE 2.1.2 *One way to think of the outer product is using distance, area, and volume elements.*

is an oriented area (two-dimensional), which has magnitude and orientation. A trivector is an oriented 3-space, etc. This is why the outer product is anticommutative; reversing the order of the defining vectors will negate the orientation. Only the subspace, orientation, and magnitude are unique, not the exact parallelogram shape; for example, the following bivectors are equal, but the defining edges are different:

$$(2\mathbf{a})\wedge(3\mathbf{b})=(6\mathbf{a})\wedge\mathbf{b}=(3\mathbf{a})\wedge(2\mathbf{b})=6(\mathbf{a}\wedge\mathbf{b}).$$

Now fix an orthonormal basis $\{\mathbf{e}_1,\mathbf{e}_2,\ldots,\mathbf{e}_n\}$ of V to simplify the presentation.

Define the geometric algebra CV associated with V to be the vector space having basis consisting of all the outer powers of the basis elements of V, along with the scalar 1. For example, if V has dimension 3, we have a basis of CV in Equation 2.1.3. We don't get any other outer products since once a basis vector appears twice, the outer product result is 0, and we can order the subscripts into increasing order using the fact that swapping adjacent $\mathbf{e}_i$ negates the answer: $\mathbf{e}_i \wedge \mathbf{e}_j = -\mathbf{e}_j \wedge \mathbf{e}_i$.

$$\left\{\underbrace{1}_{scalars},\underbrace{\mathbf{e}_1,\mathbf{e}_2,\mathbf{e}_3}_{vectors},\underbrace{\mathbf{e}_1\wedge\mathbf{e}_2,\mathbf{e}_1\wedge\mathbf{e}_2,\mathbf{e}_1\wedge\mathbf{e}_2}_{\substack{bivectors,\\ 2\text{-}blades}},\underbrace{\mathbf{e}_1\wedge\mathbf{e}_2\wedge\mathbf{e}_3}_{\substack{trivector,\\ 3\text{-}blade}}\right\} \tag{2.1.3}$$

So CV is a vector space made of all linear combinations of the basis elements in Equation 2.1.3. If the dimension of V is n, then the dimension of CV is 2^n (checking this would be a good exercise). The general vector of CV is called a *multivector* to distinguish it from the ordinary vectors in V. For example, a multivector in CV could be $\mathbf{A} = 3 + 2\mathbf{e}_1 + 4\mathbf{e}_1 \wedge \mathbf{e}_2 \wedge \mathbf{e}_3$. Any two multivectors of CV can be multiplied using the outer product with the rules given earlier. We define a few more terms. A *k-blade*[1] is the outer product of k vectors. This does not have to be a product of only the $\mathbf{e}_i$; for

[1]In other areas of math this is called a *k*-form, and CV is the exterior algebra. We use the terminology common to GA since it has a more geometric feel to it.

example, $(\mathbf{e}_1 + 2\mathbf{e}_2) \wedge (3\mathbf{e}_1 - \mathbf{e}_2)$ is a 2-blade. A *k-vector* is a sum of k-blades. Thus a k-blade is a k-vector but not vice versa. The number k is called the *step* (or *grade*) of a blade. A multivector is a general element of the geometric algebra and is a sum of k-blades, possibly for differing k values. Thus, a bivector $\mathbf{a} \wedge \mathbf{b}$ is a 2-blade and has step 2. Note a vector is also a multivector.

As an example, if $\mathbf{a} = \alpha_1\mathbf{e}_1 + \alpha_2\mathbf{e}_2$ and $\mathbf{b} = \beta_1\mathbf{e}_1 + \beta_2\mathbf{e}_2$, we can calculate, as in Equation 2.1.4,

$$\begin{aligned}
\mathbf{a} \wedge \mathbf{b} &= (\alpha_1\mathbf{e}_1 + \alpha_2\mathbf{e}_2) \wedge (\beta_1\mathbf{e}_1 + \beta_2\mathbf{e}_2) \\
&= \alpha_1\beta_1\mathbf{e}_1 \wedge \mathbf{e}_1 + \alpha_1\beta_2\mathbf{e}_1 \wedge \mathbf{e}_2 + \alpha_2\beta_1\mathbf{e}_2 \wedge \mathbf{e}_1 + \alpha_2\beta_2\mathbf{e}_2 \wedge \mathbf{e}_2 \\
&= 0 + \alpha_1\beta_2\mathbf{e}_1 \wedge \mathbf{e}_2 - \alpha_2\beta_1\mathbf{e}_1 \wedge \mathbf{e}_2 + 0 \\
&= (\alpha_1\beta_2 - \alpha_2\beta_1)\mathbf{e}_1 \wedge \mathbf{e}_2. \qquad (2.1.4)
\end{aligned}$$

Note the scalar value is the area of the parallelogram defined by vectors **a** and **b**.

For an n-dimensional space, we denote the outer product of all orthonormal basis elements as $\mathbf{I}_n = \mathbf{e}_1 \wedge \mathbf{e}_2 \wedge \cdots \wedge \mathbf{e}_n$. This is called the *pseudoscalar* and is often denoted simply as **I**.

The Geometric Product

The geometric product is the most important product, so we do not use any symbol for it; we merely place multivectors adjacent. We start by defining the geometric product of two vectors **a** and **b** from V using the dot product (also called inner product) and outer product, as shown in Equation 2.1.5:

$$\mathbf{ab} = \mathbf{a} \cdot \mathbf{b} + \mathbf{a} \wedge \mathbf{b}. \qquad (2.1.5)$$

This has the nice property that it is invertible. That is, if **a** is nonzero, we can divide **ab** by **a** to recover **b**, and likewise divide by **b** to recover **a**. Note that the inverse of **a** is $\mathbf{a}^{-1} = \mathbf{a}/(\mathbf{a} \cdot \mathbf{a})$ and satisfies $\mathbf{aa}^{-1} = \mathbf{a}^{-1}\mathbf{a} = 1$. Now we have a product we can cancel, making this product similar to the product in the complex number example.

Next in Equation 2.1.6, we extend the geometric product to arbitrary elements of CV with the following rules for scalars α, β, vectors **a**, **b**, and multivectors **A**, **B**, **C**:

$$\begin{array}{rl}
\alpha\beta \text{ and } \alpha\mathbf{b} & \text{have the usual meaning} \\
\alpha\mathbf{A} = \mathbf{A}\alpha & \text{scalars commute} \\
\mathbf{ab} = \mathbf{a} \cdot \mathbf{b} + \mathbf{a} \wedge \mathbf{b} & \text{vector and vector} \\
\mathbf{A}(\mathbf{BC}) = (\mathbf{AB})\mathbf{C} & \text{associative} \\
\mathbf{A}(\mathbf{B} + \mathbf{C}) = \mathbf{AB} + \mathbf{AC} & \text{distributes left} \\
(\mathbf{A} + \mathbf{B})\mathbf{C} = \mathbf{AC} + \mathbf{BC} & \text{distributes right}
\end{array} \qquad (2.1.6)$$

To show how to compute with these, we simplify and give formulas for an orthonormal basis—there are general formulas, but they are more involved. Any vector can be written using an *orthonormal* basis $\{\mathbf{e}_1, \mathbf{e}_2, \ldots, \mathbf{e}_n\}$. We can then expand any multivector into the basis of CV. From the vector definition, we easily compute Equation 2.1.7.

$$\mathbf{e}_i\mathbf{e}_j = \begin{cases} \mathbf{e}_i \wedge \mathbf{e}_j = -\mathbf{e}_j\mathbf{e}_i, & \text{if } i \neq j; \\ 1, & \text{if } i = j. \end{cases} \tag{2.1.7}$$

We write $\mathbf{e}_{i_1 i_2 \cdots i_k} = \mathbf{e}_{i_1}\mathbf{e}_{i_2}\cdots\mathbf{e}_{i_k}$ as shorthand for the geometric product of k basis elements. Then we claim without proof that $\mathbf{e}_{i_1 i_2 \cdots i_k} = \mathbf{e}_{i_1}\mathbf{e}_{i_2}\cdots\mathbf{e}_{i_k} = \mathbf{e}_{i_1} \wedge \mathbf{e}_{i_2} \wedge \cdots \wedge \mathbf{e}_{i_k}$ for any *k distinct* basis vectors. So now, to compute the geometric product of any two multivectors, we proceed as follows:

1. Expand multivectors into outer products of basis elements.
2. Write (as earlier) the outer products as geometric products.
3. Multiply out using associativity of the geometric product, keeping track of order.
4. In each product, swap subscripts in adjacent pairs to get the desired order. Each swap causes a sign change if the subscripts differ, and when two identical subscripts are adjacent, both terms are replaced with 1.
5. Finally, write the simplified products in terms of the outer product (this step requires unique subscripts, so we must swap and replace with 1 whenever possible in the previous step).

This computation should be mastered—it is essential. For example, consider Equation 2.1.8:

$$\begin{aligned}(\mathbf{e}_3 + \mathbf{e}_2 \wedge \mathbf{e}_3)(\mathbf{e}_1 + \mathbf{e}_1 \wedge \mathbf{e}_3) &= (\mathbf{e}_3 + \mathbf{e}_{23})(\mathbf{e}_1 + \mathbf{e}_{13}) \\ &= \mathbf{e}_{31} + \mathbf{e}_{313} + \mathbf{e}_{231} + \mathbf{e}_{2313} \\ &= -\mathbf{e}_{13} - \mathbf{e}_{133} + \mathbf{e}_{123} + \mathbf{e}_{1233} \\ &= -\mathbf{e}_1\mathbf{e}_3 - \mathbf{e}_1 \cdot 1 + \mathbf{e}_1\mathbf{e}_2\mathbf{e}_3 + \mathbf{e}_1\mathbf{e}_2 \cdot 1 \\ &= -\mathbf{e}_1 \wedge \mathbf{e}_3 - \mathbf{e}_1 + \mathbf{e}_1 \wedge \mathbf{e}_2 \wedge \mathbf{e}_3 + \mathbf{e}_1 \wedge \mathbf{e}_2. \end{aligned} \tag{2.1.8}$$

With these rules, we could construct a multiplication table for the eight basis elements of CV^3, which is a good exercise. And we can now by hand calculate outer and geometric products of any two elements in the entire algebra CV. Note the general geometric product has many terms: the geometric product of an m-blade and a k-blade potentially has terms of all grades from $|m-k|$ to $m+k$.

The Contraction Product

The final product that we use is the (left) contraction product, which generalizes the inner product (also called dot product) of two vectors to an *inner* product on general multivectors in a manner that works well for computer graphics. This is sometimes called the *left projection*; there is a right projection, the dual of the left, but we do not cover it here. This product is used to project spaces onto other spaces, much like the inner product is used to project one vector onto another. The contraction product is denoted by the symbol $\rfloor$ and expands across multivector grades in the same manner as the outer product. It is read as "a contract b" or "a left contract b."

We need some notation: for a *k*-blade $\mathbf{A} = \mathbf{a}_1 \wedge \mathbf{a}_2 \wedge \cdots \wedge \mathbf{a}_k$, we denote the *reverse* of its terms by $\tilde{\mathbf{A}} = \mathbf{a}_k \wedge \mathbf{a}_{k-1} \wedge \cdots \wedge \mathbf{a}_1 = (-1)^{k(k-1)/2}$. For a multivector **A**, we denote the grade *r* part as $\langle \mathbf{A} \rangle_r$ or sometimes $\mathbf{A}_r$ if no confusion results.

The general definition of the contraction product of multivectors is

$$\mathbf{AB} = \sum_{r,s} \langle \mathbf{A}_r \mathbf{B}_s \rangle_{s-r} .$$

What does this mean? To compute the contraction product of an *r*-blade **A** with an *s*-blade **B**, we compute the geometric product, then take the $s - r$ grade component, which may be zero. The contraction product is 0 when $r > s$, since there are no negative grade elements. To compute the contraction product of multivectors, we expand into blades and compute each combination separately. Geometrically, the contraction product $\mathbf{A} \rfloor \mathbf{B}$ of two blades returns a blade contained in **B** that is perpendicular to **A**. Figure 2.1.3 shows an example of a vector **a** contracted into a plane **B**.

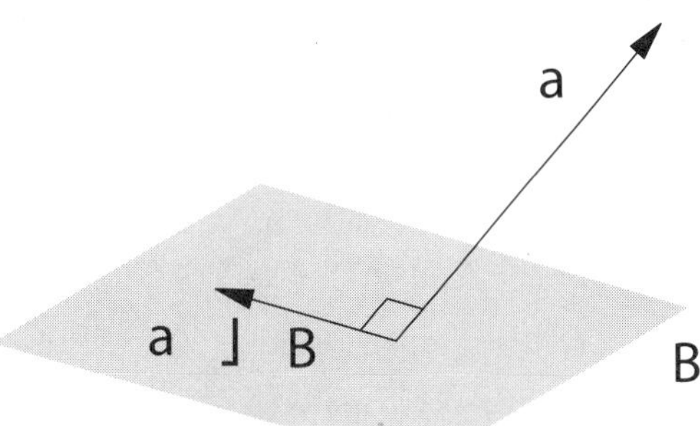

FIGURE 2.1.3 *The contraction product projects spaces onto perpendicular components in other spaces.*

We also require that the contraction product reduce to the dot product for vectors and be linear in both components. These requirements give the relations outlined in Equation 2.1.9.

$$
\begin{array}{rl}
\alpha \rfloor \beta = \alpha\beta & \text{scalars} \\
\mathbf{a} \rfloor \beta = 0 & \text{vector and scalar} \\
\alpha \rfloor \mathbf{b} = \alpha\mathbf{b} & \text{scalar and vector} \\
\mathbf{a} \rfloor \mathbf{b} = \mathbf{a} \cdot \mathbf{b} & \text{usual dot product on vectors} \\
\mathbf{a} \rfloor (\mathbf{b} \wedge \mathbf{C}) = (\mathbf{a} \rfloor \mathbf{b}) \wedge \mathbf{C} - \mathbf{b} \wedge (\mathbf{a} \rfloor \mathbf{C}) & \text{expansion formula} \\
(\mathbf{A} \wedge \mathbf{B}) \rfloor \mathbf{C} = \mathbf{A} \rfloor (\mathbf{B} \rfloor \mathbf{C}) & \text{distribution formulas} \\
\mathbf{A} \wedge (\mathbf{B} \rfloor \mathbf{C}) = (\mathbf{A} \rfloor \mathbf{B}) \rfloor \mathbf{C} &
\end{array} \tag{2.1.9}
$$

Note the contraction product is *not* associative: $(\mathbf{A} \rfloor \mathbf{B}) \rfloor \mathbf{C} \neq \mathbf{A} \rfloor (\mathbf{B} \rfloor \mathbf{C})$. So parentheses are needed to avoid ambiguity. As a simplifying notation to avoid having to parenthesize every product combination, the precedence conventions shown in Equation 2.1.10 are used:

$$
\begin{aligned}
(\mathbf{A} \wedge \mathbf{B})\mathbf{C} &= \mathbf{A} \wedge \mathbf{B}\,\mathbf{C} \quad \neq \mathbf{A} \wedge (\mathbf{B}\,\mathbf{C}) \\
(\mathbf{A} \rfloor \mathbf{B})\mathbf{C} &= \mathbf{A} \rfloor \mathbf{B}\,\mathbf{C} \quad \neq \mathbf{A} \rfloor (\mathbf{B}\,\mathbf{C}) \\
\mathbf{A} \rfloor (\mathbf{B} \wedge \mathbf{C}) &= \mathbf{A} \rfloor \mathbf{B} \wedge \mathbf{C} \neq (\mathbf{A} \rfloor \mathbf{B}) \wedge \mathbf{C}.
\end{aligned} \tag{2.1.10}
$$

This says that when there are ambiguous mixtures of types of products, outer products are performed first, then contraction products, and then geometric products.

We show an example computation before we continue. Being able to compute the following example covers most of what we have explained so far. Given multivectors $\mathbf{A} = 1 + 2\mathbf{e}_2 - 3\mathbf{e}_1 \wedge \mathbf{e}_3$ and $\mathbf{B} = 2\mathbf{e}_2 + 7\mathbf{e}_1$, compute the outer, geometric, and contraction products, as shown in Equation 2.1.11:

$$
\begin{aligned}
\mathbf{A} \wedge \mathbf{B} &= 2\mathbf{e}_2 + 7\mathbf{e}_1 \wedge \mathbf{e}_2 \wedge \mathbf{e}_3 + 4 \cdot 0 + 14 \cdot 0 - 6\mathbf{e}_1 \wedge \mathbf{e}_3 \wedge \mathbf{e}_2 - 21 \cdot 0 \\
&= 2\mathbf{e}_2 + 13\mathbf{e}_1 \wedge \mathbf{e}_2 \wedge \mathbf{e}_3 \\
\mathbf{A}\mathbf{B} &= 2\mathbf{e}_2 + 7\mathbf{e}_{123} + 4\mathbf{e}_{22} + 14\mathbf{e}_{2123} - 6\mathbf{e}_{132} - 21\mathbf{e}_{13123} \\
&= 2\mathbf{e}_2 + 7\mathbf{e}_{123} + 4 - 14\mathbf{e}_{1223} + 6\mathbf{e}_{123} - 21\mathbf{e}_{11233} \\
&= 2\mathbf{e}_2 + 7\mathbf{e}_{123} + 4 - 14\mathbf{e}_{13} + 6\mathbf{e}_{123} - 21\mathbf{e}_2 \\
&= 4 - 19\mathbf{e}_2 - 14\mathbf{e}_1 \wedge \mathbf{e}_3 + 13\mathbf{e}_1 \wedge \mathbf{e}_2 \wedge \mathbf{e}_3 \\
\mathbf{A} \rfloor \mathbf{B} &= 2 \rfloor \mathbf{e}_2 + 7 \rfloor \mathbf{e}_{123} + 4\mathbf{e}_2 \rfloor \mathbf{e}_2 + 14\mathbf{e}_2 \rfloor \mathbf{e}_{123} - 6 \cdot 0 - 21\mathbf{e}_{13} \rfloor \mathbf{e}_{123} \\
&= 2\langle \mathbf{e}_2 \rangle_{1-0} + 7\langle \mathbf{e}_{123} \rangle_{3-0} + 4\langle \mathbf{e}_2\mathbf{e}_2 \rangle_{1-1} + 14\langle \mathbf{e}_2\mathbf{e}_{123} \rangle_{3-1} - 21\langle \mathbf{e}_{13}\mathbf{e}_{123} \rangle_{3-2} \\
&= 2\mathbf{e}_2 + 7\mathbf{e}_{123} + 4 - 14\mathbf{e}_{13} - 21\mathbf{e}_2 \\
&= 4 - 19\mathbf{e}_2 - 14\mathbf{e}_1 \wedge \mathbf{e}_3 + 7\mathbf{e}_1 \wedge \mathbf{e}_2 \wedge \mathbf{e}_3.
\end{aligned} \tag{2.1.11}
$$

Inverses

The contraction product allows easy computation of inverses for many multivectors. A multivector is called a *versor* if it *can* be written as the outer product of vectors.[2] Thus, a k-blade is a versor, and a versor can be written as a k-blade. Some k-vectors are not obviously versors, and some k-vectors are *not* versors. For example, $\mathbf{e}_{13} - \mathbf{e}_{12} + \mathbf{e}_{23}$ is not a k-blade (but is a 2-*vector*) for any k as written, but it is a versor since it can be rewritten as $\mathbf{e}_{13} - \mathbf{e}_{12} + \mathbf{e}_{23} = (\mathbf{e}_1 + \mathbf{e}_2) \wedge (\mathbf{e}_1 + \mathbf{e}_3)$. A good exercise is to show that in three or fewer dimensions, every k-vector is actually a versor, although this is not true in higher dimensions. For a nonzero versor $\mathbf{A}_r$ that can be written as the outer product of r vectors, the (left and right) inverse is $\mathbf{A}_r^{-1} = \tilde{\mathbf{A}} / (\mathbf{A} \rfloor \tilde{\mathbf{A}})$, which reduces to the special case inverse of a vector $\mathbf{a}$ being $\mathbf{a}^{-1} = \tilde{\mathbf{a}} / (\mathbf{a} \rfloor \tilde{\mathbf{a}}) = \mathbf{a} / \mathbf{a} \cdot \mathbf{a}$, as we saw earlier. For fun, prove that $1 + \mathbf{e}_1$ has no (left or right) inverse in any dimension. Then find the inverse of $1 + \mathbf{e}_1 \wedge \mathbf{e}_2$. Finally, show that $1 + \mathbf{e}_1 + \mathbf{e}_1 \wedge \mathbf{e}_2$ and $1 - \mathbf{e}_1 - \mathbf{e}_1 \wedge \mathbf{e}_2$ are inverses, but neither are versors. You must be careful with inverses since there are distinct left and right inverses in some cases (or so the literature says). Keeping to inverses of versors is safe since the formula produces an inverse that works as both a left and a right inverse.

Old School Revisited

Now that we have defined geometric algebra and know how to manipulate a few products, we show how some ideas from linear algebra are already present in this formulation.

The Complex Numbers

Complex numbers exist in any plane! Given a plane, pick two orthogonal unit vectors $\mathbf{u}$ and $\mathbf{vu}$, and label the bivector $\mathbf{i} = \mathbf{u} \wedge \mathbf{v}$. Then any vector $\mathbf{a} = \alpha\mathbf{u} + \beta\mathbf{v}$ in this plane can be rotated just like the example in the Introduction, using this bivector as the imaginary unit. Multiplying by the multivector $\mathbf{R}_\theta = \cos\theta + \mathbf{i}\sin\theta$ gives Equation 2.1.12,

$$\mathbf{R}_\theta \mathbf{a} = (\alpha\cos\theta + \beta\sin\theta)\mathbf{u} + (\beta\cos\theta - \alpha\sin\theta)\mathbf{v} = \mathbf{a}\mathbf{R}_{-\theta}. \qquad (2.1.12)$$

Note that the rotation direction depends on left and right multiplication, and to make this look more like the general rotation we write $\mathbf{a} \to \mathbf{R}_{\theta/2}\mathbf{a}\mathbf{R}_{-\theta/2}$. The $\theta/2$ angles make this transform behave like quaternion rotations, which we examine next.

[2]Note a versor can then always be written as an outer product of orthonormal basis elements spanning the same subspace times a scalar "volume." This can be useful in calculations.

The Quaternions

If we define the following bivectors in 3-space

$$\mathbf{i} = \mathbf{e}_3 \wedge \mathbf{e}_2$$

then the quaternion relations apply: $\mathbf{i}^2 = \mathbf{j}^2 = \mathbf{k}^2 = -1$, $\mathbf{ij} = \mathbf{k}$ (and cyclic combinations), where the multiplication is the geometric product. The bivectors have been chosen to make $\mathbf{i}$ denote rotation about the x axis, etc., and so that there is a nice relationship between the usual notion of a quaternion and the geometric algebra notion. The set of multivectors of the form $\alpha + \beta\mathbf{i} + \gamma\mathbf{j} + \delta\mathbf{k}$ is precisely the quaternions, but when viewed as elements of the geometric algebra, extend rotations from acting only on vectors (as we usually use the quaternions) to rotations on *any* multivector! And the usual quaternion inverse, for nonzero quaternions, is exactly the geometric inverse!

The quaternion method to rotate a plane requires moving all the defining parameters one at a time with the quaternion. The geometric algebra method rotates the plane (bivector) directly by the quaternion, which is conceptually more elegant.

Now instead of thinking of a quaternion as a unit vector on a four-dimensional sphere with a continuous group law, we can picture one as a planar piece (which defines an axis of rotation), and an angle of rotation, as in Figure 2.1.4 (the axis-angle view). So it seems complex numbers give rotations in two dimensions, quaternions give rotations in three dimensions, and geometric algebra unifies them both. Rotations in any dimension use the same rules, of which quaternions and complex numbers were special cases (note they both used bivectors to rotate)!

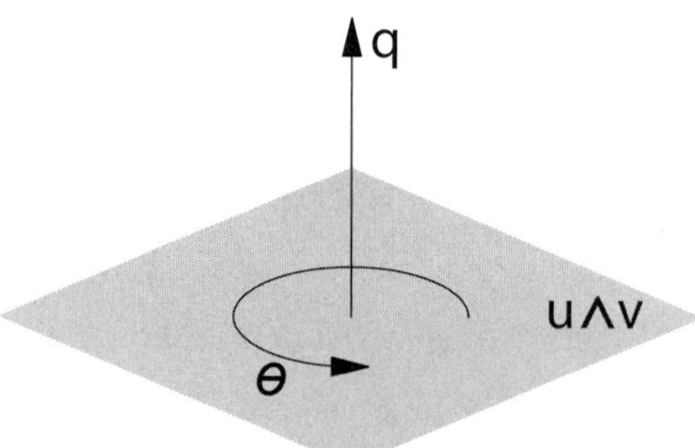

FIGURE 2.1.4 *A quaternion can be viewed as an oriented area element with a magnitude.*

Reflections and Rotations

The reflection of a multivector **K** through a k-blade **A** (both through the origin) is computed with the transform $\mathbf{X} \to -(-1)^k \mathbf{AXA}^{-1}$. This is illustrated in Figure 2.1.5, which shows how to reflect a vector $\mathbf{x}$ through a vector $\mathbf{a}$, by the transform $\mathbf{x} \to \mathbf{axa}^{-1}$. This is a useful formula, since it works in any dimension, and is the basis for rotation formulas that are dimension-independent.

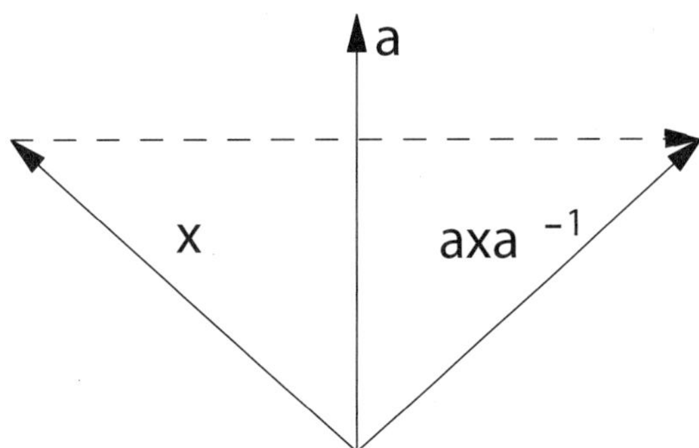

FIGURE 2.1.5 *Reflection has a simple GA notation.*

By reflecting *twice* over vectors $\mathbf{a}$ and $\mathbf{a}$ with an angle $\theta/2$ between them, we can rotate the objects encoded in multivectors by an angle θ. The object $\mathbf{R} = \mathbf{ab}$ is called a *rotor*, and performs rotation on any multivector $\mathbf{X}$ *in any dimension*, by the transformation $\mathbf{X} \to \mathbf{RXR}^{-1}$. They are more efficient to compose than matrices and are numerically more stable. And they rotate multivectors, not just vectors (see the examples that follow). In 3D, expanding a rotor in terms of basis elements shows it is just a quaternion, as we would expect.

There are several equivalent ways to construct a rotor. It is useful to take $\mathbf{a}$ and $\mathbf{b}$ to be unit vectors, since then $\mathbf{R}^{-1} = \mathbf{ba}$ is easy to compute. In 3D, a way to construct a rotor that rotates by θ around an axis $\mathbf{c}$ is to take $\mathbf{R} = \cos(\theta/2) - \sin(\theta/2)\mathbf{Ic}$. With these different and concise formulas to construct rotations, GA provides a simpler way to work out computations. And in any dimension, composition of rotors is computed with the geometric product. It's even possible to do calculus on rotors to give velocities, accelerations, interpolations, minimizing paths, camera orientation, etc., but this will require more gems. As in all mathematics, this goes much deeper than there is space to present completely. Another advantage is that the rotor also keeps track of the direction of rotation, unlike a scalar-valued angle or rotation matrix, allowing subdivision and interpolation of rotations. In three dimensions, rotor interpolation is the usual SLERP, as shown in Equation 2.1.13

$$\mathbf{R}(\lambda) = \frac{\sin((1-\lambda)\theta)\mathbf{R}_1 + \sin(\lambda\theta)\mathbf{R}_2}{\sin\theta}. \tag{2.1.13}$$

This simplifies for the midpoint between two rotations:

$$\mathbf{R}(1/2) = \frac{\sin(\theta/2)}{\sin\theta}(\mathbf{R}_1 + \mathbf{R}_2).$$

Linear Algebra Connection

Given a linear transformation $f : V^n \to V^n$ (a matrix multiplication, for example), f acts naturally on k-blades as $f(\alpha) = \alpha$. We add the rule on scalars $f(\alpha) = \alpha$ and extend linearly to get a transform $f : CV \to CV$ defined for any multivector in the geometric algebra. This extension plays nicely with our notions of geometry. For example, a linear transform moves lines to lines, planes to planes, etc. To see a linear transform move a line to another line, we apply f to both sides of the general line equation $(\mathbf{x} - \mathbf{a}) \wedge \mathbf{u} = 0$, resulting in Equation 2.1.14

$$\begin{aligned} f((\mathbf{x} - \mathbf{a}) \wedge \mathbf{u}) &= f(0) \\ f(\mathbf{x} - \mathbf{a}) \wedge f(\mathbf{u}) &= 0 \\ (f(\mathbf{x}) - f(\mathbf{a})) \wedge f(\mathbf{u}) &= 0 \\ (\mathbf{x}' - \mathbf{a}') \wedge \mathbf{u}' &= 0. \end{aligned} \tag{2.1.14}$$

The Dictionary

Before we show how GA can simplify the derivation of equations, we first list some common geometric relations and how these relations translate into GA. There is not space in this gem to derive and explain each one, so we merely list facts and simplifying computational rules that can be applied.

1. The geometric product is the most fundamental product; the others can be written in terms of it[3]. For example, consider Equation 2.1.15

$$\begin{aligned} \mathbf{a} \wedge \mathbf{b} &= \tfrac{1}{2}(\mathbf{ab} - \mathbf{ba}) \\ \mathbf{a} \cdot \mathbf{b} &= \tfrac{1}{2}(\mathbf{ab} + \mathbf{ba}) \\ \mathbf{a} \times \mathbf{b} &= (\mathbf{a} \wedge \mathbf{b}) \lrcorner \tilde{\mathbf{I}}_3 = -\mathbf{I}_3(\mathbf{a} \wedge \mathbf{b}) = -(\mathbf{a} \wedge \mathbf{b})\mathbf{I}_3 \\ \mathbf{a} \lrcorner \mathbf{b} &= \langle \mathbf{ab} \rangle_0. \end{aligned} \tag{2.1.15}$$

2. The usual 3D cross product is $\mathbf{a} \times \mathbf{b} = (\mathbf{a} \wedge \mathbf{b}) \lrcorner \tilde{\mathbf{I}}_3 = -\mathbf{I}_3(\mathbf{a} \wedge \mathbf{b}) = -(\mathbf{a} \wedge \mathbf{b})\mathbf{I}_3$. This is easy to verify by choosing an orthonormal basis for the span of $\mathbf{a} \wedge \mathbf{b}$, extending it to a 3D basis, and evaluating each expression.

[3] There is an axiomatic way to define the geometric product first, and derive the others from it, so we are not using circular definitions. This presentation way is easier to learn.

3. Vectors are perpendicular if and only if the dot product is 0. This extends to the contraction product applied to *k*-blades!
4. Linear (in)dependence: the outer product of vectors is 0 if and only if the vectors are linearly dependent. Thus two vectors are parallel if and only if their outer product is 0. This allows simple line and plane equations.
5. The equation of a line through a point **a** and with direction **u** is $(\mathbf{x}-\mathbf{a})\wedge\mathbf{u}=0$. This works in any dimension, so it is more concise than the dimension-dependent forms.
6. Similarly, a plane through a point **a** and parallel to the bivector $\mathbf{u}\wedge\mathbf{v}$ is $(\mathbf{x}-\mathbf{a})\wedge\mathbf{u}\wedge\mathbf{v}=0$. Again, this is dimension-independent.
7. The orthogonal projection of a blade **A** onto a blade **B** is given by $\mathrm{P}_{\mathbf{B}}(\mathbf{A})=(\mathbf{A}\rfloor\mathbf{B})\mathbf{B}^{-}$. This is nice since it is the same expression for any two spaces: points onto lines, lines onto planes, planes onto planes, etc., in any dimension.
8. Extending the projection, the expression $\mathbf{A}-\mathrm{P}_{\mathbf{B}}(\mathbf{A})$ must represent the perpendicular component of **A** with respect to **B**.
9. The pseudoscalar **I** commutes with all elements in odd-dimensional spaces.
10. Given a vector **n**, a plane perpendicular to it in 3-space is $-\mathbf{nI}$, and given a plane defined by $\mathbf{u}\wedge\mathbf{v}$, the normal vector is $-(\mathbf{u}\wedge\mathbf{v})\mathbf{I}$. This is shown in Figure 2.1.6. Recall this plane has an orientation, so we include the minus signs to make this agree with the "dual."

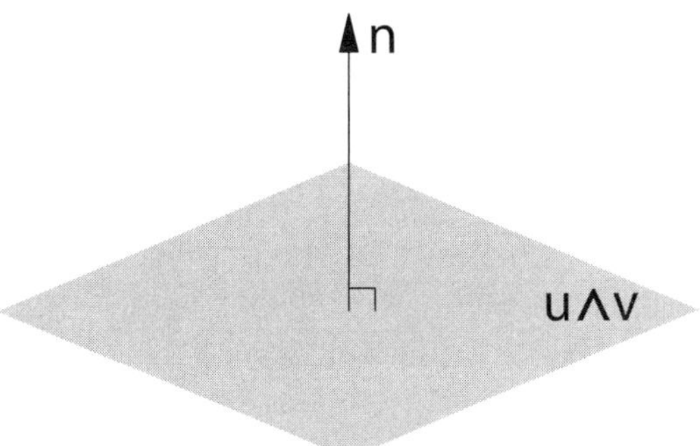

FIGURE 2.1.6 *In 3D, perpendicular vectors are "dual" to plane elements.*

11. Duality: the *dual* of a multivector **A** is defined by $\mathbf{A}^{*}=\mathbf{A}\rfloor\tilde{\mathbf{I}}$. This is useful for exchanging "spanning" relations and "perpendicularity" relations. This generalizes the previous fact. In 3D, this exchanges bivectors with normal direction vectors, so it can be used to quickly find the normal to a plane. This is shown in 3D for a normal and plane in Figure 2.1.6.
12. The *norm* of a multivector generalizes the length of a vector and is written $|\mathbf{A}|=\sqrt{\mathbf{A}\rfloor\tilde{\mathbf{A}}}$. It returns the area of a bivector, the length of a vector, etc.

13. Given two versors **A** and **B**, each defines a subspace of V; the intersection of these subspaces is called their *meet* and is denoted by $\mathbf{M} = \mathbf{A} \cap \mathbf{B}$. It can be computed via $\mathbf{A} \cap \mathbf{B} = \mathbf{A}^* \rfloor \mathbf{B} = (\mathbf{A} \rfloor \tilde{\mathbf{I}}) \rfloor \mathbf{B}$. The dual concept is the *join*, which is the smallest subspace of V containing the two subspaces, written as $\mathbf{J} = \mathbf{A} \cup \mathbf{B}$. For example, the meet of two nonparallel planes in 3D is the line of their intersection, as shown in Figure 2.1.7. The meet of two versors can be thought of as the greatest common divisor of the defining vectors, and the join as the least common multiple. Knowing one allows easy computation of the other via the relations shown in Equation 2.1.16.

$$\begin{aligned} \mathbf{J} &= \mathbf{A} \wedge (\mathbf{M}^{-1} \rfloor \mathbf{B}) \\ \mathbf{M} &= (\mathbf{B} \rfloor \mathbf{J}^{-1}) \rfloor \mathbf{A} \end{aligned} \tag{2.1.16}$$

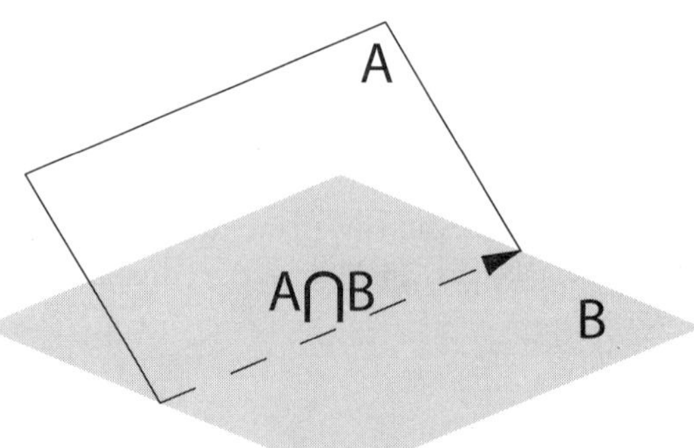

FIGURE 2.1.7 *Think of the "meet" as the intersection of subspaces.*

Examples

In this section, we present several example computations that show GA in action. The point of this gem is to show that GA simplifies hand derivations and reduces code complexity. So when working through these examples, the reader should consider the coding complexity involved for each of two geometry engines: one with basic linear algebra routines and one supporting the geometric product. In each case, these derivations are short by hand and would only involve a few lines of code in the GA engine. However, the coding work for the linear algebra methods would involve quite a bit of code for most of the examples. Quod erat demonstrandum and touché, to mix languages!

1. Given vectors **x** and **a**, suppose we want to find the component $\mathbf{x}_\perp$ of **x** that is perpendicular to the vector **a**, as illustrated in Figure 2.1.8. The perpendicular condition is $\mathbf{x}_\perp \rfloor \mathbf{a} = 0$, and magnitude conditions require another

condition: the magnitude of the area spanned by **a** and **x** is the same as that by **a** and $\mathbf{x}_\perp$ (this just says the area of the parallelogram is base times height). Thus, $\mathbf{x}_\perp \wedge \mathbf{a} = \mathbf{x} \wedge \mathbf{a}$. Adding these two equations gives the geometric product $\mathbf{x}_\perp \wedge \mathbf{a} + \mathbf{x}_\perp \rfloor \mathbf{a} = \mathbf{x} \wedge \mathbf{a} + 0 = \mathbf{x}_\perp \mathbf{a}$, and this we can divide by **x** to get $\mathbf{x}_\perp = (\mathbf{x} \wedge \mathbf{a})\mathbf{a}^{-1}$. To see how this fits into standard linear algebra, we pick a basis such that $\mathbf{a} = \alpha\mathbf{e}_1$ and $\mathbf{x} = \beta\mathbf{e}_1 + \delta\mathbf{e}_2$, plug in and expand, getting $\mathbf{x}_\perp = ((\beta\mathbf{e}_1 + \delta\mathbf{e}_2) \wedge \alpha\mathbf{e}_1)(\mathbf{e}_1/\alpha) = \delta\mathbf{e}_2$ as we would expect.

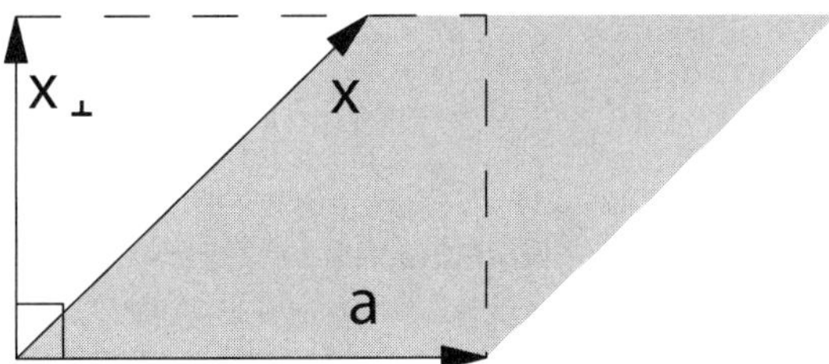

FIGURE 2.1.8 *GA has a simple notation for decomposing objects into parallel and perpendicular components.*

Now for the kicker. What if we want the vector component of **x** that is perpendicular to a plane given by a bivector **A**? We do the same math and obtain[4] $\mathbf{x}_\perp = (\mathbf{x} \wedge \mathbf{A})\mathbf{A}^{-1}$. Elegant indeed! (Or we just project **x** to the normal $-\mathbf{A}\mathbf{I}_3$ of the plane, which is equivalent by duality).

2. Next, we reflect a point through a plane. In Figure 2.1.9, **B** is the side view of a plane, and **a** is a vector that we want to reflect through the plane. We do this with the reflection through a vector idea, getting a nice formula. Let **n** be the normal to the plane. From earlier, we know the reflection of **a** through **n** is just $\mathbf{nan}^{-1}$, and from Figure 2.1.8, the reflection of the point through the plane is $-\mathbf{nan}^{-1}$. To avoid making errors by believing nice pictures, note this formula still works with the "other" normal to the plane. Computing a concrete example is instructive. So given the point and plane, it is one line of code to project like this, and the equation works in any dimension as usual.
3. We demonstrate the meet of two blades by computing the intersection of two nonparallel planes through the origin, as shown in Figure 2.1.7. We take planes that we can easily visualize, and get the answer we expect, as shown in Equation 2.1.17.

---

[4]Actually, you need to know that for any vector **x** and bivector **A**, $\mathbf{xA} = \mathbf{x} \rfloor \mathbf{A} + \mathbf{x} \wedge \mathbf{A}$ and $\mathbf{x} \rfloor \mathbf{A} = 0$ if and only if $\mathbf{X} \perp \mathbf{A}$, both of which are easy to prove. The vector case inspires this.

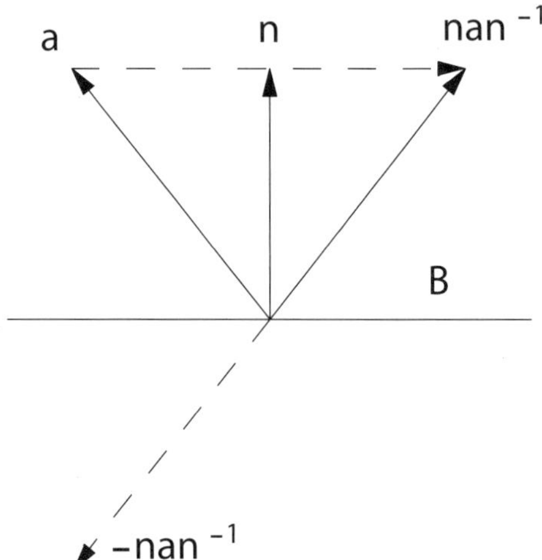

FIGURE 2.1.9 *Negating reflections of vectors gives reflection through a plane.*

$$\begin{aligned}(\mathbf{e}_1 \wedge \mathbf{e}_3) \cap (\mathbf{e}_2 \wedge \mathbf{e}_3) &= (\mathbf{e}_1 \wedge \mathbf{e}_3)^* \lrcorner (\mathbf{e}_2 \wedge \mathbf{e}_3) \\ &= ((\mathbf{e}_1 \wedge \mathbf{e}_3) \lrcorner \tilde{\mathbf{I}}) \lrcorner (\mathbf{e}_2 \wedge \mathbf{e}_3) \\ &= \langle \mathbf{e}_1\mathbf{e}_3\mathbf{e}_3\mathbf{e}_2\mathbf{e}_1 \rangle_{3-2} \lrcorner (\mathbf{e}_2 \wedge \mathbf{e}_3) \\ &= \langle -\mathbf{e}_2\mathbf{e}_2\mathbf{e}_3 \rangle_{2-1} \\ &= -\mathbf{e}_3 \end{aligned} \tag{2.1.17}$$

4. We prove a theorem of Euler stating that the product of two rotations is another rotation by obtaining a concrete formula for the resulting rotation. We view a quaternion in the normal way as a scalar β_0 plus an axis of rotation $\mathbf{q} = \beta_1\mathbf{e}_1 + \beta_2\mathbf{e}_2 + \beta_3\mathbf{e}_3$, written $\beta_0 + \mathbf{q}$. Assume that any single rotation can be represented as a quaternion.[5] Recalling the pseudoscalar $\mathbf{I} = \mathbf{e}_1 \wedge \mathbf{e}_2 \wedge \mathbf{e}_3$ and using the previous definitions, we rewrite this quaternion representation with the GA version using the transformation $\beta_0 + \mathbf{q} \to \beta_0 - \mathbf{I}_3\mathbf{q}$. Now multiply two quaternions, and one can easily read from Equation 2.1.18 both the scalar and the vector defining the resulting quaternion. This proves the theorem of Euler and also obtains a concrete answer for the resulting scalar and vector. Computing this relation is messy and ad hoc using usual quaternions but is straightforward using geometric algebra.

[5]We assume any rotation can be represented by a quaternion. I have a proof, but it won't fit in this margin.

$$\begin{aligned}(p_0+\mathbf{p})(q_0+\mathbf{q}) &\to (p_0-\mathbf{I}_3\mathbf{p})(q_0-\mathbf{I}_3\mathbf{q})\\ &= p_0q_0 - p_0\mathbf{I}_3\mathbf{q} - q_0\mathbf{I}_3\mathbf{p} + \mathbf{I}_3\mathbf{p}\mathbf{I}_3\mathbf{q}\\ &= p_0q_0 - \mathbf{pq} - p_0\mathbf{I}_3\mathbf{q} - q_0\mathbf{I}_3\mathbf{p}\\ &= p_0q_0 - \mathbf{p}\cdot\mathbf{q} - \mathbf{p}\wedge\mathbf{q} - p_0\mathbf{I}_3\mathbf{q} - q_0\mathbf{I}_3\mathbf{p}\\ &= p_0q_0 - \mathbf{p}\cdot\mathbf{q} - \mathbf{I}_3(p_0\mathbf{q}+q_0\mathbf{p}+\mathbf{q}\times\mathbf{p})\\ &\to (p_0q_0-\mathbf{p}\cdot\mathbf{q}) + (p_0\mathbf{q}+q_0\mathbf{p}+\mathbf{q}\times\mathbf{p}) \end{aligned} \quad (2.1.18)$$

5. A concrete rotation example is in order: the composition of rotation by $\pi/2$ around $\mathbf{e}_1$ preceded by a rotation of $\pi/2$ around $\mathbf{e}_2$ results in a $2\pi/3$ rotation around the vector $(\mathbf{e}_1+\mathbf{e}_2+\mathbf{e}_3)/\sqrt{3}$. The calculation uses the quaternion representation from the previous example. Recall that we divide angles by 2. The proof is provided in Equation 2.1.19.

$$\begin{aligned}\left(\cos\frac{\pi}{4}+\mathbf{e}_1\sin\frac{\pi}{4}\right)\left(\cos\frac{\pi}{4}+\mathbf{e}_2\sin\frac{\pi}{4}\right) &\to \frac{1}{\sqrt{2}}(1+\mathbf{e}_{32})\frac{1}{\sqrt{2}}(1+\mathbf{e}_{13})\\ &= \frac{1}{2}(1+\mathbf{e}_{13}+\mathbf{e}_{32}+\mathbf{e}_{21})\\ &= \frac{1}{2}-\frac{\sqrt{3}}{2}\mathbf{I}\frac{(\mathbf{e}_1+\mathbf{e}_2+\mathbf{e}_3)}{\sqrt{3}}\\ &\to \cos\frac{\pi}{3}+\frac{(\mathbf{e}_1+\mathbf{e}_2+\mathbf{e}_3)}{\sqrt{3}}\sin\frac{\pi}{3}\end{aligned} \quad (2.1.19)$$

6. An example of the rotation of an entire multivector at once is given by rotating the plane defined by the bivector $\mathbf{B}=\mathbf{e}_1\wedge\mathbf{e}_2$ by 60 degrees around the vector $\mathbf{a}=\mathbf{e}_1+\mathbf{e}_2$. There is no need to decompose the plane into component vectors first.[6] We start with the normalized rotor $\mathbf{R}=\cos(\pi/6)-\mathbf{Ia}/\sqrt{2})\sin(\pi/6)$. Then the rotated plane is as shown in Equation 2.1.20

$$\begin{aligned}\mathbf{RBR}^{-1} &= \left(\cos\frac{\pi}{6}-\frac{\mathbf{e}_{23}-\mathbf{e}_{13}}{\sqrt{2}}\sin\frac{\pi}{6}\right)(\mathbf{e}_1\wedge\mathbf{e}_2)\left(\cos\frac{\pi}{6}+\frac{\mathbf{e}_{23}-\mathbf{e}_{13}}{\sqrt{2}}\sin\frac{\pi}{6}\right)\\ &= \frac{1}{2}\mathbf{e}_{12}+\frac{\sqrt{6}}{4}(\mathbf{e}_{13}+\mathbf{e}_{23}).\end{aligned} \quad (2.1.20)$$

[6]And this avoids the problem of applying a rotation to a plane and having to recompute the normal. Recall that the normal of a rotated plane is not the rotated normal of the plane! Usually a plane is defined by a point and normal, and rotating the plane requires getting two linearly independent vectors orthogonal to the normal, rotating these two vectors, computing a new normal, and obtaining a new point.

7. Given vectors **a**, **b**, and **c** in the plane, we can find a vector **x** so that "**a** is to **b** as **c** is to **x**," as illustrated in Figure 2.1.10. If these were real numbers, we would solve $\mathbf{x}:\mathbf{c}=\mathbf{b}:\mathbf{a}$. GA behaves the same since we can now divide vectors by multiplying the ratios by **c** to obtain the answer $\mathbf{x}=\mathbf{b}\mathbf{a}^{-1}\mathbf{c}$.

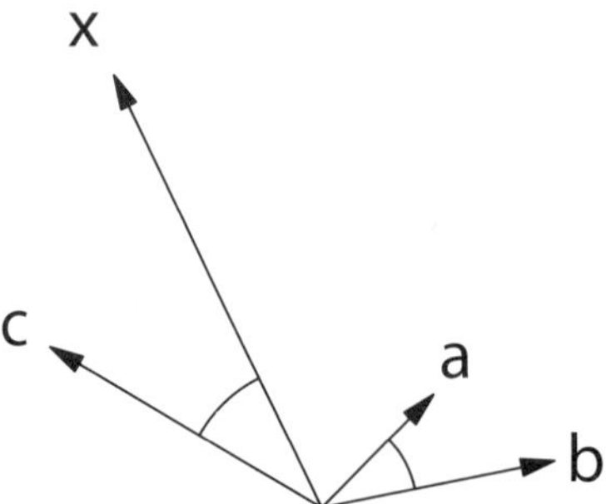

FIGURE 2.1.10 *Ratios make sense for vector magnitude and direction.*

8. Again in the plane, we find the distance from a line with equation $(\mathbf{x}-\mathbf{a})\wedge\mathbf{u}=0$ to the origin, shown in Figure 2.1.11. We find the vector **d** perpendicular to the line and passing through the origin, whose length is the distance. The same reasoning using the normal condition and area condition used in Example 2.1.1 gives $\mathbf{d}=(\mathbf{a}\wedge\mathbf{u})\mathbf{u}^{-1}$, which gives the distance $|\mathbf{d}|$. Does this work for the distance from a plane to the origin?
9. To show an example of the projection formula, we project the vector $\mathbf{a}=\alpha_1\mathbf{e}_1+\alpha_2\mathbf{e}_2+\alpha_3\mathbf{e}_3$ onto the plane $\mathbf{B}=\mathbf{e}_1\wedge\mathbf{e}_2$, where we have picked the plane so we can easily verify the answer. Since the plane is in a nice orientation, we know the answer should be $\alpha_1\mathbf{e}_1+\alpha_2\mathbf{e}_2$. Computation verifies this, as shown in Equation 2.1.21.

$$\begin{aligned}P_{\mathbf{B}}(\mathbf{a})&=(\mathbf{a}\rfloor\mathbf{B})\mathbf{B}^{-1}\\&=\langle(\alpha_1\mathbf{e}_1+\alpha_2\mathbf{e}_2+\alpha_3\mathbf{e}_3)(\mathbf{e}_{12})\rangle_{2-1}(\mathbf{e}_{21})\\&=(\alpha_1\mathbf{e}_2-\alpha_2\mathbf{e}_1)(\mathbf{e}_{21})\\&=\alpha_1\mathbf{e}_1+\alpha_2\mathbf{e}_2\end{aligned}\tag{2.1.21}$$

10. We find a general formula for the intersection of two lines in the plane (which is just Cramer's Rule, except we derive it completely intuitively and geometrically). See Figure 2.1.12; this is hard to see the first time around.

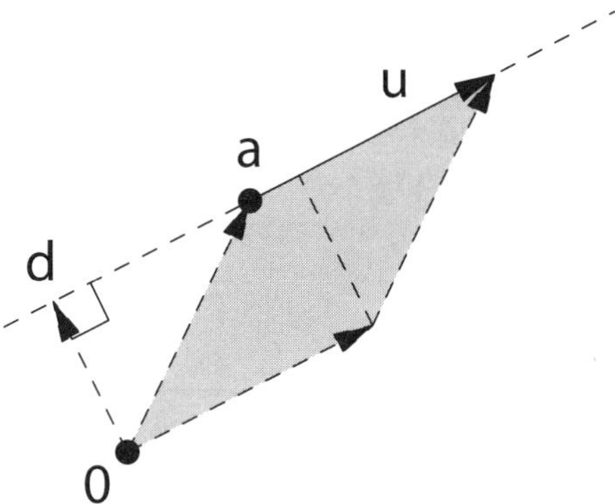

FIGURE 2.1.11 *Computing distance from a point to a line is simple.*

We can write two given lines $(\mathbf{x}-\mathbf{a})\wedge\mathbf{u}=0$ and $(\mathbf{x}-\mathbf{b})\wedge\mathbf{v}=0$ in expanded form as $\mathbf{x}\wedge\mathbf{u}=\mathbf{a}\wedge\mathbf{u}$ and $\mathbf{x}\wedge\mathbf{v}=\mathbf{b}\wedge\mathbf{v}$. Set $\mathbf{U}=\mathbf{a}\wedge\mathbf{u}$ and $\mathbf{V}=\mathbf{b}\wedge\mathbf{v}$. It is clear the intersection is a linear combination of **u** and **v**. To find the coefficients, we look at the picture. The area corresponding to **V** divided by the area corresponding to $\mathbf{u}\wedge\mathbf{v}$ gives the multiple of **u** needed, and dividing **U** by $\mathbf{u}\wedge\mathbf{v}$ gives the **v** multiple. However, since the orientation of the bivectors must be taken into account, we need to reverse $\mathbf{u}\wedge\mathbf{v}$ in the **v** direction. So the final answer must be

$$\mathbf{x}=\frac{\mathbf{V}}{\mathbf{u}\wedge\mathbf{v}}\mathbf{u}+\frac{\mathbf{U}}{\mathbf{v}\wedge\mathbf{u}}\mathbf{v}.$$

Someone fluent with geometric algebra would sketch the picture and be able to write out this equation instantly. With a GA engine, there is no need for a complicated line intersection routine—only the geometric product!

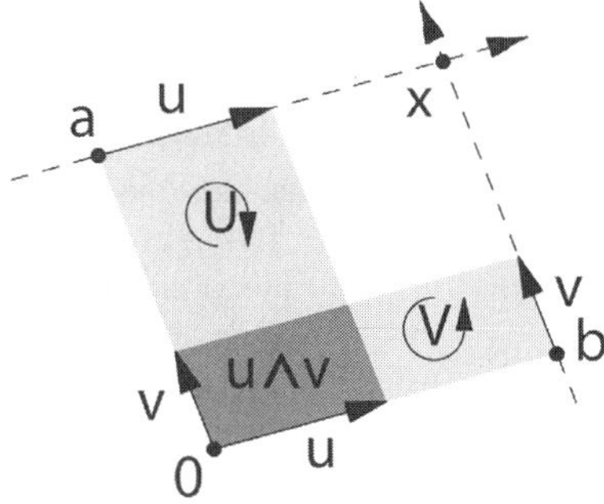

FIGURE 2.1.12 *Here is a graphical way to visualize Cramer's Rule.*

11. A do at home exercise: given a plane triangle with corners (x_i, y_i), $i = 1,2,3$, show the area is the absolute value of the determinant in Equation 2.1.22. Using only analytic geometry, this proof is a lot of work, but is very short using GA (about a half page). Hint: this is easy from using the outer product. Generalize to higher dimensions:

$$Area = \frac{1}{2}\begin{vmatrix} x_1 & y_1 & 1 \\ x_2 & y_2 & 1 \\ x_3 & y_3 & 1 \end{vmatrix}. \qquad (2.1.22)$$

12. As a final example, consider the problem of finding a rotation that will move one orientation to another, as shown in Figure 2.1.13.

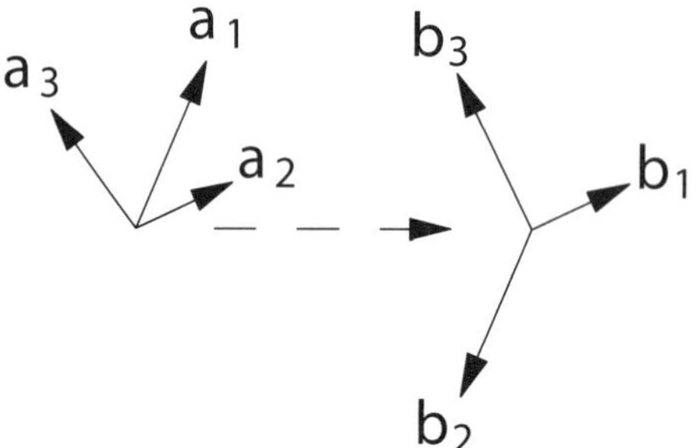

FIGURE 2.1.13 *Computing the transform to move one orientation to another is simple.*

For example, we might want to align an AI-controlled spaceship with a player-controlled one. If we have stored orientations as quaternions, then this is just an invert and multiply, but if we only have three linearly independent vectors defining each orientation, finding this rotation is a lot of work. We don't require the vectors to be orthogonal, only linearly independent. Assume there is a rotation (rotor) $\mathbf{R}$ such that $\mathbf{b}_i = \mathbf{R}\mathbf{a}_i\mathbf{R}^{-1}$ for $i = 1,2,3$. We want to solve these three equations for $\mathbf{R}$. Let $\mathbf{R} = \alpha - \mathbf{B}$ for some bivector $\mathbf{B}$ (thus $\mathbf{R}^{-1} = \alpha + \mathbf{B}$). The adventurous reader should attempt to solve this using linear algebra before proceeding. We define a reciprocal frame (which acts somewhat like an orthonormal frame) written with superscripts: set

$$\mathbf{a}^1 = \frac{\mathbf{a}_2 \wedge \mathbf{a}_3 \mathbf{I}}{\mathbf{a}_1 \wedge \mathbf{a}_2 \wedge \mathbf{a}_3 \mathbf{I}}.$$

which is a vector (easily checked), and similarly define $\mathbf{a}^2$ and $\mathbf{a}^3$. Note $\mathbf{a}^i \cdot \mathbf{a}_j = \delta^i_j$. Then we compute (carefully) the expression in Equation 2.1.23, which allows us to isolate **R**. Next, we solve for **R** in terms of the $\mathbf{a}^i$ and $\mathbf{b}_i$. To get rid of the unknown α, we normalize: set $\mathbf{T} = 1 + \sum_i \mathbf{b}_i \mathbf{a}^i$, and then $\mathbf{R} = \mathbf{T}/|\mathbf{T}|$ gives the desired rotor. The derivation is a bit of work to check, but the final answer is short, easy to compute, and takes very little code in a GA engine. Programming this given only linear algebra routines is a lot of work! As a final note on this example, one may need to check the sign of the final rotation, as shown in Equation 2.1.23, and watch out for 180 degree rotations.

$$\begin{aligned}
\sum_i \mathbf{b}_i \mathbf{a}^i &= \sum_i \mathbf{R}\mathbf{a}_i \mathbf{R}^{-1} \mathbf{a}^i \\
&= \sum_i \mathbf{R}\mathbf{a}_i (\alpha + \mathbf{B}) \mathbf{a}^i \\
&= \mathbf{R}(3\alpha + \mathbf{B}) \\
&= -\mathbf{R}(\alpha - \mathbf{B} - 4\alpha) \\
&= -\mathbf{R}(\mathbf{R}^{-1} - 4\alpha) \\
&= -1 + 4\alpha\mathbf{R}
\end{aligned} \qquad (2.1.23)$$

Conclusion and Future Directions

We have presented the definition of geometric algebra and given rules for hand computations, which can be turned into libraries for doing the work on a computer. Basic geometric ideas like projections and rotations were presented, and many examples were given to show how to use GA for geometric calculations. It should be clear GA unifies many ideas into a single framework and provides a much more concise and powerful framework than linear algebra. So what's next?

Well, there is a lot more math, computer science, and physics already developed and written in the language of GA. There is a complete description of classical mechanics in GA [Hestenes86]; GA seems very well suited for physics. You can perform calculus on GA objects, allowing minima and maxima problems to be solved and allowing differential equations to be written to describe motions, interactions, and physical properties. We saw that GA incorporates quaternions, complex numbers, projections, intersections, linear (in)dependence, and more. It also encompasses Plückerspace and unites all of the following geometries into a single framework: Euclidean, affine, projective, spherical, inverse, hyperbolic, and conformal. This unification makes moving from one system to another much easier and provides quicker access to the methods in each area.

Oddly enough, it seems GA best represents 3D geometry and interaction by embedding 3-space into a 5-space, called the "double homogeneous model" [Dorst-Fontijne04]. The power of this is that it gives spheres in a nice manner, and intersections work in a better manner among different geometric primitives. However, this topic is beyond the scope of this gem.

The most important question that the reader might still have is "Can GA replace linear algebra in my future game engines?" Realistically, GA is not ready due to performance reasons in fast action games. It took linear algebra/computer graphics 30+ years of refinement to get to the performance level it is now, and GA is just being adapted to computer graphics. Current hardware does linear algebra, making linear algebra needed for 3D engines. However the code simplicity and shortened time to create algorithms makes GA suitable for tools, testing, prototyping, and many other areas. In the same manner, subdivision surfaces were once too inefficient for real-time games but are now becoming widespread; it is possible that in the next several years GA will become an indispensable tool for developing professional games.[7] Some experimental results can be found in [Gaigen04], where they have implemented ray tracers in C/C++ using both linear algebra and geometric algebra and have done various comparisons.

The papers [Dorst-Fontijne04], [Dorst-Mann02a], [Dorst-Mann02b], and [Suter03] should provide good starting points for more information. [Hestenes98] discusses calculus with GA material and contains references. Finally, Web searches for the authors Doran, Dorst, and Hestenes yield a lot more references. As a final note, it is important to be aware of differing notation used by some authors.

References

[Dorst-Fontijne04] Dorst, Leo and Daniel Fontijne. "An Algebraic Foundation for Object-Oriented Euclidean Geometry." In preparation; available online at *http://www.science.uva.nl/ga/publications/itm.pdf.*

[Dorst-Mann02a] Dorst, Leo and Stephen Mann. "Geometric Algebra: a computational framework for geometrical applications (part 1: algebra)." *IEEE Computer Graphics and Applications*, May/June 2002. Available online at *http://www.science.uva.nl/~leo/clifford/dorst-mann-I.pdf.*

[Dorst-Mann02b] Dorst, Leo and Stephen Mann. "Geometric Algebra: a computational framework for geometrical applications (part 2: applications)." *IEEE Computer Graphics and Applications*, July/August 2002. Available online at *http://www.science.uva.nl/~leo/clifford/dorst-mann-II.pdf.*

[7]Researchers think GA will only be slightly (less than 2-fold) more costly to use than linear algebra, and since many games spend only a fraction of their time doing math, the development time and code savings should make GA an attractive alternative in many situations.

[Gaigen04] A C++ Library to generate geometric algebras. Available online at *http://www.science.uva.nl/ga/gaigen/index.html*. 2004.

[Hestenes86] Hestenes, David. *New Foundations for Classical Mechanics*. Dordrecht: Kluwer Academic Publishing, 1986.

[Hestenes98] Hestenes, David. *New Foundations for Mathematical Physics*. Two chapters are available online at *http://modelingnts.la.asu.edu/html/NFMP.html*.

[Suter03] Suter, Jaap. "Geometric Algebra Primer." Available online at *http://www.jaapsuter.com/*.

2.2

Minimal Acceleration Hermite Curves

Tony Barrera, Barrera Kristiansen AB

tony.barrera@spray.se

Anders Hast, Creative Media Lab, University of Gävle

aht@hig.se

Ewert Bengtsson, Centre for Image Analysis, Uppsala University

ewert@cb.uu.se

This gem shows how a curve with minimal acceleration can be obtained using Hermite splines [Hearn04]. Acceleration is higher in the bends and therefore this type of curve is a minimal bending curve. This type of curve can be useful for subdivision surfaces when it is required that the surface has this property, which assures that the surface is as smooth as possible. A similar approach for Bézier curves and subdivision can be found in [Overveld97]. It could also be very useful for camera movements [Vlachos01] since it allows both the position and the direction of the camera to be set for the curve. Moreover, we show how several such curves can be connected to achieve C^1 continuity between the curve segments.

A cubic Hermite curve is defined by four constraints: the two endpoints $\mathbf{p}_1$ and $\mathbf{p}_2$ and the tangents at those points $\mathbf{t}_1$ and $\mathbf{t}_2$. The idea behind this gem is to make the curve have a minimum of acceleration along the curve, and this can be achieved by modifying the lengths of the tangents. Thus, the endpoints and the direction of the tangents are the same, but the magnitude of the tangents is set to an optimal value in order to obtain a minimal bending curve. We use the variable (for this purpose. Figure 2.2.1 shows three different Hermite curves with different tangent lengths. The dotted curve with the longest tangents has a noticeable bend in the middle, while the dotted curve with the shortest tangents is rather flat in the middle but has a noticeable bend close to each endpoint. The solid curve however, has the minimal bending property. Note that the lengths of the tangents have been scaled down to 25% in all the figures so that the curve is not so small compared to the tangents.

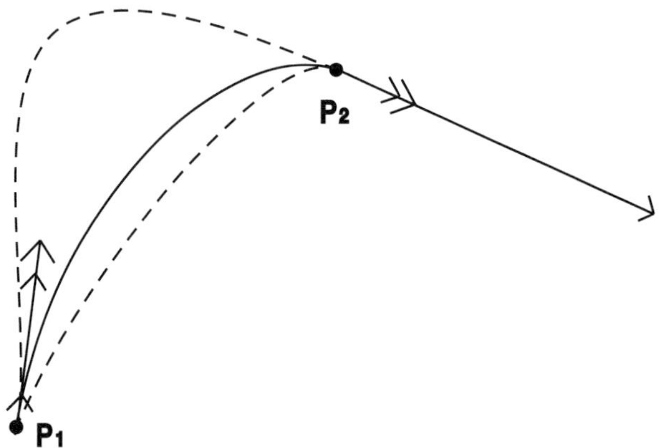

FIGURE 2.1.1 *Three different curves with different tangent lengths. The solid curve possesses the minimal bending property.*

Let a general cubic Hermite spline curve be defined as

$$\mathbf{h}(u) = \mathbf{a}u^3 + \mathbf{b}u^2 + \mathbf{c}u + \mathbf{d}. \tag{2.2.1}$$

Then the Hermite spline coefficients [Hearn04] are given by

$$\begin{bmatrix} \mathbf{a} \\ \mathbf{b} \\ \mathbf{c} \\ \mathbf{d} \end{bmatrix} = \begin{bmatrix} 2 & -2 & 1 & 1 \\ -3 & 3 & -2 & -1 \\ 0 & 0 & 1 & 0 \\ 1 & 0 & 0 & 0 \end{bmatrix} \begin{bmatrix} \mathbf{p}_1 \\ \mathbf{p}_2 \\ \alpha_1\mathbf{t}_1 \\ \alpha_2\mathbf{t}_2 \end{bmatrix}. \tag{2.2.2}$$

Note that variables α_1 and α_2 are used later to set the optimal tangent lengths. Let the vector between $\mathbf{p}_1$ and $\mathbf{p}_2$ be denoted $\mathbf{p}_{12}$. Thus $\mathbf{p}_{12} = \mathbf{p}_2 - \mathbf{p}_1$, and the coefficients for Equation 2.2.1 are given by Equation 2.2.3

$$\begin{aligned} \mathbf{a} &= \alpha_1\mathbf{t}_1 + \alpha_2\mathbf{t}_2 - 2\mathbf{p}_{12} \\ \mathbf{b} &= 3\mathbf{p}_{12} - 2\alpha_1\mathbf{t}_1 - \alpha_2\mathbf{t}_2 \\ \mathbf{c} &= \alpha_1\mathbf{t}_1 \\ \mathbf{d} &= \mathbf{p}_1. \end{aligned} \tag{2.2.3}$$

A common method for minimizing the difference between two functions is the least square approximation [Burden89]. We use the same basic idea; however, we minimize the acceleration instead. The minimal acceleration for each α_i is found by solving the pair of equations

$$\frac{\partial}{\partial\alpha_i}\int_0^1 \left\|\mathbf{h}''(u)\right\|^2 du = 0. \tag{2.2.4}$$

This equation can be interpreted as follows. The acceleration of the curve **h**, (i.e., the second derivative of **h**) is squared in order to avoid negative values, and these are summed over the whole interval by the integral. This sum depends on the different α_i. To find the optimal coefficients, the result is differentiated and set to zero. Hence, the minimum of the function is obtained, giving the minimal acceleration over the whole interval. The necessary computations are shown in Equations 2.2.5, 2.2.6, and 2.2.7

$$\mathbf{h}''(u) = 6\mathbf{a}u + 2\mathbf{b} \tag{2.2.5}$$

$$\left\|\mathbf{h}''(u)\right\|^2 = 36a^2u^2 + 24\mathbf{a}\cdot\mathbf{b}u + 4b^2 \tag{2.2.6}$$

$$\int_0^1 \left\|\mathbf{h}''(u)\right\|^2 du = 12a^2 + 12\mathbf{a}\cdot\mathbf{b} + 4b^2. \tag{2.2.7}$$

(We use the notation $a^2 = \mathbf{a}\cdot\mathbf{a}$ in order to make the equations easier to read.) Substituting the values given by Equation 2.2.3 into Equation 2.2.7 and differentiating with respect to each α_i gives Equation 2.2.8

$$\begin{aligned}\frac{\partial}{\partial\alpha_1}\int_0^1 \left\|\mathbf{h}''(u)\right\|^2 du &= 8\alpha_1 t_1^2 + 4\alpha_2 \mathbf{t}_1\cdot\mathbf{t}_2 - 12\mathbf{p}_{12}\cdot\mathbf{t}_1\\ \frac{\partial}{\partial\alpha_2}\int_0^1 \left\|\mathbf{h}''(u)\right\|^2 du &= 8\alpha_2 t_2^2 + 4\alpha_1 \mathbf{t}_1\cdot\mathbf{t}_2 - 12\mathbf{p}_{12}\cdot\mathbf{t}_2.\end{aligned} \tag{2.2.8}$$

Setting both equations to zero yields the following system of equations

$$\begin{aligned}8\alpha_1 t_1^2 + 4\alpha_2 \mathbf{t}_1\cdot\mathbf{t}_2 &= 12\mathbf{p}_{12}\cdot\mathbf{t}_1\\ 4\alpha_1 \mathbf{t}_1\cdot\mathbf{t}_2 + 8\alpha_2 t_2^2 &= 12\mathbf{p}_{12}\cdot\mathbf{t}_2.\end{aligned} \tag{2.2.9}$$

Or in matrix form after dividing by 4, we have

$$\begin{bmatrix} 2t_1^2 & \mathbf{t}_1\cdot\mathbf{t}_2 \\ \mathbf{t}_1\cdot\mathbf{t}_2 & 2t_2^2 \end{bmatrix}\begin{bmatrix}\alpha_1\\ \alpha_2\end{bmatrix} = \begin{bmatrix}3\mathbf{p}_{12}\cdot\mathbf{t}_1\\ 3\mathbf{p}_{12}\cdot\mathbf{t}_2\end{bmatrix}. \tag{2.2.10}$$

Multiplying both sides by the inverse of the first matrix gives

$$\begin{bmatrix} \alpha_1 \\ \alpha_2 \end{bmatrix} = \begin{bmatrix} 2t_1^2 & \mathbf{t}_1 \cdot \mathbf{t}_2 \\ \mathbf{t}_1 \cdot \mathbf{t}_2 & 2t_2^2 \end{bmatrix}^{-1} \begin{bmatrix} 3\mathbf{p}_{12} \cdot \mathbf{t}_1 \\ 3\mathbf{p}_{12} \cdot \mathbf{t}_2 \end{bmatrix}. \quad (2.2.11)$$

The solution is Equation 2.2.12

$$\alpha_1 = \frac{3\left(2t_2^2(\mathbf{p}_{12} \cdot \mathbf{t}_1) - (\mathbf{t}_1 \cdot \mathbf{t}_2)(\mathbf{p}_{12} \cdot \mathbf{t}_2)\right)}{4t_1^2 t_2^2 - (\mathbf{t}_1 \cdot \mathbf{t}_2)^2}$$

$$\alpha_2 = \frac{3\left(2t_1^2(\mathbf{p}_{12} \cdot \mathbf{t}_2) - (\mathbf{t}_1 \cdot \mathbf{t}_2)(\mathbf{p}_{12} \cdot \mathbf{t}_1)\right)}{4t_1^2 t_2^2 - (\mathbf{t}_1 \cdot \mathbf{t}_2)^2}. \quad (2.2.12)$$

These two values of (were used for the solid curve shown in Figure 2.2.1. Now we have the mathematical tools we need to put several curves together. Actually, we can define several curve segments where the endpoint of the first curve is the same as the starting point of the second curve. Moreover, if the tangent at the endpoint of the first curve is pointing in the same direction as the tangent of the first point of the second curve, then we have G^1 continuity [Foley97]. However, if we want the tangents to have the same length in order to achieve C^1 continuity, we have to proceed in a slightly different way, as shown in the next section.

Connected Minimal Bending Curves with C1 Continuity

If several Hermite curves are connected with C^1 continuity, as shown in Figure 2.2.2, we have to solve a system of equations generated by the integral in Equation 2.2.13.

$$\frac{\partial}{\partial \alpha_i} \int_0^1 \left\|\mathbf{h}_1''(u)\right\|^2 + \left\|\mathbf{h}_2''(u)\right\|^2 + \ldots + \left\|\mathbf{h}_{k+1}''(u)\right\|^2 du = 0 \quad (2.2.13)$$

We do not show all the calculations for this since they are basically the same as previously explained, but the system of equations has $k+1$ unknowns if there are k curves and thus $k+1$ values of α. Once again, let the vector between $\mathbf{p}_i$ and $\mathbf{p}_{i+1}$ be denoted $\mathbf{p}_{i,i+1}$. In this case we obtain

$$\frac{\partial}{\partial \alpha_1} \int_0^1 \left\|\mathbf{h}_1''(u)\right\|^2 du = 8\alpha_1 t_1^2 + 4\alpha_2 \mathbf{t}_1 \cdot \mathbf{t}_2 - 12\mathbf{p}_{12} \cdot \mathbf{t}_1 \quad (2.2.14)$$

$$\frac{\partial}{\partial \alpha_2} \int_0^1 \left\|\mathbf{h}_2''(u)\right\|^2 du = 4\alpha_1 \mathbf{t}_1 \cdot \mathbf{t}_2 + 16\alpha_2 t_2^2 + 4\alpha_3 \mathbf{t}_2 \cdot \mathbf{t}_3 - 12\mathbf{p}_{12} \cdot \mathbf{t}_2 - 12\mathbf{p}_{23} \cdot \mathbf{t}_2 \quad (2.2.15)$$

$$\frac{\partial}{\partial \alpha_3} \int_0^1 \left\|\mathbf{h}_3''(u)\right\|^2 du = 4\alpha_2 \mathbf{t}_2 \cdot \mathbf{t}_3 + 16\alpha_3 t_3^3 + 4\alpha_4 \mathbf{t}_3 \cdot \mathbf{t}_4 - 12\mathbf{p}_{23} \cdot \mathbf{t}_3 - 12\mathbf{p}_{34} \cdot \mathbf{t}_3 \quad (2.2.16)$$

and so forth, and finally we get Equation 2.2.17

$$\frac{\partial}{\partial \alpha_{k+1}} \int_0^1 \left\| \mathbf{h}''_{k+1}(u) \right\|^2 du = 4\alpha_k \mathbf{t}_k \cdot \mathbf{t}_{k+1} + 8\alpha_{k+1} t_{k+1}^2 - 12\mathbf{p}_{k,k+1} \cdot \mathbf{t}_{k+1}. \quad (2.2.17)$$

Once again we divide Equations 2.2.14 through 2.2.17 by four and rewrite them into matrix form, just as we did for Equation 2.2.8 to get the matrix in Equation 2.2.10. Note that if the tangents are normalized prior to solving the system, then $t_i^2 = 1$. This makes the matrix even simpler, but this is not done here. The system that needs to be solved looks like Equation 2.2.18

$$\begin{bmatrix} 2t_1^2 & \mathbf{t}_1 \cdot \mathbf{t}_2 & 0 & 0 & \cdots & 0 & 0 \\ \mathbf{t}_1 \cdot \mathbf{t}_2 & 4t_2^2 & \mathbf{t}_2 \cdot \mathbf{t}_3 & 0 & \cdots & 0 & 0 \\ 0 & \mathbf{t}_2 \cdot \mathbf{t}_3 & 4t_3^2 & \mathbf{t}_3 \cdot \mathbf{t}_4 & \cdots & 0 & 0 \\ \vdots & \vdots & \vdots & \vdots & \ddots & \vdots & \vdots \\ 0 & 0 & 0 & 0 & \cdots & \mathbf{t}_k \cdot \mathbf{t}_{k+1} & 2t_{k+1}^2 \end{bmatrix} \begin{bmatrix} \alpha_1 \\ \alpha_2 \\ \alpha_3 \\ \vdots \\ \alpha_{k+1} \end{bmatrix} = \begin{bmatrix} 3\mathbf{t}_1 \cdot \mathbf{p}_{12} \\ 3\mathbf{t}_2 \cdot (\mathbf{p}_{12} + \mathbf{p}_{23}) \\ 3\mathbf{t}_3 \cdot (\mathbf{p}_{23} + \mathbf{p}_{34}) \\ \vdots \\ 3\mathbf{t}_{k+1} \cdot \mathbf{p}_{k,k+1} \end{bmatrix}. \quad (2.2.18)$$

Note that nonzero entries appear only on the main diagonal and immediately above and below it. A system involving a matrix of this form is called a tridiagonal system and can be solved very efficiently using a specialized algorithm [Lengyel04].

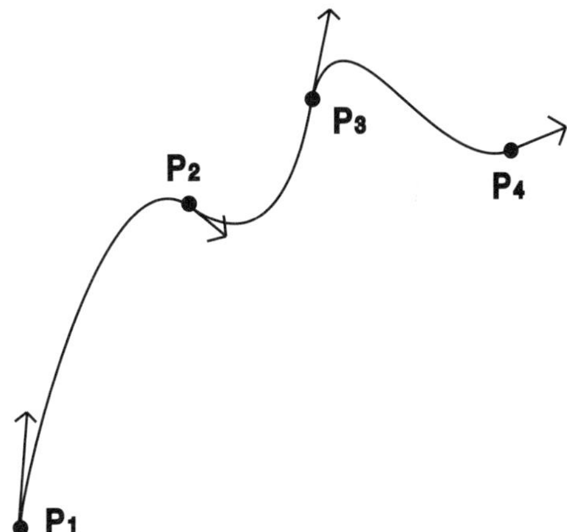

FIGURE 2.2.2 *Three connected minimal bending Hermite curves.*

A Closed Loop of Minimal Bending Curves

If a closed loop is desired as shown in Figure 2.2.3, the system can be simplified, since the first point and tangent are the same as the last point and tangent. We do not show all the computations here, but the resulting system is

$$\begin{bmatrix} 4t_1^2 & \mathbf{t}_1 \cdot \mathbf{t}_2 & 0 & 0 & \cdots & 0 & \mathbf{t}_k \cdot \mathbf{t}_1 \\ \mathbf{t}_1 \cdot \mathbf{t}_2 & 4t_2^2 & \mathbf{t}_2 \cdot \mathbf{t}_3 & 0 & \cdots & 0 & 0 \\ 0 & \mathbf{t}_2 \cdot \mathbf{t}_3 & 4t_3^2 & \mathbf{t}_3 \cdot \mathbf{t}_4 & \cdots & 0 & 0 \\ \vdots & \vdots & \vdots & \vdots & \ddots & \vdots & \vdots \\ \mathbf{t}_k \cdot \mathbf{t}_1 & 0 & 0 & 0 & \cdots & \mathbf{t}_{k-1} \cdot \mathbf{t}_k & 4t_k^2 \end{bmatrix} \begin{bmatrix} \alpha_1 \\ \alpha_2 \\ \alpha_3 \\ \vdots \\ \alpha_k \end{bmatrix} = \begin{bmatrix} 3\mathbf{t}_1 \cdot (\mathbf{p}_{k,1} + \mathbf{p}_{12}) \\ 3\mathbf{t}_2 \cdot (\mathbf{p}_{12} + \mathbf{p}_{23}) \\ 3\mathbf{t}_3 \cdot (\mathbf{p}_{23} + \mathbf{p}_{34}) \\ \vdots \\ 3\mathbf{t}_k \cdot (\mathbf{p}_{k-1,k} + \mathbf{p}_{k,1}) \end{bmatrix}. \quad (2.2.19)$$

This system gives k unknowns instead of the $k+1$ unknowns associated with a non-closed loop connected curve. The presence of the nonzero entries in the lower-left and upper-right corners make this system a cyclic tridiagonal system. It can be solved by applying the Sherman-Morrison formula to the ordinary tridiagonal system as discussed in [Press92].

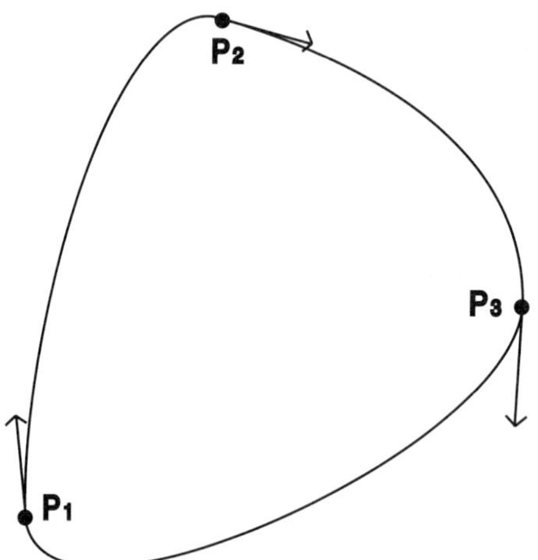

FIGURE 2.2.3 *A closed loop of three connected minimal bending curves.*

Conclusion

We have shown how a cubic Hermite spline can be modified in such a way that a minimal acceleration curve, or as it is sometimes called a minimal bending curve, is obtained. This is done by computing the least square acceleration over the curve and setting the tangent lengths to optimal values. We have also shown the necessary computations for connecting several such curves with C^1 continuity. This yields a simple system of equations to be solved. Moreover, it is possible to construct a closed loop of such connected curves. Possible uses for a minimal bending curve is for surface subdivision, and the connected version can be used for camera movements.

References

[Burden89] R. L. Burden and J. D. Faires. *Numerical Analysis*, 439, 440. Boston: PWS-KENT Publishing Company, 1989.

[Foley97] Foley, J. D., et al. *Computer Graphics: Principles and Practice*, 2nd ed, 480. Addison Wesley, 1997.

[Hearn04] D. Hearn and M.P Baker. *Computer Graphics with OpenGL*, 426–429. Pearson Education Inc., 2004.

[Lengyel04] E. Lengyel. *Mathematics for 3D Game Programming and Computer Graphics*, 2nd ed., 433–436. Charles River Media, 2004.

[Overveld97] C. W. A. M. van Overveld and B.Wyvill. "An algorithm for polygon subdivision based on vertex normals," *Computer Graphics International*, 3–12. June 23–27, 1997.

[Press92] W. H. Press, et al. *Numerical Recipes in C*, 74–75. Cambridge University Press, 1992.

[Vlachos01] A. Vlachos and J. Isidoro. "Smooth C^2 Quaternion-based Flythrough Paths." In *Game Programming Gems 2* (Mark DeLoura, ed.), 220–227. Charles River Media, 2001.

2.3

Spline-Based Time Control for Animation

James M. Van Verth, Red Storm Entertainment

jimvv@redstorm.com

One of the standard problems of animation is moving an object along a path represented by a parametric curve $\mathbf{Q}(u)$. For most curves, using the standard parameterization does not give constant speed, so it is necessary to reparameterize the curve by distance d to get $\mathbf{Q}(d)$. Then time is mapped to distance using another function, $d(t)$. For constant speed, the function $d(t)$ is a line, but we can use any function that maps time to distance.

Previous articles ([Olsen00], [Krome04]) have discussed ease-in/ease-out functions to manage velocity along a curve. This gem describes how to construct a general distance-time function using piecewise splines. Various parameters are used to constrain this function. For example, there can be distance keys requiring that a particular point must be hit at a particular time. A speed can also be attached to such a key requiring that a particular velocity be reached at the given time. Less-specific parameters can be set at each key, like fast-in/fast-out (approach/leave quickly) or slow-in/slow-out (approach/leave with zero speed), or smooth (move as smoothly as possible). The goal is to provide a flexible system for animators to use within internally built animation tools, in particular for camera animation with in-game cinematics.

To build the distance-time functions, we use piecewise Hermite splines. Some knowledge of such splines is assumed, and basic information about them is provided as a refresher, but [Burden93] and [Rogers90] cover this in more detail for those who need it.

Starting Out

The purpose of the particular functions that we create here is to control our speed as we move along a fixed path in space. This path is usually generated by a parametric curve, but for our purposes, we don't actually care whether it's a series of piecewise linear functions, a Bézier curve, or a B-spline. All we care about is that we have a general function of the form $\mathbf{Q}(u)$: we enter a value u, and out comes a point $\mathbf{Q}$ in 3D space. As u increases, the function traces out a path in space.

Before we add our own time control, we need the object that we're animating to move at a constant speed along the length of the curve, using only the parameter u. However, with cubic curves (the most common case), the relationship between distance along the curve and the parameter u is not linear. In some places, we move a short distance along the curve for a step of Δu, and in some places, we move farther. This is because to provide the curvature we want, we have to vary the first derivative and hence the speed at which we move along the curve.

Obviously, if we want to maintain constant speed, this is not desirable; in some areas of the curve we are moving faster than in others. The solution is to reparameterize the curve by distance. Rather than find a point on the curve using the parameter u, we find a point using a parameter d, where d represents the distance along the curve from the start of the curve. As we increase d at a constant rate, we move along the curve at a constant rate. In most cases, computing the reparameterization for a cubic curve is not practical with analytical methods. Handling this involves using numerical methods, usually either root finding or table-generated solutions, which are described in more detail in [Eberly01], [Parent02], or [VanVerth04]. For our purposes, we assume that we already have such a parameterization for our curve.

General Distance-Time Functions

Rather than moving along the curve by distance, we generally want to move via time; that is, determine where we are on the curve at time t. So we need some means to convert time into distance and use that as input to our reparameterized curve. We can represent this by a distance-time function $d(t)$, which varies the distance parameter based on time. A point on the curve corresponding to a time t is given by evaluating $\mathbf{Q}(d(t))$. For example, traveling at constant speed is a linear function that starts at $(0,0)$ and ends at some maximum time and distance. This is commonly normalized so that maximum time and distance are both 1 (see Figure 2.3.1), so it can be used with multiple curves. To adjust our input t to work with our normalized function, we can use Equation 2.3.1

$$\bar{t} = \frac{t - t_s}{t_e - t_s}, \tag{2.3.1}$$

where t_s and t_e are the arrival times for the start and the end of the curve, respectively. To adjust our output, we multiply the result $d(t)$ by the total length of the curve. We then plug that into our reparameterized curve to obtain our final position. For simplicity's sake, we assume that we are performing these corrections by default, and any time and distance values we refer to below lies between 0 and 1.

There is no reason to limit our distance-time function to just linear functions. Let's look at another example: the ease-in/ease-out function (see Figure 2.3.2). There are a number of ways of computing a function of this type ([Parent02], [Olsen00]), but they all have the same basic shape. Using this as our distance-time function gives the following result: we start at zero speed at the beginning of the curve, ramp up to

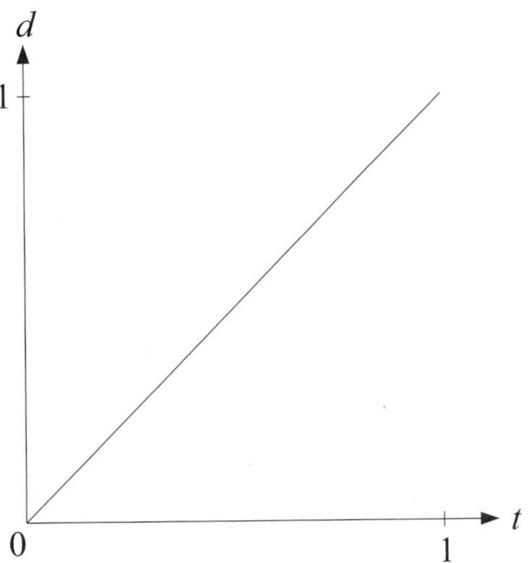

FIGURE 2.3.1 *Linear distance-time function.*

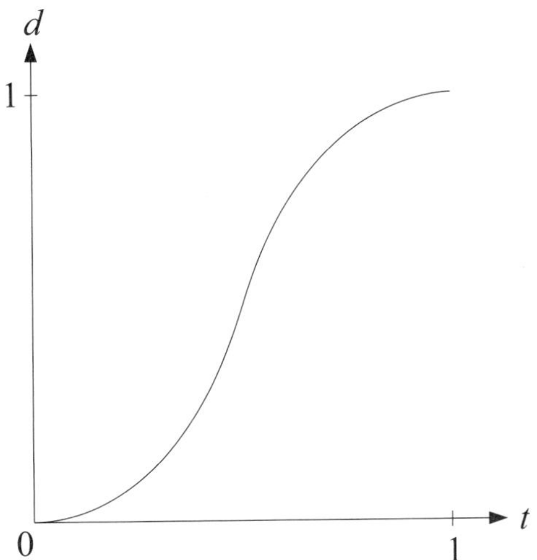

FIGURE 2.3.2 *Ease-in/ease-out distance-time function.*

maximum speed at the middle of the curve, and then slow down to zero speed at the end. This gives a very natural look to movement along the curve. Rather than starting abruptly at a given velocity, maintaining it along the curve, and then stopping abruptly at the end, it looks much more like the acceleration and deceleration needed to move a physical object.

We don't have to stop there. We can use any function of t with domain $[0,1]$ that doesn't have a range outside of $[0,1]$ (i.e., time and distance remain clamped to the normalized intervals). Beyond the basic constraints, how we lay out our function controls how we move along the curve. Figure 2.3.3 shows a distance-time function for which the slope is always nonnegative. In this case, we never move backward along the curve as t increases. If the function has negative slope at any point, we do move backward along the curve for that segment. Figure 2.3.4 shows such a curve; the gray section indicates the segment with negative slope. Note that in this function, we also delay departure, and then arrive early and wait. Using this technique gives us a great deal of flexibility for controlling speed and arrival times on our animation path.

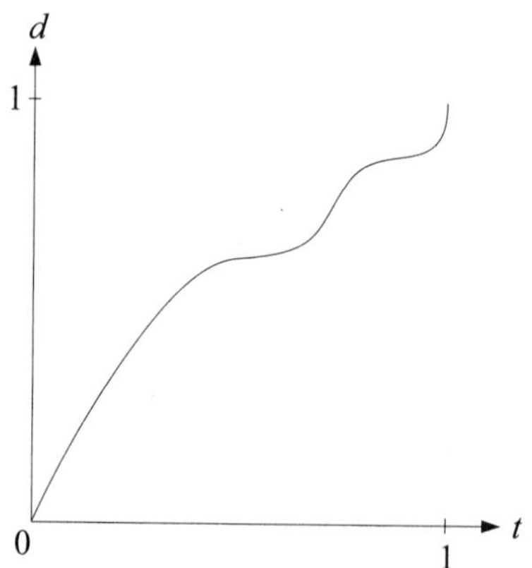

FIGURE 2.3.3 *Distance-time function with non-negative slope.*

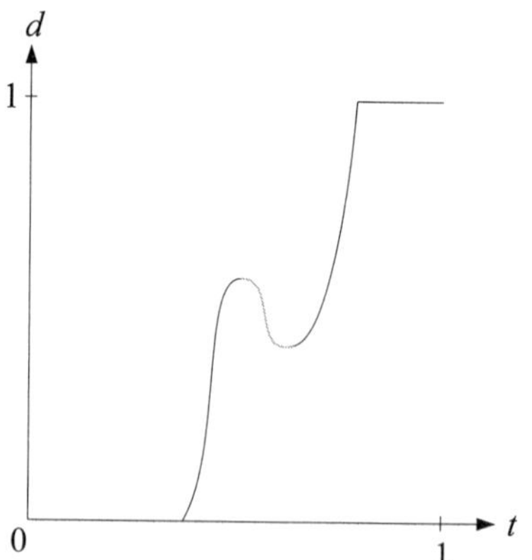

FIGURE 2.3.4 *Distance-time function with one section of negative slope and showing delayed departure and early arrival.*

Creating Distance-Time Functions with Splines

In general, we can use any function that satisfies the previously stated criteria, but for ease of construction, we use piecewise Hermite splines because they have a few advantages. They are fairly easy to compute, and they provide simple handles for control: endpoint positions and velocities. However, we use them here in a slightly different way than they are usually presented. Since we are only interpolating across distance not points in space, the positions are real numbers rather than multivalued vectors. Similarly, the tangent at each control point becomes the slope of the curve at that point, and velocity becomes speed.

The standard definition of a Hermite curve between positions p_k and p_{k+1} and slopes p'_k and p'_{k+1} is shown in Equation 2.3.2.

$$H(t)=\left(2t^3-3t^2+1\right)p_k+\left(-2t^3+3t^2\right)p_{k+1}+\left(t^3-2t^2+t\right)p'_{k,0}+\left(t^3-t^2\right)p'_{k+1,1} \quad (2.3.2)$$

This is also called a normalized Hermite curve, because the parameter t lies in the interval $[0,1]$. In our case, there are multiple sample positions $p_0,\ldots,p_n$. Each interior sample position p_k has two slopes: the outgoing slope $p_{k,0}$ and the incoming slope $p'_{k,1}$. These slopes can match if we want a smooth curve or not match if we want a "kink" in the curve. To generate a continuous function from p_0 to p_n, we create subcurves that interpolate between succeeding pairs of positions. So subcurve H_0 interpolates between p_0 and p_1, H_1 interpolates between p_1 and p_2, etc. This is called a piecewise Hermite curve. Figures 2.3.6 through 2.3.9 show examples of such curves.

In our case, the positions represent distance values along the path. Associated with each distance value p_k is a time t_k: the time at which we want to arrive at that distance. Each pair of values is called a distance key. These t_k values are in increasing order, so that $t_k \le t_{k+1}$. This means that each subcurve has a different interval $[t_k, t_{k+1}]$ for its local domain, which is not necessarily $[0,1]$. Clearly we can't use the standard definition; the solution is to use a slightly more complex but more flexible representation for our Hermite curves.

There are two parts to this. First, we have to convert our input time to something usable in the standard formula. Given a time t, we first find a subcurve for which $t_k \le t \le t_{k+1}$. We then apply Equation 2.3.1, where $t_s = t_k$ and $t_e = t_{k+1}$. As before, this will map t to a value $\bar{t}$ that lies within $[0,1]$, which we can use in the standard formula for a Hermite curve. Secondly, we must also correct the slopes at each sample position. The original slopes assume that we are moving the same number of units in t as we are in d. However, we've scaled our t value by $1/\left(t_{k+1}-t_k\right)$, so we correct for this by scaling our slopes by $\left(t_{k+1}-t_k\right)$. So for a given p'_k, $\bar{p}'_k = p'_k\left(t_{k+1}-t_k\right)$. The combination of these two adjustments allows our time inputs to be used with the standard equation for a Hermite curve.

So computing the distance-time function is fairly simple: we find the correct subcurve by searching for the time key pairs such that $t_k \le t \le t_{k+1}$. From that, we compute $\bar{t}$, and then use the result in the standard Hermite formula with the corrected slopes for that subcurve. The result is our distance value *d*. However, how do we create the Hermite spline in the first place?

Incoming and Outgoing Speeds

One way to make a spline-based distance-time function is to specify the incoming and outgoing speeds at each key, which are used as the endpoint slopes for our piecewise Hermite curve. There are a few possibilities for setting the speeds. First, the user can define them. Usually the user wants to specify the speeds in game space, so these have to be converted into an equivalent speed in the normalized distance-time function by multiplying by the total desired time for the space curve and dividing by the total length of the curve. As before, these speeds have to be corrected for the non-normalized Hermite curves by multiplying by the time interval of the subcurve. One concern is when the user sets a speed value with a large magnitude; the curve may loop outside the desired range interval of $[0,1]$ (Figure 2.3.5). However, if a graphic display and enough error feedback are provided, this can work quite well.

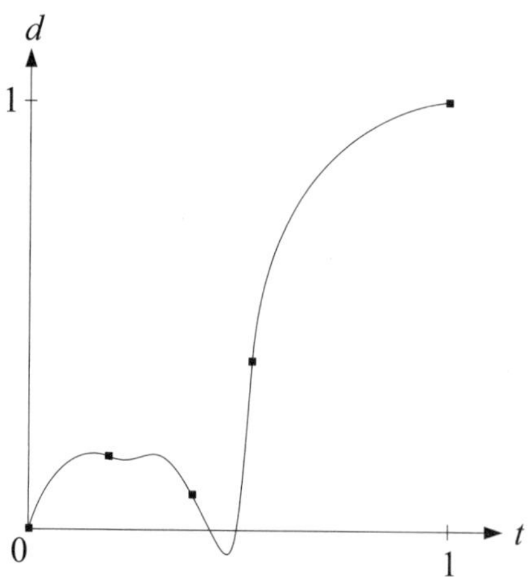

FIGURE 2.3.5 *Large user speed leads to invalid distance-time function.*

For another approach, we notice that there are some standard cases for which we can set default values, and that can be used in combination to create functions without the user needing to set slopes directly. Standard animation parlance talks about slow-in, slow-out, fast-in, and fast-out. The -in and -out parts refer to the arrival and departure speeds for the key, respectively. Slow means the speed is 0 at the key. Fast is less well defined but basically means that the object leaves the key as quickly as possible. Assuming that keys are increasing in distance and the user wants to avoid the object backing along the curve, we define "fast" so that the minimum speed along the resulting curve is 0. If the keys are decreasing in distance, we just negate that so that the maximum speed is 0. Slow-out from one key to a slow-in at another key gives us something like the familiar ease-in/ease-out curve. Fast-out to fast-in gives us the reverse: we start out fast, then slow to 0, and then speed back up again. Figure 2.3.6 shows a function that does a fast-out to a fast-in, followed by a slow-out to a slow-in.

Setting up slow-in and slow-out is simple; we just set the in or out speeds to 0 at that key. If we want something closer to the ease-in/ease-out curve, we can add an additional key at the average point between the original keys and set it to have fast-in/fast-out speed.

We can derive the speeds for fast-in and fast-out by using two constraints. First, the speed at the midpoint of the curve is 0. We can represent this by taking the derivative of a standard Hermite curve at the halfway point and setting it equal to 0, as shown in Equation 2.3.3

$$
\begin{aligned}
0 &= H'(1/2) \\
&= \left(6(1/2)^2 - 6(1/2)\right)p_k + \left(-6(1/2)^2 + 6(1/2)\right)p_{k+1} \\
&\quad + \left(3(1/2)^2 - 4(1/2) + 1\right)p'_{k,0} + \left(3(1/2)^2 - 2(1/2)\right)p'_{k+1,1} \\
&= 6p_{k+1} - 6p_k - p'_{k,0} - p'_{k+1,1}.
\end{aligned}
\tag{2.3.3}
$$

Second, the speed at the start of the subcurve needs to match the speed at the end of the subcurve. This allows us to rewrite Equation 2.3.3 as Equation 2.3.4

$$
\begin{aligned}
0 &= 6\left(p_{k+1} - p_k\right) - 2p'_{k,0} \\
p'_{k,0} &= 3\left(p_{k+1} - p_k\right).
\end{aligned}
\tag{2.3.4}
$$

This speed will be used for fast-out at key k and the same for fast-in at key $k+1$. We can use this speed with our normalized Hermite equation, so we don't have to correct it by $(t_{k+1} - t_k)$ as we did in the other cases. However, if we're correcting all speeds as a final processing step, we can set the fast-in/fast-out speed to $3(p_{k+1} - p_k)/(t_{k+1} - t_k)$ instead.

Other standard parameters exist. Linear means that the distance-time curve takes a straight line from one key to the next key. The outgoing speed at the start key and the incoming speed at the end key are set to the slope of the line specified by the two points. Step means that the distance-time curve remains at one key until the time interval has elapsed and then immediately jumps to the next key. This is not as convenient to represent with a single spline, as there is a discontinuity in the curve. One

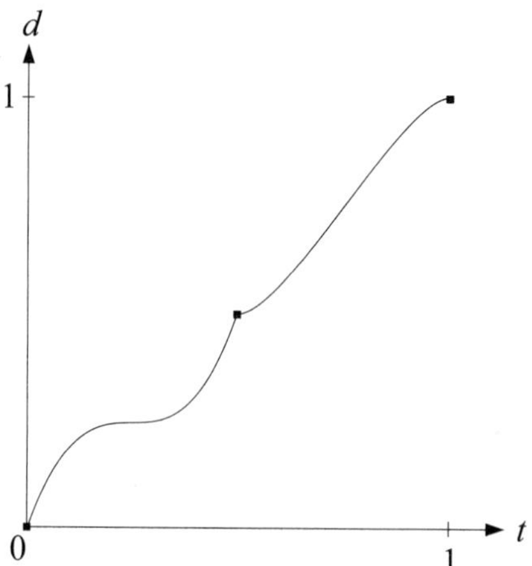

FIGURE 2.3.6 *Fast-out/fast-in followed by slow-out/slow-in.*

solution is to create a new key at the same distance as the first key but just before the second key in time, and then create two linear steps: from the first to the hidden key, and then the new key to the second key. The other is to simply break the spline at that point and start a new spline. Figure 2.3.7 shows a function with two linear sections, separated by a step.

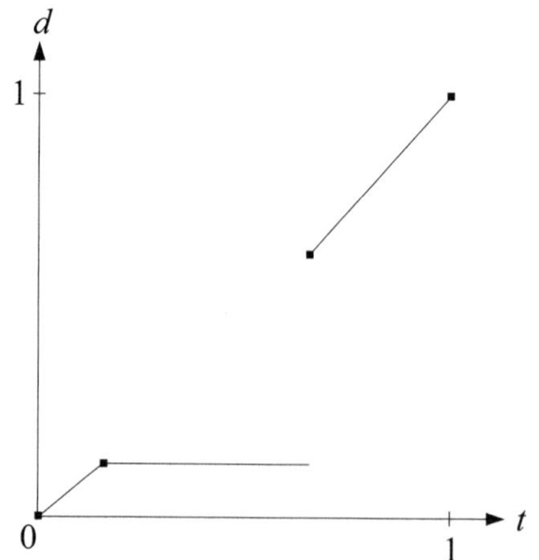

FIGURE 2.3.7 *Distance-time curve showing linear sections and a step key.*

Figures 2.3.6 and 2.3.7 show that there is no reason that the incoming and outgoing speeds at a given key have to match; while not physically realistic, it is sometimes useful to have an object arrive slowly at a point and then immediately tear off at high velocity. As another example, animators can use fast-in/slow-out to create a quick reaction time to an event and then a slow recovery. Similarly, we don't have to have matching -out and -in speeds on a given subcurve. For example, we could start off with a slow-out at one key and end with a fast-in at the next one. The end result would ramp up the object from rest from the first key to a high speed once it reaches the second. It's all up to the needs of the animator.

Automatic Curve Generation

An alternative to setting the speeds directly is to set a series of distance keys, as described earlier, and then automatically generate the subcurves that interpolate between those keys. While we have "positions" that define the ends of each subcurve, we still need speeds at each key that can be used in the piecewise spline. We'll usually want a smooth curve, so in this case, we'll assume that the incoming and outgoing speeds are the same. There are a number of approaches that can work, but the method that gives the smoothest result is to use a natural piecewise Hermite spline. This involves setting up a series of linear equations that maintain C^2 continuity for interior points on the spline and zero-valued second derivatives at the endpoints; more detail can be found in both [Burden93] and [Rogers90]. For non-normalized Hermite splines, this looks like Equation 2.3.5

$$\begin{bmatrix} 2 & 1 & & & \\ \Delta t_0 & 2(\Delta t_0 + \Delta t_1) & \Delta t_1 & & \\ & & \ddots & & \\ & & \Delta t_{n-2} & 2(\Delta t_{n-2} + \Delta t_{n-1}) & \Delta t_{n-1} \\ & & & 1 & 2 \end{bmatrix} \begin{bmatrix} p_0' \\ p_1' \\ \vdots \\ p_{n-1}' \\ p_n' \end{bmatrix} = \begin{bmatrix} \frac{3}{\Delta t_0}(p_1 - p_0) \\ \frac{3}{\Delta t_0 \Delta t_1}\left[\Delta t_0^2 (p_2 - p_1) + \Delta t_1^2 (p_1 - p_0)\right] \\ \vdots \\ \frac{3}{\Delta t_{n-2} \Delta t_{n-1}}\left[\Delta t_{n-2}^2 (p_n - p_{n-1}) + \Delta t_{n-1}^2 (p_{n-1} - p_{n-2})\right] \\ \frac{3}{\Delta t_{n-1}}(p_n - p_{n-1}) \end{bmatrix} \quad (2.3.5)$$

where $\Delta t_k = (t_{k+1} - t_k)$. Solving this set of linear equations for $p_0', \ldots, p_n'$ gives us the slopes at each key and the information we need to build our Hermite spline. Since the left matrix is sparse and tridiagonal, solving this can be done in linear time; [Burden93] has more details. Note that this solution doesn't correct our slopes for the non-normalized time interval, so we still have to multiply them by the appropriate Δt_k. An example of such a distance-time curve can be seen in Figure 2.3.8.

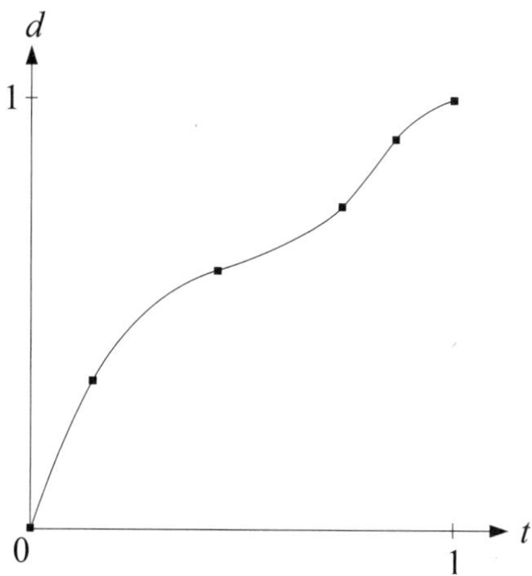

FIGURE 2.3.8 *Distance-time function created by natural spline through distance keys.*

Combining Smoothing and Speed Specification

For full generality, the user should be allowed to create a curve with fixed arrival and departure speeds at certain keys as well as automatically generated sections for the remainder. For this we add smooth-in and smooth-out keys. A sequence of smooth-in and smooth-out keys indicates a section of curve that the user wants automatically generated. If we see a smooth key, we start tracking a smooth section of curve and progressively store the parameters for our linear system until a non-smooth key is reached. Then we run the parameters through our tridiagonal matrix solver to generate the slopes for that section of curve.

Because of the flexibility of our system, we might end up with given speeds at the endpoints of our smooth section. For example, suppose we have a slow-out key followed by a smooth-in key. The curve will start at speed 0, and then smoothly blend to the following distance key. The initial endpoint is known as a clamped condition. Constructing the matrix for this is just a modification of the setup for a natural spline. We replace the first matrix row with a 1 in the diagonal, and the corresponding entry in the right vector with our given speed. If we were to end at a non-smooth key, we would do the same for the last matrix row. So for our example, the linear system looks like Equation 2.3.6

$$\begin{bmatrix} 1 & 0 \\ 2 & 1 \end{bmatrix} \begin{bmatrix} p_0' \\ p_1' \end{bmatrix} = \begin{bmatrix} 0 \\ \dfrac{3}{t_1 - t_0}\left(p_1 - p_0\right) \end{bmatrix}. \tag{2.3.6}$$

The following pseudocode shows how the tracking of the smooth sections is handled. We iterate through the keys and either set given speeds or set up parameters for the smooth sections. A Boolean inSmooth is used to indicate whether we're currently tracking a smooth section.

```
inSmooth = false
for each key do
    if current in-speed is not smooth
        if inSmooth
            finish clamped spline
            inSmooth = false
        else
            set given speed
    else
        if !inSmooth
            start clamped spline
            inSmooth = true
        if not at end and out key is smooth
            add to middle of smooth spline
        else
            finish natural spline
            inSmooth = false

    if current out-speed is not smooth
        set given speed
    else if !inSmooth
        start natural spline
        inSmooth = true
```

Some details have been skipped here for clarity. For example, we don't consider the in-speed for the first key or the out-speed for the last key, as they're not valid. The full details can be found in the sample code.

Example

As an example, let's assume that the user has set three time-distance pairs, with the following speed parameters:

Time	Distance	In-Speed	Out-Speed
0.0	0.0	—	Linear
0.45	0.60	Fast	Smooth
1.0	1.0	Slow	—

The outgoing speed at the first key is linear, so its value is $(0.6-0.0)/(0.45-0.0)$, however, we correct this by multiplying by $(0.45-0.0)$, so the final stored speed is 0.6. The incoming speed at the second key is fast-out, so its value is $3(0.6-0.0)$. The outgoing speed at the second key is smooth, so we start building a linear system. In this simple example, we stop building it immediately at the next key since it is slow-in and thus non-smooth. Our linear system for this section of curve looks like Equation 2.3.7.

$$\begin{bmatrix} 2 & 1 \\ 0 & 1 \end{bmatrix} \begin{bmatrix} p'_{2,0} \\ p'_{3,1} \end{bmatrix} = \begin{bmatrix} 3\dfrac{1.0-0.6}{1.0-0.45} \\ 0.0 \end{bmatrix} \tag{2.3.7}$$

Solving this gives us intermediate values of $p'_{2,0} = 1.09091$ and $p'_{3,1} = 0.0$. Correcting both by $(1.0-0.45) = 0.55$ gives us final values of $p'_{2,0} = 0.6$ and $p'_{3,1} = 0.0$. Our final parameters for our Hermite curves are

Time	Distance	In-Speed	Out-Speed
0.0	0.0	—	0.6
0.45	0.60	1.8	0.6
1.0	1.0	0.0	—

The resulting curve can be seen in Figure 2.3.9.

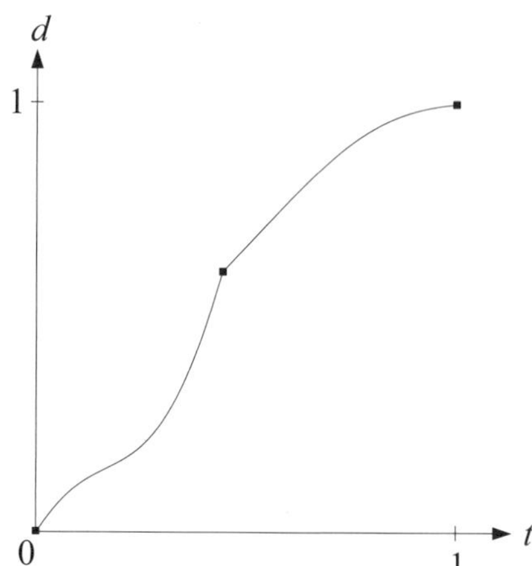

FIGURE 2.3.9 *Distance-time function created by example keys.*

Interface Choices

While the earlier material provides the mathematical underpinning for the technique, it's no good unless it can be controlled. One possibility is to provide an interface to set arrival times at each interpolating control point for the spatial curve, and then use the distance along the curve to those points to create keys for the distance-time function.

The parameters for smoothness and/or incoming/outgoing speeds can also be set at the spatial control points. Together with this, it is useful to be able to display the current distance-time graph, with the distance keys plotted as points. These can be clicked and moved left to right in the time axis. Their distance values can't be changed since they are fixed by their position on the spatial curve. Errors should be reported if the function falls outside of 0 or 1 along the range.

Alternatively, the spatial curve and the distance-time function can be set up separately, so the function has a completely independent set of keys. However, in this case it's usually wise to place icons on the distance-time display to show where the spatial control points lie, so that the user has some sense of arrival time at those points. The arrival time data can also be copied back into the display for the spatial curve.

A hybrid approach is also possible, with the starting distance keys derived from the spatial control points, and additional points added that have no correlation in the spatial domain but are only used to control the distance-time function.

Conclusion

This gem has presented a method for computing distance-time functions for animation by using piecewise Hermite splines. Hermite splines allow a lot of user input, particularly as the tangents on the curves provide an intuitive way for managing speed control. Automatic creation of splines, such as natural splines, and default settings for speed control are also useful for allowing users to quickly create distance-time functions. It may be possible to extend these ideas to other spline types, such as piecewise Bézier curves or B-splines, as long as the basic requirements for a distance-time function are maintained.

This technique can also be used for other applications. For example, the slerp function for quaternion interpolation maps a t value between 0 and 1 to two interpolants, where the result of each interpolant is also between 0 and 1. These interpolants are then used to blend two quaternions. The entire function normally requires three sines and a floating-point division. We can approximate each interpolant function instead by piecewise Hermite curves. The result won't be as exact as slerp but will be faster and will still be better than straight linear interpolation.

References

[Burden93] Burden, Richard L. and J. Douglas Faires. *Numerical Analysis*. PWS Publishing Company, 1993.

[Eberly01] Eberly, David. "Moving at Constant Speed." Available online at *http://www.magic-software.com*. January 2001.

[Krome04] Lowe, Thomas. "Critically Damped Ease-In/Ease-Out Smoothing." In *Game Programming Gems 4*, 95–101. Charles River, 2004.

[Olsen00] Olsen, John. "Interpolation Methods." In *Game Programming Gems*, 141–149. Charles River, 2000.

[Parent02] Parent, Rick. *Computer Animation: Algorithms and Techniques*. Morgan Kaufmann Publishers, 2002.

[Rogers90] Rogers, David F. and J. Alan Adams. *Mathematical Elements for Computer Graphics*. McGraw-Hill, 1993.

[VanVerth04] Van Verth, James M. and Lars M. Bishop. *Essential Mathematics for Games and Interactive Applications*. Morgan Kaufmann Publishers, 2004.

2.4

Faster Quaternion Interpolation Using Approximations

Andy Thomason

athomason@acm.org

Quaternions are used extensively in game development because they provide a simple and effective way to represent a rotation. A quaternion takes up 4/9 of the storage required for a rotation matrix, can smoothly interpolate between rotations, and has many other properties that make it useful for skinned, hierarchical animation. In particular, quaternions are used to represent the joints of characters that can only rotate about a particular point.

As games become more complex, we must move to more advanced methods similar to the linear algebra techniques used by supercomputers. Methods like the Structures Of Arrays (SOA) method can improve computational efficiency by an order of magnitude or more by grouping together similar operations, reducing memory access, and using all available ALUs (Arithmetic and Logic Units) by way of SIMD (Single Instruction, Multiple Data) instructions.

The trouble with using batch linear algebra techniques is that the trigonometric functions normally associated with quaternion interpolation cannot be used. So by using an approximation, not only can we speed up the process by sacrificing some precision, but we can enable the calculations to be done using adds, subtracts, multiplies, divides, and square roots.

In the game *Galleon*, we were able to have dozens of figures fighting hand to hand, each with cloth dynamics, real-time footstep placement, and AI. If we wanted thousands of such figures using the same hardware, the skinning and animation load would dominate, principally because of the cost of quaternion interpolation used for key expansion, animation blending, and collision.

With vertex shaders increasing in complexity, it is now possible to use quaternions for skinning [Hejl04]. We can use approximations to generate batches of quaternions from animation data and quickly feed these results to vertex shaders.

These methods should be suited for use on the specialist vector units that are becoming more common on consoles and computers alike. Examples are provided in C++, but feel free to recode them using native assembly language or intrinsics.

Using Quaternions as Rotations

Recall that a quaternion $\mathbf{q}$ is a four-component quantity that can be written as follows.

$$\mathbf{q} = \langle w, x, y, z \rangle = w + xi + yj + zk \tag{2.4.1}$$

It consists of one scalar component w and three vector components x, y, and z. Quaternion multiplication is defined using the ordinary distributive law with the following rules for the products of the "imaginary" numbers i, j, and k.

$$\begin{aligned} i^2 = j^2 = k^2 &= -1 \\ ij = -ji &= k \\ jk = -kj &= i \\ ki = -ik &= j \end{aligned} \tag{2.4.2}$$

Using these rules, the product of two quaternions $\mathbf{a}$ and $\mathbf{b}$ can be expanded to

$$\begin{aligned} \mathbf{ab} = &\left(a_w b_w - a_x b_x - a_y b_y - a_z b_z\right) \\ &+3\left(a_w b_x + a_x b_w + a_y b_z - a_z b_y\right)i \\ &+3\left(a_w b_y - a_x b_z + a_y b_w + a_z b_x\right)j \\ &+3\left(a_w b_z + a_x b_y - a_y b_x + a_z b_w\right)k \end{aligned} \tag{2.4.3}$$

Every nonzero quaternion $\mathbf{q} = w + xi + yj + zk$ has an inverse $\mathbf{q}^{-1}$ given by

$$\mathbf{q}^{-1} = \frac{\overline{\mathbf{q}}}{q^2} \tag{2.4.4}$$

where the quantity $\overline{\mathbf{q}} = w - xi - yj - zk$ is the *conjugate* of $\mathbf{q}$. For a unit quaternion, $q^2 = 1$, and the conjugate and inverse are the same quantity.

A quaternion representing a rotation through an angle θ about the unit-length axis $\mathbf{A} = \langle A_x, A_y, A_z \rangle$ is usually written in the following form.

$$\mathbf{q}_{\text{rotation}} = \cos\frac{\theta}{2} + \mathbf{A}\sin\frac{\theta}{2} \tag{2.4.5}$$

The way in which a quaternion is used to rotate a vector **v** is to treat the vector as a quaternion with zero scalar component and evaluate the product

$$Rotate(\mathbf{v},\mathbf{q}) = \mathbf{q}\mathbf{v}\bar{\mathbf{q}} \tag{2.4.6}$$

This leads to the familiar quaternion-to-matrix conversion formula:

$$\mathbf{q}\mathbf{v}\bar{\mathbf{q}} = \begin{bmatrix} 1-2q_y^2-2q_z^2 & 2q_xq_y-2q_wq_z & 2q_xq_z+2q_wq_y \\ 2q_xq_y+2q_wq_z & 1-2q_x^2-2q_z^2 & 2q_yq_z-2q_wq_x \\ 2q_xq_z-2q_wq_y & 2q_yq_z+2q_wq_x & 1-2q_x^2-2q_y^2 \end{bmatrix} \begin{bmatrix} v_x \\ v_y \\ v_z \end{bmatrix} \tag{2.4.7}$$

Note that if we don't make the usual assumption that

$$q_w^2+q_x^2+q_y^2+q_z^2=1 \tag{2.4.8}$$

then we get an alternative formula

$$\mathbf{q}\mathbf{v}\bar{\mathbf{q}} = \begin{bmatrix} q_w^2+q_x^2-q_y^2-q_z^2 & 2q_xq_y-2q_wq_z & 2q_xq_z+2q_wq_y \\ 2q_xq_y+2q_wq_z & q_w^2+q_y^2-q_x^2-q_z^2 & 2q_yq_z-2q_wq_x \\ 2q_xq_z-2q_wq_y & 2q_yq_z+2q_wq_x & q_w^2+q_z^2-q_x^2-q_y^2 \end{bmatrix} \begin{bmatrix} v_x \\ v_y \\ v_z \end{bmatrix} \tag{2.4.9}$$

and we can incorporate a scaling factor s into the quaternions as follows.

$$Rotate\left(\mathbf{v},\pm\sqrt{s}\mathbf{q}\right) = \mathbf{q}\mathbf{v}\bar{\mathbf{q}}s. \tag{2.4.10}$$

This only works because we are using the conjugate of the quaternion, not the inverse, for our rotation formula. But clearly, a negative scaling factor cannot be used. Note that negating a quaternion does not affect the rotation that is produced. That is,

$$Rotate(\mathbf{v},-\mathbf{q}) = Rotate(\mathbf{v},\mathbf{q}). \tag{2.4.11}$$

For the most part, the techniques described in the following sections assume a unit scaling factor, so be very careful how nonunit quaternions are used. However, the extra scaling factor can be very useful when using quaternions in vertex shaders.

Interpolating Quaternion Rotations

In computer games, animations consist of a series of *keys*, usually rotations representing the angles of joints of a character. To smoothly interpolate between the keys and thus to avoid using precious storage to store a key for each frame, we use a method called *spherical linear interpolation* or *slerp* for short. The goal of the slerp function is to interpolate smoothly between two quaternions **a** and **b**, sweeping a constant angle per unit time and maintaining a constant unit length.

So why can't we just use linear interpolation? The answer is that we need to maintain the unit length of the interpolated quaternion to avoid introducing a scaling factor. Even if we renormalize the result of linear interpolation, the angular velocity of the resulting animation will not be constant, resulting in jerky movement.

An example of a slerp in real life is the great circle taken by a passenger jet over the surface of the Earth. The jet keeps a constant distance from the center of the Earth and moves with a constant speed over the shortest arc. Thus, if we want to fly from Amsterdam to Berlin, we apply the function:

$$Slerp(Amsterdam, Berlin) \tag{2.4.12}$$

How do we achieve this?

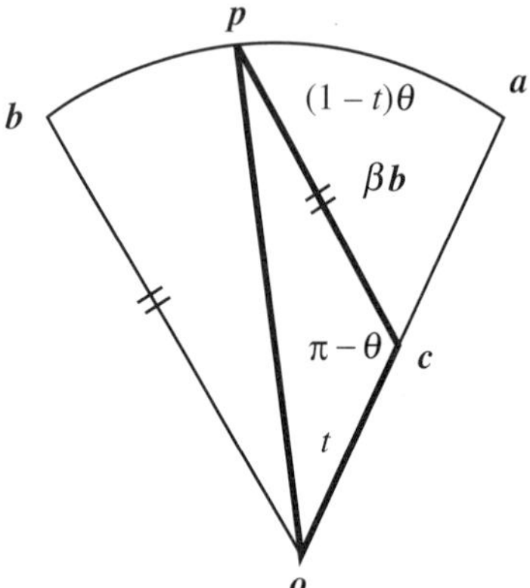

FIGURE 2.4.1 *An illustration of the slerp function.*

In Figure 2.4.1, Amsterdam is represented by the vector **a** and Berlin by **b**. The position **p** of the jet sweeps out an arc of θ radians during the journey, taking one hour. At time *t*, we have moved θt radians.

This position can be represented as a linear combination of the vectors **a** and **b**:

$$\mathbf{p}(\theta,t) = \alpha(\theta,t)\mathbf{a} + \beta(\theta,t)\mathbf{b}. \tag{2.4.13}$$

We can calculate **a** and **b** by using the triangle drawn on the diagram. Using the sine formula for triangle area in three different ways for the triangle **opc**, with $\boldsymbol{op} = 1$, $\boldsymbol{oc} = \alpha$, $\boldsymbol{cp} = \beta$,

$$\frac{1}{2}\alpha\beta\sin\theta = \frac{1}{2}\alpha\sin(t\theta) = \frac{1}{2}\beta\sin((1-t)\theta). \tag{2.4.14}$$

These equalities give us α and β leading to the well-known formula

$$\mathbf{p}(\theta,t) = Slerp(\mathbf{a},\mathbf{b},t) = \frac{\sin(1-t)\theta}{\sin\theta}\mathbf{a} + \frac{\sin t\theta}{\sin\theta}\mathbf{b}, \quad \theta = \arccos(\mathbf{a}\cdot\mathbf{b}). \tag{2.4.15}$$

So if $x = \mathbf{a}\cdot\mathbf{b}$, then

$$\alpha(x,t) = \frac{\sin((1-t)\arccos x)}{\sqrt{1-x^2}}, \quad \beta(x,t) = \frac{\sin(t\arccos x)}{\sqrt{1-x^2}}, \tag{2.4.16}$$

because

$$\sin(\arccos x) = \sqrt{1-x^2}. \tag{2.4.17}$$

Figure 2.4.2 shows a plot of $\beta(x,t)$. Notice how the graph is quite flat where $x = 1$ but curves steeply when $x = -1$. This is the source of potential problems with an approximation.

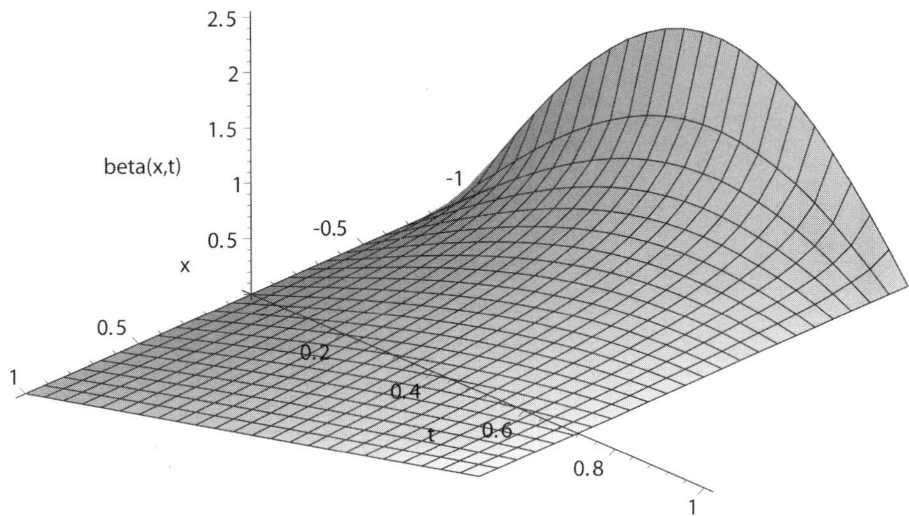

FIGURE 2.4.2 *A 3D plot of the function* $\beta(x,t)$.

Approximation Methods

Now we can discuss some methods of approximation. To illustrate the methods we can use, we use examples of Maple procedures.

We discuss several methods of approximation and summarize their strengths and weaknesses. One of the golden rules of numerical approximation is that no one method is best. The context in which the approximation is to be used must be considered when determining the specific method.

In computer games, we may have to ask ourselves a number of questions, notably:

- How many CPU cycles can we spare?
- How much precision do we need?
- Can we cheaply use functions such as `sqrt(x)` and `exp(x)`?
- Can we use SIMD instructions, like VU macro mode, paired float, SSE, or 3DNow?
- Are we going to be blending more than two quaternions at once?
- What is the maximum angle between our keys?

We present various methods here, but it is up to the reader to decide which is most appropriate for a particular application.

Direct Method

We start with the direct approach. We just examine the beta function formula and approximate the various components. This is actually the best method if very high precision is necessary, but it can be very costly, especially when evaluating large batches of slerps.

Almost every game engine contains something like the code in Listing 2.4.1, and many games spend significant proportions of their time executing it.

Listing 2.4.1 Reference Slerp Class

```
class SlerpReference
{
public:
    SlerpReference( const Quat &a, const Quat &b ) : mA( a ),
                                                     mB( b )
    {
        float adotb = a.X * b.X + a.Y * b.Y + a.Z * b.Z + a.W * b.W;
        adotb = Min( adotb, 0.99999f );
        mTheta = acosf( adotb );
        mRecipSqrt = RecipSqrt( 1 - adotb * adotb );
    }

    Quat Interpolate( float t ) const
    {
        float alpha = sinf( ( 1 - t ) * mTheta ) * mRecipSqrt;
        float beta = sinf( t * mTheta ) * mRecipSqrt;
        return Quat( alpha * mA.X + beta * mB.X, alpha * mA.Y +
                     beta * mB.Y, alpha * mA.Z + beta * mB.Z,
                     alpha * mA.W + beta * mB.W );
    }
```

```
private:
    float mTheta;
    float mRecipSqrt;
    const Quat &mA;
    const Quat &mB;
};
```

Here we have used trig functions to create a reference slerp class. The class has a constructor and a method to calculate individual interpolated quaternions. We have taken pains to avoid using branches that will cause lengthy pipeline stalls by using the `Min` function to avoid overflows. Note that although the results near `adotb` = 1 will be consistent, if the quaternions point away from each other, the result will be unpredictable.

To turn this into an approximation, we have to approximate `sin(x)` and `arccos(x)`.

The `sin(x)` component is simple, as this responds to traditional polynomial approximation tools. In Maple, there is a package called `numapprox` that contains polynomial approximation tools that can convert an arbitrary function into a polynomial over a certain range of values.

A Taylor series turns a function of x into a polynomial in x that matches the function exactly at one point. Maple has a built-in Taylor series command that gives a result like this:

$$taylorseries = x - \frac{x^3}{3!} + \frac{x^5}{5!} + O\left(x^7\right). \tag{2.4.18}$$

Unfortunately, Taylor series are not very useful for approximation as they are exact in one place only, but they are simple to calculate and are useful for showing us the general form of a function. A polynomial can be made to be exact in n or more different places, where n is the degree of the polynomial, or highest power term. This can be used to significantly reduce the error.

In the `numapprox` package, Maple has a command called `minimax` that chooses the best places to make a polynomial exact in such a way as the maximum error is minimized, hence the name.

$$minimaxSeries = \text{minimax(sin(x), x=}-\pi..\pi\text{, 3)}=\left(.824535+\left(-.08692x\right)x\right)x \tag{2.4.19}$$

Figure 2.4.3 shows a plot of *taylorseries*, *minimaxseries*, and `sin(x)`. Here we see that the Taylor series shoots off to infinity when $|x| > 1$. Figure 2.4.4 shows a plot of the error, which shows that the Taylor series is exact only at the origin, whereas the minimax polynomial is exact in five separate places, spreading out the error over the interval.

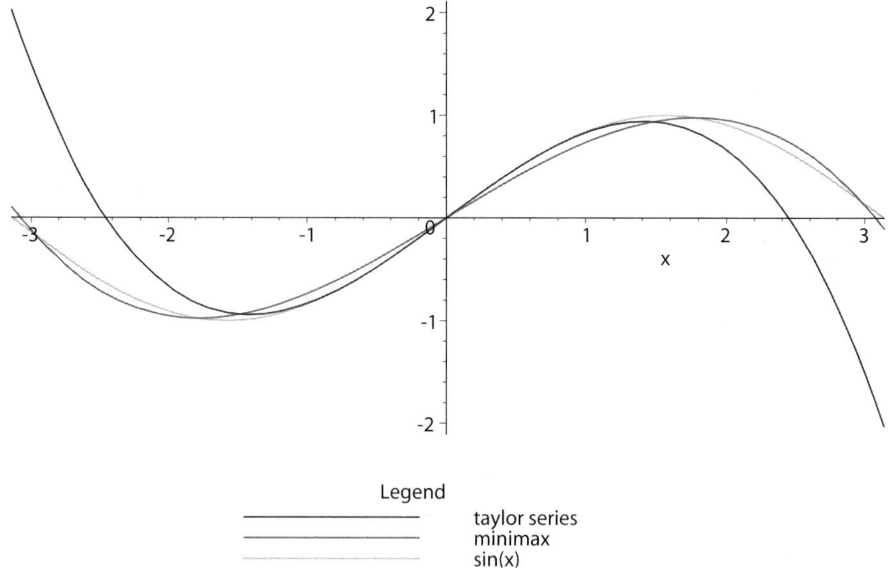

FIGURE 2.4.3 *Plot of taylorseries, minimaxseries, and* `sin(x)` *showing the differences.*

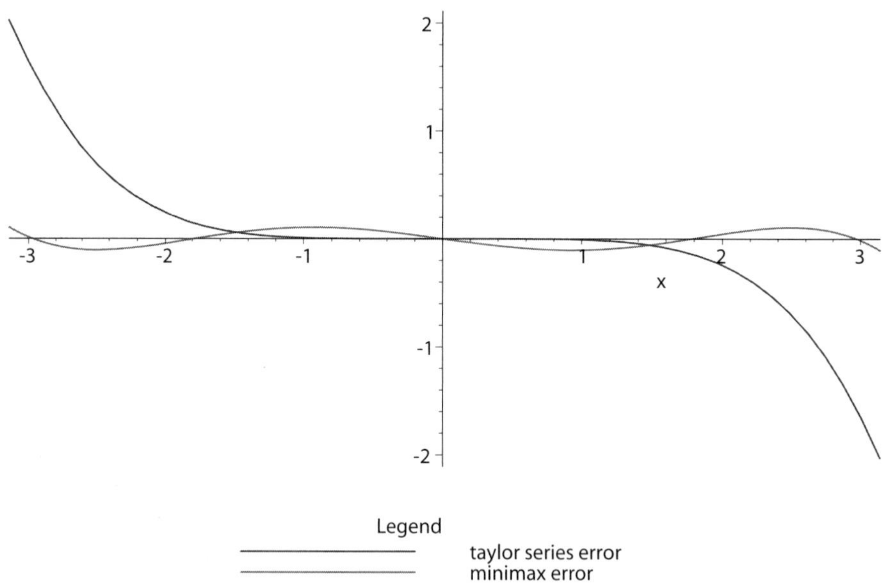

FIGURE 2.4.4 *Plot of the error of a Taylor series versus a minimax series.*

This is how the built-in functions in C++ are created. The following is an approximation to $\cos(x)$ on the interval $x \in [-\pi/2, \pi/2]$ that we can use to approximate $\sin(x)$ on $x \in [0,\pi]$. In this case, $\cos(x)$ is an easier function to approximate than $\sin(x)$, as it is even and hence uses only terms in x^2.

$$\cos(x) = \sin(x+\pi/2) \simeq 1+(-.4999991+(.416636+(-.0138537+.000231540x^2)x^2)x^2)x^2 \quad (2.4.20)$$

Figure 2.4.5 shows a plot of the error for the previous approximation.

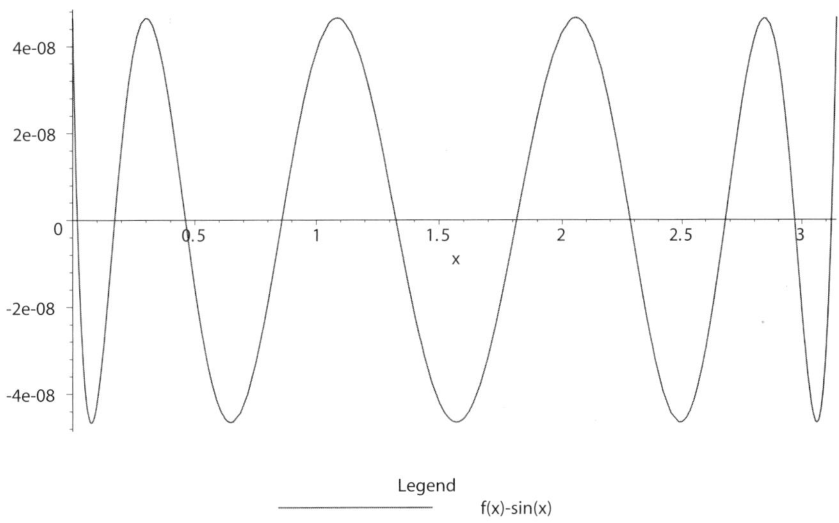

FIGURE 2.4.5 *Showing the error in the approximation to* $\cos(x)$ *shifted into the range used by the slerp function.*

The `arccos(x)` function does not respond to this kind of treatment. Figure 2.4.6 shows a plot of the error for eight terms, which is shockingly bad.

The reason for this can be seen by looking at the `arccos` function itself, shown in Figure 2.4.7. There are singularities at $x=1$ and $x=-1$ that behave as $\sqrt{1-x}$ and $\sqrt{1+x}$, respectively. It is very hard for a polynomial to approximate this kind of function. These kinds of behaviors can be discovered using the Maple "series" command.

Making an approximation in terms of nonlinear terms works much better:

$$\begin{aligned}&\arccos(x) \simeq \\ &\sqrt{2.218480716 - 2.441884385x + 0.2234036692x^2} - \\ &\sqrt{2.218480716 + 2.441884385x + 0.2234036692x^2} + \\ &\pi/2 + 0.6391287330x.\end{aligned} \quad (2.4.21)$$

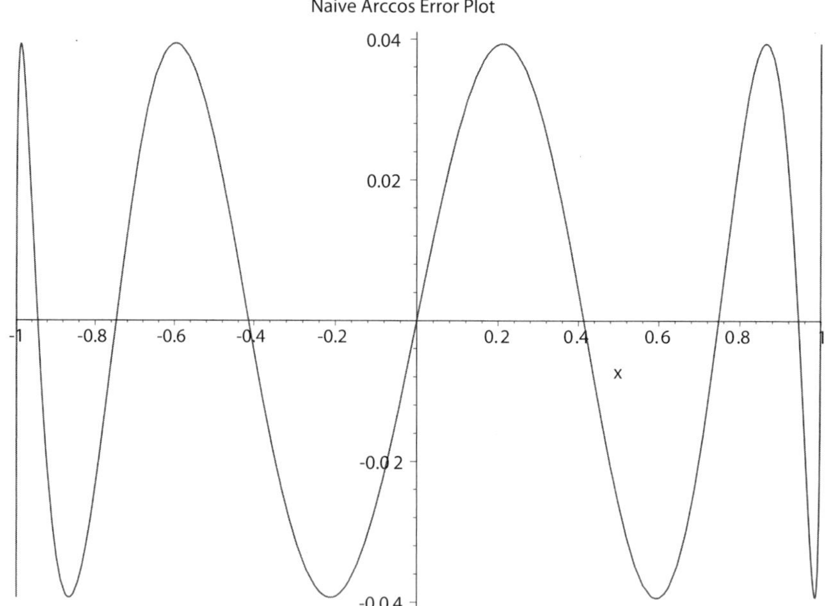

FIGURE 2.4.6 *The result of using Maple's minimax on the arccos function.*

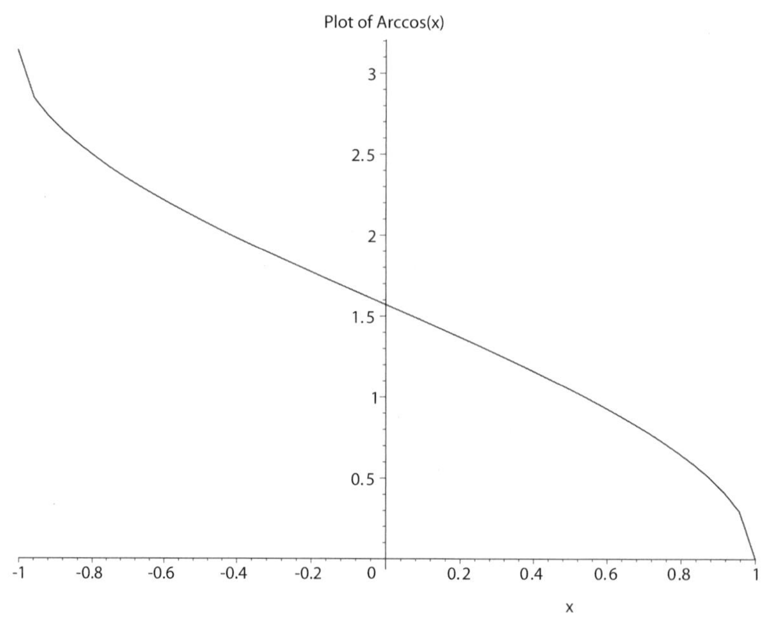

FIGURE 2.4.7 *A plot of arccos(x) showing singularities at* $x = \pm 1$.

The error for this approximation to arccos(x) is plotted in Figure 2.4.8. Note that these functions only work over our required range. If functions that work over other ranges are needed, they will have to be made separately. The accompanying CD-ROM contains some example Maple worksheets.

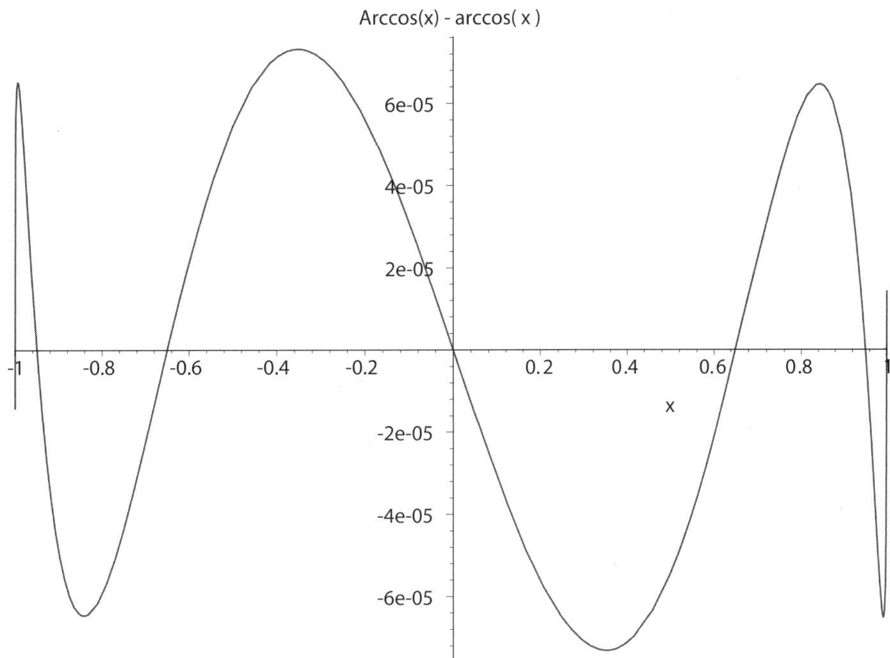

FIGURE 2.4.8 *A better approximation to arccos(x).*

The reciprocal square root is available on most modern processors using the division unit. One should be careful to allow for latency, however, and calculate this first so that the result is available later. An approximate reciprocal square root is also often available in a single-cycle form to 16 bits with SIMD instructions.

The proportional error in the rotation can be calculated to be of the same order as the error in the alpha and beta functions. To perform this calculation, we may assume an error e in the function and use the Maple "series" command. Decrease the number of series terms until the order $O(e^k)$ is the last remaining term in e.

Figure 2.4.9 shows a series of error plots of beta functions for various angles of separation of the quaternions

$$\frac{Sin(t\,Arccos(x))}{\sqrt{1-x^2}} - \frac{\sin(t \arccos x)}{\sqrt{1-x^2}}. \tag{2.4.22}$$

Where $Sin(x)$ and $Arccos(x)$ are the approximations.

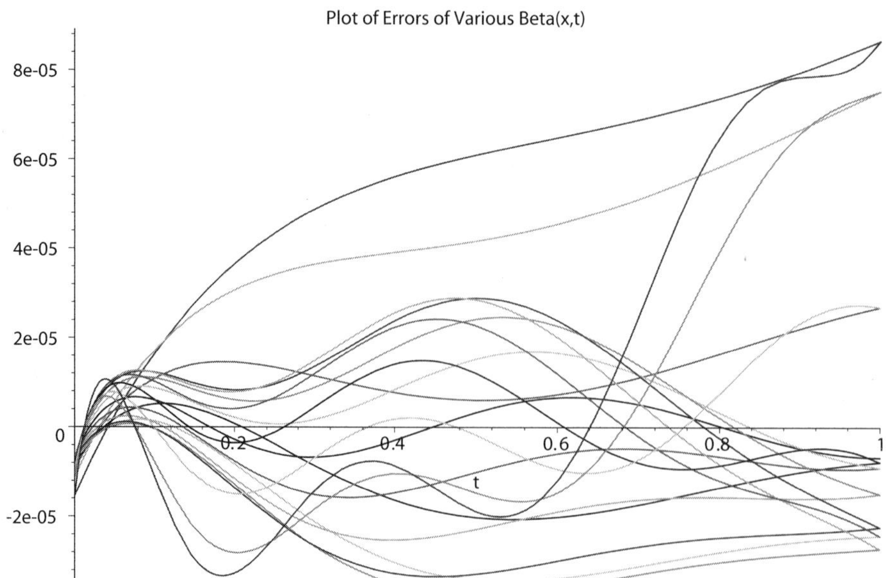

FIGURE 2.4.9 *Plots of errors in $\beta(x,t)$ for various x.*

Use of SIMD architectures enables the calculation of both sine functions together, as shown in Listing 2.4.2.

Listing 2.4.2 Direct Slerp Method Class

```
class SlerpDirect
{
public:
    SlerpDirect( const Quat &a, const Quat &b ) : mA( a ), mB( b )
    {
        float adotb = a.X * b.X + a.Y * b.Y + a.Z * b.Z + a.W * b.W;
        adotb = Min( adotb, 0.99995f );
        float even = 2.218480716f + .2234036692f * adotb * adotb;
        float odd = 2.441884385f * adotb;
        mTheta = Sqrt( even - odd ) - Sqrt( even + odd ) +
                 1.570796327f + .6391287330f * adotb;
        mRecipSqrt = RecipSqrt( 1 - adotb * adotb );
    }

    Quat Interpolate( float t ) const
    {
        float A = ( 1 - t ) * mTheta - 1.570796327f; A = A * A;
        float B = t * mTheta - 1.570796327f; B = B * B;
        float sinA = .9999999535f+(-.4999990537f+(.4166358517e-1f
            +(-.1385370794e-2f+.2315401401e-4f*A)*A)*A)*A;
```

```
            float sinB = .9999999535f+(-.4999990537f+(.4166358517e-1f
                +(-.1385370794e-2f+.2315401401e-4f*B)*B)*B)*B;
            float alpha = sinA * mRecipSqrt;
            float beta = sinB * mRecipSqrt;
            return Quat( alpha * mA.X + beta * mB.X, alpha * mA.Y +
                         beta * mB.Y,
                alpha * mA.Z + beta * mB.Z, alpha * mA.W + beta *
                mB.W );
        }
    private:
        float mTheta;
        float mRecipSqrt;
        const Quat &mA;
        const Quat &mB;
    };
```

This class shows the result we obtain when we simply approximate the component functions of the tradional slerp function.

Matrix Approximation

Because $\beta(x,t)$ is simply a function of two variables, we can, in theory, represent the entire result as a two-dimensional polynomial in *x* and *t*. That is,

$$\beta(x,t) = \mathbf{XMT} \tag{2.4.23}$$

where **M** is an $N_x \times N_t$ matrix and

$$\mathbf{X} = \begin{pmatrix} 1 & x & \cdots & x^{N_x-1} \end{pmatrix}$$
$$\mathbf{T} = \begin{pmatrix} t & t^3 & \cdots & t^{N_t-1} \end{pmatrix}. \tag{2.4.24}$$

Applying the same process as in the analysis of $\arccos(x)$, namely using the Maple series command, we see that we have a problem approximating the whole polynomial because

$$\lim_{x\to-1} \beta(x,t) = \infty. \tag{2.4.25}$$

We need to take this singularity out of the function so that we can approximate it with fewer terms.

If we evaluate

$$g(x,t) = \beta(x,t)(1+x) \tag{2.4.26}$$

instead, then we end up with a much better behaved function over the range $x \in [-1,1]$, as illustrated in Figure 2.4.10. We can then multiply by $1/(1+x)$ to obtain $\beta(x,t)$.

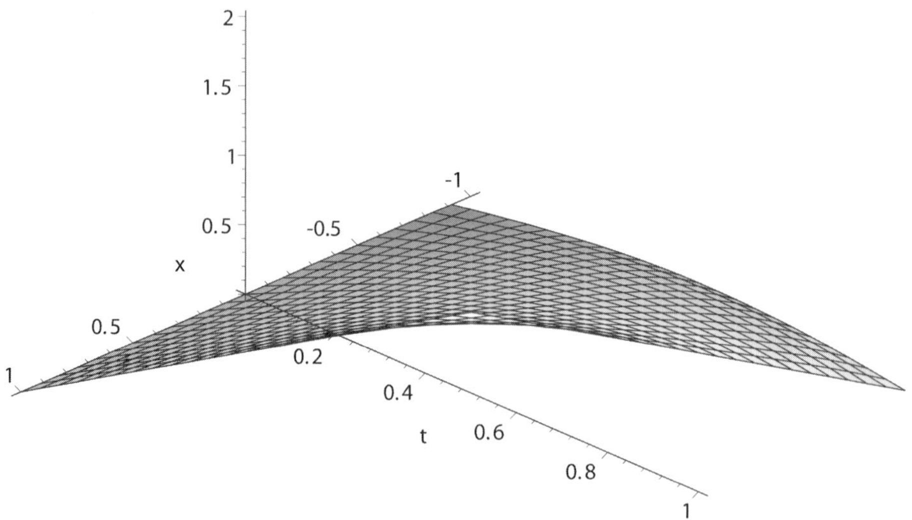

FIGURE 2.4.10 *g(x,t), a better alternative to approximating β(x,t).*

Unfortunately, Maple does not come with a 2D version of the minimax command, and besides, uniform error distribution is useful only in certain conditions.

We can make a 2D version of the Chebyshev approximation method, which constructs a function in the form

$$\sum_{j=0}^{N_t}\sum_{i=0}^{N_x} c_{i,j} T(i,x) T(j,t) \tag{2.4.27}$$

where $T(i,x)$ and $T(j,t)$ are Chebyshev Polynomials of the first kind, given by

$$\begin{aligned} T(0,x) &= 1 \\ T(1,x) &= x \\ T(2,x) &= 2x^2 - 1 \\ T(3,x) &= 4x^3 - 3x. \end{aligned} \tag{2.4.28}$$

ON THE CD

When we have constructed a function of this form, it is easy to convert it to a regular polynomial by multiplying out and collecting terms in x and t. A Maple procedure that does this is included on the accompanying CD-ROM.

Applying this to $g(x,t)$ gives

$$\mathbf{M} = \begin{pmatrix} 1.570994357 & -0.6461396421 & 0.07949824672 & -0.004354110679 \\ 0.5642929825 & 0.5945659091 & -0.1730440015 & 0.01418982936 \\ -0.1783657609 & 0.08610292588 & 0.1079287872 & -0.01567243477 \\ 0.04319948653 & -0.03465102568 & -0.01439451411 & 0.005849053560 \end{pmatrix} \quad (2.4.29)$$

for best accuracy in $0 < \mathbf{a} \cdot \mathbf{b} < 1$. Clearly, more terms can be used, and each row adds two SIMD instructions and more precision to the x expansion.

One of the most useful features of this method is that once the vector

$$\frac{1}{1+x}\mathbf{XM} \quad (2.4.30)$$

is evaluated, multiple $\alpha(t)$ and $\beta(t)$ values can be generated with simple algebra.

Listing 2.4.3 shows an implementation.

Listing 2.4.3 Matrix Slerp Method Class

```
class SlerpMatrix
{
public:
    SlerpMatrix( const Quat &a, const Quat &b ) : mA( a ), mB( b )
    {
        float adotb = a.X * b.X + a.Y * b.Y + a.Z * b.Z + a.W * b.W;
        mRecipOnePlusAdotB = Recip( 1 + adotb );
        mC1 = 1.570994357f+(.5642929859f+( -.1783657717f
            +.4319949352e-1f*adotb)*adotb)*adotb;
        mC3 = -.6461396382f+(.5945657936f+(.8610323953e-1f
            -.3465122928e-1f*adotb)*adotb)*adotb;
        mC5 = .7949823521e-1f+( -.1730436931f+(.1079279599f
            -.1439397801e-1f*adotb)*adotb)*adotb;
        mC7 = -.4354102836e-2f+(.1418962736e-1f+( -.1567189691e-1f
            +.5848706227e-2f*adotb)*adotb)*adotb;
    }

    Quat Interpolate( float t ) const
    {
        float T = 1 - t, t2 = t * t, T2 = T * T;
        float alpha = (mC1+(mC3+(mC5+mC7*T2)*T2)*T2)*T *
                      mRecipOnePlusAdotB;
        float beta = (mC1+(mC3+(mC5+mC7*t2)*t2)*t2)*t *
                     mRecipOnePlusAdotB;
        return Quat( alpha * mA.X + beta * mB.X, alpha * mA.Y +
                     beta * mB.Y, alpha * mA.Z + beta * mB.Z,
                     alpha * mA.W + beta * mB.W );
```

```
    }
private:
    float mRecipOnePlusAdotB;
    float mC1, mC3, mC5, mC7;
    const Quat &mA;
    const Quat &mB;
};
```

Here, we precalculate polynomial coefficients that enable us to simply calculate a series of interpolations. In practice, we would probably recode this using native SIMD instructions.

Renormalization

A quick and dirty approximation, where accuracy is not important, is to simply linear interpolate (lerp) the quaternions and renormalize the result. This produces a result that is good to about four to eight bits in normal use, which is quite often enough. If the angle between the quaternions is very small, the result is quite accurate.

This is the method that has been used in vertex shaders as it is possible to blend between several quaternions in a way that is superior to conventional matrix blending.

However, except for the setup time, the interpolation is slower than the Matrix slerp method presented earlier and has significantly less precision.

Listing 2.4.4 shows an implementation.

Listing 2.4.4 Simple Lerp and Renormalization

```
class SlerpSimpleRenormal
{
public:
    SlerpSimpleRenormal( const Quat &a, const Quat &b ) :
                         mA( a ), mB( b )
    {
    };

    Quat Interpolate( float t ) const
    {
        float alpha = 1 - t;
        float beta = t;
        Quat result( alpha * mA.X + beta * mB.X, alpha * mA.Y +
                     beta * mB.Y, alpha * mA.Z + beta * mB.Z,
                     alpha * mA.W + beta * mB.W );
        float recip = RecipSqrt( result.X * result.X + result.Y *
                      result.Y
            + result.Z * result.Z + result.W * result.W );
        return Quat( result.X * recip, result.Y * recip,
                     result.Z * recip, result.W * recip );
    }
```

```
private:
    const Quat &mA;
    const Quat &mB;
};
```

The simple lerp can be improved by approximating

$$\beta(x,t)=\frac{\sin(t\arccos x)}{\sin(t\arccos x)+\sin((1-t)\arccos x)},\quad \alpha(x,t)=1-\beta(x,t),\quad (2.4.31)$$

instead, and then renormalizing. Alternatively, the angle subdivision methods can be used before the lerp and renormalization operations.

Renormalization can also significantly improve the accuracy of the direct and matrix methods, but at the cost of extra time.

Listing 2.4.5 shows an implementation of the improved renormalization method.

Listing 2.4.5 An Improved Renormalization Method (Rather Cumbersome, However)

```
class SlerpRenormal
{
public:
    SlerpRenormal( const Quat &a, const Quat &b ) :
                   mA( a ), mB( b )
    {
        float adotb = a.X * b.X + a.Y * b.Y + a.Z * b.Z + a.W *
                      b.W;
        adotb = Min( adotb, 0.995f );
        float even = 2.218480716f + .2234036692f * adotb * adotb;
        float odd = 2.441884385f * adotb;
        mTheta = Sqrt( even - odd ) - Sqrt( even + odd )
            + 1.570796327f + .6391287330f * adotb;
    }

    Quat Interpolate( float t ) const
    {
        float T = 1 - t, t2 = t * t, T2 = T * T;
        float A = ( 1 - t ) * mTheta;
        float B = t * mTheta;
        float sinA =  -.67044e-5f + ( 1.000271283f +
                                    ( -.17990919e-2f
            + (  -.1621365372f + (  -.556099983e-2f +
                                  ( .1198086481e-1f
            - .1271209213e-2f * A ) * A ) * A ) * A ) * A ) * A;
        float sinB =  -.67044e-5f + ( 1.000271283f +
                      (  -.17990919e-2f
            + (  -.1621365372f + (  -.556099983e-2f +
                                ( .1198086481e-1f
            - .1271209213e-2f * B ) * B ) * B ) * B ) * B ) * B;
        float recipAB = Recip( sinA + sinB );
        float alpha = sinA * recipAB;
        float beta = sinB * recipAB;
```

```
            // renormalise
            Quat result( alpha * mA.X + beta * mB.X, alpha * mA.Y +
                         beta * mB.Y,
                alpha * mA.Z + beta * mB.Z, alpha * mA.W + beta *
                mB.W );
            float recip = RecipSqrt( result.X * result.X + result.Y *
                          result.Y
                + result.Z * result.Z + result.W * result.W );
            return Quat( result.X * recip, result.Y * recip,
                result.Z * recip, result.W * recip );
        }
    private:
        float mTheta;
        const Quat &mA;
        const Quat &mB;
    };
```

Angle Subdivision Methods

We can bisect the angle between two quaternions by noting that

$$\beta\left(x,\tfrac{1}{2}\right)=\alpha\left(x,\tfrac{1}{2}\right)=\frac{\sin\left(\tfrac{1}{2}\arccos(x)\right)}{\sqrt{1-x^2}}=\frac{1}{\sqrt{2+2x}}. \tag{2.4.32}$$

This is exact for half the angle and can be extended for any value of t that is composed of quarters, eights, sixteenths, and so on. A Maple worksheet is included on the accompanying CD-ROM that calculates the subdivision beta functions in terms of square roots using bisection.

ON THE CD

$$\begin{aligned}
\beta(x,0)&=0,\\
\beta(x,1/4)&=\frac{1+\sqrt{2+2x}}{\sqrt{2+\sqrt{2+2x}}\sqrt{2+2x}},\\
\beta(x,1/2)&=\frac{1}{\sqrt{2+2x}},\\
\beta(x,3/4)&=\frac{1}{\sqrt{2+\sqrt{2+2x}}\sqrt{2+2x}},\\
\beta(x,1)&=1.
\end{aligned} \tag{2.4.33}$$

Comparison of Methods

We compared the classes for accuracy and speed. The test data were three sets of quaternion encodings with large, medium, and tiny rotations.

We expect the small rotations to be more accurate, as the distance between the quaternions is smaller. Large rotations are less common in animation data, but an algorithm must cope with these as well. Table 2.4.1 summarizes the accuracy of the methods for different classes of input data.

Table 2.4.1 Approximate Precision in Bits Equivalent

Data set	Large angles		Medium angles		Tiny angles	
	Worst	Avg	Worst	Avg	Worst	Avg
SlerpDirect	11	13	11	11	11	11
SlerpRenormal	16	18	17	19	19	19
SlerpMatrix	13	16	14	15	15	15
SlerpSimpleRenormal	4	8	11	15	19	19

Table 2.4.2 lists the time taken (in arbitrary units) to slerp 50,000 quaternions. The test consists of one setup and 10 interpolations using a wide range of data.

Table 2.4.2 Slerp Time

SlerpReference	22906
SlerpDirect	13077
SlerpRenormal	24115
SlerpMatrix	7829
SlerpSimpleRenormal	12553

This shows that the approximate functions are quite a bit faster than the reference function, although to get real speed improvement, we would need to code using native instruction sets.

The Matrix method is the clear winner, beating even the simple lerp and renormalization method, probably because of the slow implementation of `sqrt` on the fpu.

This would work especially well on the PS2 VU0 coprocessor, where micro mode could be used to calculate large batches of quaternions for skinning.

Squad Derivative Calculation

We also investigated speeding up the "squad" or spherical quadrangle approximation often mistaken for a Bézier slerp.

Using the approximate arccos and sin functions and a nicely reduced function, we found it was possible to simplify the traditional method that uses log and exponent of quaternions.

Listing 2.4.6 shows a function that contains relatively benign components, easily codeable using SIMD instructions. The approximate functions `ArccosFast` and `SinFast` in Listing 2.4.6 are included on the accompanying CD-ROM.

ON THE CD

Listing 2.4.6 Elegant Squad Derivative Generator

```
// Squad derivative calculation, optimized by hand
// This is quite fast and gives excellent results (~16 bits)
// try to remove the branches implicit in the ? operators.
Quat DerivativeCompact( const Quat &a, const Quat &b,
                        const Quat &c )
{
   Quat bconj = Conj( b );
   Quat arel = Mul( a, bconj );
   Quat crel = Mul( c, bconj );
   float aScale = arel.W > 0.9999f ? -0.25f :
   -0.25f*ArccosFast( arel.W ) * RecipSqrt( 1 - arel.W * arel.W );
   float cScale = crel.W > 0.9999f ? -0.25f :
   -0.25f*ArccosFast( crel.W ) * RecipSqrt( 1 - crel.W * crel.W );
   float logx = aScale * arel.X + cScale * crel.X;
   float logy = aScale * arel.Y + cScale * crel.Y;
   float logz = aScale * arel.Z + cScale * crel.Z;
   float length = Sqrt ( logx * logx + logy * logy + logz * logz );
   float sinLength = SinFast( length );
   float cosLength = Sqrt( 1 - sinLength * sinLength );
   float xyzScale = length < 1e-5f ? 1 : sinLength / length;
   return Mul( b, Quat(xyzScale * logx, xyzScale * logy,
                       xyzScale * logz, cosLength
) );
}

// This function can be used like this:

Quat d1 = DerivativeCompact( q0, q1, q2 );
Quat d2 = DerivativeCompact( q3, q2, q1 );
Quat q12 = SlerpMatrix( q1, q2 ).Interpolate( fract );
Quat d12 = SlerpMatrix( d1, d2 ).Interpolate( fract );
Quat squad = SlerpMatrix( q12, d12 ).Interpolate( 2 * fract *
             ( 1 - fract ) );

// Where q0,...,q3 are a sequence of keys, fract is the
   fractional time.
```

Further Reading

The reader should read Ken Shoemake's Siggraph paper [Shoe85] for a background to the quaternion slerp process. Not only does this introduce us to the concept, but it is also a very readable introduction to quaternion rotations.

It is worth noting that $\beta(x,t)$ is almost identical to a Chebyshev polynomial of the second kind, unlike the Chebyshev polynomials of the first kind we used for the 2D approximation.

$$\beta(x,t) = U_t(x) \tag{2.4.34}$$

These are solutions of a Sturm-Louiville differential equation:

$$\left(1-x^2\right)\frac{d^2}{dx^2}\beta(x,t) - 3x\frac{d}{dx}\beta(x,t) + \left(t^2-1\right)\beta(x,t) = 0 \tag{2.4.35}$$

Normally for Chebyshev Polynomials, the parameter t would be an integer, in which case the function would be a polynomial. However, as our parameter t is a real value, we have a nonpolynomial result.

Read Chapter 11 of [Rich02] for further information. This book contains a good introduction to Maple, power series, and approximate methods.

While doing the research for this gem, we explored using forward differences to solve this equation for $\alpha(t)$ and $\beta(t)$. Although this was not a good method for evaluating the function at a spot value, it would probably be useful for evaluating a series of quaternion interpolations. It is also possible to use multiple-angle formulae to iterate successive slerp results.

Conclusion

We have explored many methods of approximating the quaternion slerp function, which is used extensively in character-based games. We have developed a simple matrix-based method that requires only a few multiplies and adds to produce accurate interpolated rotation quaternions.

Angle subdivision methods using only square roots were also discussed that enable very specific slerp values to be calculated simply.

We have also investigated the squad interpolation function and found a simple function to generate the extra quaternions required for smooth interpolation of a series of keys.

References

[Hejl04] Hejl, Jim. "Hardware Skinning with Quaternions" *Games Programming Gems 4*, 5.12. Charles River Media, 2004.

[Rich02] Richards, D. *Advanced Mathematical Methods with Maple.* Cambridge University Press, 2002.

[Shoe85] Shoemake, Ken. "Animating Rotations with Quaternion Curves," ACM SIGGRAPH, 1985.

2.5

Minimax Numerical Approximation

Christopher Tremblay

ti_chris@yahoo.com

One field of game programming that is often disregarded but ever so present is that of approximation. Approximation is extremely important in a game's perspective since the game as a whole is really an approximation of something that we want to represent. Consequently, the characters are approximated with polygons, and the physics is approximated with given models. A more mathematical, but still pretty interesting, type of approximation is that of complex functions with simpler, faster functions. For example, computations involving the sine and cosine functions are notorious for being pretty slow. It would indeed be beneficial in many cases if we could come up with a function that is faster, but perhaps a little less accurate, than that provided by the floating-point unit (FPU). Such functions can often define the movement or position of certain objects within the world, and not obtaining full accuracy typically does not significantly impair the final output. In such situations, it can be pretty useful to find faster functions that approximate the original.

Well-Known Optimizations

During the study of calculus, one typically learns a common function approximation technique known as the Taylor series. A Taylor series approximates a curve using a polynomial function of a given degree. The polynomial function is chosen for its speedy evaluation and its ease of use. A polynomial function can be quickly computed since it involves operations that are relatively fast on a CPU today (when compared to a cosine/sine or exponential function, for example). Furthermore, they can be written in the Horner form, thus making them a mere set of multiplications and additions. The Horner form of a polynomial is a form that writes the polynomial by factoring the variable x out of the polynomial. For example, the polynomial given by

$$ax + bx^2 + cx^3 + dx^4 + e \tag{2.5.1}$$

can easily be rewritten in the Horner form:

$$e + x\left(a + x\left(b + x\left(c + xd\right)\right)\right). \tag{2.5.2}$$

A Taylor series approximates a curve by copying certain properties of the curve at a given point. More specifically, it copies the position, slope, acceleration, etc. of the curve, or more precisely, it is a polynomial for which the derivatives (up to a certain level) match those of the original curve at a given point.

What Makes a Good Approximation?

The Taylor approximation unfortunately comes with several issues. Notably, the approximation converges very slowly (many terms are required to get a decent approximation). Because of that, the error on a curve at a given point can be large. If we compute a sine function approximation using a Taylor series and obtain an error of 0.5, then the approximation clearly is not really a good one since the curve has an range of $[-1,1]$. For instance, note the difference in the sine function and its fourth-degree MacLaurin series approximation (i.e., Taylor series expanded about $x = 0$) shown in Figures 2.5.1 and 2.5.2. In these figures, we see that the approximation is not terribly good near the end of the interval, while it is pretty accurate at the beginning.

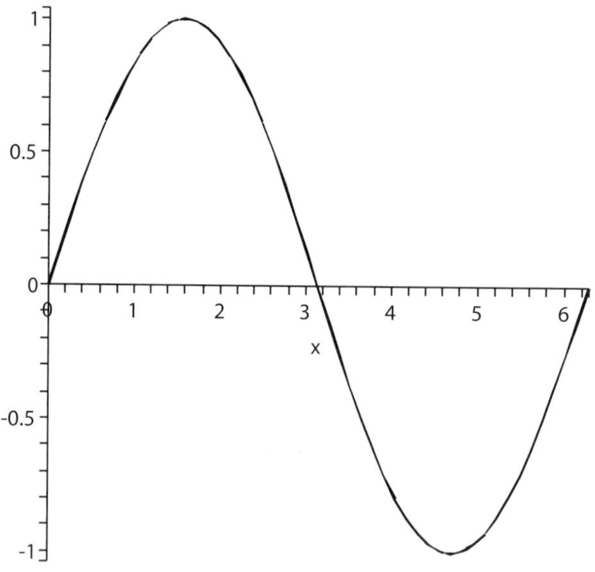

FIGURE 2.5.1 *The sine function over the range* $[0,\pi]$.

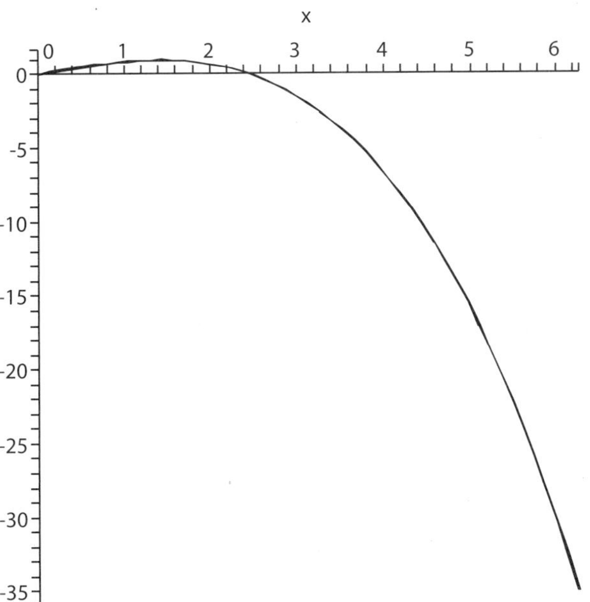

FIGURE 2.5.2 *The sine function's fourth-degree MacLaurin approximation over the range* $[0,\pi]$.

The curve is an excellent approximation at $x = 0$ but is indeed a very poor one at $x = \pi$. A better approximation to the curve would be achieved by choosing $x = \pi/2$, because the average error in the interval $[0,\pi]$ would be smaller. Thus, one thing obviously needs to be defined at this point. What exactly makes an approximation a *good* approximation? For one, it must closely resemble the initial function, and for our purposes, it must be fast. It is well known that the Taylor series approximation is more accurate if the degree of the polynomial is higher. In other words, the curve is a better approximation if more derivatives match, but this comes at the cost of greater evaluation time of the approximation. If the approximation turns out to be slower than the actual function, we do have a problem, and the approximation can't possibly be deemed "good."

Now comes the problem of actually defining what "closely resembles" really means. It is a very vague definition that needs to be specified in mathematical terms to make any sense. The first thing we want to do is to define an interval upon which the function will be approximated. We can yield a better approximation if we limit our approximation to a given domain. With this in mind, we can say that the best approximation is a function that minimizes the maximum error over an interval $[a,b]$. Furthermore, we can state that one approximation is better than another if it is more accurate for a given polynomial degree. For instance, the fourth-degree MacLaurin series for the sine function is

$$\sin x \approx x - \frac{x^3}{6} \tag{2.5.3}$$

but the Taylor series centered about $x = \pi$ is given by

$$\begin{aligned} \sin x &\approx \pi - \frac{\pi^3}{6} + \left(\frac{\pi^2}{2} - 1\right)x - \frac{\pi}{2}x^2 + \frac{1}{6}x^3 \\ &\approx \pi - \frac{\pi^3}{6} + x\left(\left(\frac{\pi^2}{2} - 1\right) - x\left(\frac{\pi}{2} + \frac{1}{6}x\right)\right) \end{aligned} \tag{2.5.4}$$

The latter in Horner form has more terms than the previous, and thus although the error is smaller in the second case but still comparable, the first approximation is better since it involves less computational complexity. If we were to add more terms to the first approximation such that it would match the number of terms of the second approximation, the first approximation would provide a smaller error for the same number of terms and thus would be deemed a better approximation than the latter.

$$\sin x \approx x\left(1 - \frac{x^2}{6}\right) \tag{2.5.5}$$

More generally, x^2 can be factored out for any degree, significantly reducing the computational complexity for a given precision since the MacLaurin approximation of the sine function has a coefficient of zero for all terms of even degree. Consequently, it is not only important to look at how a given function approximates another one very well, it is also important to look at the computational complexity. This makes it easier to speak of the best approximation as the function that for a given degree of multiplicative complexity minimizes the maximum error over an interval $[a,b]$.

Introducing the Minimax Approximation

Now that we have defined the properties for "the best approximation" as far as we are concerned, we can define the minimax approximation. The minimax approximation is the best approximation for a given polynomial degree. It has no relation or knowledge of computational complexity (i.e., how much work it takes to compute) and thus differs a little bit from our definition of best approximation. Consequently for our purposes, in a single line, the minimax approximation is a polynomial approximation of degree n that minimizes the maximum error of a given function. By construction, the minimax approximation is the holy grail of approximation for a given polynomial degree, and it is unique up to permutations of equivalent equations. Because it has no knowledge of complexity, it should be noted that some other approximations could sometimes yield "better approximations." In other words, for the same degree, the minimax approximation will still be better or equal to the better approximation, but because the amount of CPU work required to compute the better approximation makes it faster than the minimax approximation, the minimax approximation isn't the best approximation. For example, this is true for the sine function when we approximate for a total of 13 bits of accuracy. In this case, the Taylor approximation is our "best approximation" because of the Horner form that allows us to rewrite the equations in a more efficient way.

To make the notation easier, we can rewrite a general *n*th degree polynomial $f(x) = c_0 + c_1 x + c_2 x^2 + \cdots c_n x^n$ as the dot product

$$f(x) = \begin{bmatrix} c_0 & c_1 & c_2 & \cdots & c_n \end{bmatrix} \begin{bmatrix} 1 \\ x \\ x^2 \\ \vdots \\ x^n \end{bmatrix} \tag{2.5.6}$$

where we define the row vector as $\mathbf{c}$ and the column vector as $\mathbf{x}$. We are primarily interested in finding the values for the coefficients c_i in the vector $\mathbf{c}$. The key to the minimax polynomial is defined by a theorem called the Chebyshev Equioscillation Theorem. Let f be a continuous function with range $[a,b] \in \mathbb{R}$. The polynomial $p(x)$ of degree n is the minimax polynomial of degree n if and only if there exists $n+2$ points $a \le x_0 < x_1 < \cdots < x_{n+1} \le b$ for which $f(x_j) - p(x_j) = (-1)^j E$ with $j = 0,\ldots,n+1$ and $E = \pm(f - p)$. Put into words, this implies that the error function actually has $(n+2)$ extrema. As a result of the theorem's alternating sign equation, the two functions are equal exactly $(n+1)$ times for an approximation of degree n and of course, all this is true unless the error E is zero, in which case the polynomial is a perfect approximation of the original curve within its defined range.

Given that there are more extrema than times where the functions are equal as well as the previously mentioned theorems, we can easily deduce that the first and last point on the approximation are two points where the error is maximal. Furthermore for this to make sense at all, the signed error must alternate sign. Given this much information, we can actually solve simple problems with simple math. As an example, consider the case in which we want to approximate a parabola with a single line. We can solve the problem if we simply state the previously mentioned theorems and lemma in terms of mathematics. We want to find the coefficient vector $\mathbf{c} = \begin{bmatrix} a & b \end{bmatrix}$ for a line $f(t) = a + bt$ such that the error E between it and the parabola $g(t) = 3t^2$ over the range $[0,1]$ attains the same maximum absolute value at three locations (two of which are $t = 0$ and $t = 1$). This is summarized by the following equations

$$
\begin{aligned}
f(0)-g(0)&=E\\
f(x)-g(x)&=-E\\
f(1)-g(1)&=E\\
\frac{d}{dx}\left[f(x)-g(x)\right]&=0.
\end{aligned}
\tag{2.5.7}
$$

Substituting everything shows us that we are actually dealing with a system of four unknowns with four equations:

$$
\begin{aligned}
a+b\cdot 0-3\cdot 0^2&=E\\
a+bx-3x^2&=-E\\
a+b\cdot 1-3\cdot 1^2&=E\\
b-6x&=0.
\end{aligned}
\tag{2.5.8}
$$

This system can easily be solved by any method we wish to apply. Doing so reveals that the answer to this specific problem is $(a,b)=\left(-\frac{3}{8},3\right)$. We can also try the same method against any reference function $g(t)$ to notice how easy it is to compute the minimax approximation for the second level. The maximum error of a minimax approximation is always given by the difference of the original function and the approximation at either of the endpoints of the interval over which the approximation is applied. We can obtain the values for the third degree minimax approximation using the same logic expressed here. Where it becomes tricky is when we want to compute the minimax approximation for polynomials of degree higher than three. We reach a point where we have fewer knowns than unknowns, and we thus cannot solve the system. In these cases, we must resort to more sophisticated mathematical techniques to solve the problem at hand.

Solving the Minimax Approximations for Arbitrary Degrees

It is by no means trivial to obtain the coefficients of an arbitrary minimax approximation. There are no strict speed requirements in finding the solution because it does not need to be solved in real time. The Remez algorithm can help us solve the problem at hand and goes as follows.

1. Choose an initial guess for the coefficient vector **c**.
2. If the error E is satisfactory, stop. Otherwise, find the maximum vector **x** in $h(x)=g(x)-f(x)$ given **c**.
3. Find the values for the coefficient vector **c** (forget about the previous value for **c**) for the linear system $g(x)-f(x)=(-1)^i E$, given the maximum vector **x**, and go back to step 2.

In a nutshell, we choose an initial guess for the coefficient and find the values of the maxima, which we iteratively use to refine the solution (**c** finds **x**, which finds **c**, etc.). As an example of the solution, let us take the previous example and run it through the algorithm. Suppose we make an initial guess of $\mathbf{c} = (4,1)$. Now we need to find the maxima (i.e., the roots of the derivative). There are ample methods out there for finding roots of polynomials, and they are left as a reference (see [Math]). For this particular problem, the math is pretty simple and direct:

$$\begin{aligned} f(x) - g(x) &= a + bx - 3x^2 \\ \frac{d}{dx}\left[f(x) - g(x)\right] &= b - 6x = 0 \\ x &= \frac{b}{6} \\ &= \frac{1}{6} \end{aligned} \tag{2.5.9}$$

We thus find a general equation that tells us that there is a maximum every time at $x = b/6$. Quite obviously, due to the construct, there is also a maximum at $x = 0$ and $x = 1$ because they are the boundaries of the minimax approximation.

Now that we have an estimate for x (in fact the only unknown maximum for this case), we can proceed to step 2 to find our coefficient:

$$a + bx \pm E = 3x^2, x = \left\{0, \frac{1}{6}, 1\right\}$$

$$\begin{bmatrix} 1 & 0 & 1 \\ 1 & \frac{1}{6} & -1 \\ 1 & 1 & 1 \end{bmatrix} \begin{bmatrix} a \\ b \\ E \end{bmatrix} = \begin{bmatrix} 0 \\ \frac{1}{13} \\ 3 \end{bmatrix} \tag{2.5.10}$$

Solving the linear system, we find that the solution is $(a, b, E) = \left(-\frac{11}{52}, 3, \frac{11}{52}\right)$, which is not too far from the minimax solution of our previous calculations. Going through the second iteration of the loop, we find that $x = 3/6 = 1/2$, changing the equation to the following.

$$a + bx \pm E = 3x^2, x = \left\{0, \frac{1}{6}, 1\right\}$$

$$\begin{bmatrix} 1 & 0 & 1 \\ 1 & \frac{1}{2} & -1 \\ 1 & 1 & 1 \end{bmatrix} \begin{bmatrix} a \\ b \\ E \end{bmatrix} = \begin{bmatrix} 0 \\ \frac{3}{4} \\ 3 \end{bmatrix} \tag{2.5.11}$$

Solving this linear system gives the exact solution we have known for quite a bit: $\mathbf{c} = \left(-\frac{3}{8}, 3\right)$. Obviously, not all approximations are this easy to compute. Sometimes the root-finding process is tedious and requires an iterative process such as the Newton-Raphson method or Haley's method, and the linear system is sometimes tedious to process. The beauty about it is that we only need to compute the coefficient once to compute the approximation to the function; thus, there exists no true efficiency requirements. Figure 2.5.3 shows the graph of the error between the approximation and the true function. We can clearly see that it follows the theorems stated earlier in terms of extrema and null-errors.

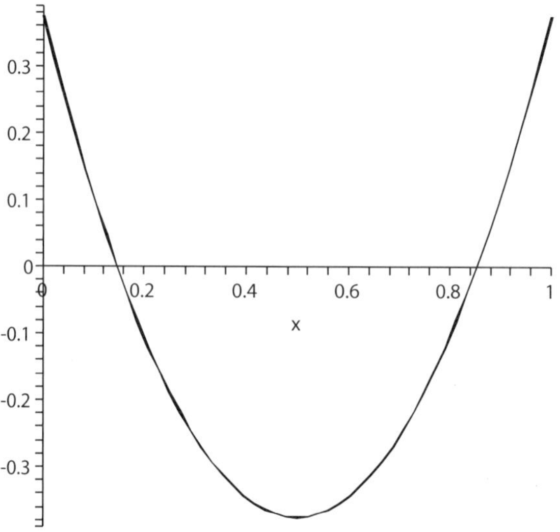

FIGURE 2.5.3 *Graph of the error between the first-degree minimax approximation of $f(x)$ and $g(x)$.*

Error Analysis

An especially true fact of approximation is that error analysis is a crucial part of the work. The minimax approximation does not directly define the best approximation. It merely defines the approximation giving the lowest maximal error for a particular polynomial degree. It does not in any way guarantee that it is the fastest method given a bit-accuracy. As a proof of this statement, suppose we wanted to approximate the sine function over the interval $\left[0, \pi/2\right]$. We can easily compute the remaining values of the function using simple trigonometric identities. The fourth-degree minimax approximation for the sine function is given by the coefficient vector

$$\mathbf{c} = (0.000107652, 0.9964223759, 0.0190787764, -0.2026644465, 0.02841900366) \quad (2.5.12)$$

In Horner form, this equation takes a total of four multiplications. On the other hand, we can write the Taylor series of the sine function for four multiplications in Horner form:

$$\sin(x) \approx x\left(1 + x^2\left(-\frac{1}{3!} + x^2\left(\frac{1}{5!} - \frac{x^2}{7!}\right)\right)\right) \quad (2.5.13)$$

If we consider that x^2 is precomputed as a single value, we have that the error function for this approximation is slightly better than the minimax approximation of equal complexity as shown in Figures 2.5.4 and 2.5.5. This all means that the minimax approximation is an excellent approximation, but others can sometimes be better depending on the bit depth. Thus, we should be careful as we go about computing this to make sure that the minimax approximation is indeed the best one for a given complexity.

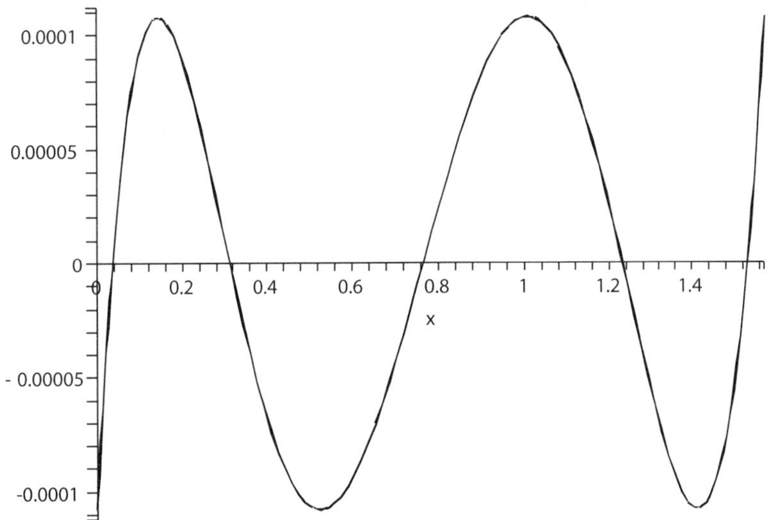

FIGURE 2.5.4 *Fourth degree minimax approximation to the sine function.*

If we compare a minimax approximation in Figure 2.5.4 with a Taylor series of similar degree in Figure 2.5.5, it is quite clear that the minimax approximation is the undisputed winner. One has a maximal error of about 0.0001 while the other hosts an error of 0.00016. The best part is that the minimax approximation offers a faster alternative to every single FPU function in existence, regardless of the precision. If we take

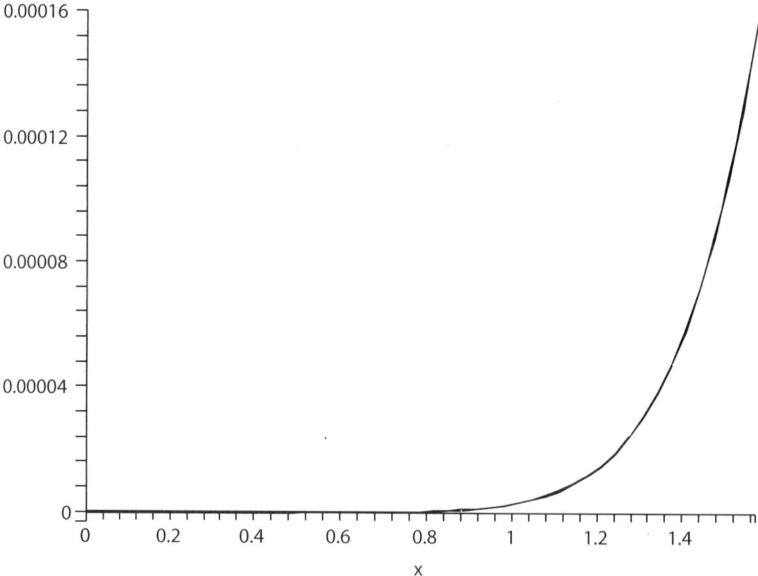

FIGURE 2.5.5 *Seventh degree Taylor approximation to the sine function.*

the previously mentioned approximation for the sine curve for example, the sine function is twice as fast as what is provided by the FPU, and in a reasonable approximation's case, the precision losses are not that high as shown in Tables 2.5.1 and 2.5.2. It gets even better if we implement this technique using a SIMD (Single Instruction, Multiple Data) processor. By doing so, we can basically compute four sine functions simultaneously, improving the speed almost seven times the speed of a single sine function, or minimally six times for a function that has full 23 mantissa bits of accuracy.

Table 2.5.1 Error for Sin(x) Taylor Series

Degree	Taylor Equations for sin x	Max Error for $\theta = [0,\pi/2]$
0	0	1
1	x	0.5707
2	x	0.5707
3	$x - x^3/6$	0.7516×10^{-1}
4	$x - x^3/6$	0.7516×10^{-1}
5	$x - x^3/6 + x^5/120$	-0.4524×10^{-2}

Table 2.5.2 Error for Minimax of Sin(x)

Degree	Minimax Equation for sin *x*	Max Error for θ = [0,π/2]
0	0.5	0.5
1	$0.1051 + 0.6366 \cdot x$	0.1051
2	$-0.1385 \cdot 10^{-1} + 1.1748 \cdot x - 0.3314 \cdot x^2$	0.1385×10^{-1}
3	$-0.1365 \times 10^{-2} + 1.0252 \cdot x - 0.7068 \times 10^{-1} \cdot x^2 - 0.1125 \cdot x^3$	0.1365×10^{-2}
4	$-0.1076 \times 10^{-3} + 0.9964 \cdot x + 0.19078 \times 10^{-1} \cdot x^2 - 0.2026 \cdot x^3 + 0.2841 \times 10^{-1} \cdot x^4$	0.1076×10^{-3}
5	$-0.7064 \times 10^{-5} + 0.9996 \cdot x + 0.2193 \times 10^{-2} \cdot x^2 - 0.1722 \cdot x^3 + 0.6097 \times 10^{-2} \cdot x^4 + 0.5721^{-2} \cdot x^5$	0.706482×10^{-5}

From this point on, computing an approximation for a function is pretty trivial. In practice, we can approximate every single FPU function, and we can almost always at least double the speed of the functions if we simply use a few identities.

Further Improving the Approximation

There are three methods for decreasing the approximation's error. The most obvious one is to increase the polynomial degree and thus increase the complexity of the computations. This is not the ideal method, since it does involve increasing the complexity. The other technique we may consider is to convert the function into a combination of other functions. For instance, if we want to compute the numerical approximation of $\sin x \cdot \cos x$, we should consider whether it is faster to compute two approximations (one for sine and one for cosine) than to compute one approximation for the entire function. In this specific case, it is not. Computing the approximation of the entire function yields faster results when compared to approximating two functions, but it is something to be considered at all times, as it may well not be the case for more complex functions. This is especially true for rational functions.

The very last method that can be used to improve an approximation is to simply reduce the range of the approximation. In the first example, the sine function was approximated only on the interval $[0,\pi/2]$, and trigonometric identities can be used to compute values outside this range. Sometimes, it may be wise to compute piecewise approximations to a function to reduce its complexity. For example, if we want to compute the approximation to the sine function once more, we could do so by computing 18 linear (first-degree) evenly spaced approximations. It is very easy to know which approximation to use if the function is evenly spaced-the range is a division of the entire curve, and we can store the coefficient in a table to compute the value. In embedded devices, sine/cosine tables are often used, and they represent the values of the functions for a given degree. If we use this technique, we can achieve a greater precision with less static footprint, given an extra multiplication/addition per computation. It is well worth the effort and rather easy to compute as was shown earlier.

Finally, the last piece of advice that can be given is to use identities or geometric relationships when possible. All transcendental FPU functions can be accelerated with the minimax approximation. It is really only a matter of knowing what geometrical relationships exist within the functions in order to reduce the range of approximation. For instance, consider the function tan x. At first view, it is a very hard function to approximate because of its asymptotic behavior. Fortunately, if we consider the identity

$$\tan x = \frac{1}{\tan\left(\frac{\pi}{2} - x\right)} \tag{2.5.14}$$

we can significantly reduce the precision issues by creating an approximation of $\tan x$ from angles 0 to $\pi/4$. As another example, consider the inverse of the tan function: the arctan function. This function is also very ugly because it is asymptotic in x and thus has an unlimited range. Fortunately with a quirky identity, we can reduce the approximation's range to a mere 0 to 1:

$$\arctan x = \frac{\pi|x|}{2x} - \arctan\left(\frac{1}{x}\right). \tag{2.5.15}$$

As long as the identity we find is not more complicated than computing the function itself with the FPU, it should not be a problem. For the two examples presented, the cost of the divisions and extra work required doesn't really hurt that much since the equivalent FPU functions for theses two functions are even slower than the sine/cosine functions, thus compensating for the more complex logic required to compute the function.

Reference

[Math] available on-line at *http://mathworld.wolfram.com/Root-FindingAlgorithm.html.*

2.6

Oblique View Frustums for Mirrors and Portals

Eric Lengyel

lengyel@terathon.com

Several techniques have been developed to render 3D images containing elements that are inherently recursive in nature. Some examples are mirrors that reflect their immediate surroundings, portals through which a remote region of the scene can be viewed, and water surfaces through which refractive transparency is applied. Each of these situations requires that part of the scene be rendered from the perspective of some imaginary camera whose position and orientation are calculated using certain rules that take into account the position of the real camera through which the user is looking. For example, the image visible in a mirror is rendered using a camera that is the reflection of the real camera through the plane of the mirror.

Once such a component of an image is rendered through an imaginary camera, it is usually treated as a geometrically planar object when rendering from the perspective of the real camera. The plane chosen to represent the image is simply the plane that naturally separates the image from the rest of the environment, such as the plane of a mirror, portal, or water surface. In the process of rendering from an imaginary camera, it is possible that geometry lies closer to the camera than the plane representing the surface of the mirror, portal, etc. If such geometry is rendered, it can lead to unwanted artifacts in the final image.

The simplest solution to this problem is to enable a user-defined clipping plane to truncate all geometry at the surface. Unfortunately, older GPUs do not support user-defined clipping planes and must resort to a software-based vertex processing path when they are enabled. Other more modern GPUs do support generalized user-defined clipping operations but using them requires that the vertex programs in use be modified—a task that may not be convenient since it requires two versions of each vertex program to be kept around.

This gem presents an alternative solution that exploits the clipping planes that already exist for every rendered scene. Normally, every geometric primitive is clipped to the six sides of the view frustum: four side planes, a near plane, and a far plane. Adding a seventh clipping plane that represents the surface through which we are looking almost always results in a redundancy with the near plane, since we are now clipping against a plane that slices through the view frustum further away from the camera. Thus, our strategy is to modify the projection matrix in such a way that the near plane is moved to coincide with the surface plane. Since we are still clipping only against the six planes of the view frustum, such a modification gives us our desired result at absolutely no performance cost. Furthermore, this technique can be applied to any projection matrix, including the conventional perspective and orthographic projections as well as the infinite projection matrix used by stencil shadow volume algorithms.

Plane Representation

Before examining the projection matrix and how it defines the six planes of the view frustum, we quickly review how planes work in 3D graphics. A plane $\mathbf{C}$ is mathematically represented by a four-dimensional vector of the form

$$\mathbf{C} = \langle N_x, N_y, N_z, -\mathbf{N} \cdot \mathbf{Q} \rangle, \tag{2.6.1}$$

where $\mathbf{N}$ is the normal vector pointing away from the front side of the plane, and $\mathbf{Q}$ is any point lying in the plane itself. A homogeneous point $\mathbf{C} = \langle N_x, N_y, N_z, -\mathbf{N} \cdot \mathbf{Q} \rangle$ lies in the plane if and only if the four-dimensional dot product $\mathbf{C} \cdot \mathbf{P}$ is zero. For points lying on the front (or positive) side of the plane, this dot product is positive, and for points lying on the back (or negative) side of the plane, this dot product is negative.

A plane $\mathbf{C}$ scaled by any nonzero scalar still represents the same plane. Likewise, a homogeneous point $\mathbf{P}$ scaled by any nonzero scalar still represents the same point. If the normal vector $\mathbf{N}$ of a plane $\mathbf{C}$ is unit length, and the w-coordinate of a point $\mathbf{P}$ is 1, then the dot product $\mathbf{C} \cdot \mathbf{P}$ measures the signed perpendicular distance from the point $\mathbf{P}$ to the plane $\mathbf{C}$.

A plane is a covariant vector and therefore must be transformed from one coordinate system to another using the inverse transpose of the matrix that transforms ordinary points (which are contravariant vectors). This is particularly important when transforming planes with the projection matrix, since it is not orthogonal. Given a camera-space point $\mathbf{P}$ and a camera-space plane $\mathbf{C}$, the projection matrix $\mathbf{M}$ produces a clip-space point $\mathbf{P}'$ and a clip-space plane $\mathbf{C}'$ as follows

$$\begin{aligned} \mathbf{P}' &= \mathbf{MP} \\ \mathbf{C}' &= \left(\mathbf{M}^{-1}\right)^{\mathrm{T}} \mathbf{C}. \end{aligned} \tag{2.6.2}$$

Inverting these equations gives us the following formulas, which transform from clip space to camera space

$$\begin{aligned} \mathbf{P} &= \mathbf{M}^{-1}\mathbf{P}' \\ \mathbf{C} &= \mathbf{M}^{\mathrm{T}}\mathbf{C}'. \end{aligned} \tag{2.6.3}$$

The Projection Matrix

We spend some time now reviewing the function of the projection matrix and its relationship to the view frustum's clipping planes. We avoid examining any particular form of the projection matrix and require only that it be invertible. This allows our results to be applied to arbitrary projection matrices that may have already been modified from the standard forms.

Recall that in OpenGL camera space (also known as eye space), the camera lies at the origin and points in the $-z$ direction, as shown in Figure 2.6.1. To complete a righthanded coordinate system, the x-axis points to the right, and the y-axis points upward. (In Direct3D, the z-axis is reversed and camera space is lefthanded.) Vertices are normally transformed from whatever space in which they are specified into camera space by the model-view matrix. In this gem, we do not worry about the model-view matrix and assume that vertex positions are specified directly in camera space.

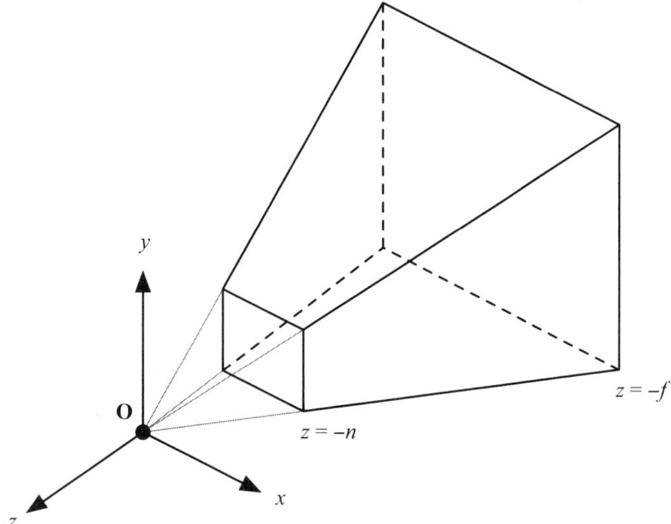

FIGURE 2.6.1 *OpenGL camera space and the standard view frustum. The near and far planes are perpendicular to the z-axis and lie at the distances* n *and* f *from the camera, respectively.*

The standard view frustum is the six-sided truncated pyramid that encloses the volume of space visible to the camera. As shown in Figure 2.6.1, it is bounded by four side planes representing the four edges of the viewport, a near plane at $z = -n$, and a far plane at $z = -f$. The near and far planes are normally perpendicular to the camera's viewing direction, but our modifications to the projection matrix will move these two planes and change the fundamental shape of the view frustum.

The projection matrix transforms vertices from camera space to homogeneous clip space. In OpenGL's homogeneous clip space, a four-dimensional point $\langle x, y, z, w \rangle$

lies inside the projection of the camera-space view frustum if the following conditions are satisfied

$$\begin{aligned} -w &\le x \le w \\ -w &\le y \le w \\ -w &\le z \le w. \end{aligned} \tag{2.6.4}$$

Performing the perspective division by the w-coordinate moves points into normalized device coordinates, where each coordinate of a point in the view frustum lies in the interval $[-1,1]$. Our goal is to modify the projection matrix so that points lying on a given arbitrary plane have a z-coordinate of -1 in normalized device coordinates.

Figure 2.6.2 shows the x and z components of a three-dimensional slice of the four-dimensional homogeneous clip space. Within this slice, the w-coordinate of every point is 1, and the projection of the view frustum described by Equation 2.6.4 is bounded by six planes forming a cube. The w-coordinate of each plane is 1, exactly one of the x-, y-, and z-coordinates is ± 1, and the rest of the components are zero, as shown in Table 2.6.1. Given an arbitrary projection matrix $\mathbf{M}$, Equation 2.6.3 can be used to map these planes into camera space. This produces the remarkably simple formulas listed in Table 2.6.1 in which each camera-space plane is expressed as a sum or difference of two rows of the projection matrix.

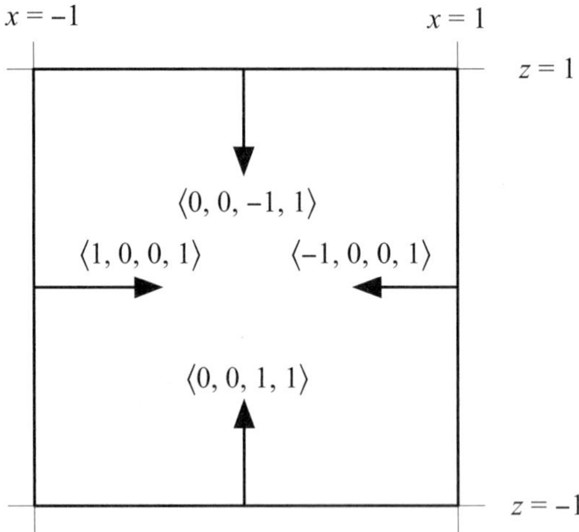

FIGURE 2.6.2 *A three-dimensional slice of OpenGL's homogeneous clip space at* $w = 1$ *and four of the six clipping planes that form a cube in this space.*

Table 2.6.1 OpenGL clip-space and camera-space view frustum planes. The matrix M represents the projection matrix that transforms points from camera space to clip space. The notation represents the *i*-th row of the matrix M.

Frustum Plane	Clip-space Coordinates	Camera-space Coordinates
Near	$\langle 0,0,1,1\rangle$	$M_4 + M_3$
Far	$\langle 0,0,-1,1\rangle$	$M_4 - M_3$
Left	$\langle 1,0,0,1\rangle$	$M_4 + M_1$
Right	$\langle -1,0,0,1\rangle$	$M_4 - M_1$
Bottom	$\langle 0,1,0,1\rangle$	$M_4 + M_2$
Top	$\langle 0,-1,0,1\rangle$	$M_4 - M_2$

Clipping Plane Modification

Let $\mathbf{C} = \langle C_x, C_y, C_z, C_w \rangle$ be the plane shown in Figure 2.6.3, having coordinates specified in camera space, to which we would like to clip our geometry. The camera should lie on the negative side of the plane, so we can assume that $C_w < 0$. The plane **C** will replace the ordinary near plane of the view frustum. As shown in Table 2.6.1, the camera-space near plane is given by the sum of the last two rows of the projection matrix **M**, so we must somehow satisfy

$$\mathbf{C} = \mathbf{M}_4 + \mathbf{M}_3. \tag{2.6.5}$$

We cannot modify the fourth row of the projection matrix, because perspective projections use it to move the negation of the *z*-coordinate into the *w*-coordinate, and this is necessary for perspective-correct interpolation of vertex attributes such as texture coordinates. Thus, we are left with no choice but to replace the third row of the projection matrix with

$$\mathbf{M}'_3 = \mathbf{C} - \mathbf{M}_4. \tag{2.6.6}$$

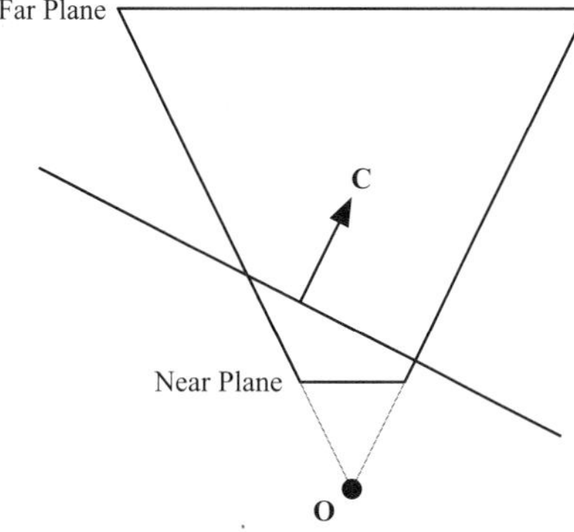

FIGURE 2.6.3 *The near plane of the view frustum is replaced with the arbitrary plane C.*

After making the replacement shown in Equation 2.6.6, the far plane **F** of the view frustum becomes

$$\begin{aligned}\mathbf{F} &= \mathbf{M}_4 - \mathbf{M}'_3 \\ &= 2\mathbf{M}_4 - \mathbf{C}.\end{aligned} \tag{2.6.7}$$

This fact presents a significant problem for perspective projections. A perspective projection matrix must have a fourth row given by $\mathbf{M}_4 = \langle 0,0,-1,0 \rangle$ so that the clip-space *w*-coordinate receives the negation of the camera-space *z*-coordinate. As a consequence, the near plane and far plane are no longer parallel if either C_x or C_y is nonzero. This is extremely unintuitive and results in a view frustum having a very undesirable shape. By observing that any point $\mathbf{P} = \langle x, y, 0, w \rangle$ for which $\mathbf{C} \cdot \mathbf{P} = 0$ implies that we also have $\mathbf{F} \cdot \mathbf{P} = 0$, we can conclude that the intersection of the near and far planes occurs in the x-y plane, as shown in Figure 2.6.4(a).

Since the maximum projected depth of a point is achieved at the far plane, projected depth no longer represents the distance along the *z*-axis, but rather a value corresponding to the position between the new near and far planes. This has a severe impact on depth-buffer precision along different directions in the view frustum. Fortunately, we have a recourse for minimizing this effect, and it is to make the angle between the near and far planes as small as possible. The plane **C** possesses an implicit scale factor that we have not yet restricted in any way. Changing the scale of **C** causes the orientation of the far plane **F** to change, so we need to calculate the appropriate scale that minimizes the angle between **C** and **F** without clipping any part of the original view frustum, as shown in Figure 2.6.4(b).

Let $\mathbf{C}' = \left(\mathbf{M}^{-1}\right)^{\mathrm{T}} \mathbf{C}$ be the projection of the new near plane into clip space (using the original projection matrix **M**). The corner $\mathbf{Q}'$ of the view frustum lying opposite the plane $\mathbf{C}'$ is given by

$$\mathbf{Q}' = \left\langle \operatorname{sgn}\left(C'_x\right), \operatorname{sgn}\left(C'_y\right), 1, 1 \right\rangle \tag{2.6.8}$$

where the sgn function returns the sign of its argument as follows.

$$\operatorname{sgn}(k) = \begin{cases} +1, & \text{if } k > 0; \\ 0, & \text{if } k = 0; \\ -1, & \text{if } k < 0. \end{cases} \tag{2.6.9}$$

(For most perspective projections, it is safe to assume that the signs of C'_x and C'_y are the same as C_x and C_y, so the projection of **C** into clip space can be avoided.) Once we have determined the value of $\mathbf{Q}'$, we obtain its camera-space counterpart $\mathbf{Q}$ by computing $\mathbf{Q} = \mathbf{M}^{-1}\mathbf{Q}'$. For a standard view frustum, $\mathbf{Q}$ coincides with the point opposite the plane $\mathbf{C}$ where two side planes meet the far plane.

To force the far plane to contain the point $\mathbf{Q}$, we must require that $\mathbf{F} \cdot \mathbf{Q} = 0$. The only part of Equation 2.6.7 that we can modify is the scale of the plane $\mathbf{C}$, so we introduce a factor a as follows:

$$\mathbf{F} = 2\mathbf{M}_4 - a\mathbf{C}. \tag{2.6.10}$$

Solving the equation $\mathbf{F} \cdot \mathbf{Q} = 0$ for a yields

$$a = \frac{2\mathbf{M}_4 \cdot \mathbf{Q}}{\mathbf{C} \cdot \mathbf{Q}}, \tag{2.6.11}$$

replacing $\mathbf{C}$ with $a\mathbf{C}$ in Equation 2.6.6 gives us

$$\mathbf{M}_3' = \frac{2\mathbf{M}_4 \cdot \mathbf{Q}}{\mathbf{C} \cdot \mathbf{Q}}\mathbf{C} - \mathbf{M}_4, \tag{2.6.12}$$

and this produces the optimal far plane orientation shown in Figure 2.6.4(b). It should be noted that this technique also works correctly in the case that $\mathbf{M}$ is an infinite projection matrix (i.e., one that places the conventional far plane at infinity) by forcing the far plane to be parallel to one of the edges of the view frustum where two side planes meet.

As mentioned earlier, modifying the view frustum to perform clipping against an arbitrary plane impacts depth-buffer precision, because the full range of depth values may not be used along different directions in camera space. It can be shown that the maximum attainable normalized device z-coordinate along the camera-space direction $\mathbf{V}$ is given by

$$-\frac{a(\mathbf{C} \cdot \mathbf{V}) + V_z}{V_z}. \tag{2.6.13}$$

In general, the depth buffer precision decreases as the angle between the normal direction of the clipping plane $\mathbf{C}$ and the z-axis increases and as the distance from the camera to the clipping plane increases. More information about depth precision issues can be found in [Leng04].

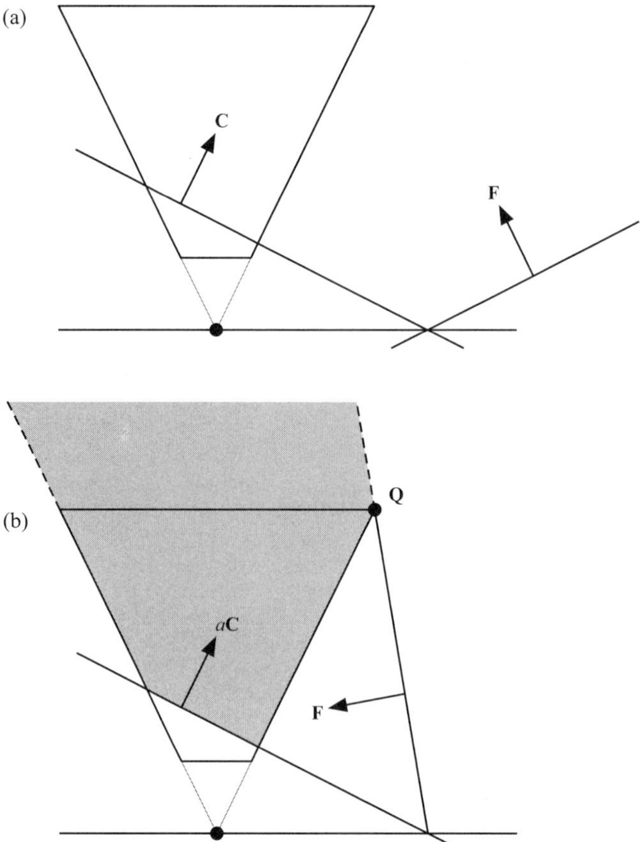

FIGURE 2.6.4 *(a) The modified far plane* **F** *given by Equation 2.6.7 intersects the modified near plane* **C** *in the x-y plane. (b) Scaling the near plane* **C** *by the value* a *given by Equation 2.6.11 adjusts the far plane so that the angle between the near and far planes is as small as possible without clipping any part of the original view frustum. The shaded area represents the volume of space that is not clipped by the modified view frustum.*

OpenGL Implementation

The standard OpenGL perspective projection matrix **M** is given by

$$\mathbf{M} = \begin{bmatrix} \frac{2n}{r-l} & 0 & \frac{r+l}{r-l} & 0 \\ 0 & \frac{2n}{t-b} & \frac{t+b}{t-b} & 0 \\ 0 & 0 & -\frac{f+n}{f-n} & -\frac{2fn}{f-n} \\ 0 & 0 & -1 & 0 \end{bmatrix} \tag{2.6.14}$$

where n is the distance to the near plane, f is the distance to the far plane, and the values l, r, b, and t represent the left, right, bottom, and top edges of the rectangle carved out of the near plane by the four side planes of the view frustum. Since $\mathbf{M}_4 = \langle 0,0,-1,0 \rangle$, Equation 2.6.12 simplifies to

$$\mathbf{M}'_3 = \frac{-2Q_z}{\mathbf{C} \cdot \mathbf{Q}} \mathbf{C} + \langle 0,0,1,0 \rangle. \tag{2.6.15}$$

The point **Q** is given by

$$\mathbf{Q} = \mathbf{M}^{-1} \langle \operatorname{sgn}(C_x), \operatorname{sgn}(C_y), 1, 1 \rangle, \tag{2.6.16}$$

applying the inverse of **M**, we have

$$\mathbf{Q} = \begin{bmatrix} \operatorname{sgn}(C_x)\frac{r-l}{2n} + \frac{r+l}{2n} \\ \operatorname{sgn}(C_y)\frac{t-b}{2n} + \frac{t+b}{2n} \\ -1 \\ 1/f \end{bmatrix}. \tag{2.6.17}$$

Listing 2.6.1 demonstrates how the modification to the projection matrix can be implemented in an OpenGL-based application for a typical projection matrix. It assumes that the projection matrix $\mathbf{M}$ is a perspective projection having the form

$$\mathbf{M} = \begin{bmatrix} a & 0 & b & 0 \\ 0 & c & d & 0 \\ 0 & 0 & e & f \\ 0 & 0 & -1 & 0 \end{bmatrix}, \tag{2.6.18}$$

where $a > 0$, $c > 0$, and $f \neq 0$. The code makes direct use of the general inverse of $\mathbf{M}$, given by

$$\mathbf{M}^{-1} = \begin{bmatrix} 1/a & 0 & 0 & b/a \\ 0 & 1/c & 0 & d/c \\ 0 & 0 & 0 & -1 \\ 0 & 0 & 1/f & e/f \end{bmatrix}. \tag{2.6.19}$$

Listing 2.6.1 Implementation of the Projection Matrix Modification for an OpenGL Projection Matrix Having the Form Shown in Equation 2.6.18 (The `clipPlane` parameter passed to the `ModifyProjectionMatrix` function represents the camera-space plane to which clipping is to occur.)

```
inline float sgn(float a)
{
    if (a > 0.0F) return (1.0F);
    if (a < 0.0F) return (-1.0F);
    return (0.0F);
}

struct Vector4D
{
    float  x, y, z, w;

    Vector4D() {}

    Vector4D(float a, float b, float c, float d)
    {
        x = a; y = b; z = c; w = d;
    }
```

```
        // Scalar product
        Vector4D operator *(float s) const
        {
            return (Vector4D(x * s, y * s, z * s, w * s));
        }

        // Dot product
        float operator *(const Vector4D& v) const
        {
            return (x * v.x + y * v.y + z * v.z + w * v.w);
        }
};

void ModifyProjectionMatrix(const Vector4D& clipPlane)
{
    float       matrix[16];
    Vector4D    q;

    // Grab the current projection matrix from OpenGL
    glGetFloatv(GL_PROJECTION_MATRIX, matrix);

    // Transform the clip-space corner point opposite the
    // clipping plane into camera space by multiplying it
    // by the inverse of the projection matrix
    q.x = (sgn(clipPlane.x) + matrix[8]) / matrix[0];
    q.y = (sgn(clipPlane.y) + matrix[9]) / matrix[5];
    q.z = -1.0F;
    q.w = (1.0F + matrix[10]) / matrix[14];

    // Calculate the scaled plane vector
    Vector4D c = clipPlane * (-2.0F / (clipPlane * q));

    // Replace the third row of the projection matrix
    matrix[2] = c.x;
    matrix[6] = c.y;
    matrix[10] = c.z + 1.0F;
    matrix[14] = c.w;

    // Load it back into OpenGL
    glMatrixMode(GL_PROJECTION);
    glLoadMatrix(matrix);
}
```

Direct3D Implementation

In the Direct3D environment, camera space is lefthanded, and the near plane corresponds to the set of points for which the clip-space *z*-coordinate is 0. Thus, the value of the near clip plane listed in Table 2.6.1 should be changed to $\langle 0,0,1,0 \rangle$ for Direct3D applications. Consequently, the camera-space value of the near clip plane is simply given by $\mathbf{M}_3$. This means that the entries of the third row of the projection matrix are exactly the coordinates of the near clip plane in camera space. The far clip plane **F** is still given by $\mathbf{M}_4 - \mathbf{M}_3$, so we have

$$\mathbf{F} = \mathbf{M}_4 - a\mathbf{C} \tag{2.6.20}$$

after replacing the third row of the projection matrix with an arbitrary plane **C**. Solving for the scale factor a that causes the far plane to include the point **Q** given by the inverse projection of Equation 2.6.8, we have

$$\mathbf{M}'_3 = \frac{\mathbf{M}_4 \cdot \mathbf{Q}}{\mathbf{C} \cdot \mathbf{Q}}\mathbf{C}. \tag{2.6.21}$$

The standard Direct3D perspective projection matrix **M** is given by

$$\mathbf{M} = \begin{bmatrix} \dfrac{2n}{r-l} & 0 & \dfrac{r+l}{r-l} & 0 \\ 0 & \dfrac{2n}{t-b} & \dfrac{t+b}{t-b} & 0 \\ 0 & 0 & \dfrac{f}{f-n} & -\dfrac{fn}{f-n} \\ 0 & 0 & 1 & 0 \end{bmatrix}, \tag{2.6.22}$$

where each value has the same meaning as it does for the OpenGL projection matrix given by Equation 2.6.14. In this case, Equation 2.6.21 simplifies to

$$\mathbf{M}'_3 = \frac{Q_z}{\mathbf{C} \cdot \mathbf{Q}}\mathbf{C}. \tag{2.6.23}$$

Equation 2.6.16 gives the value of the point **Q** in Direct3D as well as OpenGL. Applying the inverse of the projection matrix **M** given by Equation 2.6.22, we obtain the same coordinates for **Q** shown in 2.6.17, except that the z-coordinate is negated.

Listing 2.6.2 demonstrates how the modification to the projection matrix can be implemented in a Direct3D-based application for a typical projection matrix. It assumes that the projection matrix **M** is a perspective projection having the form

$$\mathbf{M} = \begin{bmatrix} a & 0 & b & 0 \\ 0 & c & d & 0 \\ 0 & 0 & e & f \\ 0 & 0 & 1 & 0 \end{bmatrix} \tag{2.6.24}$$

where $a > 0$, $c > 0$, and $f \neq 0$. The code makes direct use of the general inverse of **M**, given by

$$\mathbf{M}^{-1} = \begin{bmatrix} 1/a & 0 & 0 & -b/a \\ 0 & 1/c & 0 & -d/c \\ 0 & 0 & 0 & 1 \\ 0 & 0 & 1/f & -e/f \end{bmatrix} \quad (2.6.25)$$

Listing 2.6.2 Implementation of the Projection Matrix Modification for a Direct3D Projection Matrix Having the Form Shown in Equation 2.6.24 (The `clipPlane` parameter passed to the `ModifyProjectionMatrix` function represents the camera-space plane to which clipping is to occur. This code uses the `Vector4D` class shown in Listing 2.6.1.)

```
void ModifyProjectionMatrix(const Vector4D& clipPlane)
{
    D3DXMatrix      matrix;
    Vector4D        q;

    // Grab the current projection matrix from Direct3D
    D3DDevice.GetTransform(D3DTS_PROJECTION, &matrix);

    // Transform the clip-space corner point opposite the
    // clipping plane into camera space by multiplying it
    // by the inverse of the projection matrix
    q.x = (sgn(clipPlane.x) - matrix._31) / matrix._11;
    q.y = (sgn(clipPlane.y) - matrix._32) / matrix._22;
    q.z = 1.0F;
    q.w = (1.0F - matrix._33) / matrix._43;

    // Calculate the scaled plane vector
    Vector4D c = clipPlane * (1.0F / (clipPlane * q));

    // Replace the third row of the projection matrix
    matrix._13 = c.x;
    matrix._23 = c.y;
    matrix._33 = c.z;
    matrix._43 = c.w;

    // Load it back into Direct3D
    D3DDevice.SetTransform(D3DTS_PROJECTION, &matrix);
}
```

Acknowledgments

Thanks to Cass Everitt at Nvidia for many interesting discussions about this topic and the original idea of moving the near plane to an arbitrary orientation. Also thanks to Yann Lombard for the first adaptation of this technique to the Direct3D environment.

Reference

[Leng04] Lengyel, Eric. "Oblique View Frustum Depth Projection and Clipping." In *Journal of Game Development*, Vol. 1, No 2, 2005.

SECTION

3

ARTIFICIAL INTELLIGENCE

Introduction

Robin Hunicke, Northwestern University

hunicke@cs.northwestern.edu

Everywhere you look—at GDC and E3 or in the gaming and popular press—people are talking about "next generation" games. Pundits and players alike agree: innovation in game AI has the power to take us beyond stunning graphics and familiar genres to exciting, unexplored territories. If it's done right, AI can help diversify content, streamline development processes, and lower the production costs of games, while strengthening and broadening their overall appeal.

Easier said than done! It's clear that the "simple" or "known" AI techniques championed just a few years ago won't vault us to the next level, but when we look ahead, things get fuzzy. Preparing for new hardware (with new, unexplored capabilities), developers ask, what is the next logical step for game AI? And will we have the time and resources to take it?

A few developers have already begun experimenting with narrative, characters and emotion, procedural content, persistence, reputation, and consequence. On these teams, AI and game design tasks intertwine, and communication strategies and reporting structures change. And as new techniques are integrated, existing standards for game balance, player control, feedback, and "fun" must be met. The work is different *and* more difficult at the same time.

Experimentation and innovation are a focus, but solid engineering is a must. Beneath the investigation into game AI's new forms and roles, there is a critical push towards clarity and optimization. Programmers strive to leverage fast, predictable algorithms wherever possible, while maintaining efficient and debuggable code. Design tools must be consistent and transparent to programmers and nonprogrammers alike. Parallelization, for all its benefits, seriously impacts these concerns.

This section reflects the growing array of issues and considerations that surround modern game AI. Many of the gems are exploratory, and some present overviews of larger, complex subject areas—a bit of a break from the traditional "gems" form. To round this out, we've included some down-and-dirty discussions of familiar topics, including search and pathfinding, targeting, strategy, and combat analysis. And even here, we hope you'll find a few surprises.

Looking to the future, it's hard to say whether any of our AI dreams will pan out (though our track record, so far, is a bit discouraging). Looking beyond that, if we achieve even the simplest of our goals, what will the next crop of problems be?

As characters grow increasingly autonomous, will they also become difficult to "control" from a design perspective? Will procedural content give its games a "cookie cutter" feel that detracts from the player experience? Will persistence bite dedicated players in the butt, leading to complex but unforeseeable (and undesired) consequences, far from the incidents that initiated change? Will we see something analogous to global warming in the saved games of our future?

As AI and game design become increasingly enmeshed, how can we abstract away from game-specific issues and implementations? Do we have the right language to discuss and design broader, repeatable solutions? Can we even pinpoint the AI components of our games as such? In a few years, will this chapter have a new heading or three? There are so many unknowns, it's almost overwhelming!

Unless, of course, you're like the rest of us: the authors, developers, researchers, and players who work (and play) hard to make tomorrow's great games. For us, these questions don't depress, they excite! Because for us (as with all things), the challenge is really just part of the fun.

Hopefully you consider yourself part of our camp. And if not, consider joining us. Take that next step, beyond this chapter to other volumes, from those volumes into your practice, studies, and discussions. The work is far from over, and there's always room for fresh faces, innovative ideas, and fun!

Enjoy!

3.1

Automatic Cover Finding with Navigation Meshes

Borut Pfeifer, Radical Entertainment

borut_p@yahoo.com

In many combat-related games, NPC cover finding is implemented by placing hidden volumes, which denote areas that can be used for cover under fire. Whether separate from a navigation graph or incorporated in it, level designers must place these points manually. In very large levels and open, freely explorable worlds, this rapidly becomes a time consuming task.

This gem describes how navigation meshes can be combined with collision information, enabling NPCs to find cover points automatically. By augmenting the navigation mesh with additional information regarding the navigability of neighboring links, we can use standard, runtime search algorithms to find a valid cover position for NPCs, saving developers much time and effort.

Navigation Meshes

In his article "Simplified 3D Movement and Pathfinding Using Navigation Meshes," Greg Snook elaborates upon the use of navigation meshes in games ([Snook00]). Other gems ([Tozour02], [White02]) discuss specific techniques for simplifying meshes or speeding up searching on them. The type of mesh used in this gem is a triangle-based mesh, which is the same mesh used for in-game world collision detection.

Specifically, for each walkable triangle in the navigation mesh, there is a direct correspondence to a triangle in the collision mesh (the triangle data itself is shared), but the collision mesh may have many more nonwalkable triangles with no representation in the navigation mesh.

Building the Navigation Mesh

Each triangle in the mesh can have up to three neighbors; while only some neighbors may represent walkable triangles, all are stored for use by other applications (such as decaling). Each triangle also has a bitfield for each neighbor denoting possible traversal options (in this case, walkable, standing cover, crouching cover, and non-walkable).

To determine the flag for each link in a preprocessing step, we perform ray casts along each side of the link at the appropriate heights (Figure 3.1.1). Once we've determined the applicable cover or lack thereof for each edge, we can store that information in less than one byte per triangle (since there are only two bits of information per edge).

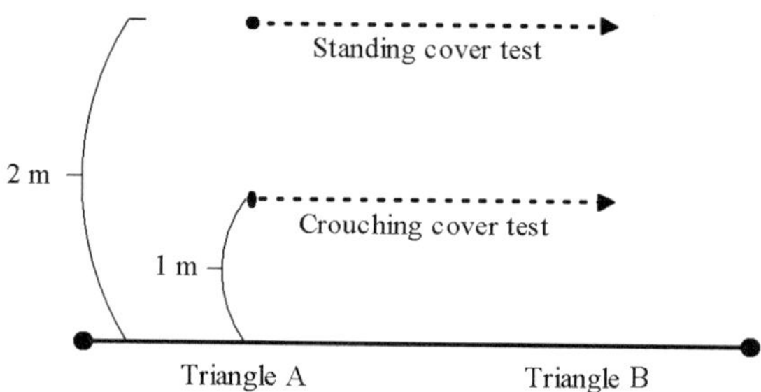

FIGURE 3.1.1 *Front view of per edge ray test during preprocessing.*

These two simple cover distinctions (standing and crouching) assume human-sized opponents. To accommodate a wider variety of heights in the NPCs searching for cover, simply increase the number of cover ranges above two (a flag for each meter of cover, for instance) or store the height of the link in the navigation graph (which has other potential applications, like determining if an NPC can climb or jump to the linked triangle).

Testing a Triangle for Cover

To determine if a given triangle is acceptable as a cover position, we have to do two things:

1. Test for a straight line path from the center of a given triangle to the target point (that we wish to be in cover from). This can use simplified two dimensional line segment intersections tests, as in Snook's article [Snook02].
2. If the triangle does not have a straight path to the target point, find the edge that is between the center of this triangle and the target; if that link was flagged in our preprocessing step as crouching or standing cover, this triangle can be considered to be in cover from the target.

Limitations

With this type of graph and cover test, we do face a couple of limitations. To start, because the navigation is preprocessed, our algorithm can only find static cover (the list of large enough dynamic objects can then be iterated through quickly for additional cover points).

In addition, the two-dimensional math for fast line-of-sight operations limits us to wall-based cover. The ground itself will never be used as cover, as in the case of a hill that lies between an NPC and its target. For many environments, such as urban settings or interiors, this is not much of a concern.

Open Goal Pathfinding

To search for a cover point, our pathfinding system needs to support the concept of open goal search. In a typical pathfinding request, the search is from a start point to a specific end point; we know the exact element that meets our goal, so it's a *closed* goal search. An *open* goal search is simply looking for an element that meets the given conditions, without knowing exactly what the element is.

We need to parameterize our search on two categories to achieve this:

The heuristic: A test that the A-star algorithm uses to weight each node.
The goal test: Defines if a given node meets the goal parameters for the search.

The pathfinding function might look like:

```
template<class PathSearch>
PathResult FindPath(NodeID startNode,
            Path* pInputPath,
            PathSearch searchParam);
```

Alternately, you could use a base class with virtual goal and heuristic functions, or function pointers, as ways of parameterizing this data, but in theory, the templates improve code locality for consoles with a small instruction cache, such as the PS2 (by avoiding per-node virtual function calls).

Some games implement these open-goal searches (such as finding cover locations) outside of the pathfinding system. However, using the previous method, you can take advantage of all the existing search code in your pathfinding engine, as well as other features (such as timeslicing).

Searching For a Cover Position

Since the notion of what defines *cover* is relative, and constantly changing, we have to test for cover given a few input parameters. The two main parameters are the *agent's position* (the start of the search) and the *target's position* (the point from which to ensure we're in cover).

Additionally, a *given direction* and *acceptable angle* within that direction allow us to weight nodes in the direction the NPC is already intending to move. A *maximum distance* allows us to limit the search to reasonable cover positions, since the NPC would only consider the area nearby in the middle of heated combat.

The template parameter PathSearch class, passed into the previous FindPath function, would look like this:

```
class PathSearchForCover
{
    PathSearchForCover(Vector start,
                Vector coverFrom,
                                  Vector inDirection,
                float angle,
                float maxDist);
```

```
        bool TestGoal(NodeID);

        float GuessRemaining(NodeID);
        ...
    }
```

The goal test is simply the cover test defined earlier. If a node qualifies as cover, we've found an acceptable end to our search (this doesn't guarantee we will find the best cover, but in practice, this was never a concern). The heuristic acts like a standard point-A-to-B path heuristic, in that it will return the straight line distance to the goal (or a similar heuristic, such as the Manhattan distance).

There are two additional rules to its method of weighting cells:

- Cells that lie beyond the target point (so we would have to travel from our starting position, past the target, into cover) are weighted much higher (10 times). This helps to prevent the undesirable behavior of NPCs running past the player to get to cover.
- Cells that lie in our given direction, within the given angle, are weighted as a third of their normal value. This ensures the search will move in the direction the NPC desires to move.

Once our search is over and we've found a cover point, we're close, but not quite finished. Since our cover test uses the center of each triangle, we need to calculate the most desirable position on the triangle for cover.

If we know the path-requesting agent's width, we can simply take the edge of the triangle that is providing us cover and offset the cover point from the vertex of the edge that is closest to the target point. See Figure 3.1.2.

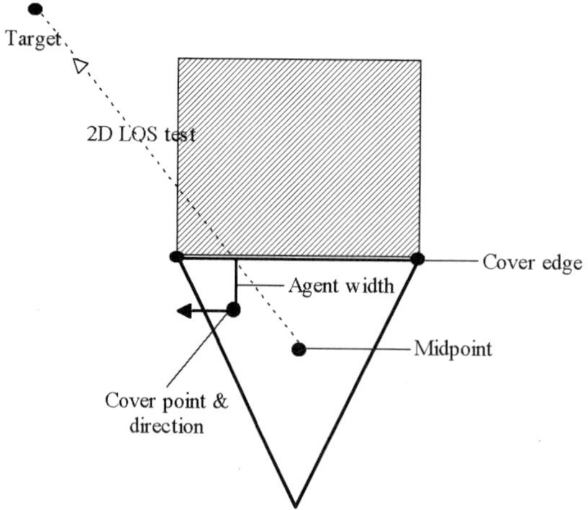

FIGURE 3.1.2 *Determining the cover point on the found triangle.*

Now we have a point offset from the wall by the agent's width, and we know the direction the agent needs to move along the wall to pop out of cover. Based on the flag of the cover edge (standing or crouching), we can adjust the cover point to be at the correct height, telling an agent if it needs to crouch to stay in cover here.

The cover test will occasionally give us false-positive results, in that it may flag a wall that is adjacent to another wall as cover. To avoid this problem, we can test adjacent triangles for cover edges that share a vertex with our current cover edge; this would indicate our edge is actually along a wall. The false-positive scenario is also dependent on the target position; it will only produce a false-positive if the target position is opposite the center of two triangles whose edges form a wall.

In practice, since the problem is by definition hidden from the player (the NPC would think they were able to move to see the player when it was actually behind a larger wall), it did not seem worth the extra per node memory retrieval costs on the PS2. The test *does not,* however, have a problem with false negatives (finding a cover position that is actually out in the open and able to be fired on from the target).

Moving through Cover

Now that we can find cover points, we can also generate paths between two points that attempt to stay in cover. This simply means we do a normal search from one point to another, but if we come across a node that is acceptable cover, we weight it much lower (so the search will consider it over other, closer nodes).

Then, in the path smoothing step, we ensure that acceptable cover locations do not get removed from the path by the regular line of sight tests. See Figure 3.1.3.

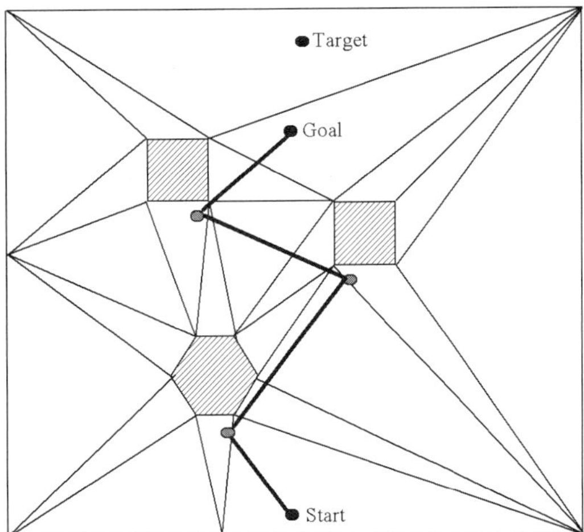

FIGURE 3.1.3 *The smoothed path with cover points kept as waypoints.*

Group Cover Behavior

It may be desirable to have NPCs use cover positions on the player as a group; for example, teammates providing covering fire or flanking the player by advancing from opposite cover points. To accomplish this, we have to modify the search slightly. We are no longer seeking one particular goal but a set of goal positions. While the search isn't normally set up for this sort of scenario, it's easy to include it as part of the open goal search.

The search itself, because we need to find all the cover points around a given point, becomes a breadth first search. There's no heuristic we can use to simplify the search, but we can use the same architecture to find the desired results.

As before, the heuristic function tests for cover from a given point. Now it also stores the valid cover points; as the search tests nearby nodes, the heuristic records applicable nodes. The goal function returns true only when the heuristic has recorded the desired number of cover points.

A team of NPCs can share these points to advance on the player and provide covering fire for each other. Once the nearby cover points have been found, one NPC can fire at the player while the others spread out to the various cover locations. Then the remaining NPC can run for cover (assuming he's still alive) as the other NPCs alternate popping out and providing cover fire.

If an NPC is looking for a player it recently lost sight of, this search can provide a list of potential hiding places. You can find all the nearby triangles that have an edge that blocks the NPC's line of sight, so the NPC can patrol its environment going from obstacle to obstacle, looking for its lost target.

Additional Functionality

The following sections describe additional functionality you may wish to add.

Reserving Cover Points

If your pathfinding system allows for simple reservation of path nodes (preventing them from being considered for other path searches), NPCs can reserve their cover points such that other NPCs will not consider them in their path searches. This prevents NPCs from bunching up at the same cover point.

More Data

It becomes trivial to embed additional collision information into the navigation mesh. Although cover is detected automatically, designers can disable/enable areas as being applicable for cover searching by using a 3D tool to paint these values on the navigation mesh. We could automatically detect other pathfinding concerns such as jumps by testing for cliff edges that have equivalent height triangles a set distance away.

Other Searches

It is also easy to extend the system by adding additional searches. For NPCs that have to run away from the player, simply forcing them to run in the direction opposite the player can cause artifacts like the NPCs getting stuck on walls. An open goal search for a position outside a certain radius of the player will give the NPC a surer path out of harm's way (although it may still need to start moving in the given direction while the path finishes processing). Additionally, we can weight this path search slightly, biasing the NPC towards cover locations if we want the NPC to avoid fire as it flees.

Conclusion

While games that are heavily focused on combat in small, tight locations may still need the use of a manual cover-placement system to allow for designer control, larger games can allow for tactical combat without requiring the same effort in the production process. The technique described here is fairly simplistic but still provides meaningful results without having the same workflow requirements for designers. In addition, such approaches allow behavior to emerge from the system, as NPCs find available cover in all manner of situations.

Thanks to Tinman, Stan Jang, Marcin Chady, Ben Geisler, and Adrian Johnston for their input and related work.

References

[Snook00] Snook, Greg. "Simplified 3D Movement and Pathfinding Using Navigation Meshes." In *Game Programming Gems*. Charles River Media, 2000.

[Tozour02] Tozour, Paul. "Building a Near Optimal Navigation Mesh." In *AI Game Programming Wisdom*. Charles River Media, 2002.

[White02] White, Stephen and Christopher Christensen. "A Fast Approach to Navigation Meshes." In *Game Programming Gems 3*. Charles River Media, 2002.

3.2

Fast Target Ranking Using an Artificial Potential Field

Markus Breyer, Factor 5

me@markusbreyer.com

Player autotargeting and AI agents often have to select a target from a number of game objects arranged arbitrarily in 3D space. Whether attacking opponents, picking up items, selecting an agent to engage in a conversation, finding the optimal place to take cover, or choosing the best landing spot, target selection is everywhere in games.

In most target-selection algorithms, items are ranked based on distance and angle: near objects are picked over those that are far away, and targets straight ahead are chosen over those at the sides or behind. This is because the observer has to spend time turning around to interact with objects behind it, making such targets somewhat less preferable. However, a target behind can be preferred to a target straight ahead if it is somewhat closer. It becomes clear here that distance and angle are two competing goals that must be properly combined into a single metric for decision making. The formula presented in this gem uses a simple and computationally inexpensive rational function to compute a 3D pseudo potential that incorporates this distance/angle trade-off in a smooth, very natural fashion and yields a single scalar value by which targets can be prioritized.

The Basic Idea

Our goal is to derive a scalar metric for objects in an arbitrary scene and use it to rank targets in order of preference. We want to find a scalar value function that takes the position and orientation of a *target* and those of the *observer* and returns a ranking (our implementation interprets lower values as higher preference, but this is simply an implementation choice).

There are two approaches to this problem. Commonly, points are *ranked by distance* (or distance squared). When the distance is interpreted as a *potential*, a 2D contour plot of such potential (i.e., a plot of isocontours comprises lines connecting points of equal potential) looks like Figure 3.2.1.

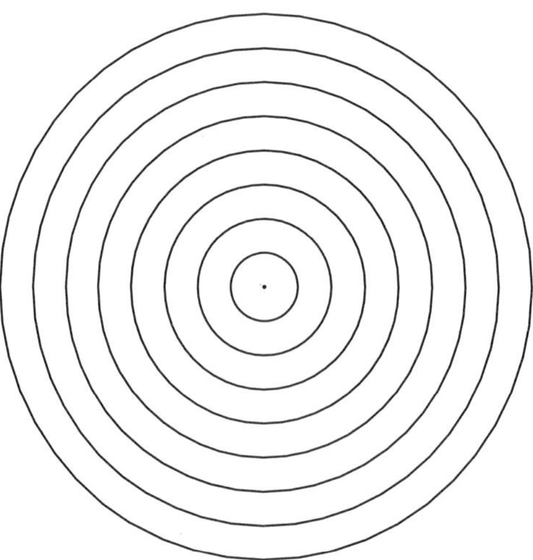

FIGURE 3.2.1 *A potential field based solely on distance. Points of equal potential form concentric circles (or in 3D, spheres) around the observer.*

Ranking based solely on distance treats targets behind the observer equal to those in front of the observer. If we would like to favor targets in front of the observer, we can select based on the angle from the view axis (or local *z*-axis) of the observer. A contour plot of a potential field ranked *by angle* looks like Figure 3.2.2.

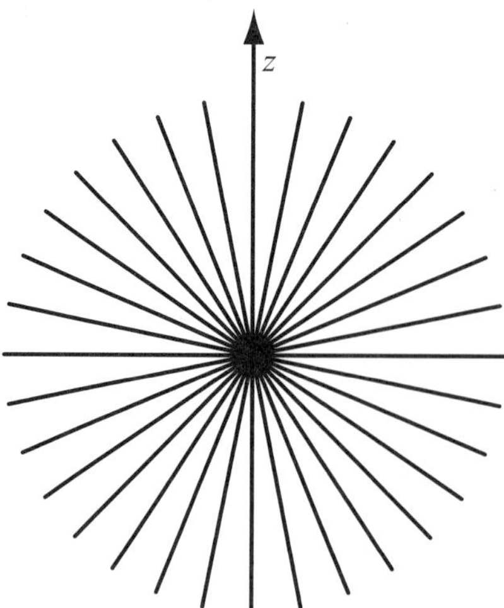

FIGURE 3.2.2 *A potential field based solely on angle. Points of equal potential form V shaped pairs of rays (or in 3D, cones) originating at the observer.*

To consider both distance *and* angle for target selection, we could compare and amalgamate the distance and angle potentials in some fashion to derive a single result. Instead, we could approach the problem from the other end: imagine that isocontours in the 2D space are connecting points of equal preference, as shown in Figure 3.2.3.

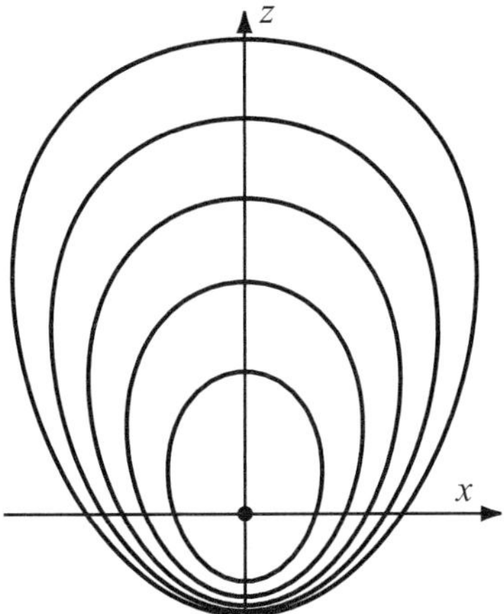

FIGURE 3.2.3 *A potential field based on both distance and angle.*

With this approach, a target far away (but straight ahead) ranks the same as a target to the side or behind (but near). That means near targets are preferred over far targets, and straight ahead targets are preferred over those by the side at the same time, as was our goal. In the following, we will examine a way to derive a function that produces such a field.

The Formula

A function to satisfy the desired requirements should have a global extremum (maximum or minimum) at the position of the observer. It should be monotonous over its entire domain, laterally symmetrical, and assume some constant value at a number of selected points along one of the equipotential curves. If the function is chosen correctly, the rest will fall into place.

To start, let us look at each of the three coordinate directions. In z direction, we would like the function to be steep behind the observer, have a minimum at the observer, and then slowly rise again. In x and y direction, the function should be symmetrical and have a minimum at the z axis ($x = y = 0$). A set of functions that accomplishes this for each axis independently is:

$$v_z = \frac{az^2 + bz + c}{pz + q}; v_x = dx^2 + e; v_y = fy^2 + g. \tag{3.2.1}$$

Adding the terms up, canceling, combining, and renaming coefficients yields:

$$\begin{aligned} v(x,y,z) = v_x + v_y + v_z &= \frac{z^2 + (ax^2 + by^2 + e)z + cx^2 + dy^2 + f}{pz + q} \\ &= \frac{z^2 + ax^2z + by^2z + cx^2 + dy^2 + ez + f}{pz + q}. \end{aligned} \tag{3.2.2}$$

Now, we need to find eight boundary conditions that will enable us to solve for the eight coefficients.

We will assume that the potential is zero and minimal at the position of the observer (i.e., smaller values of v mean a better pick) and require that the isocontour $v = 1$ (or in 3D, isosurface) goes through certain points in space.[1]

The extent of the desired isosurface bubble $v = 1$ can be defined in terms of five intuitive parameters as illustrated in Figure 3.2.4.

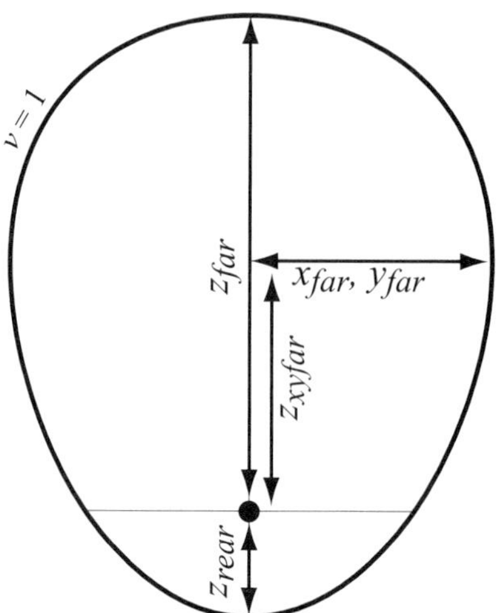

FIGURE 3.2.4 *Isosurface bubble defined by z_{far}, x_{far}, y_{far}, zxy_{far}, z_{rear}.*

[1]The value 1 is arbitrarily picked here since we need some non-zero valued isocontour to pinpoint the shape of the field.

Varying the parameters z_{far}, x_{far}, y_{far}, zxy_{far}, z_{rear}, allows us to shape the bubble as needed. We can in particular make its horizontal and vertical extents different to define a selector that is more sensitive in either horizontal or vertical direction. Experience shows that a designer can usually define the parameters right away and yield a satisfactory result that requires little or no subsequent tweaking.

Together with the requirement that the potential at (0,0,0) be zero and minimal, and have maximal lateral extent at $z = zxy_{far}$, we can then specify the following eight boundary conditions:

$$v(0,0,z_{far}) = 1 \qquad v(0,0,0) = 0$$

$$v(0,0,-z_{rear}) = 1 \qquad \frac{\partial v}{\partial z}(0,0,0) = 0$$

$$v(x_{far},0,z_{xyfar}) = 1 \qquad \frac{\partial v}{\partial z}(x_{far},0,z_{xyfar}) = 0$$

$$v(0,y_{far},z_{xyfar}) = 1 \qquad \frac{\partial v}{\partial z}(0,y_{far},z_{xyfar}) = 0$$

Solving for the coefficients yields:

$$p = z_{far} - z_{rear} \qquad a = \frac{p - 2z_{xyfar}}{x_{far}^2} \qquad c = \frac{q + z_{xyfar}^2}{x_{far}^2} \qquad e = 0$$

$$q = z_{far} z_{rear} \qquad b = \frac{p - 2z_{xyfar}}{y_{far}^2} \qquad d = \frac{q + z_{xyfar}^2}{y_{far}^2} \qquad f = 0$$

Now, v can be defined in terms of z_{far}, x_{far}, *yfar*, zxy_{far} and z_{rear}. With e and f removed, the potential function looks like this:

$$v = \frac{z^2 + (az + c)x^2 + (bz + d)y^2}{pz + q}. \tag{3.2.3}$$

Evaluating the Potential Function

When evaluating the potential function, we must pay attention to three things to ensure the function yields the expected results:

1. The denominator must not become zero or negative. Otherwise, this would not only allow the potential to assume infinity but also would make the potential field discontinuous and nonmonotonous.

2. The terms $(az + c)$ and $(bz + d)$ must not become negative. If they became negative, the potential would be allowed to fall beyond a certain *z*, which would produce inconsistent behavior, i.e., lower values even though the pick is worse.
3. The boundary contour $v = 1$ must be placed at the outmost rim of the selection volume, i.e., the maximum range of the target selector. Only values of $v \leq 1$ can be relied upon for correct ranking. A value $v > 1$ reliably tells you that the target is out of range, but values $v > 1$ cannot be relied upon for ranking, since the potential function starts losing the desired properties for values that go beyond v = 1.

With all this in mind, evaluation should go as follows:

$$R = \max(az + c, 0); \tag{3.2.4}$$

$$S = \max(bz + d, 0); \tag{3.2.5}$$

$$D = \max(pz + q, eps); \tag{3.2.6}$$

$$v = \frac{z^2 + Rx^2 + Sy^2}{D}. \tag{3.2.7}$$

Here, *eps* is some very small positive value, e.g., 0.001. This is a computationally very inexpensive formula that can be easily executed every frame for dozens of targets.

Visualization

To aid in development and debugging, a game engine is usually capable of visualizing its inner workings through graphical debug markers (boxes, spheres, etc.). Similarly, you may find it useful to visualize the potential field through one or more of its isosurfaces, in particular, the surface $v = 1$.

Even though the field is defined through an implicit formula, an explicit formula can be derived to describe an isosurface $v = v_c$. It is parameterized in distance along the view axis *z* and angle φ around the observer's view axis, consisting of a series of ellipses perpendicular to the *z* axis. Using the constants *R*, *S* and *D* defined above, compute the radii of the ellipses' principal axes for each value of *z* as follows:

$$R_x = \sqrt{\frac{Dv_c - z^2}{R}} \text{ and } R_y = \sqrt{\frac{Dv_c - z^2}{S}}. \tag{3.2.8}$$

Then render the point cloud ($z = z_{min}..z_{max}$, $\varphi = -\pi..\pi$):

$$P = \begin{pmatrix} R_x \sin\varphi \\ R_y \cos\varphi \\ z \end{pmatrix}. \quad (3.2.9)$$

Here, *zmin* and *zmax* can be found by solving the equation $Dv_c - z^2 = 0$.

In case $z_{far} > z_{rear}$, the best way to solve for z_{min} and z_{max} is defining $S = v_c p$ and $T = v_c q$, and to compute z_{min} and z_{max} by:

$$\begin{aligned} z_{max} &= \frac{1}{2}\left[S + \sqrt{S^2 + 4T} \right] \\ z_{\min} &= -T / z_{max}. \end{aligned} \quad (3.2.10)$$

Note that for $v_c = 1$, z_{min} and z_{max} are simply $-z_{rear}$ and z_{far}, so if you do not need to plot the surface for other values of v_c, then you do not need the previous formula.

The resulting point cloud can be easily tessellated if so desired. Remember that v_c must be between 0 and 1 for useful results (however, it may be possible to find applications for other values of v_c!). An example plot looks like Figure 3.2.5

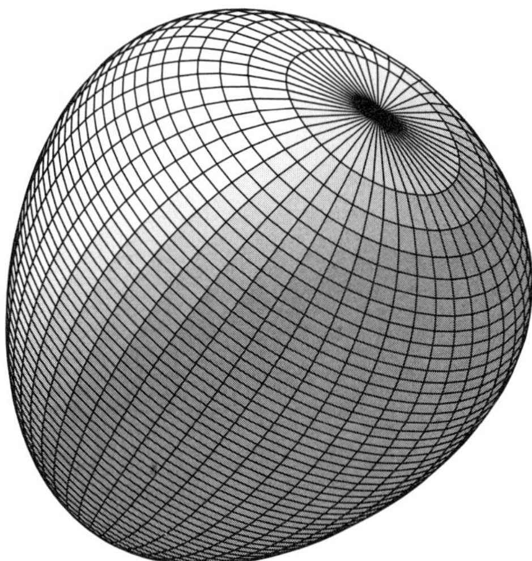

FIGURE 3.2.5 *Resultant 3D potential field.*

Use as a Directional Field

The potential function might also be used for more applications like a damage, thrust, or suction field. You might define a field magnitude by $H = \max(1 - v, 0)$, then use H (or H^2) as the damage of a flame thrower or the strength of a thrust or suction field. For direction, use the normalized gradient (negate as needed). To calculate the gradient, define two new constants as follows:

$$\begin{aligned} M &= aq - cp \\ N &= bq - dp. \end{aligned} \tag{3.2.11}$$

Then using these constants, compute the gradient of v as follows:

$$\nabla v = \begin{pmatrix} \partial v / \partial x \\ \partial v / \partial y \\ \partial v / \partial z \end{pmatrix} = \begin{pmatrix} 2xR / D \\ 2yS / D \\ [Mx^2 + Ny^2 + (pz + 2q)z]/D^2 \end{pmatrix}. \tag{3.2.12}$$

Such a suction field (in 2D) could look like Figure 3.2.6.

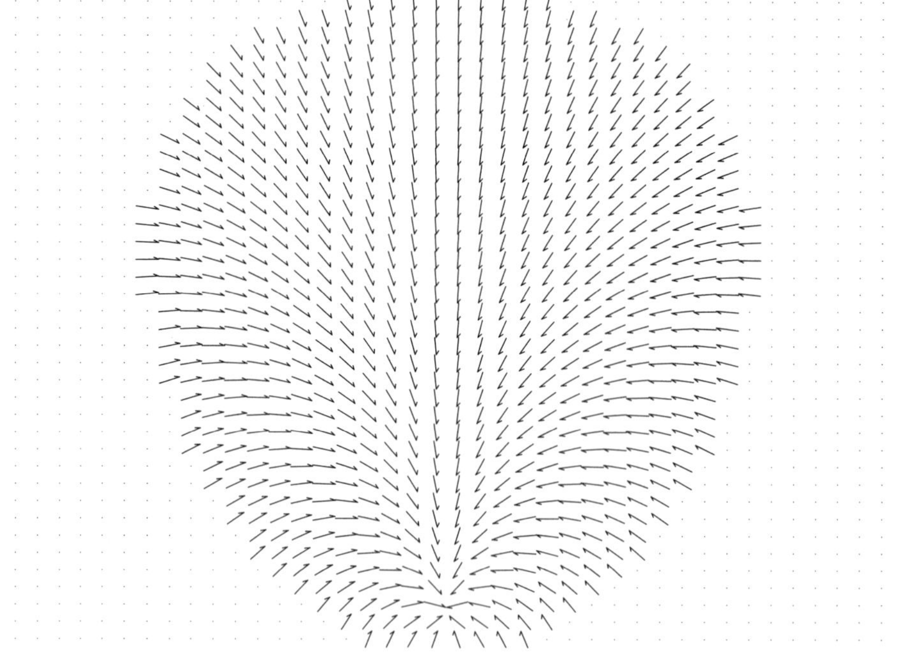

FIGURE 3.2.6 *Potential field in the case of 2D "suction."*

Expanding in More Dimensions

The application we have discussed in this gem centers around using two parameters: Distance and Angle. It is not difficult to reach the hypothesis that this could be extended to an increased number of dimensions, such as "target threat level," "target vulnerability," or any number of other examples. The use of potential fields with isosurfaces could certainly be extended into multidimensions, however, the particular rational function derived in this gem is very specific to the distance/angle problem of a 3D observer and not necessarily extensible to a general potential field approach. However, by applying a similar kind of reasoning that lead us to the particular rational function introduced in this gem, you can derive other potential functions specific to different boundary conditions.

For example, in the case of a value/threat trade off, you might find a parabolic looking potential field by requiring that even a low-threat target has to have a certain minimum value to make it worth attacking, that value should be somewhat proportional to threat, while for high-threat targets the value parameter increases more rapidly, resulting in something like v = 1/(a*value – b*threat^2). Again, here the denominator would have to be clamped to some small, positive value. Several such potential functions could then be combined, for example by simply adding them, resulting in a parabolic looking plot. This again could be represented as a simple potential function. Still, there may be some potential future application here. Experiment!

Conclusion

This gem presents a simple, computationally inexpensive method employing an artificial potential field to rank objects of interest smoothly and naturally by both distance and angle. We describe a simple method for rendering the isosurfaces of such fields, and a method for computing the gradient of the field to be used, as a direction vector of suction, thrust, or damage. An example source file with C++ implementations of all presented formulas is included on the companion CD-ROM.

ON THE CD

3.3

Using Lanchester Attrition Models to Predict the Results of Combat

John Bolton, Page 44 Studios, LLC

johnjbolton@yahoo.com

Prior to World War I, F. W. Lanchester formalized a set of basic mathematical models for describing combat in terms of the number of units and the rates at which the units are destroyed. These models are known as Lanchester Attrition models and have become a foundation for the mathematical analysis of warfare. This gem shows how these models can be used to predict the results of combat in games quickly and efficiently. The general principals of Lanchester Attrition are reviewed, and models for evaluating several combat systems and scenarios are demonstrated.

Overview

Using a system of differential equations, Lanchester Attrition models describe the rate at which units are lost in a battle. The system of equations can be solved to answer a number of questions, including

- Who wins?
- How long does the battle last?
- How many units does a side have at any time?
- How many units does the winner have at the end of the battle?

The equations are determined by the type of combat, the conditions of combat, and the combat system. In the models presented, combat ends when all the units on one side are destroyed. In general, combat is assumed to be continuous and simultaneous, and all the units on a side are assumed to be identical.

What follows are several scenarios (or combat systems) that typically occur in games. In each scenario, the appropriate model and solutions are listed. In all the scenarios, there are two armies: Blue and Red. The number of units in each army during combat is represented by the variables B and R. The initial numbers of units in each army are represented by the constants B_0 and R_0. Units of both armies have a *combat rating*, which is represented by the constants c_B and c_R. The combat rating generally represents the rate at which a unit destroys units in the opposing army. This constant can include factors such as weather and terrain, defensive and offensive capabilities. The combat rating is discussed in further detail following the scenarios.

Scenario 1: All-Out Melee

In this scenario, an army of 1,000 orcs (the Blue army) battles an army of 200 humans (the Red army) on an open plain. The humans are well equipped and well trained, and each can kill 10 orcs per minute. The orcs are slow and stupid, and each can kill only one human per minute. How does this battle play out? In this scenario, all the units are constantly fighting. The rate at which units are lost is simply the number of units in an army times the rate at which a unit destroys units in the other army. The following system of equations describes this scenario:

$$\begin{aligned} dB &= -c_R R dt \\ dR &= -c_B B dt. \end{aligned} \quad (3.3.1)$$

In our example, B_0 is 1,000, R_0 is 200, c_B is 1, and c_R is 10.

Who Wins?

To determine who wins, the equations are combined as follows:

$$\frac{dB}{dR} = \frac{-c_R R dt}{-c_B B dt} = \frac{c_R R dt}{c_B B dt}. \quad (3.3.2)$$

This is a separable first-order differential equation. Given the initial condition that $B = B_0$ when $R = R_0$, the solution is this:

$$\begin{aligned} c_B\left(B^2 - B_0^2\right) &= c_R\left(R^2 - R_0^2\right) \\ B^2 &= \frac{c_R}{c_B}\left(R^2 - R_0^2\right) + B_0^2. \end{aligned} \quad (3.3.3)$$

By our definition, Blue wins if $B > 0$ when $R = 0$, which gives the following result (noting that if $B > 0$, then $B_2 > 0$):

$$\begin{aligned} 0 &< \frac{c_R}{c_B}\left(0 - R_0^2\right) + B_0^2 \\ \therefore \quad \frac{c_R}{c_B} &< \frac{B_0^2}{R_0^2}. \end{aligned} \quad (3.3.4)$$

In this scenario, the humans lose as shown here:

$$\frac{c_{\mathrm{R}}}{c_{\mathrm{B}}}=\frac{10}{1}=10,\quad \frac{B_0^2}{R_0^2}=\frac{1000^2}{200^2}=25,\quad 10<25. \tag{3.3.5}$$

This is an important result. It shows that for open melee, while the battle outcome depends on the combat rating of individual units, it also depends on the *square* of the initial number of units in each army. That is, the Blue army needs only $\sqrt{2}$ times as many units to defeat an army whose units are twice as effective. This model is Lanchester's *Square Law*.

How Many Units Remain at Time *t*?

The number of units remaining at a particular time is given by these equations.

$$\begin{aligned} B &= B_0\cosh(\sqrt{c_{\mathrm{R}}c_{\mathrm{B}}}\,t)-R_0\sqrt{\frac{c_{\mathrm{R}}}{c_{\mathrm{B}}}}\sinh(\sqrt{c_{\mathrm{R}}c_{\mathrm{B}}}\,t)\\ R &= R_0\cosh(\sqrt{c_{\mathrm{R}}c_{\mathrm{B}}}\,t)-B_0\sqrt{\frac{c_{\mathrm{B}}}{c_{\mathrm{R}}}}\sinh(\sqrt{c_{\mathrm{R}}c_{\mathrm{B}}}\,t) \end{aligned} \tag{3.3.6}$$

Despite the superior ability of the humans, they are vastly outnumbered and losing quickly. After only three seconds (.05 minutes), nearly a quarter of the humans are gone, while most of the orcs remain.

$$\begin{aligned} B &= 1000\cdot\cosh(\sqrt{10\cdot 1}\cdot .05)-200\cdot\sqrt{\frac{10}{1}}\cdot\sinh(\sqrt{10\cdot 1}\cdot .05) &= 912\\ R &= 200\cdot\cosh(\sqrt{10\cdot 1}\cdot .05)-1000\cdot\sqrt{\frac{1}{10}}\cdot\sinh(\sqrt{10\cdot 1}\cdot .05) &= 152 \end{aligned} \tag{3.3.7}$$

How Many Units Are Left When One Army Loses?

The number of units remaining when the battle is over is given by these equations. The result is valid only for the winning army:

$$\begin{aligned} B_{\mathrm{R}=0} &= \sqrt{B_0^2-\frac{c_{\mathrm{R}}}{c_{\mathrm{B}}}R_0^2}\\ R_{\mathrm{B}=0} &= \sqrt{R_0^2-\frac{c_{\mathrm{B}}}{c_{\mathrm{R}}}B_0^2}. \end{aligned} \tag{3.3.8}$$

When the battle is over, 775 orcs remain in the Blue army ready to battle another army,

$$B_{R=0} = \sqrt{1000^2 - \frac{10}{1} \cdot 200^2} = 775. \tag{3.3.9}$$

How Long Does the Combat Last?

The amount of time it takes for the losing army to be destroyed is given by one of these equations. The result is valid only for the winning army. One important thing to note is that if the two armies are equally matched, the combat will last forever.

$$t_{R=0} = \frac{\tanh^{-1}\left(\frac{R_0}{B_0}\sqrt{\frac{c_R}{c_B}}\right)}{\sqrt{c_R c_B}}$$

$$t_{B=0} = \frac{\tanh^{-1}\left(\frac{B_0}{R_0}\sqrt{\frac{c_B}{c_R}}\right)}{\sqrt{c_B c_R}} \tag{3.3.10}$$

In this scenario, if nearly one quarter of the Red army is destroyed in three seconds with minimal losses to the Blue army, it is expected that the rest of the Red army is destroyed nearly as quickly. The actual duration of the battle is .236 minutes or 14 seconds.

$$t_{R=0} = \frac{\tanh^{-1}\left(\frac{200}{1000} \cdot \sqrt{\frac{10}{1}}\right)}{\sqrt{10 \cdot 1}} = .236 \tag{3.3.11}$$

Scenario 2: The Narrow Staircase

In this scenario, the orcs and humans instead meet on a staircase cut into the face of a cliff. Despite the size of the armies (200 humans versus 1,000 orcs), there is only room for two units to fight at a time. The difference between this scenario and the previous scenario is that only a fixed number of units (as opposed to all the units) are fighting in this scenario, so the rate that units are lost is proportional to the number of units fighting rather than the total number of units. The following system of equations describes this scenario. The model assumes that an equal number of units fight concurrently in each army, but it can be easily modified to describe a scenario with an unequal number of units fighting concurrently:

$$\begin{aligned} dB &= -c_R n dt \\ dR &= -c_B n dt. \end{aligned} \tag{3.3.12}$$

Again, in our case, B_0 is 1,000, R_0 is 200, c_B is 1, and c_R is 10. In this scenario, n is 2.

Who Wins?

Blue wins if $B > 0$ when $R = 0$, which is the case when,

$$\frac{c_R}{c_B} < \frac{B_0}{R_0}. \tag{3.3.13}$$

In this scenario, the tables are turned, and the Blue army loses:

$$\frac{c_R}{c_B} = \frac{10}{1}, \quad \frac{B_0}{R_0} = \frac{1000}{200} = 5, \quad 10 > 5. \tag{3.3.14}$$

This is also an important result. It shows that a smaller army with superior units has a better chance of winning in this scenario than in the previous scenario. This is Lanchester's *Linear Law.*

How Many Units Are Remaining at Time *t*?

The number of units remaining at a particular time is given by these equations:

$$\begin{aligned} B &= B_0 - c_R n t \\ R &= R_0 - c_B n t. \end{aligned} \tag{3.3.15}$$

After 30 minutes of battle, both armies have lost many units, but the humans are winning (70% remaining versus 40% remaining):

$$\begin{aligned} B &= 1000 - 10 \cdot 2 \cdot 30 &= 400 \\ R &= 200 - 1 \cdot 2 \cdot 30 &= 140. \end{aligned} \tag{3.3.16}$$

How Many Units Are Left When One Army Loses?

The number of units remaining when the battle is over is given by these equations. The result is valid only for the winning army:

$$B_{R=0} = B_0 - \frac{c_R}{c_B} R_0$$

$$R_{B=0} = R_0 - \frac{c_B}{c_R} B_0. \quad (3.3.17)$$

In this scenario, though half of the Red army was destroyed, it has won the battle:

$$R_{B=0} = 200 - \frac{1}{10} \cdot 1000 = 100. \quad (3.3.18)$$

How Long Does the Combat Last?

The amount of time it takes for the losing army to be destroyed is given by one of these equations. The result is valid only for the winning army:

$$t_{R=0} = \frac{R_0}{nc_B}$$

$$t_{B=0} = \frac{B_0}{nc_R}. \quad (3.3.19)$$

In our example, the Red army wins in 50 minutes:

$$t_{B=0} = \frac{1000}{2 \cdot 10} = 50. \quad (3.3.20)$$

Scenario 3: Artillery Duel

Imagine a game similar to Battleship, where neither army knows the locations of the other army's units. Each army has 100 units placed on a 100 by 100 grid, and the units can move anywhere on the grid at any time. A unit fires a shell and hits a point on the opposing army's grid. If that point is occupied by a unit, the unit is destroyed. The rate at which a unit fires is determined by an external factor and it is the same for all units in the army. For this scenario, the Blue units fire twice per second and the Red units fire once per second. The results of this scenario depend on probability. Thus, we can't compute the exact results, but we can predict the expected results.

In this scenario, the rate of loss for an army is proportional to the number and combat rating of the opposition, and also the density of its units. If A_X is the area occupied by army X, then the density of its units, ρ_X, is given by these equations:

$$\rho_B = \frac{B}{A_B}, \quad \rho_R = \frac{R}{A_R}. \tag{3.3.21}$$

In our example, both A_B and A_R are 10,000:

$$\rho_B = \frac{B}{10000}, \quad \rho_R = \frac{R}{10000}. \tag{3.3.22}$$

The following system of equations describes this scenario:

$$\begin{aligned} dB &= -c_R R \rho_B \, dt \\ dR &= -c_B B \rho_R \, dt. \end{aligned} \tag{3.3.23}$$

In our scenario, B_0 is 100, R_0 is 100, c_B is 2, and c_R is 1.

Assuming that the area occupied by an army is constant, the equations can be simplified by combining the area with the constant term. We introduce a modified combat rating constant:

$$\chi_R = \frac{c_R}{A_B}, \quad \chi_B = \frac{c_B}{A_R}. \tag{3.3.24}$$

In our example,

$$\chi_R = \frac{1}{10000} = .0001, \quad \chi_B = \frac{2}{10000} = .0002. \tag{3.3.25}$$

The simplified model is the following.

$$\begin{aligned} dB &= -\chi_R RB\,dt \\ dR &= -\chi_B BR\,dt \end{aligned} \tag{3.3.26}$$

Who Wins?

Blue wins if $B > 0$ when $R = 0$, which is the case when,

$$\frac{\chi_R}{\chi_B} < \frac{B_0}{R_0}. \tag{3.3.27}$$

In this scenario, Blue's rate of fire is twice Red's and Blue wins easily:

$$\frac{\chi_R}{\chi_B} = \frac{.0001}{.0002} = .5, \quad \frac{B_0}{R_0} = \frac{100}{100} = 1, \quad .5 < 1. \tag{3.3.28}$$

How Many Units Remain at Time *t*?

The number of units remaining at a particular time is given by these equations:

$$\begin{aligned} B &= B_0 \frac{\chi_B B_0 - \chi_R R_0}{\chi_B B_0 - \chi_R R_0 \exp\left(\left(\chi_R R_0 - \chi_B B_0\right)t\right)} \\ R &= R_0 \frac{\chi_R R_0 - \chi_B B_0}{\chi_R R_0 - \chi_B B_0 \exp\left(\left(\chi_B B_0 - \chi_R R_0\right)t\right)}. \end{aligned} \tag{3.3.29}$$

Here are the results of this scenario after the first 100 seconds. The situation does not look good for Red.

$$\begin{aligned} \chi_B B_0 &= .0002 \cdot 100 = .02 \\ \chi_R R_0 &= .0001 \cdot 100 = .01 \\ B &= 100 \cdot \frac{.02 - .01}{.02 - .01 \cdot \exp\left(\left(.01 - .02\right) \cdot 100\right)} = 61 \\ R &= 100 \cdot \frac{.01 - .02}{.01 - .02 \cdot \exp\left(\left(.02 - .01\right) \cdot 100\right)} = 23. \end{aligned} \tag{3.3.30}$$

How Many Units Are Left When One Army Loses?

As explained in the next section, the combat in this scenario always lasts forever, but as time goes to infinity, the number of units in each army approaches a value. If the armies are equally matched, the number of units remaining in both armies approaches 0.

$$\begin{aligned} B_{R=0} &= B_0 - \frac{\chi_R}{\chi_B} R_0, \quad \frac{\chi_R}{\chi_B} \le \frac{B_0}{R_0} \\ R_{B=0} &= R_0 - \frac{\chi_B}{\chi_R} B_0, \quad \frac{\chi_R}{\chi_B} \ge \frac{B_0}{R_0} \end{aligned} \tag{3.3.31}$$

In this scenario, Red loses and the number of its units approaches 0. The final number of units in Blue approaches 50.

$$B_{R=0} = 100 - \frac{.0001}{.0002} \cdot 100 = 50 \tag{3.3.32}$$

How Long Does the Combat Last?

The combat in this scenario lasts forever because as the number of units in an army gets smaller, the units are less likely to be hit. However as time goes to infinity, the number of units in one or both armies always approaches 0. A modification to this scenario that would limit the time of combat would be to declare a winner when the number of remaining units in an army is less than a certain number or less than a percentage of the army's original size.

Scenario 4: The Boss

In an RPG, a boss with 5,000 points fights three members of a party with a total of 1,000 points. In this system, the boss does a constant amount of damage, 90 points per turn, and each character does an amount of damage proportional to its health, 1 point per health point per turn.

In this scenario, the Blue side is fighting a single Red boss unit. The boss is destroyed when its "health" reaches 0, and the party is destroyed when its combined health reaches 0. This scenario is a combination of scenarios 1 and 2, except in this case, the number of units remaining is replaced by the number of points remaining. This scenario is also an example of how a combat system can be modeled when the rules are different for each side. The following system of equations describes this scenario.

$$\begin{aligned} dB &= -c_R\, dt \\ dR &= -c_B B\, dt. \end{aligned} \tag{3.3.33}$$

In this scenario, B_0 is 1,000, R_0 is 5000, c_B is 1, and c_R is 90.

Who Wins?

Blue wins if $B > 0$ when $R = 0$, which is the case when,

$$R_0 < \frac{1}{2}\frac{c_B}{c_R} B_0^2. \tag{3.3.34}$$

In this scenario, the party defeats the boss, but it is close.

$$5000 < \frac{1}{2} \cdot \frac{1}{90} \cdot 1000^2, \quad 5000 < 5556. \tag{3.3.35}$$

How Many Units Remain at Time *t*?

The number of units remaining at a particular time is given by these equations.

$$\begin{aligned} B &= B_0 - c_R t \\ R &= R_0 - \left(B_0 c_B t - \frac{1}{2} c_B c_R t^2 \right). \end{aligned} \tag{3.3.36}$$

In this scenario, after five turns, the party's health (and thus the amount of damage it does) is down to almost half, but the boss's health is down to only 20%. Still, the battle is close because the party has lost much of its ability to do damage and the boss has not.

$$\begin{aligned} B &= 1000 - 90 \cdot 5 = 550 \\ R &= 5000 - \left(1000 \cdot 1 \cdot 5 - \frac{1}{2} \cdot 1 \cdot 90 \cdot 5^2 \right) = 1125 \end{aligned} \tag{3.3.37}$$

How Much Health Does One Side Have When the Other Side Loses?

The health remaining when the battle is over is given by these equations. The result is valid only for the winning side:

$$\begin{aligned} B_{R=0} &= \sqrt{B_0^{\ 2} - 2 \frac{c_R}{c_B} R_0} \\ R_{B=0} &= R_0 - \frac{1}{2} \frac{c_B}{c_R} B_0^{\ 2}. \end{aligned} \tag{3.3.38}$$

In this scenario, the boss loses; however, the combined health of the party is now only 316 (of the original 1,000). The party is in such bad shape that perhaps it would be better to stop and recuperate:

$$B_{R=0} = \sqrt{1000^2 - 2 \cdot \frac{90}{1} \cdot 5000} = 316. \tag{3.3.39}$$

How Long Does the Combat Last?

The amount of time it takes for the losing side to be destroyed is given by one of these equations. The result is valid only for the winning army:

$$t_{R=0} = \frac{B_0 - \sqrt{B_0^2 - 2\frac{c_R}{c_B}R_0}}{c_R}$$

$$t_{B=0} = \frac{B_0}{c_R}. \quad (3.3.40)$$

In this scenario, if the boss won, it would have taken about 11 turns (1,000 points at 90 points per turn), but the party managed to defeat the boss in 7.6 turns:

$$t_{R=0} = \frac{1000 - \sqrt{1000^2 - 2 \cdot \frac{90}{1} \cdot 5000}}{90} = 7.6. \quad (3.3.41)$$

More about the Combat Rating

The combat rating constant is generally the rate at which a unit destroys opposing units. The value depends on the combat system and can include several factors. For example, units might have an attack value, a_X, which is the number of points of damage done in a unit of time, and a "health" or "hit points" value, h_X, which is the number of points the unit must receive to be destroyed. Thus, the rate at which a unit in the Blue army can destroy units of the Red army is a_B/h_R, so $c_B = a_B/h_R$ (and $c_R = a_R/h_B$).

The combat rating might include a special defensive ability that would reduce the amount of damage received by a constant percentage. Units with heavy armor or units that are highly maneuverable would modify the other army's combat rating to account for its defensive ability.

The combat rating can also include the effect of weather or terrain. Certain weather conditions might reduce the effectiveness of one army and have no effect on another. Certain types of units might be more effective on some types of terrain. As long as these factors are constant for the entire army, they can all be combined into a single combat rating.

Limitations

These models assume that combat is continuous and simultaneous. Frequently, combat in a game is implemented such that attacks occur at specific intervals rather than continuously, or each army takes turns attacking. Combat may also be implemented with no fractional units, and each individual unit fights at full strength until it is destroyed. In these cases, quantization results in a difference between the models and the actual outcome, and the model can only be used as an approximation or prediction of the outcome. However, if the number of units is large compared to the rate at which they are destroyed, the approximation will be reasonably close to the actual outcome.

Even when the attrition models are not suitable for determining the outcome of combat in the game, they can be useful aids in designing a combat system and balancing the units in the game. The models presented here could also be used for determining battles occurring out of player view or for rapidly determining battle outcomes if "fast-forwarding" through time, evolving a game world, or similar.

Conclusion

This gem has provided an introduction to Lanchester Attrition models and their use in predicting the outcome of combat in games. Several examples of the application of attrition models to combat scenarios that are common in computer war games and strategy games were given. The models described in this gem can be modified and extended to fit other scenarios and combat systems that are not listed here.

References

[Darilek01] Darilek, R., et al. "Measures of Effectiveness for the Information-Age Army." Ch. 4 Available online at *http://www.rand.org/publications/MR/MR1155/MR1155.ch4.pdf*. August 2004.

[Lanchester16] Lanchester, F. W. "Aircraft in Warfare: The Dawn of the Fourth Arm." In *Engineering 98*, 422–423; reprinted in *World of Mathematics*, ed. J.Newman, vol. IV, pp. 2138–2148. Simon and Schuster, 1956.

[Saperstein01] Saperstein, A. "Simple Models Suggest Answers to Complex Questions: Do We Need Satellite Surveillance for Land Warfare? A Lancastrian View." *Peace Economics, Peace Science and Public Policy*, Volume 8 no. 1: 21–29. Available online at *http://www.crp.cornell.edu/peps/journal.htm*. August 2004.

[Veale04] Veale, T. "Strategy and Tactics in Military War Games: The Role and Potential of Artificial Intelligence." Lecture III. Available online at *http://www.compapp.dcu.ie/~tonyv/gamesAI/war3.rtf*. August 2004.

3.4

Implementing Practical Planning for Game AI

Jamie Cheng, Relic Entertainment Inc.,

jcheng@relic.com

Finnegan Southey, University of Alberta, Department of Computing Science

fdjsouthey@uwaterloo.ca

The increasing complexity of game worlds and the growing focus on team-based gameplay have pushed the development of game AI beyond the limits of finite state machines (FSMs). FSM approaches are typically brittle with respect to changes in the game design and engine, are hard to debug, and are difficult to extend beyond their originally designed purpose. Designing multiple FSMs to interact intelligently and cooperatively is very tricky, and unforeseen situations during the game can throw the AI into disarray.

Planning addresses these issues by abstracting the reasoning to a new level and expressing them in a concise language that describes the effects of actions in the world. Using planning, most of the reasoning process is handled automatically by the planning engine. Changes to the game design can be quickly reflected in the planning domain, and because the planner reasons explicitly about the goals and subgoals to be obtained, it is able to effectively distribute tasks, allowing cooperative action between multiple agents.

This gem explains our work on the concepts and tools for implementing practical planning, including mixing planning with other types of control (e.g., pathfinding, FSMs, and scripting), communications between the game engine and the planning engine, optimizations, and other important issues.

For the purposes of this introduction, we present a *Sims*-like game, but one in which the player specifies *goals* for their simulated people instead of specific *actions*. However, the planning approach applies equally well to a wide range of games. We have given substantial thought to its use in RPGs, tactical squad-based FPSs, high-level strategy in RTSs, and stealth/espionage games; and we foresee many new types of gameplay both in and out of these genres.

The Planning Framework

Conceptually, a planning framework works with a set of *world states* that contain the essential information about the game world at a given point in time. When we are about to plan, we must provide an *initial state*, describing the world we want to reason about. For example:

- Bob is in the kitchen.
- The cabinet key is in the kitchen.
- The cabinet is in the den.
- The silver plate is in the cabinet.
- The cabinet is locked.

States are transformed into other states via *actions*, so part of our abstract description includes details on how actions alter states. Here, a `move` action would allow Bob to move between the kitchen and the den. Similarly, a `take` action would allow Bob to pick up objects in the same room as himself. If Bob used the `take` action on the key, the new state would be:

- Bob is in the kitchen.
- Bob is carrying the key.
- The cabinet is in the den.
- The silver plate is in the cabinet.
- The cabinet is locked.

Using this model, the designer can specify *goal conditions* such as "Bob is carrying the plate." We are interested in any state where Bob is carrying the plate. We will call these *goal states*. There can be multiple possible goal states, because the only condition we specified is that Bob is carrying the plate. The rest of the world can be in any state.

Planning is a search for a sequence of actions that will transform the initial state into a goal state. During the search, the planner will, explicitly or implicitly, construct many possible world states, heading toward the goal. These states do not map directly to the game engine but are instead based on the initial state fed to the planner. If the planner succeeds, it formulates a *plan*: the set of actions needed to reach the goal state. This is then executed step by step, transforming the actual game world. See Figure 3.4.1.

Planning Domains

We call the abstraction of the game world the *planning domain* for the world. Classical planning views the world as a logical construct where there are certain *facts* about the world associated with each state. It is common to introduce planning using propositional logic, which simply uses a set of propositions that are either true or false (essentially, a set of Boolean variables). A proposition might consist of a statement like "Bob is carrying the key," and that statement can be either true or false. Think of the proposition as a Boolean variable named `BOB_CARRIES_KEY`.

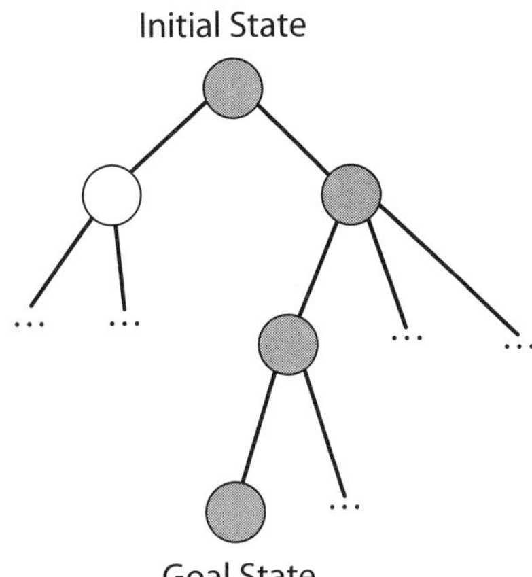

FIGURE 3.4.1 *Example of plan to reach goal state.*

Predicate logic would instead represent the same statement as a Boolean function that takes objects as arguments. Our example would become something like `carrying( Bob, key )`. This allows for a much more concise planning language and is used in most contemporary planners. Predicate logic is the basis for what is probably the best-known planner, STRIPS [Fikes71]. The STRIPS planning language is still used today, along with many variations and extensions. The most widely accepted planning language at present is PDDL, used by most contemporary research planners [McDermott98]. PDDL uses a LISP-like syntax, which is not widely used in the games industry, so we have developed our own syntax and parser, better suited to the industry at large and more readable by designers who may have only limited programming experience.

Objects

Predicate logic describes truth statements over a set of *objects*. Objects are the entities that make up the world. In our earlier example, objects would include "Bob," "key," "silver plate," "den," "kitchen," etc. These objects are not the same as objects in the object-oriented (OO) sense; they do not have methods or any associated dynamics. However, it is quite natural (and even desirable) to relate planning objects to OO game engine objects in a one-to-one fashion, so that the planner's proposed actions can be translated directly into game object manipulations.

Objects do have *types*, much as in the object-oriented framework. This mechanism affords type checking, so errors can be caught earlier in development. We allow multiple type inheritance, so types form a *lattice*. We identify one special type, "Object," often called the *universal type*, from which all other types inherit. This leads us to the first kind of statement, which declares types to the planner.

```
type Locatable;
type Location;
type Creature isa Locatable;
type Person isa Creature;
type Item isa Locatable;
type Key isa Item;
type ValuablePlate isa Item, Decoration;  // multiple inheritance
```

Once we have declared types, we can declare objects.

```
object alice isa Person;
object bob isa Person;
object cabinetkey isa Key;
object silverplate isa ValuablePlate;
object kitchen isa Location;
object den isa Location
```

Predicates

Predicates help us state facts about the objects in the world. They map tuples of objects to true or false values. For example, we can have a predicate `carrying` that takes two arguments, the first a `Creature` and the second an `Item`. We can now express ideas like: `carrying(bob, cabinetkey)` or `carrying(bob, silverplate)`.

Facts expressed as predicates make up the states in our planner. A state is simply a collection of all the facts about the world. In general, we store only the true facts in the world: the predicates that evaluate to true. Every other predicate expression is assumed to be false. This is known as the *closed world assumption* and it is motivated by the expectation that more predicates will be false than true in the world, and so it's more efficient to store the true ones.

There are a few different ways to use predicates. In some cases, we will *assert* predicates, making our expression true in the current state. So we might assert `carrying(bob, cabinetkey)` to add that fact to the state. Alternately, we may use the predicate as a *query*: "Is Bob carrying the cabinet key?" If that is a fact in the current state, the predicate will return true.

In our planning language, the arguments of predicates have types and predicates must be explicitly declared.

```
predicate carrying(Creature, Item);
predicate inroom(Locatable, Location);
```

Variables

Predicates capture relationships between objects. We can ask whether a relation exists or not, but we can go further and ask for sets of relationships. This is done with *variables*. For example, if we would like a list of things carried by Bob, we can query `carrying(bob, ?x)`, where `?x` is the notation to we use to indicate that `x` is a variable.

It's easiest to think about the process as pattern matching. The query checks all the `carrying` facts in the state, picks only those whose first argument is `Bob`, and sets `x` to each value for the second argument in succession. If the query finds one or more suitable matches, it returns true for each such match and binds the variable(s) accordingly.

Logical Connectors

Using *conjunctions* (logical AND) and *negations* (logical NOT), we can create much more interesting queries. For example, we can check whether Bob and the key are in the same room:

```
inroom(bob, ?x) and inroom(cabinetkey, ?x)
```

Here, the first `inroom()` query finds a match corresponding to `Bob` and binds `?x` to `kitchen`. The second query now becomes `inroom(key1, kitchen)`.

It is also important to allow for a special kind of predicate to represent *inequalities*, only true if its two arguments are different objects; for example: ?x != ?y.

Operators

We use *operators* to transform one state into another. In their simplest form, operators have a *precondition*, a query that must be true before the action can be performed, and *effects*, a set of changes to be made to the world. Both can be stated using simple logic expressions formed from predicates, conjunctions, and negations.

```
operator take(Creature ?c, Item ?i)
    precondition: inroom (?c, ?r) and inroom(?i, ?r)
    effect: not inroom (?i, ?r) and carrying(?c, ?r);
```

This operator takes two arguments (note their types). The preconditions state that the creature must be in the same location as the item. The effect creates a new state, identical to the original state, removing the fact that the item is in the room, and adding the fact that the creature is carrying the item.

Note that the `?r` variable is not one of the arguments of the operator. That's because it isn't really essential to the action, it's just some information we need to know to execute it. Think of it as a local variable for the operator. When the game engine needs to actually execute the action, it only needs to know the creature and the item.

Once we have operators, we can examine a state and automatically determine what actions are possible by testing the precondition for each action. Each match of the preconditions for each operator is a possible action. We now have everything we need to search for a plan except for the actual search algorithm.

A Multi-Agent Planner Example

Putting all this together, we can look at a simple example that clearly shows the power of a planner. In this example, we create a state where there is a trivial solution, and then expand the problem to one that requires two agents working together to solve the problem.

```
type Locatable;
type Location;
type Creature isa Locatable;
type Person isa Creature;
type Dog isa Creature;
type Container isa Locatable;
type Item isa Locatable;
type Key isa Item;
type Plate isa Item;
type ValuablePlate isa Plate, Decoration;
// multiple inheritance
type Food isa Item;
```

Once we have declared types, we can declare objects.

```
object alice isa Person;
object bob isa Person;
object cabinetkey isa Key;
object silverplate isa ValuablePlate;
object kitchen isa Location;
object den isa Location;
object cabinet isa Container;
object nelly isa Dog;
object lasagna isa Food;
object fridge isa Container;

predicate inroom(Locatable ?a, Location ?b);
// Object is in location
predicate carrying(Creature ?c, Item ?i);
// Creature carries item
predicate locked(Container ?c);
// Container is locked
predicate unlocks(Key ?k, Container ?c);
// Key unlocks container
predicate hungry(Creature ?c);
// Creature his hungry
predicate prepared(Food ?f);
// Food is prepared
predicate inside(Item ?i, Container ?c);
// Item is inside container

// Pick up something in the room.
operator take(Person ?p, Item ?i)
    precondition: inroom(?p, ?r) and inroom (?i, ?r)
    effect: not inroom (?i, ?r) and carrying(?p, ?r);
```

```
// move to another room
operator goto(Person ?p, Room ?r)
    precondition: inroom(?p, ?o) and ?o != ?r
    effect: inroom (?p, ?r) and not inroom(?p, ?o);

// drop something carried
operator drop(Person ?p, Item ?i)
    precondition: inroom(?p, ?r) and carrying(?p, ?i)
    effect: inroom (?i, ?r) and not carrying(?p, ?i);

// remove something from a container
operator remove(Person ?c, Item ?i)
    precondition: inside(?i, ?v) and inroom(?c, ?r) and
    inroom(?v, ?r) and unlocked(?v)
    effect: carrying(?c, ?i) and not inside(?i, ?v);

// unlock a container with a key
operator unlock(Person ?c, Container ?v)
    precondition: locked(?v) and unlocks(?k, ?v)
        and carrying(?c, ?k)
    effect: not locked(?v);

// prepare some food
operator prepare(Person ?c, Food ?f)
    precondition: carrying(?c, ?f) and not prepared(?f)
    effect: prepared(?f);

// eat some prepared food from a plate
operator eat(Person ?c, Food ?f, Plate ?p)
    precondition: carrying(?c, ?f) and carrying(?c, ?p)
        and hungry(?c) and prepared(?f)
    effect: not hungry(?c) and not carrying(?c, ?f);
```

Now we define our initial state and goal state. The trivial case is that Bob wants the plate and it is in the den while Bob is in the kitchen:

```
//define initial state
inroom(bob, kitchen)
inroom(silverplate, den)


//define goal state
goal carrying(bob, silverplate)
```

Given this, the planner returns to us:

```
goto(bob, den)
take(bob, silverplate)
```

Now watch how easily we can expand the problem, defining a new initial state where the plate is locked in the cabinet in the den and Alice carries the key. We will try to achieve the same goal:

```
//define initial state
inroom(alice, den)
inroom(bob, kitchen)
carrying(alice, cabinetkey)
inroom(cabinet, den)
unlocks(cabinetkey, cabinet)
inside(silverplate, cabinet)
locked(cabinet)
```

One possible plan is:

```
unlock(alice, cabinet)
remove(alice, silverplate)
goto(alice, kitchen)
drop(alice, silverplate)
take(bob, silverplate)
```

Now consider a new situation where Alice is hungry and we want her to be fed:

```
//define initial state
inroom(alice, den)
inroom(bob, kitchen)
carrying(alice, cabinetkey)
inroom(cabinet, den)
unlocks(cabinetkey, cabinet)
locked(cabinet)
hungry(alice)
inside(silverplate, cabinet)
inside(lasagna, fridge)


//define goal state
not hungry(alice)
```

A plan to achieve this is:

```
unlock(alice, cabinet)
remove(alice, silverplate)
goto(alice, kitchen)
remove(bob, lasagna)
prepare(bob, lasagna)
drop(bob, lasagna)
eat(alice, lasgna, silverplate)
```

These simple examples have immense ramifications. Suddenly, designers can easily create scenarios that may require the AI to cooperate to solve a problem! Even better, as the player changes the world, the AI automatically replans and acts accordingly. Over the course of the game, new predicates can be asserted or operators added that allow creatures to do more things. Other options include designers writing simple scripts that assign goals for the planner to carry out, or players asking a cooperative AI for help. The possibilities are endless.

The best way to see the possibilities is to think about them. Given the earlier domain, spend some time thinking about how you could quickly implement the following:

- Add a way for people to give items directly to each other.
- Describe the layout of the house and add doors.
- Add a thief who only steals valuable stuff and uses unlocked doors.
- Add an operator for the dog to eat food when no people are in the room.
- Make Bob not tall enough to reach the plate in the cabinet, requiring Alice to help.
- Forbid Alice from unlocking the cabinet while Bob is in the room.
- Require two people to move the fridge.
- Require food to be heated before eating.
- Create messes as a result of cooking (e.g., dirty dishes) that require cleaning up.
- Allow only trained people to cook.
- Add driving out to get food to prepare (someone needs a license).
- Require that people like each other or be in the right mood to cooperate.
- Give Alice a sword, Bob some skimpy armor, and the dog three heads to make an RPG.
- Give Alice night vision, Bob a guard's outfit, and the dog a sense of smell to make a stealth game.

Even with automated planning by the agents in our household simulation game, there's plenty of compelling gameplay here: setting a sequence of goals for agents much as actions are set in current games, dropping new objects into the world to help them, adding attributes and training the agents so they can gain new abilities, or directing the actions of one agent with the other working around it.

Planning Search

All these benefits are not without cost. There are overhead costs associated with planning, both in terms of development and machine resources. Developers must specify the planning domain, essentially a secondary description of the game world, and ensure that the actions in the domain do not produce nonsensical states (e.g., the player is in two places at once). Planning domains must be designed and debugged like regular programs. Like a compiler, the planner can only work with what it is given, and if garbage goes in, garbage is all that will come out. However, this development cost is likely to be saved by having simpler low-level mechanisms and, furthermore, we stand to gain more intelligent behavior.

The real expense of planning is search. Depending on the specific methods used, planning search may consume substantial memory. To account for this, planning search can be implemented in different ways.

The first distinction is between *forward* and *backward* planning. In forward planning, we start from the initial state and consider actions until we discover a goal state. In backward planning, we start with the goals and consider those actions that can achieve the goals. The preconditions for those actions now form a new goal, so we continue the search backward. Backward planning has the advantage that it tends to have a smaller branching factor because it never considers actions that do not satisfy some necessary goal, whereas forward planning can conceivably try all possible actions. On the other hand, forward planning is the more natural direction; it only considers states reachable from the initial state, and even an incomplete forward sequence makes sense and can be executed.

The other major difference between search strategies is whether they search in *state space* or in *plan space*. In state space, we explore states, eventually constructing a sequence of states that achieves the goal. We can then extract the plan by listing the actions necessary for each state. In plan space, we consider sets or sequences of actions directly, testing to see whether they achieve the goals, refining and extending the collection of actions as we search.

Most contemporary planners fall into one of three classes: *heuristic search planners*, *planning graph planners*, and *satisfiability planners*. We will briefly describe all three of these but focus on heuristic search planners, which we believe to be the best choice for games for a variety of reasons that will form part of the discussion.

Heuristic Search Planning

Heuristic search planning is a state space planning approach that can run forward or backward. The search is much like pathfinding. Familiar algorithms such as A* can be directly applied, and existing A* code reused. As in pathfinding, it is easy to associate costs with the actions and thus be able to compute "good" plans instead of just feasible plans. It is comparatively easy to encode specific knowledge about the game in the costs and also in the heuristics used by A*.

Another key advantages is that even if forward planning fails to find the goal, either because no sequence exists or because we have limited the running time of the planner, we can always use the best path found so far as a plan so that game characters will at least do something that is likely to reasonable. It is even likely that in subsequent re-planning, these partial actions may have helped to put us in a situation to find a complete plan.

Finally, heuristic search planning offers state-of-the-art performance, especially on nonoptimal planners (optimal planners find plans with minimal plan length or cost, whereas nonoptimal planners search for "good enough" plans; for games, we probably don't need optimal solutions) with planners like FF [Hoffmann01] among recent planning competition winners.

A good introduction to heuristic search planning [Bonet01] is available at: *http://www.tecn.upf.es/~hgeffner/index.html.*

Graph Planning and Satisfiability Planning

Graph plans are essentially backward planners that work in plan space. From a high-level perspective, they work by constructing a *planning graph*, a data structure that considers the effects of all possible actions starting from the initial state, pretending they never conflict with each other. While constructing the graph, information about mutually exclusive actions is kept, and when the graph is complete, a backward search from the goals takes place to find a set of legal actions within the graph [Weld99].

Graph planning produces *partially ordered* plans, where the exact ordering of actions is not always specified. Some actions can therefore be performed in any order or, in the case where the actions are performed by multiple agents, at the same time. This is particularly appealing when we wish to control multiple agents. However, the backward planning means that if we run out of time constructing a plan, there is no partial plan to execute. While this approach has potential for games, it not as readily adaptable as heuristic searching. However, it is worth noting that planning graphs are sometimes used to compute heuristics for other kinds of planners (e.g., the FF planner mentioned earlier).

Satisfiability (SAT) planners encode planning problems as SAT problems, which are classic NP-complete problems with lots of high-performance solvers readily available. These planners differ chiefly in how they encode the problem, but once encoded, they can simply call the latest and greatest SAT solver to generate a solution. This means that these planners can be improved from year to year using off-the-shelf components. However, SAT planning is arguably more obscure and less hackable, since the CNF instances are too large to understand and the SAT solver is essentially a black box where it is difficult to encode any extra knowledge you may have about the problem. We will not discuss this approach further here, but it is worth considering because of the rapid advance of SAT solvers.

A good introduction to both graph planning and satisfiability planning [Weld99] is available at: *http://www.cs.washington.edu/homes/weld/papers/pi2.pdf.*

Practical Issues

The following sections discuss some practical issues.

Limitations

Planning is a powerful tool, one that should be combined with our existing tools to be effective. By using planning, a lot of the complexity being built into FSMs and rules can be better expressed in the planning domain, leaving us with simpler versions of these lower level constructs. However, it also has some limitations:

1. A symbolic approach like planning is poorly suited to continuous problems (for example, one wouldn't use it to drive a car or aim at targets). Existing mechanisms should be used to handle these tasks, with the planner directing the actions. The planner is best seen as a mechanism to coordinate simple, low-level actions that are implemented in the best way available.

2. In addition to its somewhat limited scope, classical planning makes some strong assumptions. It assumes that a world behaves as described and that actions will succeed. This is clearly not the case because of randomness, because we abstract the gaming world, and above all, because of the human player. This is why we must replan periodically to reflect the changing world and the failure of earlier plans.
3. Classical planning is not adversarial. It does not take into account that someone may be working to thwart it. However, very few game AIs address this problem with more than some basic heuristics and rules. Most of these basic strategies can be reflected as goal selection, with a top-level strategy module picking overall goals that the planner figures out how to accomplish, executing the low-level behavior by instructing FSMs.
4. The symbolic approach is also not good for making value judgments, like the relative strengths of two creatures. Existing heuristic functions should be used in this case and a predicate used in the planner that calls the heuristic and applies a threshold (e.g., a `canKill(Creature, Creature)` predicate might check that one unit's strength is double that of the other unit).

Integration with the Game Engine

In addition to these concerns, it is important to consider how to integrate the planner to the game engine. This depends at least partially on how reusable you want the planning code to be, but we will address a few key points.

We first consider the initial state for planning, which must be obtained by the game engine. Subsequent states generated during planning must be copies of this initial state; we don't want to change variables in the game engine directly while planning. There are a few strategies for getting the facts for the initial state.

In a "pull" strategy, the planner requests information from the game engine to construct states. The planner examines all the predicates when we are about to plan, determines their values from the game engine, and stores them in the initial state. However, the expense of repeated copy operations here is nontrivial, and it is possible that a lot of useless state information will be stored

One solution to this is to use a *read-on-demand* approach. In this case, the value is only read when the predicate is evaluated. Another approach is to use a "push" model, where the game engine sends changes to the planner as they occur. This is a good strategy if planning occurs frequently. With infrequent planning, a lot of update operations will be performed needlessly.

It is also necessary to associate planning objects and actions with the corresponding data structures and functions in the game engine. This mapping is fairly straightforward but should be thought about carefully during design. In addition, different modules should be able to interact with the planner. We built a custom planning language to set up the planning domain (types, objects, predicates, operators) but used Lua, a popular scripting language, to drive the initial state and goals and bind objects and actions to the game engine [Lua]. Our planner can also be controlled directly via C++. Designers can use their favorite scripting language to fine tune levels and, in the same script, ask agents to solve interesting problems without resorting to loading a separate script with different syntax.

Note that it is possible to skip writing a custom parser entirely and drive the entire planner through Lua scripts (or your favorite scripting language). This gem used a custom parser, because we found it more instructional for the reader and easier to read for development, but it is not essential.

Optimizations

Planning is known to be hard in theory, and it is easy to build hard planning problems. However, games represent an instance where we have a lot of control. In robotics and industry, the world is uncontrolled. In games, the world is perfectly observable and carefully engineered. Games are built to be reliable, and a lot of the qualities QA looks for in a game lead to easy planning domains. Most games are carefully designed so that the player cannot become trapped. Every state of the game should lead to some definite outcome (even if it's just death). This lack of limbo states is good for planning.

Many games also have a lot of *monotonicity* in their actions. This means that once an action is taken, the effect it has on the world is never removed. Examples of this are objects that are never dropped once picked up, doors that can be unlocked but are never locked again, and creatures that do not respawn once killed. Think about the games you have played and you will begin to see a lot of monotonicity. This is because good game design often leads to monotonicity by attempting to keep actions simple. If there is no reason for doors to be relocked or a switch to be flipped twice, making the action monotonic simplifies the controls, the player's options in the game, and debugging/playtesting.

Monotonicity leads to easy planning domains. Moreover, many planning algorithms pretend the domain is monotonic as a heuristic. Such algorithms will be highly effective in largely monotonic game worlds. Nonetheless, nonmonotonicity is going to arise as a natural part of interesting gameplay, and contemporary planning algorithms can still perform well. Exceptionally difficult nonmonotonic subtasks that prove to be a problem can be addressed by a custom solution, a specialized algorithm that solves the hard problem. This can be treated as an action by the planner, effectively removing the hard part of the domain by ensuring that it's done as a single, special action.

For example, an agent might be required to navigate a very complicated maze of doors with switches that must be flipped and reflipped to escape. If the planner is too slow at solving this problem, a specialized algorithm or scripted solution could be associated with a `navigateMaze` action. At the planning level, the action would simply require that the agent be at the start of the maze and the effect would be to put the agent at the end of the maze. Some such problems might be puzzles, which begs the question of whether a game designer should pose puzzles for the game AI to solve. Since the usual point of a puzzle is to challenge humans, it might be better to automatically bypass the puzzle or force the player to solve it.

A lot of other optimizations are possible, such as setting an order in which to explore actions if we have some idea of which might be important. We can automatically reject certain states if they have some undesirable property, thus pruning the search. Finally, there is a large research literature and a range of excellent tutorials that can suggest good optimizations and heuristics.

Conclusion

Planning algorithms can add a new dimension to intelligent behavior in games and reduce the complexity of existing game AI implementations. Planning and games are a great match, and recent A* based strategies are both familiar to game developers and state of the art in planning research. The time is ripe to adopt planning into games.

For example, Jeff Orkin of Monolith Productions has already incorporated planning into their upcoming FPS game, *F.E.A.R.* It uses a propositional planner, planning for single agents with a small number of facts (around 20), but it provides dynamic, forward-looking AI in the fast-paced, real-time FPS setting [Orkin04]. With more sophisticated heuristics and optimizations, multiple agents and larger scenarios are within reach. Our own planner is more general, and the first iteration took about a month to implement from scratch.

In less immediate games such as RPGs, we believe that much larger environments can be modeled. Tactical and stealth-based games also stand to gain from this technology, addressing the somewhat shortsighted behavior exhibited by their characters. Whether for allies or opponents, a richer and more vivid experience can be offered to the player and a new generation of gameplay opened for designers to play with. We don't just think it's possible, we're sure it's inevitable.

A demo is available from *http://www.cs.ualberta.ca/~finnegan/planning4games.*

References

[Bonet01] Bonet, Blai and Hector Geffner. "Planning as Heuristic Search." In *Artificial Intelligence-Special Issue on Heuristic Search*, Vol. 129, No. 1–2, 2001. Available online at *http://www.tecn.upf.es/~hgeffner/index.html.*

[Fikes71] Fikes, R. and N. Nilsson. "STRIPS: A new approach to the application of theorem proving to problem solving." In *Artificial Intelligence*, vol. 2, No. 3–4, 1971: pp. 189–208.

[Ghallab04] Ghallab, Malik, Dana Nau, and Traverso Paolo. *Automated Planning-Theory and Practice.* Morgan Kaufmann, 2004.

[Hoffmann01] Hoffmann, J. and B. Nebel. "The FF Planning System: Fast Plan Generation Through Heuristic Search." In *Journal of Artificial Intelligence Research*, Vol. 14, 2001: pp. 253–302. Available online at *http://www.informatik.uni-freiburg.de/~hoffmann/ff.html.*

[Lua] "Lua The Programming Language." *http://www.lua.org.*

[McDermott98] McDermott, Drew, et al. "Planning Domain Definition Language." 1998. Available online at *http://www.informatik.uni-freiburg.de/~hoffman/ipc-4/pddl.html.*

[Orkin04] Orkin, Jeff. "Symbolic Representation of Game World State: Toward Real-Time Planning in Games." In *AAAI Workshop Technical Report WS-04-04: Challenges in Game Artificial Intelligence* (July, 2004): pp. 26–30.

[Weld99] Weld, Daniel S. "Recent Advances in AI Planning." In *AI Magazine* (1999): pp. 93–123. Available online at *http://www.cs.washington.edu/homes/weld/papers/pi2.pdf.*

3.5

Optimizing a Decision Tree Query Algorithm for Multithreaded Architectures

Chuck DeSylva, Intel Corporation

chuck.v.desylva@intel.com

Decision Trees facilitate slim, fast game AI that is easy to implement and maintain. Although Neural Nets may be better in the long term (once educated), Decision Trees are ideal for a finite set of expectations, like those defined in typical games.

This article presents a simple method for modifying an implementation of the basic Decision Tree algorithm. The method is fairly straightforward and easy to implement and more importantly can result in faster AI response. It is especially applicable to AIs with large determination sets, where many units in the game use the same tree(s) spawned from a single main thread of execution, for a given set of AI responses (e.g., attack, movement, etc.).

Overview

Essentially, a Decision Tree is a way of assessing data from a set of questions and suggesting a model that explains the data so that accurate predictions can be made. It is constructed of questions to be asked by AI characters based on data from the scene. There are numerous varieties of questions for a given set of data, and a typical game AI could (and should) have numerous Decision Trees (i.e., pathfinding, spontaneous reaction, Q&A, and to some extent, physics itself, such as avoidance and response). For more complex systems, such as agents, Decision Trees become even more important.

Decision Trees can operate on finite or infinite sets of data, though for the case of games, the finite set is of the most importance. The obvious value of Decision Trees over other algorithms is twofold: they offer a simple and discrete explanation of regression sets as well as an easy "explanation" of Decision rationale. One of the most widely used Decision Tree algorithms is Quinlan's ID3 algorithm for constructing a

Decision Tree AI. Documentation for this algorithm and how it works is readily available on the Internet.

Decision Trees are essentially computer science binary tree structures, enabling a conclusion state to be reached from a root node (which denotes the start of a decision category) via a set of Decision states. In the example used in this document, the states are 2, as shown in Figure 3.5.1. The tree provides a technique to allow a conclusion to be made based on a specified problem definition.

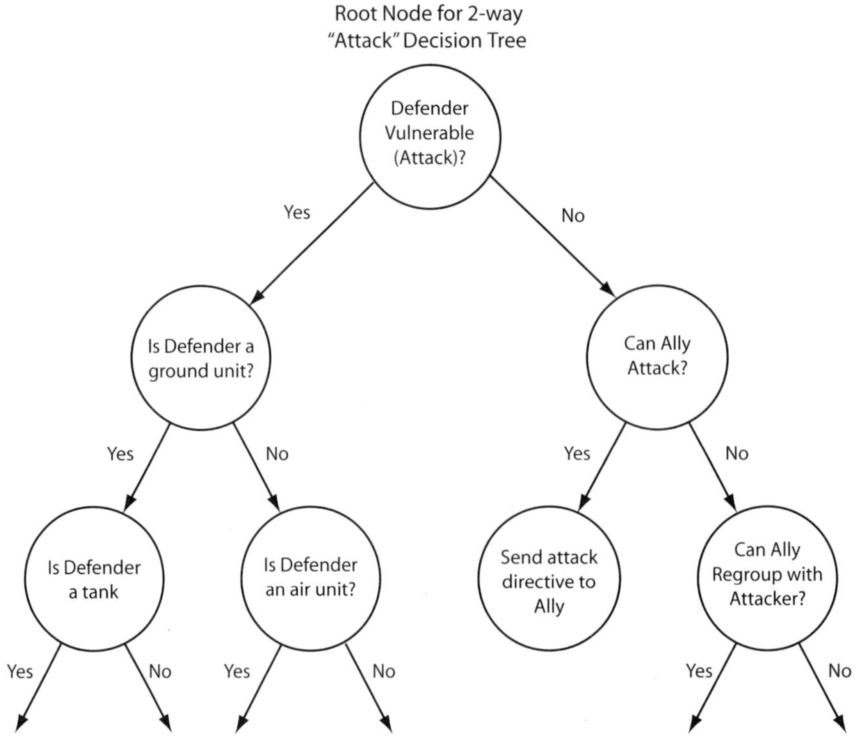

FIGURE 3.5.1 *Example 2-way based "Attack" Decision Tree.*

Since Decision Trees are a good way to turn an educated set of questions into nodes that result in answers, they are useful in classification systems as well as in computer game AI. The architecture of the Decision Tree typically requires a lot of input from the design in question and can vary from one design to the next. Although most problems in modern games are simple, the time is closely approaching where it will be possible to create game-independent AI characters that use multithreaded algorithms such as this. For now we'll constrain the topic to a simple optimization method of one implementation of this algorithm with the intent that it could be scaled to others similar to it (i.e., n-way trees, that is, more than one answer per node).

Caveats

Some Decision Trees involve decisions that can be answered in a variety of ways (in addition to the binary yes/no). In *inductive learning*, as this type of AI is referred to, the goal is to find some rule or function that lets you draw useful conclusions based on a decision case you obtain at any point in the tree. For any particular decision set, the various inputs are classified via entropy functions, typically based on logarithmic functions. Since these functions are detailed in countless sources on this subject and don't have a great impact on the performance of the algorithm (most modern compilers automatically optimize math functions with special switches[1]), we'll forego a discussion on the nuances of the inner workings of the algorithm and stick to the "biggest bang for the optimization buck."

The original Decision Tree implementation was riddled with command-line input statements. To make the algorithm more useful for the purposes of profiling, it was modified to take input from a memory-mapped file (to simulate real-time input from a typical game). Further, the tree was made significantly deep enough (as it would be in a typically robust AI) to make profiling the algorithm closer to a real-world implementation.

Optimization

Most game developers don't want their AI to assume more than ~20% of the (frame) compute cycle (depending on the game implementation) time. This is a rather liberal request given all the rigors of a robust gaming experience. If you have a well-balanced Decision Tree (one with equally distributed yes and no branches; see Figure 3.5.2) you might be able to gain that 10% back on a multithreading aware system[2] using this technique.

The algorithms detailed in this article are based on material available at the Generation 5 Web site, which details a simple yet robust and easily adaptable Decision Tree implementation.

The code modifications in this example were done using a compiler[3] that supports OpenMP (see OpenMP specification 2.0) directives. Since the majority of the (running) time spent in this algorithm is in searching for answers, the search part of the algorithm was chosen for optimization.

The algorithm itself is recursive, so some additional routines are needed. It starts by a call to the member function `DecisionTree::Query()` (see Listing 3.5.1). This in turn calls the member function `DecisionTree::QueryBinaryTree( *dt node )`. As the tree is searched, a set of recursive calls {δ: where, δ is the depth of the tree} between

[1]Intel's C/C++ Compiler (v.8.0), for example, will vectorize math functions using certain switches (i.e. /QaxW for Netburst architecture)

[2]Such as any multi-processor based system.

[3]Intel's C/C++ 8.0 Compiler. Microsoft's Visual Studio .Net 2005 is also intending to support OpenMP as of this writing.

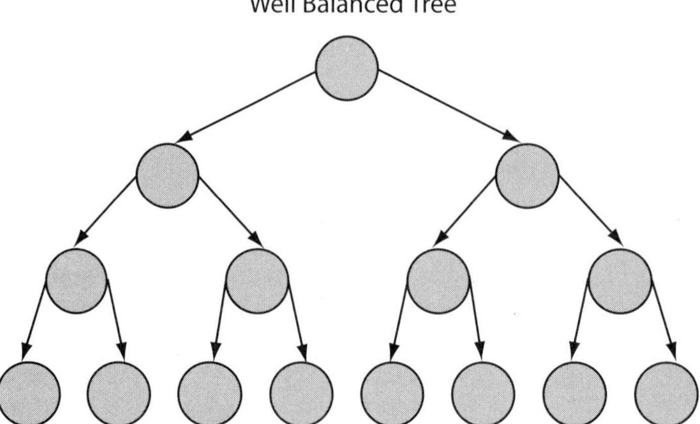

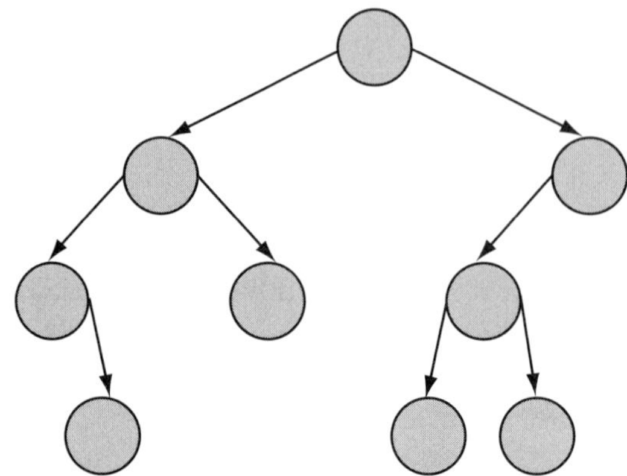

FIGURE 3.5.2 *Example of a well balanced and poorly balanced Tree, each of depth (δ) 4.*

this function and `DecisionTree::AskQuestion( *dt node )` call each other until the answer node is obtained or no answer is found.

As the desktop CPU industry moves closer to simultaneous 80 × 86-based 32 and 64 bit computing, performance is being challenged once again. Expectations are that 80 × 86 based processors[4] with these technologies will require application software to scale appropriately to maintain on-par performance with the hardware capabilities. Proper threading of applications will be critical to application performance as Dual-core and Multi-core trends redefine scalability for today's modern application software.

4 Which are expected to start shipping mid 2005 as of this writing.

Listing 3.5.1 Initial Decision Tree Search Source

```
void DecisionTree::Query() {
       QueryBinaryTree(m_pRootNode);
}

void DecisionTree::QueryBinaryTree(TreeNode* currentNode) {
      //Error Checking ... otherwise default to asking the question
      //at currentNode
      AskQuestion(CurrentNode);
         //otherwise default to asking the question at the currentN-
ode
}

void DecisionTree::AskQuestion(TreeNode *node) {
      //Error Checking
      if(answer == "yes")
            QueryBinaryTree(node->m-_pYesBranch);
      else if(answer == "no")
            QueryBinaryTree(node->m-_pNoBranch);
      else {   //Error on input
            AskQuestion(node);
      }
}
```

In keeping with this, the proposed optimization for this algorithm is targeted for a two-CPU (logical or physical) system. Branching out into 4-, 8-, 16-, etc. way implementation would mean further changes to accommodate this method by branching out and calling the first threaded routine on the Nth recursive iteration (from the root). That is, the starting point for threading is at $\delta = 2N$. The best way to do this is to base the threading starting point where the number of nodes at depth δ equals the number of available CPUs.[5]

Though the compiler determines the number of threads to generate based on CPUs, it does not determine where to spawn the threads. The new algorithm (Listing 3.5.2) breaks out the call to the threaded routine once the proper depth is attained in the query using modified data decomposition.

Listing 3.5.2 A 2-Way Threaded Decision Tree Implementation[6]

```
#include <omp.h>
...
void DecisionTree::Query() {
      QueryBinaryTreeFirstTime(m_pNode);
}
```

[5]In the Microsoft Win32 API this can be obtained by calling the Platform SDK function GetSystemInfo(...).
[6]Compiled with the Intel Compiler's /Qopenmp switch.

```
void DecisionTree::QueryBinaryTreeFirstTime(TreeNode* currentNode) {
      //Error Checking ... otherwise default to asking the question
      //at currentNode
      AskFirstQuestion(CurrentNode);
}

void DecisionTree::QueryBinaryTree(TreeNode* currentNode) {
      //Error Checking ... otherwise default to asking the question
      //at currentNode
      AskNextQuestion(CurrentNode);
}

void DecisionTree::AskFirstQuestion(TreeNode *node) {
#pragma omp parallel sections
{
      if(answer == "yes")
#pragma omp section
            QueryBinaryTree(node->m-_pYesBranch);
      else if(answer == "no")
#pragma omp section
            QueryBinaryTree(node->m-_pNoBranch);
}
      else // Wrong input
            AskNextQuestion(node);
}

void DecisionTree::AskNextQuestion(TreeNode *node) {
      //Error Checking
      if(answer == "yes")
            QueryBinaryTree(node->m-_pYesBranch);
      else if(answer == "no")
            QueryBinaryTree(node->m-_pNoBranch);
      else
      {   //Error on input
            AskNextQuestion(node);
```

In keeping with the 10% factor stated earlier for AI compute cycle, the workload was tested with a rendering load averaging 30 FPS. Doing a bit of math, this amounts to ~33 ms time per frame (neglecting the 0.3333 for extra-frame processing). 10% of 1 second is 10 ms. So, this was the allotted time per second allocated to AI cycles at 30 FPS chosen. That amounts to ~1/3 of 1 frame per second. Not a whole lot of time. So the test was run to generate one AI cycle per every 33 frames at 30 FPS. This would also allow for stabilizing the thread synchronization setup by OpenMP's internal thread pooling mechanisms.

The next step was to decide upon a coherent decision set for the workload. In an average game, there may be multiple Decision Trees active at a time per unit. Assume that each AI unit has from between 10–200 decisions (nodes) it can make. This is of course completely an assumption, as robust AIs could have more options (especially when *n*-way decisions are available). The geometric mean of this range is ~45. Given a worst case scenario of 300 AI units per scene (perhaps a large RTS), this amounts to a total of 13,500 nodes (or decisions) to be made per scene—a substantial number of nodes to parse in 1 second. Testing was performed on a Pentium 4 running at 3.2 GHz with HyperThreading enabled (see Figure 3.5.3).

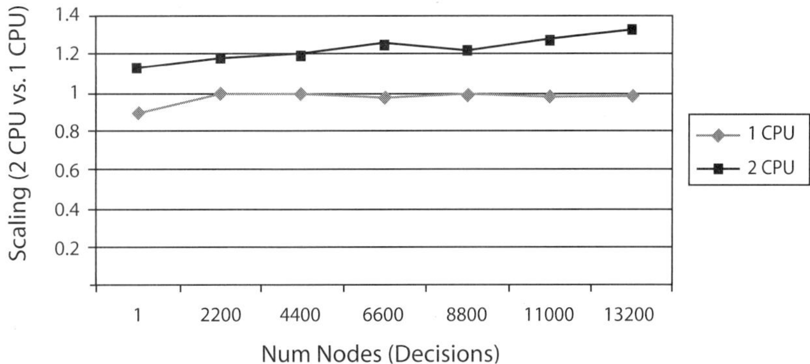

FIGURE 3.5.3 *Test results for Decision Tree workload.*

Notice the OpenMP directives for sections in Listing 3.5.2. In this case, two threads are scheduled by the OS for each section. This is done by compiling the code with the /Qopenmp switch and including the OpenMP header (omp.h). The pragma omp parallel sections informs the compiler that the following compound statement is parallelizable code, and that each work unit (function call in this case) is identified using the omp section directives. Refer to the OpenMP specification for more details on this and other directives.

Conclusion

This method illustrates a simple way to modify an existing Decision Tree search algorithm. For more information on the usage models of Decision Trees see some of the references listed. The coding techniques presented using OpenMP are applicable where data sets are significantly large enough and where the Decision Tree itself is as close to evenly balanced as possible. Performance gains will vary based on this as well as CPU cache resources and how often the search algorithm is called in a particular scene. As shown here, to gain real benefits for SMP systems, often a slight re-architecting of the algorithm with respect to load balancing is necessary. Additionally, note that there may be some trade-offs such as higher memory requirements along with code complexity.

References

Decision Trees. Available online at *http://www2.cs.uregina.ca/~hamilton/courses/831/notes/ml/dTrees.*

Generation 5 Implementation. Available online at *http://www.generation5.org/content/2004/bdt-implementation.asp*.

Intel® C/C++ Compiler Users Guide and Reference. Available online at *http://www.intel.com/software/products/compilers/cwin/.*

Microsoft Visual Studio 2005 OpenMP Support. Available online at *http://msdn.microsoft.com/msdnmag/issues/04/05/visualc2005/default.aspx.*

OpenMP Specification 2.0. Available online at *http://www.openmp.org/specs/.*

3.6

Parallel AI Development with PVM

Michael Ramsey, 2015 Inc.

miker@masterempire.com

Recent trends in chip development support the basic infrastructure for concurrent or parallel processing systems in games. The Parallel Virtual Machine (PVM) is a software system that allows an AI developer to write an AI that can run on multiple processors and systems. This gem will focus on the aspects of PVM development, primarily real-time games, with target architectures for Microsoft Windows or Linux.

While this gem is targeted toward development of an AI with PVM, many of the concepts as well as the framework, are extensible towards other areas that might benefit from parallelization and may be of use on platforms that expose multithreading concurrency technologies, such as Intel's Hyper-Threading technology or future generations of consoles.

Powerful, Not Free

A concurrent AI is usually branded as either a parallel or distributed system. PVM is both. With PVM, a game can use multiple processors on one machine or a series of computers on a local LAN for an enhanced gameplay experience.

A key proposition in PVM development is its wide use of a message-passing model to utilize a distributed environment. Retrofitting an existing system for such message passing will not yield better gameplay or a smarter AI. To reap the benefits of PVM, you must start with a general framework that will allow for the development of a concurrent AI system. This upfront work will allow for offloaded AI tasks, to communicate with and work with the core game executable. With a minimal framework in place, an AI developer can have his bots constantly evaluating the best path to take or have a separate task constantly evaluating the best tactical avenue by which to approach an elusive player. By constructing all AI queries into tasks that are executed on other processors, we allow AI tasks to be constantly executing in the background.

Any AI developer would relish the thought of not having his AI relinquished to a frame dependent clamp!

Core Terms and Concepts

Before we can discuss the details and benefits of a PVM enhanced game, we need to first define some terminology. Instead of reviewing generic parallel-programming techniques, we'll focus on the components that are needed to efficiently develop a PVM framework. See Figure 3.6.1.

For a more in-depth discussion of PVM, readers are encouraged to consult [Geist1994].

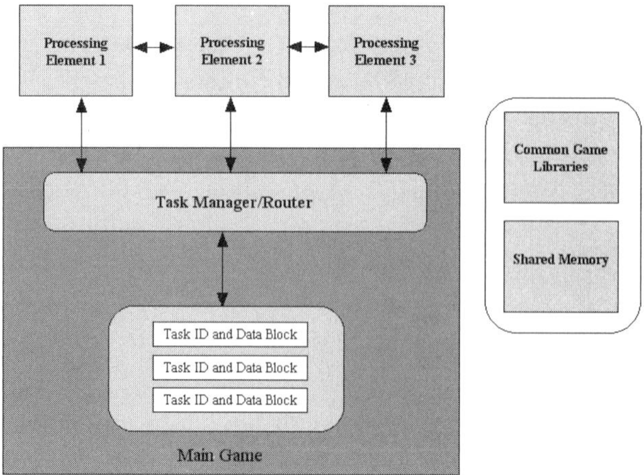

FIGURE 3.6.1 *Components of a PVM AI system.*

All tasks occur within process elements (PEs), such as on-board processors or LAN computer resources. It is easiest to visualize the relationship between the main game and the ancillary PEs by understanding that the main game is the master, and all the available PEs are its slaves. PEs do not instigate work, they are there to process tasks for the game.

Tasks are subdivided elements of a larger problem, such as path generation, influence map generation, military disposition assessment, terrain analysis, spatial determinations for unit placement, wall building, economic analysis, and other game-related actions.

Task Decomposition

A fundamental component of parallel AI development is the concept of solving a task by dividing it into a number of subtasks, each of which is processed by separate elements or workers. This infrastructure allows for a breakdown of fundamental tasks that can be easily evaluated by multiple processors.

Task decomposition generally falls into two categories: functional decomposition and data decomposition. *Data decomposition* is an algorithmic approach on task breakdown. Data decomposition is the more complex of the two categories. *Functional decomposition* is the simpler method, in that an encapsulated function can be passed off to another processor for execution. While this approach requires a shift in how we approach the design and implementation of an AI, it is the approach that our PVM system will use for game processing.

With functional decomposition, each task instigates a specific operation on another processor. For example, if you want to execute a background task to analyze potential enemy movement, you would create a task that initiates a unit analysis program with a series of prearranged parameters. These parameters would dictate things like preferred target rankings, previous diplomatic constraints, unit biases for formations, and so on. In designing the analysis task, the developer must take into consideration how *each aspect* will be executed in a concurrent system.

Creating Tasks

To illustrate how a larger problem can be decomposed into smaller elements, in Figure 3.6.2, we examine a common problem for real-time strategy (RTS) AI: distinguishing destructive short-term decisions from more cognizant long-term actions.

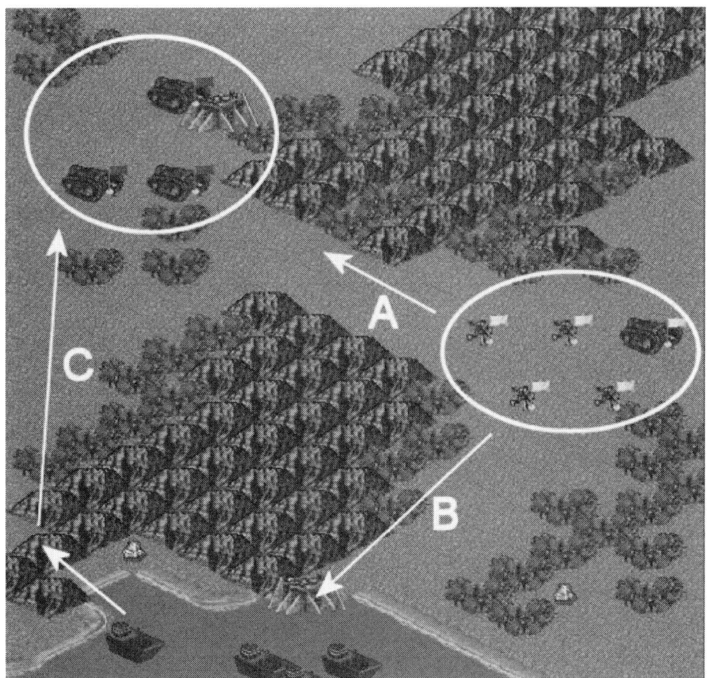

FIGURE 3.6.2 *A sample scenario from a real-time strategy (RTS) game.*

In Figure 3.6.2, we see that an AI player has discovered an enemy city with some tanks around it. In this example, we have a player massing troops on the western slope. The AI has a corresponding detachment of units on the eastern slope. The AI would like to attempt an invasion of the belligerent city. Should it use the most direct route (A) or the alternate (B–C) route?

Ideally, the AI can react with a degree of prescience. At the strategic level, we assume that the AI already *knows* it needs to take the city. To accomplish this, the AI would need to evaluate the available routes and form a plan.

Here are three possible plans:

Plan A: March forces through the mountain pass.
Plan B: March forces to the port city and then transport them around to the southern flank.
Plan C: March part of the forces through the mountain pass to occupy the enemy while the main force executes plan B.

These plans all have similar components; let's look at the components that go into plan C, as it encompasses components of both plans A and B:

Update the influence map: In this specific instance, the AI needs to know if his forces can be mobilized *through* the choke point before his forces would be engaged. This will require an up-to-date influence map.
Generate unit paths: We need paths for units that are going to enter the mountain pass and for the units that are moving via route B–C.
Provide Transportation: Tasks to either build transports at the city or route transports to help in moving the units.
Provide Attack Formations: This will direct the units once they reach the western slope of the mountain range.
Assess Diplomatic Constraints: Ascertain what type of political fallout will occur if the AI attacks the city on the western slope.

Just by deciding how the AI should attack, we've generated several potential tasks. In addition to these new tasks, we may have high-level, behind-the-scenes, strategic plans and tasks in process. Some tasks will be quick and easy to compute (usually on the local processor); others will be bulky and require assignment to other PEs. As we shall see, the size or granularity of the task will dictate how each task needs to be scheduled.

Granularity

Each task is assigned a *granularity*, which helps determine its scheduling position inside the task manager. A task's granularity is a reflection of the following:

- The size of the task
- The amount of computational effort required to accomplish the task
- The bandwidth that will be required to facilitate a solution

PVM is generally friendlier to tasks that are larger. There is an appreciable overhead that occurs during the creation of a task—its addition to the task pool—to the actual processing of that task. In attempts to maintain PVM-friendly tasks, we will generally allocate tasks that are fairly large in scope, as shown in Table 3.6.1.

Table 3.6.1 Varying Task Granularities

Sample Task	Granularity
Influence Map Analysis	Large
Generating Unit LOS	Medium
Wall building	Medium
Squad of units pathfinding	Medium
Analyzing surrounding cells	Small
Single unit pathfinding	Small
Tactical influence map analysis	Small
Combined arms formations	Small

While it is possible to hand-tune tasks for execution, we automatically assign a granularity based on task processing time, as observed during development. Execution times are cross-referenced with a master timing table, which assigns a granularity to this "type" of task. The task reference is then stored inside the task manager's granularity table, which is updated when new tasks are performed. By performing runtime analysis of task execution length, we can group or link related tasks together.

Task Management

Once created, new tasks are placed in the *task pool* data structure for distribution to the task management/routing system. Depending on the state of the tasks being executed, it may take a long time for tasks to make it from the task pool onto the appropriate number of PEs. It is important to consider this when designing your tasks, assigning granularity, and constructing distribution algorithms.

Distributing tasks among PEs depends upon two factors:

- How many processor elements are available
- The types of tasks that are suitable for distributed processing

Continuing our earlier example, lets look at the factors that will determine how our attack task will be distributed. In a system that contains just two processors, one processor should be delegated as the ancillary processor, which deals with tasks of large or medium complexity. The other processor should service small tasks, or tasks that require immediate execution. This processor will also serve as the processor that runs the main game executable.

Updating the entire influence map or generating pathing routes for an entire squad of units (which would also include dealing with potential troop formations) should be routed off to the secondary processor for execution. With something as crucial as pathfinding for a squad of units, why do we want the task offloaded to another processor for execution? Shouldn't we want the AI to immediately generate a series of paths for us? Most certainly; but this individual task is only one task in a handful of tasks that are going to be required, for a complete plan of action.

Not all your AI tasks should or will be distributed. Some instances will require immediate execution on the local PE, which the PVM architecture accounts for. For example, if our game is executing on a dual-processor system, PVM will handle the task normally, assigning it a higher priority, such that the task manager immediately schedules it for local execution. For example, if we have a lone soldier that just came under attack from an enemy, and it is unable to defend itself, the soldier should flee from the attacker. Finding a quick and dirty location to escape to takes precedence over a unit's potential long-term goals. This fight-or-flight response is purely reactionary, and this type of task should be scheduled for immediate execution. Once the danger has been avoided, the unit can then again begin to make long-term goals that are more amiable to an ancillary processor.

Dependencies

Task dependency is a potential byproduct of a task that is reliant upon a previously executed task's output. Still using our previous RTS example, the AI player needs to not only path to the opponent's city, but he also needs to be aware of any potential enemy movement surrounding the city. What is required is an enemy unit disposition analysis task, so that the most currently available influence map is used to assess and analyze the unit's strengths and movement history, as well as formulate the AI's response. One way to deal with this chain of dependencies (the simplest possible scheduling solution, in fact) is to ignore it. In this scenario, the accuracy of your AI depends on the (arbitrary) ordering of update tasks for your influence map and analysis algorithms.

Arbitrary scheduling, while simple, is inefficient and prone to errors. In a performance-critical application such as games, one must consider the myriad of possible relationships between tasks and schedule accordingly. Should we schedule tasks several frames in advance, with a reservation policy? This ensures that important tasks get completed on time and reserves bank PEs for work on tasks that are essential but large. If we reserve, should tasks be interrupted? Task interruption is discussed later.

Grouping

A simple approach is to group like tasks into execution packets when they are small enough to be lumped together on a single PE. This grouping eliminates the extraneous overhead of task setup, bandwidth wastage, and in general allows for the more efficient use of processor resources. In addition, when several similar tasks are executed on the same PE, the data required to process the tasks remains local to that PE.

This *data locality* saves us memory reads and communication overhead. See Figure 3.6.3 for an example in which similar tasks are grouped together.

The dynamic grouping of tasks requires a management class, which evaluates and groups tasks by type. This class sits between the task pool and the general task manager and serves as selection mechanism and a pump into the general task manager.

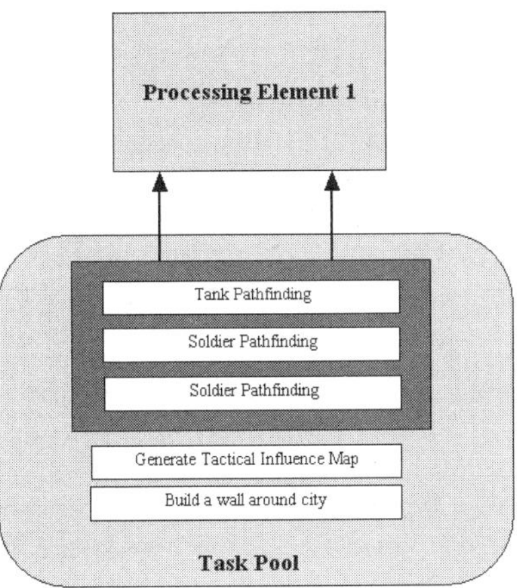

FIGURE 3.6.3 *Grouping of similar tasks before they are scheduled for distributed processing. Here, three similar pathing commands are grouped for efficiency.*

To facilitate execution, we can adjust the granularity of an operation and spread it out among available PEs. While this has benefits, some tasks (regenerating an influence map, spatial calculations for unit dispositions, and potential terrain analysis), when refactored, can lead to increased interprocess communication. In general, tasks that rely upon data that has been previously calculated and placed into shared memory will encourage the increase of interprocess communication.

Shared memory is one of the most familiar mechanisms for interprocess communication (IPC), allowing a series of processor elements access to the same memory pool. When one processor element changes the shared memory pool, the memory pool changes for all the processor elements. Within Microsoft Windows or Linux, you will have to provide your own synchronization mechanisms for accessing shared memory, using semaphores.

Linking

An ancillary variation to grouping, linking is useful when larger tasks are dependent upon smaller tasks for initialization input. Inside the task ID, an unsigned integer is reserved for linking to another task packet. The task scheduler takes note of this, and before the ancillary packet is routed to a PE, the linked packet is scheduled for execution. Linked packets should be used with care, as they are extremely susceptible to race conditions and deadlock issues that can also lead to thread leakage (discussed later).

While implementing a task scheduler is fairly straightforward, individual task selection mechanisms are highly game-specific. One key component is data processing. If the PEs are being starved (waiting for data), the AI routines that supply tasks to the pool need to take this into consideration. When starvation is observed, it is important to rework the AI routines and scheduling logic so that it is more anticipatory of potential processing holdups.

Caching or Processor Affinity

Caching or processor affinity encourages similar tasks to be executed on processors that have executed identical or similar tasks, an important consideration when offloading tasks to PEs. To accommodate this processor affinity, the task manager should contain a basic history tracking system. The basic history tracking contains a list of differing tasks and the most recent processor element that executed it.

Interruption

Once a task is routed off to a processor element for execution, it is critical that the task proceed uninterrupted. We allow any offloaded task to be completed before another task is routed to that processor element. This eliminates an entirely cumbersome mechanism of stalling processes, storing the entire state of a processor element, just because a higher priority task was entered into the task manager. If you find that a task needs to be interrupted, the task is most likely too large and needs to be broken down into smaller tasks.

A typical example from an RTS game is the generation of an influence map. A unit attacking a group of enemy tanks may not necessarily need the *entire* influence map regenerated, which can potentially become a bottleneck during normal gameplay due to the size of most influence maps. Instead, the creation of a *tactical influence map* can be used. A tactical influence map is just a smaller influence map that is focused on a particular region of interest. This allows all the normal operations of the larger influence map to occur, just on a finer scale. You don't have to limit the scope of your tasks; designing a smaller data set to work with will alleviate the possible task interruptions.

Load Balancing

When creating a task for execution, we must consider the actual size of the workload that a PE will be expected to process. If the workload is too small, the PE will be starved for data, spending more time preparing and communicating then actually processing tasks. If the task is large and takes too long to execute, it may cause data dependency issues. Worse, it may delay the delivery of a crucial result to the game, such that a gap in the decision-making process becomes evident.

To maximize the PVM architecture, it is critical that threads are kept busy. Tasks can finish out of sequence, but you want to avoid any condition where one processor element is serving as direct input into another. Dependencies can cause stalls and can turn our parallel AI system into a sequential AI system if left to proliferate unchecked.

An example of a series of tasks that could have been designed to be dependent is presented in our previous RTS example. As discussed in the dependencies section of this article, we have a series of tasks that constitute the AI's plan. These tasks are updating our influence map, assessing unit positions, analyzing the units strengths, and tracking movement history. There are definitely more tasks that could be created for a real-life RTS. If all four of these tasks are grouped as a single larger task and routed for execution, the influence map task would have to complete before the unit assessment task could start. This would then have the undesirable side-effect of a PE waiting for completion of another task before it starts its execution. This delay would have a negative impact on the other waiting tasks inside the task manager. The queued unassociated tasks would just sit there and wait, while the previous tasks stall the entire pipeline.

Threading Pools

The majority of your tasks will be managed by the task manager, which will create threads to facilitate the execution of the various PEs. A thread pool allows the runtime creation of a bank of threads, which the task manager can access for process element execution. This shifts the cost of continuous thread and stack creation to a one-time operation executed at startup.

Thread pools are subject to all the same issues that a normal parallel process can be subject to, such as deadlock, synchronization issues, resource thrashing, and thread leakage [Gerber04].

An important aspect to using thread pools is the reliance upon the thread pool being the proper size. By carefully tuning the number of threads available to game tasks, you will avoid the waste of system resources as well as reduce or eliminate thread thrashing by allowing excess thread requests to be queued.

PVM Implementation

It takes work to design and implement a parallel-friendly game. Fundamental assumptions (and often your previous experiences with AI implementation) must be re-evaluated.

Modularizing your design will facilitate the transition from serial to parallel. Create a bank of common game libraries to which all components (PEs or the main game executable) have access. The goal is to construct a modular framework in which all PEs (including the game executable) can share common code without requiring special one-off implementations.

Wrappers also facilitate the modularity of your implementation, distancing your code from any PVM-specific calls. While PVM supports the basic pack and unpacking mechanisms of strings, integers, and the like, you will have to write some of your own. These game-specific data-packing routines will increase modularity, allowing you to create data classes that can be automatically archived and unarchived by your wrapper without any direct dependencies upon the PVM system. They will also help keep the same game processes going without interruption, if the game is executed on a single processor system.

The example design includes a base class for fundamental behaviors, alongside parallel implementations. This allows the game to target single processor *or* PVM-friendly machines; see Figure 3.6.4.

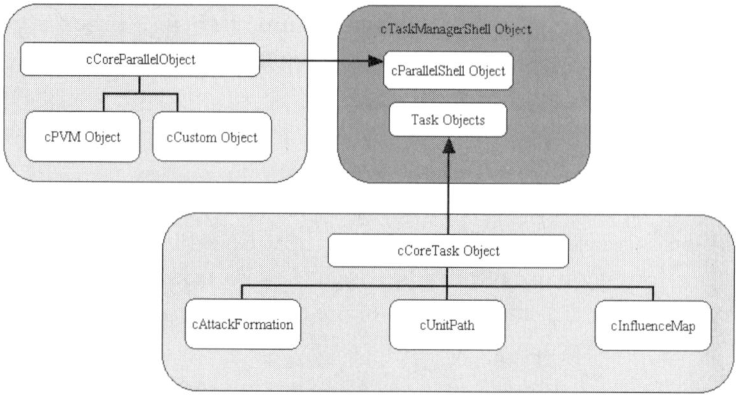

FIGURE 3.6.4 *Class diagram of a sample parallel AI. The task manager shell (*`cTaskManagerShell`*) resides inside the games AI workspace. The task manager shell holds both the parallel shell object (*`cParallelShell`*) and the core task object (*`cCoreTask`*). Both of these classes are created via simple factory methods.*

PVM has a rudimentary resource manager that will handle the placement of tasks. This simple resource manager should be used only as a simple routing mechanism to the available processors. Complex, game-specific resource management should occur within your task manager/router implementation. This will allow you to identify which processor elements have recently executed an identical or similar task, which in turn will aid in using previously cached data evaluations. Data evaluations are usually stored in shared memory to speed up processing.

PVM uses the user datagram protocol (UDP) for interprocess communication. To customize, consider adding a fault tolerance system. The addition of fault tolerance allows the game to continue executing, even if communication is lost with a PE processing a task. With a basic system in place, the task manager/router would verify if a task terminated prematurely or never failed to terminate. When this condition occurs, the current task is terminated and it is resent. The small amount of overhead required to verify a task's current state is far less than the cost of preparing an entirely new task.

Application: RTS

Now that we have all the components of our PVM, what's going to turn our normally productive AI into an AI that looks like its thinking ahead, behaving more realistically, and anticipating the player's actions? Let's look at a prototypical real-time strategy (RTS) example.

We have two belligerents facing off on a secluded island. The island is just one of many landmasses in our game world. In a typical sequential AI, level heuristics would determine if the units should attack (and if they could survive the attack), if the units need support, and where that support will come from.

In a PVM-based implementation, the AI can reason about the situation in the background, precomputing potential game situations and choosing among them when action is required. With the right prognostic actions in place, the AI can reason about the current situation and react to future player strategies and tactics more effectively.

Specifically, the AI can ask the following:

- Can I afford to lose this island?
- What will the effect be if I lose the island immediately?
- Will I be able to reclaim the island if I lose it now?
- If I want to take the island back, where can I recruit an army?
- How quickly can an army get to the island?
- Will there be political/diplomatic fallout among my allies?
- What would that look like?

Instead of performing a few serial evaluations, the AI can now "think on its feet," pursuing multiple threads of reasoning at once. As the situation changes, certain threads will bear fruit while others die, but on the whole, the AI will be much more prepared.

The real work (as with all AI programming) is in translating relatively vague strategic queries into concrete computational actions. The question, "Can I afford to lose this island?" is actually an evaluation of the AI's current military and unit power, land holdings, and diplomatic standings as they compare to the opponent's perceived rankings.

Simple in and of themselves, such comparisons are powerful in aggregate. Coupled with a dozen other guiding analysis tasks, they create an AI that is constantly evaluating the most important overall scenario: the *what-if* scenario.

Enhanced Gameplay

Just because we have an AI that executes what-if scenarios in the background doesn't necessarily mean we want an AI that exhibits a more difficult game experience for the player, though this is a definite benefit of a properly developed PVM-based AI. Another benefit of this AI system is that we can develop more complex simulators for the players to interact with. Let's look at our prototypical RTS example again.

Diplomacy

In a typical RTS when a player instigates political negotiations with an AI, the AI normally replies with preformulated responses. These responses are most often based upon limited heuristic data, generated by the enemy empire's stats (military power, proximity of enemy units to the AIs cities or bases, etc.).

If the AI could evaluate potential player actions, it might create political situations that are more responsive to individual players and more representative of real-world situations. Using the techniques discussed in this article, an AI developer can write a series of evaluation tasks, which can be executed based upon currently occurring events.

Let's say a player enters into a diplomatic negotiation with an AI opponent. The player doesn't have any of his units near the AI's bases, but he has been progressively and consistently moving towards the AI's base from multiple countries. The AI can have a background task executing that evaluates enemy troop movement. By keeping track of troop movements, the AI is able to ascertain that the player might be trying to mass groups from various positions on the map, allowing for a potential assault on the AI's base.

This type of evaluator logic would most certainly play a role in diplomatic negotiations. The AI could suggest that the player reduce military power in one of the countries that potentially threatens a strategic base. This task may be a small part of the overall diplomatic picture, one small part of a more informed and responsive negotiation logic.

A PVM-based AI can also evaluate a player's tendencies to honor long-term agreements by executing background tasks. As in real-world negotiation, the AI would evaluate what the other party has done in the past, how it could effect the current situation, and how the current decision could impact future actions.

Production

Another fairly straightforward aspect of normal RTS development is the ability for an AI to manage unit production, food harvesting, research and development, and other economic activities. These all serve as ideal background tasks that can execute on other PEs, while the central control mechanisms reside in the main game executable.

In a typical RTS, a core game unit serves as the harvesting unit for particular resources. These resources are then transported to various buildings to produce different units or supplies. A PVM task could be written that would do a flow analysis on the buildings. This flow analysis involves making sure that each building has the proper resources available for production/manufacturing of a particular unit or resource. Each building may also have a direct or indirect consumer that relies upon their output.

Consider a baker that is reliant upon the flour mill for flour to produce his baked goods. A PVM flow task would make sure that the baker is constantly supplied with flour so he may make his bread goods available for the town. The task would evaluate the past, current, and future needs and inputs for the baker. If the flow task finds a part of the production system lacking, it could have the task manager/router start a task that deals with work scheduling. This new task could produce more harvesters that would allow the flour mill a higher output.

This system is not only available for the AI but also the player. Many RTSs have ministers or governors that run or control cities and bases. The same logic that drives the AI can also run the player's town, with only a marginal CPU hit. Any one of these tasks could be accomplished with current AI systems, but the capabilities of having these systems run in the background will free traditional resources for new tasks and allow for a more immersive and complete game experience.

Other Domains

In a traditional first-person shooter, players are generally happy that bots can pathfind their way to the players and engage them in combat, perhaps executing some prescripted behavior en route, in an attempt to add some illusionary realism to the bot.

With a parallel AI system, we can in the background continuously process things like:

- The bot's threat level relative to the player
- How threatening the player is to the other NPCs in the scene
- Which NPC potentially needs backup
- Potential flanking moves
- Appropriate use of cover or distractions

The potential decisions that a bot can make are endless. With this large number of potential actions running in parallel, repeat decisions are unlikely, allowing for a truly unique, potentially emergent, nonscripted experience for the players.

Conclusion

Building intelligent, reactive, and forward-looking AI is a challenging task. In this introduction to parallel AI development, we cover the fundamental principles required to implement a PVM-based AI. We have shown how the framework can distribute AI tasks, allowing for concurrent, complete, background evaluation. With this framework, AI developers can add more depth to their opponents and agents, increase an AI's strategic opportunism, and supply users with powerful management tools.

It is often said that AI developers focus on the *artificial* aspect of AI, attempting to create the *illusion* of intelligent behavior with smoke, mirrors, and window dressing. We believe that PVM is more than just window dressing and that parallel techniques will help developers realize the *intelligence* aspect of AI. While parallel implementations require a departure from standard techniques and tools, the rise of multiprocessors in desktops and consoles makes that effort all the more feasible and worthwhile.

The time is right for PVM!

References

[Geist94] Geist, A. *PVM.* MIT Press, 1996.

[Gerber04] Gerber, Richard. *Programming with Hyper-Threading Technology.* Intel Press, 2004.

[Hughes04] Hughes, Cameron. *Parallel and Distributed Programming Using C++.* Addison-Wesley, 2004.

[Ramsey03] Ramsey, Michael. "Setting up PVM for an AI System." Available online at *www.masterempire.com/OpenKimono.html.* November 10, 2003.

[Ramsey04] Ramsey, Michael. "PVM Gotchas!" Available online at *www.masterempire.com/OpenKimono.html.* March 15, 2004.

[Tozour01] Tozour, P. "Influence Mapping." In *Game Programming Gems 2.* Charles River Media, 2001.

[Woodcock02] Woodcock, S. "Recognizing Strategic Dispositions: Engaging the Enemy." In *AI Game Programming Wisdom.* Charles River Media, 2002.

3.7

Beyond A*

Mario Grimani, Xtreme Strategy Games

mgrimani@xtremestrategy.com

Matthew Titelbaum, Monolith Productions

matt@lith.com

Most games use some form of artificial intelligence (AI), and pathfinding is usually an integral part of it. The A* algorithm is a well-known approach for solving general-purpose pathfinding problems [Stout00]. A* is a greedy algorithm [Cormen01] that combines keeping track of the cost from start, used by Dijkstra's algorithm, with the heuristic estimate of the remaining cost to target. It is the fastest known solution for finding minimal cost paths, and it works well for basic pathfinding problems.

As good as it is, A* has its limitations. For one, the algorithm performance decreases drastically as the search space grows and the demands on CPU and memory resources increase, making it impractical for problems with a large search space. To make matters worse, queries from high-level AI modules can generate numerous calls to the A* algorithm, putting even more demand on CPU resources. Because of these limitations, some games have opted for less-optimal solutions while others have used less query-intensive high-level AI.

Although there are solutions for dealing with large search space [Botea04] and other search space problems [Stout96], very little work has been done on integration of pathfinding with the rest of AI with the goal of reducing query cost. A cost reduction would allow for an increased number of queries, generating more knowledge for high-level AI. This additional knowledge would improve both tactical and strategic decision-making in many genres of games.

Defining the Problem

We begin by formally defining the problem domain as a connectivity graph with nodes representing locations and cost-bearing edges representing the cost of movement between those locations.

The A* algorithm executing in this domain would require the following parameters: start node, target node, heuristic estimate function, and agent movement criteria. The *start node* and *target node* are the nodes we are trying to connect by the minimal cost path, with the graph traversal beginning at the start node and completing when the target node is reached. As we already mentioned, the *heuristic estimate function* is a distinguishing characteristic of the A* algorithm and it represents a heuristic estimate of the remaining cost to target.

The last parameter, *agent movement criteria*, is not necessarily part of every A* analysis but it happens to be part of almost every A* implementation. It represents the ability of an agent to move across nodes and consequently the ability of nodes to obstruct agent movement. Because this ability needs to be taken into account during the graph traversal, the traversal logic needs to ignore movement-obstructing nodes.

For the purpose of this gem, we define a *query* as an inquiry or a request for information initiated by high-level AI, an answer to which is dynamically generated by underlying code. This definition is not to be confused with the usual definition of a query as a formal request to a database or search engine. Of course, the information we are requesting could be precalculated and stored in a database or cached, but those concepts are outside the scope of this gem, which is to demonstrate how to generate the information on demand.

High-level AI usually operates on and issues queries for more than one domain. In this gem, we will focus on queries that operate on the connectivity graph domain we just defined. Furthermore, we will restrict queries to the class of queries that involve pathfinding. A typical query in this class calls underlying code, which makes successive calls to the pathfinding algorithm while changing one or more parameters. Each iteration creates a unique set of parameters, which when passed to A*, produces one optimal result. After gathering all the results and selecting an optimal one, the underlying code chooses the parameter set that produced it and returns the parameter set along with the result.

A good example of one such query is a request to choose among exit locations around a building an exit location that produces the minimal cost path to a given destination location. In this case, the underlying code would make one call to A* for every exit location and return the exit location that yields the minimal cost path along with the path. As we have already discussed, making many successive calls to the A* algorithm quickly becomes a source of performance slowdown, leaving us with the need for a more efficient solution to this problem.

The Algorithm

Knowing the problem and problem domain, we are ready to start working on the solution. We plan to use the existing A* algorithm as a starting point and derive an algorithm that is more suitable for high-level AI queries we have just described. As the first step, for reference purposes, we present the A* algorithm in pseudocode form:

```
List OpenList, ClosedList

AStarPathfinder(Node               StartNode,
                Node               TargetNode,
                MovementCriteria MovementCriteria,
                Path               PathFound)
{
    Node StartNode, BestNode, SuccessorNode
    Cost NewCost

    reset OpenList and ClosedList

    if (StartNode fails MovementCriteria) return as failure
    set StartNode cost to 0
    set StartNode estimate to heuristic estimate of remaining cost
      to TargetNode
    set StartNode value to sum of cost and estimate
    set StartNode parent to NoParent
    add StartNode to OpenList

    while OpenList is not empty
    {
        remove best node BestNode from OpenList
        if BestNode is TargetNode
        {
            construct path and save it in PathFound
            return as success
        }
        for each successor SuccessorNode of BestNode
        {
            if (SuccessorNode fails MovementCriteria) continue
            set NewCost to sum of BestNode cost and cost of
              moving from BestNode to SuccessorNode
            if ((SuccessorNode is in OpenList or ClosedList) and
                (NewCost is not less than SuccessorNode cost))
                continue
            set SuccessorNode cost to NewCost
            set SuccessorNode estimate to heuristic estimate of
              remaining cost to TargetNode
            set SuccessorNode value to sum of cost and estimate
            set SuccessorNode parent to BestNode
            if SuccessorNode is in ClosedList
                remove SuccessorNode from ClosedList
            if SuccessorNode is not in OpenList
                add SuccessorNode to OpenList
        }
        add BestNode to ClosedList
    }
    return as failure
}
```

The pseudocode uses only a handful of data types. `List` is a generic data type that represents a collection of nodes and can be implemented in many different ways, as we will see later in the gem. `Node` is a data structure that contains information relevant to a single node. The node data structure includes a cost of reaching the node, a heuristic estimate of the remaining cost to target, a heuristic value equal to the sum of the cost and the heuristic estimate, and a link to parent node. `MovementCriteria` is an aggregate data structure that represents a set of variables that define an ability of an agent to move across nodes. `Cost` is an actual cost of reaching a node from the start node. In a typical implementation, the cost is represented as a floating-point number. `Path` is a data type that contains path data.

We can now set about improving the algorithm's performance. A sensible approach to finding the solution would be to bundle all instances of parameters we are planning to use and pass them to the pathfinding algorithm in one call. With this extra information, the algorithm ought to be able to execute the combined requests more efficiently.

By looking at the A* algorithm pseudocode, we can see that the most significant savings can be achieved by reducing the number of graph traversals needed to produce a solution. The parameters used inside the traversal loop are part of the logic that decides on how the traversal unravels. They cannot change during the execution of the loop without breaking the algorithm. Passing in more than one value for such parameters has no benefit since only one value can be used at a time. In fact, of all parameters passed to the algorithm, only the start node is unused by the traversal logic, making it a sole candidate for this optimization.

Improvements

How can we use these findings to modify the A* algorithm so that it accepts multiple start nodes and chooses between them as part of the single search space traversal? It turns out that the solution to this problem is rather simple. We can see from the original A* pseudocode that there is nothing in the logic of the algorithm to prevent us from using more than one start node. Instead of passing in a single start node, we pass in all of them and handle each one of them the way we would handle a single node. This means that during the initialization step, every start node becomes an open node and is added to the open list. The open list, which provides the ordering of currently open nodes by design, will assist us in the selection of a start node by returning the best one as part of the final path.

Naturally, we would like to know whether something similar is possible on the other end of the resultant path. Is there is a way to choose between multiple ending locations? If we look closely at the original pseudocode, we can see that the target node has a dual purpose. One is to provide information for the calculation performed by the cost estimate function and steer the traversal of the search space towards the target node. The other one is to act as a stopping point for the traversal. Could we split the target node functionality and relieve the target node from being the stopping point?

It turns out that is possible. We could have multiple stop nodes, which in order to be effective, need to be nodes that are encountered en route to the target node. The stop nodes, very much like the target node, can be used only after they have been removed from the open list and not before. After taking all the changes in consideration, we are ready to present a derived pathfinding algorithm in pseudocode form:

```
List OpenList, ClosedList

BeyondAStarPathfinder(List             StartList,
                      List             StopList,
                      Node             TargetNode,
                      MovementCriteria MovementCriteria,
                      Path             PathFound)
{
    Node StartNode, BestNode, SuccessorNode
    Cost NewCost

    reset OpenList and ClosedList

    for each StartNode in StartList
    {
        if (StartNode fails MovementCriteria) continue
        set StartNode cost to 0
        set StartNode estimate to heuristic estimate of remaining
          cost to TargetNode
        set StartNode value to sum of cost and estimate
        set StartNode parent to NoParent
        add StartNode to OpenList
    }
    while OpenList is not empty
    {
        remove best node BestNode from OpenList
        if BestNode is in StopList
        {
            construct path and save it in PathFound
            return as success
        }
        for each successor SuccessorNode of BestNode
        {
            if (SuccessorNode fails MovementCriteria) continue
            set NewCost to sum of BestNode cost and cost of
              moving from BestNode to SuccessorNode
            if ((SuccessorNode is in OpenList or ClosedList) and
                (NewCost is not less than SuccessorNode cost))
                continue
            set SuccessorNode cost to NewCost
            set SuccessorNode estimate to heuristic estimate of
              remaining cost to TargetNode
            set SuccessorNode value to sum of cost and estimate
            set SuccessorNode parent to BestNode
            if SuccessorNode is in ClosedList
                remove SuccessorNode from ClosedList
            if SuccessorNode is not in OpenList
                add SuccessorNode to OpenList
```

```
            }
            add BestNode to ClosedList
        }
        return as failure
    }
```

When compared to the A* algorithm, the derived algorithm has a few major differences: its parameter list accepts multiple start and stop nodes, multiple start nodes all become open nodes, and any stop node can stop the algorithm traversal.

How can we know that the derived algorithm is guaranteed to produce minimal cost paths? Although proving this is beyond the scope of the gem, we will give a few pointers on the subject. First, we need to define any algorithm guaranteed to find an optimal path to the goal as *admissible.* Next, we need to look at the admissibility of the A* algorithm [Nilsson98] and use that as a starting point. The key to our proof would be introducing an extra node that connects to all start nodes. This new node acts as a single start node and essentially changes our derived algorithm into the standard A* algorithm.

Details of Implementation

A typical implementation of the derived algorithm is not drastically different from a typical A* implementation. Since the nuances of A* implementation are well known [Pinter01], we will focus on how to implement features unique to the derived algorithm.

The derived algorithm passes in multiple start and stop nodes. As we would expect, passing multiple start and stop nodes as parameters increases the amount of data involved and adds extra overhead to the performance. To reduce this overhead, we store the multiple node data in arrays, which themselves are passed by reference. Many practical implementations dealing with similar problems, in addition, store the node data separately and use the arrays to store references, handles, or object Ids for accessing the actual node data.

The derived algorithm also uses multiple stop nodes to halt execution of the algorithm. It is advisable that stop nodes are explicitly tagged as such. The tags should be stored in some sort of node data structure, which also contains all other node runtime data (cost values and a link to parent node). By tagging nodes, we no longer need to compare each traversed node with the entire list of stop nodes. Instead, the node tag can be checked immediately. When traversing m nodes looking for one of n stop nodes, an implementation with untagged stop nodes would require $m \times n$ comparisons. Using tagged nodes cuts the number of comparisons to m, one for every traversed node.

Practical Examples

Put into practice, the derived algorithm allows for some advanced functionality. Let's consider a typical RTS game with game objects that may garrison units and assign rally points to which the garrisoned units should move upon exit. For the purpose of this gem, we will refer to these game objects as *containing game objects*. In the actual game, containing game objects are usually implemented as buildings or a variation of transport vehicles.

Examples with Multiple Start Nodes

One of the common problems related to garrisoning is how to choose where, among all the exit locations around the containing game object, to place the exiting unit. The simplest and the fastest approach would be to use a predefined order of exit locations and choose the first unobstructed location. Since this approach does not take into consideration the location of the rally point, more frequently than not the exiting unit is forced to move around the object it exited before heading towards the rally point.

In an attempt to avoid this problem, we might choose the exit location with the shortest straight-line distance to the rally point. Although this is clearly a better approach, it still has its problems. For one, it does not take into account any obstructions that might lie between the exit locations and the rally point. As a result, there is no guarantee that the chosen exit location is the optimal exit location that is a starting point of the minimal cost path leading to the rally point. Worse still, sometimes the obstructions cut off the chosen exit location from the rally point, stalling the exiting unit and thoroughly diminishing the unit's usefulness to the player.

One way to account for the obstructions is to find minimal cost paths between every exit location and the rally point and choose the exit location that yields the path with the lowest overall cost. Unfortunately, with the exception of situations with very few exit locations, the performance cost of this implementation is prohibitive.

This problem can be avoided if, instead of making many successive calls to the A* algorithm, we make a single call to our derived algorithm. Possible exit locations will provide us with multiple start nodes, and the rally point will provide us with a target node, which will act as a stop node as well. By using these parameters, the derived algorithm will find an optimal exit location and an associated minimal cost path to the rally point in one search space traversal.

Figure 3.7.1 shows an example with a building as a containing object, a dozen or more exit locations, a rally point obstructed by a wall-like structure, and an optimal exit location as a starting point of a minimal cost path leading to the rally point. The example also demonstrates how an exit location that has the shortest straight-line distance to the target, which in this case is the location in the lower-right corner of the building, is not necessarily an optimal exit location.

There are other practical uses for the pathfinding algorithm with multiple start nodes. One of them is determining, among several possible buildings, which one would be the best choice to produce units needed at a given target location, such as a hotly contested area. The chosen building would be the one that can produce units capable of getting to the battlefield the quickest. A call to the derived algorithm can

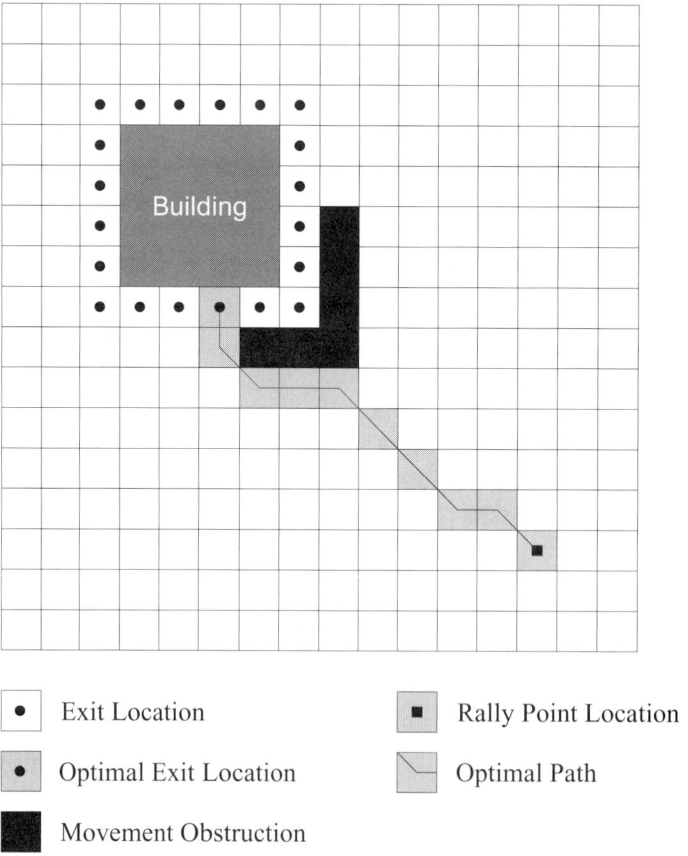

FIGURE 3.7.1 *An example of using multiple start nodes to find an optimal exit location.*

provide a quick answer to this request. The exit locations of all the buildings will provide us with multiple start nodes, and the target location will provide us with a target node. With these parameters, the derived algorithm will have no problems finding a minimal cost path to the target location, which will also give us an optimal exit location and the building associated with that location.

Figure 3.7.2 shows an example with the buildings A, B, and C as candidates for production of units needed at the target location. Building B happens to have an optimal exit location that is a starting point for the path with the minimal cost. It is important to notice that building A has the exit locations that have a shorter straight-line distance to the target location, but because of the wall-like obstruction to the right of the building, those exit locations are nonoptimal.

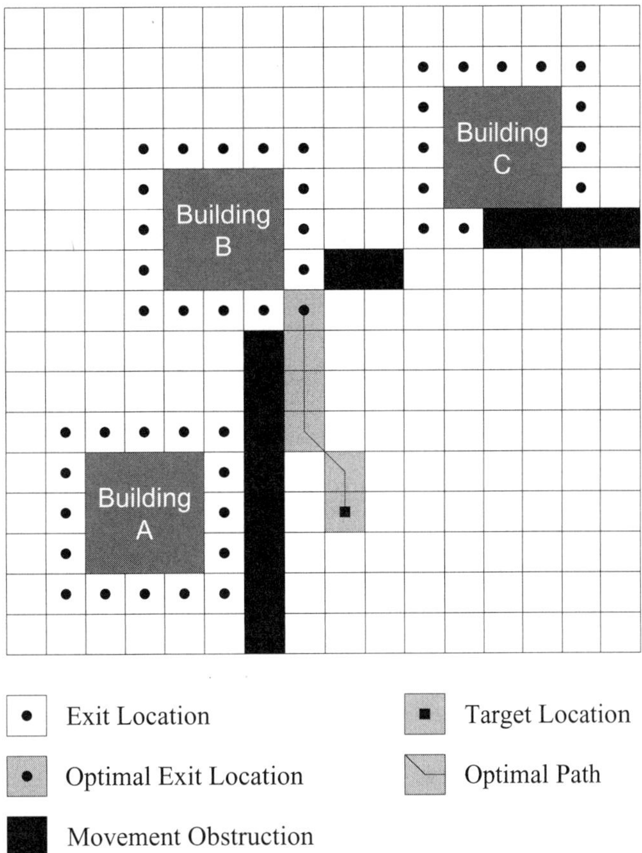

FIGURE 3.7.2 *An example of using multiple start nodes to find the best building to produce units.*

Examples with Multiple Stop Nodes

Now let's change things around and assume that there is a unit ordered to garrison in a given containing game object. Our task is to choose the entry location, among all the entry locations around the containing game object, from which the unit will enter the object. Choosing the entry location with the shortest straight-line distance to the unit is a possibility, but this approach is plagued with the same obstruction problems that we encountered when we were dealing with exiting units moving towards a rally point. Another possibility, not available when we were dealing with exiting units, is to ignore the containing game object as an obstruction during this pathfinding traversal and make the unit just enter when it collides with the object. Unfortunately, this approach works only for containing game objects of convex shape. In any other case, we may not be able to find an optimal solution.

A better and more general solution is to consider paths between the unit and every entry location. As we have done with exiting units we need to forgo making successive calls to the A* algorithm and make a single call to our derived algorithm. The unit's location will provide us with a start node, and possible entry locations will provide us with multiple stop nodes. To make sure the algorithm converges on the containing game object, we will need a target node inside the containing game object, preferably close to the center location of the object. Passing these parameters to the derived algorithm will give us a minimal cost path leading to the optimal entry location.

Figure 3.7.3 shows an example with a building as a containing object, a dozen or more entry locations, an initial location of the unit looking to garrison, and a mini-

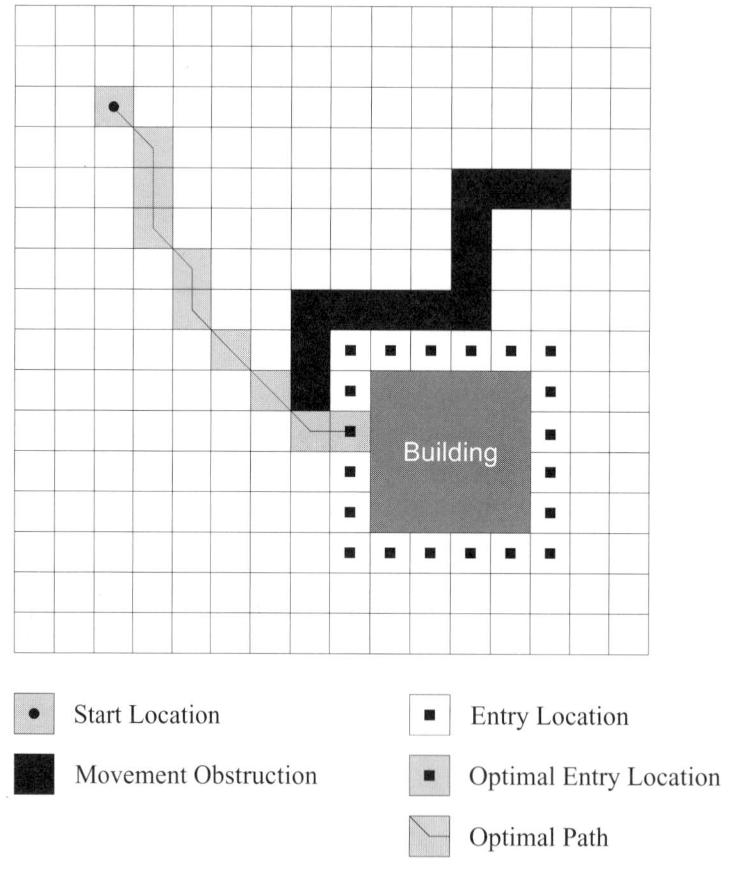

FIGURE 3.7.3 *An example of using multiple stop nodes to find an optimal entry location.*

mal cost path ending in optimal entry location. Similar to the example in Figure 3.7.1, this example also demonstrates how an entry location that has the shortest straight-line distance to the unit's location—in this case, the location in the upper-left corner of the building—is not necessarily an optimal entry location.

Examples with Both Multiple Start and Stop Nodes

Now that we have seen how multiple start nodes and multiple stop nodes work on their own, it is time to examine how they work together. Consider a situation when there is a unit garrisoned inside a containing game object. The unit is ordered to exit the containing game object and immediately enter another. It is our task to find a minimal cost path between the two objects while taking into consideration potential obstructions.

Using what we have learned from the previous examples, it is obvious that the exit locations around the first object will provide us with multiple start nodes, and the entry locations around the second object with provide us with stop nodes. In addition, a target node needs to be placed inside the second object, close to the object's center point. Using these parameters, the derived algorithm can determine where the unit exits the first game object, where it enters the second game object, and the path it should follow in the process. The algorithm guarantees that the path found is a minimal cost path.

The situation presented is not necessarily an unusual situation, and we can find it in many games. For example, we could have a unit producing building that automatically sends units into a defensive structure that allows garrisoning, such as a bunker or a tower. To set this up, a player could set a rally point from the unit producing building to the defensive structure.

Figure 3.7.4 shows an example of two buildings, A and B, and a minimal cost path connecting them. As with previous examples, there are wall-like structures obstructing the direct path between the buildings, demonstrating that the straight-line approach does not work.

The techniques we have presented so far also prove very useful when applied to a search space represented by a waypoint graph [Tozour03]. In such a system, points in continuous 2D or 3D space, known as waypoints, define nodes of the graph. The placement of waypoints is usually rather sparse, due to the nature of the world and the graph data used to represent it.

When trying to find a path in this search space, the main problem is pathing object's current location, which can be quite far from the graph. Because of this, choosing proper start and stop nodes becomes a bit of a challenge. If we use the node with the shortest straight-line distance to the pathing object as the start node, the unusual results might happen. The movement of the object onto the start node can render the actual path to be suboptimal, which would manifest itself as an object moving away from the target location before moving towards it. Figure 3.7.5a shows an example of a situation where this kind of movement happens.

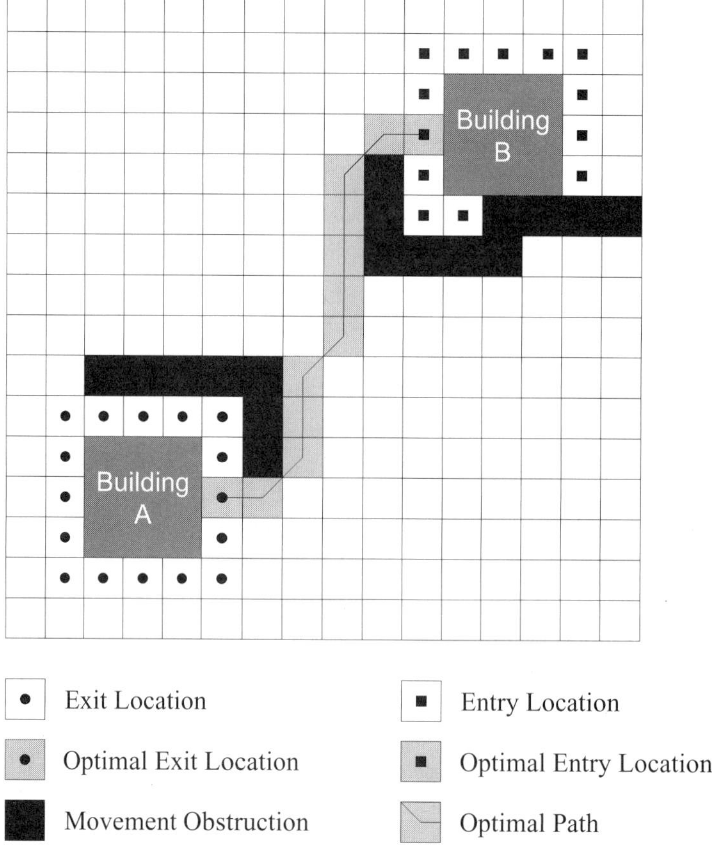

FIGURE 3.7.4 *An example of using multiple start nodes and multiple stop nodes to find a minimal cost path between two buildings.*

We could attempt to find a solution to this problem by searching for the nearest point on the nearest edge of the graph to the pathing object, but the performance cost associated with this search is prohibitive. These issues are present on both ends of the desired path. Using our derived algorithm with multiple start and stop nodes solves this problem rather nicely by allowing the submission of several good candidate start and stop nodes. The algorithm accepts the candidate nodes and, as part of the pathfinding process, it figures out which should be the actual start and stop nodes of the resultant path. Figure 3.7.5b shows the same situation as Figure 3.7.5a, but this time we are using our derived algorithm, so the awkward movement is gone.

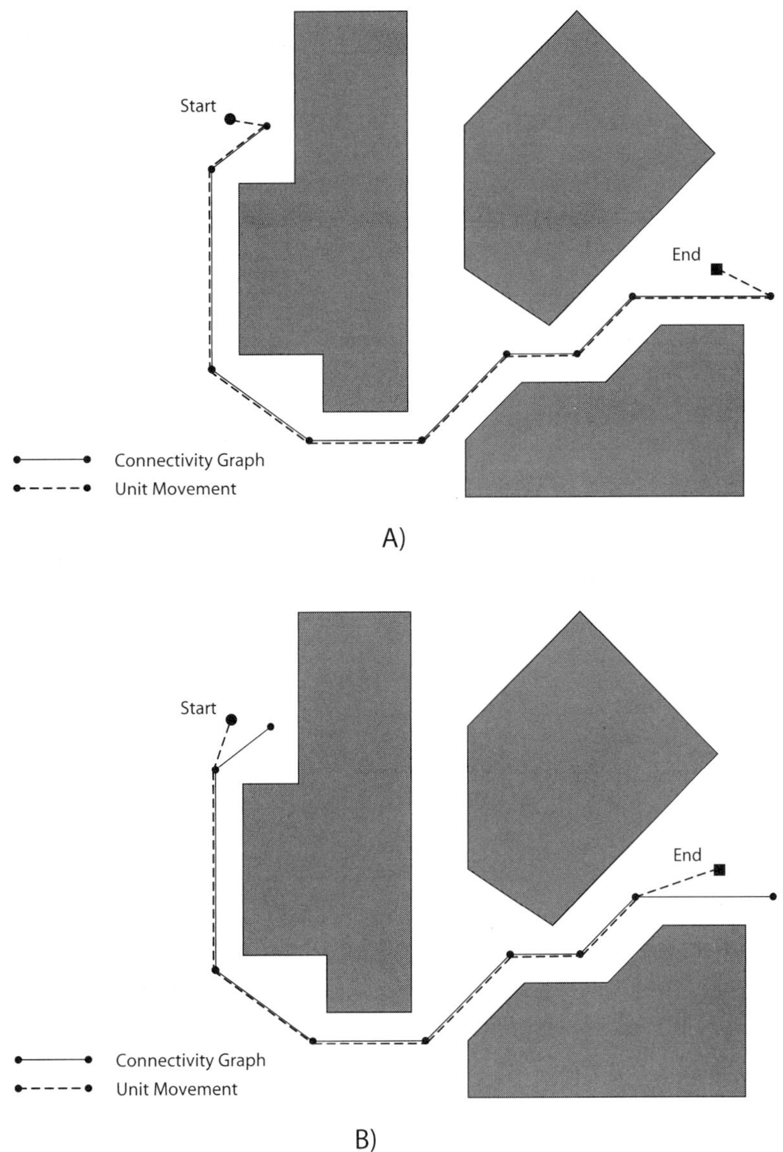

FIGURE 3.7.5 *(a) An example of a unit using a waypoint graph (b) and how our derived algorithm can improve a unit's selection of start and stop nodes.*

Performance Considerations

To make a fair overall comparison, we will contrast the performance of a single iteration of the derived algorithm with the performance of multiple iterations of the original A* algorithm. This functionality is typical of high-level AI queries. For querying purposes, this derivative A* traversal takes the place of multiple calls to the original A* algorithm and is comparable in functionality to multiple iterations of the original A* algorithm. Unlike the original A* algorithm, though, since multiple inputs are used simultaneously and the nodes between start and stop nodes are traversed only once, the overall performance improvement can be an order of magnitude or larger.

Given a set of start nodes l, a set of stop nodes m, and the set of nodes that need to be examined between l and m, n, one can really begin to see the real difference that this derived algorithm makes. Using multiple consecutive iterations using the original A* algorithm, a query will require $l \times m \times n$ individual nodes to be examined to find the solution to what the shortest path is between l and m. Each node in n will be examined roughly $l \times m$ times, one for each permutation of start and stop nodes. Using the derived algorithm, though, since it aggregates the inputs, will require only n individual nodes to be examined to find the same solution.

To drive this point home, we can look at the performance improvements for some of the examples we have presented earlier. For the example in Figure 3.7.1, the derived algorithm yields a 20-fold performance increase; for the example in the Figure 3.7.2, the performance increase is 45-fold; and for the example in the Figure 3.7.4, it is an impressive 208-fold increase.

Advanced Issues

The following sections address some advanced issues.

Multiple Start Nodes with Heuristics

As we can see from the algorithm pseudocode, as part of the initialization step, all start nodes become open nodes and are added to the open list. Since every open node in the list has to have a cost and a heuristic estimate associated with it, start nodes get those values assigned to them as well. For all new open nodes, the cost value is set to zero and the heuristic estimate value is set to the estimated cost to target.

By using the same cost value for all start nodes, which in this case is a zero, we are assuming that all of them are of equal importance to the high-level AI. In the actual game, this is rarely true. The high-level AI not only looks at start nodes with different importance, but their importance varies depending on the situation. For example, in some cases the AI might be looking for nodes that are less vulnerable to attack, while in the others it might be looking for nodes closer to resources. In situations that are more complex, the AI might be even looking at the combination of several different traits.

To accommodate the AI needs, we should allow start nodes to have different initial cost values. This feature lets us attach heuristic values to the start nodes and rank them by importance. As it is case with all heuristic values, these values need to be picked carefully and with regard to the other costs the algorithm will use during the execution. Otherwise, the initial cost values might render the algorithm heuristics useless. We can implement this feature by attaching the initial cost values to every start node passed to the algorithm and using those values during the initialization.

Returning Multiple Solutions

So far, we have assumed that queries using the algorithm require a solution with a single stop node. That is why the algorithm, as presented, terminates when it reaches the first stop node. In practice, some queries might prefer to receive the results for all stop nodes and combine them with some other data before deciding which stop node to choose.

To accommodate this new requirement, we modify the current algorithm so when it reaches the first stop node, it stores the path to that first stop node and continues looking for the other stop nodes. When the next stop node is reached, the path to it is saved as well, and the algorithm continues until all stop nodes produce a result or the algorithm runs out of open nodes. Running out of open nodes would indicate that one or more stop nodes are unreachable. The result returned by this modified algorithm is an array of paths, one path per reachable stop node.

One potential pitfall worth pointing out is the danger of a severe performance hit. Our derived algorithm, very much like the original A* algorithm, now has a bad worst-case scenario. Because the algorithm is designed to keep traversing the search space until a path is found, the algorithm will traverse the entire search space if no stop can be found. By attempting to reach more than one stop node, the likeliness of the worst-case scenario happening increases significantly. This pitfall is substantial, and we should take it into account when deciding whether to use a version of the algorithm that returns multiple solutions.

Conclusion

The A* algorithm is an important part of many AI implementations and a proven solution for basic pathfinding needs. Unfortunately, queries from high-level AI modules can generate a large number of calls to the A* algorithm and have a negative impact on performance. One way of solving this problem is to design a pathfinding algorithm that performs the work of many calls to the A* algorithm in a single performance-efficient call. In this gem, we have presented one such algorithm.

The algorithm presented here is an A* derivative, which accepts multiple start and stop nodes. By taking advantage of this additional information, the algorithm manages to find a query solution in a single search space traversal. This efficiency is reflected in performance improvements that can be as large as a couple of orders of magnitude. The presented algorithm has many practical applications, some of which were discussed in this gem. The material presented is a good reference and a starting point for writing further derivative A* algorithms that can be used by high-level AI.

References

[Botea04] Botea, A., M. Müller, and J. Schaeffer. "Near Optimal Hierarchical Path-Finding." In the *Journal of Game Development.* March, 2004.

[Cormen01] Cormen, Thomas H., et al. *Introduction to Algorithms, Second Edition,* 370–404. MIT Press, 2001.

[Nilsson98] Nilsson, Nils J. *Artificial Intelligence: A New Synthesis,* 145–150. Morgan Kaufmann Publishers, Inc., 1998.

[Pinter01] Pinter, Marco. "Toward More Realistic Pathfinding." In *Gamasutra.* Available online at *www.gamasutra.com/features/20010314/pinter_01.htm.* March 14, 2001.

[Stout00] Stout, Bryan. "The Basics of A* for Path Planning." In *Game Programming Gems,* 254–263. Charles River Media, 2000.

[Stout96] Stout, Bryan. "Smart Moves: Intelligent Pathfinding." In *Game Developer Magazine.* October 1996. Available online at *www.gamasutra.com/features/19970801/pathfinding.htm.*

[Tozour03] Tozour, Paul. "Search Space Representation." In *AI Game Programming Wisdom 2,* 85–102. Charles River Media, 2003.

3.8

Advanced Pathfinding with Minimal Replanning Cost: Dynamic A Star (D*)

Marco Tombesi

baggior@libero.it

Pathfinding is one of the most famous theoretical problems in game development. There is vast documentation in literature covering many aspects of the problem. This is because pathfinding issues are present not only in computer science but also in robotics, mining, and automation technology.

In games, our maps approximate reality. In most cases, maps are graphs that represent the environment using a regular grid, where each node matches a point in the map with a particular scale or resolution (see Figure 3.8.1).

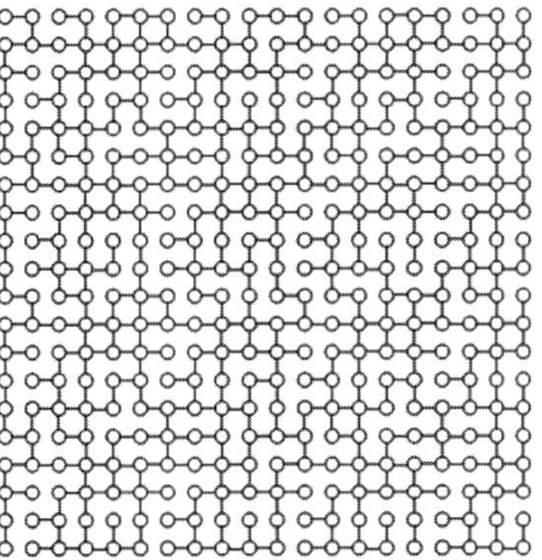

FIGURE 3.8.1 *A regular grid graph representing a map with a one foot resolution.*

Given a start point and a goal point in the map, how do we find the shortest path between them? The most common algorithm used to solve this problem is A*, whose performance is far better than Dijkstra, or any other SSSP (Single Source Shortest

Path) algorithm [Stout96]. While A* works very well in static environments, it is inefficient on dynamic maps, where any map modification requires replanning.

Because there is a high probability that a given change affects only a small portion of the already computed path, it is a waste of time to recompute the entire path. A dynamic version of A* (known as D*) helps solve this problem.

The D*Algorithm

As stated previously, we have to use a graph that represents a real map. If two points in the map are connected, there is an edge from the two nodes representing them in the graph. Generally (but this is not mandatory) every edge has associated a cost that represents the price we have to pay for passing over it.

In Figure 3.8.2, we assume that if the cost associated to a particular edge is > *n*, then that arc is not drawn in the graph representing the map.

In this gem, we assume that if from point A we can reach point B, we represent that as $Cost\left[Edge\left(A,B\right)\right] \leq n$*, where n is the number of nodes on the map. If the two points are not connected, we represent that as* $Cost\left[Edge\left(A,B\right)\right] > n$.

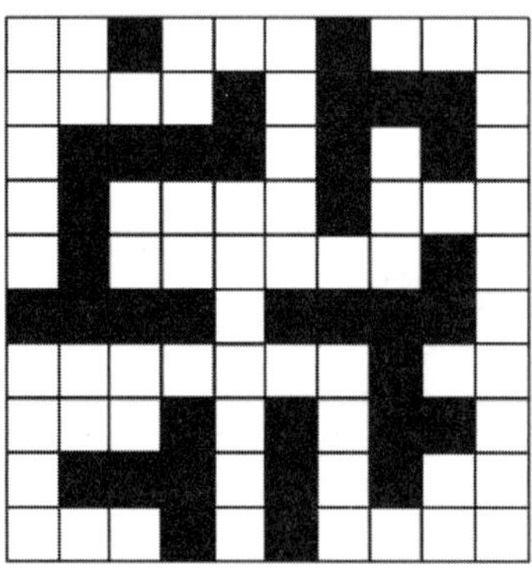

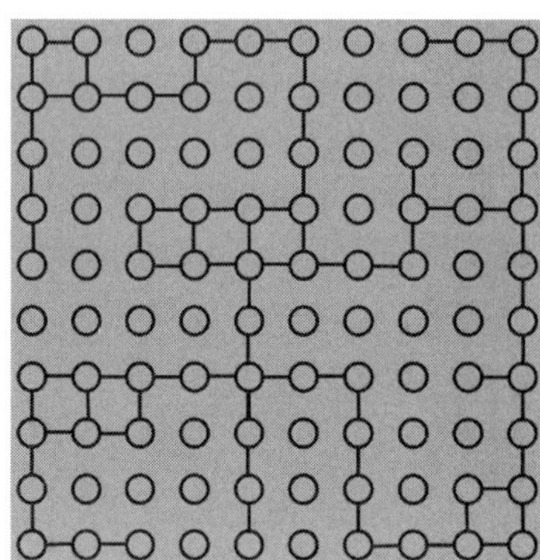

FIGURE 3.8.2 *A map with obstacles and the resulting graph.*

The D* algorithm takes a map graph as input. During traversal, the algorithm checks to see if there have been any modifications in any points of the map. When a modification in the graph is detected, D* starts from the node in which there has been a change and modifies the proposed path only in the affected area.

In essence, the algorithm focuses replanning within a very small area. Real-time tests [Stentz94] show clearly that the advantage of D* over A* increases exponentially with the number of points in the map.

D* in Detail

Suppose that the environment is a square with edge *M*, and that the input of D* is a graph that maps the ambient environment. (We assume without loss of generality that only horizontal and vertical movements are allowed between nodes—no diagonals.)

D* maintains a list of open states, which is used to process states and to expand the computing to the affected neighbors of the current examined node. At the beginning, all nodes are marked NEW. They become OPEN when they are inserted in the open list. After their computation, they are marked CLOSED.

D* maintains an explicit list of these tags for each node; we will refer to it as *Tag(x)*.

Backpointer(x) is intended as the direction to follow to arrive to the goal. From each node *x*, if we follow *Backpointer(x)*, we arrive at the goal following a shortest path (in fact, there can be more paths with the same cost). The cost of a path is the sum of all edges traversed when following it.

H(x) is defined as the estimated distance from *x* to the goal. After a replan, *H(x)* is the minimal distance from the goal.

The key function *K(x)* is defined as the minimum between:

- *H(x)* before a modification occurs
- All *H(x)* values since *x* was placed in the open list

This is an important threshold in classifying the nodes in two classes. Based on *K(x)* value and *H(x)* value, we consider two types of nodes:

Raise $K(x) < H(x)$**:** The class of nodes used when there is a *cost increase* in the graph and we must propagate this information to all nodes affected.

Lower $K(x) = H(x)$**:** The class of nodes used when there is a *cost decrease* in the graph and we must propagate this information to all nodes affected.

As we will see shortly, the algorithm treats each type of node in a different way.

An Example

ON THE CD

Now that we have focused the practical key issues of the algorithm, it should be useful to see how it works on a real example. In the accompanying CD-ROM there is an easy algorithm implementation that you can check to understand how it works in detail. There is a win32 demo application, too.

Suppose (for simplicity) that we have a 5 × 5 map with obstacles (Figure 3.8.3). Each square can be FREE (white) or OBSTACLE (black). This ZERO-ONE choice is again made to better clarify the steps of the algorithm. We start in the upper-left corner; our goal is at lower-right corner.

The algorithm performs an initial pathfinding by calling `ProcessState()` repeatedly. In Figure 3.8.4, the arrows show the backpointer of each node. Remember that the backpointers tell us which direction we should follow to minimize the total cost of our path.

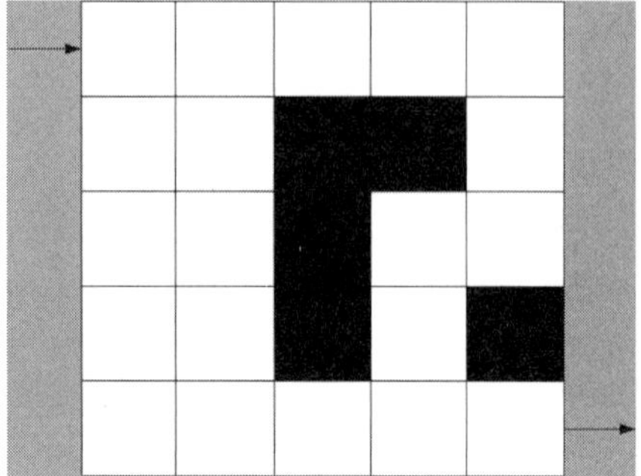

FIGURE 3.8.3 *A 5 × 5 map with obstacles.*

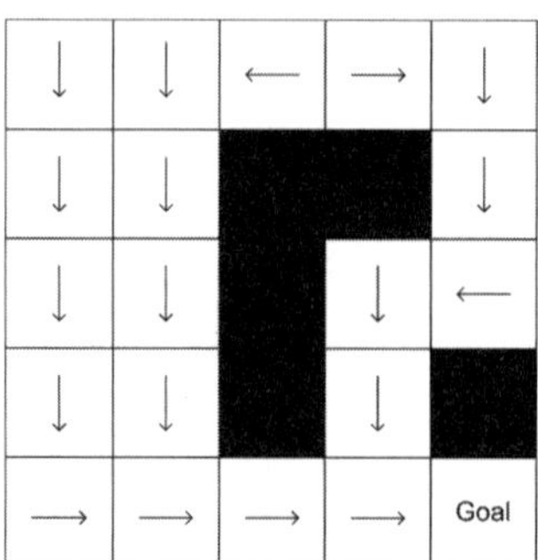

FIGURE 3.8.4 *Initial backpointers configuration.*

In Figure 3.8.5, we show the path that is followed if we start from upper-left corner ([0] [0] if we use a C notation and read the map as a matrix).

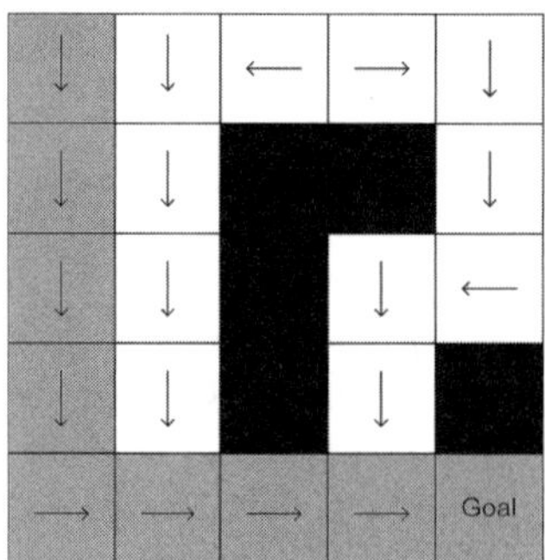

FIGURE 3.8.5 *The path from start to goal.*

Our agent starts following the path depicted. Suppose that when it is at location [4][1], the square at [4][2] becomes an OBSTACLE. Let's see how D* handles this.

When the algorithm detects that there has been a change in the environment, it calls the function `ModifyCost(x, y, value)`; it changes the arc cost from x to y and then inserts the node x in the open list if it's a closed node. Next, the function `ProcessState()` is called while there are nodes on the open list whose distance from the goal is lower than the one of the current node. In this way, D* modifies only the *backpointers* of affected nodes, saving the already computed work where possible.

In Figure 3.8.6, we show in dark gray only the recomputed nodes after the algorithm detected a change in the environment. Figure 3.8.6 should convince you that D* analyzes only the minimum number of nodes needed to correctly compute a new shortest path. The strength of the algorithm is made clear here.

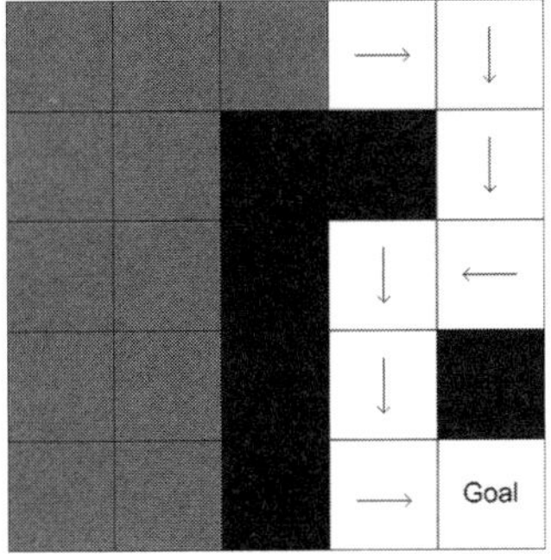

FIGURE 3.8.6 *Affected nodes by the modification.*

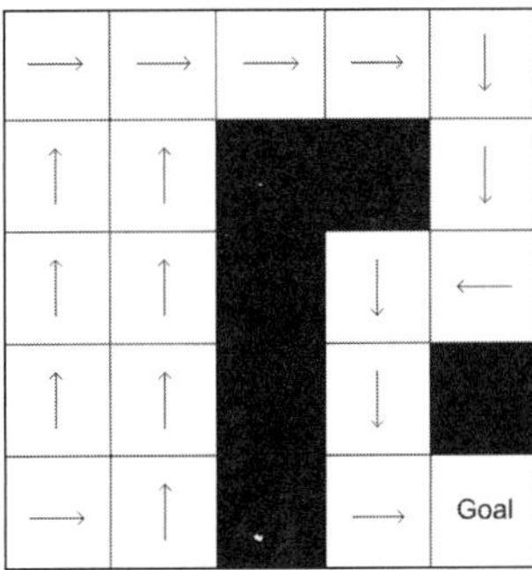

FIGURE 3.8.7 *New backpointer configuration after modification in [4][2].*

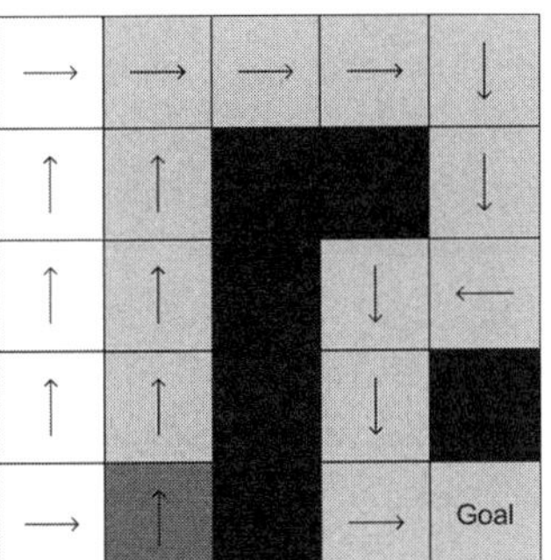

FIGURE 3.8.8 *New path computed from [4][1].*

Let's see how the *backpointers* configuration changes after the modification (Figure 3.8.7). Starting from [4][1] (depicted in darker gray), Figure 3.8.8 shows the new path computed.

And in the Game?

Actually there aren't many real games that uses D* in any way to perform any sort of pathfinding algorithm. This is due to the intrinsic nature of the game simulation, which privileges the illusion of the AI over the real AI, so is far simpler to find a pseudonatural way to get a unit move between two points in a well-known (a-priori) environment than let it discover the best path during the way. The search maps actually in use are spatially limited and not very detailed, letting A* be efficient enough. Obviously, this is an AI limitation caused by the minimal CPU resources allocated to AI in current and past games.

D* is ideal for each situation where the programmer wants to give some learning capabilities to a game agent. In this scenario, the agent doesn't know anything a priori about the surrounding environment: all information is detected from its sensors during its lifetime.

D* agents can move on larger maps, because the environment needs to be scanned only locally to perform a path search and when any perturbation occurs (a new obstacle is discovered or removed), the replanning only affects a small search area. Thus, CPU resources allocated for agent path planning would be enough.

Currently, many game developers think that the next generation of games will spend more time performing AI, because the focus will be on the behavioral realism, so more sophisticated algorithms like this will come into the game development world.

Conclusion

This gem has analyzed the basic D* implementation. As you can see in [Stentz94] the benefit of using D* instead A* becomes stronger as the size of the environment increases. This is simply because the computational cost of replanning from scratch increases as the number of nodes in the graph becomes higher, and D* avoids as much recomputation as possible.

It is possible to use a focused D*, which can lower the number of examined node in case of a world change; this is achieved by using a heuristic to drive the research only for promising nodes. Interested readers should consult [Stentz95].

A final note on the demo included with the book: it makes use of the Leonardo Library [Leonardo03], which is mentioned in the references, for interested readers.

References

[Leonardo03] Leonardo Computing Environment. Available online at *www.leonardo-vm.org*.

[Stentz94] Stentz, T. "Original D*." In ICRA 94. Available online at *www.frc.ri.cmu.edu/~axs/doc/icra94.pdf*.

[Stentz95] Stentz, T. "Focused D*." In IJCAI 95. Available online at *www.frc.ri.cmu.edu/~axs/doc/ijcai95.pdf.*

[Stentz96] Stentz, T. "Map strategies for using D*." In AAAI 96 workshop. Available online at *www.frc.ri.cmu.edu/~axs/doc/aaai96.pdf.*

[Stentz01] Stentz, T. "Constrained D*." In AAAI 02. Available online at *www.frc.ri.cmu.edu/~axs/doc/aaai02.pdf.*

[Stentz98] Stentz, T. "Framed Quad-trees with D*." In ICRA 98. Available online at *www.frc.ri.cmu.edu/~axs/doc/icra98.2.pdf.*

[Stout96] Stout, B. "Smart Moves: Intelligent Pathfinding." In *Game Developer Magazine*. October, 1996.

SECTION

4

PHYSICS

Introduction

Mike Dickheiser, Red Storm Entertainment

mike.dickheiser@redstorm.com

The next time you are outside, pause for a moment to take in the sights around you. Everywhere you look the world is full of motion on both grand and subtle scales, from the great, mechanized products of human ingenuity to the dancing of nature's freshly fallen leaves. Each movement pervades our senses, adding to our understanding of the world and defining our expectations of reality.

It is natural for us to use the real world as a basis for comprehension, experimentation, and enjoyment of other, fictional, worlds. After all, this world is what we know, and everything we see, feel, or imagine is filtered through our understanding of the familiar. If a fictional world fails to meet the standard (in the ways that matter), we are led to boredom, confusion, or disappointment. As creators of such worlds, this simply won't do. Thus, we seek to meet the standard, so that we may immerse ourselves in new worlds that keep us amazed, excited, and absorbed.

Returning our attention to computer games, we see how far we have come. This year marks another step in the evolution of realism achieved in the virtual worlds we create as game developers. More than ever, physical simulation in games approaches a degree of fidelity that eerily matches much of what we see around us. Clearly, our craft has advanced considerably over the past several years. In the following section, several gems demonstrate the progress that has been made and offer ideas for getting to the next level.

Graham Rhodes starts things off at full speed by presenting a solid and intuitive look at aerodynamics and its various applications in games. From the airborne to the wind swept, we next move to Rishi Ramraj's discussion of dynamic grass simulation and other effects, including water surfaces and the motion of leaves. Our realism toolset is then rounded out with Juan Cordero's look at cloth animation, followed by Maciej Matyka's discussion of an innovative technique for animating soft bodies.

The next gems remind us that the art of computer game development is a dichotomy: a simultaneous effort in maximizing the degree to which we can emulate the real world but also our skill at creating masterful illusions. Michael Mandel manipulates the puppet strings of game characters by adding feedback control systems to rag doll simulation. We then reach the opposite end of the rich spectrum of physical realism with two gems on prescripted physics. The basic architectural considerations are handled by Dan Higgins, and Shawn Shoemaker presents a variety of applications.

The section closes where it begins: with a good look at the world. This time the view is provided by Barnabás Aszódi and Szabolcs Czuczor, who present several ideas for realistic control of camera motion in 3D car simulations.

The gems in this section cover a wide variety of topics and illustrate the tremendous progress that has been made in computer game physics. At the same time, they only hint at the exciting possibilities that have yet to be realized, teasing us with still just-out-of-reach capabilities that will immerse us even deeper. With every closer glance at the real world, we notice more details of reality that defy our imitative efforts and challenge us to go to the next level. The hope is that these gems will serve as stepping stones on the exciting path up that next level and will inspire new entrants to the discipline to take up the cause.

4.1

Back of the Envelope Aerodynamics for Game Physics

Graham Rhodes, Applied Research Associates, Inc.

grhodes@nc.rr.com

In real life, aerodynamics enable heavier-than-air vehicles to fly, make the curve ball possible, and cause palm trees to sway above beautiful girls on exotic beaches. Aerodynamics have long played a role in gaming, primarily in flight simulators, and in some cases have been used to improve the realism of effects such as particle systems. Many game developers take an ad-hoc approach to aerodynamics that is based more on numerical experimentation than on sound principles. This gem will provide a portfolio of simple, low-CPU/GPU-cost, back-of-the-envelope formulas, derived from sound engineering principles and strictly controlled wind-tunnel experiments, that game programmers can use to support a wide variety of aerodynamic effects in many game genres. While we use the term *aerodynamics*, in fact the formulas here work equally well for objects moving through a fluid such as water, as long as velocities are fairly high.

The gem is developed in two sections. The first section describes how different *aerodynamic primitives* can serve as proxies to game geometry and presents simple equations for calculating aerodynamic forces on those primitives. You can reasonably use these equations for objects that are moving through the air or other fluids at a Mach number of less than approximately 0.75. While the presentation is short on theory due to limited print space, certain key principles from aerodynamics theory are present. The second section of the gem focuses on applications of back-of-the-envelope aerodynamics to achieve way cool effects in action games, complete with source code.

Background

The following sections provide some background on the topic of aerodynamics.

Aerodynamic Loads and Rigid Body Dynamics

The formulas presented herein will help you to calculate approximate aerodynamic loads—forces and moments (also known as *torques*)—that can be applied to rigid bodies. The loads calculated with these formulas can simply feed your existing rigid body physics system!

In the engineering world of aircraft flight dynamics, there are six standard aerodynamic load quantities: three forces (lift, drag, and side force, which is perpendicular to the other two) and three moments (pitching moment, yawing moment, and rolling moment). However, the manner in which this gem treats geometry allows us to simplify the situation, modeling only lift, drag, and a single moment. The full set of three forces and three moments is simply a generalization. Figure 4.1.1 illustrates the orientation of these three load quantities.

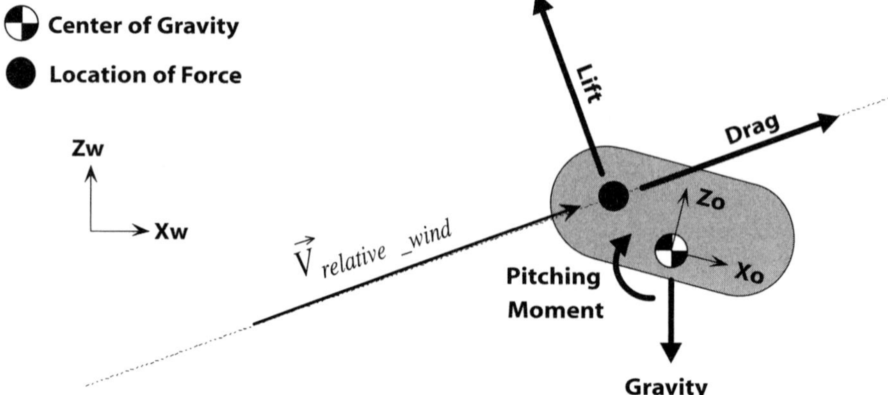

FIGURE 4.1.1 *Location and orientation of lift, drag, and pitching moment. Drag acts in the direction of the relative wind, and lift acts perpendicular to the relative wind—both often through a location other than the center of gravity. Pitching moment acts about an axis through the center of gravity and perpendicular to the lift/drag plane.*

Here, the axis system *Xw*, *Zw* represents the world space coordinate system, and the axis system *Xo*, *Zo* represents an object-aligned coordinate system. For 3D objects, there are of course *Yw* and *Yo* directions, and the two coordinate systems will often be more arbitrarily oriented. The object's orientation is unimportant as long as it is known. The orientation of the relative wind, defined later, is critical to calculation of the forces.

The orientation of these loads, which are defined here in the so-called *wind axes*, may surprise you. You may have been expecting the lift force to act vertically straight up (opposite gravity) and the drag force to act horizontally—both acting through the center of gravity, since many simplistic introductions to aerodynamics present the forces in this way. You may have never heard of pitching moment. Be assured, the wind axis representation is both realistic and fundamental to simple aerodynamic theory.

The force calculations depend only on the object's orientation relative to the wind and not to the world. While lift on airplane wings normally does have a vertical component that balances the object's weight, causing the object to move horizontally or with a constant vertical velocity, lift can in fact act in any direction, even horizontally! It is recognition of this that makes it reasonable for us to ignore the side force, for example, as a special case, since side force is often just a horizontally oriented lifting force.

Dimensionless Forms

It is common practice to represent all the aerodynamic loads in terms of dimensionless coefficients. Equations 4.1.1 through 4.1.3 are equations for computing the loads given the value of a dimensionless coefficient.

$$D = \text{Drag} = \frac{\rho V^2 S_{ref} C_D}{2} \tag{4.1.1}$$

$$L = \text{Lift} = \frac{\rho V^2 S_{ref} C_L}{2} \tag{4.1.2}$$

$$M = \text{Pitching Moment} = \frac{\rho V^2 S_{ref} l_{ref} C_M}{2} \tag{4.1.3}$$

Here, C_D is the drag coefficient, C_L is the lift coefficient, and C_M is the pitching moment coefficient. The variable S_{ref} is a constant reference area, usually taken to be a projected area of the geometry, such as a cross-section area or a top-down projected area. The variable l_{ref} is a reference length, usually taken to be one of the physical dimensions of the object, such as the chord width of a wing or the diameter of a sphere-like object. The variable ρ *is the fluid density, which for gaming applications will most often be taken to be constant.*

Finally, the variable V is the speed of the fluid, measured *relative to the object*; that is, it is the speed of the fluid moving past the object, measured in world space. Given the velocity of the point on the body where the force is applied to an object, $\vec{V}_{location-of-force}$, in world space, and a wind velocity in world space, $\vec{V}_{wind}$, it is easy to find the wind velocity relative to the object, $\vec{V}_{relative\_wind}$, using Equation 4.1.4. The geometry of this situation is illustrated in Figure 4.1.2. The quantity V in Equations 4.1.1 through 4.1.3 is simply the magnitude of $\vec{V}_{relative\_wind}$. When calculating $\vec{V}_{location-of-force}$, be sure to include the translational velocity due to object rotation, since this will affect the forces. Specifically, let $\vec{V}_{location-of-force} = \vec{V}_{point-of-rotation} + \left(\vec{\omega} \times \left(\vec{r}_{location-of-force} - \vec{r}_{point-of-rotation}\right)\right)$, with $\vec{r}$ being the location of a point, measured in world space, and $\vec{\omega}$ being the rotational velocity about an axis through the point $\vec{r}_{point-of-rotation}$, measured in radians per second, as shown in Equation 4.1.4.

$$\vec{V}_{relative\_wind} = \vec{V}_{wind} - \vec{V}_{location-of-force} \tag{4.1.4}$$

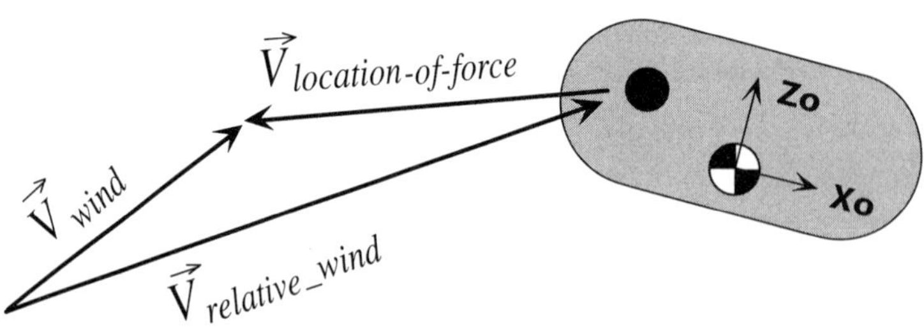

FIGURE 4.1.2 *The geometry of relative wind.*

Fluid Properties and the Standard Atmosphere

The equations presented herein are dependent on the fluid properties, be that fluid air, water, or something else. At sea level, air has an average density, ρ, of 1.225 kg/m^3 (23.77 × 10–4 slugs/ft^3), and dynamic viscosity, μ, of 1.789 × 10–5 Newton-seconds/m^2 (3.737 × 10–7 lb-seconds/ft^2). At 20 degrees Centigrade, pure water has an average density of 1000 kg/m^3 (1.94 slugs/ft^3) and a dynamic viscosity of 1.0 × 10–3 Newton-seconds/m^2 (2.09 × 10–5 lb-seconds/ft^2).

For air, at any given moment in time, the properties vary with altitude, as well as with weather conditions, etc. There is a model, called the *Standard Atmosphere* (U.S. and International versions exist), which represents the average air properties over a range of altitudes. An Internet search on that phrase will produce numerous links, including table listings of the properties and software for querying the tables.

Aerodynamic Primitives

While there have been a few developments that simulate variants of the *Navier-Stokes* equations of fluid flow in real time [Stam03, Lander02], for the purpose of simulating smoke, clouds, and water flow in games, these methods are usually overkill when the goal is to find the net force and moment on a rigid body object. For games, in many cases, a *very* approximate solution is realistic enough. To that end, the remainder of this gem will discuss aerodynamic load calculations for a number of *aerodynamic primitives*. These primitives have simple shapes for which the engineering world long ago has developed closed form, simple algebraic equations. Some of these developments date back centuries. To apply these equations in your game, you simply need to choose the most appropriate aerodynamic primitive—usually the one whose shape is closest to your in-game object—and apply the equations associated with that primitive. You can also represent a more complex shape as a composite of several aerodynamic primitives (e.g., a sphere plus a simple wing, linked together as a rigid set) to approximate the loads. To be sure, this approach often produces *very* approximate, first or zeroeth order estimates that ignore object-to-object interference effects, among other things. Fortunately, these estimates are extremely cheap to compute and are often absolutely convincing!

Forces on Bluff Bodies

We define a *bluff body* to be any object that is not slender or streamlined, and that does not contain wings for generating lift. For the purposes of this gem, consider anything that is shaped somewhat like a sphere, or a cylinder whose center axis is perpendicular to the relative wind, to be a bluff body. This includes arbitrary blobs, cubes, tubes, etc. Consider the location of the force of a bluff body to be located at the object's centroid.

Drag (Aerodynamic Primitive: The Sphere)

For bluff bodies, C_D is largely a function of a dimensionless parameter called the *Reynold's Number*, defined by Equation 4.1.5. The Reynold's Number represents the ratio of inertial to viscous forces in the fluid.

$$\text{Reynold's Number} = R_e = \frac{\rho V l_{ref}}{\mu} \tag{4.1.5}$$

Three of the variables you recognize. The fourth, μ, is the dynamic viscosity of the fluid (units are force-time/length-squared). Figure 4.1.3 illustrates the variation of C_D for a sphere over a large range of Reynold's Number values.

To calculate the drag on a sphere-like bluff body: first calculate its R_e, with l_{ref} set to be the diameter; next, pick a C_D value from Figure 4.1.3; finally, plug the C_D into Equation 4.1.1, with S_{ref} equal to a representative, front-projected area for the body.

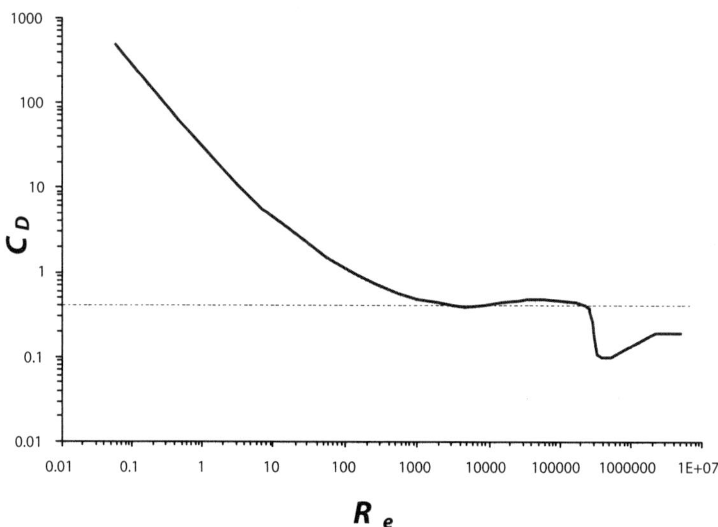

FIGURE 4.1.3 *Variation of C_D on a spherical bluff body over a range of Reynold's Numbers.*

For convenience, White [White74] presents a simple equation, reproduced as Equation 4.1.6, for estimating drag on a sphere that is fairly accurate for R_e below approximately 200,000. This equation was produced as a curve fit to experimental data.

$$C_{D,\,sphere} = \frac{24}{R_e} + \frac{6}{1+\sqrt{R_e}} + 0.4 \tag{4.1.6}$$

For R_e values between approximately 2,000 and 200,000, just pick C_D equal to 0.4. For higher Reynold's Numbers, use whatever works best between 0.1 and 0.4.

In some cases, a sphere is not the best way to represent a given shape. While C_D versus R_e charts aren't often available for other shapes, there are resources that will provide you with a reasonable guess at a C_D for different shapes. In particular, the JavaScript-based *Bluff Body Drag Calculator* provided by Professor M. S. Cramer of Virginia Tech [Cramer98] is an excellent and recommended resource.

Bet You Thought Drag Varied Linearly with Velocity, Didn't You?

As presented earlier, by definition, drag and the other aerodynamic forces are proportional to a dimensionless coefficient multiplied by the *square* of velocity. This relationship is *always* correct, no matter what the fluid, no matter what the speed of travel, no matter what the object. It is a definition! But, as you may have read, it is also true that in some circumstances, drag varies linearly with velocity. How are both possible? The truth lies in the variability of C_D. It turns out that for R_e below approximately 1,000, C_D varies approximately proportional to the inverse of R_e, which effectively puts an extra V in the denominator of Equation 4.1.1, thus making drag a linear function of V. But, the relationship defined by Equation 4.1.1 also remains perfectly valid!

Lift on Spinning Bluff Bodies (Aerodynamic Primitive: The Cylinder)

Lift is a force that acts perpendicular to the relative wind, caused by fluid pressure differences that result from flow acceleration and deceleration over the surfaces of an object. The fine details of the physics that ultimately cause this to happen are beyond the scope of this gem; however, we can take advantage of one of the early developments in theoretical aerodynamics to obtain a handy equation for estimating the lift force on bluff bodies. One of the classical simplifications of the *Navier-Stokes* equations of fluid flow is the so-called *linearized potential flow* model. With this model, it is possible to represent a full flow field as a superposition (summation) of elemental flow fields. The flow about a general object in a fluid can be approximated as a background flow in which the fluid velocity is balanced (and no lift is generated) plus a so-called *circulation* flow, which represents an acceleration of the fluid on one side of the object and a deceleration on the other side. The easiest way to begin to understand circulation is to consider it to be a concentric flow, a vortex, superimposed on top of a background flow. The vortex flow is additive, incrementing the fluid velocity on one side of the object, producing lower pressure, and decrementing the fluid velocity on the other side of the object, producing higher pressure. The pressure difference between the sides causes the lift force.

In the early 1900s, two scientists, Kutta and Joukowski, each independently determined that if the relative wind is nonzero and if there is a circulation, then a lift force exists and can be quantified with a simple equation. Equation 4.1.7 is a generalization of the *Kutta-Joukowski Theorem*, which defines the lift force in terms of a known circulation.

$$\vec{L}_{per\_unit\_length} = \rho\vec{V}_{relative\_wind} \times \vec{\Gamma} \tag{4.1.7}$$

Here, $\vec{\Gamma}$ is a vector representing circulation per unit-length, oriented in a certain direction, and the resulting force, $\vec{L}_{per\_unit\_length}$, is the lift force per unit-length, with length being the object length along the circulation direction. In real life, the circulation is a variable along the length, and Equation 4.1.7 must be integrated along the length to obtain the total lift force.

Circulation can be the result of geometric asymmetry in the curvature of an object (e.g., an airfoil that has more curvature on the top than on the bottom), and can also result due to rotational motion—spinning. The curve of a curveball is due largely to lift caused by circulation flow around a spinning baseball. The circulation is due to skin friction on one side of the ball accelerating air molecules faster in the direction of the relative wind (lower pressure), while skin friction on the other side of the ball decelerates the air molecules against the relative wind (higher pressure). The direction of circulation for a spinning ball is the ball's spin direction, as shown in Figure 4.1.4.

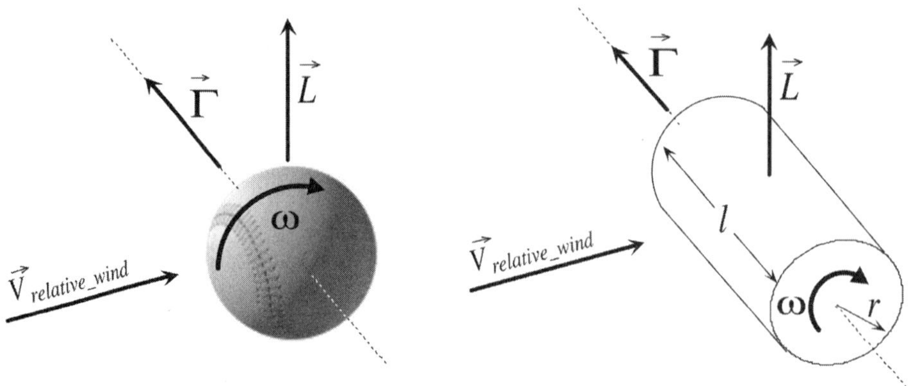

FIGURE 4.1.4 *Circulation generated on a spinning baseball and a cylinder, due to circulation caused by skin friction.*

The real-world fluid flow around any general object is quite complex, and its circulation situation is nontrivial. To *greatly* simplify matters for games, simply treat the object as a *cylinder*. The aerodynamic primitive is a bounding cylinder, aligned with the spin axis. In this case, the circulation per unit length is approximated for a cylinder. The total lift can be approximated by multiplying the result of Equation 4.1.7 by the length of the bounding cylinder. For such a cylinder, with radius r and spinning at a rate of ω radians per second (positive or negative), the circulation per unit length is given by Equation 4.1.8.

$$\Gamma_{cylinder} = 2\pi\omega r^2 \tag{4.1.8}$$

From here, the total, approximate lift on the bluff body with bounding cylinder length l can be calculated using Equation 4.1.9. Here, $\vec{e}_{spin}$ is a unit vector indicating the axis of spin, and $\omega\vec{e}_{spin}$ is the rotational velocity in radians per second. The extra factor of 0.785 approximates three-dimensional losses that occur for finite length cylinders. The equation is more accurate for longer cylinders.

$$\vec{L} = 0.785 l\rho\vec{V}_{relative\_wind} \times (2\pi\omega r^2\vec{e}_{spin}) \tag{4.1.9}$$

If you consider the force associated with the spin of a baseball as being due to the so-called *Magnus Effect* (also called the *Robin's Effect*), you are quite correct. These are terms given to the phenomenon long before Kutta and Joukowski formulated the math, though in reality, there are factors other than circulation at play.

Forces on Streamlined Bodies

In the following sections, we'll look at a number of forces affecting the behavior of streamlined bodies.

Lift and Drag on Wing-Like Bodies (Aerodynamic Primitive: Quadrilateral Plate/Wing)

Objects that are shaped like airplane wings are especially good at generating circulation, and hence, lift. For our purposes, consider any object that is basically flat, and aligned within 10–15 degrees of the relative wind, to be a wing—an efficient lifting body. The engineering world derived *thin wing theory*, which led to the development of convenient equations for C_D and C_L of thin wings. These equations are perfectly fine for many gaming applications outside of realistic flight simulation. Figure 4.1.5 illustrates a number of geometric parameters required to evaluate the following equations.

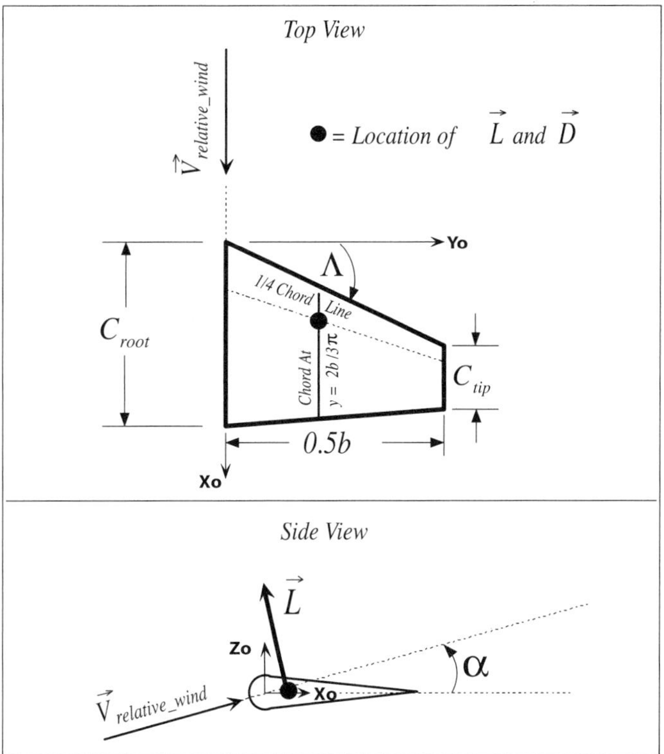

FIGURE 4.1.5 *The geometry of wing-like bodies. The XY plane of the object-aligned coordinate system is aligned with a representative center plane of the object.*

Here, Λ is the leading edge sweep angle, the C values are the chord lengths at the root and tip of the wing, $0.5b$ is the semi span length, and α is the angle of attack of the wing, measured relative to $\vec{V}_{relative\_wind}$. There is a simple formula, due to Hale [Hale84], for approximating the lift on such wing-like bodies at small (less than 10–15 degrees) angles of attack, given by Equation 4.1.10.

$$C_L = C_{L,0} + \frac{\pi A \alpha}{1 + \sqrt{1 + \left(\frac{A}{2\cos\Lambda}\right)^2}} \tag{4.1.10}$$

Note that the equation requires α in radians. Here, $C_{L,0}$ is the lift generated when the wing is at zero angle of attack. This is nonzero when the wing curvature is different on the top and bottom surfaces. For approximate solutions in games, assume it is zero. A is the aspect ratio, equal to the span, *b*, divided by the average chord length. For α greater than 10–15 degrees, the variation of C_L with α will become nonlinear. See Bertin and Smith [Bertin79] or Raymer [Raymer92] for information on the more realistic behavior of CL for higher values of α.

Drag on wing-like bodies consists of two primary components: a parasite drag component that is the same drag as that encountered by bluff bodies and a vortex-induced drag that is a side effect of the generation of lift. From thin-wing theory, drag on wings can be approximated by a parabolic *drag polar*, given by Equation 4.1.11.

$$C_D = C_{Do} + \frac{1}{\pi A e} C_L^2 \tag{4.1.11}$$

Here, C_{Do} is the parasite drag component, and the remaining term is the induced drag component. Normally, since wings are streamlined, C_{Do} is quite small. A reasonable value is 0.045, though certainly you can tweak this as needed. *A* is the wing aspect ratio, and *e* is the so-called *Oswald span efficiency factor*. Outside of flight simulation games, just pick *e* equal to 0.8.

It is important to pay careful attention to the location where the lift and drag forces act, since these forces will contribute to moment loads. To locate the center of lift and drag, first find the chord along the location $y = 2b/3\pi$. This location assumes a semi-elliptic, span-wise lift distribution. The lift and drag act approximately at the intersection point of that chord and the *quarter-chord line*, which occurs one quarter of the chord length behind the leading edge, along the entire span. It is also critically important that you include the translational velocity at the force location due to object rotational velocity. This velocity component contributes to physically based pitch damping. Without it, your simulation may exhibit instabilities.

There are a couple of important observations to make. First, Equation 4.1.10 was developed under the assumption that the wing is symmetric across the XZ plane, e.g., there are two halves. Regardless of this fact, if you only have half a wing, e.g., a quadrilateral fin stuck to the side of a missile, Equation 4.1.10 will work perfectly as long as you choose S_{ref} in Equation 4.1.2 to be the area of the portion of the wing that exists in your model. Second, if you have a full wing that is symmetric about the XZ plane, you need to include the lift and drag for both halves, doubling the net force. Notice that the net lift and drag for the two halves will act at a point that has the same X coordinate value as the individual halves, but a Y coordinate value of 0, e.g., lift and drag act at a point down the centerline between the two wing halves.

Raymer [Raymer92] provides a much more comprehensive introduction to the lift and drag of wing-like bodies, and provides a wider range of still-simple formulas. This is a highly recommended resource that should be available in most major engineering university libraries.

Pitching Moment

In reality, lift and drag are not generated at the center of gravity of an object. They are the integrated result of a pressure and friction force distribution over the surface of the object. The actual centroid of the forces almost never coincides with the center of gravity of the object. We merely use center of gravity for our rigid body simulations for convenience of the time integration of the rigid body equations of motion. If you apply lift and drag at the location given earlier, you will have a reasonable approximation to the pitching moment produced by the wing.

Moments in General

When you think about it carefully, you will realize that any of the aerodynamic forces (lift, drag, side force as a variant of lift) can produce a moment about the center of gravity of the object that must be applied during a simulation. If an object has a bluff body component producing drag, and the vector from the object's center-of-gravity through the bluff body component's center is not parallel to the relative wind, then the drag will produce a moment about the center-of-gravity. Lifting forces in any direction usually produce the largest moments. Bottom line: if you ensure that your forces are applied at the correct locations, approximations to the aerodynamic moments will result naturally.

Forces on Slender Bodies (Aerodynamic Primitive: Slender Ellipses of Revolution, or Missiles)

Some objects are neither bluff bodies nor are they shaped somewhat like airplane wings or flat plates. Among these are the so-called *slender bodies*, objects that are shaped similar to capsules or missiles, with a high length-to-diameter ratio (the *slenderness* ratio), which fly through the air with their length axis approximately aligned with the relative wind. These objects can in real life generate lift, drag, and pitching moments. Unfortunately, due to space limitations, it is not possible to delve into a detailed discussion of slender body aerodynamics here; however, Karamcheti [Karamcheti80] presents a comprehensive theoretical introduction in his book. In a pinch, you can approximate a pitching moment using the following variant of the formula presented by Karamcheti, which is fairly realistic for α less than approximately 10 degrees. Equation 4.1.12 defines the magnitude of the pitching moment coefficient.

$$C_{M,\ slender\_body} = |2\alpha| \qquad (\alpha \text{ in radians}) \tag{4.1.12}$$

Here, α is the angle between the axis of the slender body and the relative wind. In this case, the product Sreflref in Equation 4.1.3 is taken to be the volume of the slender body. The pitching moment acts about the center of gravity of the body, and the orientation of the moment is given by the cross product, $\vec{V}_{relative\_wind} \times \vec{A}_{slender\_body}$, where $\vec{A}_{slender\_body}$ is an axis from the nose to the tail of the slender body, through its center of gravity. Note that this moment is destabilizing, e.g., if the slender body ever becomes misaligned with the relative wind, the pitching moment will seek to push the slender body further out of alignment. To make a slender body stable, add fins behind the center of gravity. Fins are wings that will counteract the pitching moment to stabilize the object.

For the quick-and-dirty case, slender bodies generate no lift, and so you can choose $C_L = 0$. For drag, try a C_D value of 0.1 or less, and use the maximum cross-section area perpendicular through the body axis for S_{ref}.

Sample Applications

ON THE CD

Let's look at applying the principles covered thus far in three different examples: a wind-driven particle storm, a curve-ball simulation, and a simple airplane simulation. Impementations of all three are included on the CD-ROM.

A Wind-Driven Particle Storm

This example uses the equations for drag on a spherical bluff body to simulate particles in a windstorm, a simple tornado. In this case, we model the windstorm using a so-called *potential vortex*, with a strength that varies quadratically with altitude. The center, base point of the vortex is (0, 0, 0). The world Z direction represents altitude. The storm is assumed to have a strength that varies quadratically from *So* at sea level to S_{500} at 500 meters, as given by Equation 4.1.13.

$$S(z) = S_0 + \left(S_{500} - S_0\right)\frac{z^2}{500^2} \tag{4.1.13}$$

From this, the local wind velocity, $\vec{V}_{wind}$, at any point in space due to the storm is given by Equation 4.1.14.

$$\vec{V}_{wind,x}(x,y,z)=\frac{yS(z)}{2\pi r};\ \vec{V}_{wind,y}(x,y,z)=\frac{-xS(z)}{2\pi r};\ \vec{V}_{wind,z}=0 \qquad (4.1.14)$$

Here, r is the perpendicular distance from the point to the core axis of the vortex. In this case, $r=\sqrt{x^2+y^2}$, since the vortex is located at the origin. Care must be taken when r is very small. Bertin [Bertin79] provides a more comprehensive introduction to the potential vortex.

The drag force on each particle is evaluated by first calculating $\vec{V}_{wind}$ at the location of the particle, due to the storm, then computing the relative wind, and finally by calculating C_D and the actual drag force. The drag force is then added with the object's weight to obtain the total force acting on the particle. This total force is applied within a simple particle physics simulator.

A Simulated Curve Ball

This example uses the equations for drag on a spherical bluff body and lift on a spinning bluff body to simulate a curve ball pitch in a baseball game. In this case, we assume that the wind velocity is zero, so that the relative wind is simply the opposite of the ball's current velocity. This example is illustrated earlier in Figure 4.1.4, with the exception that the spin axis is vertical, resulting in a horizontally oriented lift force. You can vary the pitch speed from 70 to 90 miles per hour (a/s keys), and you can vary the spin rate from –100 revolutions per minute to 100 revolutions per minute (+/– keys). The pitch always begins horizontally, along the –X axis (towards home plate), and the spin axis is the Z axis. Gravity acts along the negative Z axis (straight down). Press the g key to begin the simulation, p to pause, and r restart.

A Simple, Longitudinal Airplane

This example demonstrates the calculation of lift and drag on a very simple airplane (see Figure 4.1.6). This airplane is of the canard style, meaning its main wing is behind the horizontal stabilizer, and the center of gravity lies between the two wings. The purpose of this example is to demonstrate the stabilizing nature of the pitching moment that results from wing lift when the centers of lift of the two wings are positioned properly relative to the center of gravity. For simplicity, this example ignores the phenomenon known as *downwash*, which causes the angle of attack of the rear wing to be reduced by the presence of the forward wing. The simulation does include airplane rotation when calculating the relative wind for each wing, and the physically based pitch damping that results helps make the airplane dynamically stable for small angles of attack. The pitching oscillations that occur are realistic—they occur in life and damp themselves out naturally.

In this example, you can adjust the orientation angle of the forward wing relative to the rear wing (+/– keys). As you adjust the parameters, notice that the airplane orientation changes but over time finds rotational equilibrium. This is due to the balancing of the pitching moments of the two wings. This is a longitudinally stable airplane.

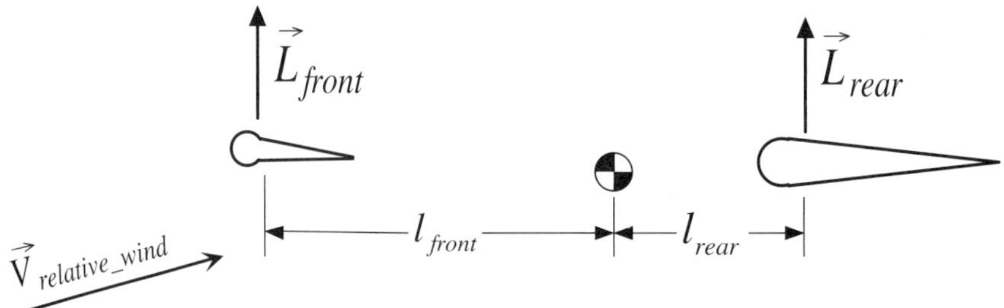

FIGURE 4.1.6 *A simple, canard style longitudinal airplane configuration.*

Conclusion

This gem introduces a series of fundamental aerodynamic concepts and provides simple equations that you can use to quickly calculate interesting aerodynamic effects within your game. Depending on your gaming platform, you may have a number of options available for implementing aerodynamics. If you use a custom, freeware, or licensed physics engine, you will need to implement callback functions that can compute the aerodynamic loads about the center of gravity of a rigid body, given its current state and the current wind velocity. Once the loads are computed in the wind axes, map them into world space and apply them to the rigid body. The physics engine will simply incorporate the additional loads into its numerical time integration with no additional work on your part. With the advent of programmable graphics hardware, it has become possible to perform limited physics calculations on the GPU. The formulas presented herein are simple enough that they can be implemented in a vertex shader using current or emerging GPUs. This is an especially compelling approach when adding aerodynamics to a particle system. These simple formulas are cheap enough that you may be able to use them, limitedly, on handheld gaming platforms. The challenge here will be optimizing the formulas to run quickly using fixed-point math or on floating-point capable-but-limited CPUs.

Though these equations are based on occasionally severe assumptions and ignore many higher-order effects, including object-to-object interference and ground effects, you can reasonably use them to provide extremely cheap illusions that will make your game worlds appear more realistic to your players. Aerodynamics alone cannot make a game, but can contribute to a much richer gaming experience when used in conjunction with other more traditional visual, physical, and animation effects. The most interesting results are often obtained via experimentation and play. For this reason, feel free to apply the techniques described here in unexpected ways. Make your next game world live, with aerodynamics!

References

[Bertin79] Bertin, John J., and Michael L. Smith. *Aerodynamics for Engineers*. Prentice Hall, 1979.

[Cramer98] Cramer, M.S. Bluff Body Drag Calculator. Available online at *http://www.fluidmech.net/jscalc/cdcal26.htm*. 1998.

[Hale84] Hale, Francis J. *Introduction to Aircraft Performance, Selection, and Design*. John Wiley & Sons, 1984.

[Karamcheti80] Karamcheti, Krishnamurty. *Principles of Ideal-Fluid Aerodynamics*. Robert E. Krieger Publishing Company, 1980.

[Lander02] Lander, Jeff. "Taming a Wild River." Presented at the Game Developers Conference 2002. Available at *http://www.darwin3d.com/confpage.htm*.

[Raymer92] Raymer, Daniel P. *Aircraft Design: A Conceptual Approach*. AIAA Education Series. American Institute of Aeronautics and Astronautics, Inc., 1992.

[Stam03] Stam, Jos. "Real-Time Fluid Dynamics for Games." Presented at the Game Developers Conference, 2003. Available online at *http://www.dgp.toronto.edu/people/stam/reality/Research/pdf/GDC03.pdf*.

[White74] White, Frank M. *Viscous Fluid Flow*. McGraw-Hill, 1974. Available online at *http://hyperphysics.phy-astr.gsu.edu/hbase/fluids/kutta.html*.

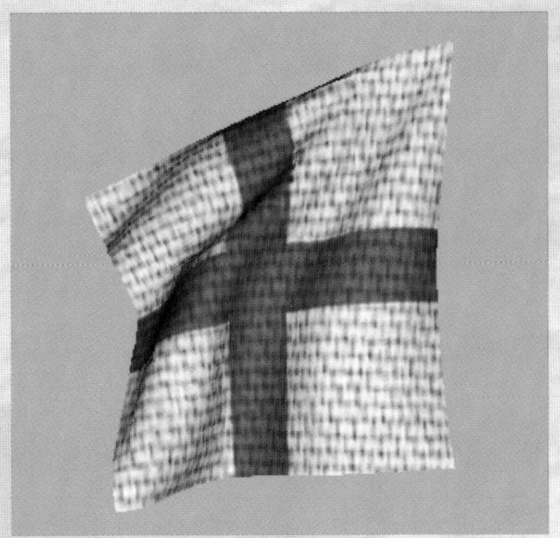

COLOR PLATE 1A *Physically animated cloth from Article 4.3.*

COLOR PLATE 1B *Physically animated cloth from Article 4.3, draped over a sphere.*

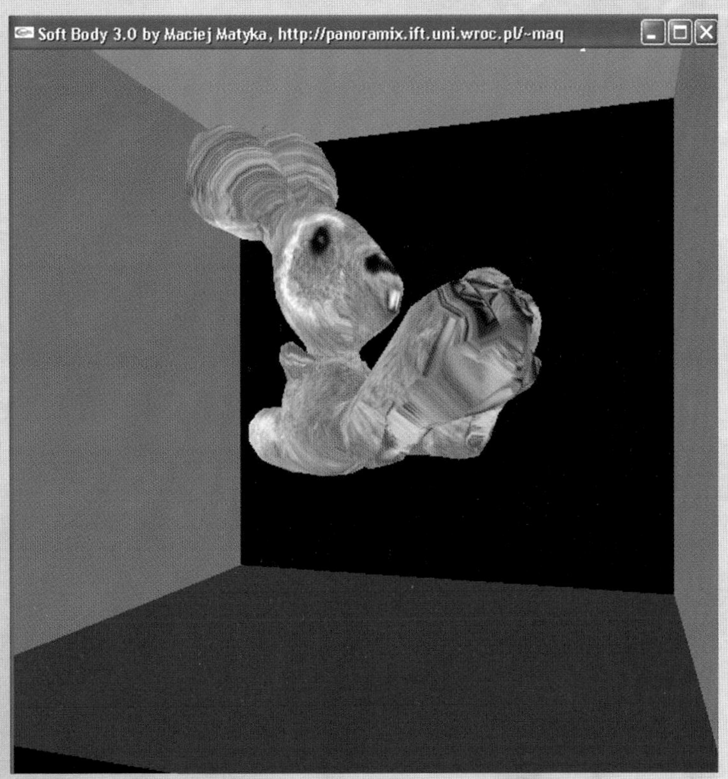

COLOR PLATE 2 *A deformable rabbit model showing Article 4.4's practical animation of soft bodies.*

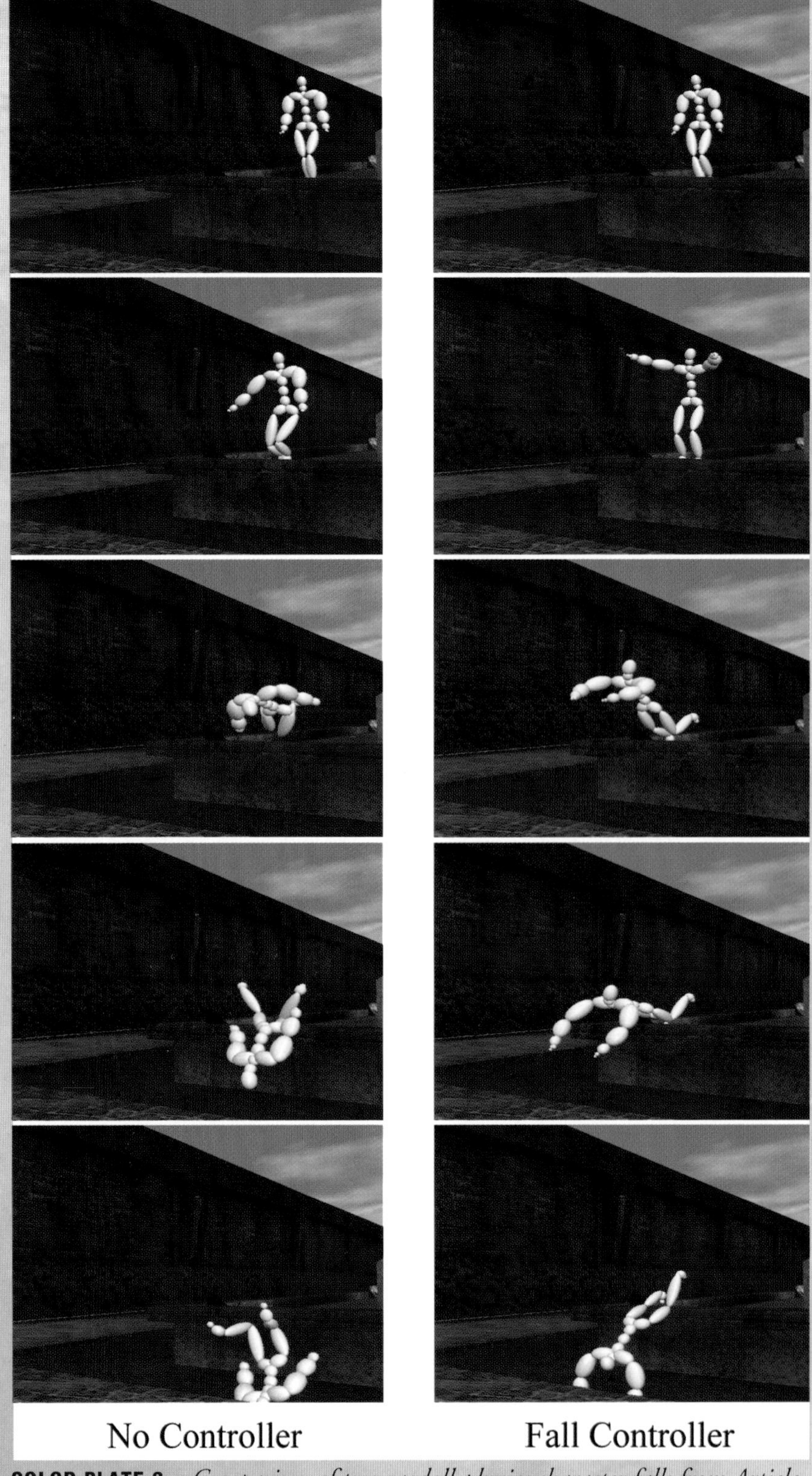

COLOR PLATE 3 *Comparison of two ragdoll-physics character falls from Article 4.5, on the left without feedback control, on the right with feedback control.*

COLOR PLATE 4A *Applications of prescripted physics from Article 4.7.*

COLOR PLATE 4B *Applications of prescripted physics from Article 4.7.*

COLOR PLATE 5 *Procedural Cloud techniques from Article 5.1. These four images are rendered at 640 × 480 and run at 60 frames per second on a GeForce6800 using ps.3.0. The top left image gives high weighting to the high frequency octaves. The top right image uses typical settings and includes a lens flare. On the bottom left, we choose a sharpness value which gives very thick clouds. In the bottom right image we show typical settings.*

COLOR PLATE 6 *Screenshot of snow moving at high velocity from technique presented in Article 5.2.*

COLOR PLATE 7 *Gridless fire technique from Article 5.5.*

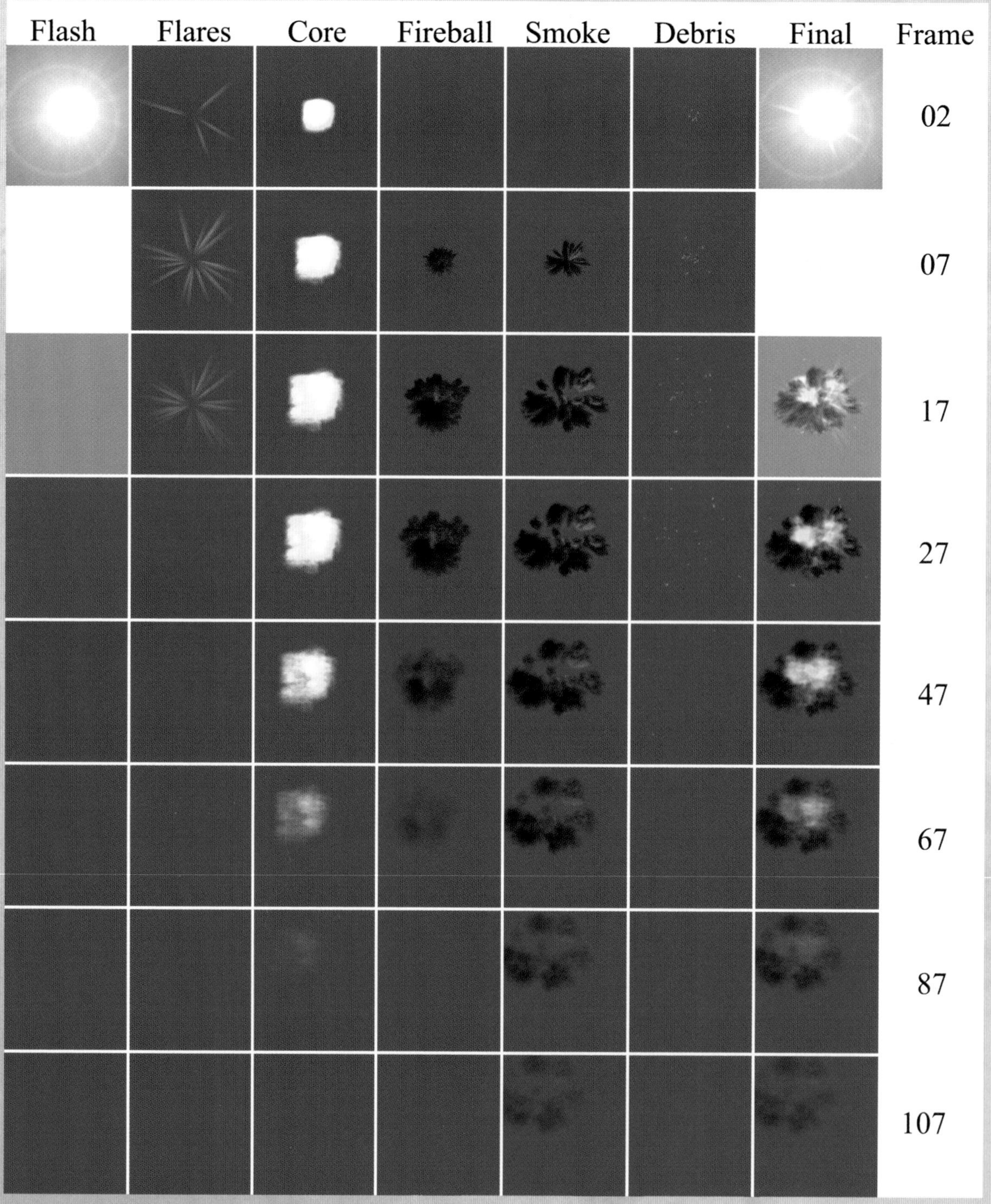

Flash Flares Core Fireball Smoke Debris Final Frame

02

07

17

27

47

67

87

107

COLOR PLATE 8A *Components of explosions used in technique from Article 5.6.*

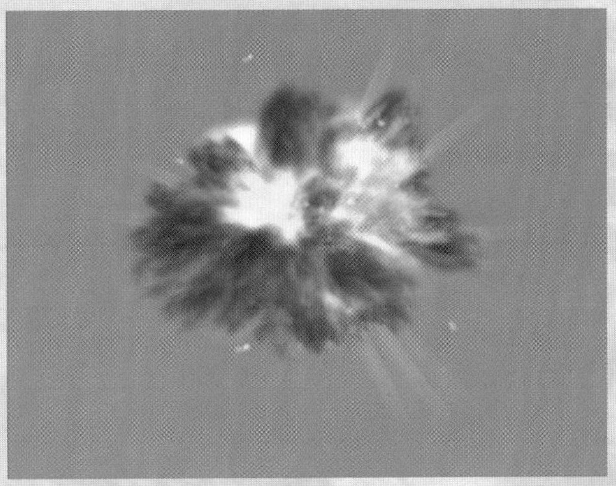

COLOR PLATE 8B *Final effect of explosion in Article 5.6.*

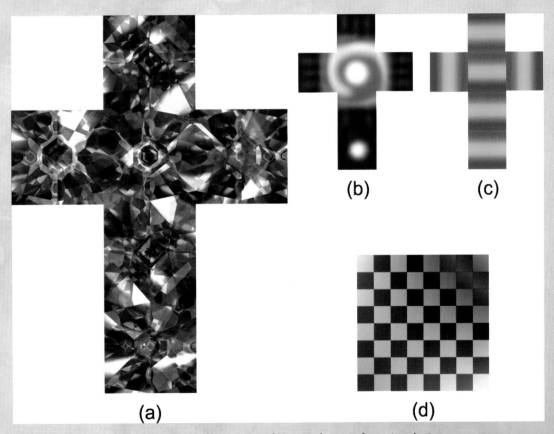

COLOR PLATE 9A *Components used in gem rendering technique from Article 5.7.*

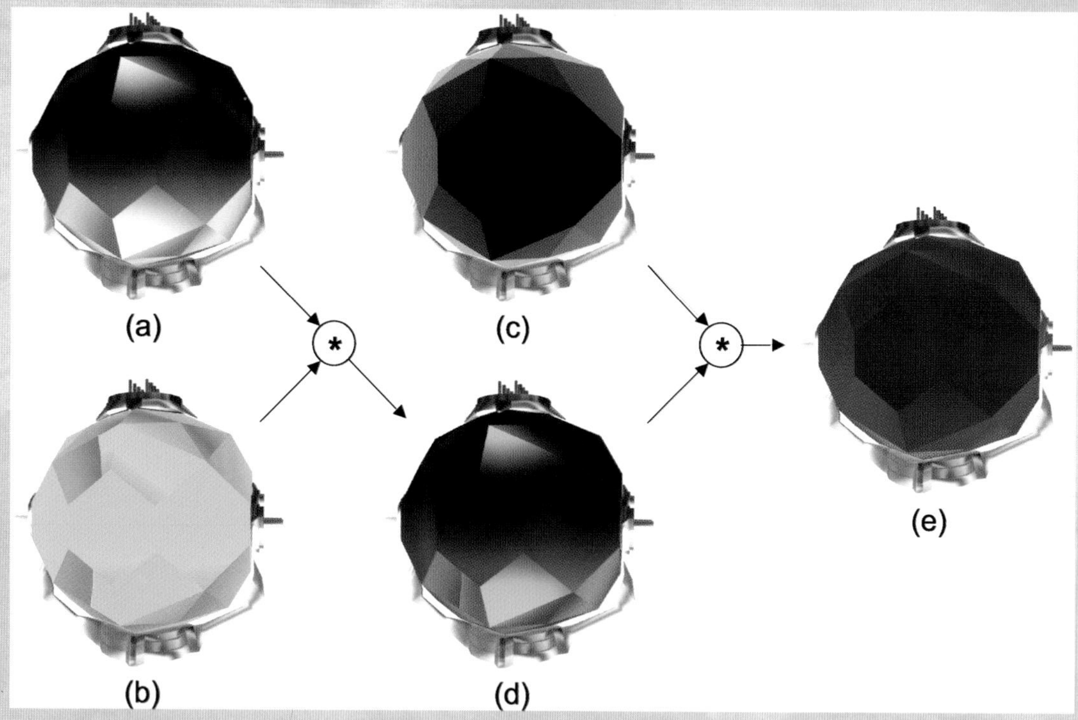

COLOR PLATE 9B *Components used in gem rendering technique from Article 5.7.*

COLOR PLATE 9C *Screenshot from ATI's demo "Ruby: The Double Cross" showing the gem rendering technique from Article 5.7 in action.*

4.2

Dynamic Grass Simulation and Other Natural Effects

Rishi Ramraj, The University of Waterloo

thereisnocowlevel@hotmail.com

Developments in games like *Half Life 2* have demonstrated that the physical behavior of a game's environment plays a large role in providing an immersive feel to the user. However, simulating complex natural effects involves significant computational overhead.

Overhead can be reduced by examining an existing algorithm used for water simulation. The memory requirements of this methodology can be reduced by up to 50%, while still maintaining (if not enhancing) the quality of the simulation. This methodology can then be extended to simulate effects such as wind blowing over grass and through leaves.

This gem has three goals. First, a method is presented for optimizing the memory requirements of water simulation under certain circumstances. The resulting model is then used to provide a robust and easily implemented algorithm for simulating dynamic grass. Finally, these methods are generalized to provide an approach for simulating effects involving the impact of change through a network of similar or dissimilar objects.

The Water Effect

The approach to natural effects described in this article was derived from an algorithm outlined in *Game Programming Gems 4* called "iWave" [GPG04]. A simplified version of the algorithm can be found at [Willemse00]. Both algorithms described are essentially the same, but for simplicity's sake, we will discuss the latter.

The Algorithm

The iWave algorithm approximates a planar body of water by a grid of points. The vertical motion of each point on the grid simulates ripples moving over the water, as depicted in Figure 4.2.1.

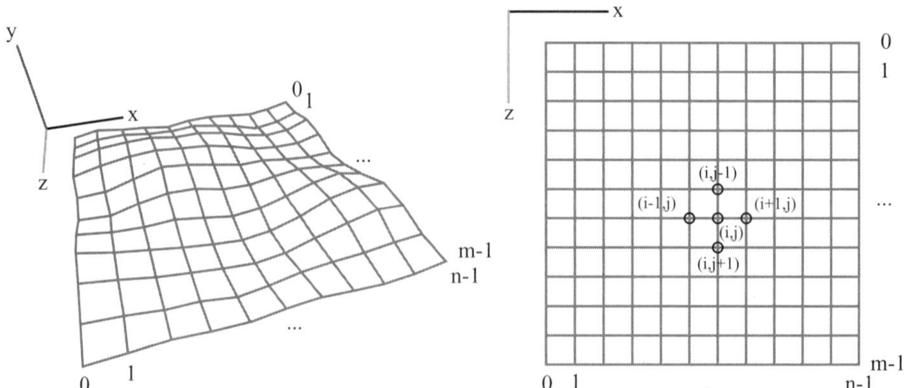

FIGURE 4.2.1 *The iWave approximation of a planar body of water. Three-dimensional (left) and two-dimensional (right) depictions are shown.*

To animate the system, two grids are used, representing the pre and post state of a time step. One grid stores the current height values of the system. It is then used to calculate the values of the next time step, stored in the other grid. Using two grids ensures the calculations performed on the $(i - 1, j)$ point for example, do not bleed over onto point (i, j).

To make waves move through the system, we look at each point (i, j) individually. The resulting height at that point is calculated by summing the heights of the point around it, dividing the result by two, and subtracting the height of the current point:

```
res_h[i,j] = (src_h[i-1,j] +
                 src_h[i+1,j] +
                 src_h[i,j-1] +
              src_h[i,j+1] ) / 2 – src_h[i,j];
```

The result is a system where waves move through the grid. The waves maintain the same amplitude, so energy has to be removed from the system. The solution is to simply remove a portion of the energy from the system every update by subtracting a portion of the height:

```
res_h[i,j] -= res_h[i,j] * damp_factor;
```

To create a ripple on the surface, simply set the height point on the surface to a value other than 0. The effect is that the change produced moves throughout the system, affecting points around the selected point. A wave, in turn, ripples out from the selected point.

Specifics as to how and why these formulas are used and why they work are found in [Willemse00] and are more thoroughly discussed in [GPG04] (including how to animate over a variable time step). The effect conserves water mass; as a surface rises in one location, it falls in another. [GPG04] also discusses how obstacles that cause waves to rebound are modeled.

These specifics, however, exceed the scope of this gem. Next we will look at the aspects of this simulation that relate to change propagation.

Analyzing the Approach

Intuitively, we view this system as an approximation using a planar mesh because that is how it is rendered. If, on the other hand, we view the system as a network, we can make several interesting observations.

The network is composed of several nodes, each the same, with at most four and at least two connections to other nodes. Each node is used to store a height value, and their logical position in the network is used to determine their physical position in the render.

Links used in the network tell the system that change occurs between the linked nodes. Nodes on either side of this link can mutually affect each other. Thus, if we change the height of one node in the system, it would affect the heights of its neighbors during a time step, and would later be affected by its neighbors in the succeeding time step. The result, over a period of time is a rendition of the affect of change in one node on the entire system.

The function defined earlier is part of each link. It defines how the properties of one node affect the properties of its neighboring node and characterizes how change propagates throughout the network. The function is integral to the operation of simulation. For example, the entire effect can be changed into a blur (as mentioned in [Willemse00]) by averaging the heights of the nodes. It also characterizes the stability of the simulation. Without the aforementioned `damp_factor`, for example, the entire simulation would become very sporadic; waves would never fade out.

Optimization

[GPG04] mentions that iWave is not very effective at generating ambient ocean waves. This optimization creates a simple approximation of ambient waves, while reducing the memory requirements of the effect, making an ocean feasible. It also adds an interesting quirk to the change propagation model.

The optimization is simple: use one planar grid instead of two. This approach keeps the concept of a time step between calculations while eliminating half the bulk memory requirement of the system. As the update proceeds through this one grid, the point (i, j) is calculated with a mix of updated points, $(i - 1, j)$ for example, and current points like $(i + 1, j)$. Instead of waves radiating outwards from a point in all directions, they radiate from a point in the direction of the update. The result is a water simulation that seems as though it is being blown by the wind; it resembles the large ambient waves of an ocean. The result is presented in Figure 4.2.2.

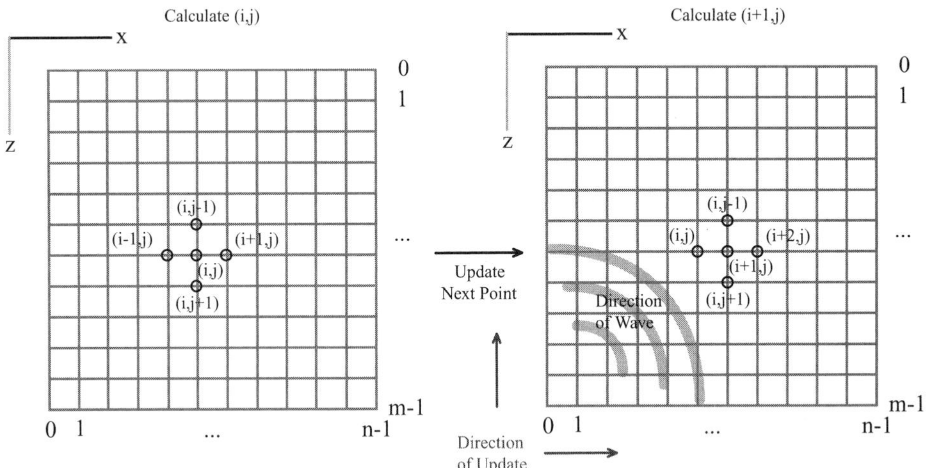

FIGURE 4.2.2 *The iWave approximation with optimization. As the update proceeds through the mesh, a point (i, j) is calculated. It is then used to calculate (i + 1, j).*

Why is this happening? We are of course removing the "double buffering" approach the initial algorithm used. The original algorithm used double buffering to ensure one time step's data wasn't polluted by interim calculations of the next time step. However, this is only problematic depending on the goal of the simulation. If the goal is accuracy, which is required for certain simulation, then eliminating the second buffer is not an option. If the goal is a simulation that looks "good enough," then eliminating the second grid is not only beneficial to memory, it can also look good as in the case of iWave.

There are many situations where an accurate time step is necessary. This is not the case in most natural effects because the simulations are usually cosmetic. The remaining effects discussed in this gem do not use a second buffer to accommodate for an accurate time step. The next example, grass simulation, starts to exploit aspects of network analysis.

Simulating Grass

There is very little difference between simulating grass and the water effect. In a large field of grass, when energy is applied to one stalk, it in turn affects those around it. It should be noted that the term *energy* is used colloquially. In this sense, it describes a quantity that affects or is possessed by an object. It is used as such for the remainder of the gem. If sufficient energy is applied, like a gust of wind, then a wave of energy moves through the field of grass.

The Algorithm

If we analyze the water effect using the previous network approach, we can pick out elements that we can preserve. Grass, like water, uses the same planar grid to represent its elements. Each node can represent a stalk of grass and is surrounded by up to four other stalks. Energy moves through both systems similarly, so the function we use between links does not change. The only difference between the systems is the way the property of the node is interpreted. In the case of a water simulation, each node represents a height value. In the case of grass, it is more complex. When energy affects a stalk of grass, the stalk rotates (e.g., bends) in the direction of the energy flow. This process requires two things: a direction of the application of this energy and a scalar representation of energy to determine the extent to which the stalk is affected.

We can use the value at each node as a representation of energy. That is, the height of a wave instead becomes the degree to which the grass rotates. We can define a vector as the direction of the energy. This lets us control which way the wind blows. The vector is scaled by the energy scalar. It is then divided into components along the x and z axes. Rotation along these axes is proportional to the resulting components. There are different ways to convert the components of the vector into angles, the easiest being to simply scale the components. The result is demonstrated in Figure 4.2.3.

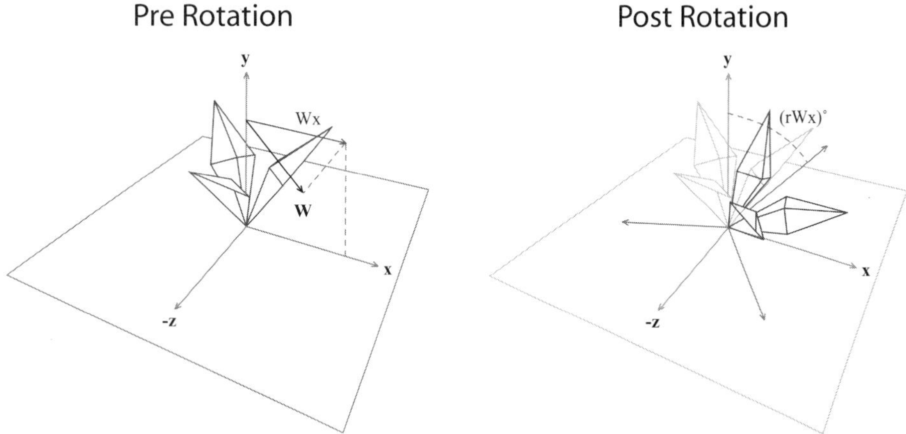

FIGURE 4.2.3 *The rotation or "tilt" of a stalk of grass. The vector Wx is calculated from* **W***. It is then scaled with a value r to produce (rWx)° of rotation. A similar rotation is preformed in the z direction.*

Repeat this process for a large amount of grass over a field, and you create the illusion of a plain of grass being blown by the wind. We are now capable of converting a water simulation to a grass effect with little effort. Next, we will take a look at the rules of the change propagation model.

The Change Propagation Model

Over the past discussion, we have highlighted several components required for a change propagation model. It is composed of a network of nodes connected to other nodes, each used to store some value. These nodes are linked together if they change each other and the change that occurs is controlled by some function. Next, we will take a look at each component of the model to identify the essential parts.

The Network

The networks described so far have all been girded matrices. In both examples, the logical arrangement of the network (i.e., a grid) maps directly to the physical representation. However, these examples are simply implementations of an abstract concept. We can generalize the concept; the network is responsible for defining the interconnections between nodes. It is not restricted by architecture or any physical mapping to reality (as the next effect will demonstrate). The architecture of the network can also change over time.

The Nodes/Interpretation

Nodes in previous examples have all been composed of one value. This value has been some floating-point scalar that has been mapped to a physical element. Every network presented has been a collection of the same node.

In general, a node can be considered a thing that can be changed. It can represent any quantity, from a single floating-point variable to a linked list of arbitrary classes. Nodes do not have to be mapped to any physical quantity; they can just as easily represent something abstract, like the weights of a neural network [Buckland01]. Furthermore, nodes do not have to be replicas of their neighbors, so long as they fulfill the requirements of the links and functions, which we will discuss next.

The Functions

The functions presented have worked with scalar values to produce scalar values. iWave, for example, uses the heights of a mesh to produce a new height. In general, however, we can say that a function, in this model, is a relation that maps the output of a node to the input of another node (or back to the original node). To address the earlier problem with dissimilar nodes, a function could be written to convert the output of one node to the input of another. Further, these functions do not have to be bidirectional.

The relevance and derivation of functions have been in part influenced by the application that uses them. iWave, for example, derived its function from the *linearized Bernoulli equations* [GPG04], functions that describe fluid dynamics. Although we cannot totally avoid the end application, it should be noted that the function does not have to be justified mathematically. It is a relation between the causal input and the resulting output. Approximations and arbitrary associations are acceptable, provided they produce the desired effect.

The Links

The previous examples have not covered the concept of links. In general, a link is the set of functions between nodes and acts as a bridge between nodes where changes occur. One link may use more than one function. Functions can in turn be swapped between nodes as the simulation continues. If the architecture of the network changes, then a standard input/output type is required. The conversion could be preformed by a function inserted in the middle of a link.

Simulating Leaves: Applying the Model

In the next exercise, we will use the change propagation model to simulate the effect of wind blowing through leaves. In this effect, the leaves of a tree react more violently on the side of the tree facing the wind. As energy moves through the tree, leaves closer to the source of energy obstruct leaves farther away. To reproduce this effect, we will take a look at individual components of the change propagation model and decide on reasonable solutions to the problems they pose.

The Network

The network is responsible for defining the interconnections between nodes. In reality, the effect between leaves on a tree is fairly minimal. Leaves do not regularly make contact with each other. However, leaves do obstruct each other from wind, which implies that they induce change. In this case, the architecture of the network does not change over time.

Ideally, each leaf would affect all others; the wind could come from any direction such that each leaf could obstruct others. The function would be based on the flow of wind around the leaf. It is obvious that this is overkill. Instead, we can simplify the simulation by making a few observations. The basis of the simulation is that energy is dissipated from one or several points in the network. We can say that a node is connected to three of its closest neighbors and the energy transferred between nodes is proportional to the distance between them. The value three is arbitrary and in practice has proven to be a fairly good compromise between an accurate fully meshed simulation and a mesh of single links.

The Nodes/Interpretation

A node is a thing that can be changed. In this case, we want to store some sort of scalar, which represents how much the leaf blows in the direction of the wind. Each leaf must be aware of its current orientation and the overall orientation of the wind so that it can be blown in the proper direction. Note that we could design the system so that the leaves would be blown in random directions. In this case, the orientation of the wind could be inferred by the way energy flows through the system.

Interpreting the energy scalar poses several interesting problems. We have two vectors, one defining the orientation of the leaf and the other defining the orientation of the wind. The energy scalar indicates how closely the leaf rests on the wind vector. When there is no energy, the leaf settles back into its original position. When there is a lot of energy, the leaf moves violently in the direction of the wind.

There are several mathematical ways to tackle this problem. We could use quaternion and spherical linear interpolation [Wattenberg97]. Using this approach, we would run into problems when trying to introduce randomness to the behavior as well as problems rendering the leaves in the desired directions. Instead, we could consider the problem in spherical coordinates [Bobick03]. The initial orientation of each leaf and the orientation of the wind are specified by an azimuth and an inclination. The energy scalar is used to specify how much of an angle we add from the current leaf orientation towards the wind orientation. We will also be adding small random angles to produce noise. The algorithm for calculating the new orientation for the leaf is presented in Figure 4.2.4.

Step 1
The first step is to determine the angle between the leaf's current orientation and the wind's orientation.

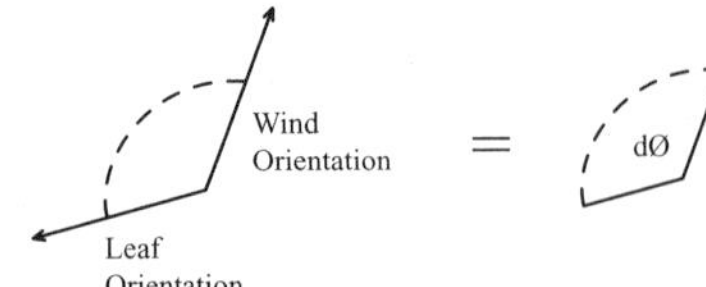

Step 2
We then multiply this value, dØ, by the energy scalar to produce dE.

dØ X ENERGY = dE

Step 3
A random value R is added to dE to produce dF.

dE + R = dF

Step 4
dF is then added to the Leaf's original orientation to produce the Final orientation, which is rendered.

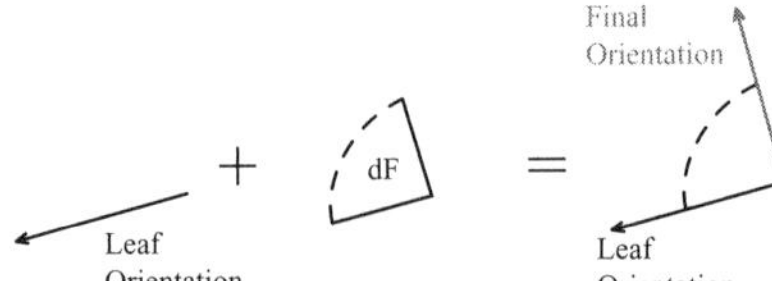

FIGURE 4.2.4 *Algorithm for calculating the new orientation of a leaf.*

The Function

When wind blows through a tree, the leaves closer to the source of the wind are affected the most. When the wind stops, the energy affecting the leaves dies off.

Energy on those affected the most dies off last. This type of behavior is best reproduced by a blurring algorithm, as discussed in the water effect portion of the gem. In a typical blur, the point (i, j) results from taking the average of points around it and itself.

Although this function emulates the behavior we seek, over time, the energy of the system increases permanently as more energy is added. Take, for example, a grid that uses this function. If we apply an increase in energy at (i, j), then when the distribution of energy settles over a time t, all points in the grid will possess some of the initial energy. The energy applied to the system initially will be evenly divided among the points in the grid.

We want a system where energy fades back to zero: a return to equilibrium. We can make the interchange of energy proportional to the distance between nodes. This way, only a portion of energy is transferred between nodes; as the distance between nodes increases, the energy transfer decreases. The result is then summed. Distances between nodes will be constantly reducing the amount of energy in the system over time, and as a result, the system will return to equilibrium.

The Links

In this particular simulation, the role played by the links is minimal. Analysis using links becomes important when considering networks with dynamic architecture.

Conclusion

Throughout this gem, we have considered three simulations: water, grass, and leaves. Each simulation uses the same basic idea: the change propagation model. The intent is for the reader to consider the examples presented and use them along with the change propagation model to create new effects.

References

[Bobick03] Bobick, Nick. "Rotating Objects Using Quaternions." Available online at *http://www.gamasutra.com/features/19980703/quaternions_01.htm*. June 3, 2003.

[Buckland01] Buckland, Mat. "Neural Networks in Plain English." Available online at *http://www.ai-junkie.com/ann/evolved/nnt1.html*. June 12, 2001.

[GPG04] Tessendorf, Jerry. *Game Programming Gems 4*. Charles River Media, 2004.

[Wattenberg97] Wattenberg, Frank. "Spherical Coordinates." Available online at *http://www.math.montana.edu/frankw/ccp/multiworld/multipleIVP/spherical/body.htm*. May 21, 1997.

[Willemse00] Willemse, Roy. "The Water Effect Explained." Available online at *http://www.gamedev.net/reference/articles/article915.asp*. February 15, 2000.

4.3

Realistic Cloth Animation Using the Mass-Spring Model

Juan M. Cordero, Dep. de Lenguajes y Sistemas Informáticos, Universidad de Sevilla

cordero@lsi.us.es

Although cloth is a common object, the physical laws that govern its dynamics are complex. Continually, algorithms for cloth animation are improved by focusing on two main aspects: the efficiency of the models and the search for realistic results.

Since the mid-eighties, several cloth simulation models have been proposed based on geometric [Weil86], physical [Provot95, House00], and hybrid [Tsopelas91] properties. For the moment, only models based on physics provide realistic results. However, physical models are time-consuming processes due to the complexity of calculations and the difficulty of creating user-friendly methods for specifying material characteristics.

In recent years, the Kawabata Evaluation System (KES) [Kawabata75] has been used in cloth simulation models to empirically obtain parameters intrinsic to a particular type of cloth. However, KES is a costly technique, and in most cases, relatively few of the obtained results are used in the simulation models.

This gem details a new simulation method based on the mass-spring model that achieves high-quality results with a low computational cost. In the next section, we describe a computational model for cloth based on masses and springs. After that, we present the forces involved in cloth dynamics. We then outline the equations of the dynamic system and provide an approach to resolve them. Finally, we present our conclusions and identify directions for further research.

A Discrete Representation of Cloth

A rectangular piece of cloth can be represented by a mesh of $n \times m$ mass particles linked by springs, as shown in Figure 4.3.1.

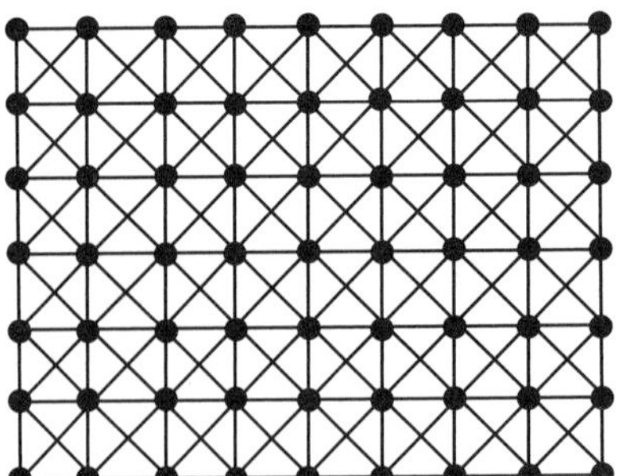

FIGURE 4.3.1 *A discrete representation of cloth using a mesh.*

The mass of each particle represents the mass of the material situated around the particle. Springs, linking particles, generate forces that make the distances between the particles constant. A mesh is oriented such that for every particle of the mesh, a normal vector to the surface is defined. The normal vector that describes the orientation of the mesh has the expression shown in Equation 4.3.1.

$$\vec{n}_{ij} = \frac{\vec{N}_1 + \vec{N}_2 + \vec{N}_3 + \vec{N}_4}{\| \vec{N}_1 + \vec{N}_2 + \vec{N}_3 + \vec{N}_4 \|} \tag{4.3.1}$$

where $\vec{N}_k$ is the normal vector of each triangle that defines the mesh around the particle (see Figure 4.3.2).

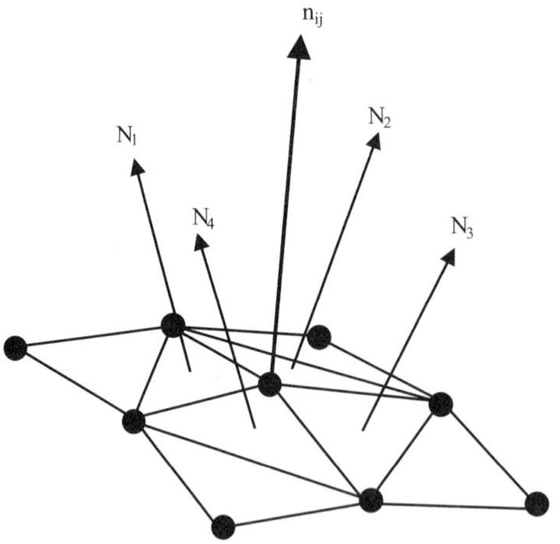

FIGURE 4.3.2 *The normal vector of the mesh at a particle position is a combination of the normal vectors of the triangles that surround the particle.*

As we will show, it is important to know the surface normal for each particle in order to decide if a force is internal or external to the plane of the mesh. For every particle of the mesh, there are three sets of neighboring particles: *stretching* (or structural) neighbors, *shearing* neighbors, and *bending* neighbors. The internal forces of the mesh will be described once the sets of neighboring particles are defined. Starting from a particle of the mesh situated at (i, j), the stretching neighbors are described in Equation 4.3.2

$$V_T = \left\{ P_{i+1,j}, P_{i-1,j}, P_{i,j+1}, P_{i,j-1} \right\}. \tag{4.3.2}$$

for the case involving four neighbors. If the particle is localized at the edge of the mesh, it will have three neighbors, and if at a corner of the mesh, it will only have two (see Figure 4.3.3).

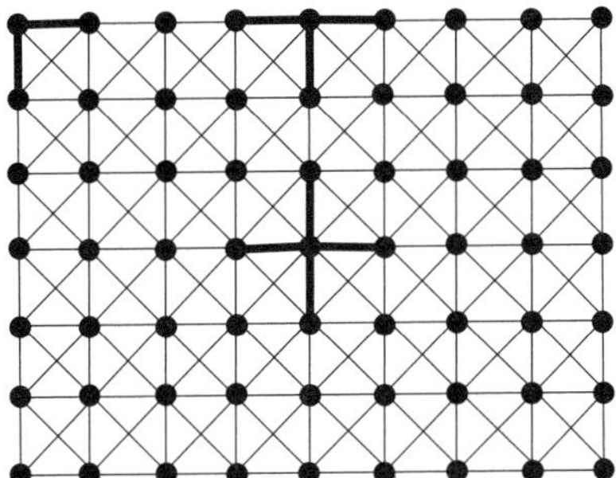

FIGURE 4.3.3 *Stretching neighbors representation.*

The set of stretching neighbors, V_T, is divided into two subsets that correspond to the principal directions of the mesh:

$$V_{T^{wp}} = \left\{ P_{i+1,j}, P_{i-1,j} \right\}$$
$$V_{T^{wf}} = \left\{ P_{i,j+1}, P_{i,j-1} \right\},$$

where V_T^{wp} is the subset of stretching neighbors in the direction of the warp and V_T^{wf} is the subset in the direction of the weft.

The set of shearing neighbors is expressed as in Equation 4.3.3 (see Figure 4.3.4).

$$V_S = \left\{ P_{i+1,j+1}, P_{i-1,j+1}, P_{i+1,j-1}, P_{i-1,j-1} \right\} \tag{4.3.3}$$

Note that there are one, two, or three neighbors, depending on the situation of the particle under study.

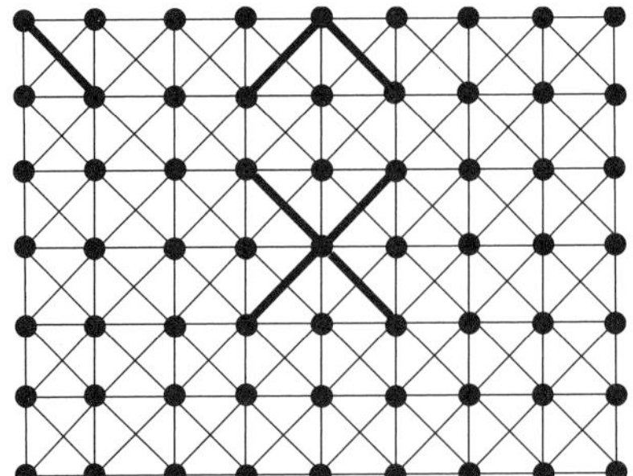

FIGURE 4.3.4 *Shearing neighbors representation.*

We will later show that the set of shearing neighbors does not need to be divided.

The set of bending neighbors is expressed as:

$$V_B = \left\{ P_{i+2,j}, P_{i-2,j}, P_{i,j+2}, P_{i,j-2} \right\}. \tag{4.3.4}$$

As with stretching neighbors, the set can consist of four, three, or two elements, depending on the position of the particle within the mesh (see Figure 4.3.5).

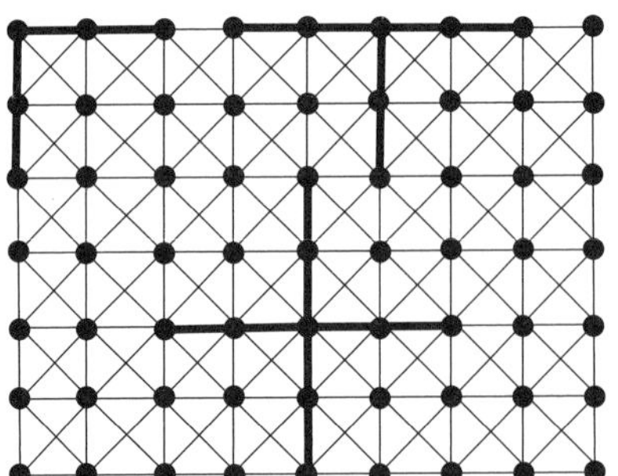

FIGURE 4.3.5 *Bending neighbors representation.*

The set *VB* is also divided into two subsets:

$$V_{B^{wp}} = \{P_{i+2,j}, P_{i-2,j}\}$$
$$V_{B^{wf}} = \{P_{i,j+2}, P_{i,j-2}\}.$$

These represent the neighbors in the directions of the warp and the weft of the cloth, respectively.

To simplify the notation, we use R to designate the set of subindexes related to sets 1, 2, and 3 along with their respective subsets:

$$R_T = \{(i+1,j),(i-1,j),(i,j+1),(i,j-1)\}$$
$$R_{T^{wp}} = \{(i+1,j),(i-1,j)\}$$
$$R_{T^{wf}} = \{(i,j+1),(i,j-1)\}$$
$$R_S = \{(i+1,j+1),(i-1,j+1),(i+1,j-1),(i-1,j-1)\}$$
$$R_B = \{(i+2,j),(i-2,j),(i,j+2),(i,j-2)\}$$
$$R_{B^{wp}} = \{(i+2,j),(i-2,j)\}$$
$$R_{B^{wf}} = \{(i,j+2),(i,j-2)\}$$

Forces

Once the mesh of the cloth is obtained and the orientation of the particle is defined along with its set of neighbors, we can express the forces related to each particle. Two different groups of forces will be determined: internal forces and external forces.

Internal Forces

The internal forces relate to the quasi-elastic behavior of the cloth. There are stretching forces, bending forces, and shearing forces. Stretching and shearing forces are in-plane forces while bending forces are out-of-plane forces. This means that stretching and shearing forces follow the directions defined by the mesh, while bending forces are normal to the surface of the mesh. Therefore, to define the forces, we must first know the orientation of each particle within the mesh.

The stretching force is predominant among the internal forces. Due to the similarity of the stretching properties of cloth in general, this force does not discriminate against different types of cloth during the simulation. Therefore, many authors do not consider the effect of the stretching force, and instead they impose a fundamental assumption on the mesh: the distance between stretching neighbors is constant [Witkin90]. This paper takes into account stretching forces. *Hook's Law* gives the following expression for the stretching force of a mesh particle P_{ij}:

$$F_{ij^T} = -\sum_{(k,l)\in R_{T^{wp}}} K_{T^{wp}}(\xi)\vec{1}_{ijkl} - \sum_{(k,l)\in R_{T^{wf}}} K_{T^{wf}}(\xi)\vec{1}_{ijkl}, \tag{4.3.5}$$

where

$$\vec{1}_{ijkl} = \vec{P}_{ij} P_{kl}$$

$$\xi = \frac{\left\|\vec{1}_{ijkl}\right\| - 1_{ijkl^0}}{1_{ijkl^0}},$$

where

l_{ijkl^0} is the length of the spring that links P_{ij^0} to P_{kl^0} when the mesh is at rest. That is:

$$1_{ijkl^0} = \left\|P_{ij^0} P_{kl^0}\right\|,$$

where $K_{T^{wp}}(\xi)$ and $K_{T^{wf}}(\xi)$ depends on the elongation, ξ. Together $K_{T^{wp}}(\xi)$ and $K_{T^{wf}}(\xi)$ model the quasi-elastic behaviour of the cloth.

The other in-plane force is the shearing force. This force represents the lateral deformations of the cloth. The force over a particle P_{ij} is:

$$F_{ij^S} = -\sum_{(k,l)\in R_S} K_S(\xi)\varphi_{ijkl}\vec{1}_{ijkl}, \tag{4.3.6}$$

where

$$\vec{1}_{ijkl} = \vec{P}_{ij}\vec{P}_{kl}$$

$$\xi = \frac{\left\|\vec{1}_{ijkl}\right\| - 1_{ijkl^0}}{1_{ijkl^0}}$$

$$1_{ijkl^0} = \left\|P_{ij^0} P_{kl^0}\right\|$$

$$\varphi_{ijkl} = 1 - \left|\frac{\vec{1}_{ijkl}}{\left\|\vec{1}_{ijkl}\right\|}\vec{n}_{ij}\right|.$$

and n_{ij} is the normal vector at P_{ij} particle, as seen earlier.

The parameter φ_{ijkl} can be explained as follows: the shearing force is an in-plane force that attains its maximum value when φ_{ijkl} is 1. This occurs when the normal at P_{ij} and the vector $\vec{l}_{ijkl}$ are perpendicular. When the vectors are not perpendicular, the value of φ_{ijkl} decreases as the force changes from a shearing force to a bending force, as shown in Figure 4.3.6.

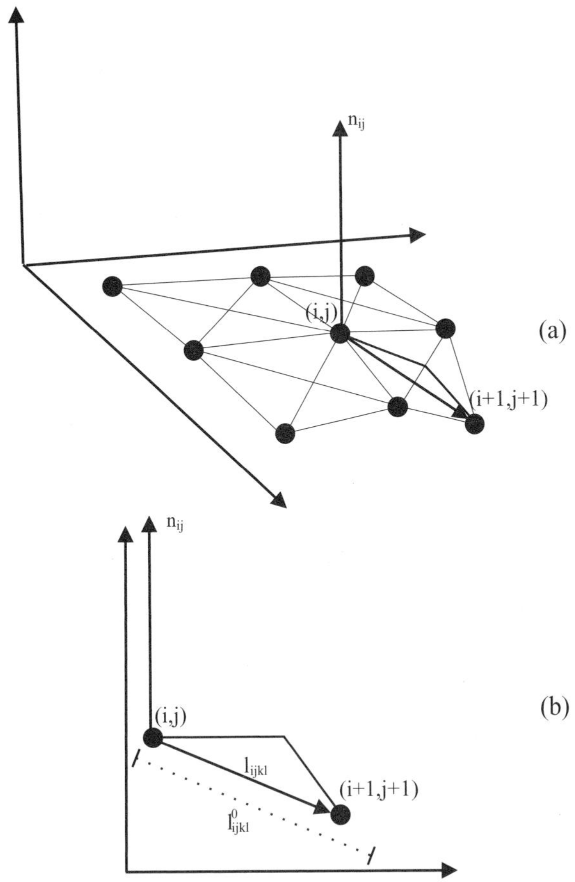

FIGURE 4.3.6 *The longitude of a shearing spring has been modified (a). The elongation of the spring is applied perpendicular to the plane of the mesh, so there are no shearing forces (b).*

There is no absolute coordinate system for the mesh, so we cannot express shearing forces based on the warp and the weft of the cloth. Therefore, when a lateral deformation occurs, we assume both directions are equally affected. So, instead of $K_S{}^{wp}$ and $K_S{}^{wf}$, a combination of both functions K_S is used.

Bending forces are the only out-of-plane forces and can be expressed as:

$$F_{ij^B} = -\sum_{(k,l)\in R_{B^{wp}}} K_{B^{wp}}(\xi)\psi_{ijkl} - \vec{1}_{ijkl} - \sum_{(k,l)\in R_{B^{wf}}} K_{B^{wf}}(\xi)\psi_{ijkl} - \vec{1}_{ijkl} \tag{4.3.7}$$

where

$$\vec{1}_{ijkl} = \vec{P}_{ij}\vec{P}_{kl}$$

$$\xi = \frac{\left\|\vec{1}_{ijkl}\right\| - 1_{ijkl^0}}{1_{ijkl^0}}$$

$$1_{ijkl^0} = \left\|P_{ij^0}P_{kl^0}\right\|$$

$$\psi_{ijkl} = \left|\frac{\vec{1}_{ijkl}}{\left\|\vec{1}_{ijkl}\right\|}\right|\vec{n}_{ij}.$$

The value of the parameter ψ_{ijkl}, similar to φ_{ijkl}, represents the force applied out of the plane. Then, when $\psi_{ijkl} = 0$, the normal $\vec{n}_{ij}$ and the vector $\vec{l}_{ijkl}$ are perpendicular and the force is applied within the plane. However, if $\psi_{ijkl} = 1$, the vectors are parallel and the force is applied out of the plane, as shown in Figure 4.3.7.

Elongation Functions

The $K(\xi)$ functions, previously introduced, determine the force variation due to elongation. If we consider these functions linear, the springs' behavior will also be linear. This would mean that stretching forces, lateral deformations, or flexions of the cloth obey *Hook's Law.* However, the elastic behavior of cloth is nonlinear. When elongation extends beyond a certain limit, the force opposing the motion increases exponentially (as seen in the graphics of KES). This way, the functions $K(\xi)$ introduce the quasi-elastic behavior of cloth into the force expressions. Therefore, to obtain coherent results in the animation, $K(\xi)$ has to meet at least two conditions:

$$K(0) = 0$$

$K(\xi)$ is monotonically non-decreasing

External Forces

The set of forces that are not produced by the quasi-elastic behavior of the cloth are known as external forces. These forces are gravity, air friction, and others. In the proposed model, every particle mass corresponds to the mass of the area over which that

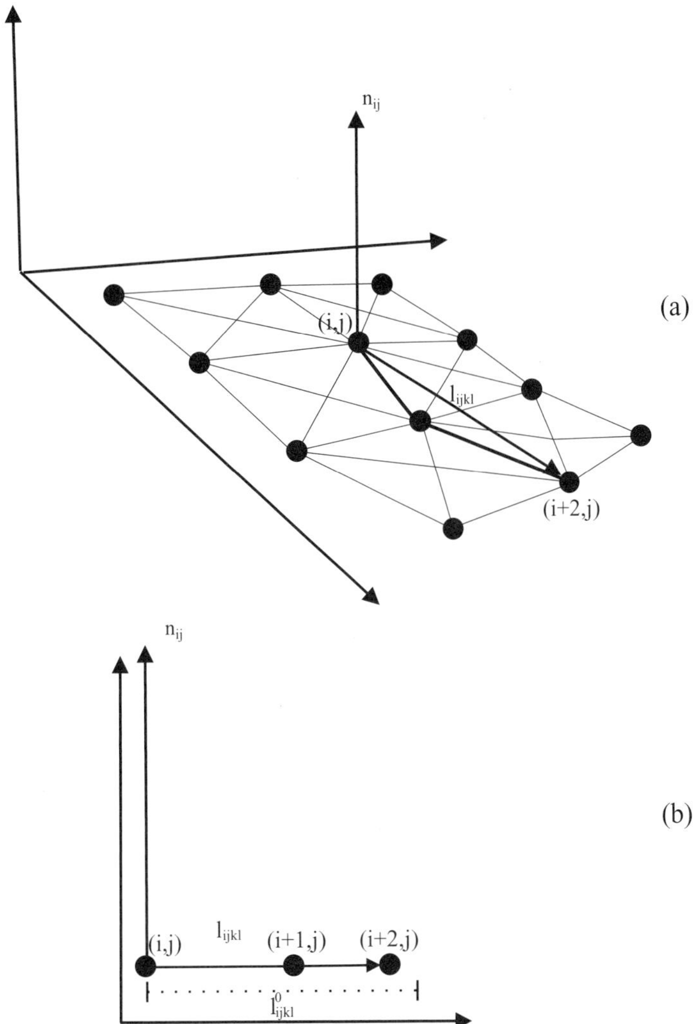

FIGURE 4.3.7 *The length of a shearing spring has been modified (a). The spring elongation is applied within the mesh plane, so no bending forces exist (b).*

particle dominates. Thus, gravity is applied over all the particles. We use the common expression for gravity:

$$F_{ij}^{G} = m_{ij}\vec{g}$$

where m_{ij} is the mass of the particle P_{ij} and $\vec{g}$ is the acceleration due to gravity. The influence of air over the cloth depends on the speed and direction of the air as well as the speed of the cloth itself. This force is estimated as:

$$F_{ij}^{A} = C_a\left[\vec{n}_{ij} \cdot \left(\vec{u}_a - \vec{v}_{ij}\right)\right] \cdot \vec{n}_{ij} \tag{4.3.8}$$

where C_a is the air viscosity constant, $\vec{u}_a$ is a vector that defines the speed and direction of the air, $\vec{v}_{ij}$ is the speed of the particle P_{ij} and $\vec{n}_{ij}$ is the normal vector of the particle P_{ij}. When the air speed vector $\vec{u}_{ij}$ is equal to 0, the air remains immobile and the previous expression can be considered as air friction. Many other forces that are applied over the cloth are categorized as external forces. Examples of such forces are: the resulting force when manipulating the cloth and the force produced when hanging the cloth from one corner.

Dynamic System Approach

After obtaining the forces applied over the particles of the mesh, we can formulate a dynamic representation of the system. To accomplish this, the particles must follow *Newton's Second Law*, as shown in Equation 4.3.9.

$$\sum F_{ij} = m_{ij} a_{ij} \tag{4.3.9}$$

where F_{ij} represents the forces applied over each particle P_{ij}, m_{ij} is the mass of the particle, and $a_{ij} = \ddot{P}_{ij}$ the acceleration. From Equation 4.3.5, for each particle of the mesh we can obtain the differential equations in Equation 4.3.10.

$$\begin{cases} \ddot{P}_{ijx} = \dfrac{1}{m_{ij}} F_{ijx} \\ \ddot{P}_{ijy} = \dfrac{1}{m_{ij}} F_{ijy} \\ \ddot{P}_{ijz} = \dfrac{1}{m_{ij}} F_{ijz} \end{cases} \qquad \begin{matrix} i = 1,\ldots,n \\ j = 1,\ldots,m \end{matrix} \tag{4.3.10}$$

The computational methods used to solve differential systems can also be employed to resolve the cloth dynamics problem [Volino00]. In this particular case, due to the use of elongation functions instead of elongation constants, time-step techniques are recommended for solving the previous equations. In most cases, forces will not increase much, but they may increase to oppose the effects of severe elongations. By using the *Runge-Kutta-Fehlberg* method of fourth-fifth order, good results can be obtained.

Simulation

After presenting the model and the equations that describe the dynamic behavior of the mesh, we can outline the description of the cloth animation method (see Figure 4.3.8).

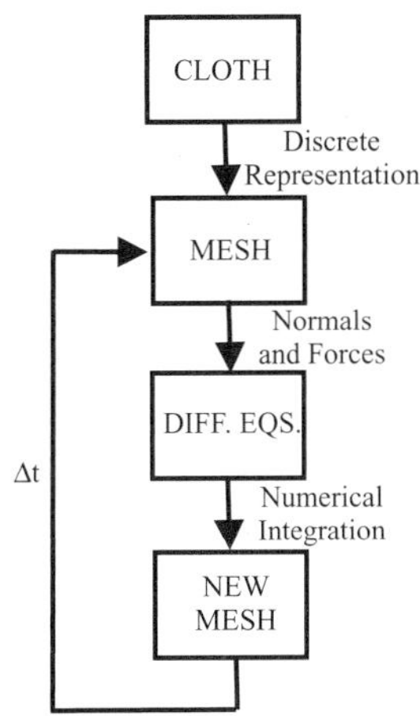

FIGURE 4.3.8 *Scheme of the proposed simulation method.*

First, we model an associated mesh from a cloth object. A suitable mesh is chosen that will have an adequate number of particles to allow the representation of the surface to be as smooth as possible.

Second, we calculate the normal vectors of the surface at each particle. We then obtain the internal and external forces applied to each particle and formulate the differential equation system as previously shown.

Finally, we resolve the system by applying an incremental interval of time, with which a new position of the mesh can be obtained. Repetition of these steps results in a real-time animation of the cloth system.

Conclusion

We have proposed a model for realistic cloth animation. The advantage of the model resides in the simplicity of its implementation. The mesh representation is based on a familiar mass-spring system and provides an efficient computational system viable for computer game application.

By considering the behavior of cloth as quasi-elastic, rather than perfectly elastic, we increase the realism and avoid undesired effects such as super-elastic effects [Cordero01].

Furthermore, distinguishing between in-plane and out-of-plane forces produces a more accurate simulation, avoiding (for example) the appearance of bending forces when only shearing forces exist.

Figures 4.3.9 and 4.3.10 (see Color Plates 1A and 1B) have been generated using the proposed method.

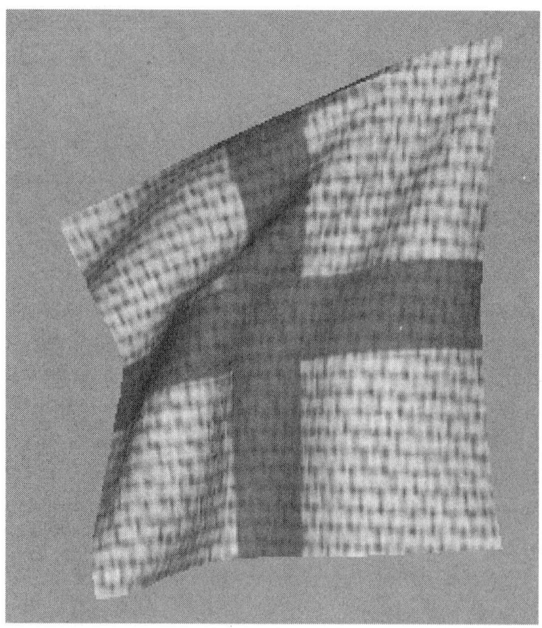

FIGURE 4.3.9 *A flag flying.*

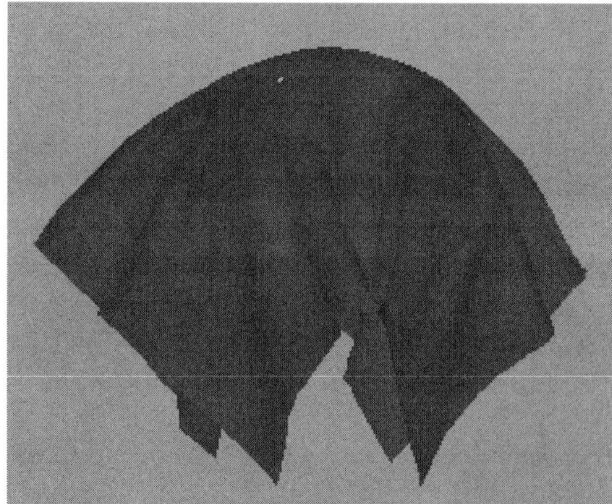

FIGURE 4.3.10 *A cloth draping over a sphere.*

Any future work proposed should strive to find the $K(\xi)$ *functions capable of simulating cloth more realistically. That is, to find the best parametric function* $K(\xi)$ and the value of its parameters, to minimize the error between the real motion of a cloth and its simulation. Also, the method we have presented uses a mesh of a rectangular cloth. Future models should strive toward the mesh representation of any cloth, independent of its form.

References

[Cordero01] Cordero, J.M., J. Matellanes,, and J. Cortés. *Corrección del Efecto Superelástico en Dinámica de Telas.* XI Congreso Español de Informática Gráfica (CEIG'2001), Girona, pp:141–147. 2001.

[House00] House, D.H. and D. E. Breen. *Cloth Modeling and Animation.* A K Peters, Ltd, 2000.

[Kawabata75] Kawabata, S. *The Standardization and Analysis of Hand Evaluation.* Committee of the Textile Machinery Society of Japan, 1975.

[Provot95] Provot, X. *Deformation Constraints in a Mass-Spring Model to Describe Rigid Cloth Behavior.* Graphics Interface '95 Proceedings, 147–154. Quebec, Canada, 1995.

[Tsopelas91] Tsopelas, N. *Animating the Crupling Behavior of Garments*, 11–24. Proc. 2nd Eurographics Workshop on Animation and Simulation. Blackwell, UK, 1991.

[Volino00] Volino, P., N. Magnenat-Thalmann. *Virtual Clothing. Theory and Practice.* Springer-Verlag, 2000.

[Weil86] Weil, J. *The Synthesis of Cloth Objects.* Computer Graphics (Proc. Siggraph), 20:49–54, 1986.

[Witkin90] Witkin, A., M. Gleicher, and W. Welch. *Interactive Dynamic.* Computer Graphics (Proc. Symposium on 3D Interactive Graphics), 24(2):11–21. 1990.

4.4

Practical Animation of Soft Bodies for Game Development: The Pressurized Soft-Body Model

Maciej Matyka, University of Wrocław

maq@panoramix.ift.uni.wroc.pl

In Computer Graphics (CG) research, a number of approaches for simulating soft bodies exist. Generally, these can be divided into two primary models: geometric and physically based. Fast and simple geometric models (known as *free form deformations* [Sedenberg86]) are not feasible in game development because of limited control. For purposes of realistic computer animation, other methods—particularly physically based—have been proposed.

Physically based application of the theory of elasticity gives a mathematically complicated and complex solution for the problem of soft body motion. Using finite volume methods [Irving04], we are able to simulate the behavior of viscoelastic bodies accurately. Unfortunately, use of these engineering methods results in non real-time animation, and is therefore inappropriate for games. Even classic computational fluid dynamics (CFD) found its place here; in [Nixon02] the authors build a model of compressible fluid enclosed by a mesh that introduces additional forces into the model. That approach is discussed further because of its similarity to our model of pressurized soft bodies. Note that the CFD approach is not considered here because it is not a real-time solution due to the complexity of solving the Navier-Stokes equations.

We will not go deeper into non–real-time soft body models. We mention them because it is important to know that more accurate and physically correct models exist in current CG research that may serve as basis for future game development application.

Several different approaches have been proposed for the application of real-time soft body simulation, but none of them seem to be particularly suitable for game development. Simple spring-mass (SM) models were introduced mostly because of their ease of implementation and computation speed (see [Lander03]). However, SM models do not generally yield very good realism, and increasing the number of springs with the hope of increasing realism does not automatically result in an ideal solution; it comes with its own problems. Using a large number of springs typically creates difficulties with the "stiffness" of the simulation. Also, animators working with SM models will have to play with a large number of physics constraints, which involves dubious changes to the simulation model (imagine an object with 1,500 springs and an animator attempting to anticipate the effect of changing the properties of a single spring).

Simplified Spring Mass Models

Because of the problems with SM models in deformable body simulation, some modifications have been proposed to avoid introducing additional spring connections.

Consider the geometric object shown in Figure 4.4.1a. Its construction would be nearly useless in a typical SM simulation; running the simulation in the presence of gravity would cause the object to immediately collapse. We need some kind of internal system of forces that will keep the object stable. The easiest and most intuitive way to do that is to add supporting springs between all vertices in the object.

A model constructed in this manner is presented in Figure 4.4.1b. Such a model should behave reasonably well as a deformable body in a typical SM simulation. Note the addition of connections between all pairs of points. This means that for N points we will need to do N^2 spring calculations. This is really too much for objects composed of more than a few thousand vertices, and in fact, we are probably quite close to precluding real-time SM simulation altogether. By increasing the number of springs, we have also increased the difficulty of maintaining rigidity and managing unwanted internal motion. There are two ways to reduce this "stiffness" problem. One way is to use implicit integration that is applied for calculation of the motion equations [Baraf98]. Another is to use inverse dynamics constraints as corrective measures for the explicit integration method [Lander03, Provot95]. Both methods would help to some degree, but they of course incur additional costs in processing speed.

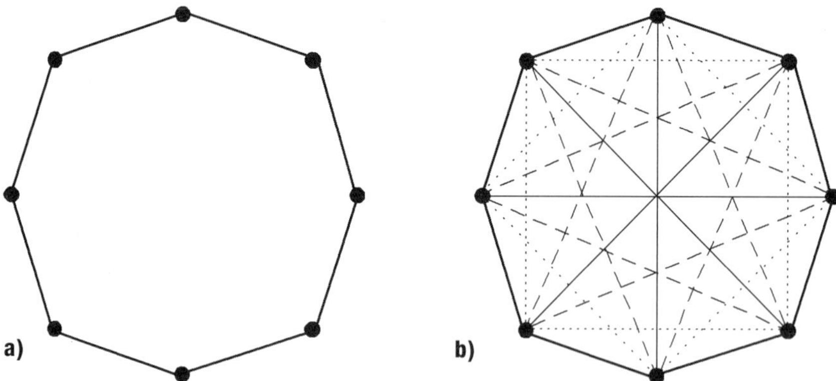

FIGURE 4.4.1 *Typical Spring-Mass models showing a) a simple hull without internal support and b) a hull supported with internal connections.*

These issues have been successfully avoided in computer graphics research involving models composed of simplified spring-mass constructions (see [Matyka03, Nixon02, Meseure00]). Nixon et al. [Nixon02] build a three-dimensional mesh filled with compressible fluid, and they solve Navier-Stokes equations inside of the object. This approach seems to be an accurate and very interesting new idea for physically based models. Unfortunately, the solution is completely inappropriate for efficient real-time simulation because of the complexity of the solutions to the Navier-Stokes equations and the need to construct a time-dependent grid.

The fields of medical imaging and virtual reality have also delved into real-time deformable bodies and have produced very interesting results. Meseure et al. [Meseure00] claim that models composed only of springs are not viable for surgical applications because of the complexity of geometric construction for objects containing a large number of points. They built an SM mesh in the same way Nixon et al. did, but without filling the object with fluid. Instead, the object is filled with a "virtual rigid component." The rigid component is called "virtual" because it does not interact with the simulation environment.

The idea of a virtual rigid component introduced by Meseure et al. seems to be interesting for game development. However, one disadvantage is that it introduces some complications over the simple model. For example, the physics background of the model is somewhat abstruse. Of course, in results-oriented game development we are only interested in getting a good deformable body simulation, but when working with a model of physically based animation, we should be reasonably up to speed about the physics behind it.

Physics behind the PSB Model

In the Pressurized Soft Body (PSB) model, we consider a geometric object consisting of a mesh made of nodes (mass material points) and spring connections (Hooke linear springs), as shown in Figure 4.4.1. We assume that the shape of the object is closed, which means that there are no holes (discontinuities) occurring in it. Because of the similarity to SM construction of cloth-like objects [Barraf98, Provot95], we generally consider it to be similar to an object sewn out of cloth.

To get deformable body behavior out of the "sewn cloth" object we introduce the PSB model. The basic idea is illustrated in Figure 4.4.2, in which a small pipe has been inserted into the object.

The pipe has been connected to a gas container. Inside the container, a gas with pressure $P_c > 0$ exists. Because of the difference between the pressure inside the body ($P_b = 0$) and pressure inside the connected container ($P_c > 0$), gas will flow from the container to the object as long as P_c is not equal to P_b. The pipe is then removed. After that, the simulation model will be slightly different from that shown in Figure 4.4.1. It will have been reshaped (expanded) due to the fact that the gas inside of it is under a pressure that exceeds that of the atmosphere ($P_b > P_a$).

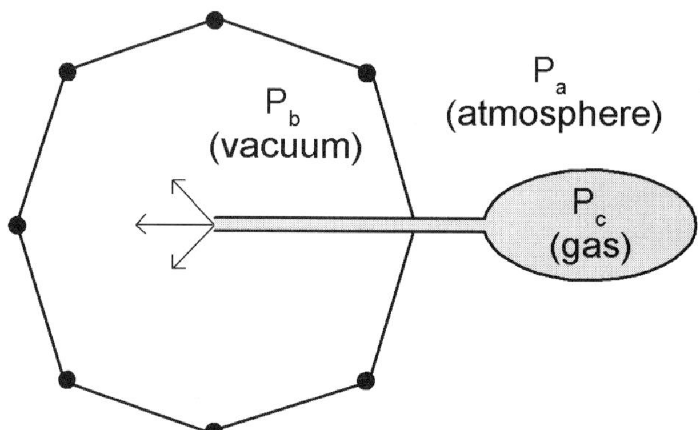

FIGURE 4.4.2 *A pipe has been put inside of the object with an initial pressure, P_b, of zero. It is connected to a container of a gas under pressure P_c in an environment with atmospheric pressure P_a.*

An Ideal Gas Approximation

Because of the macroscopic size of the simulated object and microscopic size of the particles in the gas, we can neglect the interactions between gas particles and use an approximation of an ideal gas with non-colliding particles [Callen85]. This means that we will be able to use the familiar *ideal gas law*, shown in Equation 4.4.1.

$$PV = nRT \tag{4.4.1}$$

where:

- $P\left[\frac{N}{m^2}\right]$ is the pressure of the gas.
- $V\left[m^3\right]$ is the volume occupied by the gas.
- n is the number of moles of the gas.
- R is the gas constant.
- T is the gas temperature.

In this expression, we assume that n, R, and T are constant and will not change during the simulation. We also assume that we know how to calculate the volume of the body. As a result, we will get a simple expression for the calculation of the pressure inside of the object that changes only according to changes in the volume, as shown in Equation 4.4.2.

$$P = \frac{nRT}{V} \tag{4.4.2}$$

On the right side of Equation 4.4.2, we have three constants (n, R, T) and one variable quantity, V. The volume calculation will be discussed later.

We will use the pressure calculated directly from the ideal gas law to calculate the forces acting on the mesh nodes. It is a straightforward and rather easy procedure; however, it is useful to review the physics and math behind it.

Because of the physics dimension of pressure $P\left[\frac{N}{m^2}\right]$, we will need to determine the force by using a pressure value calculated from Equation 4.4.2. Pressure roughly entails a dimension of the force acting on a unitary field.

By considering one triangular face of the three-dimensional object as shown in Figure 4.4.3, we can write a simple expression for the force that acts on mesh node material points.

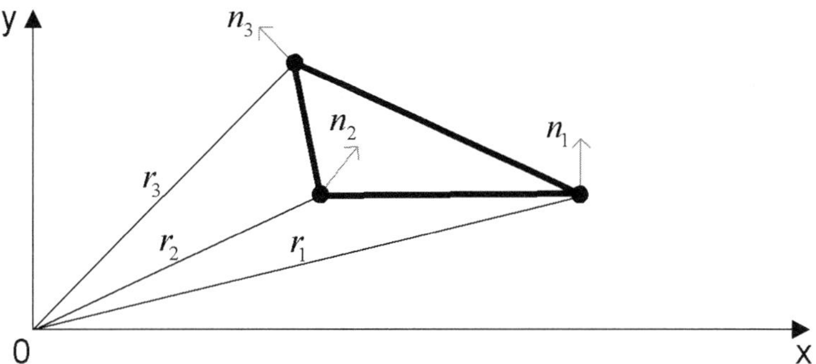

FIGURE 4.4.3 *A triangular face consisting of three mass nodes and three spring connections. The light gray vectors represent point normal vectors.*

Using the notation given in Figure 4.4.3, we express the force acting on a triangle by Equation 4.4.3:

$$\vec{F}^{P} = P \cdot \vec{n}_i \cdot A \tag{4.4.3}$$

where:

- P is the pressure calculated using an equation (4.4.2)
- A is a field of the face
- $\vec{n}_i$ is the normal vector to the i-th point

At this point, two things need to be addressed. First, we must determine how to calculate the normal to the point. This is simply the sum of the normal vectors of all faces to which the point belongs.

To calculate the field of the face we use simple vector multiplication. Using notation from Figure 4.4.3, the field of the triangular face from that figure can be expressed as in Equation 4.4.4.

$$A = \left|\left(\vec{r}_1 - \vec{r}_2\right) \times \left(\vec{r}_1 - \vec{r}_3\right)\right| \tag{4.4.4}$$

Equation 4.4.4 expresses the length of a vector generated by multiplying two vectors that lie on two of the edges of the triangulated face.

PSB Model Implementation

In [Matyka03] the *pressure based model* is introduced, and the basis of its implementation is presented. A brief outline of the proposed algorithm will be presented here in subsequent sections. We will introduce the reader to the PSB model by giving a full description of the workings of the simulation program. We refer the reader to [Matyka03] for further reading. However, we believe that the code can be written from scratch with the descriptions that follow.

First, let us summarize where we are so far. We have defined the physical model of the deformable body that is filled by an ideal gas. In the previous section, we outlined the mathematical model but we still did not explain how to use those equations and where they fit in the overall scheme.

Understanding how the model works requires the reader to be familiar with the spring-mass simulation ideology. We see no need to introduce it in detail here, due to the wealth of documented research available to the reader (see [Lander03, Provot95, Barraf98]). However, we briefly outline the technique used in soft body application later.

We start with a model of a closed 3D mesh composed of triangles with mass points placed at every node of the mesh as in Figure 4.4.1. All edges of the mesh represent spring connections. (We leave it up to reader to determine how to keep the object in computer memory. For simplicity of the code, we use STL vectors.)

Typical Spring-Mass Model

The procedure for the typical SM engine is straightforward. The object being simulated is presented as input to the procedure, and after processing one time step, the updated (changed) object is produced as output. The new version of the object is then presented again to the procedure and the cycle continues.

The high-level algorithm for an SM system can be expressed in three simple steps:

1. Calculation of the forces acting on all material points
2. Integration of equations of motion with collision detection and response
3. Results visualization

The first of these steps requires closer examination. It can be further broken down into the following steps:

1. External force calculation. We first iterate over all the material points (represented by mesh nodes), calculate the external forces, and store them in the material point force accumulator. By assuming that only one external force (gravity) exists in the system, the total force acting on *i*th point at this level will look like Equation 4.4.5.

$$\vec{F}_i^T = m_i \cdot \vec{g} \tag{4.4.5}$$

   where m_i is the mass of the point, and $\vec{g}$ is the gravity vector.
2. Node interaction forces. Loop over all spring connections and calculate mesh node-to-node interaction forces. We use an expression for Hooke's force with damping, which can be written in the form of a force vector, as shown in Equation 4.4.6.

$$\vec{F}_{12}^H = -k_s \cdot \left(\left|\vec{r}_1 - \vec{r}_2\right| - d\right) \cdot \hat{n}_{12} + k_d \cdot \left[\left(\vec{v}_1 - \vec{v}_2\right) \cdot \hat{n}_{12}\right] \cdot \hat{n}_{12} \tag{4.4.6}$$

   where the normal vector can be expressed by Equation 4.4.7.

$$\hat{n}_{12} = \frac{\vec{r}_1 - \vec{r}_2}{\left|\vec{r}_1 - \vec{r}_2\right|} \tag{4.4.7}$$

   Here, k_s is the spring elasticity factor, and k_d is the spring damping factor. Typical values for these are given in the results section. Note that vectors calculated with Equation 4.4.6 are accumulated by two interacting points with opposite signs.
3. The PSB model step is discussed in a later section.
4. Integration. The integration step should be applied now. Note that even a first-order Euler integrator works quite well for some limited set of physics properties. We refer to [Ancona02] as a reference for numerical integration.

   The simple Euler integrator gives us an expression for the movement of all the points of the geometrical model that make up the deformable body. By looping over all points, assuming that we have accumulated all the forces acting on them, we can write a discrete form of Newton's second law, as shown in Equation 4.4.8.

$$\begin{cases} \vec{v}_i^{n+1} = \vec{v}_i^n + \dfrac{\vec{F}_i^T}{m_i} \cdot \Delta t \\ \vec{r}_i^{n+1} = \vec{r}_i^n + \vec{v}_i^{n+1} \cdot \Delta t \end{cases} \tag{4.4.8}$$

Here, $n / n + 1$ enumerates the time step (n indicates "at the previous time step"). By applying this simple integrator, we can simulate deformable bodies using a PSB model. Later, we will present an application of the predictor-corrector Heun integrator in the deformable body simulation.

As we can see in the previous algorithm, the deformable body simulation we present is based strongly on SM simulation (see Figure 4.4.4). Note that this model can be viewed as an enhancement of the general SM system and is therefore applicable to any physical system that currently handles simple SM simulations.

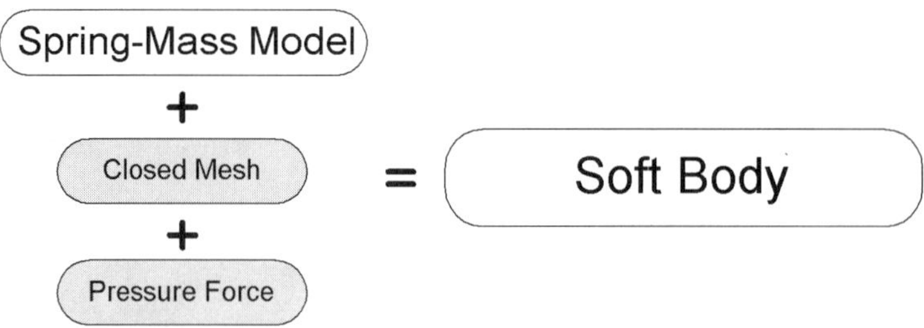

FIGURE 4.4.4 *Summary of the PSB model; two enhancements added to cloth dynamics yields real-time deformable bodies.*

PSB Step

In the previous section, we noted that following the force calculations we should call a PSB step procedure. That procedure is called together with all the other force calculation functions because it also calculates the result force of the gas that has been put into the object.

We discussed earlier how the pressure value should be calculated using Equation 4.4.2. By assuming that the reference atmospheric pressure is zero, we can reuse the pressure value in Equation 4.4.3. We simply iterate over all the faces of the object, determining the pressure value for each and distributing the pressure over all nodes that belong to each face.

Volume Calculation

In order to calculate the forces, we will need to determine the volume of the simulated body. For purposes of [Matyka03], we use the simple idea of generating bounding boxes for the object and calculating the total volume from those boxes.

However, it turns out that such an approximation introduces a number of problems into the simulation. Unexpected oscillations and object growth to infinity (as well as growing pressure) are examples of the errors that can come from a naïve approximation of the volume. We pointed out in [Matyka03] that we are looking for a good approximation of the exact volume of the body, and we found that for closed shapes without holes or integral faces (for example, balloon-shaped objects) we could use Gauss's theorem to find an elegant, fast, and very accurate value for the volume. We will skip mathematical derivation of Equation 4.4.9 and leave the reader with a reference to [Feynman01], where Gauss's theorem is well explained. For those who are going to derive the volume integration equation, we simply assume that our object has been placed in a vector field (for example) in the form $f(x,y,z) = x$. We are then able to calculate the divergence of that field, which is equal to 1. If we put these results into Gauss's integration theorem in specified vector fields, we end up with a simple expression for volume that can be written as in Equation 4.4.9.

$$V = \sum_{i=1}^{NUMF} \frac{1}{3} \cdot \left(\vec{r}_{i1}.x + \vec{r}_{i2}.x + \vec{r}_{i3}.x \right) \cdot \vec{n}_i.x \cdot A_i \tag{4.4.9}$$

where r_i is the node position, n is the normal to the triangle, A_i is the field of the ith triangle, and $NUMF$ is number of faces.

Predictor-Corrector Heun Integration

Euler integration is the simplest means of integrating equations of motion and generally requires small time steps. The stiffness problem occurs, too, and is a well-known disadvantage of low-order schemes of ODE integration. To make the solution more accurate and stable, we consider using more complex integrators. This may be an explicit scheme from the Runge-Kutta family (second-order mid-point method could be good choice, see [Matyka03, Ancona02]) or one of several unconditionally stable implicit schemes, such as Backwards Euler.

We propose using something between explicit and implicit schemes. A semi-implicit predictor-corrector Heun integrator will give us second-order accuracy and will still be somewhat as simple as the explicit schemes. We will not go very deeply into the derivation of that scheme, which the reader can find in any book about numerical computation, e.g., [Ancona02].

The semi-implicit Heun integrator consists of two main steps, and for a typical problem is given by Equation 4.4.10.

$$\frac{dy}{dt} = f\left(y^n, t^n\right) \tag{4.4.10}$$

The first step of the integration (called the "predictor") is exactly the same as in the Euler integrator and is used to calculate the estimated value of y in the next time step, as shown in Equation 4.4.11.

$$\hat{y}^{n+1} = y^n + \Delta t \cdot f\left(y, t\right) \tag{4.4.11}$$

Normally, the procedure ends here and the next time step is ready to start. However in the Heun integrator, some of the values are used in the next step (called the correction step), as shown in the second term of Equation 4.4.12.

$$y^{n+1} = y^n + \frac{\Delta t}{2}\left(f\left(y^n, t^n\right) + f\left(\hat{y}^{n+1}, t^{n+1}\right)\right) \tag{4.4.12}$$

The entire semi-implicit integration scheme has been written with two equations: Equations 4.4.11 and 4.4.12. Note that the "dashed" y is distinct from the normal y, as it is retained separately between the two steps.

Time Step Calculation Speed

To give the reader an idea how fast the presented method is, we performed a benchmark test similar to the one presented in [Meseure00]. We performed a simulation of a toroid falling to the ground without any additional collision detection (only collisions between deformable body and the ground were taken into account). Figure 4.4.5 presents a comparison between the PSB model and that presented by [Meseure00]. The simulation was performed on an AMD Athlon with a 1.4 Ghz processor. It should be noted that test performed by [Meseure00] was run on a R10000, 194 Mhz processor, so the comparison in Figure 4.4.5 is qualitative only.

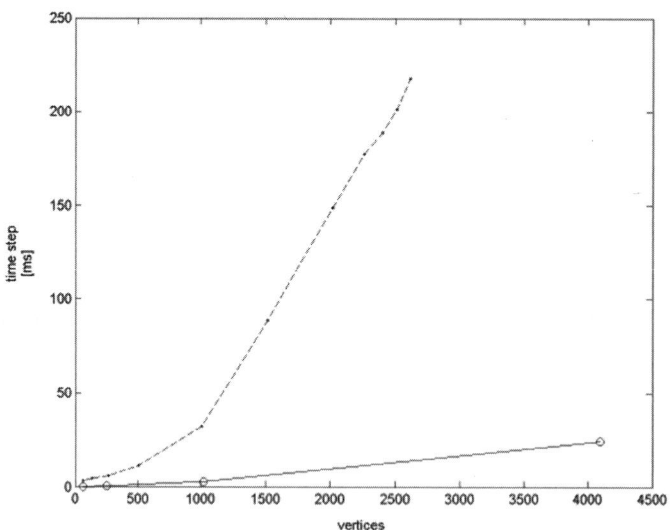

FIGURE 4.4.5 *Time calculations for one full simulation step of a toroid falling to the ground. The PSB model (indicated with circles with straight line) is compared with results presented in [Meseure00] (dashed line with black points).*

As Figure 4.4.5 indicates, using the PSB model, we obtain real-time performance (less than 25 ms per time step) for the simulation of objects containing up to 4500 nodes.

Examples

Figure 4.4.6a shows the initial state of a rabbit object without internal pressure. In Figure 4.4.6b, we have this same rabbit with some internal pressure $P > 0$. Figure 4.4.6c shows the same object after the user has captured it during motion. Finally, Figure 4.4.6d shows the rabbit with one mesh node fixed in place while still under the force of gravity. These pictures are from the Soft Body 3.0 application. The simulated object has 690 vertices and 1,376 faces. The physical constants used in that simulation are: $k_s = 350000$, $k_d = 10$, $P = 53000$, and single node mass $m = 1.0$. The simulation runs at 50 fps on an Athlon 1.4 Mhz computer with a Radeon9200 graphics card.

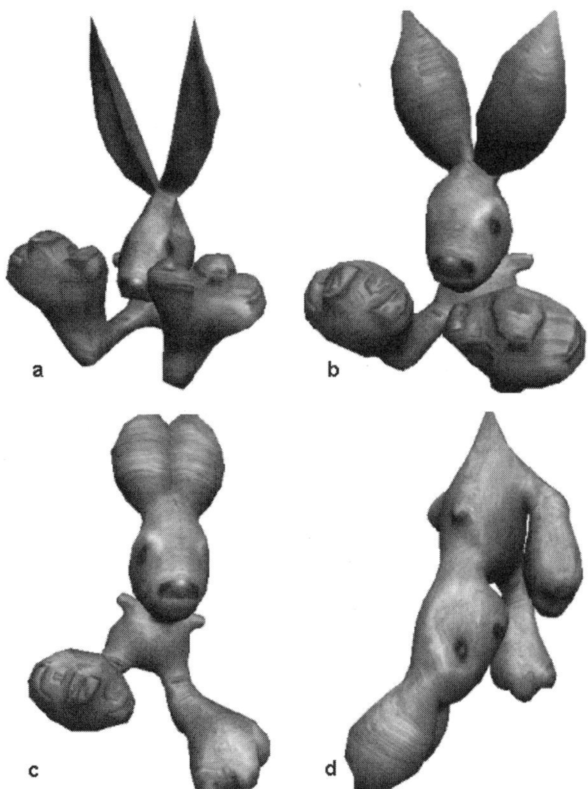

FIGURE 4.4.6 *Simulation snapshots of a deformable rabbit object.*

In Figure 4.4.7, we present a second example of real-time animation using the PSB method applied to a ball containing 642 vertices and 1,280 faces. The ball is dropped and allowed to collide with the ground. In this example, collision detection is simply performed between the mesh nodes and the ground ($y = 0$), using the following physical parameters: $k_s = 121100$, $k_d = 110$, $P = 611120$, and node mass $m = 1.0$. The simulation runs at 50 fps on an Athlon 1.4 Ghz computer with Radeon9200 graphics card.

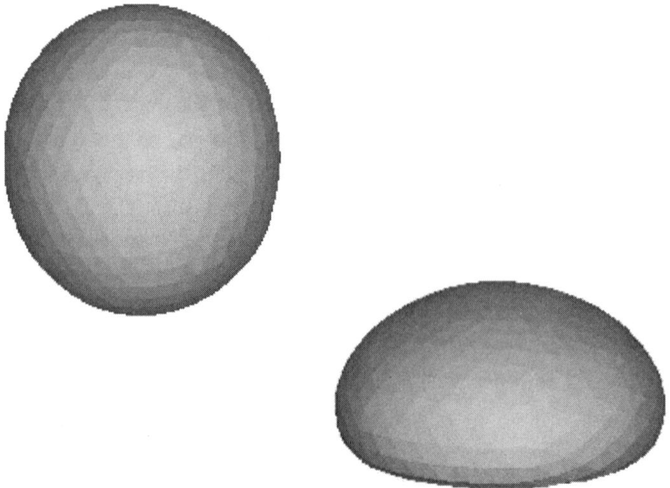

FIGURE 4.4.7 *Simulation of a bouncing deformable ball.*

Future Development

The PSB model of deformable body simulation is in the early stages of development. Several projects have been created that are based on this model [OpenCAL, Jello, MotionPlan] and attempt to develop the model in a variety of ways. We see a lot of ideas for improving the PSB model, including the following:

- Implementation of implicit integration as done previously in "Large Steps in Soft Body Simulation" [Barraf98]
- Application of inverse dynamics constraints as done before in [Provot95], including experimentation with the behavior parameters
- Separation of the physical model from its graphical representation, which allows more focused work on simulating simple models as the basis for more complicated shapes (see [Meseure00])
- Implementation of object-object collision detection and response, a "detail" omitted here to facilitate presentation of the material (see [Matyka03])

- Application and testing of the use of nonlinear springs in the object mesh
- Real-time PSB simulation with collisions computed on the GPU

These ideas represent possible ways for future developments of the presented model. It should be noted that a lot of research in cloth animation could be used here as background material and developed further according to specific geometric shape of the simulated PSB objects.

Conclusion

We have presented a system for real-time deformable body simulation. The main reasons why it is worth it to go more deeply into development of this model is that it is based on the well-known spring-mass model, which can be easy updated and extended to handle soft bodies. We also have observed that objects simulated with our method behave very well in comparison to other previously developed systems.

Because of the model simplicity, we lose little computational time by calculating the additional forces used beyond those in the simple spring-mass model. All the effort during development of the system has been focused on proper object construction and selection of the simulation parameters.

We hope that the model will fit the requirements of those in the game development community. All the updates, new versions of the source code, and applications will be available on the home page of the author [Matyka05].

Source Code

The source code for this gem contains portions of the Soft Body 3.0 program. It has been developed using MS Visual C++ compiler. Updates of the code can be found on the Web page of the authors (see [Matyka05]). The code provides the solution to three-dimensional deformable body real-time simulation with user interaction.

Acknowledgments

Special thanks to Jos Stam, who contributed an idea about volume calculation of soft bodies using Gauss's theorem. Thanks also to Mariusz Jarosz for providing the 3D renderings presented as illustration.

References

[Ancona02] Ancona, M. G. *Computational Methods for Applied Science and Engineering: An Interactive Approach*. Rinton Press, 2002.

[Barraf98] Baraff, David and Andrew P. Witkin. "Large Steps in Cloth Simulation." Proceedings of SIGGRAPH 98, pp. 43–54, 1998.

[Callen85] Callen, H.B. *Thermodynamics and an Introduction to Thermostatistics*. New York: John Wiley & Sons, 1985.

[Feynman01] Feynman, Richard P. "The Feynman Lectures on Physics, Vol. 2.1." PWN, Warszawa, 2001.

"Geometric Models." Computer Graphics (Proceedings of SIGGRAPH 86), 20(4), pp. 151–160, 1986.

[Irving04] Irving, G., J. Teran, and R. Fedkiw. "Invertible Finite Elements for Robust Simulation of Large Deformation." ACM SIGGRAPH/Eurographics Symposium on Computer Animation (SCA), 2004.

[Jello] Mecklenburg, P. and C. Miller. *Jello Simulation*. Available online at *http://vorlon.cwru.edu/~prm8/eecs466/overview.html.*

[Lander03] Matyka, M. "Inverse Dynamic Displacement Constraints in Real-Time Cloth and Soft-Body Models." In *Graphics Programming Methods* (edited by Jeff Lander). Charles River, 2003.

[Matyka03] Matyka, M. and M. Ollila. "A pressure model for soft body simulation." Proc. of Sigrad. UMEA, November 2003.

[Matyka05] Matyka, M. *http://panoramix.ift.uni.wroc.pl/~maq/eng/.* Author's home page.

[Meseure00] Meseure, P. and C. Chaillou. "A deformable body model for surgical simulation." J. Visual. Comput. Animat., pp. 197–208, 2000.

[MotionPlan] Gayle, R. *Motion Planning for Physically-based Deformable Objects.* Available online at *http://www.cs.unc.edu/~rgayle/Courses/Comp259/MPDO/mpdo.html.*

[Nixon02] Nixon, D. and R. Lobb. "A fluid-based soft-object model." *Comp. Graph. and App., IEEE,* Vol. 22 Iss. 4, pp. 68–75, 2002.

[OpenCAL] Dierckx, J. *Open CAL Project.* Available online at *http://sourceforge.net/projects/opencal/.*

[Provot95] Provot, Xavier. "Deformation Constraints in a Mass-Spring Model to Describe Rigid Cloth Behavior." *Graphics Interface* '95, pp. 147–154, 1995.

[Sedenberg86] Sederberg, Thomas W. and Scott R. Parry. "Free-Form Deformation of Solid Geometric Models," *Computer Graphics* (Proceedings of SIGGRAPH 86) 20(4), pp. 151–160, 1986.

4.5

Adding Life to Ragdoll Simulation Using Feedback Control Systems

Michael Mandel, Apple Computer

mmandel@gmail.com

Characters in games sometimes look unrealistic when interacting with dynamic environments, because their movements are predetermined by an animator's keyframes or a motion capture actor's movements. *Ragdoll physics* has been used to combat this problem by modeling the physics of the body as it collides with the environment and other characters. At their best, ragdolls can be applied in games to allow players to send enemies hurling through the air, reacting quite dynamically to objects they encounter in the environment. Unfortunately, their usefulness is limited to the lifeless, flopping motion seen in these death animations, because they lack control systems to produce more realistic behavior. If developers could control the muscles of the ragdoll, they could direct the arms to protect the body from injury before impact, much as a real person would do.

This gem looks at how to control a character's body during simulation, while still retaining the realistic qualities obtained by enforcing physical laws between the body and its environment. We cannot yet hope to replace all our animation data with simulation due to the complex and coordinated movements required for many human behaviors. We can, however, produce better results in many situations by using simple feedback controllers to generate muscle torques that naturally direct simulated limbs. Color Plate 3 shows a side-by-side example of how controllers can improve the human-like nature of a fall over ordinary ragdoll simulation. The tools presented in this gem provide a generic means to drive the movements of a typical ragdoll simulation, enabling you to generate protective falling behaviors, balancing reactions, and even jumping or tackling motions. You can be as inventive as you like, provided you can model the underlying control laws of a particular behavior.

Motivating Work

A number of researchers have used physical controllers to generate motion for a variety of human behaviors. Hand-tuned feedback controllers have been demonstrated for simulating athletic behaviors including running, vaulting, and bicycling [Hodgins95]. Faloutsos further developed the idea of creating *composable controllers* by stringing together many behaviors like falling, standing, and balancing to create a virtual stuntman [Faloutsos01]. Interactively controlling a physically simulated character has the potential to open up doors to new gameplay mechanics. Laszlo et al. explored using intuitive interfaces to allow players to take direct control of a simulated human to produce running, climbing, and gymnastics movements [Laszlo00].

It is also important to have the ability to interface your physically controlled behaviors with existing motion data. Techniques have been developed that allow characters to react physically to external forces followed by a smooth return to existing animation through trajectory tracking [Zordan02]. There are other methods that allow simulation and animation data to vie for control of the character, using either approach in a context-dependent way [Mandel04], [Shapiro03]. The biomechanics literature is another starting point for a low-level understanding of how the body performs a particular movement. Capable rigid body simulators like Open Dynamics Engine [Smith04] are freely available to enable you to experiment with controller development. The methods presented in this gem are the low-level control mechanisms crucial to many of the works referenced earlier.

Controlling the Simulation

Ragdoll characters are represented as an articulated figure consisting of a series of rigid links connected by joints. A rigid body simulation engine is supplied with a set of primitives to represent each body part, each with mass and inertial properties, joints of appropriate type connecting the parts, and constraints to keep the movement of each joint to human physical limitations. The basic building blocks for controlling a ragdoll simulation are target poses for the joints, as well as a method to compute the joint torques that drive the motion towards these desired targets. For computing the muscle torques, this gem will cover the commonly used proportional derivative (PD) controller. One option for specifying target poses is to use sparse artist-directed poses separated by time or event-based transitions. Known as a pose controller, these target poses guide the simulation to key elements of a behavior, such as the twist and tuck positions of a diving motion [Wooten96]. A continuous controller generates target poses automatically from the current state of the system (positions and velocities of limbs). This tight coupling with feedback from the simulation allows continuous controllers to be more dynamic than pose controllers but is potentially harder to specify. A continuous falling controller might look at how the shoulder and hip velocity evolve during the simulation and constantly adjust the target position of the arms to break the fall.

Isn't This Just Keyframing?

While controlling the simulation with guiding sequences of target poses may sound like keyframing, there are a number of important distinctions. First, the inputs to the controller are *desired* joint angles, not *actual* joint angles. The controller computes muscle torques to drive the joints towards the desired values, but the limb's motion remains the result of all the applied forces, including those from the environment. The joints may never reach the desired values because of the environmental forces. For example, an arm might be pinned by the body to an object in the world causing the joint controller to be unable to generate enough force to move to the desired position. Second, the character's global position and orientation is not specified directly but evolves from the natural interactions between the character and the environment. The character will always fall under gravity, for example. Finally, the desired pose isn't always predetermined as static keyframes are. When using continuous control, the pose is adaptively determined as a function of the system's state.

Computing Torques with a PD Controller

The PD controller is a valuable tool, representing the low-level control system that drives the desired movements of a simulated character. For a more thorough introduction to control systems, see Dorf [Dorf89]. The inputs to the controller are the desired joint angles q_{des}, the state of the system $x = \begin{bmatrix} q\dot{q} \end{bmatrix}$, and various sensor data such as the contact state of the hands. The output of the controller is the internal muscle torques τ_i applied to each joint, driving it towards the desired value. This is the classic setup for a closed-loop system (closed because it requires feedback of the system's state). Figure 4.5.1 is a graphical representation of this basic controller feedback loop.

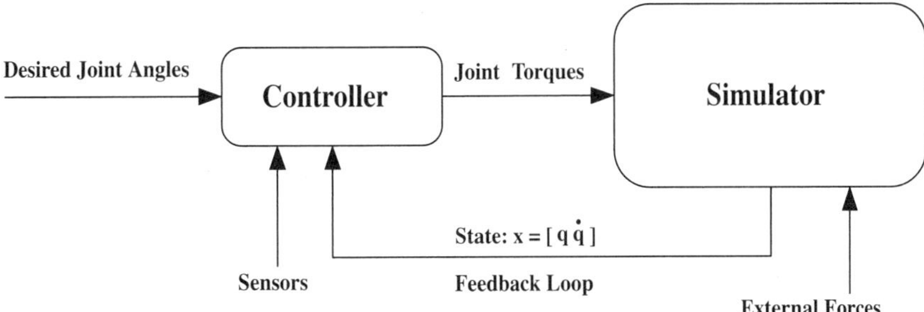

FIGURE 4.5.1 *Structure of a basic closed-loop feedback system.*

For each joint, the PD controller computes the required torque using the equation:

$$\tau_i = k_p(\theta_{des} - \theta) - k_d\dot{\theta},$$

where k_p and k_d are the proportional and derivative gains θ and θ_{des} are the current and desired joint angles, and $\dot{\theta}$ is the current velocity of the joint (generates angular velocity in its attached bodies). Clamping the torque at a reasonable maximum value is a good idea to maintain a stable simulation. The following code snippet implements the computation made by the PD controller:

```
void ApplyPDControlTorques(Vec3 *Kp, Vec3 *Kd, Vec3 *des,
                            int numJoints)
{
     for(int i = 0 ; i < numJoints ; i++)
     {
          Vec3 torque;
          Vec3 vel = GetJointVelocity(i);
          Vec3 cur = GetCurrentAngleForJoint(i);
          torque[0] = Kp[i][0]*(des[0] - cur[0]) - Kd[i][0]*vel[0];
          torque[1] = Kp[i][1]*(des[1] - cur[1]) - Kd[i][1]*vel[1];
          torque[2] = Kp[i][2]*(des[2] - cur[2]) - Kd[i][2]*vel[2];

          if(torque.length() > MAX_TORQUE)
               torque = MAX_TORQUE*torque.normalize();

          ApplyTorqueAtJoint(i, torque);
     }
}
```

Tuning Controller Gains

The PD controller behaves like a spring and damper, with the proportional and derivative gain parameters, k_p and k_d, controlling the resulting response curve. Tuning these parameters is critical to achieving natural looking movement. The proportional (stiffness) gain controls the strength of the spring while the derivative (damper) gain adjusts how smoothly the joint arrives at the desired value. Under-damp and you will get an oscillating response as the joint overshoots the desired value, while over-damping will give an overly slow progression towards the desired value. Somewhere in the middle, you will achieve critical damping, the perfect balance where the joint arrives at the desired value quickly, with little to no overshoot. Traditionally, the gain values are hand-tuned, and this process can be somewhat time-consuming. If you plan on hand-tuning the gains, a good rule of thumb is to start with a 10:1 ratio between the proportional and derivative gains.

One technique that can drastically reduce the number of hand-tuned parameters is to scale the computed torques by the effective moment of inertia of the chain of bodies affected by each joint [Zordan02]. For instance, the shoulders would be affected by the relative moment of inertia of the upper arm, lower arm, and hand, as illustrated in Figure 4.5.2. Using this technique, the number of tuned parameters can be reduced to one stiffness and damping parameter for the entire body because the final gains will be adjusted by the affected chain of bodies for each joint. Collect the affected bodies per joint and compute the relative moment of inertia according to this equation:

$$H = \sum_i (m_i r_i \times v_i + I_{CM_i} \omega_i),$$

where m_i is mass of the body, r_i is the relative center of mass (CM) of the body compared to the chain's CM, v_i is the relative velocity of the body CM compared to the chain's CM, I_{CMi} is the inertia tensor of the body about its CM, and ω_i is the angular velocity of the body (see [Kwon98]). In addition to this technique, you may also try learning the appropriate gains for a given behavior using optimization techniques like simulated annealing or genetic algorithms; see [Sims94].

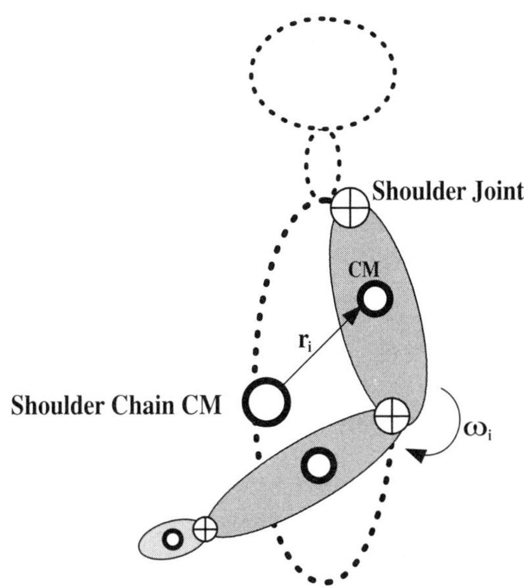

FIGURE 4.5.2 *An example chain of bodies affecting the movement of the shoulder joint. By estimating the relative moment of inertia of these bodies to the shoulder, its controller gains can be tuned efficiently.*

Building Behaviors

Now that you have a low-level mechanism for controlling the joints of a simulated character, you can begin developing specific behaviors. Finite state machines are a common representation for managing transitions between motor control states. Transitions between states are typically time or event based, and may ease in new controller gains or desired values tailored to the state's goals. For instance, a fall controller may have a number of states that throw one or both arms in the direction of a fall, requiring the gains to keep the body somewhat rigid, but still give the arms a rapid response. When the arms contact the ground, a transition is made to a controller state that will absorb the impact and reduce the velocity of the hips and upper body. Figure 4.5.3 demonstrates an example of a fall controller simulating a backwards fall.

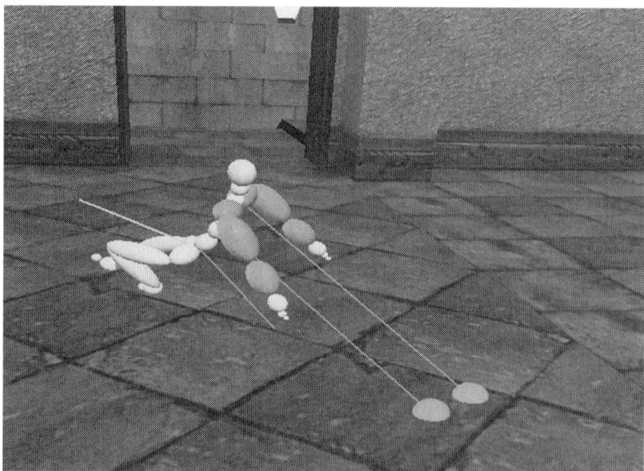

FIGURE 4.5.3 *An example fall controller. The predicted shoulder landing positions, indicated with spheres, are used as reference points to compute desired arm positions. The forward velocity and facing direction are indicated with vectors and are used to determine the current state, based on fall direction.* © *2004 Reprinted with permission from Iikka Keranen & Rich Carlson.*

Observing the raw state of the simulation may not provide controller states with the most useful information. It is helpful to implement sensors that provide information to controllers such as support polygon, center of mass, body part contacts, and facing direction. Using this information, personal intuition, and perhaps some biomechanical knowledge, you can break down a behavior into its fundamental control states. Plan ahead to make sure your controller can robustly respond to the variety of inputs that could occur during gameplay. Keep your goals manageable; building a controller that generates a stable running gait is much more difficult than one that simply needs to make sure the body ends up on the ground. Building simulated behaviors is difficult, but as a game developer, this is where your creativity and ingenuity greatly impacts the results.

Conclusion

This gem presents techniques to augment your existing ragdoll characters with more interesting behavior. PD controllers allow you to drive the limbs of your characters in a physically grounded way. While computing the desired joint values and tuning the controller gains can be tricky, the methods described can lower the number of manually tuned parameters. Being creative with this technology is up to you, but the possibilities are endless as we discover better ways to model human behaviors.

Acknowledgments

Thanks to David Cherry, Iikka Keranen, and Rich Carlson for providing the world geometry appearing in some of the figures.

References

[Dorf89] Dorf, R. C. *Modern Control Systems*. Addison-Wesley, 1989.

[Faloutsos01] Faloutsos, Petros, et al. "The Virtual Stuntman: Dynamic Characters with a Repertoire of Autonomous Motor Skills." In *Computer Graphics*, Vol. 25, no. 6: pp. 933–953.

[Hodgins95] Hodgins, Jessica, et al. "Animating Human Athletics." In *Computer Graphics*, Vol 29, Annual Conference Series: pp. 71–78.

[Kwon98] Kwon, Young-Hoo. "Mechanical Basis of Motion Analysis." SIGGRAPH 2000, *Computer Graphics Proceedings:* pp. 201–208.

Available online at *http://kwon3d.com/theories.html.*

[Mandel04] Michael, Mandel. "Versatile and Interactive Virtual Humans: Hybrid use of Kinematic and Dynamic Motion Synthesis." Master's thesis, Carnegie Mellon University, available online at *http://www.city-net.com/~amandel/portfolio/masters.html.*

[Shapiro03] Shapiro, Ari, et al. "Hybrid Control for Interactive Character Animation." In *Pacific Graphics* 2003: pp. 455–461.

[Sims94] Sims, Karl. "Evolving Virtual Creatures." SIGGRAPH 1994, Computer Graphics Proceedings: pp. 15–22.

[Smith04] Smith, Russell. "The Open Dynamics Engine." Available online at *http://ode.org/.*

[Wooten96] Wooten, Wayne, et al. "Animation of Human Diving." *Computer Graphics Forum*, Vol 15, no. 1: pp. 3–14.

[Zordan02] Zordan, Victor, et al. "Motion capture-driven simulations that hit and react." In *ACM SIGGRAPH Symposium on Computer Animation*: pp. 89–96.

4.6

Designing a Prescripted Physics System

Daniel F. Higgins

webmaster@programming.org

Game development is, without a doubt, an intense, high-endurance sport. Its leading developers have seasoned teams who dominate genres because of their incredible focus, innovation, and fierce passion. As if playing a game of high-stakes poker, developers tend to gather around the same no-limit table and constantly raise the pot to the sky. We hold our cards close, counting on our new game's technology, "fun factor," and the love of our fans to win the hand. Therefore it's no surprise that when a competitor reveals a winning hand, we watch slack jawed as our chips disappear in the blink of an eye.

To strengthen our hand of cards, we have to look everywhere for inspiration. It can be found in the battle for Helms Deep in *The Two Towers*, watching silly skateboard tricks at the skate park, or observing a border collie's leap for a slimy tennis ball.

This gem describes an engine born from inspiration. That inspiration served as a challenge to design a system that could produce the illusion of a big-budgeted physics engine, allow for rapid development, and avoid a large development price tag. Additionally, it should be designed to be usable by novice and expert programmers alike while still maintaining enough flexibility to be integrated into an out-of-game physics tool. Eventually, that system was created, and its name is *prescripted physics*.

What Is Prescripted Physics?

On a typical day, a conversation with a game developer about physics will include words like velocity, friction, rigid body, gravity, and acceleration. You'll also probably hear the term "ragdoll." In the old days, game physics operated mostly as a vehicle, drearily moving objects from point A to point B along a path like a painfully dull merry-go-round. In today's competitive game development arena, kiddy rides are no longer cutting the mustard. Today's engines not only move objects along paths, they hurl them through the air, crash them through walls, and cause cascades of bricks to come loose and eventually pile up in dynamically formed rubble. Our competitors, armed with big-budget engines, can be scary to face in hand-to-hand combat on the fields of game development. How can we rush into the melee against powerful adversaries who are so well armed? Simple; we fake it by creating the illusion of complicated physics when in actuality, we're just moving these objects on a preplanned track like a roller coaster.

Even if using a "real" physics system, prescripted physics may be useful to drive the behaviors of some of the more "ambient" elements of the simulation. For example, arcing and bouncing bits of debris from explosions might be prescripted while vehicles are not.

How Prescripted Physics Works

Prescripted physics works by connecting a series of 3D points together using a curved path. A simple way to visualize it is to think of each point as a clothespin on a clothesline. Now imagine that the clothesline was on the ground with a dozen or so pins stuck at fairly regular intervals along it. If that clothesline is slack, the line between the clothespins looks curved. In prescripted physics, we use waypoints for our clothespins and use splines as our clothesline.

The first step in creating a prescripted physics event begins with the artistic skill of observation. The creator has to observe the event they wish to duplicate by either seeing it on screen, in real-life, or in the mind's eye. Next, they break it down into keyframes of movement such as a head turning here, rotation there, an explosive start, or bouncy ending. Once the keyframes have been identified, the programmer then has to "reverse engineer" how the event took place by coding the physics from a time perspective instead of one using the traditional velocity accumulation. In simple terms, for each keyframe (or waypoint), the programmer records what the object's orientation and 3D position should be for that point as well as how much time has passed since the event started. The list of waypoints is then passed to the physics engine. The engine is responsible for ensuring that the object appears at each point at the given time, that it moves correctly in both orientation and position between points, and finally that it possesses all the properties specified (e.g., final orientation and animation).

To demonstrate how this works, let's make a physics event. In this event, we want to hurl Edgar the Chicken dramatically through the air. Our event begins by identifying what we want the outcome of the physics to look like, then marking waypoints along the flight path.

The simplest physics event we could make for Edgar would be to just move him along a path as seen in Figure 4.6.1. Besides being possibly the world's most boring physics, anyone watching it would boggle in confusion as to why something so "fake" was allowed into the game. We can cure this problem by fixing one of the most unnatural things about the physics: Edgar is still maintaining fantastic posture. Great posture is no doubt an admirable trait, however since were going more for the "under nature's force" look, we'll need to pitch him forward a bit as he flies (Figure 4.6.2).

FIGURE 4.6.1 *Edgar on a boring ride.*

FIGURE 4.6.2 *Edgar tilting on his journey.*

That was an improvement, but it's still not very believable. Let's try changing Edgar into a panic animation as he hits one of the early waypoints. The animation will make a big difference, but we can't stop there. The battle is won or lost in the details! An interior decorator knows the job isn't finished without lots of pillows and a throw on a sofa; likewise, we need that extra something that brings the hurling Edgar to life. That extra something could be a graphical effect like random feathers erupting into the air as he transitions from a casual animation to one of panic (see

Figure 4.6.3). Finally, playing a loud "SQUAWK" as he transitions should make it just right. Let's stop here, even though we could continue to embellish on the event.

FIGURE 4.6.3 *Animation and other effects help to sell the illusion of Edgar's flying.*

Thanks to Edgar, we can see how moving an object through a series of points can have the same end result as more traditional physics engines. Remember that while prescripted physics simulates more complex, "real" physics by reducing an object's movement into simple keyframes and the lines that connect them, it's all about the details you add to the event that make it come alive and mask the simplicity of the underlying technology.

Prescripted Physics Pros and Cons

Like almost everything in life, prescripted physics has its ups and downs. Those peaks and valleys are due in large part because the system doesn't compute physics in real-time; instead, it's done at the start of the event. Understanding this difference is the key to realizing the strengths and weaknesses that come with prescripted physics.

Following is a list of the strengths of prescripted physics:

Ease of use: Prescripted physics systems are built from the ground up with the intention of being used by people who aren't versed in the complex math of more advanced physics systems.

Rapid development: Building the prescripted physics engine takes less than a weekend to prototype and under a week to develop to its game-ready state. The real benefit of rapid development becomes evident when creating new custom physics events. Instead of days implementing complicated math for new physics, most should take only a few hours and require little code from the programmer.

Tools: Prescripted physics can be made into a tool that artists and designers use to generate "physics files" for objects in the world. This can take the programmer completely out of the loop once the engine is built and game-ready.

Performance: A common barrier people face when using physics is the fear of performance. Since prescripted physics events are by definition precomputed, the real-time performance cost can be very light on the CPU.

Replay: The prescripted physics engine is ideal for "rewinding" an object's movement through the game world as if it were in a sports "instant replay."

Following is a list of the weaknesses of prescripted physics:

Reactions: If you want prescripted physics to interact with other objects in real time, like a baseball being interrupted by a baseball bat, then it requires extra code to support that reaction. Since this system computes the path the object will travel at the beginning of the physics event, reactions can only work if the engine supports both collision detection and the ability to morph the event into a reaction event. Coding this functionality can potentially take as much time as coding the prescripted physics engine itself.

Unique and unfamiliar: If a tool isn't built for artists or designers to use, you must rely on programmers to produce the physics events. Programmers need to understand that they have to think differently to use prescripted physics. It doesn't take a math genius to write these events, but it does take skills in observation and the ability to transfer those observations into steps. With such a foreign system of physics, it's not surprising that some of the most mathematically gifted programmers struggle with this system at the beginning or outright refuse to use it. Once they toss aside their calculus books and think of the physics as if they were watching a movie, it generally "clicks."

Compound physics: Compound physics, like reactions, requires extra effort to get right. As a general rule, when an object is under the influence of prescripted physics, no other physics in the world should be affecting the object unless you write special code to support it.

The Engine

The most basic prescripted physics engine has two main parts: the movement of 3D points and the changing of an object's orientation. Both the movement and orientation use a percentage value computed using time as the basis for interpolation. For location, the time converts to a percentage indicating where an object is on the spline from point A to point B. As for orientation, that same percentage is used to determine the object's yaw, pitch, and roll. For example, if a waypoint started at world time 100 ms and went until 250 ms, giving us a total of 150 ms in length, at world time 175, we would be 50% complete: (175–100)/150. Using that percentage, we can determine both its position and orientation by using splines and quaternions.

Movement of 3D Points

Think of the physics event as if you were going to play connect-the-dots. In this version of the game, the dots are already numbered in order, and you already know that the shape you're tracing is a person's face. Since most faces aren't square, when you trace between the dots, you decide to put in an artistic touch by making the lines between the dots have gentle curves instead of harsh straight lines. The end result is that the curves make the face look natural and far more pleasing than if you had simply used a ruler.

Like playing connect-the-dots, the manner in which you draw the lines between the dots (or waypoints) determines the overall picture that the customer will see. Most prescripted physics engines can easily support multiple connect-the-dot movement algorithms, including basic linear methods and several implementations of splines. In this gem, we'll focus on just using Catmull-Rom splines [Dunlop00] to move our objects from point to point.

Velocity is a great example of how topsy-turvy this new physics can be. Velocity is determined based on where we place our waypoints and how much time we allow for an object to travel between a pair of waypoints. It's one of the many backward-thinking hurdles programmers face when using this method of physics. We're so used to giving an object acceleration and velocity, then sending it off into the world, that it can get confusing when we realize that an object traveling *X* distance for *T* amount of time plugs nicely into the old velocity formula.

Listing 4.6.1 is a basic function that uses percent complete, percent squared, percent cubed, our *X*, *Y*, or *Z* position for spline points at $n - 2$, $n - 1$, and $n + 1$ intervals, and our given *X*, *Y*, or *Z* position to generate our current position.

Listing 4.6.1 Catmull-Rom Computation for a Given X, Y, or Z

```
inline float GetSpline(float inOurPoint, float inPercent,
                    float inTSquared, float inTCubed,
                    float inBack2, float inBack1, float inNext)
{
    return (0.5f * (2.0f * inBack1 +
              ((-inBack2 + inOurPoint) * inPercent) +
              ((2.0f * inBack2 - 5.0f * inBack1 + 4.0f *
               inOurPoint - inNext) * inTSquared) +
              ((-inBack2 + 3.0f * inBack1 - 3.0f * inOurPoint)
              + inNext)* inTCubed)));
}
```

Listing 4.6.2 is a simplified function that advances an object to its next waypoint given a percentage. It uses the GetSpline method with this waypoint's ending world position to determine the current 3D location. For example, if inPercent is 0.5, the object's current position will end up halfway between the last waypoint and the current waypoint.

Listing 4.6.2 Advancing a Point Along a Spline Path

```
void AdvanceSpline(float inPercent, GE3DPoint& ioPoint, const
GE3DPoint& inBack2, const GE3DPoint& inBack1,
const GE3DPoint& inNext)
{
inPercent = min(1.0F, inPercent);
float theTSquared = inPercent * inPercent;
float theTCubed = theTSquared * inPercent;

/* Spline for X */
ioPoint.mX = ::GetSpline(mPoint.mX,
                  inPercent, theTSquared, theTCubed,
                  inBack2.mX, inBack1.mX, inNext.mX);

/* Spline for Y */
ioPoint.mY = ::GetSpline(mPoint.mY,
                  inPercent, theTSquared, theTCubed,
                  inBack2.mY, inBack1.mY, inNext.mY);

/* Spline for Z */
ioPoint.mZ = ::GetSpline(mPoint.mZ,
                  inPercent, theTSquared, theTCubed,
               inBack2.mZ, inBack1.mZ, inNext.mZ);
}
```

Listing 4.6.3 shows AdvanceSpline using mostly precomputed splines. If you want to use faster spline calculations, precompute most of the math into a look-up table as shown. (Note, you'll see in later sections of this gem that it's possible to affect an object's physics path during runtime. In that case, go with the normal, slower spline calculations since you will end up recomputing the splines every time the physics path changes.).

Listing 4.6.3 Cached Spline Calculations

```
/* uses a precomputed array to compute a fast spline */
inline float GetFastSpline(float* inArray, float inSquared,
          float inCubed, float inPercent)
{
return (0.5f * (inArray[0] + (inArray[1] * inPercent) +
         (inArray[2] * theTSquared) + (inArray[3] * theTCubed)));
}
```

```
/* simplified Advance spline method */
void AdvanceSpline(float inPercent, GE3DPoint& ioPoint)
{
ioPoint.mX = GetFastSpline(mOptimizedSplines,
                          theSqd, theCube, thePercent);
ioPoint.mY = GetFastSpline(mOptimizedSplines + 4,
                          theSqd, theCube, thePercent);
ioPoint.mZ = GetFastSpline(mOptimizedSplines + 8,
                          theSqd, theCube, thePercent);
}
```

Orientations and Quaternions

Orientations describe an object's yaw, pitch, and roll. In short, orientation is not an object's location, but rather which direction it is facing while at that position. If the object is facing upside down, angled sideways, or head over heels, that refers to its orientation. Luckily for us, quaternions are great for orientations. Quaternions not only do an amazing job of modifying an object's orientation smoothly, they also fit neatly into the time-percent paradigm that we use with our 3D movement and splines. If that wasn't enough, using quaternions to advance orientation is so simple it should be a crime. Quaternions work their magic on an object's orientation by using a spherical linear interpolation, known as "slerping," which smoothly scales its orientation along a curve (see [Svarovsky00]).

Start Your Engines!

Time to put all the pieces together into a roaring engine that will thrill our game fans. The heart of a basic engine is simple. Its job is to process all the physics nodes, advance object positions using splines, and then advance orientations using quaternions. Finally, the correct orientation is applied and the object's location is set.

Walking through Listing 4.6.4, we can see what the update code of the prescripted physics engine looks like. The first operation in the update is to pop off our nodes until we are in the correct time range. For example, if world time is 200 and node 3 goes from 195 to 220, we will pop off nodes 1 and 2 to ensure we are ready at node 3 for processing. Once we have the current node, we advance the orientation (using time and quaternions), followed by advancing the 3D position (using time and splines). Lastly, we ensure that we are rotating around the correct point on the object (feet, head, middle, wherever) before finishing our update. It's simple, it's fast, and it's almost too easy.

Listing 4.6.4 Update Method of the Prescripted Physics Engine

```
float       thePercent;
bool        theResult = true;
bool        thePointMatches;
```

```
/* Ensure our next point is the right one (time-wise) */
AdjustToCorrectPointUsingTime(inWorldTime);

/* any physics nodes? */
if(mPhysicsNodes.empty() == false)
{
GE3DPoint thePoint;

        /* get our point */
        inCurrentLocation.GetPosition(thePoint);

        /* get the first item */
        FPNode& theNode = mPhysicsNodes.front();

        /* compute the percent(it will be 0-1.0F because
       of the "AdjustToCorrectPoint method" */
        thePercent = ((float)(inWorldTime –
theNode.mStartTime)) * theNode.mInverseTotalTime;

        /* advance Orientation */
        theNode.AdvanceOrientation(thePercent,
                                mQuatOrientation);
        outResultOrientation = mQuatOrientation;

        /* Advance our location */
        theNode.AdvanceSpline(thePercent, thePoint,
        theNode.mSplines[0], theNode.mSplines[1],
theNode.mSplines[2]);

        /* Rotate it at the correct spot. (head/middle/etc) */
        ApplyRotation(theNode, outTransform, thePoint);
}
else
{
        theResult = false;
}
```

Polish It to a Shine!

As with almost everything in the games industry, the details are where you can pull away from the crowd or fall back with the pack. Some polish items that make a large impact on how well the physics appears to our customers come from adding acceleration ramps, animations, and effects to waypoints. Other items include mapping points onto objects or terrain, rotating about an arbitrary point on the object, rewinding physics, or causing reactions to occur.

Ramps and Rewind

At almost every turn, prescripted physics seems to be battling the traditional notion of physics. How can we possibly move an object through a series of points naturally without using acceleration? It's lucky for us that quaternions needed a percentage from 0% to 100% to orient things correctly, because it's the secret that makes custom ramps so useful for us.

"Normal physics moves objects from point A to point B by applying forces that result in acceleration, which in turn changes their velocity and acceleration over time until a desired velocity or position is reached. In prescripted physics, we use ramps to affect our percentage from 0–1, which in turn tells us how far along the path we are.

Imagine pushing Edgar the Chicken in a straight line from point A to point B. If we use no ramps, Edgar will move along the path at exactly the same speed. However, if we apply a sine or cosine ramp that affects the current percentage, Edgar can be moved quickly away only to slow as he approaches his destination, or moved slowly at first, only to speed up at the end. The net result of a ramp might be, given a percentage of 25%, to modify it and return 12%. We then execute our spline and orientation thinking that we are at 12% along instead of 25%. We can also use a ramp modifier that can be used as a scratch variable for our ramps. Let's say we want to use a cosine ramp, we might only want to use half of the curve, so by using a floating-point modifier we control how our ramp changes the percentage. Naturally, these ramps must be integrated into our AdvanceSpline and AdvanceOrientation methods as seen in Listing 4.6.5. Don't forget to use different ramps for orientation and movement since they advance independently.

Listing 4.6.5 AdvanceOrientation with a Ramp

```
void AdvanceOrientation(float inPercent, Quaternion& outQ)
{
/* Change the incoming percent by using a ramp */
inPercent = ProcessRamp(inPercent, mOrientationRamp,
                        mOrientationRampModifier);

/* slerp to my-lou my darling. */
      mStartQuat.Slerp(mQuaternion, inPercent, outQ);
}
```

Rewinding is a simple feature to add and operates in much the same fashion as ramps. If all the event nodes are stored after they are fully executed, then either by flipping the percentages (25% ends up at 75%) or rewinding time, we can watch Edgar rewind his movement and orientation, going from the ending waypoint all the way back to the first.

Mapping to Terrain and Objects

One of the big fears of applying prescripted physics is that if we plan a path for the object during the beginning of the event, any time something unexpected happens in the world that affects the object's path, the physics event breaks. For example, imagine that an object falls off a high-rise building, and we determine that the final resting place would be a nice grassy hilltop. Halfway down, an explosion annihilates the hill leaving it a deformed pile of dirt far below where we expected our object to land. All hope is not lost! We can change our path during real time, but doing so requires that we adjust our times and splines for the surrounding (or all) waypoints in the event. This is not the pinnacle of CPU efficiency, so overall we don't like surprises during prescripted physics events.

One of the tools we can use to get out of this jam is mapping waypoints onto terrain or other objects. When we map a point to terrain during the creation phase, we know that whatever else happens during prescripted physics, this waypoint will be firmly on the ground. Likewise, mapping a point onto an object means that wherever the mapped-to object moves, the waypoint will remain locked onto it. If you decide to use mapping, remember that when waypoints move, they must have their time scaled so their perceived velocity doesn't change. That requires that you adjust the ending time and possibly the start and end times of all future nodes. It's very important to also adjust the waypoint spline positions for the current waypoint (as well as the next two waypoints), because spline calculations use the positions of waypoints ($n - 2$) in reverse.

Rotations

When we apply rotations in the engine, they happen about the 3D position of the object. If the object is at the exact position we want to rotate, perfect for us! Otherwise, we have an object whose defined center isn't at the center of its geometry, and we may have to do some transformations to ensure that we rotate about the right area. For example, in an RTS game, you might have the 3D point of an object be at its feet, but you probably want to rotate objects from its center instead. Perhaps you even want to make something flip lopsided by starting the rotation point at the feet and sliding up to the head over the lifetime of the physics event. Listing 4.6.6 is an unoptimized function that demonstrates how we can rotate using transformations:

Listing 4.6.6 Using the Current Quaternion to Rotate about the Desired Point on the Object

```
GETransformation      theRotateCenter;
GETransformation      theRotateCenterInverse;
GETransformation      theTranslation;
GETransformation      theRotation;
GETransformation      theResult1;
GETransformation      theResult2;
GE3DPoint             thePoint;

/* put it into transform. */
this->mQuatOrientation.ConvertToTransform(theRotation);
```

```
/* set the translation */
theTranslation.SetPosition(inPoint);

/* set the rotation center (adjusting for Z, not XY) */
theRotateCenter.SetZ(mHeight * ioNode.mRotationModifier);

/* make inverse (cache this and the main transform) */
theRotateCenter.MakeInverse(theRotateCenterInverse);

/* apply the rotation center to the world translation */
theTranslation.Apply(theRotateCenter, theResult1);

/* apply the world/rotated to the result */
theResult1.Apply(theRotation, theResult2);

/* convert from local space to world space. */
theResult2.Apply(theRotateCenterInverse, ioFinalTransform);
```

Reactions

Reactions are the weakest part of prescripted physics compared to using traditional physics. It's all planned out ahead of time, so the engine doesn't take well to surprises unless you code in the ability for it to handle them. In general, reactions should focus on creating "reaction events" in response to things like collision with walls or other objects. When the collision happens, a special reaction event should examine the current situation, create the appropriate reaction physics event, and follow the path of the reaction instead of the old physics event. Like mapping to terrain and objects, reactions affect the path in real time but cause more catastrophic changes.

Imagine we're using prescripted physics to pitch a baseball. As the ball flies towards the catcher, a bat pops into its way and hits it. That is a catastrophic change to the object's path that causes a reaction. The reaction is handled by creating a new physics event, taking into account things like velocity, current position, bat swing strength—you name it—then giving it to the physics engine, which kills the old event and continues life with the new one.

Optimization tip: Collision detection can be expensive, so try turning it on and off on a per-waypoint basis when you know that it's safe to skip.

Out-of-Game Tool

Even though prescripted physics events are easy to create for a programmer, it's inevitable that changes from an artist or designer will likely be needed. Ideally, once prescripted physics has demonstrated its value to a game engine, an out-of-game tool should be written to allow artists and designers the ability to generate descriptions of physics events. This can be a very complicated tool to design since so much of the creation needs to involve examining the world in which the physics event is created. It is generally a good idea to make a few simple physics events in code to prove that prescripted physics works in your game engine before embarking on tool creation. Otherwise, the "days" estimate to get a prescripted physics engine up and running could easily turn into weeks as the programmer tweaks user interface details, such as ways for artists and designers to "simulate gravity" or "add points around a circle."

Twister: Right Foot on Red

After putting together the prescripted physics engine, it's finally time to have some fun writing a physics event! As a quick example, if we were to write a tornado event, we could derive a class from a physics event base, overload the Create method, and have our own tornado in one simple function. Listing 4.6.7 provides a very simple version of a tornado that swirls an object about in the air.

Listing 4.6.7 A Simple Tornado Physics Event

```
/* using velocity and distance, get the time */
unsigned long theTimePerIteration =
::FloatToUnsignedLong((kPI * (2.0F * inRadius)) / inVelocity) *
1000;

/* compute the iterations needed */
long theTornadoWaypointsPerPI = 35;
float theFloatIters = ((float)inTime /     (float)theTimePerItera-
tion);
float theInterval = (theTimePerIteration / theTornadoWaypointsPerPI);
float theIncPerLoop = (1.0F / theTornadoWaypointsPerPI);

/* set the starting point. */
thePNode.SetStartingQuat(inCurrentQuat);
theRotationTransform.SetPosition(inCenter);
theNewPoint = inStartPoint;

/* animation */
thePNode.SetAnimation(inAnimation);

/* set the point */
thePNode.SetPoint(theNewPoint);

/* Start NEW POINT */
long theNextYPRCounter = 0;
long theZCounter = 0;

/* Rotation amount we'll use */
float theRotationAmount = -((kTwoPI / 35.0F) * 2.0F);
theZCounter = (theTornadoWaypointsPerPI / 4);
```

```
/* Loop over all the points */
for(theFLoop = 0.0F;
    theFLoop < theFloatIters;
    theFLoop += theIncPerLoop,
    theZCounter—,     theNextYPRCounter—)
{
/* Cache the last Z for use later */
        theLastZ = theNewPoint.GetZ();

        /* Reset yaw/pitch/roll increments? */
        if(theNextYPRCounter == 0)
        {
                /* setup next */
                theNextYPRCounter = 4;

                /* Inverse instead of dividing 3 times */
                theInverse = 1.0F / (float)theNextYPRCounter;

                /* compute the change range */
                theYaw = GetRandom(-TwoPI, TwoPI) * theInverse;
                thePitch = GetRandom(-TwoPI, TwoPI) * theInverse;
                theRoll = GetRandom(-TwoPI, TwoPI) * theInverse;
        }

        /* Orientation setup */
        thePNode.SetOriYPR(theOri.mYaw + theYaw,
            theOri.mPitch + thePitch,
            theOri.mRoll + theRoll);

        /* Vector/destination point */
        theRotationTransform.RotateByYaw(theRotationAmount);
        theRotationYaw = theRotationTransform.GetYaw();

        /* Tip: Tweak radius and time to make a funnel */
        /* Compute the local point spacing in relation to the
      radius and transform into world space */
        theLocal.SetY(inRadius);
        theRotationTransform.Apply(theLocal, theWorld);

        /* Rotate world. */
        theFloatPoint = theWorld;
        theFloatPoint.RotatePointAroundZero(theRotationYaw);
        theFloatPoint.SetZ(theWorld.GetZ());
        theNewPoint = inCenter;
        theNewPoint += theFloatPoint;

        /* Get a new Z? */
        if(theZCounter == 0)
        {
                /* reset it */
                theZCounter = (theTornadoWaypointsPerPI / 4);
```

```
    /* compute Z Change (0.0F = TERRAIN Z) */
    theZChange = GetRandom(0.5F, 5.0F) + 0.0F;
    theZChange = (theZChange - theLastZ ) /
                    (float)theZCounter;
    }

        /* Set the position, and add the Z to our current Z */
        thePNode.SetPoint(theNewPoint.GetX(),
       theNewPoint.GetY(),
                    theLastZ + theZChange);

        /* Time this will take. */
        theCurrentTime = thePNode.SetTime(theCurrentTime,
      theCurrentTime + theInterval);

        /* add to our list of waypoints we'll use later */
        theNodes.push_back(thePNode);
    }

    /* add those waypoints to the physics event, your done! */
    AddPoints(theNodes);
```

Conclusion

The key points from this gem you should remember include the following:

Physics is important: Today's market demands game physics that can rival movies and special effects software. Don't be afraid to take the challenge! There is almost always a solution that is off the beaten path. It just has to be found.

Prescripted physics has strengths: Use prescripted physics for special physics events like throwing objects, recoil physics, and other cinematic moments.

Prescripted physics has weaknesses: Don't use prescripted physics where traditional linear physics is superior such as walking soldiers in an RTS world.

Quick to code: The prescripted physics engine is quick to create, and it's even quicker to program events. Don't be afraid to use all that extra time to experiment with new ramps, splines, and other polish items.

Wait on the tool: Don't create a physics tool until you have created the engine and in-code events. After all, getting it up and running is the first step.

Optimize splines: If you're not applying real-time forces to your physics points (like an object being carried off in a moving tornado), then cache your splines into an array to reduce math computations.

Quaternions are incredible: If you don't already have one, write a quaternion class for your application and slerp your orientations for smooth rotations.

Modify those rotations: Change how you rotate an object by using a floating-point modifier from 0.0F (feet) to 1.0F (head). Otherwise all rotations for the object will occur about the actual 3D position, which could be anywhere.

Polish it: This gem details a basic prescripted physics engine, but there are many ways to improve it. Be sure to add ramps, rewinding, animations, sounds, graphical effects, or whatever else you can think of that will add excitement to your game.

In today's competitive game industry, physics is just as important as graphics. Graphics draws the world the user sees, but if we don't make a world worth looking at, no amount of graphics will help. Prescripted physics can be a great solution for developers who want exciting physics in their game at a fraction of the time needed to create a traditional big-budget physics engine.

Every year we sit at the World Series of Poker for game developers, guarding our hands, feeling both nervous and confident at the same time. What will you do with your next hand of cards? Will you play tight and aggressive? Will you stick to what you know? Will you be innovative, and work on building those cards? Whatever style you choose, be sure to keep raising the pot for all of us. In the end, it's what keeps us pushing the envelope and making our customers happy.

Thanks to Richard Woolford for the use of Edgar the Chicken. (No chickens were actually harmed in the writing of this gem).

References

[Bourg01] Bourg, David, M. "Physics for Game Developers." 2001.

[Dunlop00] Dunlop, Robert. "Introduction to Catmull-Rom Splines." Available online at *http://www.mvps.org/directx/articles/catmull.* 2000.

[Svarovsky00] Svarovsky, Jan. "Quaternions for Game Programming." In *Game Programming Gems,* Charles River Media, 2000.

4.7

Prescripted Physics: Techniques and Applications

Shawn Shoemaker

shansolox@yahoo.com

Real physics simulation in games provides robust results but can be quite expensive in terms of processing, especially on more modest platforms and in Web applications. Also, "true" physics simulation generates arbitrary locations and orientations for units, which can result in unexpected (and undesirable) situations. Many games require that units obtain a particular location and orientation as a result of physics motion, and some also require hundreds of units to be simulated simultaneously. This gem describes the merits of implementing a prescripted physics system to generate the illusion of actual physics, and demonstrates how Hollywood effects normally available to games with sophisticated physics engines can be achieved inexpensively and quickly while sticking to the rules of the game world.

While there are many published articles on rigid body physics and general dynamics, there are few devoted to prescripted physics systems. This gem discusses an actual game example of a prescripted physics system, detailing the physics used for the paratrooper drop in the RTS game *Empires: Dawn of the Modern World* developed by Stainless Steel Studios. It is assumed that the reader has some knowledge of basic game physics, quaternions, and splines, and has become familiar with the mechanics of a general prescripted physics system, such as that described by Dan Higgins [Higgins05].

Why Prescripted Physics?

Why not just stick to real physics in a game? Often, real physics does not allow the designers to specify exactly what should happen in the game, because often what *should* happen does not actually follow the laws of physics. Most games prefer the look of Hollywood physics: explosive, fantastic, and exaggerated. Usually this is hardly what real physics simulation will result in. For example, consider an explosion near infantry units. Actual physics simulation would toss all the units away from the explosion location, with a bit of rotation for some of the units. By contrast, the Hollywood model calls for all of the infantry units to fly high in the air, flip a few times, and then crash to the ground—a much more dramatic and visually pleasing effect.

Some may argue that a solid, working knowledge of physics and the underlying equations allow the programmer to alter environment parameters to result in the desired look of the system. While this is true, the prescripted physics route gives the programmer—and more importantly, the designers (who may not be fully versed in physics simulation)—complete control. Further, altering global physics parameters can throw the physics simulation off unpredictably in other areas, as the system is typically tuned for one particular result. If the programmer is stuck tuning the physics simulation for each particular behavior, there is no good reason to have run on a realistic system in the first place. Instead, the exact desired results for each situation may be attained every time with a prescripted system.

Not only does prescripted physics help attain the desired visual look, it also provides for a known end state of the simulation. In true physics simulation, the initial state and inputs are known, but the final result usually is not known, leading to some complicated possible situations. This is not the case in a prescripted system; the programmer or designer determines what the end result will be and plans the physics route accordingly. This is much more flexible in games with thousands of units, where some of the more computationally expensive techniques are not feasible, and units are restricted in their pathfinding.

The final selling point is the big benefit that the producer will enjoy: short development time. A simple prescripted physics system can be up and running in two weeks. A robust rigid body system would require considerably more time, perhaps several months. The prescripted system avoids some of the challenges of rigid body simulation, such as integrator instability, friction, resting constraints, and penetration issues. The bottom line is, prescripted physics is very inexpensive to implement, debug, and maintain.

The Prescripted Physics System

A detailed design of prescripted physics is beyond the scope of this gem, but the basic mechanics are worth mentioning here. Briefly, a combination of Catmull-Rom splines and quaternions make up the chief components. Units are moved along the spline segments at a particular rate, rotating and animating as they go.

Each spline *control point* has various parameters that can be set to control the motion. First, each control point has the total time for the unit to traverse that particular segment. Next, each control point has a time function, used to control the "acceleration" of the motion along the spline segment. This time function can simply be linear, or based on some higher-order function of time. The total time combined with the time function dictates the *speed* of the spline segment.

The control points also specify a goal rotation in the form of a quaternion. This allows units to rotate towards an explicit orientation as they move along the spline segment, with the orientation at any given point along the spline coming from interpolation between control points. Finally, each control point specifies a particular animation that is to be played while the unit is traveling along the segment. The control point parameters may be set in real time or predetermined by design. All that matters is that "good" values are chosen.

Choosing "Good" Prescripted Values

For a prescripted physics system to work, it needs to look believable. For example, units should appear to fall realistically and bounce when they hit an obstacle. To sell the look of the system, it's important that it has some of the same properties of a real simulation. The problem, then, is determining how to partially model the effects of a realistic system in the prescripted world.

Dynamics provides all the equations that are needed for a realistic simulation. Typically, an examination is made of the real-world equations that are necessary to model particular effects, such as gravity, buoyancy, drag, and friction. The equations are then combined, and some time points are chosen for motion and are plugged into the appropriate parameters. The equation is then solved for each time point, and the resulting table of time inputs and equation outputs can be fed right into the prescripted simulation. Note that increasing the granularity of the time points will increase the approximation of the real system.

Another way to arrive at the input values for the prescripted system is to run a real simulation "offline" and record the position data over time. The "fake" simulation can then be made to match the real simulation data, resulting in a natural look and feel to the motion.

Once a prescripted physics system has been developed and a method for selecting values has been chosen, it's easy to use the system to cover a variety of situations. What follows are a number of examples of prescripted physics applications.

Application: RTS Building Destruction

In 3D RTS games, buildings generally build up out of the ground and fall back into the ground once they are destroyed. This simple behavior can easily be modeled using prescripted physics. A number of short spline segments are needed, positioned from the building's center point to a point below the terrain, at a total distance sufficient to hide the top of the building under the terrain. Each control point's quaternion contains a small pitch or roll amount, to simulate the building's shaking. The speed of the control points should increase as they go down, so that the building appears to accelerate on its way to the ground. Figure 4.7.1 shows five control points for building destruction. In this example, five points are sufficient to show the varied speed and rotation for the destruction.

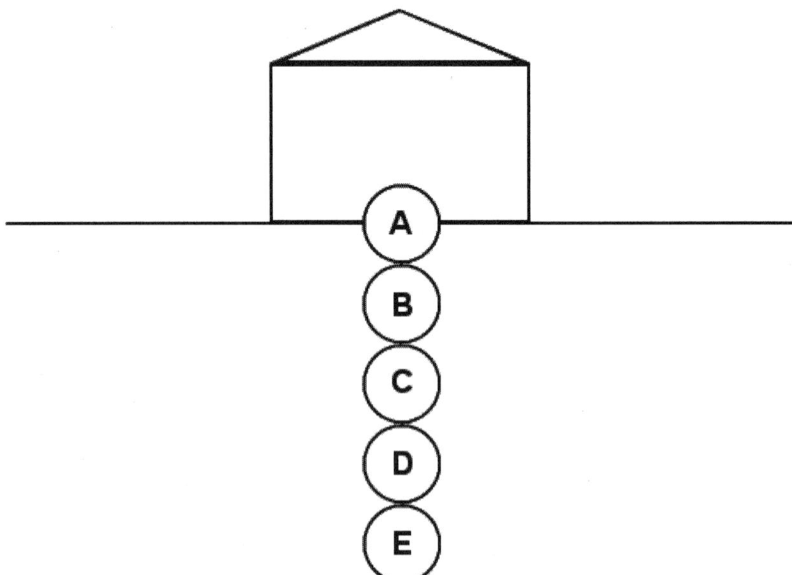

FIGURE 4.7.1 *Spline control points for building destruction.*

Application: Jumping

Jumping is another straightforward application for a prescripted physics system. From a stop, a unit runs a small distance, bends down, and leaps up. After a small amount of time, the unit comes down and lands. As shown in Figure 4.7.2, the unit should play a run animation and accelerate from control point A to B. At point B, the unit should play a "jump into the air" animation and begin with high velocity towards point C. The velocity should slow towards point D. While it is not possible to alter vertical and not horizontal velocity in this system, this simulation does not need such accuracy to look convincing. There is a slight pause in velocity about point D, at which point the acceleration due to gravity overcomes the unit's upward velocity. The unit accelerates through point E and quickly arrives at point F. At point F, the unit plays a landing animation, which is accompanied by an appropriate visual effect for the terrain on which the unit lands. Point G completes the effect, allowing room for the unit to recover or stutter following the jump.

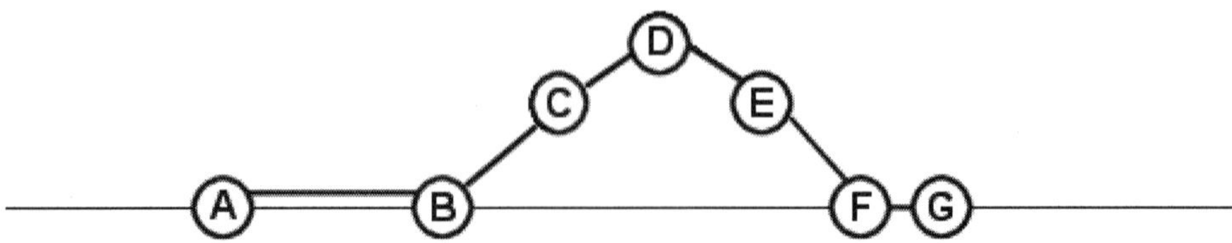

FIGURE 4.7.2 *Spline control points for a jumping effect.*

Application: Explosion Displacement

Explosions are another great application for a prescripted physics system. As shown in Figure 4.7.3, units follow a somewhat parabolic spline. However, as opposed to actual physics, units will flip as they fly through the air. All units fly away from the center of the explosion. Units choose from a number of predetermined splines based on both their distance to the center of the explosion and some randomization factor. This, along with control point height and rotation randomization, provides for a lot of variety in the flight taken by units.

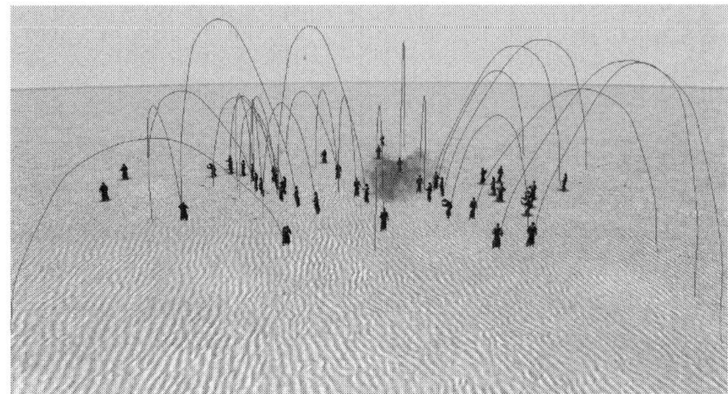

FIGURE 4.7.3 *Units following a parabolic path following an explosion. © 2004. Reprinted with permission from Stainless Steel Studios.*

Rotations are broken up over a few control points so that no single spline segment has too much rotation for its spline segment length. Breaking up the rotation also allows for the units to flip completely over. A unit should only rotate in one direction throughout the spline. While flips are a Hollywood effect, changing direction mid flight would be an obvious red flag to the player. At the end of the spline, any rotation must leave the unit on its back or on its stomach in preparation for the landing animation.

Animations are added to show the unit flying up off of the ground. Units can either fly forward on their stomach, or backward on their back. Once airborne, units play a mid-air flailing animation. For landing, "land-on-stomach" and "land-on-back" animations are used, as appropriate. The landing animation will sell the physics effect even better if it includes some amount of bounce for the unit on impact. Finally, an appropriate visual effect for the terrain collision should be added when the unit hits the ground, such as a dust cloud or tossing of other debris.

Application: Buoyancy

The effect for buoyancy is easy to simulate. What is really needed to convince a player of buoyancy? Units must fall to the water, at which point their descent is greatly reduced. After falling down through the water, the unit will stop, and then begin to rise. The unit rises faster and faster, until it breaks the surface of the water. Perhaps the unit breaks the water plane again on the way down and then resurfaces before coming to a resting position on top of the water. This is all that needs to be shown to sell the idea of buoyancy.

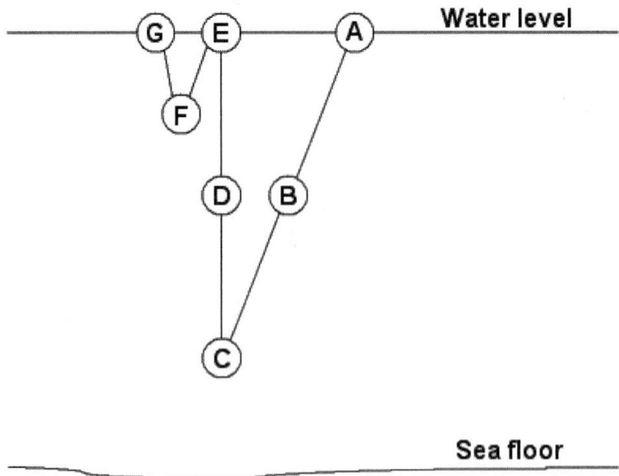

FIGURE 4.7.4 *Spline control points for a prescripted buoyancy effect.*

Figure 4.7.4 shows additional details of the buoyancy described. The speed between splines control points A and B should greatly reduce. This deceleration should continue to point C, at which point the buoyancy of the unit has overcome the force of gravity. The unit accelerates from a stop up to point D, with additional increases in speed to point E. From point E, the unit again accelerates from a stop. Points F and G repeat the process of gravity and buoyancy for the secondary splash-down but with greatly reduced time durations for each control point.

To add realism, as usual some animations are added. Units should use a tread water animation for points G and E, and a swim animation for points C, D, and F. Points A and B call for a falling animation. Each break of the water's surface should be accompanied by a visual splash effect. To add variety to the physics, a unit's density and mass should affect the depth of control points as well as the speed. Finally, should the unit have sufficient velocity, or if the water is shallow enough, the unit should kick off of the sea floor, and thus have an increased speed for points D and E.

Application: Paratroopers

For *Empires: Dawn of the Modern World*, some number of paratroopers were required to drop out of their C-47. The paratroopers needed to follow a realistic-looking path to the ground. Further, the paratroopers needed to land near the player-specified landing zone. Paratroopers were not allowed to land on illegal map locations, as this would frustrate players.

Each paratrooper had six spline control points created to move the paratrooper to its pre-calculated landing location. The positions of the spline control points were slightly randomized per paratrooper, creating unique flight paths for each. Further, subsequent splines would move the paratroopers in opposite directions, to further distribute their descent.

Figure 4.7.5 (also Color Plate 4A) shows these six spline control points for one paratrooper. Control point 1 is the location from which the paratrooper begins his descent and is located on a tag point on the C-47 airplane model. As mentioned previously, control points 2, 3, and 4 are slightly random, so that subsequent paratroopers have varying flight paths. This variation is easier to see in Figure 4.7.6 (also Color Plate 4B), which provides a better perspective on the scene and features a whole stick of paratroopers. Control points 5 and 6 add a hook at the end of the spline. This hook ensures that the paratrooper intersects the terrain at the correct predetermined location. Note that control point 6 is actually below the terrain.

FIGURE 4.7.5 *Control points for one trooper. © 2004. Reprinted with permission from Stainless Steel Studios.*

Each physics tick, the amount of time passed combined with the paratrooper's acceleration, was used to calculate the distance the paratrooper had traveled. Each spline segment had its length calculated before the simulation began. In this manner, the paratrooper could determine which segment of the spline it was currently following. Once the trooper knew its current spline segment, its new position along that

FIGURE 4.7.6 *Line of troopers with variance. © 2004. Reprinted with permission from Stainless Steel Studios.*

particular segment was determined based on the distance traveled and the total length of that particular segment.

To help make the motion of the paratroopers more believable, animations were combined with the prescripted physics paths. A "snap" animation was added for the point at which the units left the C-47. A wobble animation was used for most of the descent through the air. Two different animations were used for landing, including one in which the unit raised its legs in preparation for landing and an animation in which it absorbed the shock of landing with its legs. The look of the paratroopers along the spline benefited from the combination of the prescripted motion and the animations. For example, the "raising legs" animation was combined with a nearly smooth path over the terrain, yielding a natural looking glide that is often seen in real life landings.

Random rotation of the paratroopers was also added to help simulate the effects of wind. This rotation slowed as the units got closer to the ground. Also, as the units approached the ground they were scaled up in size. This was due to the fact that the scale of the C-47 was accurate to that of the buildings and paratroopers. Hence, the paratroopers begin very small and actually get larger as they fall to the ground.

Conclusion

This gem demonstrates some applications for a prescripted physics system for use in RTS and other games. A few points are worth reiterating. A prescripted physics system can provide many benefits including low implementation time, a Hollywood look, and a final result that matches designers' vision. Actual physics simulation can be measured to produce starting values for a prescripted system. Further, splines and quaternions are the key elements driving movement in such a system. But movement alone is not enough; it's also crucial to combine animation with the prescripted motion.

There are obviously some drawbacks to a prescripted physics system. It is preplanned and therefore not reactive. Units may not collide with other units if that possibility has not been accounted for. Further, a prescripted system requires that each particular path of motion is either programmed or created in some sort of application. For example, if a path of motion is created for a unit falling from a 40-story building, a different path of motion will be necessary for a unit falling down a flight of stairs.

These issues aside, the prescripted system is very useful in RTS games or any other genre in which hundreds of units are in need of exciting Hollywood physics. It can also be applied to many other areas of the game wherever units require motion that is not covered by simple object dynamics. All of this can be achieved in a very short amount of time, allowing developers to spend more time creating interesting behaviors for their games.

References

[Higgins05] Higgins, Dan. "Designing a Prescripted Physics System." In *Game Programming Gems 5*. Charles River Media, 2005.

4.8

Realistic Camera Movement in a 3D Car Simulator

Barnabás Aszódi, Szabolcs Czuczor, Budapest University of Technology and Economics, Department of Control Engineering and Information Technology, Computer Graphics Group

ab011@hszk.bme.hu, cs007@hszk.bme.hu

In a car simulator or driving game, there can often be several different camera positions used throughout the course of the game, with most of the virtual cameras attached to the moving car (i.e., internal cameras in the cockpit, on the top of the hood, etc.). In the case of an internal cockpit camera, it is not only acceptable but also desirable that every little car movement also causes movement of the camera, in order to enhance the realism. In other cases, such as when the virtual camera is placed beside the path of the car, it can be very disturbing if every little movement of the car shakes the camera. Additionally, in a collision that stops the car very rapidly, the camera stops rapidly as well, which can be quite jarring. In this gem, we propose a camera model that can enhance the realism of our virtual camera movement. Our virtual camera could have weight and inertia, but primarily its behavior is based on human nature. As a result, the car, due to its movement in the world, may not always be in the center of the screen, but may fall behind or go ahead, enhancing the realism of the representation.

What Do We Need? Physical Principles

In reality, every object follows the rule of continuity, meaning that a real object cannot change its position with sudden jumps through space. Without this, the object's speed would need to be infinite, which is impossible. Therefore, when we define our object's position as a function of time, it should be continuous if it is a simple straight line or a path with lots of curves or angles, as in Equation 4.8.1.

$$\mathbf{r} = \mathbf{r}(t) \tag{4.8.1}$$

Here, r is the actual position of an object, which is represented as a three-dimensional vector whose actual value depends on time. A real object can change its speed just as continuously as its position, as defined in Newton's second axiom, provided in Equation 4.8.2.

$$\vec{\mathbf{F}} = m \cdot \vec{\mathbf{a}} \Rightarrow \vec{\mathbf{a}} = \frac{\vec{\mathbf{F}}}{m} \tag{4.8.2}$$

F (force) and a (acceleration) are vectors, and m (mass or weight) is a scalar. The speed can change with a jump only when the acceleration is infinite. This expression means that it can happen only when the force is infinite or the mass is zero. Of course, both are impossible in real life, so when we want to control a virtual camera in a virtual scene, we have to care about these two major rules, otherwise, its movements will be unrealistic.

A real camera has mass and, as a result, inertia. To simplify our task in calculating our camera's movement, we represent it with two points: an *eye* and a *target*. The camera looks from the eye to the target, which means that the target will be always in the center of the screen. We define the orientation of the camera based upon the relative position of these two points. Because the eye and the target have mass, and because the acceleration must be finite, the speed of a real object cannot change discontinuously. We cannot change the force discontinuously either, so the function that represents the force can only be continuous. Let us see this problem in reverse.

Using Figure 4.8.1, we will review what we mean when we talk about different degrees of continuity. This will be important when discussing the continuity of Equation 4.8.1, which defines the position of an object in time. On the far-left column of Figure 4.8.1, we show a discontinuous motion that fails the laws of physics. If there are no instantaneous jumps in the function, as shown in the second column of Figure 4.8.1, we can refer it as a C^0 continuous curve. To calculate the velocity of the object

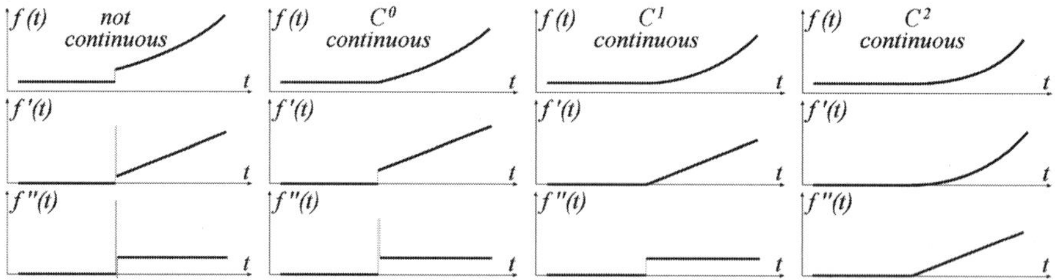

FIGURE 4.8.1 *Curves with discontinuity, C^0 continuity, C^1 continuity, and C^2 continuity. The top row is the initial function of time. The second and third rows are the first and second derivatives of each function.*

on its path, we take the derivative with respect to time. If the derivative is also continuous, as shown in the third column of Figure 4.8.1, it is referred to as a C^1 continuous curve. Finally, if we examine the second derivative of our path, which is the *acceleration* of the moving object on the path, and find that it is also continuous, then our path can be referred as a C^2 continuous curve as shown on the far-right column of Figure 4.8.1. If we want to make the movement of our virtual camera realistic, its path must be at least C^0 continuous, but it would be better if it could fulfill the requirements of a C^2 continuous path as well.

What Do We Get? Sometimes Unrealistic Movements

There is a huge variety of 3D driving games on the market today. Some of them invite the player into a realistic world, while the others transport the player into fictional places. In some games and simulators, we need to observe traffic laws, while in the others, we can drive with reckless abandon. In either case, however, it is generally expected that the virtual cars have realistic movement.

Even for racing games that offer the player a cockpit view, there is often a race replay mode, during which we can review details of our race from external points of view. In addition to inside views, we can often watch our race from stable cameras placed beside the speedway. Imagine that you are a camera operator whose task is to follow a racing car with his TV camera. The camera is fixed on a tripod and you can rotate it around a vertical (Y) and a horizontal (X) axis. In this case, we can say that the *eye* position is stable and the *target* is moveable. These two points can be defined as two 3D vectors. There is also a third vector, called *up*, which defines the default vertical axis of the camera as shown in Figure 4.8.2. By default, you can pitch and yaw your camera. If you want to roll it too, you need to change this assumed up vector and use another formulation such as the Euler angles shown in Figure 4.8.3.

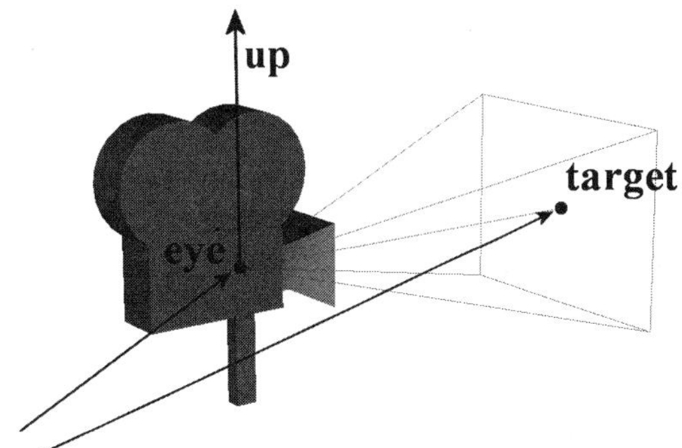

FIGURE 4.8.2 *A camera and its important vectors. The eye defines the viewpoint, the target defines the orientation (it will be in the center of the rendered screen), and the up defines the vertical axis of the camera.*

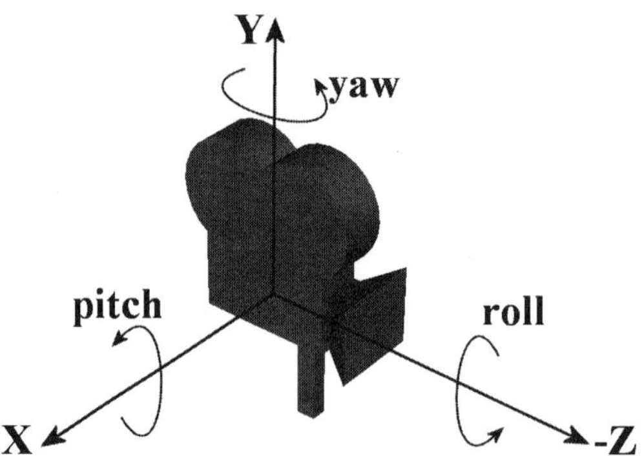

FIGURE 4.8.3 *An object can be rotated around three axes: pitch (X), yaw (Y), and roll (Z). These rotations are defined by Euler angles.*

Now, your job as a camera operator in a fantasy race has already begun, and the cars are coming towards your viewpoint, as shown in Figure 4.8.4. The car that you need to record appears on the horizon and you start following it with your camera's target point. It comes with very high speed, but the driver accelerates even more. You knew that he would likely accelerate since your assigned section of the track is a long straightaway, so you keep right up. Eventually, the car is nearly in front of you, when a giant creature made of stone suddenly appears just in front of the car! The creature is too stupid to jump away and the driver does not have enough time to step on the brake to avoid the collision. CRASH!!! The creature seems to have felt nothing but the car is in pieces on the track. Because of the mass of the camera and the unexpected accident, your rotation of the camera continues. After you recognize what happened, you rotate back to the car wreck.

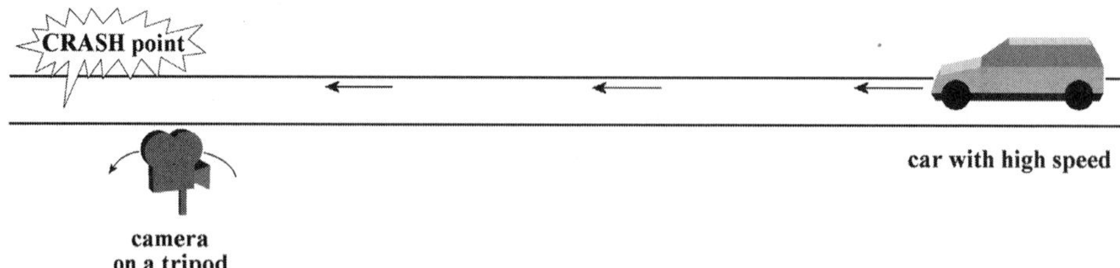

FIGURE 4.8.4 *An example situation where a roadside camera tries to follow a racing car, which stops suddenly.*

Examining the Camera Control

As we discussed earlier, we would like to define the path of a camera as a C^2 curve. In a car racing game, a stable camera beside the road always looks at the car no matter what kind of maneuvers the player of the driving game makes. As we know, computer games do their physics and graphics calculations at a series of discrete points in time. As a result, we must process the paths of the moving objects and cameras as sampled curves. But how do we define a C^2 continuous curve based on discrete samples?

Working with Parametric Curves

What if we define parametric curves aligned to the actual positions of the given object? This solution results in several problems. As mentioned earlier, the followed object (i.e., the car) can have unrealistic movements, yet we need to use its sampled path to create the C^2 continuous path of our camera. One of the problems is that the sudden movements, which may have discontinuous jumps, cannot result in a C^2 curve. Besides, how could we generate a curve from the sample points of an object's position that is controlled by the player in real time if we don't know the future? Expanding the curve with a new point might change the whole shape of the curve. We could partition the path to several smaller curves, but the problem of adding a new point to it would still exist. We will put aside this mathematical approach and start again from another point of view.

Observing Human Behavior

Recall the camera movement described in the previous story. Of course, there are the mass and inertia of the camera, but the most important source of our fictional camera's behavior is human control. In fact, hereafter we will refer to realistic camera movement as *human camera control.* If we had a bigger and heavier camera, its movement would be much smoother, according to Newton's second axiom. That is, even though we have limited force to accelerate the camera, reaching a given speed is just a question of time. So, we can move or rotate our heavy camera as fast as a handy cam but with not so much detail in the movement. Smoothness means that we can follow the slow and the fast movements well (sometimes with some delay), but we cannot follow sudden direction changes. The frequency is a typical parameter of movements that can be described by curves, thus smoothness can be represented by a frequency limit. This limit can be applied by some kind of low-pass filtering method.

Human behavior means not just smoothing the movement of the camera, but also taking the thinking of the camera operator into account. First, he sees something in the viewfinder and starts following it. Then, he recognizes the speed of the object, but still follows it. If the object is accelerating, the camera operator notices it and tries to keep it in the screen. The overshooting in case of a sudden movement of the object can be explained with both properties: *thinking*, because the camera operator wants to be too smart and he has some delay after an unexpected event, and *smoothing*, because the bodies of the camera operator and the camera have mass and the muscles of the camera operator can apply finite force.

Actually, if we are able to create smooth paths having the ability of human prediction on the future shape of the path, we can approximate C^2 continuous curves properly enough.

Final Decision: Realizing Human Behavior

We saw that the mathematical approach is very proper and scientific. However, it needs much time to explain, to understand, and to implement. Besides, we thought that the theory of human behavior represents the problem that we want to solve much better. Additionally, its implementation is not too difficult. So, let us find out which algorithms can be used to implement the two main human behaviors of *smoothing* and *thinking*.

Smoothing Curves with Inertia

As we mentioned earlier, the main result of inertia is smoothing of the paths of motion. How do we apply this to our discrete set of sample points? How do we smooth them or apply low-pass filtering on them? If you are familiar with digital signal processing, you are aware that because of Shannon's sampling theorem (also known as the Nyquist criterion), a waveform can store components only up to half of the sampling rate. For example, if we have 120 samples in a second, we can store sounds up to a maximum 60 Hz frequency.

Let us take the average of two neighboring samples of a signal, keeping the original sampling rate, as shown in Figure 4.8.5. This procedure is similar to downsampling the waveform to 60 samples per second, limiting the maximum frequency to 30 Hz. If we take the average of three neighboring samples, the maximum frequency will be 20 Hz, and so on.

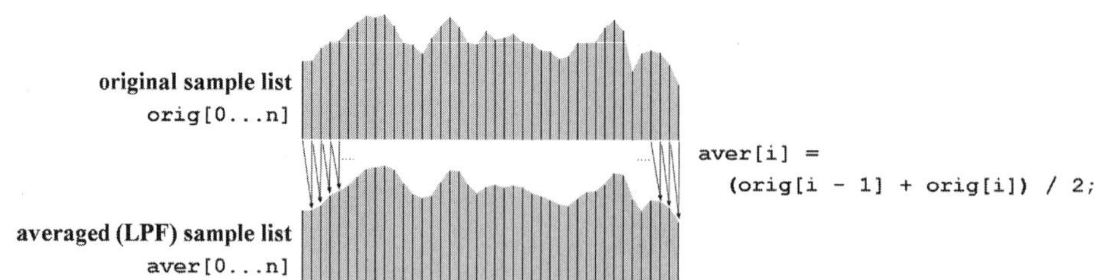

FIGURE 4.8.5 *Averaging neighboring samples of a list.*

Of course, in camera control we have three-dimensional position vectors coming one after another, frame by frame. The sampling rate in the previous example corresponds to the frame rate in the case of motion control. First, we need a list where we can store the position vectors of the target object. We need another list, into which we can calculate the low-pass filtered values of the input position list. This smoothing is one step toward human camera control.

Thinking: Extrapolating Position Samples

Remember your behavior as a camera operator. You tried to anticipate where the target object will be and how fast it will be moving. During the preceding step of interpolation, we had two or more key-samples and we tried to find out what would be between them as shown in Figure 4.8.6a. During extrapolation, we have the same two or more samples and we will try to find out what the next sample point will be, as illustrated in Figure 4.8.6b. Taking just the differences of the known position samples into account, we can predict a new position. Taking the differences of differences into account, we can also predict velocity, and with this, we can correct our first prediction for the new location. In addition, taking the differences of these differences of differences into account, we can make a prediction for acceleration, so we can correct our speed and, in turn, the location prediction. While the first extrapolation needs at least two samples, the last one needs at least four. However, if we have just few samples, the result of our prediction can be somewhat inaccurate. To improve this, we can consider even more samples. We can also weight the samples to define their importance. For example, the recent past can be taken into account with more weight than the distant past.

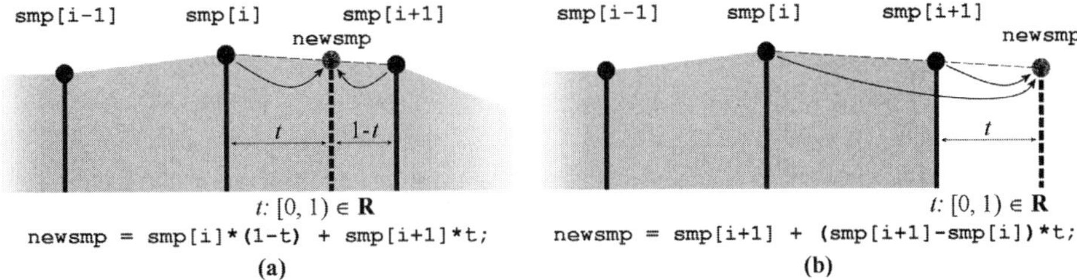

FIGURE 4.8.6 *Interpolation (a) and extrapolation (b) of sample points.*

By choosing the length of the extrapolation, we can define the "watchfulness" of our virtual camera operator. As mentioned earlier, we need at least two samples to extrapolate the next position of the target object. This newly predicted position will be used in the very next moment. In this case, we can tell that our camera operator is very watchful and fast, because a tiny little sudden change in the movement of the followed object is taken into account just in the next frame. If the frame rate is high, for example 120 frames per second, this speed is too fast for a human. It would mean that our camera operator perceives changes in movement in 8.3 milliseconds. Generally, people can perceive sudden changes in 0.7 seconds, which causes some delay in motion. To compensate, the prediction about the actual position of the followed object is born 0.7 seconds earlier. Therefore, the sample buffer holding the extrapolated positions needs to store samples from the last 0.7 seconds, which is easy to solve in case of a constant frame rate. However, the frame rate of a computer game is always changing depending on the complexity of the rendered scene. As a result, we must use a variable length sample buffer for extrapolated positions.

Programming Issues

This gem was implemented in C++ language using OpenGL and GLUT graphics support in the Win32 environment. In this section, we will present our virtual camera model and other helper data structures, which are applicable to OpenGL easily.

Camera in OpenGL

First of all, let us see how we can define a perspective view in OpenGL using GLUT. We used two functions to define a view. The first is

```
gluPerspective(fov, width/height, nearDist, farDist);
```

The `fov` (field of view) is the vertical viewing angle of a camera in degrees. This can be a small value when using a telephoto lens and can be large in the case of a wide-angle lens. If you want to simulate zooming, you have to change this variable from time to time. The value `width/height` defines the aspect ratio of the rendered view, which should be the same as the screen to avoid distortion. The last two parameters, `nearDist` and `farDist`, define the distance of the camera's eye from the near and far clipping planes. The scene appears between these two planes.

The basic function for the camera definition is as follows:

```
gluLookAt(eye.X(), eye.Y(), eye.Z(),
          target.X(), target.Y(), target.Z(),
          up.X(), up.Y(), up.Z());
```

With this call, we can define the actual position of the camera's eye, the target point, and the camera's up vector. In a computer game, the scene is always changing. If the camera is changing too, we need to recalculate these variables frame by frame in both functions.

Changeable Field of View, Auto-Zoom

Our camera model has an auto-zoom feature. Our camera can take into account the size of the followed object and its distance from the camera, allowing it to calculate the `fov` at every time step:

```
fov = 2.0 *
      atan((targetSize / 2.0) / (target - eye).Length()) *
      180.0 / M_PI;
```

You can notice that in our code snippet, we used the distance between the camera's eye and its target instead of the distance between the camera's eye and the object itself. The argument for doing this is that the camera's target always represents the *direct* or *indirect* position of the followed object. An indirect case occurs when the target deviates from the actual position of the object after applying low-pass filtering and extrapolation.

Implementing Human Behavior

We will now discuss the implementation of our human camera movement model in our camera model. The `Camera` has a variety of data members and member functions. Here, we will introduce the most important ones.

At the beginning of the camera.h header file, where the `Camera` class is defined, there are some global constants. One of them defines the maximum length of arrays that are used in extrapolation of the camera's target. It is called `MAXEXTRAPOLLENGTH` and its value, used by us, is 1000. This value should be greater then the maximum frame rate of the rendered scene in the used computer, because the lists defined with this length should store vectors of a second collected frame by frame.

Other important members of the `Camera` class are the `Vector3f` variables, which define the camera itself (`eye`, `target`, and `up`). The `Vector3f` arrays (`objPosList`, `objPosDifList`, `objPosDifDifList`, and `lpfObjPosList`) and `float` arrays (`objFrameWeightList` and `sumWeight`) are used in the extrapolation. The first three arrays are the collections of position, speed-like, and acceleration-like samples, while the fourth one is reserved for the low-pass filtered position samples. The first `float` array stores weights where we define the importance of the corresponding `objPosDifList` and `objPosDifDifList` elements, while the second list contains a precalculated sum of weights for each element number used in averaging.

These arrays store data chronologically. The elements indexed by 0 correspond to the actual frame, while another indexed by *n* represents the past, *n* frames ago.

Here you can see the spirit of the human behavior for our virtual camera model. This function (called `placeObjectHereToFollow()`) gets the actual position (`objPos`) of the followed object with a flag (`lookAtItExactly`) to know that the target should follow it directly or with human nature.

```
void placeObjectHereToFollow(Vector3f objPos,
                             bool lookAtItExactly = false) {
   if (actualFPS == 0.0) return;}
```

The function starts with a control. If the actual frame rate is zero, which can happen for a while when the application first starts, we skip this execution to avoid malfunction.

Then we define those time-dependent parameters, which are calculated from the actual frame rate (`actualFPS`). The floating-point variables `lengthForExtrpl` and `lengthForLPF` and their integer versions (called `iLengthForExtrpl` and `iLengthForLPF`) contain the number of samples used in extrapolation or low-pass filtering. In other words, they represent the time constant of extrapolation (in our example, it is 0.7 seconds) and low-pass filtering (0.4 seconds, which is the 2.5 Hz limit frequency of LPF).

```
float lengthForExtrpl =
      min(actualFPS, (float)MAXEXTRAPOLLENGTH) * 0.7;
float lengthForLPF =
      min(actualFPS, (float)MAXEXTRAPOLLENGTH) * 0.4;
```

In the next part of the code, we calculate the next low-pass filtered sample using a set of the original samples of the followed object stored in `objPosList`.

```
Vector3f lpfObjectLastPos = objPos;
for (int i = 0; i < (iLengthForLPF - 1); i++)
    lpfObjectLastPos += objPosList[i];
if (iLengthForLPF != 0)
    lpfObjectLastPos *= (1 / (float)iLengthForLPF);
else lpfObjectLastPos = objPos;
```

Whatever happens, we always shift the previously mentioned lists frame by frame in full length.

```
for (int i = MAXEXTRAPOLLENGTH - 1; i > 0; i–)
{
    objPosList[i] = objPosList[i - 1];
    lpfObjPosList[i] = lpfObjPosList[i - 1];
    objPosDifList[i] = objPosDifList[i - 1];
    objPosDifDifList[i] = objPosDifDifList[i - 1];
}
```

After shifting, insert a new value into the 0 position. Notice that the list, which stores the speed-like data, has the differences of LPF samples as new element.

```
objPosList[0] = objPos;
lpfObjPosList[0] = lpfObjectLastPos;
objPosDifList[0] = lpfObjPosList[0] - lpfObjPosList[1];
objPosDifDifList[0] = objPosDifList[0] - objPosDifList[1];
```

Here, we calculate the weighted average of the speed-like and acceleration-like data.

```
Vector3f averageTargetStep;
Vector3f averagePosDifDif;
for (int i = 0; i < iLengthForExtrpl - 1; i++)
{
    averageTargetStep +=
        (objPosDifList[i] * objFrameWeightList[i]);
    averagePosDifDif +=
        (objPosDifDifList[i] *
        objFrameWeightList[iLengthForExtrpl - i - 1]);
}
averageTargetStep *= (1 / sumWeight[iLengthForExtrpl - 1]);
averagePosDifDif *= (1 / sumWeight[iLengthForExtrpl - 1];
```

If we want to follow directly, we just leave the function "attaching" the target onto the object. Else, we take the element of the low-pass filtered position list at the beginning of the extrapolation (by 0.7 seconds in the past) and increment it with the average speed multiplied by the time of extrapolation and the half of the low-pass filtering. As a final correction, add the average acceleration to it.

```
    if (lookAtItExactly) { target = objPos; return; }

    target = lpfObjPosList[iLengthForExtrpl] +
                 averageTargetStep *
             (lengthForExtrpl + lengthForLPF / 2.0) +
             averagePosDifDif;
}
```

You could ask why exactly the half of the LPF time constant was used in the calculation. The answer is simple: generating the low-pass filtered position data, we performed averaging. Let us examine a straight-lined, even-paced movement of an object that we need to follow with the target of our camera. Take `iLengthForLPF` pieces of neighboring position samples and get their average. This results in the arithmetic mean of those samples. In the case of such movement, the arithmetic mean of vectors will be the center of the section defined by those sample vectors. Chronologically, that center point is in the center of that section in time, too. If we take the first element of `lpfObjPosList` (indexed by 0), which was generated during such movement, it points to a location that was passed by a half of `lengthForLPF` time ago. Therefore, the delay is (`lengthForLPF/2`). If we take the element of this list indexed by `iLengthForExtrpl`, the summed delay will be (`lengthForExtrpl + lengthForLPF / 2`). This time multiplied by the average speed will result in the actual position of the followed object in case of straight-lined, even-paced movement. This is the reason why the algorithm is able to keep up with the object in straight sections. In other kinds of movements, the nature of following will be more human-like.

Conclusion

We have described an algorithm for adding human camera control to driving applications. The algorithm is straightforward to implement and simulates the inertia and the struggle of the camera operator to keep up with the movement of a virtual car. The performance of our algorithm does not depend on the frame rate or the speed of the car. The main advantage of this algorithm is that it demands very little processing time, so it does not degrade the performance appreciably.

Sample Application

We have implemented our algorithm in a simple demo application, which can be found on the companion CD-ROM. The demo shows a car in a three-dimensional environment followed by a camera on a tripod. The car can be controlled using the arrow keys. The camera follows the car as if it were controlled by a virtual camera operator. Pressing the Q key toggles the human behavior of the camera.

SECTION

5

GRAPHICS

Introduction

Jason L. Mitchell, ATI Research
JasonM@ati.com

With GPU processing power increasing at a rate that outstrips the ability of the rest of the system to feed it—not to mention the increasing cost of authoring content—you will notice a trend toward data amplification through instancing and proceduralism in the coming years. As a result, we have chosen to focus on both data amplification and natural phenomena in the graphics gems in this fifth edition of the *Game Programming Gems* series.

In the first graphics gem, "Realistic Cloud Rendering on Modern GPUs," Jean-François Dubé of UBISOFT discusses a technique that uses advanced pixel shaders and precomputed noise textures to generate procedural clouds with sophisticated dynamic illumination. In the gem "Let It Snow, Let It Snow, Let It Snow (and Rain)," Niniane Wang and Bretton Wade describe the technique they developed for rendering precipitation in the game *Microsoft Flight Simulator 2004: A Century of Flight*. This technique is both efficient and controllable, allowing artists to tweak the model to suit the desired look of the game.

We then move from the sky to the ground, with a focus on efficient and realistic foliage rendering. In his gem, "Widgets: Rendering Fast and Persistent Foliage," Martin Brownlow describes techniques for using current graphics hardware to efficiently render large numbers of instanced objects to act as ground cover. This includes both GPU and CPU techniques for maintaining maximum performance. In the gem "2.5 Dimension Impostors for Realistic Trees and Forests," Gábor Szijártó discusses a technique that uses dynamic depth sprites to render realistic tree canopies.

Interactive virtual worlds with procedural skies and foliage may be beautiful, but you can't make a game without a little destruction, right? To that end, Neeharika Adabala and Charles E. Hughes present a technique in "Grid-less Controllable Fire" that enables the simulation and rendering of highly realistic flames. Sometimes you want something even more dramatic, with that over-the-top Hollywood flair. In his gem, "Powerful Explosion Effects Using Billboard Particles," Steve Rabin of Nintendo describes a technique for creating powerful over-the-top explosions that are realistic, controllable, and efficient to render.

For the first time in the *Game Programming Gems* series, we have an article on rendering—you guessed it—*gems*! In the gem, "A Simple Method for Rendering Gemstones," Thorsten Scheuermann of ATI Research describes the technique used in the ATI demo *Ruby: The DoubleCross* to efficiently render a realistic diamond. Dominic

Filion and Sylvain Boissé then present a method for integrating realistic refraction and heat haze effects into 3D scenes in their gem, "Volumetric Post-Processing."

As noted earlier, the cost of content creation is increasing with the ability of GPUs to consume large data sets. In their gem, "Procedural Level Generation," Timothy Roden and Ian Parberry present a framework for generating game worlds procedurally—drastically reducing the tedium of creating certain classes of game levels. In our final graphics gem, Dominic Filion presents a technique in "Recombinant Shaders" that enables graphics application programmers to effectively manage the large numbers of shaders that must be generated to effectively render increasingly complex game worlds.

The ideal gem is one that is quick and easy for you to drop into an existing game programming project without a major rewrite. As a result, we have chosen topics that meet this need and address the increasingly important topics of data amplification and natural phenomena.

5.1

Realistic Cloud Rendering on Modern GPUs

Jean-François Dubé, UBISOFT

jfdube@ubisoft.qc.ca

With the new generation of rendering hardware, games are becoming more and more realistic. Per-pixel lighting and shadowing, volumetric lighting, and atmospheric effects are now possible. Despite these advances, if you take a look at any modern game, you'll notice something that they all have in common: a static (and sometimes ugly) cubemap for the sky. More advanced solutions add a moving layer of clouds, which helps but is still not as realistic as we would like. In this chapter, we'll discover how to render and light realistic, dynamic clouds all on the GPU, using shader model 3.0.

In this gem, we'll see how to procedurally generate an animated noise texture that looks like real clouds, all on the GPU. This texture will then be mapped on a plane over the camera, similar to a skybox. Finally, we'll see how to add realistic lighting by actually integrating along rays through the clouds with ps3.0 shaders with loops, as we see in Figure 5.1.1.

FIGURE 5.1.1 *Realistic real-time procedural clouds.*

Making Noise

The basic idea behind cloud rendering is to generate and animate noise over time to make the clouds change shape in a plausible way. As we want to perform all our computations on the GPU, current implementations of 3D Perlin Noise aren't well suited for our task. Instead, we will composite multiple precomputed noise textures at different octaves and weights. Each octave of noise adds detail to the final texture—the first octave gives the rough shape, and the more octaves we use, the more details we add. We have found that using eight octaves of noise is a good trade-off between performance and visual quality.

Octave Compositions

Each noise octave is represented by a smoothed 128 × 128 noise texture. This noise is generated with random numbers, and smoothing is performed with simple neighborhood filtering. Because the noise is signed, you may have to perform some scaling and biasing to pack the data into the textures and when you sample from them in your pixel shaders, depending on the texture format you're using. In our pixel shader, all eight octaves are added together with different scales and weights to achieve the desired effect. That is, the first octave is not tiled, giving the rough shape of the final composite noise. As we continue to add in higher octaves, they are repeated more frequently and weighted less, giving more and more fine detail, as shown in Figure 5.1.2. Playing with the tiling rates and weight factors allows you to tune the look of your clouds. Giving more weight to higher octaves results in smaller cloud formations, but still provides the rough shape defined by the lower octaves. Good starting values are 1, 2, 4, 8, and so on for octave scales, and 1, 1/2, 1/4, 1/8, and so on for octave weights.

Animating the Noise

Animating the noise texture is simply a matter of animating the octave textures over time, as discussed in [Elias] and [Pallister01]. Low octaves should animate more slowly than high octaves. This way, the basic shape of our clouds will change slowly, while finer details will change faster. For each octave, we keep two noise textures and interpolate slowly between them at different rates. We will return to this step later when we discuss optimizations.

Cloud Density

So far, we have created our basic building block: dynamic noise with controllable octaves. A typical image of eight octaves of noise is shown in Figure 5.1.3a. We must now perform a few more steps to make this noise appear more cloudlike. For example, we need to be able to control the percentage of clouds in the sky. To do this, we sub-

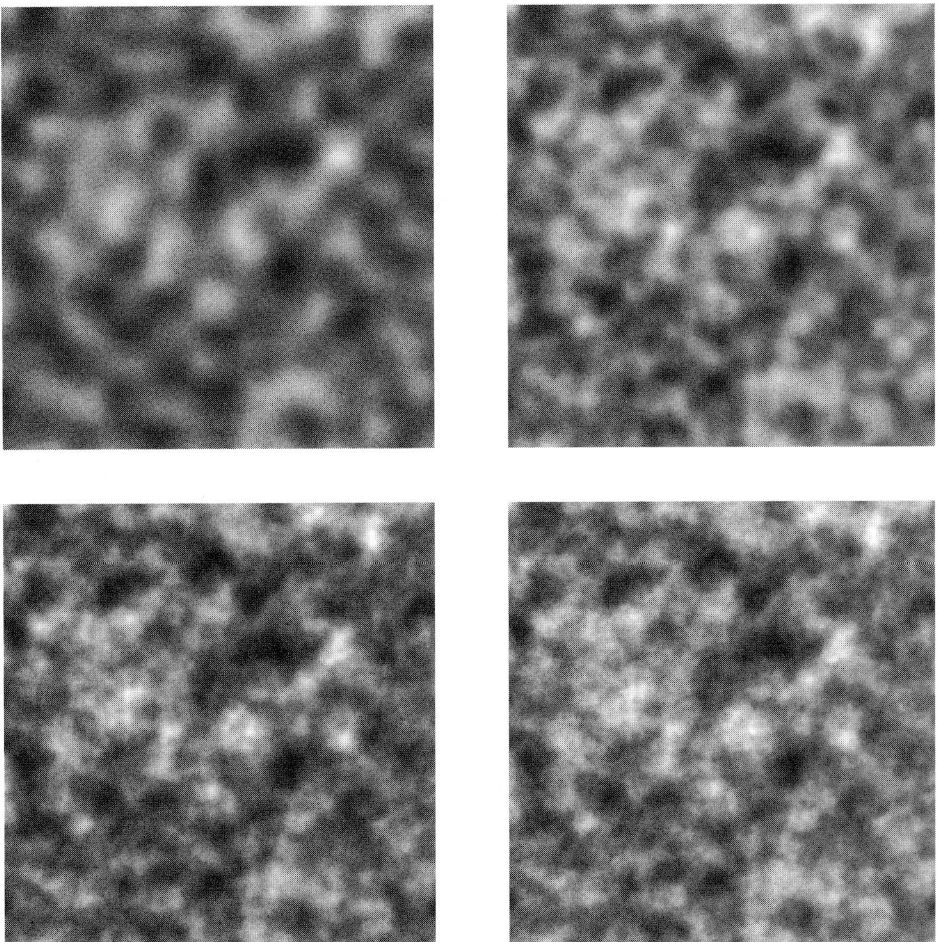

FIGURE 5.1.2 *(a) First octave gives the rough shape of the clouds. (b) Second octave adds detail. (c) Third octave adds finer detail. (d) Fourth octave and higher add more detail but are more and more subtle.*

tract a value called "cloud cover" from the noise and clamp the result to zero, thus removing a certain quantity of noise, as shown in Figure 5.1.3b. The cloud cover variable ranges from [0..1] and represents the amount of blue sky that we want to see (0 creates a fully clouded sky, and 1 creates a fully clear blue sky). At this point, we still don't quite have clouds, so we exponentiate our current result to obtain the fluffy look of clouds that we're looking for, as shown in Figure 5.1.3c.

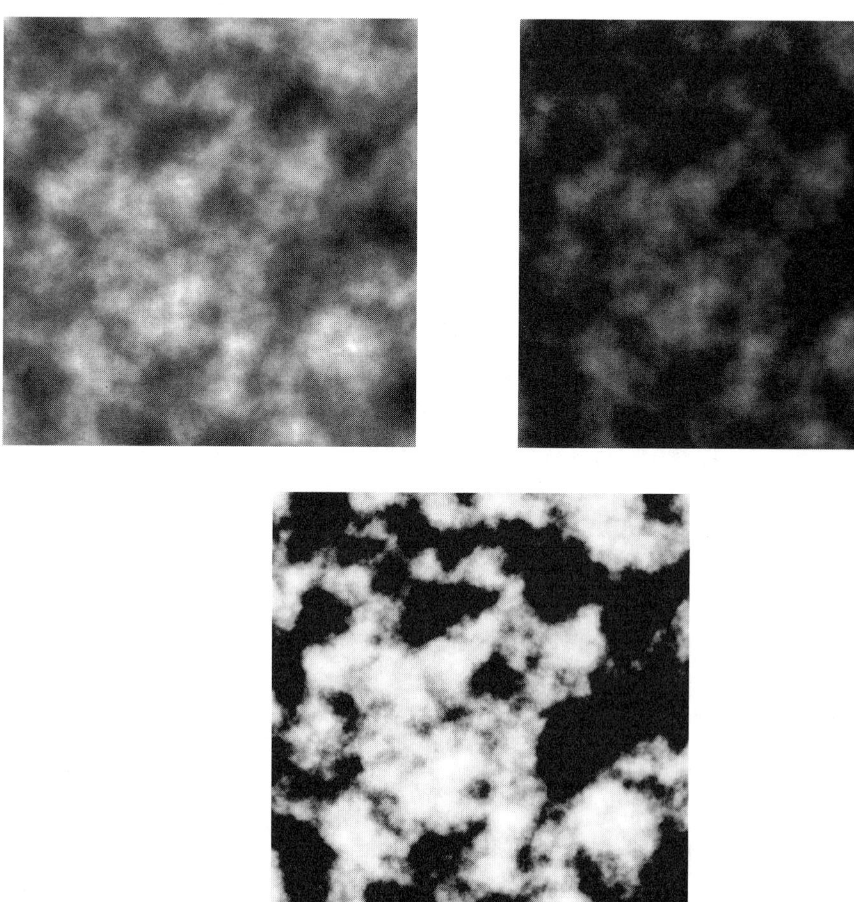

FIGURE 5.1.3 *(a) The eight octaves noise texture. (b) The same noise texture after we subtracted the cloud cover value and clamped it. (c) The same noise texture, after exponentiation. Notice how it starts to look like clouds.*

The following HLSL code performs the computations described earlier (the rest of the shader will be given later in the article):

```
float cloud_cover = 0.45f;
float clouds_sharpness = 0.94f;
float3 tex = tex2D(Octave0, uv * OctavesScales0.x) * OctavesWeights0.x;
tex += tex2D(Octave1, uv * OctavesScales0.y) * OctavesWeights0.y;
tex += tex2D(Octave2, uv * OctavesScales0.z) * OctavesWeights0.z;
tex += tex2D(Octave3, uv * OctavesScales0.w) * OctavesWeights0.w;
tex += tex2D(Octave4, uv * OctavesScales1.x) * OctavesWeights1.x;
```

```
    08. tex += tex2D(Octave5, uv * OctavesScales1.y) *
OctavesWeights1.y;
    09. tex += tex2D(Octave6, uv * OctavesScales1.z) *
OctavesWeights1.z;
    10. tex += tex2D(Octave7, uv * OctavesScales1.w) *
OctavesWeights1.w;
    11. tex = max(tex * 0.5f + 0.5f - cloud_cover, 0.0f);
    12. tex = 1.0f – pow(clouds_sharpness, tex * 255.0f);
```

Lines 3 to 10 perform the compositing of the eight octaves of noise. The value `uv` contains the texture coordinates of the cloud plane, which get scaled prior to sampling. The values fetched from the noise textures are weighted as well. This shader assumes that the noise is stored in a signed texture format, hence the value of `tex` is signed. As a result, Line 11 converts the noise range from [–1..1] to [0..1], subtracts the cloud cover value, and clamps the result to zero. Line 12 performs the exponentiation.

So far, we have used fairly traditional methods to compute plausible cloud density in real time. To fully integrate our animating clouds into our game worlds, however, we must light them in a realistic way.

Cloud Lighting

Real cloud lighting is very complex, exhibiting light scattering, which is difficult to evaluate in real time. Even sophisticated solutions still leave much to be desired [Harris01], [Harris02]. As a result, we have chosen to ignore physically correct computations and tried to approximate the desired look.

Light Scattering

In real life, clouds receive light from the sun. What we see from below is the amount of light coming out of the underside of the clouds. As light travels in the cloud volume, it is scattered in all directions as it hits water particles, resulting in dark gray portions in the bottom of clouds. Ideally, for every pixel rendered in our cloud plane, we would like to trace a ray from the sun to the pixel, accumulating the distance traveled within the clouds to approximate the light scattering integral. This would be quite expensive to do in real time, so we have come up with approximations that make this usable for games.

Cloud Density Field Tracing

To perform the trace from the sun through the clouds to a given pixel on the underside of the clouds, we use the noise composited previously as a density field very similar to a height field. To reduce aliasing, our cloud lighting is performed using only the first four octaves of noise. At the beginning of every frame, we render the first four octaves of the cloud density into a 512×512 render target, which will be used in the final shader as the density field. The following HLSL code performs the path tracing. This code follows the previous code and `tex.r` is the current cloud density.

```
01. float Density = 0.0f;
02. float3 EndTracePos = float3(uv, -tex.r);
03. float3 TraceDir = EndTracePos - SunPos;
04. TraceDir = normalize(TraceDir);
05. float3 CurTracePos = SunPos + TraceDir * 1.25f;
06. tex = 1.0f – pow(clouds_sharpness, tex * 255.0f);
07. TraceDir *= 2.0f;
08. for(int i=0; i<64; i++)
09. {
10.     CurTracePos += TraceDir;
11.     float4 tex2 = tex2D(DensityFieldTexture, CurTracePos.xy)
        * 255.0f;
12.     Density += 0.1f * step(CurTracePos.z*2, tex2.r*2);
13. }
14. float Light = 1.0f / exp(Scattering * 0.4f);
15. return float4(Light, Light, Light, tex.r);
```

In line 2, notice that we use –`tex.r` as the end position of the sun to cloud ray. This is because in real life, clouds aren't mapped on a plane: they are three-dimensional. So in the trace loop, the cloud height field is going in both directions (equal distances above and below the cloud plane). Also notice that we perform the exponentiation after computing the ray information: this is because exponentiation is only a trick to make clouds look better. Lines 7 to 13 are the heart of the shader: the actual sun to cloud density field tracing loop. As you can see, we perform ray marching in 64 increments of 2 units, accumulating the density traversed during the trace. Line 12 performs the actual check to see if the current ray position is inside the clouds. Essentially, we're checking to see if the current trace *Z* position is inside the clouds. On line 14, we roughly approximate light scattering, and then return the final lit cloud pixel in line 15. The complete shader and a demo are included in the companion CD-ROM—including videos for people without shader model 3.0 video cards.

ON THE CD

Performance

This technique is highly fill-rate dependent, due to the tracing loop. Development was done on a GeForce6 graphics card, and the sky runs at 60 frames per second at a resolution of 640 × 480. As the resolution increases, performance drops dramatically. It is also possible to run this technique on ps2.0 hardware by replacing the tracing loop by direct illumination: this is left as an exercise for the reader.

Optimization

Some steps of this algorithm can be precomputed each frame, notably the animation of noise octaves. Instead of interpolating from two textures for each octave at every pixel, it is possible to precompute them using a render target for each octave. We slowly interpolate between the two, and we use the render targets as input textures for our cloud shader. Also, as we render the first four octaves in the density texture each frame, we do not need to compute them again in the final cloud shader: we simply fetch them from the density texture and add the final details with the last four octaves.

Conclusion

Simulating clouds that look realistic is very difficult, but we showed that it is possible, with modern graphics hardware, to get very good results in real time. We anticipate that the coming generation of game consoles will have enough rendering power to perform techniques like the one described in this gem at the target HDTV resolutions.

References

[Elias] *http://freespace.virgin.net/hugo.elias/models/m_clouds.htm.*

[Harris01] Harris, Mark J. and Anselmo Lastra. "Real-Time Cloud Rendering." *Computer Graphics Forum (Eurographics 2001 Proceedings),* 20(3):76–84. September 2001.

[Harris02] Harris, Mark J. "Real-Time Cloud Rendering for Games." *Proceedings of Game Developers Conference.* March 2002.

[Pallister01] Pallister, Kim. "Generating Procedural Clouds Using 3D Hardware." In *Game Programming Gems 2* (edited by Mark Deloura). Charles River Media, 2001.

5.2

Let It Snow, Let It Snow, Let It Snow (and Rain)

Niniane Wang, Google Inc.
niniane@gmail.com

Bretton Wade, Microsoft Corporation
brettonw@microsoft.com

Whether you're creating a driving game, a first-person shooter, or the next big RPG, realistic-looking rain and snow can add realism to your outdoor scenes. Your cars, armored soldiers, and two-headed monsters can all benefit from being viewed through a sheet of rain or dense snow.

Many games have modeled precipitation with particle systems [Reeves83], which produce realistic motion by simulating every drop of rain or snow. For example, each snowflake can travel on its own path, caught in flurries of wind. However, this is often expensive, and the cost increases with denser precipitation since that requires simulating more particles.

In this article, we present a technique for rendering precipitation with less performance overhead by mapping textures onto a double cone and then translating and elongating the flakes or drops via hardware texture transforms. Our approach, which was implemented in *Microsoft Flight Simulator 2004: A Century of Flight* as shown in Figures 5.2.1 and 5.2.2, also yields more artistic control over motion factors and drop appearance than typical particle systems.

Modeling Particle Bundles Using a Texture

We build upon the basic idea of using a texture to simulate precipitation, with low performance overhead. The textures consist of a bundle of drops created by our artists, an example of which can be seen in Figure 5.2.3.

FIGURE 5.2.1 *A scene of snow in Seattle—a rare sight.*

FIGURE 5.2.2 *Screenshot of snow moving at high velocity.*

We need to apply translation to the texture so that the precipitation appears to be falling over time. We started with the obvious approach of translating the texture at a rate proportional to the desired speed of precipitation according to the game clock.

FIGURE 5.2.3 *An example rain texture.*

This simple approach produced two visual artifacts. First, when the translation is much larger than the size of an individual raindrop, the eye does not connect the raindrop in one frame with the same translated raindrop in the next frame, due to the lack of motion blur and large spatial separation. Thus, it looks as though disconnected raindrops are randomly flitting past the camera, rather than one raindrop making a continuous movement. If the texture coordinate translation is even larger—so that it is almost the length of the entire texture from one frame to the next—the rain can appear to move backward, much like the typical wagon-wheel effect in old western movies. To fix this, we translate the texture by a fixed size of one raindrop width each frame. This ensures the eye will connect the movement of each raindrop across frames.

Note that the translation is constant regardless of precipitation speed and also of framerate. Since we want the precipitation to appear to fall at a constant rate regardless of framerate, we must account for varying frame times—otherwise, it will fall faster with higher framerates and slower with lower framerates. To this end, we scroll the texture each frame by D_{precip}, described in Equation 5.2.1:

$$D_{precip} = S_{streak} * \frac{t_{delta}}{t_{const}} \tag{5.2.1}$$

where t_{const} is a fixed frame time, e.g., $\frac{1}{30}$ seconds.

To simulate motion blur, we use the aforementioned stretch factor. This factor is proportional to the speed of movement, such that longer streaks occur when the camera is moving quickly.

We compute the stretch factor, described in Equation 5.2.2, based on Vec_{precip}, S_f (a precomputed scale factor to scale down successive textures so they appear further away), C_{pixel} (a conversion factor specifying the world space equivalent for each pixel in the texture), and S_{streak} (an artist-controlled scale factor to give different lengths of streaks to different types and intensities of rain, e.g., light rain has longer streaks than heavy rain).

$$E = \frac{S_{streak}}{S_f * \left(C_{pixel} * S_f * Vec_{precip} + S_{streak}\right)} \tag{5.2.2}$$

Rendering Snow or Rain in Parallax

In addition to providing the sense of particles moving past the player, we want to provide a sense of depth and parallax. Raindrops or snowflakes in the distance should look smaller and fall slower than ones close by [Langer03]. To simulate this, we apply our texture scrolling technique to multiple textures. Our system used four textures, scaling down the texture coordinates progressively on each one to produce smaller precipitation drops and slower scrolling. We use Direct3D fixed function multitexturing to blend the four textures together.

The amount of scaling down depends on the type and intensity of precipitation, and is controlled by our artists.

Although this produces the parallax effect, the *Z* information is incorrect. The textures are designed to look far from the camera, but they are actually rendered on a plane at a close distance. When the drops are small enough, however, this is not a noticeable artifact.

Simulating Camera Movement with a Cone

When the camera is traveling forward, the rain or snow should tilt so that it appears to be shooting at and past the camera. Similarly, when the camera moves sideways, the precipitation streaks are expected to have a sideways component to their motion. To simulate these effects, we map the four precipitation textures onto a double cone, as shown in Figure 5.2.4. Our textures are designed to tile so that no seams are visible when they are repeated across the cone surface, or as they scroll across the cone.

To reduce the visibility of the singularities at the cones' tips, we make the cones more transparent at those points, gradually fading in toward the circle at which the cones meet. We also select an appropriate cone height to tune the angle at which the rain appears to fall. If the cone is too short, when the camera is stationary, the rain will fall at an unrealistic slanted angle rather than straight down due to the cone's steep edges. On the other hand, the cone must not be too tall. This ensures that when the camera is moving and the cone is rotated, the rain will fall from the middle of the screen toward the edges as desired.

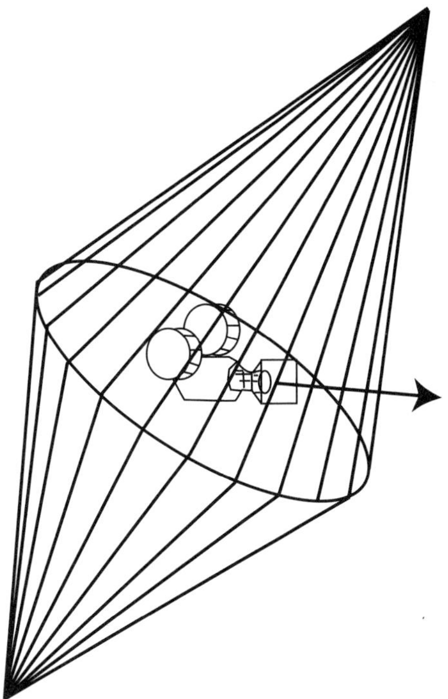

FIGURE 5.2.4 *Double cone onto which we mapped textures.*

As the camera moves, we pivot the double cone so that precipitation appears to fall toward the camera from the direction of movement. We do this by setting the cone's world matrix to look along the precipitation travel vector Vec_{precip}, described in Equation 5.2.3.

$$Vec_{precip} = \left(C_f * Vel_{camera} + Vel_{gravity}\right) * t_{delta} \tag{5.2.3}$$

where Vel_{camera} is the camera velocity, C_f is an artist-controlled damping constant to limit the tilting of the cone, $Vel_{gravity}$ is the velocity of the precipitation due to gravity, and t_{delta} is the time elapsed since the last frame.

Together in One Matrix

Dprecip and the elongation factor E are combined in the texture transform matrix shown in Equation 5.2.4. D_{precip} is represented in pixel space and converted to real-world space by E, which also slows down scrolling in successive textures.

$$\mathbf{M} = \begin{bmatrix} S_f & 0 & 0 & 0 \\ 0 & \dfrac{S_{streak}}{S_f * \left(C_{pixel} * S_f * Vec_{precip} + S_{streak}\right)} & 0 & 0 \\ 0 & S_{streak} * \dfrac{t_{delta}}{t_{const}} & 1 & 0 \\ 0 & 0 & 0 & 1 \end{bmatrix} \quad (5.2.4)$$

We can also simulate different precipitation intensities by varying the scaling and translation on the matrix. For example, heavy precipitation is modeled with larger drops (less scaling down) and faster movement (larger translation). A big advantage to designing a system with so many tweakable variables is that it can be controlled by the artists.

Adding Artist Control

We designed our system to give our artists fine-grained control over the final look and feel. First, the artists create the textures, so they control the distribution of raindrops and snowflakes. We use a different set of textures for light rain versus heavy rain, and the artists can adjust the drop density for each intensity. The artists can also add a haze or fog into the texture, which obscures objects in the scene. The fog can be heavier in some parts of the textures to add variety.

We also grant artists control in the rainfall/snowfall equations by allowing them to adjust damping and scaling factors at several points. We wrote a tool that interfaces with our in-game rendering engine that allows tweaking of visual parameters using sliders.

Artists can adjust S_f to change the drop size and scrolling speed. They can also adjust S_{streak}, the streak length (to give lighter rain longer streaks than heavy rain, for example) and C_f to limit the cone tilting.

For each intensity of rain and snow, our artists experimented with parameter settings until they found the right combination of streak length, drop size, speed, and cone damping. Immediate visual feedback and artistic control over the parameters was key to creating a high-quality end result.

Conclusion

Our system looks most realistic for rain and heavy snow. In real life, light snow tumbles and flutters as it falls, which is not well simulated with our current system. Shifting around the texture coordinates over time may approximate the effect and is an area for future work.

The system is also more suited for games with relatively steady framerates. When the game framerate stutters drastically, the scrolling of the precipitation texture also stutters, which is more noticeable than the rest of the frame. In particular, the stretch emphasizes stutters, possibly causing the effect to appear to run backward.

Our technique has negligible impact on the game's overall framerate and has the same performance overhead for heavy precipitation as light precipitation, unlike a particle system. It ships with *Microsoft Flight Simulator 2004: A Century of Flight*, which maintains framerates of 15 to 60 fps across a range of consumer PCs.

References

[Langer03] Langer, Michael and Linqiao Zhang. "Rendering Falling Snow Using an Inverse Fourier Transform." *SIGGRAPH Technical Sketch,* 2003.

[Reeves83] Reeve, William T. "Particle Systems—A Technique for Modeling a Class of Fuzzy Objects." *SIGGRAPH 1983, ACM.* Detroit, Michigan.

5.3

Widgets: Rendering Fast and Persistent Foliage

Martin Brownlow

martinbrownlow@msn.com

Games that render outdoor environments face a common problem: to look realistic, vast amounts of foliage must be drawn. For the purposes of this gem, foliage includes such features as plants, bushes, boulders, grass stalks, and other low-to-the-ground objects. These objects serve to obscure the ground textures in complex layers, lending a more realistic, voluminous appearance to the ground.

The objects used as foliage, which we shall refer to as *widgets*, are generally inert (they cannot be interacted with) and are there just to give the ground depth. Although these widgets could be randomly generated as new areas of the world are activated, an astute player might notice any differences when revisiting a previous location. Additionally, artists generally want control over everything that affects the look of their levels, and so prefer to define which types of foliage appear in which areas and how often they appear. In extreme cases, an artist might even want to go in and individually place several widgets to achieve a specific look.

Another consideration is that of destructibility: although widgets are essentially inert, it is often desirable to have world events affect them. For instance, if your game has huge explosions that change the underlying landscape textures to represent damage to the ground, it would be ridiculous for all the little tufts of grass to survive the blast unscathed. Some method of temporary or permanent removal of individual widgets or groups of widgets from the world will help the sense of immersion.

For efficient rendering of foliage, we need to address two distinct problems: we need to be able to quickly generate only those widgets that fall within the view frustum, and then to efficiently draw the resulting list of models.

Meshes for Widgets

Although our intent is to render highly complex scenes covered with foliage, the individual meshes that make up the widgets need not be complex at all. In fact, the most effective models used as widgets generally use only a handful of double-sided polygons and a single texture. This simplicity allows us to render many more instances than we otherwise could, and so adds to the overall complexity of the scene. Figure 5.3.1 shows a simple example mesh that can be used as a widget, consisting of eight double-sided triangles and a texture map.

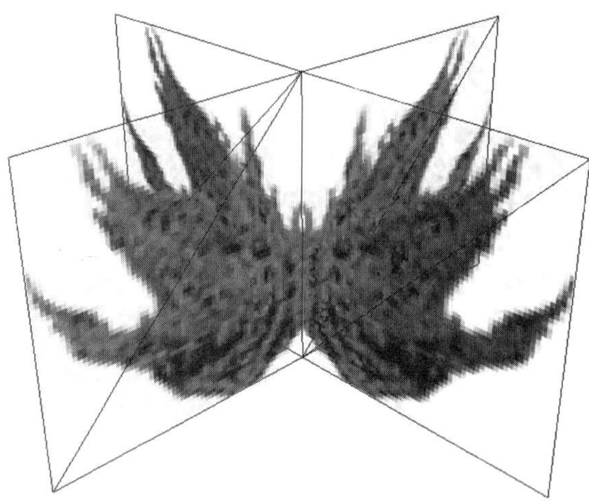

FIGURE 5.3.1 *A simple ground cover mesh.*

Unfortunately, although the meshes themselves are simple, drawing them efficiently is not. Today's graphics hardware is designed to render huge amounts of triangles but performs best when rendering in blocks consisting of thousands of vertices. Rendering a thousand different copies of our eight triangle mesh is not going to be making the best use of graphics hardware.

Drawing Widgets Efficiently

If we put aside for the moment the question of how to generate a list of the widgets that are to be drawn, we can look at how we are to efficiently draw a large number of tiny models. We have already determined that our widget meshes are to consist of a small amount of triangles and a single, simple material. We can further insist that each widget mesh should consist of exactly one triangle strip of indeterminate length.

To get the best throughput from our graphics hardware, we must submit as few batches of triangles to the hardware as possible, with each batch being as large as we can make it. This, then, is our objective: to find some way to batch together a large number of small models whose positions can change independently of one another from frame to frame (as the view changes, different sets of widgets will need to be drawn). This obviously rules out a large vertex buffer containing pretransformed widgets, since we would need to keep editing this buffer as the viewpoint moves around the world.

Widget Batches

Although filling a vertex buffer with pretransformed widgets is out of the question, can we find a way to make the graphics hardware transform each widget by the correct matrix for us? In fact, we can; this is a similar problem to skinning, where each vertex indexes into a palette of matrices for its transform. By adding a matrix index to each vertex in the widget, we can make each widget index its own transformation matrix, then add multiple copies of the same widget to the buffer. Each individual widget must have the same index value for every vertex it contains, but consecutive widgets can and should have different values. Using an indexing system like this, we can place as many widgets in a single vertex buffer as there is room for matrices in the vertex constants. This method was employed by Gosselin, et al. for rendering large crowds of characters, but due to the skeletal animation, only four characters could be rendered in one API call [Gosselin04]. For foliage, we can render more widgets per API call. The following structure shows a possible vertex format for describing widgets:

```
typedef struct
{
    float    position[3];
    float    uv[2];
    u32      mtxIndex;

} WIDGETVTX;
```

Now that we have created a vertex buffer containing several copies of the same widget, each with its own matrix index, we must figure out how to draw them in a single batch. We already know that each widget consists of a single triangle strip; we just need to stitch together the strips of consecutive widgets. This is done through the use of degenerate triangles; triangles that have two or more vertices that are coincident. To join two triangle strips together, we need to add four degenerate triangles, in the form of two indices. For example, to join the two strips, (1,2,3,4) and (8,9,10,11) we would repeat the last vertex of the first strip and the first vertex of the second strip to form the strip (1,2,3,4,4,8,8,9,10,11). In this example, our four degenerate triangles are (3,4,4), (4,4,8), (4,8,8), and (8,8,9). Each degenerate triangle produces no pixels, and so the net result is the appearance of drawing two disconnected strips of triangles but with a single draw call.

However, joining strips in this fashion requires that the first strip be of an even number of indices. If the first strip is not an even number of indices in length, the winding order for the second strip will be wrong, since the winding order of the triangles in a strip is reversed for every other triangle. To get around this, if the first strip is an odd number of indices in length, we must first make it an even length by repeating the last vertex. For example, joining the two strips (1,2,3,4,5) and (8,9,10,11) results in a single strip of 12 vertices: (1,2,3,4,5,5,5,8,8,9,10,11).

Along with the vertex buffer containing multiple instances of a single widget, we must also create an index buffer containing a single strip to draw all these widgets. When creating this buffer, we must remember that the base vertex for each consecutive widget must be incremented by the number of vertices in a single widget in order to address the correct set of vertices. The following code will generate a single strip for nw widgets, each consisting of nv vertices and ni indices, and returns the number of indices generated in the strip:

```
u32 CreateWidgetIndices(
                    u16 *pOutput,    // ouput buffer
                    u32 nw,          // number of widgets
                    u32 nv,          // # verts per widget
                    u32 ni,          // # indices per widget
                    u16 *pIndices ) // ptr to indices for 1 widget
{
    u32 i,basev,j;
    u16 *pout;

    // base vertex = 0
    basev = 0;
    pout = pOutput;

    // for each widget
    for( i=1;i<=nw;i++ )
    {
        // copy the widget's indices, offset by base vertex
        for(j=0;j<ni;j++ )
        {
            pout[j] = pIndices[j] + basev;
        }
        pout += ni;

        // if the widget is an odd length
        if( ni&1 )
        {   // repeat the last index
            pout[0] = pout[-1];
            pout++;
        }

        // if we're not the last widget, add degenerates
        if( i!=nw )
        {
            // create degenerate tris:
            // repeat the last index
            pout[0] = pout[-1];

            // increase the base vertex
            basev += nv;

            // repeat the first vertex of the next widget
            pout[1] = pIndices[0] + basev;
            pout += 2;
        }
    }
    // return the # of indices
    return pout – pOutput;
}
```

Drawing Widget Batches

Once we have our vertex and index buffers, we can now draw multiple widgets in a single draw call. To do this, we must first generate a list of widgets that must be drawn and their respective transformation matrices. We will then send the transformation matrices for the first batch of widgets to the corresponding vertex shader constants and draw the primitive. If there are more widgets than can be sent in a single batch, we simply send multiple batches containing as many widgets as possible.

As long as we draw full widget batches, this is relatively simple, but what happens when we cannot completely fill a batch? In cases like this, we simply reduce the number of indices that we render from the strip to cut out some widgets. If a widget is n indices long, and we want to draw m copies of the widget, then we need to draw $(((n + 1) \& (\sim 1))*m + ((m - 1)*2))$ indices. That is, we need to draw the number of indices required for a single widget, rounded up to an even number, times the number of widgets to be drawn, plus two extra indices between each drawn widget.

Compressing Widget Transforms

As we have previously seen, we can now draw as many widgets in a single batch as we have room for transformation matrices in the vertex shader constant registers. Generally, a matrix transform takes up three vertex constant registers, but we can impose some limitations on our widgets that help reduce this to two constant registers, increasing the number of widgets that can be drawn. We know that our widgets are supposed to lie on the ground; therefore, we can restrict the degrees of freedom given to each widget. Specifically, we will restrict the widget to five degrees of freedom; a 3D position, a single rotation around the vertical axis, and a scale factor. The matrix for such a transformation is as follows:

$$\begin{pmatrix} \sin(\alpha)\cdot scale & 0 & \cos(\alpha)\cdot scale & x \\ 0 & scale & 0 & y \\ \cos(\alpha)\cdot scale & & -\sin(\alpha)\cdot scale & z \\ 0 & 0 & 0 & 1 \end{pmatrix}$$

As we can see, this matrix contains very few distinct values. Given a vertex processor with arbitrary element swizzling capabilities, we can easily compress the needed values into the following two vertex constants:

$$\begin{pmatrix} x & y & z & scale \end{pmatrix}$$
$$\begin{pmatrix} \sin(\alpha) & \cos(\alpha) & -\sin(\alpha) & 0 \end{pmatrix}$$

As we will see when we look at the HLSL vertex shader code in the next section, it is a simple matter to reconstruct the transformation matrix from these constants. By compressing the transformation matrix for each widget in such a fashion, we can draw 50% more widgets in a single batch than we otherwise could if we had used a 4×3 matrix to represent a more general transform for each widget.

Widgets in Practice

Now that we've looked at the theory of drawing widgets, let's look at an example implementation. On the companion CD-ROM in the directory containing the FoliageDemo (/chapter5-Graphics/5.03-widgets_Brownlow) is the source for a simple foliage demo. The files widgetmesh.h and widgetmesh.cpp define a class, `CWidgetMesh`, which handles all the steps involved in optimally rendering a number of instances of a given widget.

The FoliageDemo program requires PC graphics hardware capable of running vertex and pixel shader programs compiled for Version 1.1 or later. It must also be capable of displaying four simultaneous textures. If your graphics hardware is not capable of this, the FoliageDemo program will not execute.

The member function `Create` is responsible for creating a widget mesh from a regular mesh. It takes as parameters a pointer to an array of vertices, a pointer to an array of indices, the number of vertices and indices in the arrays, and the name of a texture. This function creates a vertex buffer and an index buffer with enough space in them for `WIDGET_MAXINSTANCES` (defined in 'widgetmesh.h') copies of the input data, and then fills the buffers as described earlier in this gem.

To draw a series of instances, we must first call the `Begin` member function. This function sets up the rendering pipeline to render the widgets. It sets the vertex and index buffers associated with the mesh as well as the vertex and pixel shaders, vertex format, and texture. After calling `Begin`, we can then iterate through the instances that we want to be drawn, calling `AddInstance` for each. Each time that `AddInstance` is executed, it stores a record of the instance in a static array. If at any point this array becomes full, `FlushInstances` is automatically called.

The `FlushInstances` member function is responsible for drawing a batch of widgets. It first sends the array of instances created by `AddInstance` to the appropriate vertex shader constants. After this, a `DrawIndexedPrimitive` command is issued, using the appropriate number of indices and vertices, as calculated from the number of instances in the array. Finally, it clears the count of instances in the array and returns. The final function of interest in the `FoliageDemo` class is the `End function`. This function simply issues a `FlushInstances` call to ensure that all the instances added are drawn.

The vertex shader program for drawing widgets is located in the file widget.hlsl. It is a fairly basic vertex shader; the only real point of interest lies in the transformation of each vertex by the compressed instance's matrix. The shader uses swizzling to recreate the first and third rows of the uncompressed rotation matrix (the second row contains only a single element, *scale*, and so is trivial to implement) and uses them to rotate the input point, adding the instance position afterwards. This is represented by the following code fragment:

```
float4 pos;

pos.x   = dot(vtxin.pos,mtxInstances[vtxin.index+1].xwy);
pos.y   = vtxin.pos.y;
pos.z   = dot(vtxin.pos,mtxInstances[vtxin.index+1].ywz);
pos.w   = 1;
pos.xyz = pos.xyz*mtxInstances[vtxin.index].w +
            mtxInstances[vtxin.index].xyz;
```

Once the rotated and scaled position has been calculated, the point is transformed into clip space and passed to the pixel shader as usual.

Culling Widgets

Now that we can efficiently draw a large number of instances, we must look at ways to generate the relevant instances from a constantly changing viewpoint. There are two main ways to approach this. In the first, instances are generated semirandomly (but deterministically!) as new areas of the world are revealed and instances that are no longer visible are deleted. The second method—the one that this gem will concentrate on—involves precalculating the positions of all the widget instances in the world and creating an efficient representation of them that can be used to quickly generate a visible set of widgets.

Although more memory intensive, the main advantage of this method is that the position of these widgets will be constant—players can leave an area and return later to find the foliage in the same position as earlier. Moreover, using this method, widgets can be deleted when necessary with little effort on the programmer's part. This allows players to leave their mark on the foliage of the world with explosives and whatever else they care to fire at it.

BSP Trees

The method that we will use to store the positions for the widget instances in the world is a modified BSP tree. The use of a BSP tree over a quad- or octree allows the world to be irregular in shape without using any extra memory for empty nodes. For those unfamiliar with BSP trees, they consist of a hierarchy of planes. Each plane cuts the world into two pieces, with each object in the world ostensibly falling on one side or the other of each plane. Figure 5.3.2 shows an example of the first two planes of a BSP tree. The first plane separates the world into two halves, while the second plane separates one of those halves into two more halves. In this way, the objects in the world are arranged into a binary tree.

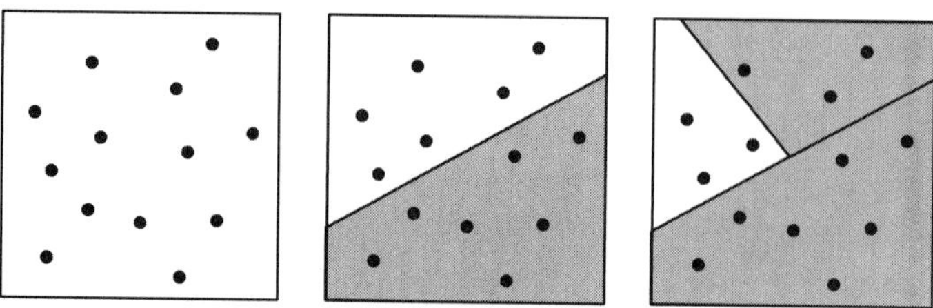

FIGURE 5.3.2 *BSP tree construction.*

A typical BSP node can be represented by the following structure:

```
typedef struct
{
    float   plane[4];     // the cutting plane
    BSPNODE *front;       // nodes in front of the plane
    BSPNODE *back;        // nodes behind the plane
    BSPLEAF *coplanar;    // elements that are coplanar

} BSPNODE;
```

This structure is 28 bytes long (assuming, for now, that the target machine's pointers are 32 bits in length), which is a little excessive. Additionally, because the structure contains three pointers that may need dereferencing, the data access pattern for any code using this representation of a BSP node will be erratic at best, causing havoc with the data cache. Finally, the length of the structure, in addition to being excessive, is not a multiple (or even a divisor) of the cache line size. This means that each time the CPU pulls this structure into the data cache, it has to fill at least one, and possibly two, cache lines, depending on the memory address of the node. Figure 5.3.3 illustrates these two possibilities for a machine with 32-byte cache lines.

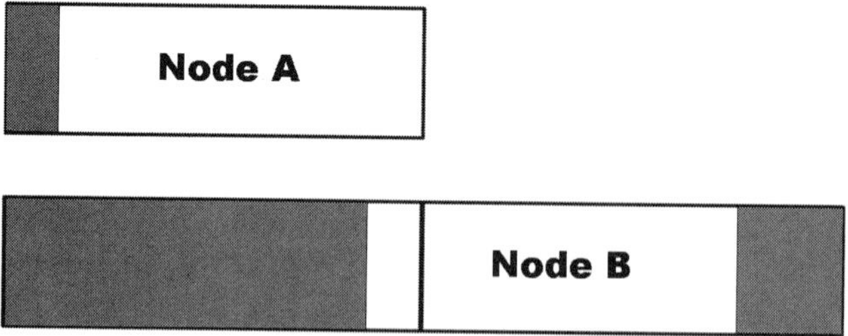

FIGURE 5.3.3 *Cache line usage for two unaligned BSP nodes.*

In each of the large blocks in Figure 5.3.3, the white area represents the memory taken up by the BSP node and the gray area represents memory that is read into the cache whose contents are not known. Upon examination of Figure 5.3.3, it is easy to see that there is potentially a lot of unused data being pulled into the data cache when randomly accessing a BSP node. Even if nodes are stored consecutively in memory, we are still going to be accessing them randomly (from the point of view of the memory controller; the actual access pattern is defined by the view position and BSP tree layout). This means that we will be pulling almost as much unused data into the data cache as used data, with a commensurate loss in performance. Clearly, we would like to modify our algorithm and our data structure in some way to avoid this poor cache behavior.

A Memory-Efficient BSP Tree

The two most obvious ways to improve our CPU cache usage are to reduce the size of the BSP node structure and to impose some kind of predictable pattern on the memory accesses. Examining our initial definition of the node structure, we can see that it is divided into two, roughly equal sections. The first of these sections contains the cutting plane and the second contains the locations of the child nodes.

We can greatly reduce the memory required to store the cutting plane of each node by ensuring that each plane chosen is axis-aligned to one of the three ordinal axes. By doing this, we can reduce the 16 bytes required by the plane to 4 bytes (to store the plane's distance from the origin) and 2 bits (representing which axis to use). This leaves us with 30 more bits to use to store the tree pointers, in order to occupy a measly 8 total bytes. Let's look at how we can do this.

In addition to reducing the memory taken by pointer storage, we also need to impose some sort of memory access pattern on tree searches. If we always ensure that the front child of a given node is stored immediately after the parent, then we remove the need for a front node pointer at all. Additionally, we can use an extra two bits to record whether the front and back nodes are leaf nodes, containing only data (in this case, widget instances). Finally, to reduce the memory required to store the pointer to the back node, we can store it instead as a positive offset from the current node. These changes result in a definition of a BSP node that takes only 8 total bytes, as shown by the following structure:

```
typedef struct
{
    u32     axis              : 2;
    u32     numFrontLeaves    : 4;
    u32     numBackLeaves     : 4;
    u32     backNodeOffset    : 22;
    float   distance;

} WIDGETNODE;
```

If we can ensure that any code searching through the BSP tree always visits the front child of a node before the back node, we make maximal use of the data cache. This is because the data for the front child is very likely to be located in the data cache due to its proximity to its parent node.

Creating the BSP Tree

Creating this BSP tree is almost trivial, especially if we treat each widget instance as a point. After creating an array of all the widget instances in the world, we calculate an axis-aligned bounding box for them. At each node, we find the longest axis of this box. This axis becomes the splitting plane. After sorting the nodes by their position along this axis, we then position the plane between the two median widgets. That is, if there are 63 widgets in the world, the cutting plane would be placed between the 31st and 32nd widgets.

We continue creating nodes in this fashion until there are only a small number of widget instances remaining in each node; the node is then said to be a leaf node. A leaf node in this instance is considered to be an array of `WIDGETLEAF` structures. The count of widgets remaining in the array is located inside each element of the array. The `WIDGETLEAF` structure as described also takes only 16 bytes of memory, maintaining efficiency and cache-friendliness.

```
typedef struct
{
    float   position[3];    // position of the widget
    s8      sinAngle;       // sin of its orientation (*127)
    s8      cosAngle;       // cos of its orientation (*127)
    u8      scale;          // scale of this widget (*32)
    u8      pad;

} WIDGETLEAF;
```

The `FoliageDemo` application included on the CD-ROM contains the files widgetbsp.cpp and widgetbsp.h, which describe the `CWidgetBSP` class. This class is responsible for the creation and management of a widget BSP tree. The `CreateTree` member function takes an array of WIDGETLEAF structures as a parameter and creates a BSP tree from them, as described in this section. Once the tree has been created, we can efficiently search it to find the list of widget instances that must be drawn.

Searching the BSP Tree

Now that we have a compact, memory access-efficient BSP tree definition, we can look at how to calculate the set of widgets that should be rendered. To do this, we must retrieve from the BSP tree all the widgets within the view frustum that are within a certain distance of the view position. We can use the size of the viewport, the camera matrix, and the field of view to construct an axis-aligned box that encloses the area of interest, as shown in Figure 5.3.4.

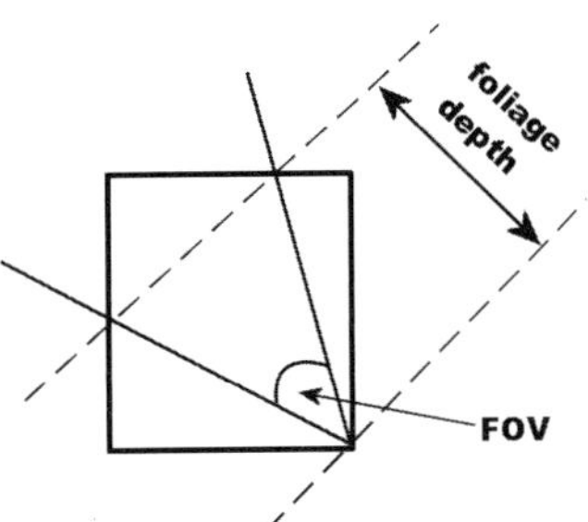

FIGURE 5.3.4 *An axis-aligned view box.*

Armed with this box, searching the BSP tree becomes trivial; at each node, we can compare the distance associated with it with the precalculated minimum and maximum values of the view box in the relevant axis to determine which child or children to visit. We must remember that, to maintain cache coherency, if the front child of a node is to be visited, it should always be visited before the rear child of the node.

When passed the view parameters and a maximum draw distance, the `Draw` member function of the `CWidgetBSP` class will construct a view box and then perform a view-based search of the widget BSP tree. For each widget instance that is found within the view box, the `AddInstance` member function of the appropriate `CWidgetMesh` class is called.

Conclusion

We have seen in this gem that by reducing the number of API calls required to draw a set of models, we can greatly decrease both the CPU and GPU cost involved in processing and rendering these models. This premise forms an efficient way to draw a large number of small models, which also works well with older (vertex shader 1.0) graphics hardware.

We also saw how to construct a memory-efficient and cache-friendly version of a BSP tree. These optimizations allow us to create and navigate a BSP tree that can contain enough foliage to cover a sizable world. The memory layout and access patterns of this BSP tree allow it to function efficiently even on systems where memory speed is relatively slow, such as the Sony Playstation 2 console. With selective use of any available cache prefetch instructions, the efficiency of this BSP tree can be further increased.

Combining these two techniques allows us to populate a world with a large number of foliage models and be able to efficiently draw views from anywhere within the world.

One possible avenue of advancement is to create an algorithm to deterministically place foliage in a small area, and then create BSP trees for these areas as they approach the viewpoint. Such an algorithm would allow us to take advantage of the memory cache efficiency of the BSP tree while keeping actual memory usage to a minimum. This would give us the ability to populate worlds of increasing size with foliage for a constant memory cost, since only BSP trees that could possibly be rendered with the current viewpoint need to exist at any given time.

References

[Gosselin04] Gosselin, David, Pedro V. Sander, and Jason L. Mitchell, "Drawing a Crowd: Instancing in Current Hardware." In *ShaderX*^{3} (edited by Wolfgang Engel). Charles River Media, 2004.

5.4

2.5 Dimensional Impostors for Realistic Trees and Forests

Gábor Szijártó, Technical University of Budapest

szijarto.gabor@freemail.hu

One of the major challenges in developing techniques for realistic and high-performance visualization of outdoor environments is the rendering of vegetation. Convincing modeling of trees and bushes requires a very large number of polygons that exceed the limits posed by the current rendering hardware. A number of methods have been proposed in the past to address the issue, most of which are variants of multiresolution modeling and level-of-detail algorithms.

In this gem, a 2.5 dimension impostor based method [Szijarto03] is developed for high-resolution tree rendering, which uses the structure of conventional trees. Moreover, it takes advantage of the programmable rendering pipelines available on the recent video cards. The algorithm uses view-dependent 2.5 dimensional impostors to visualize convincing trees in most levels of detail. Due to the use of impostors, the performance depends heavily on the fill rate of the video card.

Introduction

It is often useful to define specific scales of simulation at which a vegetation-rendering algorithm should provide the required level of realism. Most applications can be assigned to one or more of the following categories:

Insect scale: The level of simulation where a consistent, realistic depiction of individual branches and leaves is expected. (The avatar can climb the tree.)

Human scale: Scenes must look realistic at distances ranging from an arm's reach to some tens of meters away. Consistency is desired but not required. (The avatar can bump into trees, even dash through bushes, but does not focus on specific details.)

Vehicle scale: At this level, vegetation serves as little more than a backdrop. Individual trees are almost never focused upon, and consistency is not required. Viewing distance may exceed several hundred meters. (The avatar is usually moving through the environment at some altitude above the ground at faster than running speeds.)

The focus of this research has been an algorithm for human and vehicle scale simulation, with possible application in low-altitude (helicopter and glider) flight, land vehicle simulators, and first person shooters.

Vegetation visualization seems to be a hard nut to crack. There are two general approaches: geometry- and image-based methods. As its name suggests, techniques of the former group use geometric representations of the foliage. As it takes roughly one hundred thousand triangles to build a convincing model of a single tree, some form of Level of Detail (LoD) rendering technique must be applied to reduce the polygon count for a given frame to a reasonable level ([Remolar03], [Puppo97]). Visually pleasing results can only be achieved with complex algorithms or significant memory overheads. At this point in time, geometry-based methods are not acceptable for real-time applications. Image-based methods represent a trade-off of consistency and physical precision in favor of more photorealistic visuals.

Previous Image-Based Methods

The simplest of all image-based methods is sprite rendering, shown in Figures 5.4.1 and 5.4.2. This technique is analogous to using a cardboard cut-out with a tree-like image painted on it that always faces the camera. Though the resulting visuals are far from satisfactory, the technique is often used to depict smaller plants.

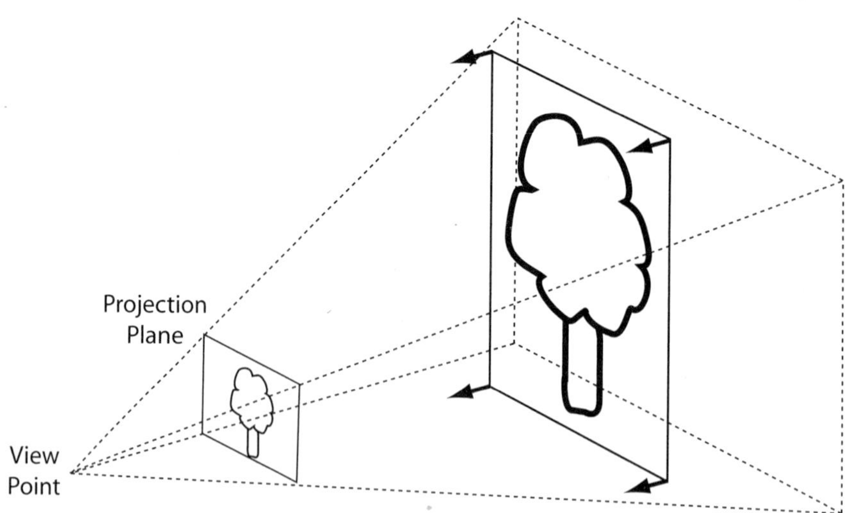

FIGURE 5.4.1 *Sprite rendering. The textured polygon is always facing the camera.*

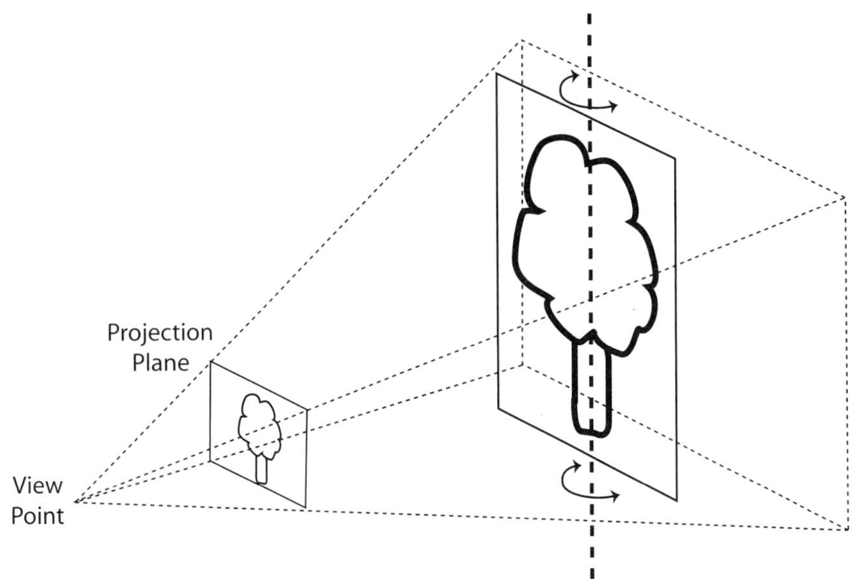

FIGURE 5.4.2 *Billboard with arbitrary position and orientation.*

Two obvious improvements introducing some form of view dependence are sets of view-dependent sprites and more complex cutouts. The view-dependent sprite method simply pregenerates a finite set (usually 4 or 8) of views and, at runtime, presents the one closest in alignment with the viewing direction. A popping artifact is visible when there is an alignment change and another view is selected. The complex cutout approach uses texture transparency and blending to render more than one view at the same time onto properly aligned surfaces, as shown in Figure 5.4.3. Both methods yield surprisingly acceptable results in vehicle scale simulations but fail to deliver quality in close-up views. It is also not trivial to introduce varying shapes and sizes of trees without overtaxing memory. Lighting is also a concern with this method.

One of the most advanced methods actually implemented in commercial entertainment software is the basic freeform textured tree model with some LoD applied, as shown in Figure 5.4.4. Though the idea is quite straightforward, only in the last few years has hardware become powerful enough to handle the task. Resulting visuals are satisfactory, although, due to the simple geometric model used, close-up views usually look artificial and variations are usually introduced through new models or through combining model parts. Increasing the number of trees in a scene quickly reduces performance. Most recent human scale simulators rely on this technique, and on the raw hardware power to cope with it.

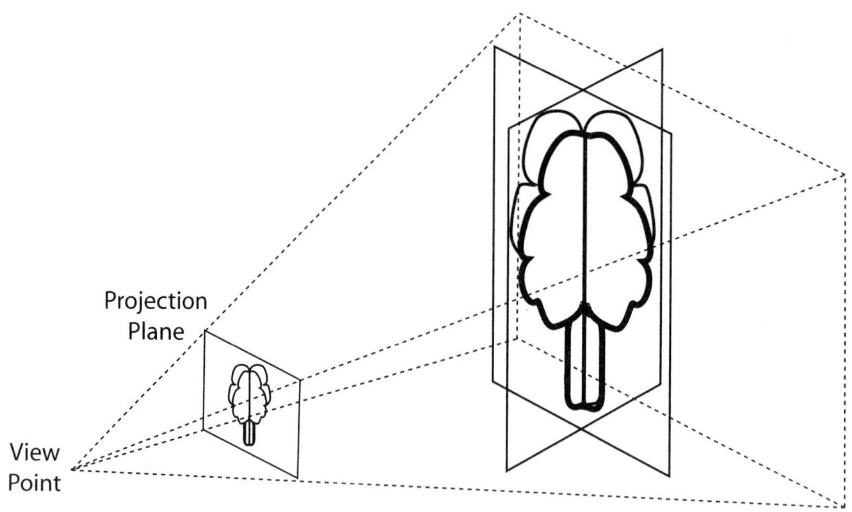

FIGURE 5.4.3 *Complex cutout with two faces.*

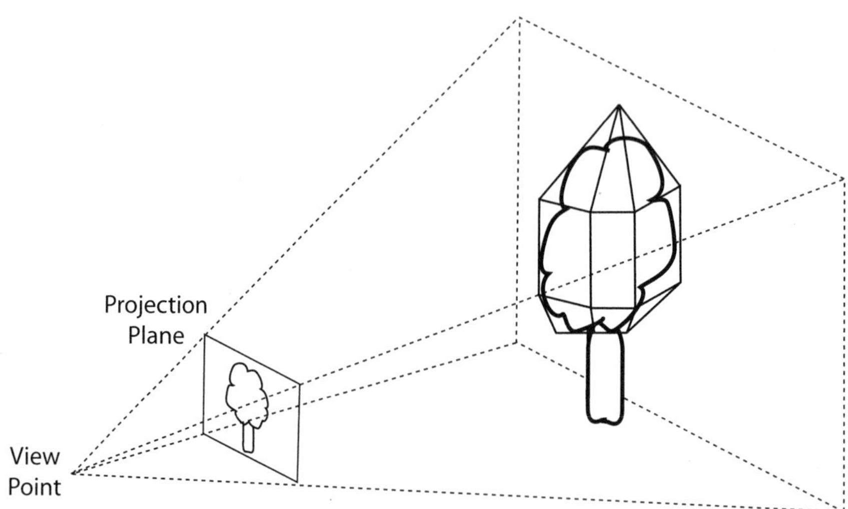

FIGURE 5.4.4 *Freeform textured tree model.*

Improving on Previous Methods

The techniques described so far all take advantage of the fact that it is much faster to render a recorded image of a tree than to actually process the geometric information describing the tree model. There are two key reasons for this:

- A leaf on a tree is usually mapped to only a few pixels. On today's hardware, rendering a pixel is much faster than transforming a triangle.
- The number of obscured leaves is very large. Thus, a significant number of transformations would be performed in vain.

Image-based methods suffer from two significant drawbacks: fixed perspective and invariance to motion and rotation. Fortunately, in tree rendering, the fixed perspective is not so disturbing. The tree canopy is a fairly irregular structure, and the human eye is far less sensitive to perspective distortions of irregular shapes than regular ones. The other problem is far more disturbing. Leaves are static as the camera moves, while it would be expected for some leaves to appear and others to become obscured as the viewer moves relative to the tree. This issue has to be addressed in some way to raise rendering quality to an acceptable level. Popping artifacts are about as disturbing to the human eye as static textures in motion. Thus, we can conclude that to achieve convincing visuals, the geometry of leaves has to be processed to some extent.

The algorithm described in the following sections renders the tree canopy as a collection several small leaf clouds. A leaf cloud consists of only a fraction of the total leaves needed to model the entire tree. The amount of geometry needed to render a leaf cloud is small enough to handle on a per-frame basis. The idea is to process a leaf cloud, render it to a texture, and apply that texture multiple times to render the tree canopy, thus introducing the motion parallax missing from previous image-based methods. However, because the leaf cloud textures overlap, artifacts will occur unless depth information is handled correctly. Introducing depth-consistent impostor rendering results in images where leaf clouds can correctly overlap with other leaf clouds, branch geometry, other trees, or any other object in the scene.

The Algorithm

The proposed technique is an improvement to traditional impostor rendering. Impostor rendering has two stages. The first stage is a view-dependent render-to-texture operation (drawing the impostor), the result of which is used in the second stage usually as sprite or billboard texture (see Figures 5.4.5 and 5.4.6).

The idea is to represent the tree canopy with more than one sprite, as shown in Figure 5.4.5. Sufficient variations can be introduced by the perturbation of the relative positions of the sprites in space. Rendering two or three different textures for sprites can introduce even more diversity. Individual sprites can also be blended using different colors, again to introduce variations, and even lighting. A canopy depicted using 10 to 100 sprites can look very convincing in still images, as shown in Figure 5.4.8, even if the same texture is repeated over all sprites.

However, the view independence of sprites makes the previous method quite useless for real-time rendering when the viewer is in motion. As sprites are always facing the camera, if their appearance is constant, they upset the motion parallax, producing very unrealistic results. The introduction of view dependence through the use of

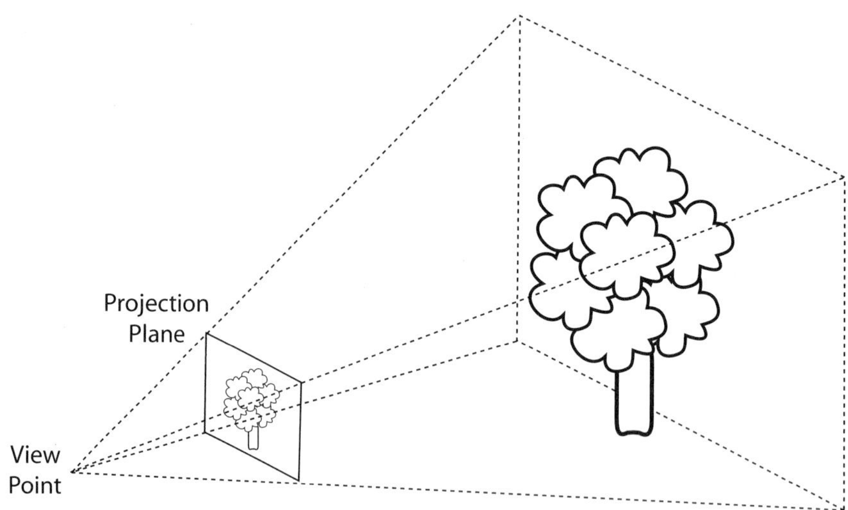

FIGURE 5.4.5 *Using multiple sprites to render the tree.*

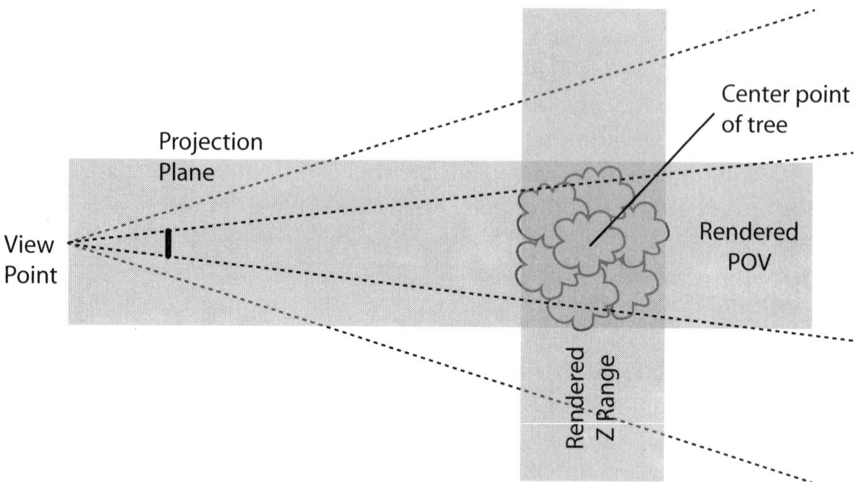

FIGURE 5.4.6 *Rendering the impostor texture from a group of leaves assumed to be positioned at the center point of the tree.*

impostors updated every frame instead of static sprites successfully eliminates this problem.

In the stage of impostor rendering, depth and color information are stored in target textures. The result is a 2.5 dimensional impostor. The *z*-near and *z*-far planes are adjusted to approximate a reasonable bounding box for the rendered group of leaves, as shown in Figure 5.4.6. In the final phase of rendering, the stored depth values are appropriately scaled and clipped to the final depth buffer before depth testing is performed, yielding a volumetric feel to the textured sprites, which can overlap in a spatially coherent manner.

The artificial look resulting from repetition of the same image over many sprites is almost completely eliminated, as volumetric overlapping obscures this arrangement to the point where it is almost impossible to discern any single impostor.

Implementation

The proposed technique produces very convincing results and can be efficiently implemented using the GPU of recent video cards, as shown schematically in Figure 5.4.7. Figure 5.4.8 shows the tree canopy rendered using impostors.

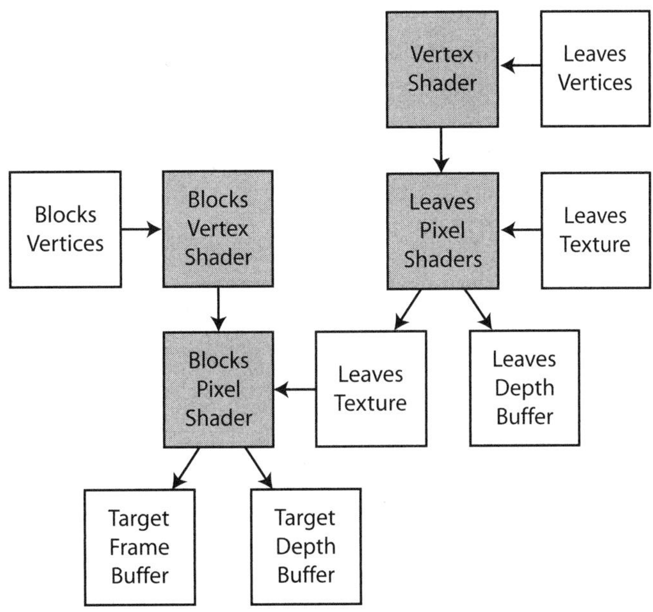

FIGURE 5.4.7 *Block diagram for implementation using two vertex and two pixel shaders.*

The implementation assumes Version 2.0 vertex and pixel shaders and uses only standard techniques. The code is written in C++ with DirectX 9 [Microsoft04]. The shader program is written in Cg [NVIDIA02]. The example program shows a tree equivalent to 1.6 million polygons.

Leaves are rendered into an impostor texture at the resolution of the final image to avoid resizing artifacts and performance overhead. Allocating impostor textures every frame would have large performance overhead, thus it is recommended that applications pre-allocate big enough impostor textures for all cases.

FIGURE 5.4.8 *Tree canopy rendered using impostors.*

Depth Precision

Current graphics cards do not provide efficient access to the depth buffer because of internal optimization considerations. Because of this, the pixel program of the first pass stores depth information in the alpha channel, thus enabling the next stage to access it. Since the alpha channel has 8-bit precision, the projection matrix should be set carefully to minimize information loss.

The front clipping plane is moved to the front of the leaf cloud, and the far clipping plane is moved to its back. Additionally, the center of the window is moved to the center of the foliage. In the Direct3D rendering pipeline, the corresponding projection matrix is [Szirmay95]:

$$\mathbf{M}'_{\mathrm{Pr}} = \begin{bmatrix} w' & 0 & 0 & 0 \\ 0 & h' & 0 & 0 \\ x_{offset} & y_{offset} & \dfrac{z'_f}{z'_f - z'_n} & 1 \\ 0 & 0 & \dfrac{-z'_n \cdot z'_f}{z'_f - z'_n} & 0 \end{bmatrix}$$

$$w' = w \cdot a_{impostor}$$
$$h' = w' \cdot a_{impostorXY}$$
$$z'_n = z_{center} - r_{impostor}$$
$$z'_f = z_{center} + r_{impostor}$$

where w is the half window width (which can be computed from the horizontal field of view as $w = 1/\tan(fov/2)$), $a_{impostor}$ is the ratio of the number of pixel columns in the frame buffer, and in the impostor texture, z_{center} is distance along axis z between the eye position and the center of the foliage, and $r_{impostor}$ is the radius of leaf cloud.

To move the leaf cloud to the center of the impostor texture, x_{offset} and y_{offset} are determined. These values are calculated by transforming the center of the foliage with the standard model, view, and projection transformations, which determines the center of the foliage in screen coordinates. The computed x_{offset} and y_{offset} values are the first two screen coordinates multiplied by -1.

Rendering the Impostors

As mentioned earlier, this rendering algorithm has two passes. The first pass computes the impostors and uses the following vertex shader:

```
vertout main(appin IN,
             uniform float4x4   mModelViewProj,
             uniform float4     invTrSunDir,
             uniform float4     colorParam)
{
    vertout OUT;

    float4 pos     = IN.Pos.xyzz;
    pos.w          = 1;

    pos            = mul( pos, mModelViewProj);
    pos            /= pos.w;

    OUT.Pos        = pos;
    OUT.Col.a      = pos.z;

    float light    = max( 0, dot(IN.Normal.xyz, invTrSunDir.xyz));
    OUT.Col.rgb    = IN.Col * (light * colorParam.x +
                     colorParam.y);

    return OUT;
}
```

The leaf cloud will be rendered into the impostor using this vertex shader. Each vertex has a position, normal, and color. The vertex shader also gets two additional parameters defining the direction of the sun and its directional and ambient intensities. The diffuse illumination model is applied to compute the reflected intensity.

The output of the vertex shader is the transformed position and the lit color value. The color value contains the pixel color and the depth in the alpha channel.

The pixel shader program of impostor rendering is very simple. Since in this case, the alpha channel contains depth values, we have to disable alpha blending before executing this code.

```
void main( vertout      IN,
           out float4   color    : COLOR)
{
    color.rgba     = IN.Col.rgba;
}
```

Mipmaping of impostors is unnecessary, because the impostor texels have the same orientation and approximately similar size as the pixels. The effect of rescaling the impostors due to perspective correction is not significant.

Using the Impostor

The second pass that renders the tree canopy into the final image as a collection of impostors is far more interesting. The vertex shader is used to calculate the projected size and the position of the impostor texture. The application loads these values into the vertex shader constant store as if the impostor were located in the center of the foliage. The vertex program makes the appropriate corrections based on the actual location of the leaf cloud in the image and passes the associated depth value to the pixel shader. The pixel shader is responsible for rendering the impostor texture, including correct depth information.

Two triangles are needed to draw each impostor to the screen. At first, the vertex shader calculates the impostor center. The impostor texture contains the depth of leaves from the impostor's front clipping plane. Thus, we add the *z* distance of the leaf cloud to the *z* coordinates stored in the impostor. Additionally, the impostor is scaled according to the perspective distortion.

```
vertout main(appin IN,
             uniform float4x4    ModelView,
             uniform float4x4    Proj,
             uniform float4      constans,
             uniform float       impostorSize,
             uniform float       centerBlockSize,
             uniform float       impostorZSize,
             )
{
    vertout OUT;

    float4 pos      = IN.Pos.xyzz;
    pos.w           = 1;
```

```
    // calculate center point of the impostor from view
    Pos             = mul( pos, ModelView);
    float4 scl      = float4( 0, impostorSize, pos.z, 1);

    // projection transformation
    pos             = mul( pos, Proj);
    pos             /= pos.w;
    pos.z           -= impostorZSize;

    // calculate size of the impostor
    scl             = mul( scl, Proj);
    scl             /= scl.w;

    // calculate scale factor
    float scale     = scl.x / centerBlockSize;

    // calculate impostor corner
    float2 uvp      = (IN.uv - 0.5) * constans.xy * scale;
    pos             = pos + float4( uvp.x, uvp.y, 0, 0);

    // calculate impostor uv parameter
    float2 uv       = IN.uv * constans.z + constans.w;

    OUT.Pos         = pos;
    OUT.Col.rgb     = IN.Col;
    OUT.Col.w       = 0;
    OUT.uv          = float4( uv.x, uv.y, pos.z, 1);

    return OUT;
}
```

The pixel program has to determine the real depth of impostor texels and ignore any invisible ones. If the scaled z value of a texel is greater than 1, it is not visible. Current pixel shaders do not support pixel pipeline breaking, thus the final depth values of these invisible texels have to be set big enough to let the z-buffer hardware ignore them. The pixel shader gets constant `depthScale`, which scales the depth values of the impostors. Finally, the scaled depth value is added to the depth of the front clipping plane used in the impostor computation.

```
void main(  vertout IN,
            uniform sampler2D    impostorTexture,
            uniform float        depthScale,
            out float4           color           : COLOR,
            out float            depth           : DEPTH)
{
    float4 texCol = tex2D(impostorTexture, IN.uv.xy);
    if (texCol.a >= 1.f) {
        depth       = 1;
    } else {
           depth            = IN.uv.z + texCol.a * depthScale;
    }
    color.xyz       = texCol.xyz * IN.Col.xyz;
    color.a         = 1;
}
```

Conclusion

In this gem, depth impostors were used to render foliage. The power of the technique becomes obvious when the objects are in motion, as there are no popping artifacts, no obvious flat sprites turning, etc. We can obtain a high level of detail since the number of leaves perceived can easily surpass one million for an average forest canopy.

The algorithm presented can be used in vehicle and human scale simulators to render realistic looking trees and forests in real time. The technique takes full advantage of the programmable rendering pipeline available on recent graphics accelerators.

References

[Microsoft04] Microsoft Corporation. *DirectX 9.0.* Available online at *http://www.msdn.com/directx.*

[NVIDIA02] NVIDIA Corporation. *C_g Language Toolkit.* Available online at *http://www.nvidia.com.*

[Puppo97] Puppo, E. and R. Scopigno. *Simplification, LOD, and Multiresolution—Principles and Applications.* Eurographics'97. Tutorial Notes, 1997.

[Remolar03] Remolar, I., M. Chover, J. Ribelles, and Ó. Belmonte. *View-Dependent Multiresolution Model For Foliage,* 370–378. WSCG 2003, 2003.

[Szijarto03] Szijártó, G. and K. József. *High Resolution Foliage Rendering for Real-time Applications.* Budmerice, Slovak Republic: SCCG, 2003.

[Szijarto032] Szijártó, G. and K. József. *High Resolution Foliage Rendering for Real-time Applications.* Budapest, Hungary: GrafGeo, 2003.

[Szijarto04] Szijártó, G. and K. József. *Real-time Hardware Accelerated Rendering of Forests at Human Scale.* Plzen, Czech Republic: WSCG 2004.

[Szirmay95] Szirmay-Kalos, L. *Theory of Three-Dimensional Computer Graphics.* Budapest: Akadémia Kiadó, 1995. Available online at *http://www.iit.bme.hu/~szirmay/book.html.*

5.5

Gridless Controllable Fire

Neeharika Adabala, School of Computer Science, University of Central Florida

nadabala@cs.ucf.edu

Charles E. Hughes, School of Computer Science and School of Film and Digital Media, University of Central Florida

ceh@cs.ucf.edu

Gaming scenarios often involve fire: objects/vehicles/buildings on fire, torches of fire, fireplaces, etc. Fire is a phenomenon created by glowing combustion products in turbulent motion. Fire simulation techniques used in computer graphics usually involve solving the equations for dynamics of fluids on grids. These approaches are often computationally intensive and do not work in real time [Nguyen01]. Other approaches [Wei02] work in real time; however, they are based on computations on three-dimensional grids that introduce significant design issues in terms of choice of grid size, resolution, and position. For example, what should be done when a wind blows on a fire? Should a grid be defined so that it encompasses the whole region that may ever contain the fire or should it be designed to move *with* the fire? In the latter case, knowledge of the possible regions the fire could flow into is required. Also, grid-based computations are often not guaranteed to be stable and relate to the resolution of the selected grid, adding to the complexity of applying these approaches. Thus, grid-based simulations of fire demand skillful choice of grid size, position, and resolution in every scenario that involves fire, which can be a tedious task.

In this chapter, we present a gridless technique for modeling fire, based on a stochastic Lagrangian process [Pope00]. In this approach, the equations for dynamics simulation define the trajectory of each particle. As a result, they can be directly evaluated to yield the position of each particle at successive time steps. The stochastic nature of the approach makes the computations relatively stable.

Most fires that are created in gaming scenarios are diffusion fires, or fires in which the oxidizer and fuel are not premixed (unlike the steady flame of a burner where the fuel and oxidizer *are* premixed). The fuel or object that is burning has to evaporate and come in contact with the oxidizer before it can burn. Since this process does not occur uniformly, fires flicker and exhibit a characteristic "jumping" behavior. Most of the existing approaches do not allow us to capture this distinctive property of fire. In this chapter, we present a simplified approach to modeling flickering fire in order to enhance realism. The work of Lamorlette and Foster [Lamorlette02] identifies the intermittent flame region in fire, but their model is designed for an offline production environment rather than real-time applications. In this chapter, the flickering of fire is captured by creating a simplified model for the "global extinction" behavior of fire. Global extinction refers to the moment when the combustion in the fire is so low that no flame is visible. Our technique also models "flame brushes," which are regions of greater brightness in flames that occur in areas of the flame where there is higher rate of chemical reaction.

An additional issue in modeling of fire in games is the need to have parameters to control the appearance of fire. The approach presented in this chapter, enables control of the flicker rate, flame height, and number of flame regions in the fire. In addition to the simulation, a technique for real-time fire rendering that uses the programmability of graphics hardware is described.

Our fire model is presented in the next section. There are two main aspects to our model: the stochastic Lagrangian model for the dynamics and the chemical evolution model that represents the combustion accompanying the fire. The rendering of the model using programmable graphics hardware is then detailed. This is followed by a discussion with examples demonstrating the capabilities of the technique. Conclusions are given in the final section.

Model of Fire

The key aspects that have to be modeled while simulating fire are turbulent dynamics and the chemical reaction accompanying them.

Dynamics Model

The flow of hot gaseous products in a diffusion flame can be modeled as an incompressible turbulent flow. The equations that define this flow are the equation for conservation of mass, shown in Equation 5.5.1.

$$\nabla \cdot \mathbf{u} = 0 \qquad (5.5.1)$$

and the Navier-Stokes equation, shown in Equation 5.5.2.

$$\frac{D\mathbf{u}}{Dt} = -\frac{1}{\rho}\nabla p + \upsilon\nabla^2\mathbf{u} + \mathbf{F} \tag{5.5.2}$$

where $D\mathbf{u}/Dt$ is the material derivative $\partial/\partial t + u\partial/\partial x + v\partial/\partial y + w\partial/\partial z = \partial/\partial t + \mathbf{u}\cdot\nabla$, $\mathbf{u}$ is the velocity vector (u, v, w), p is the pressure, ∇^2 is the Laplacian operator, ρ is the density, υ is the coefficient of kinematic viscosity, and $\mathbf{F}$ represents the external and body forces.

These equations can be solved by the *Eulerian approach*, where one solves for the vector fields that define the flow at fixed points of a grid, or by the *Lagrangian approach*, where one solves for the trajectory of a set of particles evolving in the flow. In the case of turbulent flow, the chaotic nature of the flow makes the problem of defining the size, shape, placement, and resolution of the grid tricky. Also grid-based techniques require significant insight into the expected behavior of the flow. For example, the grid should be shifted in the direction of an external wind field to keep the solutions on the grid points relevant. Because of these issues, we choose a Lagrangian approach because it is gridless.

When computations are applied for real-time simulations, they must be stable. Turbulent flows are chaotic and notoriously sensitive to small changes in initial conditions. Therefore, the stability of the computations cannot be guaranteed. However, this sensitivity of flow to small changes in initial conditions makes it suitable to stochastic modeling. The stochastic Lagrangian approach to maintain the gridless nature of the computations is used here. In this approach, the fluid flow is modeled by a set of particles whose statistical characteristics are the same as those of particles that evolve based on the equations of flow. These approaches are numerically more stable than the deterministic solutions to the equations.

The turbulent motion of the particles is simulated by using a stochastic Lagrangian approach. Equations 5.5.3 through 5.5.5 define the evolution of the *ith* particle in the simulation [Pope00].

$$d\mathbf{X}^{(i)} = \mathbf{U}^{(i)}dt \tag{5.5.3}$$

$$d\mathbf{U}^{(i)} = \frac{3}{4}C_0\langle\omega\rangle\mathbf{U}^{(i)}(t) - \langle\mathbf{U}\rangle dt + \sqrt{C_0 k\langle\omega\rangle}d\mathbf{W} \tag{5.5.4}$$

$$d\omega^{(i)} = -(\omega^{(i)} - \langle\omega\rangle)C_3\langle\omega\rangle + \sqrt{(2\sigma^2\langle\omega\rangle\omega^{(i)}C_3\langle\omega\rangle)}dW^* \tag{5.5.5}$$

Equation 5.5.3 defines the position of a particle based on its velocity. The computation of velocity is based on the simplified Langevin model for stationary isotropic turbulence with constant density. The details of the derivation are beyond the scope of this chapter and can be found in the book on turbulent flows by Pope [Pope00]. The terms that are enclosed in $\langle\ \rangle$ represent the local mean values of the enclosed variables. In combustion studies, they are evaluated by dividing the region occupied by the particles into a grid and considering the particles that lie in the same grid cell as the ith particle. In our approach, we use a *kd* tree to store the particle system and evaluate these local mean values on n nearest neighboring particles of the ith particle. The value of n used in our work typically falls in the range of 10 to 20. This approach of storing particles in a *kd* tree was introduced earlier in [Adabala00] and is called the particle map approach. The constant $C_0 = 2.1$ is the standard value used in turbulent flow simulations, and k is the turbulent kinetic energy. In the simulations presented in this work, the value of k is taken as 1.5. d and **W** represents an increment in the isotropic Wiener process $\mathbf{W}(t)$. It is implemented as a vector of three independent samples of the standard normal distribution. The next equation represents the evolution of the turbulent frequency. The value of the constant C_3 is 1, and $\mathbf{W}^*$ represents an increment in a scalar Wiener process $\mathbf{W}^*(t)$, which is independent of the Wiener process in the previous equation.

The previous equations enable us to model the *turbulent motion* of fire. We will now describe our model of the *chemical* aspects of fire.

Chemical Evolution Model

The chemical evolution model simulates the changing composition of fuel in the fire as the reaction progresses. Modeling of global extinction requires identification of the stage in the reaction's progress when it is no longer able to sustain a visible flame. At this stage, global extinction occurs. After global extinction, the diffusion of fuel and oxidizer continues, and the conditions for combustion are again met and a flame reappears. The whole process occurs in a fraction of a second. Therefore the actual moment when no flame exists is not actually perceived but rather a flicker in the flame is observed. This phenomenon has not been modeled by the typical approaches to fire modeling in computer graphics that concentrate on modeling the variation of temperature in the flame.

Various approaches to model the chemical aspect of fire exist in combustion studies. Many of these results are based on empirical studies of fire [Drysdale99]. There is still a large gap between models of combustion and the actual phenomena, as several simplifying assumptions have to be made. For example, each fuel has its own unique way of burning, depending on its chemical composition, diffusivity of fuel, oxidizer, and products. The Euclidian Minimum Spanning Tree (EMST) mixing model, proposed by Subramaniam and Pope [Subramaniam98], is a general model for modeling evolution of composition of fuel during combustion in a turbulent flow. This model is compared with other approaches to model combustion in [Subramaniam99]; the comparison is done by applying the techniques to simulate the evolution of composition in a simple periodic thermochemical model [Lee95]. The fundamental concept of this model is to associate chemical composition parameters with the particles involved in the combustion process. The composition of the particles is initially defined using a periodic thermochemical model. The composition of the particles is subsequently evolved by constructing an EMST in composition space and updating the composition by considering the particles' neighboring nodes in the tree. This approach of updating the composition helps to maintain the locality of chemical composition evolution with combustion. Visually, this results in the ability to simulate flame brushes. In this approach, global extinction is estimated by computing the expected value of the reaction progress variable and comparing it with a threshold. If the value is less than the threshold, global extinction occurs.

We formulate a simplified model that mimics the main aspects of the EMST model for real-time applications. In the EMST model with the simplified thermochemistry, the initial composition of the particles at equilibrium is as shown by the solid line in Figure 5.5.1. The composition then evolves with time to a distribution along the dotted line in Figure 5.5.1. The extent to which it evolves towards the dotted line depends on the nature of the combustion. When the combustion is steady, the time for mixing of oxidizer and fuel is comparable to the time of combustion. Hence, the line remains close to the equilibrium state indicated by the solid line. However, when the reaction is *not* steady (when there is global extinction), the time taken for diffusion is significantly larger than the time for chemical reaction. As a result, the composition of particles evolves to the dotted line in Figure 5.5.1. The exact distribution of the compositions may vary significantly, depending on the value of several parameters that define the EMST mixing model [Subramaniam99]. The essence of the composition evolution in the EMST model can be summarized as a shift from the solid curve to the dotted curve in Figure 5.5.1 while maintaining the neighborhood in composition space.

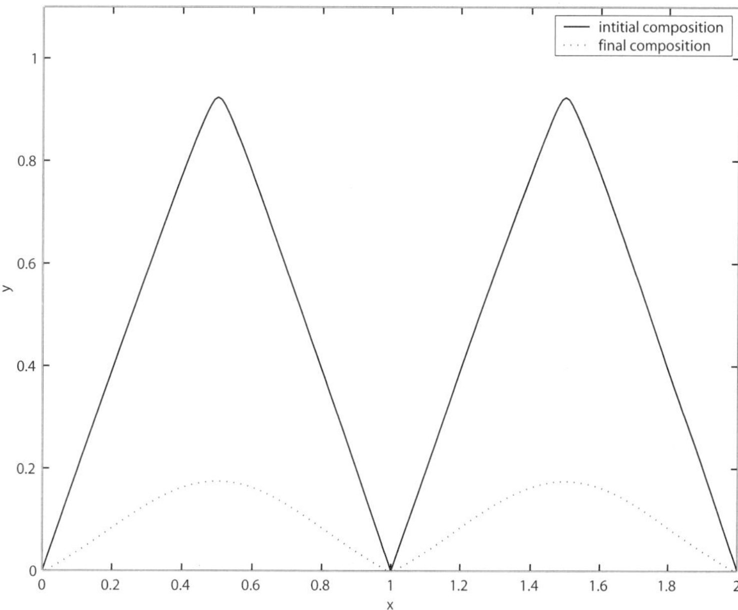

FIGURE 5.5.1 *Plots of main curve along which composition values are distributed at the initial and final (before global extinction) time step for the EMST mixing model simulation. The x axis is the mixture fraction $\xi(X,t)$, and the y axis is the reaction progress variable $Y(X,t)$.*

The x axis in Figure 5.5.1 is the mixture fraction $\xi(X,t)$, and the y axis is the reaction progress variable $Y(X,t)$. Here X is the position vector of the particle (x_1,x_2,x_3). The reaction progress variable is the mass fraction of product where the chemical reaction considered is fuel + oxidant $\longleftrightarrow$ product [Subramaniam99].

In our simplified model, we do not evolve the values of the mixture fraction. Therefore, we represent it by $\xi(X)$ by removing its dependence on time. The values of $\xi(X)$ for a particle are defined such that the gradient $\partial\xi/\partial x_1$ is a constant as in the case of [Subramaniam99]. We defined a constant as a parameter $\eta \in (0.0,\infty]$ in our approach. This parameter is used to control the number of flame brushes. The number of flame brushes that occur in a spatial region where the value of x_1 varies by one unit is equal to the value of η. Therefore when $\eta = 1.0$, there is a single flame brush in the spatial region, where the value of x_1 varies by one unit. The value of $Y(X,t)$ at $t = 0$ in our model is defined in Equation 5.5.6.

$$Y(\mathbf{X},t) = Y(\xi(\mathbf{X})) = \exp(-(\xi(\mathbf{X}) - \lfloor \xi(\mathbf{X}) \rfloor) - 0.5)^2 / \lambda). \tag{5.5.6}$$

This is the representation of adjacent overlapping Gaussian distributions. The parameter $\lambda \in (0.0,\infty]$ controls the overlap between two neighboring flame brushes. Lower values result in less overlap and well-separated flame brushes, while higher values result in greater overlap. Figure 5.5.2 gives the plot of the values of $Y(X,t)$ with $\eta = 1.0$ and $\lambda = 0.8$.

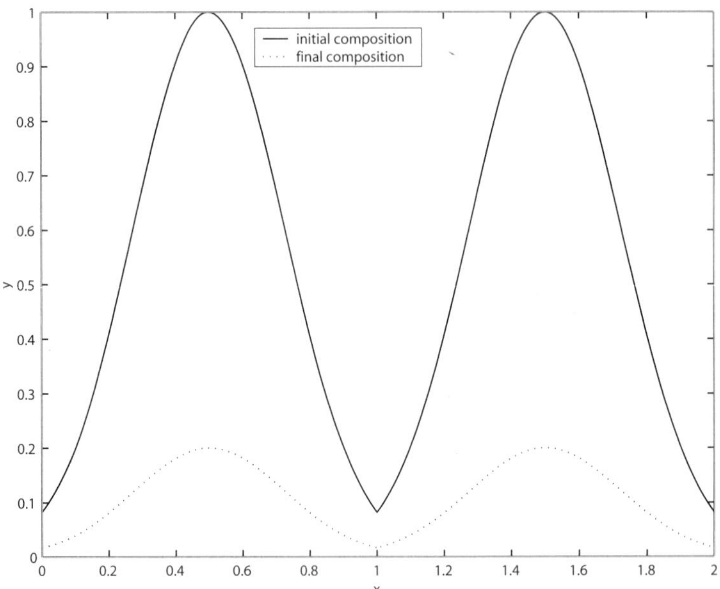

FIGURE 5.5.2 *Plots of main curve along which composition values are distributed at the initial and final (before global extinction) time step for our model that mimics the EMST mixing model. The x axis is the mixture fraction ξ(X), and the y axis is the reaction progress variable Y(X,t).*

In our model, we begin by distributing the composition of particles as a Gaussian distribution as given by Equation 5.5.6 and illustrated in Figure 5.5.2. We then evolve the composition to values about the curve shown in dotted lines in Figure 5.5.2. We choose the Gaussian distribution as the starting distribution, because it has been shown empirically and numerically that the distribution of composition should relax to a Gaussian with time. The EMST model is formulated so that the composition distribution relaxes to a Gaussian with successive updates of composition. In our simplified approach, we start the fire visualization from the first step of simulation. There are no preprocessing simulation steps that allow the distribution to relax to a Gaussian. Therefore, the distribution of composition should be a Gaussian from the start. This is ensured by the use of Equation 5.5.6 to initialize the composition.

We evolve the composition $Y(X,t)$ with Equation 5.5.7:

$$Y(\mathbf{X},t) = (\chi + rd) * Y(\mathbf{X},t-1), \tag{5.5.7}$$

where χ is the rate of decrease of the reaction progress variable. $rd \in [0, 0.01 * \chi]$ is a small random perturbation in the value of χ. This simple approach to updating the composition mimics the essence of the EMST mixing model as the neighborhood regions are maintained in composition space and there is an evolution between the initial and final curves that have a similar appearance. The value of χ can be in the range (0, 1.0]. It was found that values of χ in the range [0.85, 1.0] give visually realistic results. Values of χ tending towards 1.0 result in high flames, as the reaction progress of the particle remains in the visible range for more time steps of the dynamics simulation.

Global extinction is identified as the stage during combustion when the overall reaction progress is not enough to sustain the flame. At this stage, the flame reduces in intensity and reappears in the next time step when the compositions of the particles are redistributed at thermochemical equilibrium (the values at $Y(X,0)$. In the EMST model, the stage of global extinction is predicted by computing an extinction index that relates directly to the expected value of the reaction progress variable. The extinction index is compared with a fixed value. If the index is less, global extinction is said to occur. In our simplified approach, we compute the mean value of the reaction progress variable of all the particles involved in the simulation. If it is less than a threshold value, global extinction occurs and we restart the simulation with new particles and composition, as the old particles are no longer visible after global extinction. Thus, Equation 5.5.8:

$$\text{if mean } (Y(\mathbf{X},0)) < \theta \text{ global extinction}, \tag{5.5.8}$$

where θ is a threshold parameter that can be adjusted to control the frequency of global extinction. The justification for varying the value of threshold θ is that various fuels produce different kind of flames, and depending on the fuel, a different value of minimum reaction progress is needed to sustain a flame. The value of θ is chosen in the range [0.0, 0.4] for a visually realistic appearance. We use the $mean\left(Y\left(X,0\right)\right)$ rather than the sum of the reaction progress values to estimate the overall reaction progress in the system so that the threshold value is independent of the number of particles involved in the simulation.

A model of flickering fire that works in real time is achieved with the techniques described in this section. In the following section, we describe a method for rendering the particle system that evolves according to the model presented thus far.

Real-Time Rendering

A programmable graphics card is used to realize the rendering of the particle system evolving based on the model presented in the previous section. Specifically, the approach exploits the ability to render to an OpenGL p-buffer.

The particle system is rendered as streaks of light extending from the current position of the particle to its previous position. This approach is adopted because when a bright light-emitting particle moves with high velocity, we perceive a streak due to persistence of vision. The composition parameter is used to define the texture coordinates of the line. The current value of composition is used as the texture coordinate at the current particle position, and the composition at the previous time step is used for the other end of the line. Since a particle composition and location represent the characteristics of a small volume of the fuel located at a given position, a thickness is associated with these lines. These lines are rendered into the p-buffer. A blur/halo is created in the upward direction to represent the scattering of particle light by hot gaseous products resulting from combustion. Two random textures are used to obtain offsets to the texture coordinates for blurring. The result of the computation is stored back in the p-buffer that is being used as the source to obtain the texture coordinates. This enables creating a cumulative blur.

The blurred texture is then used as a texture coordinate index into a one-dimensional texture that represents the variation of light emitted with the progress of combustion.

Examples and Discussion

The examples presented here are implemented in C++ and OpenGL and run on machines with the Linux operating system. The algorithm performs at the rate of approximately 60 frames per second on both a 2.2 GHz Pentium 4 with 768 MB of RAM and GeForce 5800 graphics card and a 1.46 GHz Athlon XP with 512 MB RAM with a GeForce 5900 Ultra graphics card. The number of particles used in all the images and animation is 300.

Figure 5.5.3 shows some images of fire between two stages of global extinction. The fire in the image is generated with $\eta = 2$, and the spread of the fire is two units in the x_1 direction. Therefore there are four flame brushes. The value of λ is one and χ is 0.97. The threshold θ is 0.1. Values of θ in the range 0.1 to 0.4 give the most visually appealing results.

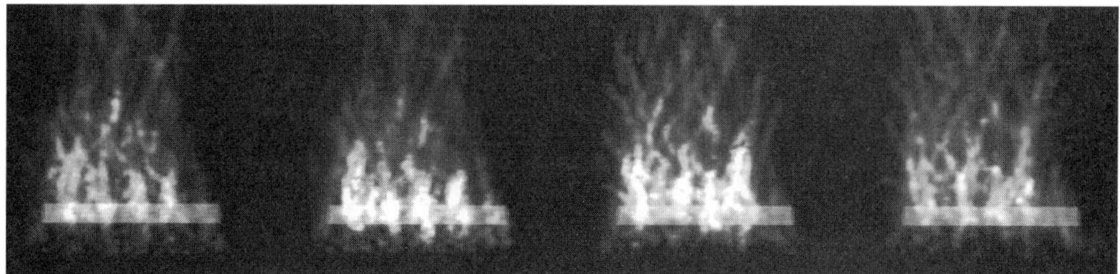

FIGURE 5.5.3 *Images of fire between two stages of global extinction. Several frames exist between two time instances of global extinction; these are not consecutive frames.*

Figure 5.5.4 shows fire generated with $\eta = 1.0$ and $\eta = 2.0$. In both cases, λ was chosen to be 1.0. This creates an overlap of flame brushes that gives the fire a realistic appearance.

FIGURE 5.5.4 *Comparison of fire with different numbers of flame brushes. The fire on the left has two main regions (η = 1.0) while the one on the right has four regions (η = 2.0).*

Figure 5.5.5 shows fires of different heights created with our model. For the tall flames, the value of χ is close to 1. Tall flames undergo little or no global extinction. When the value of χ is lower, global extinction occurs more frequently. This is consistent with the intuitive idea that when a flame is extinguished frequently, it has to start again from the fuel source and cannot propagate to a great height before it is extinguished again.

In this implementation, the particles are introduced into the simulation by assigning an initial velocity in the upward direction to represent the initial upward velocity due to thermal buoyancy. Apart from controlling with the parameter χ, the height of the flames can also be controlled to some extent with the value of upward

FIGURE 5.5.5 *Comparison of fire with different heights of flames. Left image created with χ = 0.99999, middle image created with χ = 0.97, and right image generated with χ = 0.9.*

velocity assigned to the particles as they are introduced into the simulation. Higher initial upward velocity results in greater flame height. This is consistent with the fact that a larger flame results when a fuel is injected or introduced into an oxidizer with greater velocity. It should be noted that particles evolved with the turbulent flow (Equations 5.5.3 to 5.5.5), are not always guaranteed to move upward. When a particle moves significantly in the outward direction, it is deleted from the system and a new particle is introduced for every deleted particle. When the composition of a particle reduces so that it no longer emits enough light to be visible, such a particle is deleted from the simulation. In the examples, we have not simulated smoke. A technique for simulating smoke can be introduced on top of the fire as described in [Lamorlette02]. In that case, a particle that is no longer emitting light can be introduced into the smoke simulation system.

These images are created with constant threshold θ value. The examples demonstrate that it is possible to design fires with desired visual properties using the simple intuitive parameters η, χ, and θ.

Conclusion

In this chapter, we have presented an approach to synthesize fire in real time for computer graphics applications. The features of this work include:

- A gridless stable numerical simulation technique for turbulent flow in the form of a stochastic Lagrangian approach-based solution.

- A model for the phenomena of global extinction that enables capture of flicker in fire. This property of fire was not previously included in computer graphics models of fire.
- A parametric model such that flicker rate, flame height, and number of flame brushes can be controlled in the model.
- A hardware accelerated technique for rendering the fire particle system.

The dynamics technique is implemented with particle maps, making the approach gridless, and thus overcoming the problem of addressing grid design related issues like choice of grid size, grid resolution, and grid placement in space. The technique proposed is inspired by the physics and thermochemistry based models, however it is tailored for computer graphics and gaming applications where control of the visual aspects of fire is more important than physical accuracy.

References

[Adabala00] Adabala, N. and S. Manohar. "Modeling and rendering of gaseous phenomena using particle maps." *Journal of Visualization and ComputerAnimation*, 11:279–293, 2000.

[Bentley75] Bentley, J. L. "Multidimensional Binary Search Trees Used for Associative Searching." In *Communications of the ACM*, 18(9):509–517, 1975.

[Drysdale99] Drysdale, D. *An introduction to fire dynamics.* Chichester, New York: John Wiley and Sons, 1999.

[Lamorlette02] Lamorlette, A. and N. Foster. "Structural modeling of natural flames." *Proceedings of ACM SIGGRAPH 2002*, pages 729–735, July 2002.

[Lee95] Lee, Y. Y. and S. B. Pope. "Nonpremixed turbulent reacting flow near extinction." *Combustion and Flame*, 101:501–528, 1995.

[Nguyen01] Nguyen, D. O., R. Fedkiw, and H. W. Jensen. "Physically based modeling and animation of fire." *Proceedings of ACM SIGGRAPH 2002*, 21:721–728, July 2002.

[Pope00] Pope, S. B. *Turbulent Flows.* Cambridge: Cambridge University Press, 2000.

[Subramaniam98] Subramaniam, S. and S. B. Pope. "A mixing model for turbulent reactive flows based on Euclidean minimum spanning trees." *Combustion and Flame*, 115(4):487–514, 1998.

[Subramaniam99] Subramaniam, S. and S. B. Pope. "Comparison of mixing model performance for nonpremixed turbulent reactive flow." *Combustion and Flame*, 117(4):732–754, 1999.

[Wei02] Wei, X., W. Li, K. Mueller, and A. Kaufman. "Simulating fire with texture splats." *IEEE Visualization 2002*, pages 227–237, August 2002.

5.6

Powerful Explosion Effects Using Billboard Particles

Steve Rabin, Nintendo of America Inc.

steve_rabin@hotmail.com, steve@aiwisdom.com

Explosion effects are common in games, but often they lack punch or intensity. This article explains how to create an impressive fuel explosion effect out of billboard particles on any 3D hardware platform, including portable devices. Since computers and video game consoles are currently not powerful enough to simulate real explosions or even replay precanned explosion simulations consisting of thousands of particles, game explosions must be caricatures of the real thing. Therefore, the goal is not to directly simulate an explosion, but rather to convey the impression that a powerful explosion has taken place. This requires a careful blend of approximation and caricature. The in-game explosion must attempt to look like a real explosion, but also exaggerate certain aspects to sell the effect.

The explosion effect in this article is a combination of seven different particle effects: initial flash, radial flares, white hot inner core, intense fireball, expanding smoke, and debris. The effect is shown in Color Plates 8A and 8B, as well as in several videos on the CD-ROM. While the explosion does not resemble any kind of simulation, research in simulating both explosions and smoke inspired many of the techniques [Fedkiw01, Feldman03, Stam03].

ON THE CD

Initial Flash

When an explosion occurs, there is a moment at the very beginning when the viewer is blinded by light. While this effect is missing from most video game explosions, it is a critical cue that the explosion was both intense and powerful.

One way to simulate the initial flash is to create a single semitransparent particle with a very bright yellow/white glow that falls off completely at the edges. An effective method is to place a Photoshop lens flare in the alpha channel of the texture, as shown in Figure 5.6.1. The color component of the texture should be a solid yellow/white.

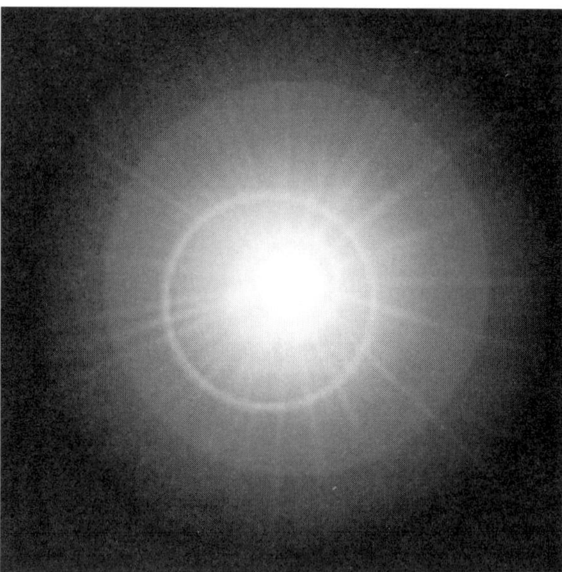

FIGURE 5.6.1 *Alpha channel of a flash texture.*

At the time of the explosion, the particle should spawn from the center of the explosion and uniformly scale up very quickly, taking up the entire screen. Starting at fully transparent, it should fade up quickly, then after about 0.3 seconds, it should fade down very quickly until it is fully transparent (at which time it can be destroyed). This sequence is shown in the far left column of Color Plate 8A.

This technique works best for explosions taking place in the sky, since the rapidly expanding flash particles will intersect with the ground, buildings, and other objects, causing the familiar *z*-buffer intersection of the billboard particles with the scene geometry. If this artifact is unacceptable, another option is to create the flash using a post-processing effect on the entire rendered image.

Radial Flares

As you can see in Figure 5.6.1, the initial flash contained some radial flares. However, this technique is so effective that it's worth emphasizing in the explosion. The effect involves creating 10 to 30 pointy flares that are randomly placed around the explosion, as shown in Figure 5.6.2.

These flares won't be scaled but should protrude out enough so that they are seen sticking out of the initial explosion, with each being a random length. Each flare should be started randomly between 0 and 0.2 seconds after the start of the explosion. They should be fully visible on initialization and then start fading out after 0.1 seconds. Note that the explosion will seem cartoonish if the flares are long or if they fade out more slowly than this. If the flares are short and fade out quickly, the effect is

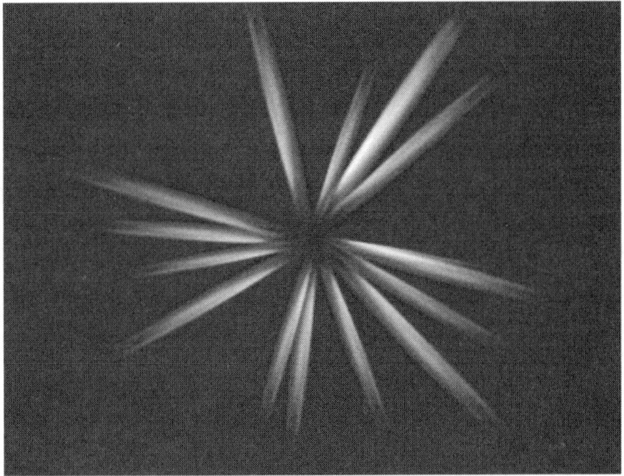

FIGURE 5.6.2 *Radial flares randomly pointing away from the center of the explosion.*

almost subliminal yet very effective in conveying the intensity of the explosion. This sequence can be seen in the second column of Color Plate 8A.

Each radial flare billboard should be a narrow quad that points in the direction of the explosion, as shown in Figure 5.6.3. A solid colored texture with a cloud-like blob in the alpha channel works well for these billboards. A good color scheme is for the flares to be a dusty light gray at the center and then blend to a dirty light yellow at the tips. This colorization and gradient can be easily achieved by using a monochrome texture map blended with interpolated vertex colors to provide the yellowish tint.

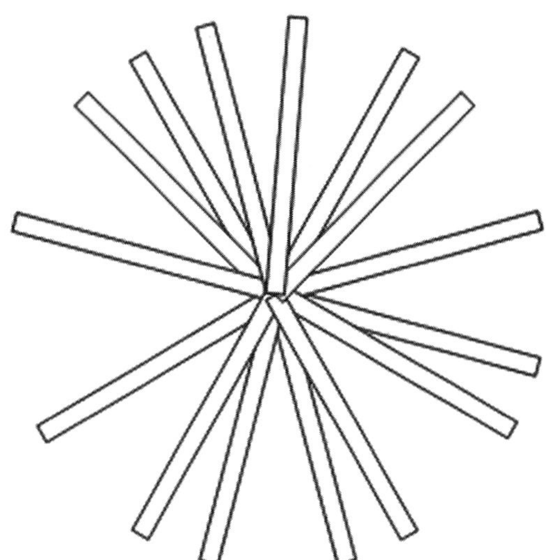

FIGURE 5.6.3 *Radial flare billboards made up of quads.*

White Hot Inner Core

The white hot inner core is a key component of the explosion effect. It starts out as a small fully opaque white circle fringed in yellow and orange. It then expands at a very high rate, yet the expansion exponentially decays over time until it ceases to grow. At its largest, the white hot inner core is a cloud-like white, yellow, and orange mass, as shown in the third column of Color Plate 8A.

From the time of creation, the core should remain at full visibility for about one second and then start fading out very slowly. This effect will act as a backdrop for the fireball and smoke effects, which will be described shortly. As the smoke and fireball expand, this white hot inner core will show through any empty spots and add to the mottled look of the explosion.

There are two ways to render the inner core. The first method is the cheapest, both for the CPU and GPU, and only requires one particle. The second method is more expensive and requires about 100 particles. As we will see later, games can choose between the cheap and expensive methods in order to scale performance depending on the platform or the complexity of the scene.

The cheap method uses a single texture shaped as an amorphous solid white blob with a very thin fringe of yellow and orange around the edges. The texture should have a sharp but smooth edge in the alpha layer. This single particle will start off rapidly expanding (scaling up), but then slow down exponentially until it stops growing. Then it will fade out slowly after one second.

The expensive method uses about 100 solid white particles, each with a cloud-like blob in the alpha channel. By coloring the vertices of each particle yellow-orange and rendering them using an additive blend, hot white spots will appear on overlapping particles, fading out to yellow-orange at the edges. One effective color scheme is to use bright yellow-orange on the top-right vertex, medium yellow-orange on the bottom-right vertex, medium gray on the top-left vertex, and dark gray on the bottom-left vertex. It also helps to make different octants of the explosion have different intensities of the color scheme so that the core appears less uniform.

With the expensive method, each particle will remain the same size during the entire effect. However, the particles shoot out randomly from the center with a high velocity, exponentially decaying until the particle is motionless. Once all particles have stopped moving, the core will have reached its full size. After about one second, the particles should begin to fade slowly.

In reality, a lingering explosion will rise slowly due to its thermal buoyancy in the air and then drift in a given direction due to the wind. Both of these effects can be simulated by defining a wind force that blows softly in some horizontal direction with a slight vertical component to represent the thermal buoyancy. This wind should be applied to any hot inner core particles. This small touch helps to sell the effect.

Intense Fireball

The fireball is a secondary effect that kicks in after the first three effects. It starts at about 0.1 seconds after the start of the explosion and shoots outward from the center of the explosion. The fireball should start fully opaque and then fade out slowly after 0.3 seconds (as seen in the fourth column of Color Plate 8A).

As with the hot inner core, there are two ways that you can choose to render the fireball component of this explosion effect. The first method is the cheapest and involves a single particle. The second requires about 50 particles and is more expensive.

The cheap method uses a single texture shaped as an amorphous blob, similar to the cheap hot inner core step. The texture itself should be a mottled red fireball with black cloud-like edges within the texture, while the alpha channel should have a cloud-like density and amorphous shape. This particle will basically crossfade with the white hot inner core, scaling up at a similar rate with the exponential decay. After 0.3 seconds, the particle should slowly fade out.

The expensive method involves spawning roughly 50 particles in the center of the explosion. Each uses a texture similar to the cheap effect and each starts off very small and scales up slowly to a capped size. Each particle shoots from the center at a very high velocity in a random direction. The velocity will then exponentially decay until the particles are still, with only the combined wind and thermal buoyancy causing them to drift. Each particle should then fade out slowly after 0.3 seconds. To make the fireball more mottled, it helps to darken particle vertex colors in particular octants of the explosion.

An important aspect of the expensive method is stretching of the fireball particles in the direction of motion. As each fireball particle moves away from the center, it relaxes into a square shape. This effect is very important in creating the feeling of power bursting from the center. Figure 5.6.4 shows how the billboard quad transforms over the particle's lifetime. Note that the particles become larger and more square as they expand outward and slow down.

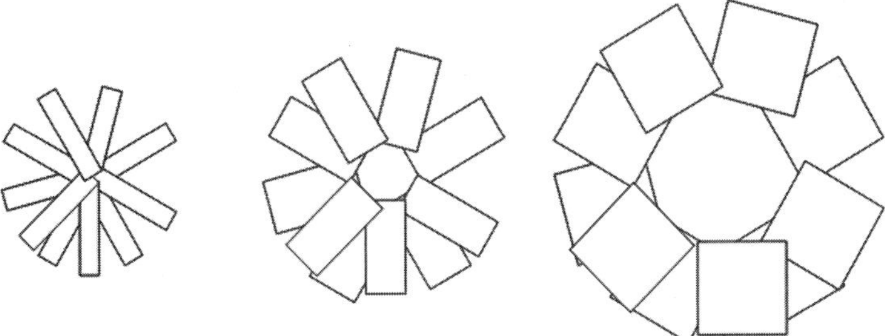

FIGURE 5.6.4 *The transformation of the fireball billboard quad over its lifetime. Note how the quad starts out narrow in the direction of the explosion and then relaxes into a square shape.*

Expanding Smoke

The expanding smoke is another secondary effect that occurs after the flash, flares, and core. It happens at about the same time as the fireball and generally overlays on top of all the previous effects. Starting at 0.1 seconds, about 30 to 50 smoke particles shoot from the center of the explosion (as seen in the fifth column of Color Plate 8A). The particle's texture should be a light gray smoke cloud with lots of billowing detail. The alpha channel should have a cloudlike density and amorphous shape.

The smoke effect is fairly important to the explosion since it will expand the farthest and linger the longest. There is no cheap way to create the smoke effect, especially since it provides the cover for the cheap core and fireball effects, masking their simplicity. Even with the expensive core and fireball, the smoke needs to be rather detailed to sell the effect. Many game explosions ignore smoke, but it is a rather convincing detail.

As the smoke shoots out of the center, it will use the same basic technique as the fireball. Each particle will shoot in a random direction with a very high velocity and exponential decay. Each particle should start out stretched in the direction of its velocity and then relax into the shape of a square over time as shown in Figure 5.6.4. After about 0.3 seconds, the smoke should begin to fade out very slowly (slower than the fireball step).

During the course of each smoke particle's lifetime, it should be carried by the wind and thermal buoyancy just like the core and fireball. However, there is one more effect that can add a nice touch. Normally, smoke has lots of billowing and interesting turbulence. This can be caricatured by rotating the smoke particles. The trick is to determine the wind direction as projected to screen space and rotate the particles to simulate subtle vorticity. All smoke particles on the left side of the wind direction should rotate counterclockwise, and all smoke particles on the right side of the wind direction should rotate clockwise, as shown in Figure 5.6.5. The rotations should be very slow, and each particle should have a different randomly determined angular velocity.

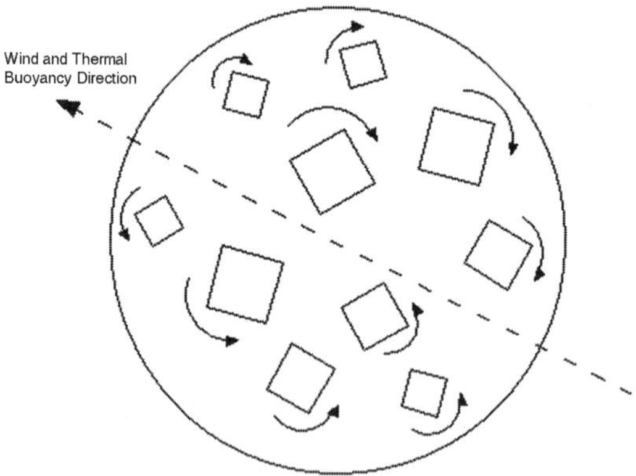

FIGURE 5.6.5 *Faked rotational turbulence based on the wind and thermal buoyancy direction.*

Debris

No explosion would be complete without debris flying from it. The debris can be embers, small dark chunks of dirt/metal, pieces on fire leaving smoke trails, or whole pieces of whatever just blew up. The debris should be given a high initial velocity and should not decay like the other gaseous effects. Instead, the initial velocity coupled with gravity should drive its motion.

Dark debris is quite effective, since it has a high contrast with the explosion itself. A cartoonish look can be achieved by having chunks of debris give off smoke trails as they sail away from the explosion. Usually these smoke trails give off smoke particles that start off hot white and change over time to yellow, orange, light gray, then finally dark gray. Of course, these smoke trails require rendering of even more particles, so the effect has to be used judiciously to maintain acceptable performance.

Effects Table

The previous effects involved many precise timings, velocities, and forces. Table 5.6.1 lists each effect with all the relevant data so that you can easily compare and recreate the explosion effect. Referring to Color Plate 8A will also help you understand the precise timing of each effect.

Table 5.6.1 Comparison of the Timings, Velocities, and Forces Involved for Each Effect

Effect	Particles	Start Time (sec)	Fade Up	Fade Down	Scale Up	Outward Velocity	Other Forces
Initial Flash	1	0.0	quickly	very quickly	very quickly	none	none
Radial Flares	10 to 30	0.0 to 0.2	instantly	quickly after 0.1 seconds	none	none	none
White Hot Inner Core (cheap)	1	0.0	instantly	very slowly after one second	quickly with exponential decay	none	wind and thermal buoyancy
White Hot Inner Core (expensive)	100	0.0	instantly	very slowly after one second	none	very fast with exponential decay	wind and thermal buoyancy
Intense Fireball (cheap)	1	0.1	instantly	slowly after 0.3 seconds	quickly with exponential decay	none	wind and thermal buoyancy
Intense Fireball (expensive)	50	0.1	instantly	slowly after 0.3 seconds	slowly until square	very fast with exponential decay	wind and thermal buoyancy
Smoke	30 to 50	0.1	instantly	very slowly after 0.3 seconds	slowly until square	very fast with exponential decay	wind and thermal buoyancy
Debris	10 to 100	0.0 to 0.2	instantly	depends	none	fast with exponential decay	gravity

Extra Touches

The billboard effects presented so far will create a nice explosion, but the following extra touches can help make the explosion really come alive.

Randomness

While this article presented a great deal of timing information for start times, fading rates, and velocities, the entire effect is much more effective if each particle is unique and isn't in lockstep with the others. Randomness should be used to tweak all these times, rates, and velocities, but it helps to keep the randomness within narrow ranges. Most of the particles need to behave similarly, so the randomness shouldn't introduce any large variations.

Screen Shake

When a powerful explosion takes place, the perceived intensity can be amplified by briefly shaking the camera up and down (not left and right). Not every explosion might warrant this effect, but close or powerful explosions will certainly be enhanced by the brief shaking.

Efficiency Concerns

There are several efficiency concerns that are raised when many explosion effects occur at the same time. The following explains how to deal with three such concerns.

Controlling the Number of Particles

In a game, it is typically difficult to control how many near-simultaneous explosions occur at a time, due to the unpredictability of the players or AI. Therefore, the cost of each explosion effect should be relatively small since the cumulative cost can skyrocket quickly. Not only must each particle be updated every frame, but all particles from all explosions must be sorted on the CPU in order to blend correctly with the frame buffer. As more particles are drawn, the sorting cost will rise exponentially.

The explosion effect described in this article showed how to make a cheap white hot inner core and a cheap fireball in order to limit the number of particles. The cheaper explosion effect uses about 43 particles (not including optional debris). The more expensive explosion effect uses about 230 particles (not including optional debris) and has considerable overdraw, which can be expensive for the GPU.

Choosing whether to use cheap or expensive explosions is one way to limit particles, but an equally important technique is to put a hard limit on the number of drawn particles and recycle the oldest ones when the limit is about to be hit. For example, a limit of 1,000 particles may be imposed so that the fifth overlapping explosion will start to recycle particles from the first explosion. Since the first explosion is probably far into its lifetime and already fading out, the removal of these older particles is generally not noticeable, especially since new explosions are very distracting to the eye.

Optimizing Billboard Orientation

During gameplay, it might be common to see half a dozen simultaneous explosions represented by thousands of particles. Each particle must recalculate its orientation in order to face the camera each frame. This represents some serious computation, but it isn't necessary or even desirable.

Within a single explosion, if each particle faced the camera based on its center point, the particles would intersect with each other and cause ugly artifacts. Therefore, the particles within an explosion must all be oriented in the same direction. The solution is for each spawned explosion to have a single center point that travels with the explosion during its lifetime (affected by wind and thermal buoyancy). This orientation can be calculated once per frame for each explosion. All particles belonging to a given explosion then use this same orientation, reducing the number of orientation calculations from over a thousand to less than a dozen.

Sorting Particles within Framerate Constraints

With thousands of potential semitransparent particles, all must be sorted with respect to the camera so that they can be rendered properly. Unfortunately, this task falls on the CPU, so efficiency is a major concern.

It is well known that the quicksort algorithm is ideal for this type of sorting, taking on average $O(n \log n)$. However, the time that quicksort takes can fluctuate wildly each frame, even up to $O(n^2)$ in the worst case. This can be a big problem for games that are trying to maintain a fixed or respectable framerate.

One solution is to use a sorting algorithm that can be stopped after taking a specified amount of time, thus ensuring that it will never take too long. Obviously, this will cause some artifacts, as not all particles are properly sorted on every rendered frame, but this is a concession that may be acceptable in practice. The chosen algorithm must be incremental in that whenever the sorting is interrupted, the list is more sorted than when it started. Since explosions stay confined to small areas and don't move quickly, the sorted list of particles will be relatively unchanged from frame to frame.

One sorting algorithm that can solve the problem is the infamous bubblesort. This very simple sorting algorithm is well known to perform poorly, but it has two nice properties. First, it can steadily sort a list and be interrupted at any time while leaving the list intact and partially sorted. Second, if the list is sorted, it can escape early with as little work as $O(n)$. Therefore, the bubblesort algorithm can be capped, for example, to never take more than 3% of the frame time.

Conclusion

The combined explosion effect presented in this article is a detailed account of one type of explosion, performed completely with billboard particles. Since there are many types of explosions, it will take some careful tuning and creativity to caricature the explosion that you're interested in for your particular game, but hopefully many of the techniques presented in this article can be applied. The key is to study the type of explosion you're trying to recreate. This can be done by looking at reference material from the Internet, movies, and military documentaries.

Many game explosions focus on the white hot core or the fireball but could be enhanced by considering the other effects such as the flash, smoke, and camera shake. One of the key innovations in this article, shown in Figure 5.6.4, was applied to the fireball and smoke. This innovation of making the fire and smoke forcefully explode from the center is very convincing in showing a sense of intensity and power. Without it, the fireball and smoke just seem to be static puffs that quickly move away from the center. This disparity can best be seen in two of the example movies on the CD-ROM. The file explosion1.mpg uses the pointy fireball and smoke technique, while explosion2.mpg does not. The other explosion movies on the CD-ROM are supplied to show different variations.

ON THE CD

Creating good explosions for games is a balancing act of trying to get the best effect within the limits of the hardware. Until we can simulate or replay explosion simulations with tens of thousands of particles per explosion, it will surely take both programming wizardry and artistic creativity to get the most bang for the buck.

References

[Fedkiw01] Fedkiw, R., J. Stam, and H. W. Jensen. "Visual Simulation of Smoke." *The Proceedings of ACM SIGGRAPH*, 2001.

[Feldman03] Feldman, B. E., J. F. O'Brien, and O. Arikan. "Animating Suspended Particle Explosions." *The Proceedings of ACM SIGGRAPH*, 2003.

[Stam03] Stam, Joe. "Real-Time Fluid Dynamics for Games." *Proceedings of the Game Developers Conference*, 2003.

5.7

A Simple Method for Rendering Gemstones

Thorsten Scheuermann, ATI Research

thorsten@ati.com

Many games require players to find or earn treasure in order to advance in the game environment. This article discusses a technique for rendering gemstones that could be used to reward successful treasure-hunting players with neat eye candy.

The beautiful and complex appearance of gemstones is mainly due to their transparent material that has a high index of refraction. This causes chromatic dispersion and total internal reflection of light rays traveling through the gem.

The gem-rendering technique for this article was used in ATI's Radeon X800 launch demo *Ruby: The Double Cross* (see Figure 5.7.1).

FIGURE 5.7.1 *A screenshot from ATI's demo Ruby: The Double Cross showing the gem rendering technique in action. © ATI Technologies, Inc. 2004.*

Overview of the Technique

Our gem-rendering technique combines lighting terms for light transmitted through the gem, reflections (using a cubic environment map), and specular highlights. For the transmitted lighting term we render the back and front faces of the gem separately. The reflections and specular highlights are only computed for the front-facing geometry.

The appearance of a gem is dominated by light traveling through the gem and bouncing around its interior due to total internal reflection, which unfortunately is expensive to simulate properly. The gem-rendering technique described in [Guy04] performs fairly accurate simulation of light transmission in gemstones at interactive frame rates, but its performance is not acceptable for a game scenario on current-generation hardware. We use a "refraction" cubemap for computing a simple approximation of the transmitted lighting term. Several samples from this cubemap are accumulated to give the appearance of total internal reflection and several light bounces inside the gem.

Finally, to make the gem look very shiny, we render a number of light flares over its brightest regions using screen-aligned billboards.

Normals and Cubemap Sampling Issues

Cut gemstones have flat facets and hard edges, which introduce shading discontinuities. However, when using gem geometry with unshared vertices and vertex normals set to face normals, the reflected and refracted view vector will not change much over each face. When these vectors are used to look up into the reflection and refraction cubemaps, only small regions of the cubemaps are sampled and magnified over the gem's facets (Figure 5.7.2a). Using smooth vertex normals improves cubemap sampling coverage, but the shading discontinuities along face edges disappear (Figure 5.7.2b). As a compromise, our gem geometry contains both face and smooth normals. For reflection and refraction vector computations, we use the average of both normals which results in a reasonable rate of change for normals interpolated across faces. This improves cubemap sampling coverage while still maintaining edge discontinuities (Figure 5.7.2c).

Transmitted Light

To compute the transmitted lighting term, we use a very simple approximate form of precomputation: an offline renderer that can account for total internal reflection through raytracing generates a cubemap from inside the gem looking out. Figure 5.7.3a shows the refraction cubemap used in the screenshots of this article. It was generated in Maya using raytracing with the recursion depth set to four bounces. The lighting environment in the offline renderer was approximated with an environment map. Although the gem geometry is simple, the cubemap captures a lot of the visual complexity due to the complex path light rays follow when traveling through the gem.

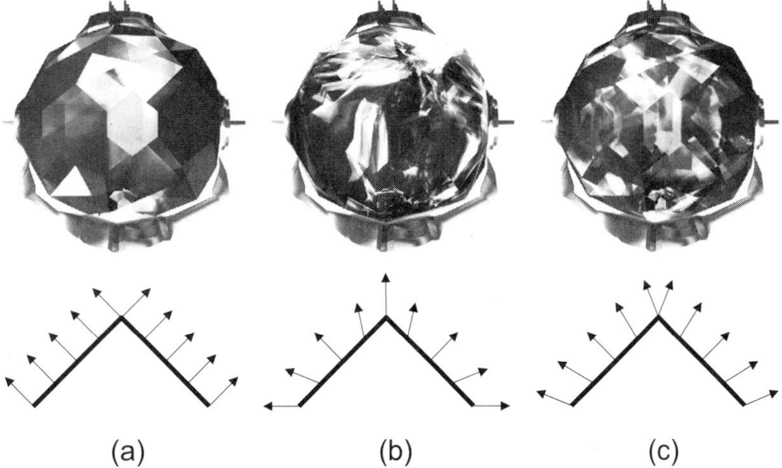

FIGURE 5.7.2 *Visual effect of using different normals: (a) face normals, (b) smooth normals, (c) averaged normals.*

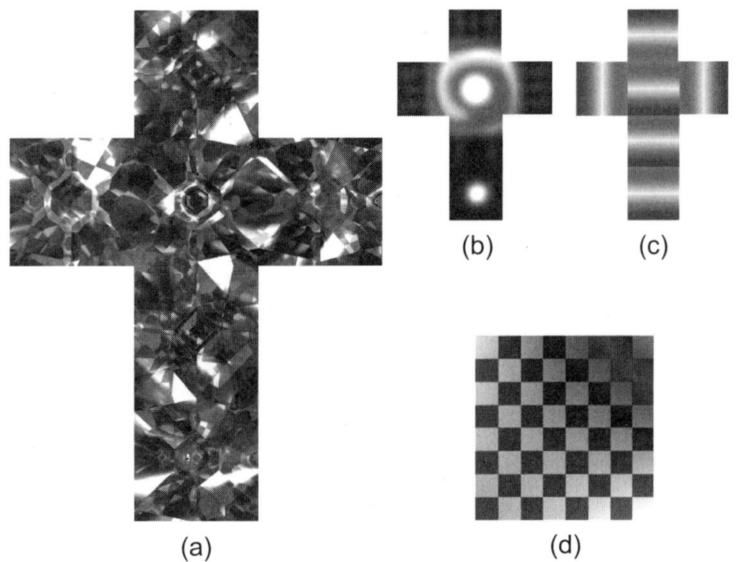

FIGURE 5.7.3 *Textures used in the examples: (a) refraction cubemap, (b) environment cubemap, (c) rainbow cubemap, (d) edge map.*

The gem pixel shader performs two lookups from the refraction cubemap and accumulates them. The gem's back and front faces are rendered in separate passes with the front faces using additive blending, so that ultimately a total of four refraction cubemap samples are accumulated for the final image. Figure 5.7.4 illustrates how the transmitted lighting term is computed.

For each pass, the vectors used to look up into the refraction cubemap are two refraction vectors computed with a different index of refraction. Additionally, the second refraction vector undergoes a reflection in a per-face random direction and an additional arbitrarily chosen swizzle. The random reflection direction is looked up in a 1D texture containing random values with a texture coordinate computed in the vertex shader based on the face normal in model space:

```
rndTexcoord = dot(N_face_model, float3(1, 1, 1));
```

The semirandom reflection and swizzling causes the two vectors to look up into different regions of the refraction cubemap, which results in a more complex appearance of the transmission term. Rendering two passes instead of just performing four cubemap lookups on just the front-facing geometry has the advantage that different normals are used in the computation on back and front faces, which yields more diverse sampling locations in the cubemap.

An additional way to increase visual complexity is by mapping a texture with hard edges (the "edge map") on the gem's geometry and modulating it with the transmission term (see Figure 5.7.4). In our example, we use a simple colored checkerboard pattern (see Figure 5.7.3d). The colors of the edge map help to give the illusion of chromatic dispersion (light splitting into a color spectrum due to the physics of refraction). The strength of this effect is controllable by a parameter that blends the edge map to white.

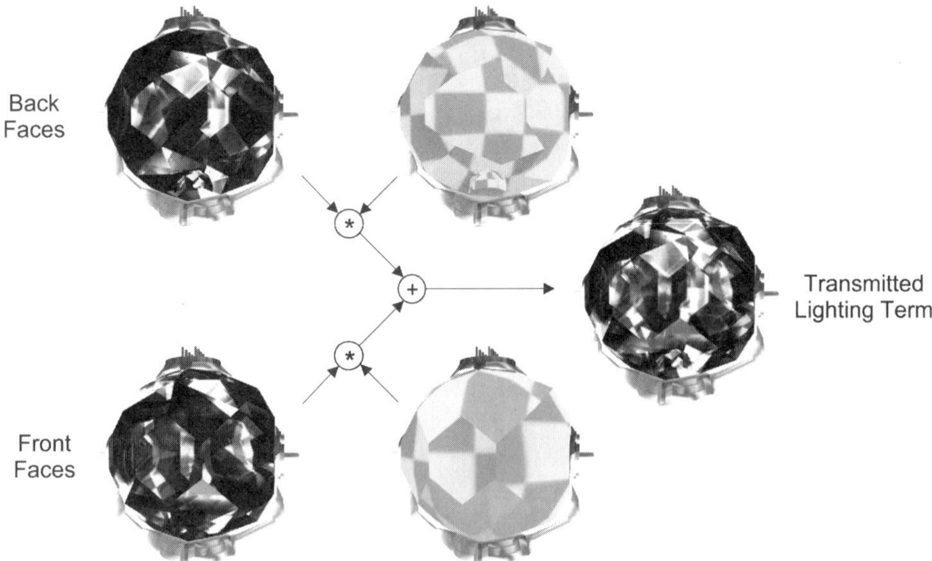

FIGURE 5.7.4 *Breakdown of the steps for computing the transmitted lighting term.*

Here is the HLSL function for the transmitted light term:

```
sampler tRefraction; // refraction cubemap
sampler tEdge;       // edge map
sampler tRandom;     // 1D texture with random RGB values

float3 TransmissionTerm (float3 N_curved,     // averaged normal
                         float3 V,            // view vector
                         float2 edgeUV,
                         float rndTexcoord,
                         float brightness,
                         float edgeStrength)
{
  // Compute refraction vectors
  float3 vTransmission1 = refract(V, N_curved, 2.4);
  float3 vTransmission2 = refract(V, N_curved, 1.8);

  // Reflect second vector by a unit vector random to each face.
  // rndTexcoord is computed in the vertex shader based on the
  // face normal in model space.
  float3 rnd = tex1D(tRandom, rndTexcoord);
  rnd = normalize(2.0 * rnd – 1.0);
  vTransmission2 = reflect(vTransmission2, rnd);

  // Lookup into refraction cubemap and apply gamma
  float3 cRefract = texCUBE(tRefraction, vTransmission1);

  // Look up again, swizzling the vector for additional
  // "randomness"
  cRefract += texCUBE(tRefraction, vTransmission2.yxz);

  // Apply gamma curve to cubemap to bring out bright regions
  // (this could be folded into the cubemap)
  cRefract = pow(cRefract, 4.0);

  // Edge term
  float3 edge = tex2D(tEdge, edgeUV);
  edge = lerp(1.0, edge, edgeStrength);

  // Modulate with edge term and scale overall brightness
  return cRefract * edge * brightness;
}
```

Reflections

The reflection term of the gem shader is a combination of a specular highlight from a point light source and reflections from an environment cubemap modulated by a Fresnel term. To increase the dispersion effect, we use a cubemap in which each face contains a rainbow color gradient and modulate it with the environment map (see Figure 5.7.3). Together with the Fresnel term, this creates discolorations around the edge of the gem (see the final result in Figure 5.7.5e). As with the dispersion from the edge map, the strength of this effect can be controlled by brightening the rainbow cubemap.

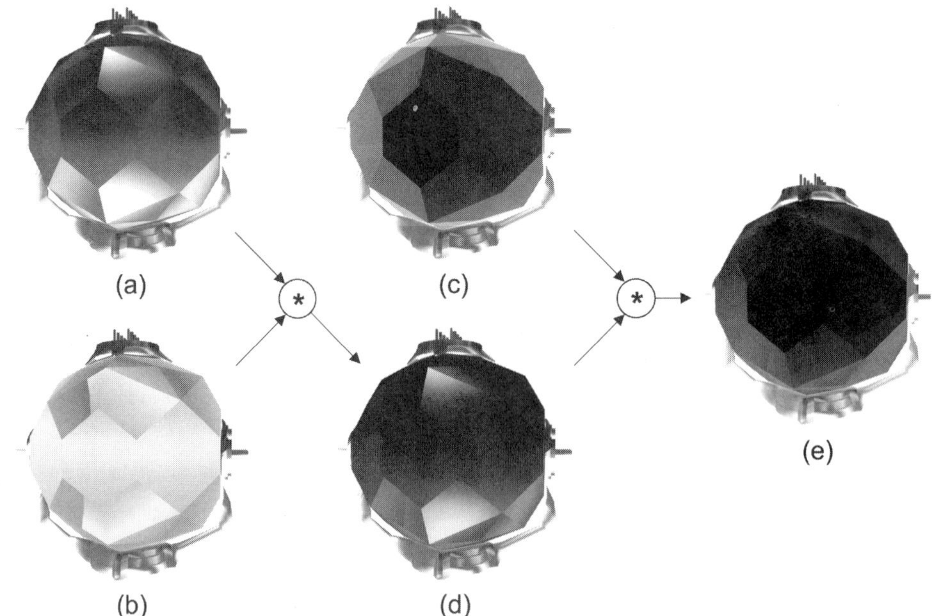

FIGURE 5.7.5 *Breakdown of the steps for computing reflections with dispersion. (a) Environment map reflections, (b) rainbow cubemap samples, (c) Fresnel term, (d) product of (a) and (b), (e) final result.*

Here is the HLSL code to compute the reflection term:

```
sampler tEnvironment;      // environment cubemap
sampler tRainbow;          // rainbow cubemap

float3 ReflectionTerm (float3 N_curved,        // averaged normal
                       float3 N_face,          // flat face normal
                       float3 V,               // view vector
                       float3 L,               // light vector
                       float3 lightColor,
                       float shininess,        // specular exonent
                       float dispersionStrength)
{
  // Reflection vectors
  float3 R_face = reflect(V, N_face);
  float3 R_curved = reflect(V, N_curved);

  // Specular highlight
  float RdotL = clamp(dot(R_face, L));
  float3 specular = pow(RdotL, shininess) * lightColor;

  // Fresnel term approximation
  float fresnel = pow(1.0 – clamp(dot(N_face, V)), 2.0);
```

```
    // Look up in environment map
    float3 cEnv = texCUBE(tEnvironment, R_curved);
    float3 cRainbow = texCUBE(tRainbow, R_curved);

    // Modulate environment map by fresnel term and dispersion
    cRainbow = lerp(1.0, cRainbow, dispersionStrength);
    cEnv = cEnv * cRainbow * fresnel;

    return saturate(specular) + cEnv;
}
```

Light Flares

Rendering light flares over the gem's brightest regions can give it a more brilliant look. We place static flare billboard geometry on the gem's surface and throughout its interior (see Figures 5.7.6b and 5.7.6c). The flare centers stay fixed relative to the gem while the flare geometry is screen-aligned in the vertex shader.

The flares are rendered with additive blending on top of the final image as a post-processing effect. Before rendering the flares, the frame buffer contents must be copied into a texture so that they are accessible in the flare pixel shader. The flare intensity is chosen in the shader depending on the luminance of the frame buffer at the flare's center position. If the luminance is below a threshold, all fragments of the flare are discarded. This causes flares to only appear over the brightest spots on the gem. Moreover, they will rapidly turn on and off as the viewing angle and the position of the gem change, which hides the fixed position of the flares relative to the gem. Additionally, the flare intensity can be modulated by a noise value dependent on the flare's screen space position and the current view direction for a more sparkly appearance.

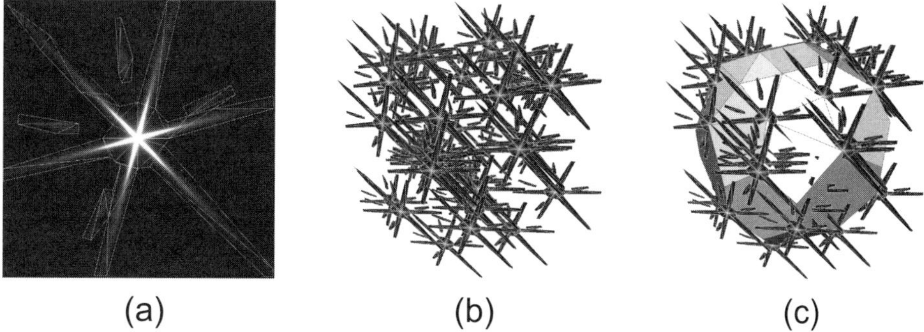

FIGURE 5.7.6 *(a) Flare geometry, (b) and (c) flares distributed throughout the gem.*

Rendering a lot of flares—most of which will be faded out at any time—can be expensive because of the high overdraw involved. To save fill overhead, it is advisable to create flare geometry that tightly bounds the nontransparent area of the flare texture (as shown in Figure 5.7.6a), which can result in better performance when compared to simple billboarded quads, which would have large empty areas.

For the billboarding vertex shader that follows to work properly, all vertices that belong to a flare have to have the same vertex position located at the flare center. The flare's shape is determined by the 2D texture coordinates, as shown in the shader code.

Following is a flare vertex shader:

```
float4x4 mWorldViewProj;
float4x4 mWorld;
float4x4 mView;
float3 worldCamPos;
float flareRadius;

struct VsInput
{
  float4 pos      : POSITION0;
  float2 uv       : TEXCOORD0;
};

struct VsOutput
{
  float4 pos          : POSITION0;
  float2 uv           : TEXCOORD0;
  float2 noiseUV      : TEXCOORD1;
  float2 screenUV     : TEXCOORD2;
};

VsOutput main (VsInput i)
{
  VsOutput o;

  // Screen-align billboard geometry and transform
  // Note that all vertices of one flare must be set to the flare
  // center position. The shape of the flare is determined by the
  // texture coordinates.
  float2 pos2D = i.uv – 0.5;
  float4 pos = i.pos + (pos2D.x * mView[0] +
                        pos2D.y * mView[1]) * flareRadius;
  o.pos = mul(pos, mWorldViewProj);

  // Compute screen space position of flare center
  float4 flareCenterPos = mul (i.pos, mWorldViewProj);
  o.screenUV = flareCenterPos.xy/flareCenterPos.w;
  o.screenUV.y = -o.screenUV.y;
  o.screenUV = 0.5 * o.screenUV + 0.5;

  // View vector to flare center
  float3 V = normalize(worldCamPos – mul(i.pos, mWorld));

  // Pass along texture coordinate
  o.uv = i.uv;
```

```
    // Compute some "random" texture coordinates depending on the
    // position and view vector, which are used to look up into a
    // noise texture in the pixel shader.
    o.noiseUV.x = fmod(abs(dot(pos.xyz, float3(1, 1, 1))), 2.0);
    o.noiseUV.y = fmod(abs(2.0 * dot(V, float3(1, 1, 1))), 2.0);

    return o;
  }
```

Following is a flare pixel shader:

```
  sampler tFlare;            // flare texture
  sampler tNoise;            // 2D noise texture
  sampler tScreen;           // back buffer contents

  float flareIntensity;

  struct PsInput
  {
    float2 uv       : TEXCOORD0;
    float2 noiseUV  : TEXCOORD1;
    float2 screenUV : TEXCOORD2;
  };

  float4 main (PsInput i) : COLOR
  {
    // Sample flare texture
    float fAlpha = tex2D(tFlare, i.uv);

    // Get noise value for flare intensity
    float noise = tex2D(tNoise, i.noiseUV);
    noise = lerp(0.6, 1.0, noise);

    // Get screen luminance at flare center
    float3 cScreen = tex2D(tScreen, i.screenUV);
    float lum = dot(cScreen, float3(0.3, 0.59, 0.11));

    // Discard fragment if luminance is less then 0.8
    clip(lum - 0.8);

    // Pull luminance for visible flares into [0, 1] range
    // and apply a gamma
    lum = smoothstep(0.8, 1.0, lum);
    lum *= lum;

    float4 o = 0;
    o.rgb = noise * lum * fAlpha * flareIntensity;
    return o;
  }
```

Conclusion

This article described a technique for rendering gemstones that performs well on current graphics hardware. This method largely ignores physical accuracy and instead concentrates on an interesting look that would fit in a typical game environment. Transmitted light is approximated using lookups into a precomputed refraction cubemap. The reflection term is a combination of a reflection cubemap and specular lighting. The illusion of chromatic dispersion is created by simple blending of different textures. Flares are rendered over bright spots on the gem using billboards in a post-processing pass.

Our rendering technique uses tricks that could be applied in other scenarios: averaging face and smooth normals can be useful for shaders on geometry with hard edges. The flare post-processing technique can be generalized to cover the complete image and used for special effects. Finally, complex particle geometry that bounds the nonempty regions of a particle texture—as used for the flares—might help improve performance on fill-bound particle systems.

Reference

[Guy04] Guy, Stephane and Cyril Soler. "Graphics Gems Revisited." *ACM Transactions on Graphics (Proceedings of the SIGGRAPH conference)*, 2004.

5.8

Volumetric Post-Processing

Dominic Filion, Artificial Mind & Movement

dfilion@hotmail.com

Sylvain Boissé, Motorola

sylvainboisse@hotmail.com

With the ubiquity of programmable graphics hardware, we are seeing increasing interest in customized post-processing effects. Effects such as pixel displacements, blooms, and glows are common post-processing effects in today's games. Typically, post-processing effects are inherently 2D. Pixel displacement effects, for example, will transform pixels so as to warp the image, simulating refraction due to heat or some special effect. This process is typically applied to a specific subregion of the image and does not take into account issues of object ordering and shape. As an example, consider a heat shimmer effect shown in Figure 5.8.1. The heat given off by the fire should warp objects seen through it, displacing pixels to form an undulating wave pattern. Done naïvely, the heat shimmer effect will warp not only objects behind the fire but also objects *in front* of it, which is incorrect. Clearly, the post-processing effect needs some form of depth awareness. This gem will discuss how we can integrate depth information into our image-space operations using *volumetric post-processing.*

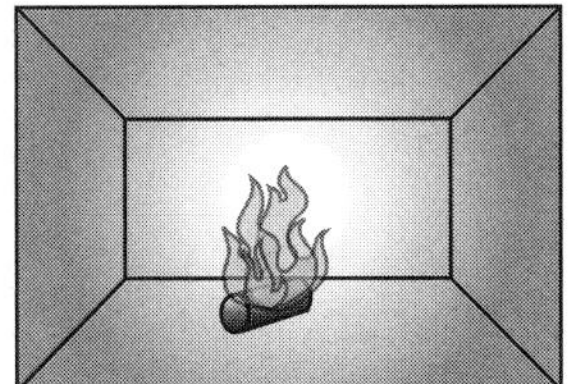

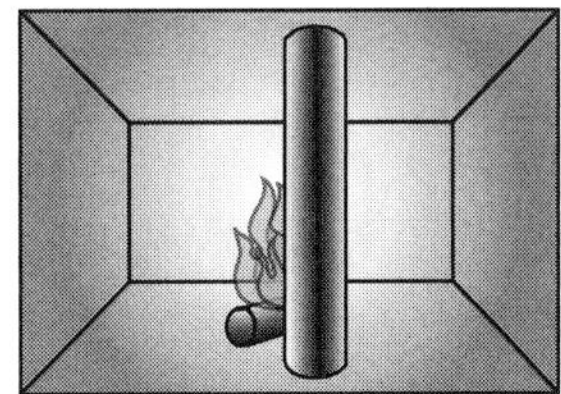

FIGURE 5.8.1 *Correct post-processing. The heat from the fire should distort the wall seen behind it. However, if an object such as a column is put in front of the object, the column should not be affected by the heat shimmer.*

Volumetric Post-Processing

To apply our volumetric post-process, we will define the concept of a post-process volume. The *post-process volume* is a 3D object that will affect any scene pixels that are behind it. Figure 5.8.2 shows an example of a post-process volume.

FIGURE 5.8.2 *The post-process volume.*

Unlike standard post-processes, we are using a 3D shape, not a 2D image-space rectangle, as our post-process region. The post-process volume defines a region—it is not meant to be rendered directly. The post-process volume could be a simple cube as shown in Figure 5.8.2 or it could be defined by a more arbitrary shape as discussed in [Oat04]. Naturally, some scene objects may penetrate the post-process volume, causing only a portion of the object to be distorted.

Depth Awareness

With our post-process volume defined, we can classify our scene in two sets: regions that are behind the front of the volume and regions that are in front of it. We could simply sort the objects in our scene to try and figure out the spatial relationship with the post-process volume; however, this would not work for objects intersecting the volume and would not be robust in general for arbitrary scenes.

In effect, we need to:

- Render only objects that are behind or contained by our post-process volume to an offscreen render target.
- Apply the post-process effect (i.e., a warp to simulate refraction due to heat) to the render target.
- Render objects that are in front of the post-process volume.

The first problem is how to render only objects that are behind the post-process volume in image space. We would like to compare the z-values of the pixels of the scene that we render to the *z*-values of the pixels of the post-process volume and only allow those *z*-values that are greater than the post-process volume's *z*-values.

This would suggest that using a simple *z*-buffer greater-than comparison mode would do the trick; unfortunately, changing the *z*-buffer test from its normal less-or-equal value to greater-than will ruin the hidden surface removal for the scene in general. Essentially, we want the nearest pixel that is behind the front of the post-process volume to remain in the frame buffer. Having two *z*-buffer tests that would each compare values from separate source frame buffers would do the trick (greater-than post-process volume and less-or-equal current frame buffer *z*-value) but no such concept exists in hardware depth buffering.

Using Shaders for *z*-Compares

Since the graphics card does not natively support multiple depth buffer tests, the solution is to add this functionality to the videocard through the use of vertex and pixel shaders. We will implement the comparison with the post-process volume this way.

Naturally, we first need a value with which to compare. The post-process volume's *z*-values must be calculated and stored in an image buffer that will be the same size as the main framebuffer. We cannot use the *z*-values in the videocard *z*-buffer directly, since these values are typically encoded or compressed in a hardware-specific format.

Instead, we can use a vertex shader to compute these *z*-values ourselves. These values can be passed to a pixel shader through an interpolator and stored in a texture. Since high precision is needed on values computed, it is necessary to use a floating-point texture. We only need to store a single floating-point value per pixel, so we use a `D3DFMT_R32F` format texture in Direct3D. Since not all hardware supports float textures, a standard color texture still can be used as a fallback. This can result in precision limitations that create subtle artifacts on screen, though this can be reduced using workarounds such as reducing the Far/Near ratio when computing the depth values.

Storing the *z*-values of our post-process volume into a single-component floating-point texture gives us the values we need so we can find objects that are behind the post-process volume. We will refer to this texture with the post-process volume's *z*-values as the *volume's depth texture*. We want only objects behind and *within* our post-process volume to be affected by the post-process.

Pixel-Perfect Clipping

The volume's depth texture can now be compared with the pixels of the scene. The depth texture is first selected as an active texture. As before, a vertex shader will compute the *z*-values in the scene and transfer them to a pixel shader.

We will also need to know which pixels in our frame buffer correspond to which pixels in the depth texture. To achieve this, the vertex shader will perform the perspective transformation to screen space. The screen space coordinates will then be normalized by the vertex shader to a normalized 0..1 range so that the screen coordinates correspond to UV coordinates on the depth texture. These UV coordinates are passed to a pixel shader using an interpolator. The pixel shader can then use these UV coordinates to look up the post-process volume's z-value in the depth texture, as illustrated in Figure 5.8.3.

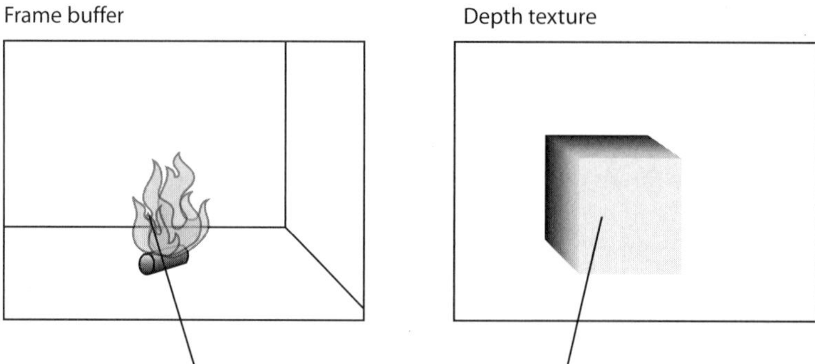
Frame buffer
Depth texture
Pixel in frame buffer image is compared with corresponding pixel in depth texture. In this image, darker pixels in the depth texture correspond to larger depth values.

FIGURE 5.8.3 *Looking up the depth value.*

These two z-values are compared in the pixel shader, and alpha testing is used to mask which pixels get written to the frame buffer. If the z-value of the scene pixel is greater than the post-process volume's, the alpha of the resulting pixel is set to 1, otherwise, it is set to 0. With an alpha test compare function of greater-than and an alpha reference value of 0, this allows us to kill pixels that are in front of the post-process volume. We could alternatively use the assembly `texkill` (or HLSL `clip()` intrinsic) to perform this conditional pixel killing.

After our rendering pass, what we will have is a rendered scene that is "clipped away" by our post-process volume mesh at the pixel level. The post-process volume mesh used for this clipping operation can be arbitrarily complicated, as shown in Figure 5.8.4.

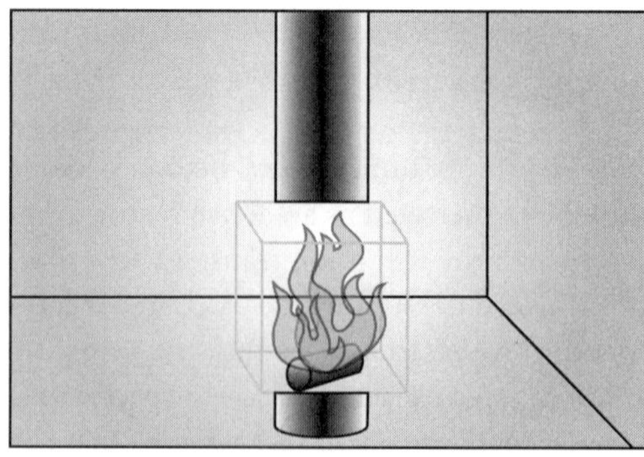

FIGURE 5.8.4 *The "clipping" operation.*

The Post-Process

As mentioned earlier, there are many post-process transforms such as distortions, blurs, and color transforms that can be applied in image space. In our example, we are modeling a heat shimmer effect, which can be suitably modeled by a traveling sine wave distortion with a slight blur. Please refer to the sample code included on the companion CD-ROM for a detailed implementation. The effect is applied by selecting the proper post-process shader (blur, displacement, bloom, etc.) and re-rendering the post-process volume. This will apply the post-process only to pixels within the volume.

ON THE CD

The Final Pass

At this stage, we will have rendered what is behind the post-process volume and applied our effect to our post-process area. We now must render the undistorted polygons that are in front of the post-process volume. This is exactly the reverse of the operation conducted in the first pass of the algorithm. Here, pixel alpha will be 1 when the *z*-value of the scene polygon is *less* than the post-process volume's and 0 otherwise. At this point, the image will be completed.

Multiple Volumes

Our technique could be used with multiple post-process volumes as long as the volumes are nonintersecting and are easily sortable by their *z*-order. Given these conditions, our algorithm extends to:

1. Clear frame buffer.
2. Clear depth texture to zero.
3. Select greater-than *z*-buffer comparison test and render all post-process volumes into depth texture, storing *z*-values as floating-point values in depth texture.
4. Set *z*-buffer test to *less*, not *less-or-equal*, to save on fillrate (we will be rendering the same polygons multiple times) and render the scene with a vertex shader calculating *z*-values and a pixel shader filtering out pixels that are in front of *z*-values calculated in depth texture.
5. Apply post-processing effect of farthest post-process volume to screen.
6. Go back to step 2, this time excluding the post-process volume that is farthest away from the viewer. Loop through steps 2 to 5 multiple times, removing the next farthest post-process volume on each loop until there are no volumes left.

For an example of how this process works with multiple volumes, refer to the top-down view shown in Figure 5.8.5. Say a scene contains nonintersecting post-process volumes A, B, and C. On the first loop, all three volumes are rendered into the depth texture. This will cause our pixel shader to only render pixels that are behind all three volumes (region 1). Setting the *z*-buffer test to *greater-than* will ensure that the farthest front-facing polygons from the set of three volumes are stored in the depth texture. The post-process effect for C is then applied to the scene.

On the second loop, the depth texture is cleared and post-process volume A and B are rendered in the depth texture. We re-render the scene, allowing pixels that were behind A and B but were in front of C (region 2) to be written to the scene. We then apply the post-process for volume B (the farthest away in the current post-process volume set). On the third loop, only post-process volume A is rendered into the depth texture, thus adding pixels that are behind A but were in front of B and C (region 3). The post-process for volume A can then be applied. Finally, objects that were in front of all three post-process volumes are rendered (region 4). No post-process effect is applied on these.

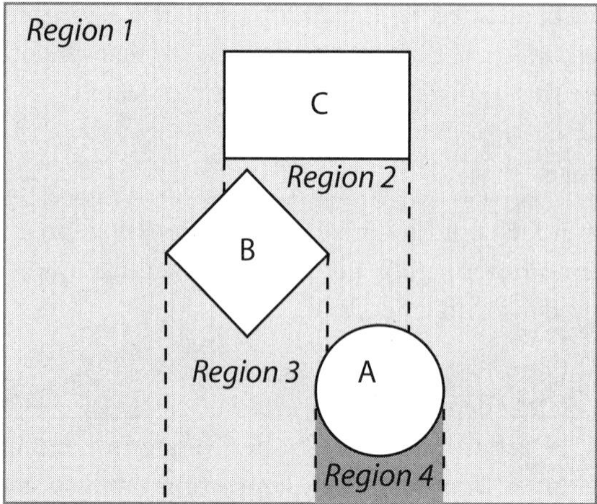

FIGURE 5.8.5 *Multiple post-process volumes.*

Conclusion

The technique presented in this gem allows an arbitrary 3D volume to be affected by a post-process effect. This can be used for dramatic effect with localized image filters.

The algorithm does rely on some recent features of videocard hardware such as shader functionality and, most importantly, floating-point textures. There can be some overhead as the scene geometry is rendered multiple times, but this can be alleviated through clever culling and a good visibility system.

The technique can also be used in many other situations where pixel-perfect 3D clipping with a volume must be achieved. One could easily imagine using this technique to provide "cutaway" views of objects or to perform voxel based processing.

References

[Isidoro02] Isidoro, John, Guennadi Riguer, and Chris Brennan. "Texture Perturbation Effects." In *Direct3D ShaderX: Vertex and Pixel Shader Tips and Tricks*, 337–346. Available online at *http://www.ati.com/developer/shaderx/ShaderX_TexturePerturbationEffects.pdf*.

[Michell02] Mitchell, Jason L. "Image Processing with 1.4 Pixel Shaders in Direct3D." In *Direct3D ShaderX: Vertex and Pixel Shader Tips and Tricks*, 258–269. Available online at *http://www.ati.com/developer/shaderx/ShaderX_ImageProcessing.pdf*.

[Oat04] Oat, Christopher and Natalya Tatarchuk. "Heat and Haze Post-Processing Effects." In *Game Programming Gems 4*. Charles River Media, 2004.

5.9

Procedural Level Generation

Timothy Roden and Ian Parberry, University of North Texas

roden@cs.unt.edu
ian@cs.unt.edu

Traditionally, a typical 3D game development project proceeds concurrently on two fronts. Programmers design, code, and test a game engine at the same time that artists create content for the game. There are compelling reasons to suggest that this paradigm may no longer be desirable or even feasible for some projects. Technical advances in hardware have enabled the use of art assets that are much more detailed than ever before. Increased storage and available RAM translates into larger game worlds. Some games require an enormous amount of content such as online multiplayer games and games that aim to provide a high level of replay. Still another factor is the increased availability of licensed engines and other high-quality middleware, which can cut engine development time significantly. What this means is high-definition art assets, which take artists longer to create, will likely be needed sooner rather than later in the development cycle. One obvious solution to this problem is to create art assets procedurally. This gem presents the ideas and techniques behind a procedural level generator. We illustrate its use to create a simple 3D dungeon.

General Methodology

We have several goals for the level generator. First, we want a prototype system to create an integrated collection of portal-rendered indoor 3D geometry—a level. The system should be as generic as possible so it can be adapted to specific needs. We want to generate levels of arbitrary size and complexity. We want the system to run fast so we can use it to generate levels dynamically during program execution. Finally, we want the level generator to rely upon human-created artwork as little as possible. Ideally, the entire level will be synthesized by the computer. In practice, however, a small amount of human-created artwork will be required to make a better quality level.

Creating a level consists of five steps:

1. Design the level.
2. Create a set of prefabricated 3D geometry.
3. Procedurally generate a 3D graph.
4. Procedurally map the prefabs to the nodes of the graph.
5. Procedurally add content (details) to the level.

Level Design

Designing a procedurally generated level has some strong similarities to designing a level by hand, at least initially. Questions have to be answered such as, what is the theme of the level? What is the general size and shape of the level? How many rooms are there? How many corridors? Since the level will be created procedurally, we get to specify some of this information parametrically. For the purposes of this gem, we create a simple dungeon consisting of corridors, stairs, and rooms.

Out of necessity, we envision our dungeon positioned on a 3D grid that partitions world space into cubic sections called cells, as shown in Figure 5.9.1a. Using a grid will simplify many implementation details, including welding of geometry, mapping world coordinates to local coordinates, automatically generating portals, and instancing of geometry. Each grid cell will be 90 feet high, 90 feet wide, and 50 feet high, as shown in Figure 5.9.1b. Each cell can contain either a corridor or a room. Geometry in each cell can connect with the geometry of up to four adjacent cells (north, south, east, and west). We allow connections between cells at either the same height or in a sloping manner. For example, we allow a corridor to connect to an adjacent corridor that is higher or lower, as shown in Figure 5.9.4. In such cases, we generate stairs to connect the two cells.

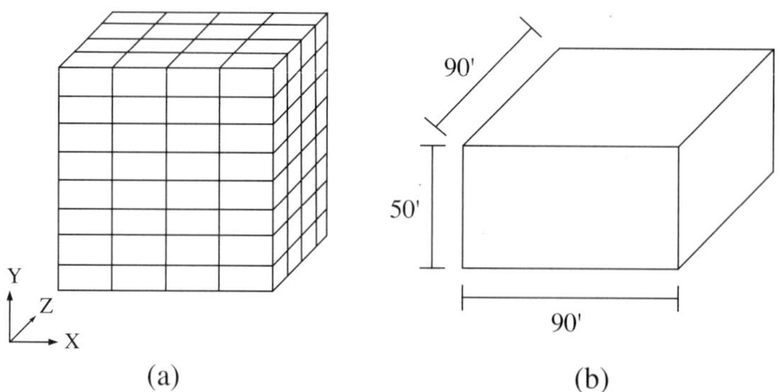

FIGURE 5.9.1 *(a) World space partitioned into cubic cells by means of a 3D grid. (b) One 3D grid "cell."*

Corridors, both flat and with stairs, are 10 feet wide. Flat corridors have 10 foot ceilings while stairs have 15 foot ceilings. Rooms are 30 by 30 feet square with 10 foot ceilings and have 10 foot open entrances (no doors). All horizontal connections between corridors are at right angles. Given these dimensions, we could lay out a 4-connected corridor in a cell, as shown in Figure 5.9.2a, or a 4-connected room, as shown in Figure 5.9.2b.

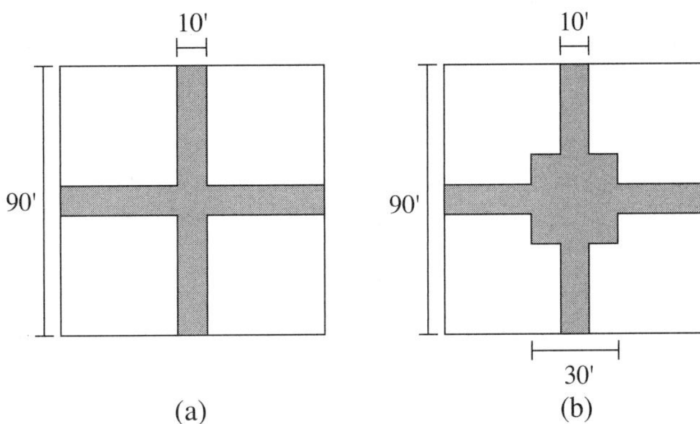

FIGURE 5.9.2 *(a) Top view of cell containing a 4-connected corridor. (b) Top view of cell containing a 4-connected 30'× 30' room.*

Using Prefabricated Geometry

In contrast to a purely procedural approach that would take our preceding definition of the level and generate the geometry for each cell, we add a human element. We want the level to look as good as possible, so it's a good idea to have an artist create portions of the actual level geometry. We use a modeling program to create a set of prefabricated geometry pieces. Using prefabs as building blocks for more complex geometry is a straightforward approach already in use in more conventional human-centered level design [Perry02].

The goal is to create a prefab for each possible cell layout. The problem with this is that even with the simple dungeon we've described so far, there is a large number of possible cell variations. Consider a cell containing a corridor. The cell could be 1-connected, 2-connected, 3-connected, or 4-connected. With 1-, 2-, or 3-connected cells, there are four different orientations. For example, a 1-connected cell could be connected to another cell to the north, south, east, or west. To make matters worse, connections can occur between cells at the same or different heights. A 2-connected cell, for example, has nine different variations, which when multiplied by its four possible orientations, gives 36 possible layouts. A 4-connected cell has 80 possible layouts, and so on.

To make the job of creating prefabs more manageable and to reuse as much geometry as possible, we subdivide each cell horizontally into 3 × 3 sub-cells, each 30 × 30 × 50 feet in dimension. Our aim is to populate a cell with geometry by welding together several smaller prefabs at execution time. As it turns out, we only need the nine small prefabs shown in Figure 5.9.3 to do this. To augment this set of sub-cell prefabs we could optionally create one or more full-cell (or sub-cell) "special" prefabs. This could be useful if our design called for the inclusion of special rooms or locations in the dungeon that couldn't be readily constructed using only the nine smaller prefabs.

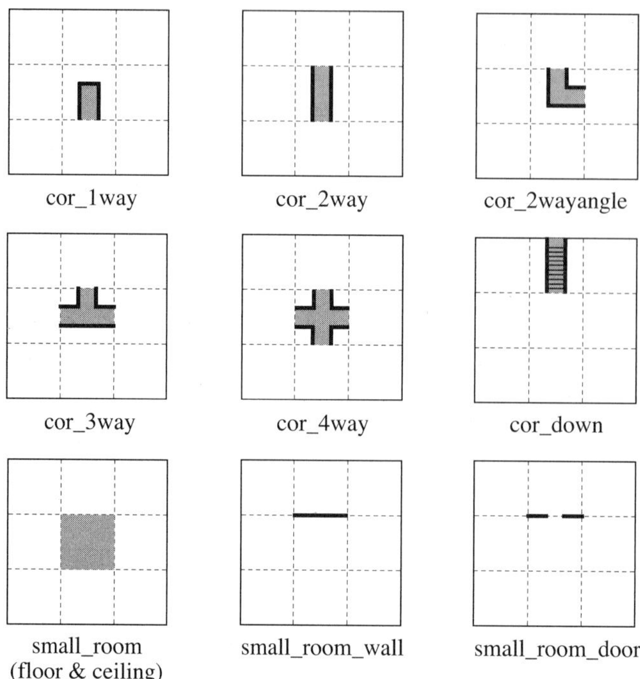

FIGURE 5.9.3 *Top view of nine prefabs needed for basic dungeon level, each shown on a 90' × 90' cell, subdivided into 3 × 3 sub-cells, each 30' × 30'.*

Graph Generation

With a design in hand and a set of prefabs to work with, we're now ready to implement the procedural part of the level generator. We generate a 3D graph data structure as a high-level representation of the procedural game level. Each node in the graph will correspond to one cell of geometry in world space. We store the nodes of the graph in an array. Each node in the graph contains the following data:

```
struct GraphNode {
  int x, y, z;  // in graph coordinates, (0,0,0 = start node)
  int dir[4];   // array index of 4 adjacent nodes (0=none,
                //   else connect to node
};              //   dir[x]-1 in array)
```

Generating a random graph presents myriad possibilities. Whatever method we devise should be driven by the design. Our design may include constraints to be placed on the graph generator. For example, we may want to enable specific sequences of rooms in the dungeon that can only be visited in a particular order.

For the purposes of this article, we generate a graph with a tentacle-like topology that radiates from the starting node in the graph (the entrance to the dungeon). With knowledge of the intended geometry, we place one constraint on the graph generator—a new node in the graph cannot be created directly under an existing node that has a connection to a lower node. The reason for this can be seen in Figure 5.9.4. In case a cell needs to connect to a lower cell, the actual geometry for the cell will drop below the cell into the adjacent lower cell. We therefore require this lower cell to remain empty since we will assume the geometry if a descending cell occupies not only the space contained by the cell but also the cell directly beneath it.

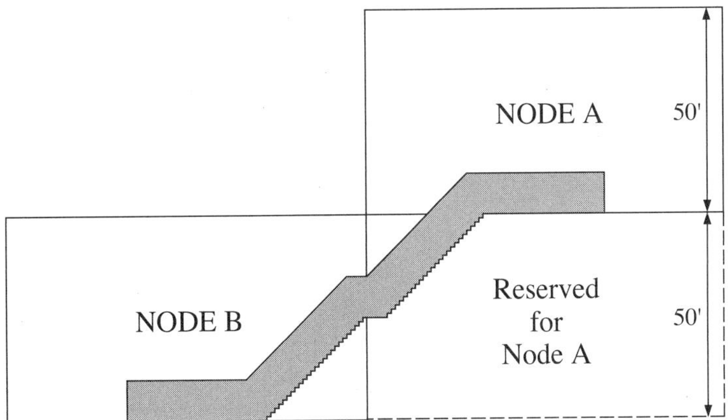

FIGURE 5.9.4 *Side view showing how two corridor nodes (cells) can connect to each other diagonally using stairs. The graph node below Node A is reserved for use by Node A.*

We begin by specifying a minimum and maximum number of nodes for the graph. We control the height of the graph by supplying a parameter that specifies the percentage of connections between nodes that will be at different heights. For example, using a value of 25% means each new node added to the graph will be at the same height as the node it is connected to about 75% of the time and at a different height about 25% of the time.

The basic algorithm works as follows. We generate a starting node that becomes the entry point into the dungeon. Since this node can have up to four connections to other nodes, we add four entries into an "available" list. Then, in a loop that executes once for each additional node we want to generate, we do the following:

1. Create a new node.
2. Randomly select from the available list an existing node as the attachment point.
3. Verify that all constraints remain satisfied.
4. Attach the new node to the graph.
5. Remove one entry in the available list for the existing node.
6. Add three entries in the available list for the new node.

If we find that attaching the new node will violate any constraints, we select another attachment point. For very complex constraints, there may not be a valid attachment point. In that case, we can either terminate the algorithm, if the minimum number of nodes have already been generated, or optionally, restart the algorithm from the beginning. When implementing a new graph generation algorithm or modifying an existing algorithm, automated testing should always be done to prove the algorithm works reasonably well.

When selecting a new node from the available list, we prefer to choose nodes created more recently as attachment points. This allows the graph to grow outward, producing a more interesting graph. A simple method for selecting an available node is to generate a random number between 1 and the number of entries in the available list. Call this value *r*. Next, generate a second random number between *r* and the number of entries in the available list. Use this second number as the index into the available list.

After the graph is created, we save the graph in both binary and text file formats. Along with the graph data, the files contain some statistics including seed values used by the random number generator. The seed values can be very useful. For example, given a fully generated level, we can regenerate it again at any time using only the seed values. An example text file is as follows:

```
num_nodes: 99
max_level: 5
adjacency: 4
min_nodes: 50
max_nodes: 100
percent_vertical_connects: 0
percent_sloping_horizontal_connects: 25
random_type: 0
random_start_seed: 1076104227
random_end_seed: 1359372770

Node: 0
  location (x,y,z): 0,0,0
  connected to nodes: 1(N)
```

```
Node: 1
  location (x,y,z): 0,-1,1
  connected to nodes: 0(S) 2(E) 3(W)
...
```

The companion CD-ROM contains the source code for the graph generator.

Mapping Prefabs to the Graph

The next step in generating the level is to cycle through each node in the graph, mapping geometry to it. We tag each node according to the type of geometry we want in the corresponding cell. Some nodes become rooms while others are tagged as corridors. We can enforce additional constraints at this point such as no two rooms are adjacent to each other.

Mapping prefabs to the graph is purely mechanical. We initialize an empty list of full-cell models. This cell-model list, when built, stores every possible variation of cell geometry found in the level. It is highly possible that multiple cells will be of the same type (room, corridor) and have the same spatial connectivity. In this case, we don't want to duplicate actual model geometry. Instead, we allow multiple nodes in our graph to instance the same geometry in the cell-model list as shown in Figure 5.9.5. Potentially, we end up with a fairly large list of models, but it is likely a smaller set than all possible variations.

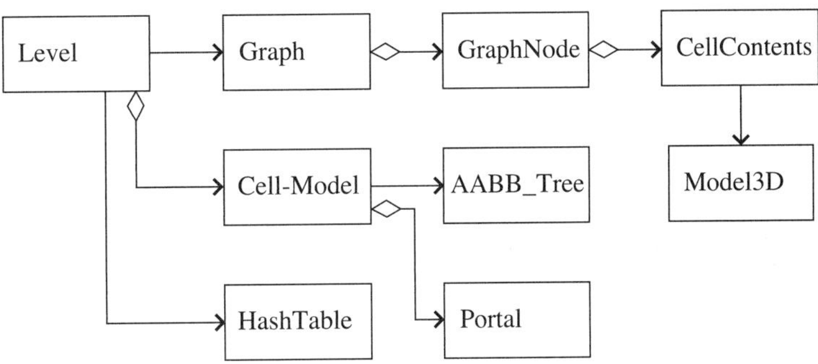

FIGURE 5.9.5 *The major data structures that make up a level.*

Using the sub-cell prefabs, we have basically shifted work from the artist to the computer by eliminating the need to generate all possible variations of cell geometry ahead of time. We also reduce the run-time storage requirements of the level by only storing the cell geometries used in the level.

For each node in the graph, we examine its connectivity information and look for previously generated geometry in the cell-model list. If identical geometry is found, we instance this geometry. Otherwise, we create the geometry for the cell and place it in the cell-model list. Creating new cell geometry proceeds as follows:

1. Gather the sub-cell prefabs needed.
2. Translate/Rotate each prefab as necessary.
3. Weld all the prefabs into a single model (see Figure 5.9.6).
4. Add this new model to the cell-model list.

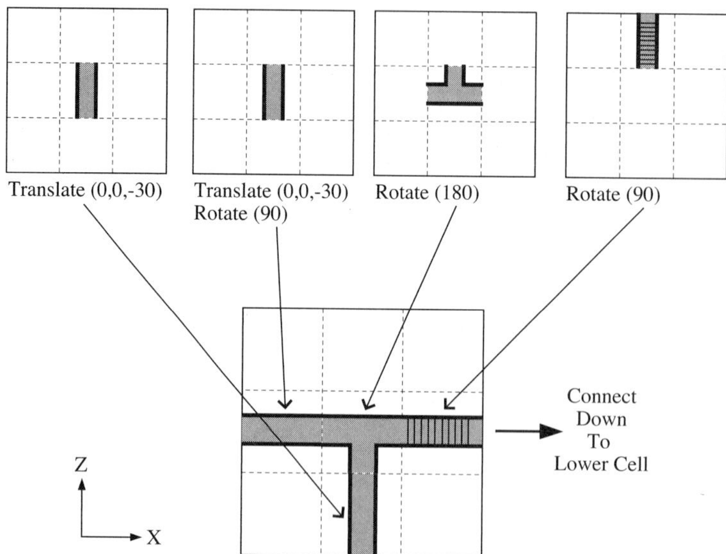

FIGURE 5.9.6 *Welding four sub-cell prefabs into a single model.*

Since our sub-cell prefabs tend to be small in terms of number of vertices, we prefer not to render them as distinct models with individual API draw calls. Instead, for efficiency and for simplicity, we want to treat the geometry of each cell in the level as a single model. To combine several smaller models into one, we must reorient and weld the geometry of all the sub-cell prefabs together into a single model for each cell, as illustrated in Figure 5.9.6. This sufficiently reduces the API overhead and allows for efficient rendering.

Visibility and Collision Detection

Once all cell geometries have been built, we dynamically generate data needed for rendering and collision detection. For each model in the cell-model list, we create an associated set of up to four portals, depending on the connectivity of the cell. Each portal is a 2D rectangle that encloses all vertices of the cell's geometry that lie on the plane connecting the cell to the adjacent cell. We use these portals to enable portal rendering of the level [Luebke95]. In contrast to the standard portal rendering philosophy of using convex cells connected via portals, we place no restrictions on the geometry in each cell. A disadvantage of using non-convex cells is that it can result in overdraw during rendering. This is outweighed, however, by the flexibility we gain from placing no limits on the cell geometry and the ease with which we can automatically create the portals.

To enable collision detection, we create a binary tree of axis-aligned bounding boxes (AABBs) for each model in the cell-model list in a manner similar to [Schroeder01]. Finally, since there is no direct relationship between a cell in the level (in world space) and its corresponding node in the graph, we create a hash table that maps world coordinates to nodes in the graph. Making the hash table efficient is vital since every reference to data in the level, using world coordinates, maps through the hash table. Some general knowledge of the potential layout of the level is helpful to make the hash function fast.

Adding Level Content

At this point, we have a basic level, perhaps large but nonetheless empty, as shown in Figure 5.9.7. Using a rule-based system, with rules derived from the design, several types of content can be added. Nodes in the graph can be annotated with environmental audio properties and other sound effects based on the size, shape, and content

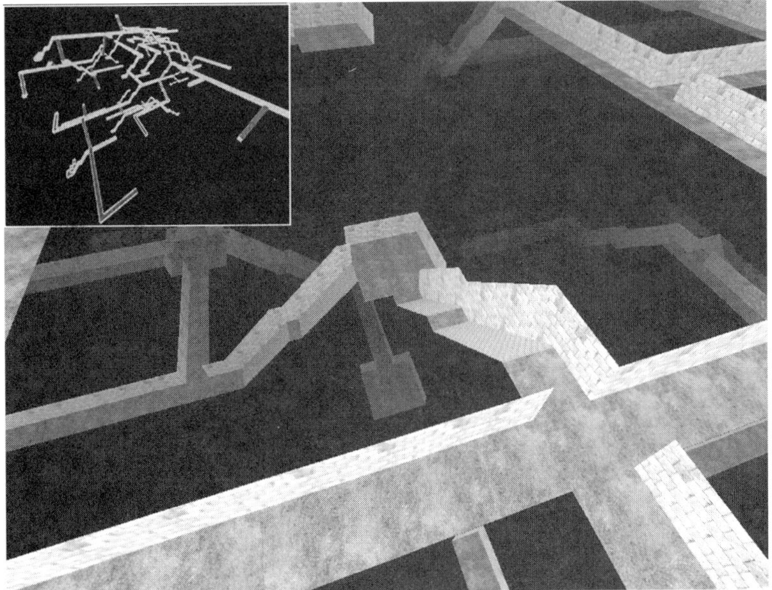

FIGURE 5.9.7 *Basic dungeon of corridors and rooms generated using a "tentacle" graph (inset). Entrance to the dungeon is via a small corridor shown at the top of the graph.*

of each node's geometry. Adding actual geometry falls into two categories. Static geometry includes augmentations to the level geometry such as pillars or statues. These are items we may want to weld to the existing cell geometry. If so, we need to make sure the cell geometry is not being instanced by more than one node in the graph. If it is, we will need to create a separate version of the cell geometry before we weld any new geometry to the cell. Welding new geometric features also requires an update to the cell's AABB tree and possibly the recalculation of portals. Nonstatic geometry can simply be added at the node level without welding.

Conclusion

We have presented a process for generating procedural game levels to address the large amount of content required by growing game genres such as massively multiplayer online games. Given an appropriate set of rules, our algorithm provides amplification of a simple data structure into a complex geometric game level [Roden04]. Our process begins by generating a 3D graph with appropriate rules. Prefabricated 3D geometric level pieces are then mapped to nodes of our graph. Identical geometry is instanced instead of being copied, taking care to weld sub-cell prefabs into a single model to reduce the number of redundant vertices and save on rendering time. We then compute visibility and collision detection information for later use by our portal algorithm. Finally, we add level content such as static geometry and environmental audio.

The method presented should be considered as a foundation for the reader in building their own level generator. One important issue we have not touched upon is lighting. A procedure for adding realistic lighting would depend not only on the design but also on how the level generator is used. If levels are generated as a pre-process, lighting can be computed using pre-processing techniques, whereas for dynamically generated levels, a different set of lighting techniques would be employed.

References

[Luebke95] Luebke, David and Chris Georges. "Portals and Mirrors: Simple, Fast Evaluation of Potentially Visible Sets." In (Pat Hanrahan and Jim Winget, editors) *ACM Symposium on Interactive 3D Graphics* (April 1995): pp. 105–106.

[Perry02] Perry, Lee. "Modular Level and Component Design." In *Game Developer Magazine* (November 2002): pp. 30–35.

[Roden04] Roden, Timothy, and Ian Parberry. "From Artistry to Automation: A Structured Methodology for Procedural Content Creation." *3rd International Conference on Entertainment Computing* (September 2004).

[Schroeder01] Schroeder, Tim. "Collision Detection Using Ray Casting." In *Game Developer Magazine* (August 2001): pp. 50–56.

5.10

Recombinant Shaders

Dominic Filion, Artificial Mind & Movement

dfilion@hotmail.com

Graphics Processing Units (GPUs) were recently brought much closer to their CPU counterparts with the introduction of shaders. GPUs went from rigid graphics processing devices to more general chips, as can be seen in the increasing amount of research being put into using shaders for physics, math computations, and raytracing.

It was only a matter of time before the advent of GPU compilers would make shaders even more useful. GPUs are indeed seeing the same evolution as their CPU counterparts (specialized chips, evolution to general purpose, compiling tools, and optimizers) but at a much faster pace.

GPUs are at this time, however, very far behind their CPU counterparts when it comes to flexibility and ease of integration.

Some issues with GPUs include:

Limited length of programs: Limited length of microprograms means that the whole application's graphics pipeline cannot be put into a single program or function, as it may have been for a software renderer.

Limited or missing branching: Lack of branching instructions in most programming models is a severe limitation that inhibits flexibility in the pipeline.

No general scatter-gather: GPUs don't have a general memory model, as their memory is not randomly accessible.

No interaction with fixed pipeline: On an API-level, shaders run on a completely different path than the standard fixed pipeline. An effect implemented in a shader must supply its own implementation for skinning, lighting, and other features that may already be present in the fixed pipeline. There is no way to effectively make "calls" into fixed pipeline circuits.

Combining Effects

In practice, the very linear nature and limited scope of the graphics pipeline along with the limitations of shader programming models described earlier tend to force applications to treat shaders as a fairly hardcoded, precanned process. This is exactly what shaders were designed to prevent!

Consider the collision of a technique like matrix palette skinning and a typical special effect. It is quite common for special effect shaders to only affect lighting, texture coordinates, or any other vertex component besides position. Yet, to be combined with skinning, the vertex shader implementer must write specialized *variants* of an effect for skinned and unskinned versions. The combinatoric explosion that this implies for even a moderately complex graphics engine means that it becomes impossible to write a single shader that will work for all situations. In fact, just supporting the full fixed-function pipeline as specified in DirectX® 9 is not possible using a single shader [Sander03]. Thus, for maximum optimality, a different vertex shader would have to be written for every possible fixed pipeline setting combination.

In this gem, we will explore ways to handle the problem of multiple shader variants, along with effective techniques to generate the variants, store them, and generally integrate a flexible shader pipeline into a 3D engine. One specific approach for flexible shader integration is presented here, but this gem will also provide many starting points that could be used for further research into novel approaches to shader integration.

Dealing with Combinatoric Explosion

First, let's categorize some of the approaches to dealing with this proliferation of shader variants.

Close-ended: This is the most common approach to the problem. Most games will write between 5 and 60+ highly specialized shaders that will handle the most common effects a game will implement. It is a viable approach when the feature set of the graphics pipeline is very clearly defined, but it does limit creativity and makes any engine code rather inflexible to changes in the game design. With this strategy, the shader variants problem is side-stepped by simply not allowing an arbitrary number of effect types to be applied in the game.

Open-ended. Generate shader variants at runtime: The most flexible approach is to actually build the shader variants at runtime. The engine renderer must analyze the current renderer settings, determine the appropriate vertex shader code fragments needed, and assemble this into a single shader. There are several ways to approach this.

- Nvidia's NVlink
- DirectX Fragment linker
- HLSL

Methods to generate shader variants can be classified as additive or subtractive. Additive methods work by adding, copying, or linking fragments of code, while subtractive methods will take a large generic shader and refine it to create a specialized variant with only the relevant subset of functionality. Here, we present a brief overview of these methods so that we can understand and point out the advantages of the novel method that we will propose.

NVIDIA'S NvLink

The NvLink tool provided by NVIDIA is an older additive method used to sew together assembly language vertex shader fragments. The `#beginfragment` and `#endfragment` keywords are placed within the shader code to delimit fragments. The INVLink interface (obtained from a library provided by NVIDIA) can then be used to link the fragments together at runtime. We will not dwell more on this technique, as its restricted use for assembly shaders severely limits its usefulness; it is mostly of historic value.

D3DX Fragment Linker

The D3DX fragment linker consists of a set of sparsely documented functions in the D3DX library. The key entrypoints are `D3DXAssembleFragments()`, `LinkShader()`, and `LinkVertexShader()`. These functions can be used to additively link shader fragments written in DirectX assembly language or compiled from HLSL.

To use the linker, a semantic prefixed with `r_` is assigned to some function parameters. These parameters then act as the glue between the shader fragments, serving as their communication channel. The vertex fragment also has to be declared with a special `vertexfragment` keyword, as shown in the following example:

```
void Transform(
    float4 vPos : POSITION,
    float4 vNormal : NORMAL,
    float3 vPositionResult : r_TransformedPosition,
    float4 vNormalResult : r_TransformedNormal )
{
    vPositionResult = mul( vPos, mWorldView );
    vNormalResult = mul( vNormal, (float3x3)mWorldView );
}

Vertexfragment Transform = compile_fragment vs_1_1 Transform();
```

`D3DXAssembleFragments()` can then be used to load all shader fragments from a given file, and `LinkShader()` can be used to combine them to construct shaders [Boyd].

Using the fragment linker is a lightweight process that can be done at runtime. The linker will resolve symbol tables, optimize register use, and remove dead code.

Generating Shader Variants through HLSL

Since shaders can be written in a high-level language, it is only natural to use the shader compiler to concatenate shader code strings together to build a more complex shader. Generating shader variants through a high-level shader language can be done using either additive or subtractive methods.

Additive Methods

Through additive methods, the shader code is built from smaller fragments of shaders. This has the advantage that small shader fragments can be written without the need to know the complete shader pipeline. In the simplest form, we are merely pasting HLSL strings together. To be truly effective, however, a strict set of rules should be defined to allow the shader fragments to interoperate.

We can view the shader pipeline as a set of atomic component blocks operating together, not unlike hardware component blocks. These blocks have input and output ports that can be used for communication. Adding fragments to HLSL code is quite simple, since they can be written as separate functions. A runtime shader combiner can then paste in the code to call the function at the relevant point in the code.

Subtractive Methods

Subtractive methods use a completely different approach to generating shader variants. A large generic shader that describes a game's *complete* pipeline, including skinning, effects, uv animations, etc., is written. Specialized versions of this generic shader are then derived through the use of constants and/or defines, as shown in the following example:

```
struct Input
{
    float4    Position        : POSITION;
    float4    Normal          : NORMAL;
};

struct Output
{
    float4     Position        : POSITION;
    float4    Color0          : COLOR0;
};

// Parameters
float4     Diffuse[8];
float4     LightDir[8];

void Main( in Input In, out Output Out )
{
    // Insertion Point

    Out.Position = mul( view_proj_matrix, In.Position );

    float3 NormView = mul( (float3x3)view_matrix, In.Normal.xyz );

    // Lighting
    Out.Color0 = AmbientCol;

    for ( float i = 0; i < LightCount; i++ )
    {
        // Directional light
```

```
            {
                Out.Color0.xyz +=     Diffuse[i] * dot( NormView, -
                                      LightDir[i].xyz );
            }
        }
    }
```

The previous example shows sample HLSL code for a simple lighting pipeline using a variable number of point lights. The previous example would actually not compile using the vs_1_ compile target since loops and conditionals are not supported.

We can prefix the code right where the `Insertion Point` comment is with:

```
LightCount = 3;
```

We have just generated a specialized variant of the code, taking a generic vertex shader and specializing it as a shader for three point lights. The shader compiler will analyze the code and find out the loop can be unrolled three times. Also notice that if we were to set `LightCount` to zero instead, the shader compiler would optimize out the whole lighting loop as well as the calculation of `NormView`.

This allows us to write a single, monolithic shader for our game. We can ignore limitations of shader microprogram length and limited registers in this generic shader as the specialized variants will weed out any unused elements.

Both additive and subtractive methods have their advantages. The additive method is closer to the true concept of *recombining* shaders as it glues shader fragments together and allows each shader fragment to be developed independently, as well as being more flexible. The subtractive approach is much simpler to use and facilitates debugging by having the programmer preassemble all fragments together early on.

Some code may need to be "switchable" through the use of `#defines` and `#ifdef` in the HLSL code. Vertex structure members that are not needed (extra uv coordinates, etc.) can be culled out through the use of `#ifdef` statements. The shader combiner can then add the necessary `#define` to include the necessary vertex components as needed.

Hybrids

One good compromise is to use a hybrid of the two methods. The subtractive method is used for the common, standard parts of the pipeline—skinning, lighting, uv animations, and so forth—while a large, generic shader is written that supports all the main pipeline features, as shown in Figure 5.10.1. Multiple *attachment points* are defined in this generic shader code where the shader code can inject function calls to *pipeline plug-ins*. These pipeline plug-ins are specialized, optional effects such as toon shaders and shadow volumes. Such pipeline plug-ins can be exposed through the art package and eventually be written by tech-savvy artists as well as programmers.

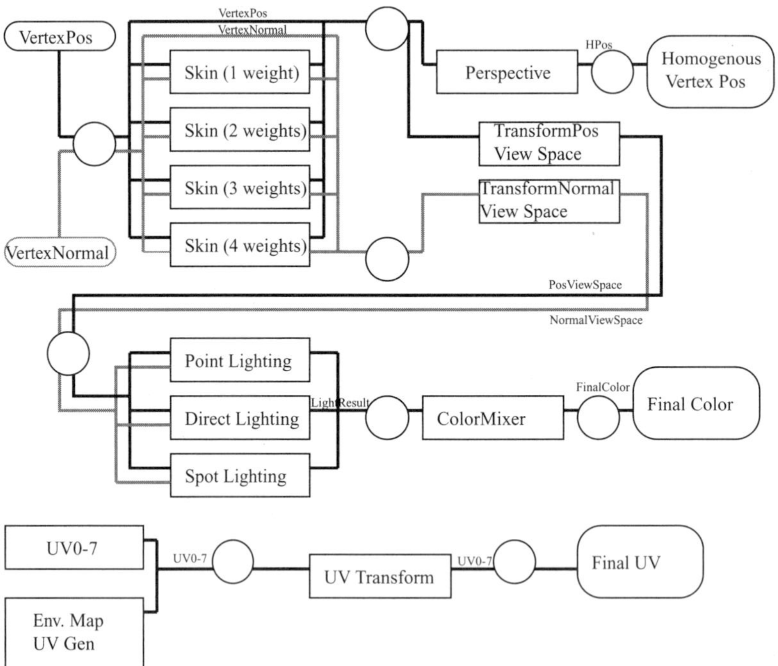

FIGURE 5.10.1 *An example pipeline using the hybrid approach.*

For the technique to work in a generalized fashion, the communication channels (function parameters and variables) between all components of the pipeline must be clearly defined and have standardized names. These are indicated in the diagram on top of the communication channel lines.

In the example, the lighting subcomponent needs the vertex position in view space. It could compute it itself, but to avoid recomputing it for each light, this task is delegated to a `TransformPosViewSpace` component that performs the transformation. The lighting subcomponent can then retrieve the view space position through the `PosViewSpace` communication channel coming out of `TransformPosViewSpace`. Components of the pipeline must be carefully planned and thought out to maximize reuse cases such as this one.

The circles in the diagram represent attachment points where "external" shader pipeline plug-ins can be attached, effectively pasted in the generic shader code at specified injection points.

Integrating Recombinant Shaders

Having described ways in which shaders can be combined together at runtime, we can examine what would be an effective setup for tying this system into a 3D engine.

Most graphics API such as Direct3D and OpenGL are mainly state machines. Several render states are set and a batch of polygons is sent to the hardware using the specified render states. Our shader system rendering interface will use the same mechanism. States will be set by an interface to our graphics subsystem and stored by the shader system until a call is made to prepare a shader to render the next batch of polygons.

Having recorded all active states, the shader system can gather all the relevant states and encode them in bit field with 64 or 128 bits. For example, the lowest 2 bits may encode the number of skinning weights that need to be used while the next 3 bits may contain the number of lights, etc. This shader *key* only describes what effects need to be activated. It does not contain specific parameters such as light positions, direction, color, etc., as these do not affect which shader fragments need to be linked in.

The shader system can then look up the key value in a STL Map. If the key is found, that particular combination of effects was used recently and thus the precompiled shader can be retrieved from the map immediately. Otherwise, a new shader variant must be generated. This generated shader can be built by taking the generic shader code, finding a proper insertion point, and using code specialization for subtractive shader combining: setting number of lights as a constant, number of skinning weights, and so forth. The shader key can be used to derive all code specialization.

To add fragments using the additive method, the shader combiner must find which shader functions it will graft to at which attachment points. Each shader fragment has a standard *callform* string for each compatible attachment point, which will be pasted into the main shader body at the specified attachment point in the main shader code's body.

After the shader is compiled, we can query the shader compiler to find which shader parameters are needed for this shader. These parameters can be uploaded to the GPU in succession, retrieving them from the active render states.

The generated shader is added to the map and associated with its key, thus giving us a cache of recently used shaders. As we generate shaders, their compiled binary size is computed. If a newly compiled shader causes the cache to exceed a threshold, the least recently used shader will be destroyed.

At this point, the shader has been compiled and activated, and the parameters have been set up. The renderer can proceed to rendering the polygon batch.

Building a Complete Pipeline through Shaders

The approach described herein allows us to achieve a flexible, unified pipeline where all shader effects can be combined together. It is actually possible using this approach to have a 3D engine using shader variants for 100% of all rendering. At the moment, this may not be ideal on all cards, as older video cards still use a specialized hardware path for fixed function transform that may make the standard fixed pipeline faster than the shader pipeline. Video cards such as the ATI RADEON™ 9600 and above, however, actually use shaders internally for all rendering, whether the fixed function pipeline API is used or not.

The sample CD-ROM contains an example of a typical fixed-function style pipeline, completely built using recombinant shaders. The sample pipeline supports:

- Skinning with one to four weights
- Arbitrary number of lights
- Point, spot, and omnidirectional lights with specular component
- Environment mapping
- UV transformations
- Multiple coloring modes: white, material color, vertex colors, dynamic lighting, vertex color + dynamic lights, vertex color * dynamic lights

Other Issues

The following sections address some other issues you should be aware of.

Shaders Version 2.0 and Beyond

It could be tempting to think that a recombinant shader system is overkill for a system that is planned to support shaders 2.0 and above only. Shaders 2.0 and above support longer shaders, some forms of branching, conditions, and loops.

Although migrating to a higher version of the shader model implies a certain amount of performance headroom, the fact remains that a short shader will still outpace a longer shader. Recombinant shaders can still be relevant for shaders above 2.0 by optimizing out major shaders variants that are often used.

Optimizing Combinations

The shader system makes all effects combinable in myriad ways. Care must still be taken to watch for excessive generation of shader variants, as any machine will buckle when handling thousands of shader variants. Compiling shaders takes time, and any steps taken to pregenerate shader variants for static assets at export time will help reduce the load. Certain similar shader variants can also be regrouped into a slightly suboptimal shader variant representing a whole shader category.

The recombinant shader system gives complete control to artists over creative aspects of special effects in games, but they should be made aware that "one effect per polygon" is not the way to go. Switching shaders often takes some time, thus polygons using the same shader keys should be batched up together.

Conclusion

Centralizing an engine around shaders without falling into the pattern of precanned effects and inflexible setups is not an easy task. However, a well-built recombinant shader system can pay off in the long run by allowing those hard-earned effects to be assembled in new and creative ways. Artists can insert small, specialized effects without requiring a complete knowledge of the shader pipeline or can even create new effects by starting from basic shader building blocks that can be recombined. Instead of having a programmer build a specialized ice shader, artists can be set loose to make their own effects by assembling more complex shaders from more elementary building blocks of the pipeline. Through recombinant shaders, the artist is truly given total control of the graphics pipeline.

References

[Bean04] Bean, Scott. *ShaderWorksXT*. Available online at *http://www.shaderworks.com/shaderworks/shaderworks-main.html*. 2004.

[Boyd02] "Direct3D Tools." Available online at *http://www.microsoft.com/korea/events/directx/ppt/Direct3DTools.ppt*. 2002.

[Frick02] Frick, Ingo. "Visualization with the Krass Game Engine." In *Direct3D ShaderX: Vertex and Pixel Shader Tips and Tricks*, 453–462.

[Lake02] Lake, Adam. "A programmable vertex shader compiler." In *Game Programming Gems 3*, 404–412. Charles River Media.

[O'Rorke04] O'Rorke, John. "Integrating Shaders into Applications." In *GPU Gems*, 601–616. Charles River Media.

[Pharr04] Pharr, Matt. "An Introduction to Shader Interfaces." In *GPU Gems*, 537–550. Charles River Media.

[Sander03] Sander, Pedro. "A Fixed Function Shader in HLSL." ATI Whitepaper, October 2003. Available online at *http://www2.ati.com/misc/samples/dx9/FixedFuncShader.pdf*.

SECTION

6

NETWORKING AND MULTIPLAYER

Introduction

Shekhar Dhupelia

sdhupelia@gmail.com

The number of networked, online games is growing. Some titles offer discrete "offline" and "online" modes, while more and more are unfolding entirely online. While the hardware and low-level technology has stayed fairly constant over the past few years, the quality of services found on each platform, and within each game, is getting better and better every year. For evidence, witness the growing number of people playing Massively Multiplayer Online Games (MMOs), or look to the popularity of Sony and Microsoft's respective online console services.

As more and more games are designed from the beginning to take advantage of this community of players, more and more teams have taken on full-time network engineers and online game designers, to exclusively focus on these gameplay aspects. While many problems have been solved, and have been neatly wrapped up for some time now, there are many new lessons to be learned every day.

This section tries to address the myriad types of online games, and should have something for everyone. Starting with MMOs, Shea Street breaks down how to use a distributed service approach to better handle the server side. Patrick "Gizz" Duquette continues with an article on implementing seamless world servers, without the zone-to-zone transitions found in titles today. This is followed by a brief look at various schemes of vulgarity filtering, applicable to all types of online games. Hyun-Jik Bae then gives a detailed explanation of how to use RPC calls for the network layer of a client/server game.

Many people with broadband connections have installed NATs in their homes; Jon Watte takes a look at how to best get through this restriction. Martin Bromlow then describes how to design a reliable messaging layer for game communication, followed by a demonstration of a random number system that is safer to use for online gameplay than standard C/C++ calls. Finally, Adam Martin returns to the series to look at how to design your game with a focus on security, no matter the type of game, to provide a better player experience.

Whether you're a commercial game developer, implementing online features in a big-budget title, or an independent developer hoping to add networked gameplay to your next great demo, these articles will both stimulate and serve as a reference for years to come.

6.1

Keeping a Massively Multiplayer Online Game Massive, Online, and Persistent

Shea Street, Tantrum Games

shea.street@tantrumgames.com

In our world of fast food, fast cars, and even faster Internet, we struggle to keep things mass produced, always available, and high quality. Creating and hosting a massively multiplayer game is no different. Our players demand the game to be just that: massive, always online, and never miss a beat. Unfortunately, we live in a world always short on time and full of unforeseen events. However, up to a certain level, we can provide these things to the player. In this article, we will discuss how to achieve these levels of uptime, by expanding on the distributed services approach [Street05].

Quick Review

The distributed services approach is a system of services distributed across multiple servers all connected to a unified network (see Figure 6.1.1).

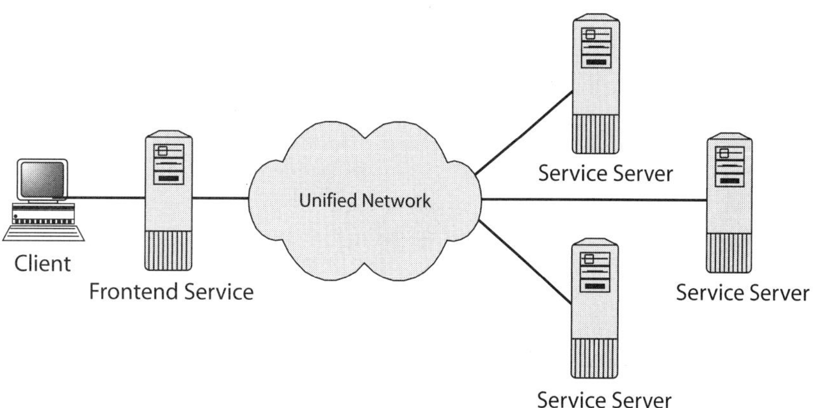

FIGURE 6.1.1 *Distributed service system diagram.*

These services provide task-specific game functionality to the entire game world. Services provide a way for the game world to distribute its load on an individual task-by-task basis. Examples of typical game services include chat services, item services, position services, AI services, and combat services (See Figure 6.1.2). By using distributed services, the entire simulation of the game is now no longer run on just a single server.

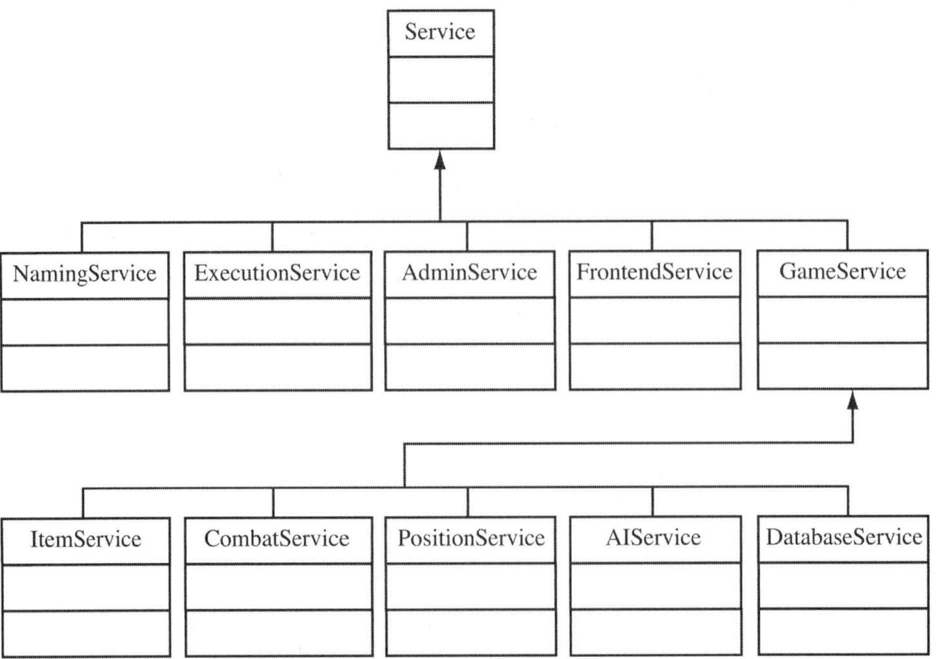

FIGURE 6.1.2 *Distributed services example breakdown.*

Being Massive

As the total number of online gamers grows, the need to support greater amounts of concurrent players also increases. There are a number of ways to tackle this obstacle.

Streamline the Frontend Service

The *frontend service* is secretly the hardest worker in the entire distributed services system. At first glance, it may appear to be just another generic gateway into an online game, but in actuality, it is so much more than that. It is important to understand the full scope of the frontend service and the best approaches to optimizing this process.

But before it could ever be optimized, its operating goals need to be properly defined. These goals and their implementations will always be game specific but are still built upon a common underlying framework of ideas. These include:

- Being an entry point for all players
- Serving as the first line of defense
- Performing sanity and error checking
- Managing and balancing bandwidth usage
- Ensuring proper routing of game information
- Providing the fastest response times possible

The frontend service acts as a middleman between the clients and the game's backend. It concentrates data from all the backend services into a single filtered usable stream for all its connected players, and vice versa. By using game specific knowledge, the frontend service can provide faster player response times while saving the backend from unwanted traffic. Creating flow charts and use cases can greatly help target, study, and develop these potential optimizations (See Figure 6.1.3).

One possible optimization is with the addition of a local spatial database. This database can merely be a sphere tree [Ratcliff01] that holds positions, state data, and static statistical information. Since this database can end up holding data on all the players, items, and NPCs that are currently active in the game, it is best to keep this information as simple as possible. When designed right, the spatial database will take up very few resources and allow the frontend service to do more optimal work. The reason for this database and the local caching of this amount information is to allow for a quick out. If the system never has to go beyond the frontend service to provide a client with information, it never will. Also, when a player performs an action, it can be quickly perceived by everyone else connected to that same frontend service, while it is still being propagated through the rest of the system. Performing sanity checking and keeping communications to a need-to-know basis can prevent the backend from being flooded and overworked. This is true in the case of all services; once these guidelines have been implemented, there are subsequent methods to further guarantee quality and stability.

Increasing and Upgrading Servers

When talking about increasing or upgrading servers, we primarily concern ourselves with dealing with the machines upon which the frontend services are run. The number of players supported by a distributed services system is directly proportional to the number and power of these frontend services. The system is designed in such a way that more players can be supported just by adding more frontend services, without ever having to touch the backend. This by no means suggests that the backend will never have to be changed. As a game matures and evolves, it may need more services to accomplish its goals, and thus need additional and more powerful servers to be able to reach this.

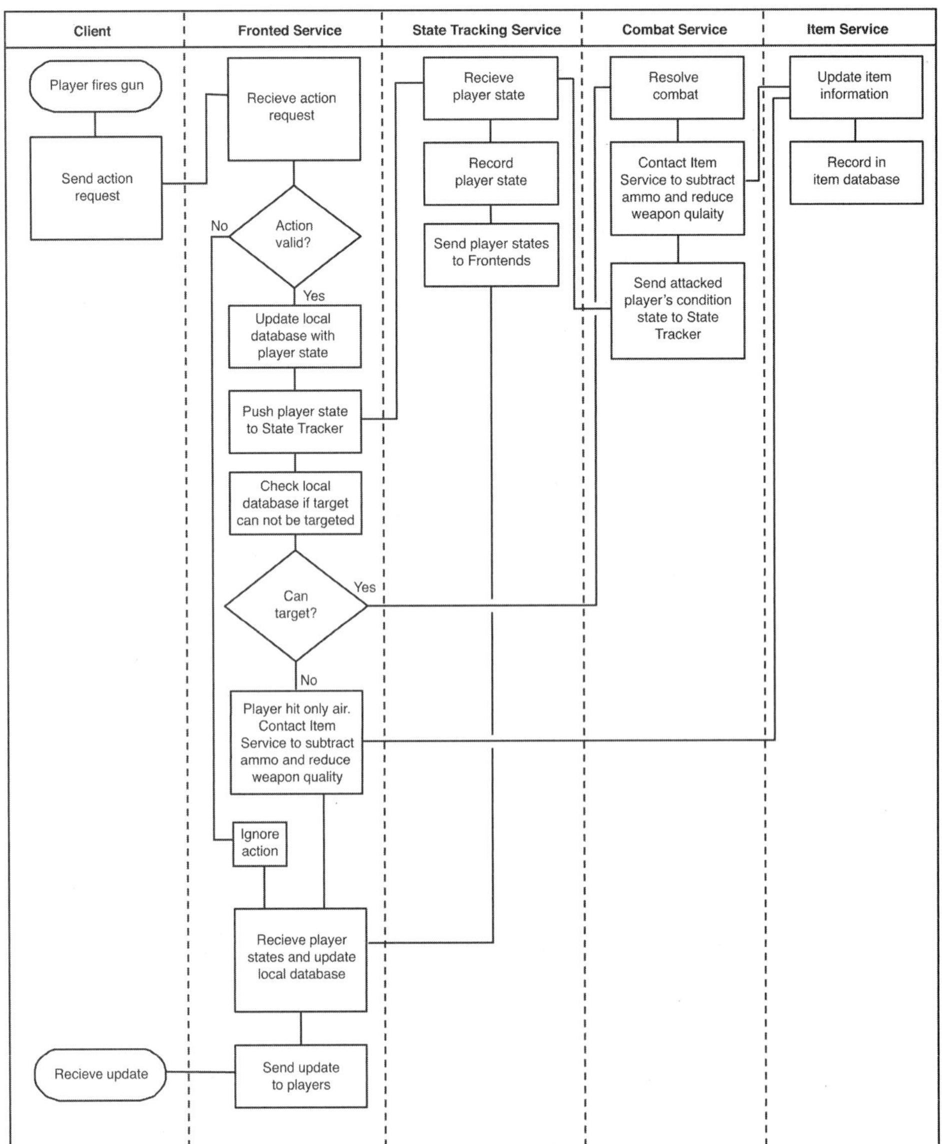

FIGURE 6.1.3 *Example of a frontend service optimization flow chart.*

Overall, this process is quite simple. Typically, all it takes to add or upgrade a piece of hardware is to install the needed services and set up the admin service to designate when and how these services should be run on this specific machine. It has always been the goal of the distributed services approach to be able to use consumer off-the-shelf hardware, but the sheer amount of required servers may get out of hand. At some point, it may be more fruitful to move to an enterprise server solution or a hybrid approach to save on space. This design ensures that a game never has less or more than what it absolutely needs to properly function. The whole concept of increasing and upgrading servers in general is obvious, but it needs to be remembered when dealing with a distributed services system.

Staying Online

There is no way to guarantee bug-free code. The important thing is to prevent a crash from taking down the entire game. When a system crashes, it must be transparent to the players. This involves monitoring for crashes, keeping track of buggy service versions, and very fast resumption of the game execution.

Watchdog and Shadow Services

If any part of the game ever goes down, you need to know when it went down and how to get it back up and running as fast as possible. The best way to do that is by using automated processes that can handle the most common causes of downtime.

The *watchdog service* is a program that keeps an eye on other running services in case of any unscheduled termination. In some cases, the service being watched will be able to catch the terminating signal and perform some form of a shutdown procedure. As a precaution, the watchdog looks after this service, so even if there is an abrupt termination that cannot be handled by that program, the watchdog will still notice. When this happens, the watchdog will launch the waiting *shadow service* into action.

Shadow services are copies of whatever service programs they are shadowing. Every time a service is started, a shadow of that program is created as a clone of that service. Though the shadow service is a copy of its partnered service program, it sits idle, waiting to take its place if any critical, abrupt termination of that service occurs. The watchdog and shadow services can be consolidated into the same program.

Hot Swappable Services

In the event of hardware failure, the watchdog and shadow service become irrelevant. There may be a need to have a separate piece of hardware waiting in standby to pick up the dropped service as soon as a failure is detected.

The admin service will determine if this is the case, and is responsible for telling the execution service (running on the spare server) to start the necessary service. If a spare service server is not available, the admin service could tell a service server that isn't as heavily loaded to become the temporary backup for that service.

Service Version Control

If a critical event happens that causes a termination of a service, there needs to be a way to flag it and revert back to a stable version. In the event of a service's terminating unexpectedly, the version would be flagged, and after a set number of flagged crash occurrences, a reversion to a previous build would begin. A *service version table* would be kept to distinguish between the current, stable, unstable, and unusable versions (see Table 6.1.1).

Table 6.1.1 Service Version Table

Service Name	Version	Flags
Chat Service	1.32	Current, Stable
Chat Service	1.24	Unstable
Chat Service	1.11	Stable
Chat Service	1.0	Stable, Not Usable
Item Service	2.23	Unstable
Item Service	2.0	Current, Stable

When a service is reverted to a previous version, the shadow service loads the previous stable version of that service and takes control of its responsibilities. The shadow service will never revert to a previously flagged unstable version or a version marked unusable. Instead, the shadow service will make sure to always run a revision known to be stable.

Live Updates

With the previously mentioned methods in place, we are now able to ingeniously handle live updates. We push the updates to the revision tables, have the service servers launch the new services in standby, switch control from the old services to the new services, and then shut down the old services to clear up resources.

Keeping Persistent

To resume functionality in the event of a crash, data must be stored persistently, and in more than just a statistical database. We need valid game state data in order to continue from where we left off. Currently, some online games write the entire game state to disk about every 20 minutes. If a crash were to occur, that saved game state would be reloaded. The problem with this is, since we do not know when a crash will occur, the state may be up to 20 minutes old.

Backing up Game States

The solution to this is *shared memory.* Anything loaded into shared memory stays around until you explicitly destroy it, so it is safe for each service to store its game state data in this memory block. In the event of a non-hardware crash, the shadow service can simply attach to its shared memory segment and have all its previously available data. In addition, a snapshot of that shared memory can be taken every few minutes and copied to another segment of memory as a backup. Normally, this process should be very fast and take up few resources. The backing up to disk could then be done at leisure in the background from these backup segments of memory. Synchronizing these game state snapshots across the services can be done with a simple message sent to all the services. Since each service performs a specific task, and those tasks are done in small steps, they are allowed to process their current event, queue all incoming events, copy current shared memory, and then resume normal operation. Once this has taken place, the new active service can begin sending its own snapshots to other servers. This is done so that a game state backup can always be found on the network and easily retrieved when needed.

Restoring Saved Game States

Depending on the game's architecture, there are two methods to restoring a saved game state when a service goes down. The first method is appropriate when the game's state requires it to be time synced; all services would then need to be reverted. The second method is used when your services are structured to be independent enough to allow only single services to be reverted.

When only one service needs to be reverted, the system finds the service server that failed, locates a server with enough spare resources to run the needed service, and then tells it to start that service up. A running server with the dead service's most recent snapshot then pushes its snapshot to that new server, and the system instructs that service to load its previously saved snapshot.

However, in a game architecture that requires all services to be reverted on failure of a single service, the process is basically a domino effect. As before, the system locates a spare service server, has the dead service's saved game state pushed to it, and then instructs the server to load that previously dead service in an idle state. After the service is loaded, the system takes down each individual service, has them restarted, and loads a snapshot of the same timestamp. When all services have been restarted, the system then resumes normal game operation. The restoration of the game state is based on the frequency that the snapshots are saved and sent to other servers.

Conclusion

Online games are rapidly maturing and evolving and so are the players. Their demands and expectations will always continue to increase just as fast. As with any progress, the problems of the past will no longer be viewed as acceptable. The distributed services approach and the improvements discussed in this article are just the tools to help keep up with this pace. With all these tools in place, we can now meet the current demands of these players. In the end, size, duration, and continuity are just a few of the keys to winning their hearts.

References

[Ratcliff01] Ratcliff, John W. "Sphere Trees for Fast Visibility Culling, Ray Tracing, and Range Searching." *Game Programming Gems 2*. Charles River Media, Inc., 2001

[Street05] Street, Shea. "Massively Multiplayer Games Using a Distributed Services Approach." In *Massively Multiplayer Game Development 2*. Charles River Media, Inc., 2005

6.2

Implementing a Seamless World Server

Patrick Duquette, UBISOFT Entertainment Inc.

gizmo@gizz-moo.com

In [Beardsley03], the author provided an introduction to seamless world servers and their pros and cons. He did a great job of making us think of the many issues inherent with a seamless world. This article relates a journey, in the world of a too-many-times-shunned server design. It will focus on the actual implementation of a seamless world server, complete with world nodes, a proxy, and a login server. In the course of the article, we will look at the design decision normally encountered with this type of server and wrap the article with a "where to go from here" section outlining some areas for further exploration.

The Mandatory Definition

By definition, a *seamless world* is a world where the player is free to roam, explore, and travel to his heart's content. No physical barriers between "zones" to hinder your travel and no loading screen while transitioning between the zones. Designers no longer need to put mazes between zone borders in a seamless world and, having fewer constraints, they can let their imaginations run free.

Although seamless worlds can benefit any game genre since it's the core of the server and the game specific world should reside on top of it, the immersive gains will vary depending on genres and gameplay designs. RPG games benefit from having a huge, continuous world through which the player can travel. And FPS games can now have wars that can unroll on vast expanses of terrain. Taking away the physical zones greatly boosts the player's immersion in the game.

Of course, this level of freedom comes at a cost. The artists need to create transition areas to join different climates, just like in real life. While in traditional zoned worlds, you could have sub-tropical zones next to zones with frosty mountain ranges without disorienting the player, because you expect the hard cut between the two parts of the world and you have time to "disconnect" from the game when changing zone or loading. It's like loading a new map and you expect something different when it will finish loading.

From a programmer's perspective, the challenge resides mostly near the borders. When a player moves from one server to another or is exchanging items in the border area, having players managed by different servers can lead to many potential problems if not handled correctly. Another problem is the loading of visual assets as we move around between servers. It needs to be done in the background, if you don't want the player noticing.

And since we can have interactions between players, NPCs, objects, etc. that are on different servers, we have to keep an eye on the number of messages that are sent internally, server to server. Those can skyrocket in no time if care is not taken while working out the inter-server communication details. Even if today's network hardware is more than able to manage our expected LAN traffic, we have to keep in mind that we not only need to send the packets, the recipient must process them, too. Fewer data exchange between servers means less processing.

The Implementation

A brief explanation of the different types of servers found in our seamless world:

RemoteController: The login coordinator and the process giving the okay to the ProxyServer to start accepting client connections.
ProxyServer: The bridge between the outside world and our server layout.
LoginServer: Authenticates the clients.
NodeServer: Manages a segment of the world.
WorldManager: Distributes the world segment to the NodeServers.

From the start, you will have a minimum of three servers: ProxyServer, LoginServer, and NodeServer. Since the number of NodeServers could vary, and we don't want to manually add lines in an ini file, we will use an autoregister system. The different servers will register themselves with the ProxyServer upon starting up (well, actually it's with the WorldManager, but that will be discussed later). This strategy lets us change the number of NodeServers as often as we like without changing a single line in an ini file.

The RemoteController, or How to Manage the Server's Startup Period

Of course, this way of doing things led us to another potential problem. When do we start to accept incoming connections? The naïve solution would be to put a wait delay on the proxy before it starts accepting connections. Although it could work, it isn't flexible and it's quite dangerous, as you don't know if everything will be booted before it goes online.

The second option is to have the proxy wait on a special packet containing a "go online" command. This way you can control precisely when is the proxy server goes online. This packet will be sent only when all the conditions of the RemoteController are met. Some conditions are: making sure that the LoginServer is up, that the WorldManager has handed all the world segments to the NodeServers, etc.

The RemoteController is more than just a convenience, it is an invaluable tool to schedule the server boot up period. The alternative would be to manually control the ProxyServer, which can lead to human error and everything that comes with it.

ProxyServer

As with many online games, you don't want to expose your server architecture to the outside world. One way to achieve that is to make all communication pass through a proxy server that will relay the packets to the right recipient. This technique has the advantage of having only one external entry point and hiding the actual servers' layout from the client. If you need to change your server layout, number, or internal protocol, you can do so and the client will be none the wiser, since the only thing it knows is the proxy.

This server will handle all the incoming and outgoing packets between the clients and our servers and thus handle the most traffic. With that in mind, the proxy server can be implemented using IO Completion Port (IOCP), since it doesn't take much resource, while being able to service many concurrent clients' connections. For a good introduction to IOCP and other relevant windows socket paradigm, please refer to [Jones02].

On a live setup, you would want to have many ProxyServers to spread the load. The client would connect to a master redirector, which will tell the client which ProxyServer to use based on current work load and latency (ping time) from the client. This will enable you to have ProxyServers distributed in the world while maintaining a single connection point for the client.

When the ProxyServer receives an incoming connection from an unknown client, it forwards it to the LoginServer for authentication. Once the credentials of the client are verified, the LoginServer notifies the ProxyServer of the client's spawn point and NodeServer handling the spawn location.

The client connections are internally maintained via a simple array that does the translation between the ClientID and the NodeServer to which it should connect. The ClientID is the index of the array and is handed by the ProxyServer when it receives the authentication confirmation from the LoginServer. The ProxyServer allocates at boot time the array, knowing the maximum number of connections it will support. It also keeps a list of unused connections for fast management of client connections and disconnections. To minimize the possibility of a malicious user spoofing a client while it is connected, we store the connection details alongside the NodeServer to which it will connect. Once in a while, we check that the packet we received is really coming from the legitimate client.

LoginServer

The LoginServer handles client authentication. The LoginServer take up the matter of checking the player profile for his spawn point coordinate and looking up the correct NodeServer to switch the connection to. This is done by asking the WorldManager which NodeServer handles this part of the world. The LoginServer handles the database lookup and calling up the WorldManager, since we want to have the ProxyServer as lightweight as we can.

The player's information is stored in a standard SQL database. For simpler implementations, mySQL [mySQL] might be a good choice, as it is more than capable of handling smaller needs, and it is free. Other database solutions for a live setup that you might want to look at are [Oracle] and [SQLServer]. In a production environment, you might also consider having a proxy/queue server in front of the database to queue the query/update by order of importance. Also, if you are able, keep your database in memory; it will greatly speed up your transactions with the database if it doesn't need to access the disk. Of course, schedule physical dumps once in a while to have a physical copy of the database in case the server crashes. However, keep it to a minimum, and if possible, do it on another server (using replication).

NodeServer

The NodeServers are the keepers of the world, the final arbiter of conflicts between the client representation of the world and the one kept internally. They perform sanity checks on player interactions with his surroundings, making sure everything is kept tidy, but also giving a life to the many parts of the world. For example, while it might not control directly the gust of wind that moves some leaves near the player's feet, it will notify the client that a 5 km/h wind is blowing in a certain direction.

Since online games tend to have huge open worlds for player exploration, each NodeServer has a small segment to manage. Alas, with this splitting of the game world comes a non-negligible complexity cost for a seamless world implementation that is not present in a traditional zoned online world (at least, not in this magnitude). Interactions between players and/or with NPCs take a new meaning, as they now can be on two different servers when the interaction is initiated. This can lead to various exploits, and great care has to be taken when designing the transaction system used when the player is acquiring/exchanging/giving "items." For the sake of clarity, anything that can be exchanged between players or with an NPC and that has a repercussion in the game like physical items, quest parts (physical or "spoken"), etc., will be put in the "item" category.

To manage across border interactions, the NodeServers not only need to manage what is in their segment of the world, but they also need to be aware of things just outside it, in what we call the *BorderZone*. The BorderZone stretches a little past the border between two segments. This space, while really belonging to another server, will let the NodeServer tell his client situated near the border what is in their awareness area, even if it's situated in a part of the world managed by another NodeServer.

To have the same object on two servers at the same time, we must introduce the concept of proxy objects, a server-side object representing a ghost of the master object, which is on another NodeServer. When a transaction between two players is initiated and each one is on a different side of the border, the server will perform the transaction with the proxy object instead of the real copy situated on another NodeServer.

One last thing on BorderZones: as noted in [Beardsley03] and other articles on the subject, the minimum BorderZone size has to be at least the size of the player awareness radius to circumvent problems where two players, each one on different sides of a border, may not see the same things, or worse, one might not see the other, and thus open the door to exploit. Also, having the BorderZone slightly larger than the player awareness radius will lessen the possibility of visual popping as new objects are replicated as proxy on the neighboring NodeServers.

Performance Consideration

This server will need to process a lot of packets, both from the outside world (via the proxy server) and the inside (inter-server communication). It will also need to manage a large object base and moving characters (players and AI). It will also need to update things that are game specific, like weather modification and quests/missions handed out by NPCs or even other players. Astral objects like stars and the sun(s)/moon(s) should be managed by a global server and not by a NodeServer, if your online world does not span more than one solar system.

Looking at all this, it adds up to quite a lot of processing per server. To alleviate the NodeServer from some extra processing, at the cost of taking more inter-server bandwidth, the game AI entities can be managed on separate dedicated server(s) and be treated as normal clients by the NodeServer.

The world is divided in many segments, which lead to many borders and more importantly, many border junctions. For simplicity, an easier starting point might be a stripped world, with only two border junctions per NodeServer, with no "T" or "cross" junctions. See Figure 6.2.1 for a visual representation.

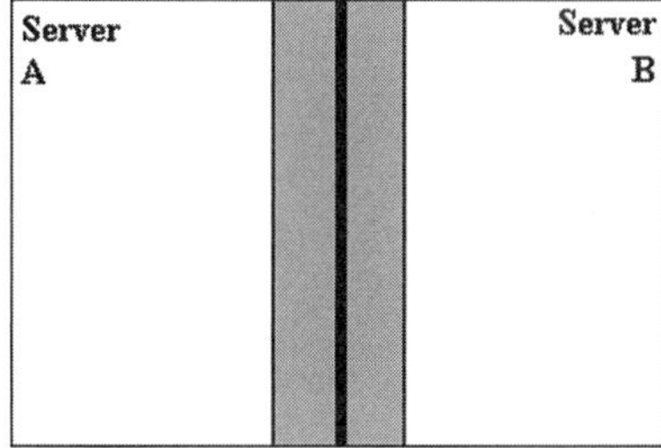

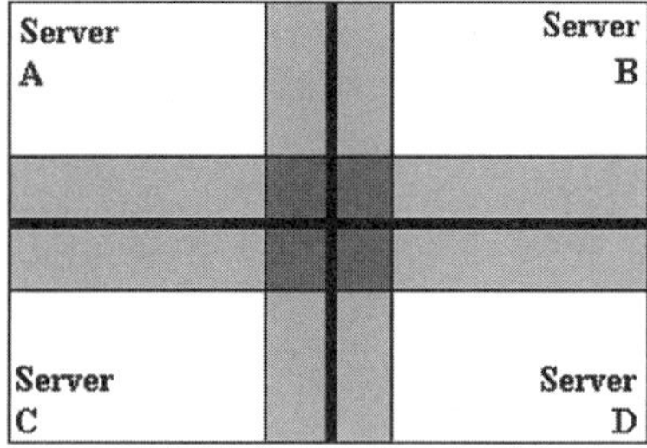

FIGURE 6.2.1 *Two border junctions and "cross" junctions.*

Registering with the ProxyServer

When registering with the ProxyServer, the NodeServer is only telling it "I'm online and ready to serve." Nothing has been decided concerning which portion of the world is to be managed by this server. Of course, an ini file could solve the problem but that means that you will have to manually manage the file, for all the servers, every time. Instead, the servers get their "work order" from another server, the WorldManager. Upon booting up, before registering with the ProxyServer, the NodeServer negotiates with the WorldManager for a segment of the world to take care of. The NodeServers each have a copy of the complete world. While this causes a burden when updating the game content since it has to be replicated on all the NodeServers, it also alleviates us of having all the NodeServers trying to fetch the world data at the same time during the boot process. Having everything locally will also permit dynamic resizing of the NodeServer borders, a technique discussed in the "Where to Go from Here" section.

The bulk of the work of this server is the validation of the player input. Be it item exchanging/acquiring, player navigation in the world, or the rate-of-attack during a combat, the NodeServer has to look over everything that comes from the player. This is the old networking idiom, "never trust the client" at its best.

To do so, the server has to keep a simulation of the world, and this simulation acts as the reference when a disparity between the client and the server representation happens. If anything isn't as in the master copy kept by the node server, the client must be notified and action should be taken to correct the situation.

Handling the Communication with the Outside World

Knowing that this server will need a quick way to associate incoming network traffic to the managed object it is destined to, we must make sure that it is as efficient as possible. A map of the objects in the managed world might be in order, as a list traversal might be too time consuming for our needs. The drawback with mappping is that insertion may turn up as being one of the bottlenecks in the connection processing, but since we shouldn't have too much object creation/deletion at any one time, we shouldn't experience any slowdown. Another possibility is to have every object have a unique ID throughout the world and use the same technique as for the ProxyServer. This would even be faster than the map search, without the insertion/deletion penalties but at a greater memory footprint. (Imagine an array for all the world objects.) If the objects are handed a new ID when crossing borders, you only need to keep an array for the maximum number of objects that will be present at any time on the NodeServer. Add to that the possibility to grow the array in an emergency situation, and we should be okay.

Each object is represented on the server, and network messages can be addressed to them. When a player interacts with an NPC, the player's actions are sent to the server and validated. When a player tries to hit a monster, it actually sends a message to the NodeServer telling it "I target MonsterX." The NodeServer validates that the player is able to see the monster, to target it from where he stands, and that he is allowed to target it. The player then sends an "I swing at MonsterX" message. The NodeServer validates that the player is near enough to swing at MonsterX and tells the monster if it was hit, and if so, tells the player how much damage he has caused. If any of these steps fail, the NodeServer might log the attempt for later review. It could be a latency issue or a player's trying to fool the NodeServer.

The client should always receive the world information on a need-to-know basis. Only when a player is near a game object should its relevant information be sent to the player. For example, only when a beast is slain and searched should the server send the loot description.

While the AI is updated often on the server, a message containing the current status/position of the AI will only be sent once in a while to the client, once per 10th of a second, maybe less often when there's no situation asking for more frequent update. The client will use dead reckoning to extrapolate the AI position based on the last update. Of course, the client will have to make a correction when it receives an update from the server. For more information on dead reckoning, please refer to [Aronson97].

X Proxy Objects for a Master

How do we keep in sync an unknown number of proxy and a master? Since we can have an unknown number of proxy objects for any given "master object," we need to keep track of everyone to update them whenever the internal states change. Luckily, a design pattern is designed just for that: the Observer pattern (also known as the Publish-Subscribe pattern). For a formal explication of this pattern (and many others), please refer to [Gamma95]. Briefly, this pattern defines a one-to-many relationship between objects and is used to synchronize the objects between them. The beauty is that you don't need to know beforehand how many objects there will be.

Our application of this pattern has the proxy notify the master of change, and the master replicates those change to the registered proxy's objects. While not really relevant to our current implementation, it was done in prevision of having border junctions with more than two node servers. The master object is the final arbiter in case of discrepancy between the proxy objects and the master.

Proxy Objects Notification

Since the proxy objects can be created and deleted as the master moves throughout the world, we need a sure way to manage their life span on the node server. Sure, the proxies are part of a observer pattern, which will cover the death of un-needed objects when the master moves outside the border zone, but what happens when the master moves from the center of the managed segment of the world to the border zone between two servers? No proxies are created at this time. The master object, when crossing a border zone threshold, notifies the correct neighbor that a proxy should be created. The proxy, once created, registers itself with the master, which will then send the updated state of the object and start the Observer relation.

Neighbors

The NodeServer can request from the WorldManager its neighbors. This can be done at boot up or every time you need to check if you have dynamic borders (see the "Where to Go from Here" section at the end of the chapter). In the simpler "strip world" example, we can only have two neighbors. Our implementation is simplified greatly by this, and as such, we only have two member variables keeping the information associated with the neighbors. If the info is not set, we ask the WorldManager who they are and then we initiate a communication channel with them that will be kept until the server is shut down.

The WorldManager

The WorldManager server is responsible for splitting the world into different manageable segments and giving each segment to a different NodeServer. When the manager has handed out all the world segments, it sends a message to the RemoteController, telling it that the world is distributed. This will ensure that we can't start receiving player connection while segments of the world won't be managed and thus inaccessible.

Subsequent connections to the WorldManager asking for a piece of the world are ignored in a Strip World implementation, as there's no provision for backup NodeServers; this is discussed in the "Where to Go from Here" section. Also, the number of segments of the world is already known at boot time, so that when the node servers connect, they are handed a segment of the world immediately.

Another task of the WorldManager is to answer requests from the LoginServer and NodeServers as to which NodeServer handles a certain part of the world. This is vital since from one player session to another, if the server was shut down, we can't guarantee which NodeServer will handle the part of the world from which the player disconnected. This may seem strange and inefficient, but it does free us from having to manually specify world boundaries for each NodeServer, and it makes an automated process when introducing new NodeServer in our layout, be it from expansion or because a server crashed.

Where to Go from Here

Dynamically managing the world segments, instead of statically, is one area for improvement. If a NodeServer is overcrowded, the WorldManager could receive a request for backup processing. By resizing the borders or splitting the current world segment in two, giving the other half to a backup NodeServer would alleviate the server if the need arises. The NodeServer will have to support direct transfer of managed entities without going through the ProxyObject creation normally associated with entities crossing the NodeServers border.

Having backup NodeServers registered to take the load of a dying NodeServer could also help recover from hardware fault without interrupting the service. If a NodeServer monitors the hardware notifications, it can react to them. Instead of clos ing the game service for maintenance because one of the redundant power supplies died, the NodeServer tells the WorldManager its status. The WorldManager takes one of the backup NodeServers and assigns it to the world segment managed by the dying server. When the transfer of all the managed entities is done, the dying NodeServer can be safely removed.

Because of the sheer size of the entity transfer, we might want to do it progressively. If we transfer the entire load from NodeServer A to NodeServer B, doing it in one operation may be noticeable. Instead, by moving the NodeServer borders and migrating only a part of the total world segment area at a time, the transitions, albeit the fact that many proxy objects will be created and destroyed while the borders are moving, will be smoother.

With dynamic borders, the RemoteController could also act as a world segments interface, giving the administrators the capacity to control their exact layout and size, enabling concrete management of the world division. No longer confined to static division, the administrators could modify the world segment's size before planned game events where a large number of players are expected.

Instead of computing the AI directly on the NodeServer, it can be done on dedicated servers. While the NodeServer will treat the AI like a normal client, having them connected through a dedicated port (the port used for inter-server communication) will give us the possibility for further optimization, since they can be considered "trusted" clients. Some double-checking for physics with the world or AI action validity could be skipped. Some might wonder if this doesn't lead to a possibility for exploits, and they would have been right if the AI server wasn't connecting through another port than the one used by the communication with the outside world. (On a live server, that would have been through another network card altogether.) Only at the time of connection, when the server will start to manage the AI entity, will the flag "trusted entity" be set.

Some of these "next steps" can be found on the [Gizz04] Web site, where they are continuously implemented.

IOCP

While IOCP was discussed in this article, please keep in mind that it is Windows-specific. For information on the difference between the IOCP concept and its *nix counterpart, "dev/poll," please refer to the article by Ian Baril [Baril04].

References

[Aronson97] Aronson, Jesse. "Dead Reckoning: Latency Hiding for Networked Games." Available online at *http://www.gamasutra.com/features/19970919/aronson_01.htm*. September 19, 1997.

[Beardsley03] Beardsley, Jason. "Seamless Servers: The Case For and Against." *Massively Multiplayer Game Development*. Charles River Media, 2003.

[Baril04] Baril, Ian. "I/O Multiplexing & Scalable Socket Servers." *Dr. Dobb's Journal* (February 2004): pp. 42–45.

[Gamma95] Gamma, Erich, et al. *Design Patterns: Elements of Reusable Object-Oriented Software*. Addison-Wesley, 1995.

[Gizz04] *http://www.gizz-moo.com/*.

[Jones02] Jones, Anthony and Jim Ohlund. *Network Programming for Microsoft Windows,* Second Edition. Microsoft Press, 2002.

[mySQL] *http://dev.mysql.com/*.

[Oracle] *http://www.oracle.com/*.

[SQLServer] *http://www.microsoft.com/sql/*.

6.3

Designing a Vulgarity Filtering System

Shekhar Dhupelia

sdhupelia@gmail.com

With online usernames and chat rooms more and more prevalent in recent online games, so too becomes the problem of adult content (especially when trying to ship an E-rated game!). Everyone at this point would acknowledge that it's impossible to catch every possible use of vulgarity while also trying to remain efficient and user friendly. However, there are methods that will catch a lot of the more obvious cases.

This article discusses the components that go into a fast word-search vulgarity filter, including how to organize the "bad words" in a data source, how to search through all of this data, and the various options for what to do with the violating text. Also discussed are some best practices and additional points of reference when building such a system.

Syntax Versus Context

It's important to keep in mind that most games cannot afford to attack the problem of "context." Context suggests the actual *meaning* of a sentence, or a full thought. While some standard sentences might be blocked in their entirety, a very high level of artificial intelligence would be needed to determine the meaning of a sentence and refuse potential rule violations; this is especially true since the AI would need to be running in real time.

Further, it is far beyond the scope of this gem to discuss voice chat. While it is admirable to want to provide a "family friendly" environment within a game, especially one geared towards all age levels, it is far beyond the scope of our average game hardware to monitor voice chat and do anything particularly useful with it.

The discussion here is of *syntax*. Syntax refers to the words themselves; while "^#$% YOU!" still confers quite a bit of meaning, the point is that the effect is still dulled from not allowing full expletives to be transmitted back and forth.

Dictionaries

A dictionary, or data dictionary, is where the lookup table of bad words exists. The options here are endless; the application might already have a database system or filesystem in place, probably using some sort of relational or token lookup. The goal is to have a consistent, easy-to-manage data source that can store all the designated "bad words" in one place.

If constructing from scratch, a good place to start is XML files. For the uninitiated, XML is a form of information identification, assigning tokens to data that can quickly be searched and referenced. A good reference for XML can be found at the O'Reilly Network's XML.com [Oreilly01].

Parsers

Having a dictionary to store the bad words is only a start. The more resource-intensive part involves searching through the data dictionary for matches against a string. While most C/C++ programmers and Java programmers will be familiar with string manipulation, parsing can be slow and turn into a bottleneck for the game if not implemented carefully.

Again, this is a subsystem that may already be in place with many existing game engines. Parsing through a data source is useful in many other areas of a game besides this one feature. When building a new engine with XML in mind, however, Xerces is a good place to start [Xerces01]. The Xerces library is an open source C++ library that allows very fast searching through XML file sources.

Filtering

So far, the game will have a lookup dictionary for bad words and strings, and a parser to actively go through and root out any violations against this dictionary. The next step is to filter the text and either block it or change it accordingly. However, the method used in the game is dependent on the specific design in mind, as there are several different ways to filter the violating strings.

Search-and-Replace, Predetermined Strings

The first filtering method is to do a search-and-replace operation on the string, with a predetermined string. This involves setting up a second word or list of words that act as suitable replacements. An example predetermined string might be:

```
char szReplacementText[] = "[censored]"
```

In this case, the bad word would be replaced with `[censored]`. To add variety in a place where there might be many violations, you might loop through a list of 10 or 20 variations, such as `banned`, `blocked`, and `not allowed`.

Search-and-Replace, Random Strings

This method is similar to the previous, except that it uses random characters to provide variety. For example, English-speaking comic strips often use something like `&^*$` to designate a curse word. However, there's no set standard on the number of symbols to use, or even what particular symbols to draw from. With that in mind, more variety could be presented by choosing a random number of letters, as well as choosing randomly from a list of characters or substitute words. This might look like the following process:

1. Define a list of substitute characters.
2. Get the violating string.
3. Choose a random number of characters.
4. Loop through the bad string, character-by-character.
5. Choose random replacement characters from the list.
6. Return the filtered string.

Word Stripping

Word stripping is useful in that it helps remove some of the meaning from a block of text. Sometimes, a sentence such as `I want to %#@$@%` might still confer some meaning in the context of the conversation or situation. However, word stripping might change this into `I want to`, which just eliminates the violating string completely, with no substitutions. Of course, this doesn't stop the user from simply entering the string with substitute characters in place; this is where human intervention is sometimes necessary, a topic discussed further later.

Block-and-Refuse

This is the most forceful method, but does the most to try and automatically block violating *context*, instead of just the syntax. Block-and-refuse detects the violating string, then refuses the entire submission. For example in a chat room construct, the user entering a sentence `word word2 word3 violator` would not even get to send `word word2 word3` or `word word2 word3 %#$^`. Instead, they would get an error message informing them of the violation, with the string thrown away.

Best Filtering Practices

While the various filtering methods can be implemented efficiently, either alone or together, there are several key practices that will help make the process quicker and less frustrating for the end user, as well as provide efficiencies to the game servers. These are described in the following section.

Use Both an Offline and Online Dictionary

While not possible for some embedded systems (such as game consoles without large local storage), it's a good idea to use an offline dictionary, in addition to the server-side dictionary file. This allows some checks to be performed quickly and locally, without spending extra bandwidth to verify every string. The online dictionary might serve as a second form of protection; for example, a static offline dictionary might do a quick first check on every string, while the dynamic, updateable online dictionary can do another pass on the strings as they are transmitted.

Filter Offline First

As mentioned previously, don't waste large amounts of bandwidth unnecessarily on anything that is not part of the core gameplay. Filtering offline first can save a lot of time and cost, and actually make some processes more user friendly. An example of this might be during user registration; as the player enters a username or an avatar tagline or some other string, a quick check can be made against the offline dictionary. This could at least let the user finish the registration process and then proceed online. The online portion might simply check the suspect strings again without requiring re-entry of the entire form.

Again, while not possible for all systems, a dynamically updated dictionary file is a great tool; as players come up with new or overlooked vulgarity or questionable jargon, the dictionaries should be updated regularly with these additions. Even in cases where the offline dictionary cannot be modified, the online dictionaries should have regular review periods.

Dictionary Change Control

While it's established that regular dictionary updates are important, care should be taken to control these changes and track them, similar to source code changes or source art modifications. Updates should be scheduled on regular time intervals (while necessary), tracked and revised similar to source code, and done with a minimal impact on users (if not in real time, than as part of other updates such as bug fixes or content changes).

Continually Monitor Any Workarounds

When filtering is based on a dictionary, there will always be words that fool the systems you have in place but still convey some illicit or angry tone. Regular Internet users have grown accustomed to writing their words with symbols or numbers in place of standard characters. For an example, pretend that the word "FOOL" was in the dictionary file. Now, if the user instead types "F00L" or "F@@L," the meaning is still clear, but the word escapes the attention of the system.

If these modified words are not addressed, the entire vulgarity filtering system is rendered useless. Unfortunately, no automated method has shown itself to date that can efficiently handle all the possible word permutations from a given dictionary. This reality suggests the need for constant, vigilant human intervention.

Human Intervention

After all this technology, there's still the major concern that none of these tactics will fully provide a "safe," family-friendly environment. The fact is, any one or combined approach to filtering that fits within reasonable CPU/memory constraints will have easy workarounds.

Unfortunately, the best one can hope for is to make a reasonable effort from a technology standpoint, and hope that it covers a large majority of potential violators. But this technology will fail under many cases. If the game is still likely to suffer heavy abuse despite these safeguards, there is often no choice but to add a layer of human intervention. There are two often-used methods that help weed out a large majority of the worst-case users: the in-game supervisors and player feedback.

In-Game Supervision

In-game supervision refers to an actual moderator or team of moderators, who actively play and patrol the online game, basically looking for any sort of violation. These moderators may choose whether to be listed as administrators, versus serving "undercover." While the consequences for bad behavior may include a ban from future play, often a looser punishment might solve the problem (for instance, a 30-day ban on chatting).

Player Feedback

Player feedback can be quite powerful if handled correctly. With this technology, the other players themselves have a means to report unruly behavior. This allows the community to actively police themselves and potentially weed out more cases of unwanted actions than a team of moderators could hope to find. While this still requires people to read the feedback and act accordingly, as well as handle cases of fraudulent feedback, this also allows more active reporters to become "senior" members of the community, and likely will serve as the game's staunchest advocates.

Conclusion

This article discussed a couple of different ways to implement vulgarity filtering in an online game. Further, this article talked about ways in which this filtering can—and will—fail, and where human intervention is still necessary. Fortunately, the methods discussed here will severely blunt the blow of a malicious user, to the point where it may become too difficult or frustrating for the user to try and continue his bad behavior. Between combinations of these methods, users can be assured of a safer, protected game environment.

References

[Fepproject01] The Free Expression Policy Project. "Fact Sheet on Internet Filtering." Available online at *http://www.fepproject.org/factsheets/filtering.html.*

[IGN01] IGN Xbox. "Xbox Live Etiquette." Available online at *http://xbox.ign.com/articles/377/377569p1.html.*

[Oreilly01] O'Reilly Network. "XML.com: XML from the Inside Out." Available online at *http://www.xml.com/.*

[Xerces01] "Xerces C++ Parser." Available online at *http://xml.apache.org/xerces-c/.*

6.4

Fast and Efficient Implementation of a Remote Procedure Call System

Hyun-jik Bae

imays@hitel.net

There are many articles on network game development focused on aspects such as dead reckoning, distributed game servers, throttling, load balancing, smart seeds, and so on. These are very useful and important ideas and can be applied to many projects. All these techniques share a common characteristic in that they all require sending and receiving at least one message; this code is typically one of the greatest sources of redundant network code.

Many network game programmers tend to write redundant code that treats every network message the same but could easily be consolidated. Sending and receiving messages involves many switch-case statements and structure definitions. This redundancy only grows as messages are added or changed during the development process.

This article introduces a solution to reduce this burden, focusing on a code-level perspective.

First, let's take a look at a typical problem area for most network games. Listing 6.4.1 shows an example that processes two messages: "move knight" and "attack enemy."

Listing 6.4.1 Our Familiar Networking Code

```
/////// on both sides
#define Message_Knight_Move_ID 12
#define Message_Knight_Attack_ID 13

struct Message
{
    int m_msgID;
};
```

```
struct Message_Knight_Move:public Message
{
    int m_id;
    float m_x,m_y,m_z;
};

struct Message_Knight_Attack:public Message
{
    int m_id;
    int m_target;
    int m_damage;
};

/////// on sender side

void Knight_Move(int id,float x,float y,float z)
{
    Message_Knight_Move msg;
    msg.m_msgID=Message_Knight_Move_ID;
    msg.m_id=id;
    msg.m_x=x;
    msg.m_y=y;
    msg.m_z=z;
}

void Knight_Attack(int id,int target,int damage)
{
    Message_Knight_Attack msg;
    msg.m_msgID=Message_Knight_Attack_ID;
    msg.m_id=id;
    msg.m_target=target;
    msg.m_damage=damage;
}

void DoReceivedMessage(Message* msg)
{
    switch(msg->m_msgID)
    {
    case Message_Knight_Move_ID:
        {
            Message_Knight_Move* msg2=
                (Message_Knight_Move*)msg;
        }
        Do_Knight_Move(
            msg2->m_id,
            msg2->m_x,
            msg2->m_y,
            msg2->m_z);
        break;
        // ... cases for other message types
    case Message_Knight_Attack_ID:
        {
            Message_Knight_Attack* msg2=
                (Message_Knight_Attack*)msg;
```

```
                }
                Do_Knight_Attack(
                    msg2->m_id,
                    msg2->m_target,
                    msg2->m_damage);
                break;
                // ... cases for other message types
            }
        }
```

Let's now assume a case where we must add another message type. We must modify four spots in Listing 6.4.1 for the new message: a new message ID, a new message structure, a new function sending the message, and a new case for reading the message. This cumbersome work can be reduced by using streaming classes, such as `Carchive` or `std::istream`, or by writing your own. With these classes, Listing 6.4.1 can be simplified to look like Listing 6.4.2.

Listing 6.4.2 Another Style of Our Familiar Networking Code

```
//////// on both sides
#define Message_Knight_Move_ID 12
#define Message_Knight_Attack_ID 13

//////// on sender side

void Knight_Move(int id,float x,float y,float z)
{
    Message msg;
    msg<<(int)Message_Knight_Move_ID;
    msg<<id<<x<<y<<z;
}

void Knight_Attack(int id,int target,int damage)
{
    Message msg;
    msg<<(int)Message_Knight_Attack_ID;
    msg<<id<<target<<damage;
}

/////// on receiver side
void DoReceivedMessage(Message* msg)
{
    int msgID;
    (*msg)>>msgID;
    switch(msgID)
    {
    case Message_Knight_Move_ID:
        {
            int id;
            float x,y,z;
            (*msg)>>id>>x>>y>>z;
            Do_Knight_Move(id,x,y,z);
```

```
                }
                break;
            case Message_Knight_Attack_ID:
                {
                    int id,target,damage;
                    (*msg)>>id>>target>>damage;
                    Do_Knight_Attack(id,target,damage);
                    break;
                    // ... cases for other message types
                }
            }
        }
```

Either way, we can send, receive, and process messages by calling `Knight_Move()` on the send side and calling `Do_Knight_Move()` on the receiver side, as well as the messages `Knight_Attack()` and `Do_Knight_attack()`.

Notice the pattern in these examples, in that they're very redundant. They can be abstracted for now to just read as one-line declarations, such as Listing 6.4.3, which is the goal for how we want our actual game code to look.

```
Knight_Move(int id,float x,float y,float z);
Knight_Attack(int id,int target,int damage);
```

Listing 6.4.3. The ultimate style we desire

We can refer to Listings 6.4.1 and 6.4.2 as the *manual send- receive-switch-case* code and refer to Listing 6.4.3 as the *automatic send-receive-switch-case* code. Later in this gem, we'll discuss how these send-receive-switch-case codes can be generated automatically, which is one of the major benefits of *Remote Procedure Calls (RPC)*.

RPC: Introduction

RPC is a message-passing facility that is independent of the underlying network layer and allows a distributed application to call services available on various computers in that network. Put more simply, RPC abstracts the technique of a program on one computer requesting a function call on another computer. For a complete introduction to generic RPC usage, refer to an operating system textbook [Silberschatz02].

There are many RPC implementations, some available by several major companies. Some of the more well known are MS-RPC, DEC-RPC, DCOM, CORBA, and Java RMI. (DCOM, CORBA, and Java RMI have object-oriented behavior, but their concepts are also based on RPC.) In this article, let's call these implementations *legacy* RPC systems. Legacy RPC systems are stable and support many features such as security, authentication, and many protocol compatibilities. However, because many of these implementations have some drawbacks for game programming, we want to write our own RPC system and avoid the following problems with legacy RPC:

- Hard to understand and use
- Too redundant and cumbersome for game applications

- Do not allow for complete control of message formats
- Do not allow for complete control of message transmission, such as with throttling
- Legacy asynchronous models are much more complex than synchronous models in practice

In this article, we introduce a guide to implementing an RPC system for game programming, composed of an *RPC compiler* and a *runtime engine*. Because this RPC system is fully under application control, it can be optimized or streamlined as necessary.

The example presented here is very simple and should be fast enough for a quick start. For further simplicity, we'll intentionally ignore some lower-level topics such as the actual socket code and error recovery with this RPC system, because the more features we add, the more complicated the examples will become.

We refer to a module that makes RPC calls as an *RPC client*, while a module receiving these RPCs is an *RPC server*. Note that the RPC client and server are different from the game client and server. Ordinarily, a game server and a client have two heterogeneous RPCs for calling client-to-server and server-to-client in their program modules, while a game peer has a homogeneous RPC, calling and receiving mutually. The included example *RPCDuel* is a case of the latter.

There are two networking models of RPC: asynchronous and synchronous. Synchronous RPC has output parameters. If your RPC client program sends a synchronous RPC to your RPC server, the RPC client will wait until the RPC server accomplishes execution and the return values are received. On the other hand, asynchronous RPC differs in two aspects:

- Asynchronous RPC doesn't wait for return calls.
- Asynchronous RPC cannot have output parameters.
- Asynchronous RPC allows for unreliable messaging. Since some messages may be lost during transmission, RPCs with unreliable messages may be missing as well.

Game programs rarely require synchronous RPC; most RPC server programs have no case that waits for execution on the RPC client by design, because it may be a cause of bottleneck or deadlock. Instead, they define two messages for requests to the RPC server and replies from it. Moreover, RPC client programs have a few cases that wait for execution on the RPC server. Many games have to wait for replies from the RPC server, showing a wait animation and permitting users to push a Cancel button. Moreover, synchronous RPC is hard to implement, for reasons we'll explain later.

The example code with this article contains a compiler as well as parser. There are some further readings about grammar definitions, parsers, and lexical analyzers [Sebesta02].

RPC: Design

Here is a simplified presentation of a well-known sequence design of a generic RPC implementation. In short, it works like Figure 6.4.1.

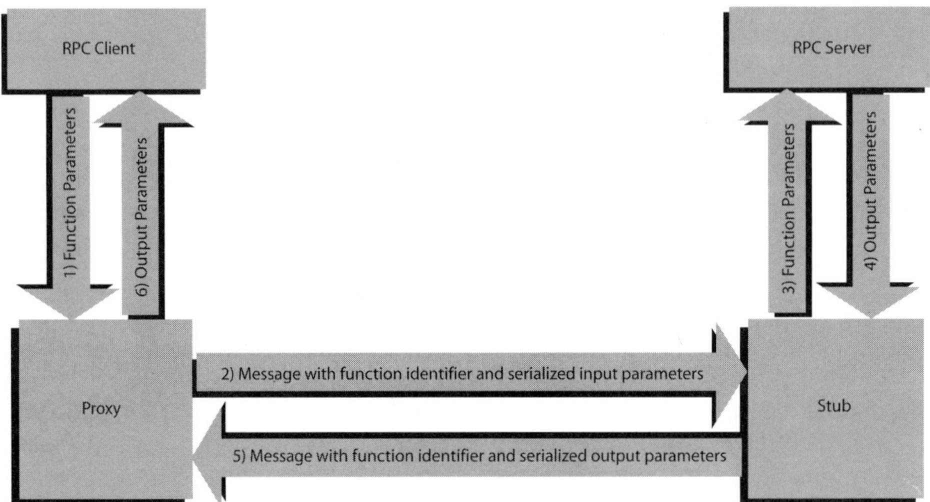

FIGURE 6.4.1 *RPC sequence diagram with reply.*

As we are just interested in the asynchronous model, we do not need phases that wait for replies. After trimming them, it works like Figure 6.4.2.

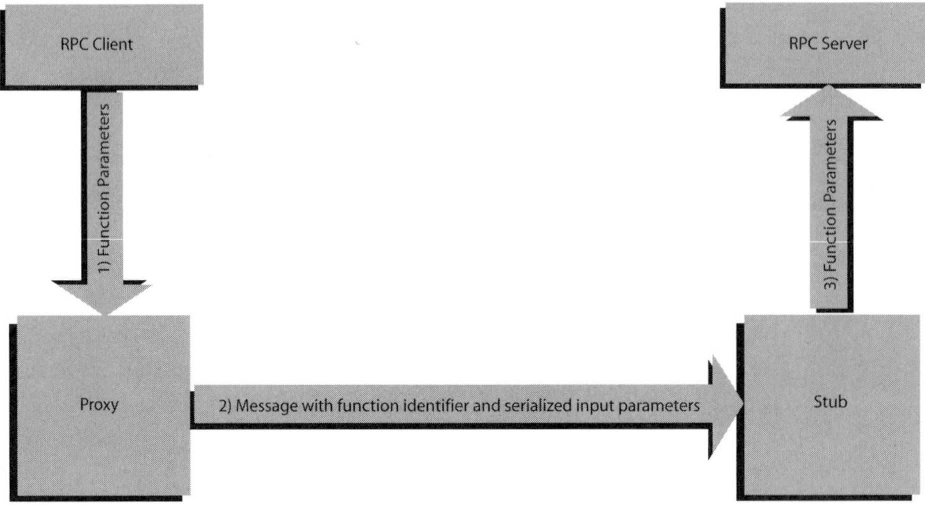

FIGURE 6.4.2 *RPC sequence diagram without reply.*

When an RPC function is called from an RPC client, it cannot directly execute the function body on the RPC server, of course. Instead, it collects function parameters and adds these parameters into a message, as well as a message header, to identify the desired function call. The code that performs this phase is called the *proxy*, because it runs another function with the same name, which *serializes (marshals)* function identifiers and parameters to a data stream and sends a message, instead of calling the actual function.

When a message is received on an RPC server, it passes the message to a function that reads the message, determines which RPC body should take the control, extracts message data into parameters, and calls an RPC function body. This is called the *stub*, due to its role of selecting one of many functions and invoking the appropriate call. Notice that we are only discussing asynchronous RPC here, so we can safely ignore the RPC response phase.

As an RPC call is converted to a message and analyzed at the other side, every RPC message should be formed in a specific manner. When an RPC is called on the proxy side, the generated message must include all needed information about the function call. This includes:

- Function Identifier tag
- Serialization of function parameters

The *Function Identifier* is a predefined number whose value is incremented whenever another RPC function is declared. This is necessary to detect where the message is serialized.

Serialization of function parameters is basically a concatenated data block of each parameter listed one by one, built by the proxy. Ignoring error detection and recovery for now, only the parameter values themselves are needed, because we can deduce how many parameters and which type they are when we look at the Function Identifier.

There are several ways to serialize parameters of various data types. The example presented with this article shows an example of a message class and several serialization functions with the same function name and different parameter types (function overloading), like the following example:

```
void Message_Read(CMessage& m,double &val);
void Message_Read(CMessage& m,std::string &val);
void Message_Write(CMessage& m,const double &val);
void Message_Write(CMessage& m,const std::string &val);
```

Figure 6.4.3 shows how developers adopt RPC for their own networking applications.

We want to generate all our networking code with simple, one-line declarations. RPC introduces *Interface Definition Language (IDL)* for this type of declaration. The IDL file is where we write RPC function declarations, as well as these one-line declarations. Keep in mind that the IDL file cannot be directly identified by our application source files. Instead, IDL files should be compiled by the *IDL compiler*, which generates the proxy and stub code files. The proxy code is then linked to a program

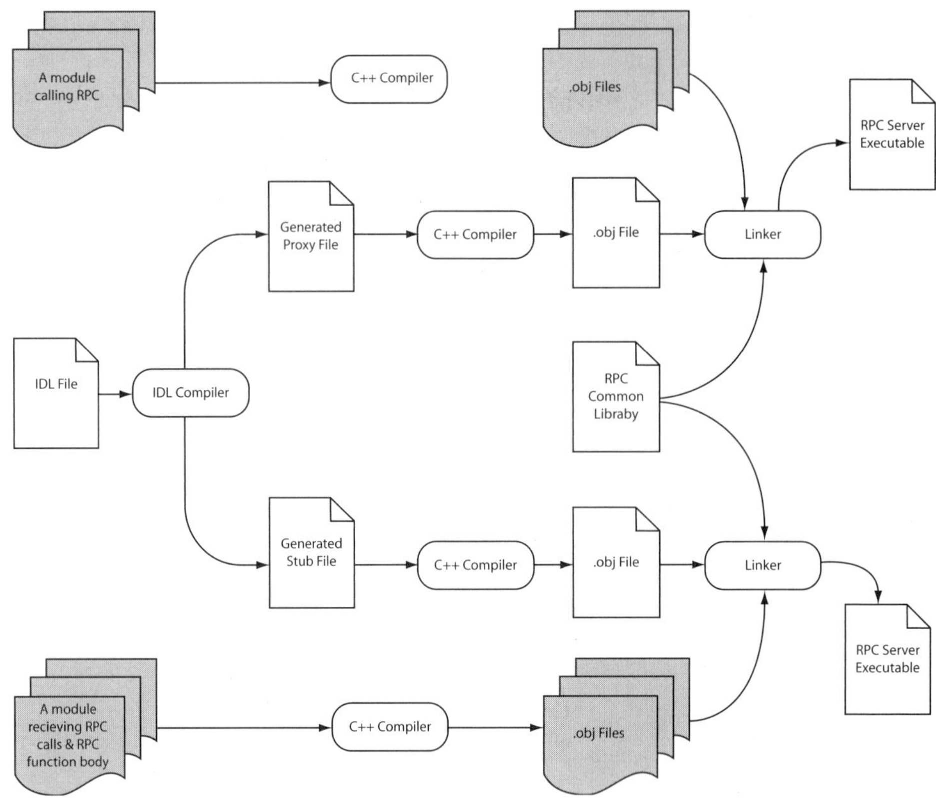

FIGURE 6.4.3 *Design-time sequence diagram.*

where RPC functions are remotely called; meanwhile, the stub code is linked to the program where they are invoked.

As at least one helper function or class exists for both the stub and the proxy, we may want to move them into a library, which we call the common runtime.

Do not include the generated proxy and stub code in your source control system, however. As the IDL compiler overwrites the proxy and stub code when an IDL file is modified, it may cause a build error when the proxy and stub codes are not checked out and are read-only.

RPC: Implementation

The following sections detail RPC implementation.

Proxy and Stub

An RPC function cannot be called directly, since its actual body is on another process. However, the local function with the same prototype should be available. It surrogates the call by creating a message and sending it to the remote process, where the actual function body exists. These local versions of the remote calls are what we refer to as *proxy code*.

The IDL compiler is responsible for generating the proxy code. Our IDL compiler generates proxy code using a code pattern that we specify. One easy way of defining this specification is to write an example proxy code, deduce code patterns from it, and use this model within our IDL compiler.

When a message is received, it should be passed to a function that will have a giant switch-case. At first, we identify what the receive message is requesting by reading the Function Identifier in the message header. Then, we go to one of the switch-cases. Each switch-case routine *deserializes* (unmarshals) the messages into each parameter value. Then we call the RPC function body. Our stub code consists of only a function with many switch-cases inside it. The function bodies are outside the stub code. The IDL compiler can also be responsible for generating the stub code. Like our proxy code patterns, we feed stub code models to the IDL compiler.

IDL Compiler

To start the IDL compiler, we have to make a compiler that takes IDL files as input and then generates output code of stub and proxy. Let's start with the parser, which analyses what RPC functions the IDL file declares. We choose ANTLR [Parr04] for our implementation here, which is more comprehensive and easy to use than Lex and Yacc. ANTLR is a top-down parser generator written in Java, but we can generate parser code in C++ as well.

For simplicity, we'll stick to a basic grammar for our IDL files. When you look at IDL files of legacy RPC systems, they have more parameters such as network protocols, parameter-passing directions, and unique IDs. For now, let's see a basic example:

```
Knight_Move(int id,float x,float y,float z);
Knight_Attack(int id,int target,int damage);
```

With this model in mind, Listing 6.4.4 provides an example of a complete grammar in ANTLR format.

Listing 6.4.4 A Snippet of Our IDL Grammar

```
// an RPC function definition
functionDefinition :
    IDENT // function name
    LPAREN
    ( parameterDefinition
        ( COMMA! param=parameterDefinition  )*
```

```
    )?
    RPAREN
    SEMI
    ;
// an RPC parameter
parameterDefinition :
    IDENT // type
    IDENT // name
    ;
```

The first function identifier number can be defined anywhere, even outside of the IDL file, but it's usually less confusing to keep the definition within the IDL file.

The backend of our compiler should generate these files based on the semantic information from the frontend (discovered by the parser). In general, an IDL output consists of several source code files:

- Proxy source code and its header
- Stub source code and its header

Going back and looking at Listings 6.4.1 and 6.4.2, we can see that these code patterns correlate to Listing 6.4.4, where `FunctionName` stands for an RPC function name, `ParameterDeclarations` stands for C++ declarations for all the function parameters in the RPC function, and `Parameters` stands for the parameter list separated by commas. See Listing 6.4.5.

Listing 6.4.5 Our Proxy and Stub Code Pattern

```
// common
static const RPCHeader RPC_ID_FunctionName=(10+0);
FunctionIdentifierDefinitionsForOtherFunctions

// proxy
RPCResult FunctionName(RPCSendTo sendTo,RPCSendContext
                       sendContext,ParameterDeclarations)
{
    CMessage m;
    Message_Write(m,RPC_ID_FunctionName);
    Message_Write(m,FirstParameter);
    ...
    Message_Write(m,LastParameter);
    return RPC_Send(sendTo,sendContext,m);
}

ProxyDefinitionsForOtherFunctions

// stub
RPCResult RPC_DoStub(RPCSendTo recvFrom,RPCSendContext
                     recvContext,CMessage& m)
```

```
{
    RPCHeader msgID;
    m.SetCursor(0);
    Message_Read(m,msgID);
    switch(msgID)
    {
    case RPC_ID_FunctionName:
        {
            FirstParameterDefinition;
            Message_Read(m,FirstParameter);
            ...
            LastParameterDefinition;
            Message_Read(m,LastParameter);
            FunctionName(
                recvFrom,
                recvContext,
                Parameters);
        }
        break;
    CasesForOtherFunctions
    }
}
```

Note that `RPCHeader`, `RPCSendTo`, and `RPCSendContext` are just our own local type definitions. In these examples, they're defined as `unsigned int`.

For simplicity, the backend code described here uses `printf()` or `cout`, with several `for{}` statements. However, this will get cumbersome when the code patterns get more complex. So it will be helpful to adopt a text generator based on text templates such as eNITL [Breck99].

It may be hard to keep maintaining and modifying the IDL compiler as we add more functionality to our RPC system. We can drive some parts of them into a common library, which contains several `typedefs`, helper functions, and some classes. The example in this article has a very little common library called `MyRPC`. `MyRPC` has a class `CMessage` and several read and write functions for the most frequently used primitive data types such as `int`, `float`, and `std::string`.

RPC: Usage

To use our RPC implementation within our application, we should add the IDL file to our project and configure custom build options for the IDL files. In the case of Visual Studio.Net, we may configure these per Figure 6.4.4.

In addition, the compiled output files and common library need to be added to our project configurations. As the generated proxy and stub code is a kind of compilation output, it is recommended to add generated proxy and stub .h and .cpp files indirectly to your source code using `#include` clauses.

`RPCHeader`, `RPCSendTo`, and `RPCSendContext` are used for sending and receiving tasks via your networking module. If the number of RPC functions defined is under 255, a traffic conservation trick would be to change `RPCHeader` to `unsigned char`.

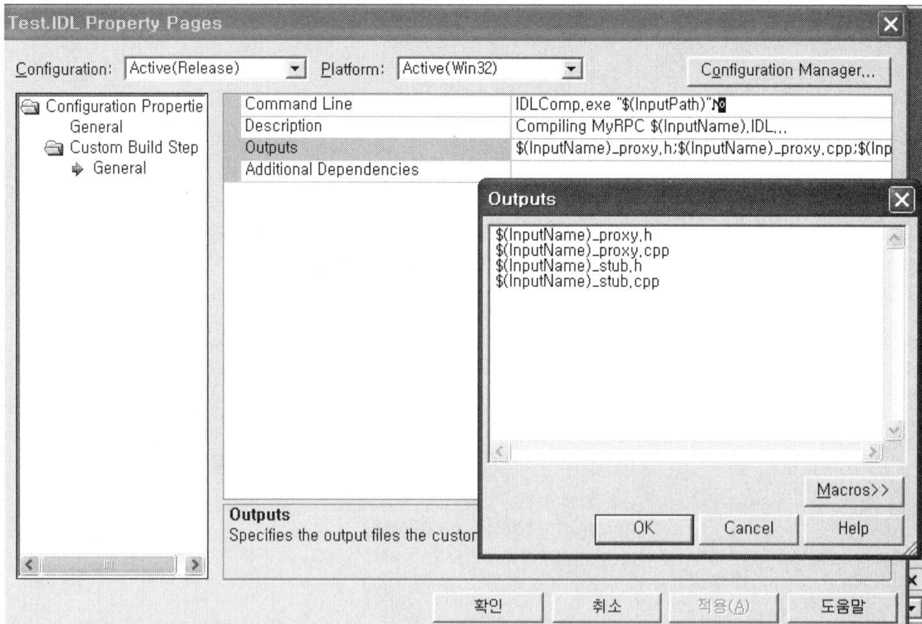

FIGURE 6.4.4 *Configuration of Test.IDL.*

`RPCSendTo` identifies the remote computer that receives the messages. `RPCSendContext` defines other parameters such as protocol selection (TCP or UDP), timeout options, or invocation identifiers for multiple asynchronous responses. You may change these `typedefs` as you wish. This RPC implementation automatically adds `RPCSendTo` and `RPCSendContext` into generated RPC functions' declarations as the first and second parameter, respectively.

You then need to add a networking module to the application, because our RPC system itself doesn't have any. When the proxy constructs a message, it calls `RPC_Send()` to pass it to your network modules. Meanwhile, when a message is received at your network modules, it should pass the message to the stub through `RPC_Stub()`, which exists in the generated stub file.

Sample Programs

There are two executable examples with this article: *SimpleTest* and *RPCDuel*. SimpleTest is basically a Hello World application. It has an IDL file and a `main()` function, which calls some RPC proxy functions, which just saves the generated message to its local memory. Then assuming it has already received the message sent by the proxy, it calls a stub function, which resolves the message and calls the appropriate RPC body. While trivial, it should serve as a quick example of how the more complex RPC samples work.

RPCDuel is a modified version of a simple game called *Duel* in the Microsoft DirectX SDK sample. RPCDuel is an example of RPC based on DirectPlay, which *Duel* is also based on. The original application messages have been changed to `MyRPC` ones, while commenting out the original portions. You can examine how RPC works by searching for the comment before RPC in the RPCDuel source files.

Further Features

There is a proverb in Korea, "A journey of a thousand miles starts with but a single step." Although the implementation here, as a first footstep, is written in a simple manner and only begins to show the practical use of RPC, it should be easy to improve and extend the system based on your needs. Here are some areas for improvements worth investigating.

Allow Multiple Proxy/Stub Instances of an IDL in a Program

This implementation generates global functions and `typedefs`. This means there's a limitation on multiple instantiations of the RPC functions for multiple game sessions or other re-use. One solution is to have the IDL compiler generate a proxy class and an abstract stub class, capable of handling several clients at once.

Error Detection and Recovery

Most online game servers or peers have to program in a tolerance against erroneous messages, which may cause various exceptions such as buffer overrun, invalid message format, and networking failure. One of the solutions is to add boundary checking to our serialization and deserialization functions. Of course, if you enable your IDL grammar to accept value ranges specified by the game programmers, it may reduce having to write vulgarity checking codes.

More Data Types

In our example, only some primitive data types such as integer, floating number, and strings have serialization and deserialization functions. However, we may want to support more data types in our RPC functions, even arrays and structures. There is a serializable class `Vector3D` in the SimpleTest example. It has these two functions.

```
void Message_Write(CMessage& m,const Vector3D &val);
void Message_Read(CMessage& m,Vector3D &val);
```

We can continue defining as many serialization and deserialization functions as necessary. Some C++ template functions might be more convenient for generic structures such as `array` and `list`, however.

Message Encryption

In many online games, not all the messages need highly secured encryption, and due to performance issues, only a few types of communicated messages are made secure.

When we add an encryption option to our IDL grammar, and IDL output code pattern and encryption facilities to our streaming class, we can make use of encryption easily just with one definition such as:

```
[encrypted] RequestLogin(string id,string password);
```

Message Compression

Message compression is easily implemented by enhancing our streaming class and our IDL grammar. For example, we may want to add a "number of bits" option for each parameter, which we can define like this:

```
Knight_Attack(int type:4,int magicBuff:7,int critical:1);
```

Variable `type` takes four bits and `magicBuff` takes seven bits, while `critical` takes one bit. Of course, we would then need to modify our streaming class for bitwise manipulation.

Switch-Case Optimization

For better performance, it is also a good approach to substitute switch-cases in RPC stub to a binary search tree, to get $O(\log n)$ for n as number of RPC functions.

Debugging and Profiling Tools

It may be easier to profile servers by adding some probe code to the RPC proxy and stub code templates. For example, when we want to trace every incoming or outgoing message, we can do so just by adding code that prints the function name and parameter values to console or debug output. Of course, we can also view the trace log records showing what functions and parameters have been passed. This is a great way to help detect vulgarity received from a bad game client or RPC body functions that cause long process times.

Synchronous RPC

Most games will typically not require synchronous RPC; however, if it is needed for your programs, you can add this faculty to your RPC at runtime.

Adding synchronous RPC to our example requires some more work:

- We need to define more sequences that wait until the RPC body returns and passes the return values to the RPC function caller.
- Only guaranteed messages are acceptable with synchronous RPC.
- We need to add a parameter direction option, which are input parameters (*inparam*) and output parameters (*outparam*). Inparam is sent to the RPC server

while Outparam is received from the RPC server after the RPC body executes. For this difference, we should add parameter direction grammar to our IDL compiler and add code that serializes outparams at the stub and deserializes inparams at the proxy. Here is one example of synchronous RPC.

```
UserLogin([in] string id,[in] string password,
        [out] int loginResult);
```

- We need to consider exceptional cases such as timeouts and exceptions, to prevent deadlock.
- We need to manage function call sequence number. When RPC outparam messages are received by the proxy, it can determine which thread is waiting by the call sequence number. To only wake a thread that corresponds to that sequence number, we need to prepare a queue containing outstanding RPC calls waiting for outparam messages.

Conclusion

Writing an RPC implementation normally has some prerequisites not associated with game programmers. This gem was an attempt to guide you towards getting started with your own RPC system, and you're encouraged to explore and see the productivity and efficiency, as well as performance, you can get via RPC systems. To get the best understanding from this article, you may want to look at some of the references. Now it is your turn!

References

[Breck99] eNITL. *The Network Improv Template Language*. Available online at *http://networkimprov.com/enitl/enitl.html*.

[Parr04] Parr, Terence. *ANTLR Parser Generator v2.7.4*. Available online at *http://www.antlr.org*.

[Sebesta02] Sebesta, Robert W. *Concepts of Programming Languages 5th Edition*, 109–123, 155–159. Addison Wesley, 2002.

[Silberschatz02] Silberschatz, Galvin, and Gagne, *Operating System Concepts 6th Edition*, 121–124. Wiley, 2002.

6.5

Overcoming Network Address Translation in Peer-to-Peer Communications

Jon Watte

hplus-gpg5@mindcontrol.org

Peer-to-peer computing revolutionized the way we compute. From the early research Internet of the late 1970s through the dial-up Internet revolution in the early 1990s to today's bonanza of fat broadband pipes, everyone is using computer networking for fun and for profit. More than 50% of all Internet users will have broadband when this gem is published. Although, with this popularity comes all kinds of problems: self-replicating worms, pings of death, and Windows security problems, coupled with heavy vendor scare tactics, cause most users to set up firewalls to protect their computers. Connection-sharing firewalls are a hot selling item, as homes with multiple computers find that sharing a single broadband connection is the easiest route; prices having fallen to under $100 for a feature-rich wireless access point with router, switch, and firewall.

Online games are maybe one of the more exciting applications of computer networking technology, where the ability to compete with players from all over the world from the comfort of your own office, living room, or coffee shop has subtly changed how we view the term "buddy" and how we choose to interact online. Companies like Sony Online Entertainment and NCSoft make it their business to run large server clusters where players from all over the world can meet and play together. However, these big server clusters come with big leasing, power, and networking bills, and such services usually come with a monthly price tag for the end user. Thus, another popular form of online gaming is *peer-to-peer gaming*, where one player's computer also serves as the server for the game, and all the other players connect to this player, who is said to be hosting the game.

Unfortunately, some games are not as good at supporting this model of connection as others. Frequently, firewalls and connection sharing software get in the way of hosting games, and sometimes even joining games. While some users may be technical enough to configure a DMZ or port forwarding in their firewalls, many are not. And even for the technical users, pleading with a Starbucks® employee to give you access to their wireless access "hot spot" is unlikely to make that hosted game of *Warcraft® III* come any closer. As a developer of a networked game, you would like to do better, and this gem will show you how.

Audience

This chapter is intended for all game programmers who want their game to work as well as possible on the Internet. It is especially important for programmers who want their games to use peer-to-peer, player-hosted servers, and want to extend to as many users as possible without telling users to configure port forwarding, set up a DMZ, or remove their firewall.

We assume that you are familiar with general Berkeley sockets programming (Unix) or Windows WinSock Version 2 (Windows). The technique shown will work equally well under either operating environment. For purposes of this gem, MacOS X (and higher) works a lot like Unix, but the code has not been verified on MacOS X. This chapter uses C++ for its code samples, but the techniques can be expressed in any language capable of using networking at the sockets layer.

IP Addresses

At the core of all networking is the network address. The Internet at large uses an address format called IPv4, which is short for Internet Protocol Version 4. What the first three versions looked like has long since lost its relevance. There is also an up-and-coming version called IPv6 that has so far failed to gain mainstream acceptance. In this article, "IP address" is synonymous with "IPv4 address."

An IP address is simply a series of four bytes. Typically, it will be written out in dotted notation, such as 192.168.1.2. An IP address identifies a specific network card or modem connected to a specific device on the Internet; these individual hardware devices are called *network interfaces*.

Devices connected to the Internet may run multiple services; for example, a Web server will often also run a Secure Shell Daemon (SSHD) that allows administrators to access the command-line interface of the server for monitoring and maintenance. To distinguish network packets destined for the Web server from network packets destined for the SSHD, the two most common Internet protocols add the concept of a port number. Each service uses its own port; for Web servers, the port is 80 unencrypted services and 443 for encrypted services. For the SSHD, the port is 22.

For games, the developer will often choose an arbitrary port within the allowable range. Ports in TCP and UDP addresses are two bytes, and thus the range is between 0 and 65535 inclusive, although tradition dictates that the port number is chosen in the range 1024–49151, inclusive. This tradition likely started with the arbitrary implementation choice on Unix, where ports 1 through 1023 are reserved for the special administrative user "root" on the machine, and only root may open new sockets listening for traffic on these ports. For more information, see [Man3rresvport] and [RFC793].

A UDP or TCP address thus consists of six bytes: four single-byte numbers in the range 0–255, inclusive, called the IP address, and one two-byte number in the range 0–65535, inclusive, called simply the port. The IP protocol suite specifies that all numbers larger than a single byte be sent with the high-order byte first (big-endian), and most sockets implementations supply functions or macros named `htonl()`, `htons()`, `ntohl()`, and `ntohs()` to convert between the local machine representation and the well-defined network representation of numbers.

Sockets Usage

A program running on a machine (we will call these programs "processes" and the machines "nodes" in the rest of this chapter) will typically play one of two roles: server or client. A server process will create a socket using `::socket()` and bind it to a local port and one of many local addresses if the node has multiple network interfaces, using `::bind()`. If the socket is used for TCP connections, the server will then call `::listen()` and enter a loop where it calls `::accept()` to wait for and accept incoming connections from clients. `::accept()` returns a new socket for each new client, and data is exchanged using `::send()` and `::recv()` using this socket. To tell the different connections apart, each TCP connection on the client side automatically allocates a new, unused port for the specific server connection.

If the socket is instead used for UDP connections, the process will enter a loop where it calls `::recvfrom()` on the socket directly after `::bind()`. All incoming traffic from all clients will arrive at the same socket. The network layer has no notion of connectedness, so if multiple, related packets are to be exchanged over UDP, some higher layer software (such as the process itself) has to take care of the coordination thereof. Return traffic for servers using UDP is usually sent using `::sendto()`.

For a client of a TCP service, after calling `::socket()`, the process will call `::connect()` to establish a connection to the intended recipient; once connected, `::send()` and `::recv()` are used for data exchange. The argument to `::connect()` is a TCP address that may have been looked up from a textual name (such as "www.there.com:80"), using name server functions such as `::gethostbyname()`. Meanwhile, clients of UDP just call `::sendto()`, passing in the IP address (again, possibly derived from textual form using the name resolution library), and receive data back using `::recvfrom()`.

In a typical process, many things will be going on at the same time, so thinking of "send" and "receive" as sequential events is usually misleading. Physics simulation, graphics drawing, audio mixing, and disk I/O are examples of other actions often happening at the same time as networking in a typical action-oriented networked computer game. The approach to managing these overlapping tasks is usually either to poll the network using `::select()` to determine what can be productively done, or to spawn multiple threads to deal with operations in different parts of the program. The supporting code for this article uses `::select()`(or on Linux, the `::select()`-like function `::poll()`), because it causes less synchronization overhead and leads to fewer threading bugs; the techniques presented are equally useful in either world view.

A specific process can be a server and a client at the same time. For TCP, this usually means creating at least two sockets; one that is listening and accepting new incoming connections and a separate socket that is connected as a client to some server on the other end. For UDP processes, multiple sockets are not necessary, because it is possible to `::sendto()` and `::recvfrom()` on a socket to and from an arbitrary number of peers. In fact, when using UDP, the concept of "client" and "server" is only visible at the application level, not in the network layers below.

Purists will note that the TCP protocol doesn't specify "clients" and "servers," but in reality, a process that calls `::accept()` is a server, and a process that calls `::connect()` is a client. See [Stevens94] for more details.

Routers, Peers, Protocols

A few more preliminaries are needed to flesh out the background against which to examine peer-to-peer networked gaming.

First, the Internet does not work like a telephone, where a wire is hooked up to the handset on one side and, conceptually, is hooked up through switches to a wire leading to the handset on the other side, forming a closed electrical circuit. Instead, from the point of view of the Internet infrastructure, each IP packet is separate from each other packet. When a process causes a packet to be sent, the local node makes a determination on which interface to send the packet; the packet then makes it through that interface to a router on the other end of that specific connection (the first router along this path is referred to as a gateway for the local node). That router then makes a determination as to where to forward the packet among its possibly many interfaces, passes it along, and so on. The process is repeated until the packet makes it to one of the interfaces on the recipient node and is delivered to the receiving process, or delivery fails. It is important to keep in mind that each router inspects all incoming packets and follows some kind of rule to figure out which interface to forward the packet to, or whether to just ignore the packet (known as "dropping the packet").

Second, because every node participating in the Internet has its own IP address (and, for most services, a socket listening on a specific port), there is no way to inspect just the IP address of a packet and know whether the packet is sent by a client or a server. On the Internet, all nodes are logically equivalent; they are said to be peers of each other. The notion of client and server is something that is constructed by the users of the Internet, typically implemented into the software running the processes on each node.

Third, there are a large number of protocols in use on the Internet. Some of the more common ones include 802.3 (for regular wired Ethernet), IP (packets containing an IP address), UDP (specifying a source and destination port number), and DNS (used for querying name servers to resolve textual node names to IP addresses). A given packet will usually make use of many of these protocols at the same time; a DNS query will be sent on port 53 in a UDP packet to some name server IP address, transmitted over Ethernet through the first jump to the DSL or cable modem. Each protocol is layered on top of the underlying protocols, so UDP is layered on top of IP, and DNS is layered on top of UDP (in this case).

UDP Packet Diagram

An example DNS query packet, as explained earlier, is shown in Figure 6.5.1 at the IP layer. Below IP, there will be additional framing, such as Ethernet, ATM, or PPP, which we have excluded for clarity because this gem deals only with phenomena observable at the IP protocol layer and above. We also disregard minutiae like packet fragmentation or van Jacobsen header compression, which do not modify the basic operation of IP networks at the level visible in this gem.

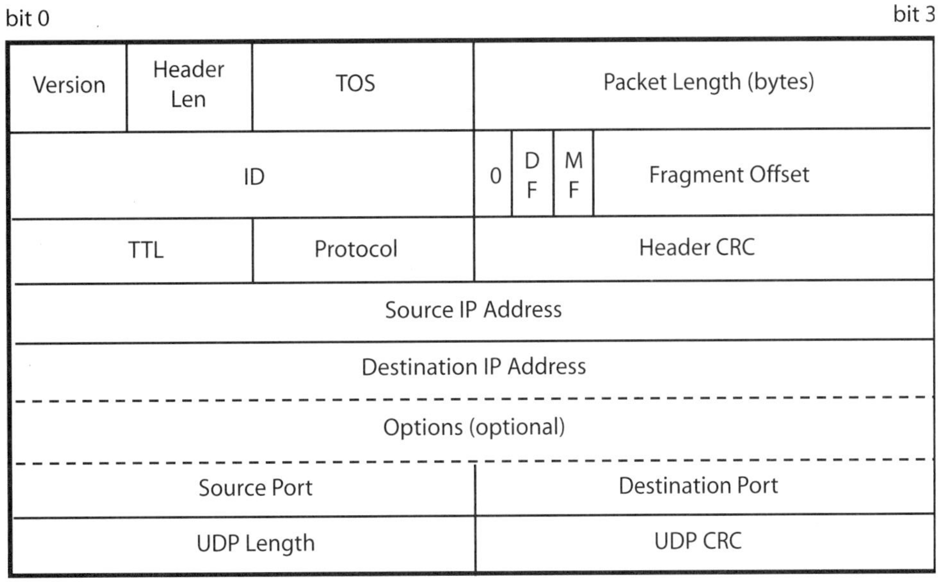

bit 0 bit 3

Version	Header Len	TOS	Packet Length (bytes)			
ID			0	D F	M F	Fragment Offset
TTL		Protocol	Header CRC			
Source IP Address						
Destination IP Address						
Options (optional)						
Source Port			Destination Port			
UDP Length			UDP CRC			

FIGURE 6.5.1 *Anatomy of a UDP packet, with IP header, UDP header, and payload data.*

Given all this knowledge, you should be able to write a networked game that works over the Internet as it looked in the early '90s. However, time has moved on, and the introduction of NAT (Network Address Translation) changed all that.

What Is NAT?

The Internet started growing rapidly in 1992 and has kept on growing ever since. Because it is a peer-to-peer network, each node on the Internet needs its own, unique address. These addresses take the form of four bytes, so there is a total available of a little over four billion addresses in the world.

The Problem (IP Address Space)

At some point, we are going to want to add more nodes (or at least interfaces) in the world than supported by four-byte addresses, and even worse, the way that addresses are used at the routing level causes a certain amount of waste. In addition, the allocation between different parts of the world is sometimes grossly skewed; it is said that MIT has more Internet addresses allocated for its internal use than the entire country of China! Whether this is true or not, the Internet has been facing an address crunch, growing faster than the ability to allocate addresses.

Another Problem (Security)

Nodes connected to the Internet are peers to all other nodes. This means that you can type in any URL in a Web browser, and send network traffic to whatever other node that URL resolves to. Unfortunately, it also means that any peer on the Internet can send your node whatever network packet it wishes. Some network services are designed with more careful attention to this fact than others are, and a number of remote exploits (security holes) have been found, using bugs in networked software or even in an OS like Windows itself to take over virtually any node on the Internet, bypassing the need for a password.

Most users will be unable to fix application bugs on their own, and a better way of avoiding security holes through application bugs than just unplugging the machine from the network is necessary.

The Fix

A popular fix to the dual problems of IP address space shortage and keeping unwanted network traffic away has emerged; it is known as *Network Address Translation* or *NAT* for short. Most DSL routers, cable modems, and Internet Connection Sharing devices use NAT to work their magic.

The idea is simple: most network protocols use UDP or TCP for their underlying transport. A port number and an IP address identify the endpoints communicating in those protocols. If multiple nodes can share a single IP address but use different port numbers, and the network could somehow distinguish which node to forward a packet to, based on the port in addition to the address, then you would only need a single IP address per household, company, or other subnetwork using less than 65,000 simultaneous connections.

The low-level network protocols like ARP that make the packets flow between nodes do not work well if more than one node share the same IP address, but there's a higher-level entity that fits the bill perfectly to implement this address sharing: the gateway router. If all nodes wishing to share one address (from the point of view of the Internet) sit on one end of the router, and the router is the only visible node to the Internet, then everything will be happy, assuming we can find some addresses for the internal nodes to use when talking to each other and to the router.

Luckily, some address ranges of the IP address space are reserved for experimental or private use. These ranges are `10.x.x.x` (with space for 16 million internal nodes), `172.16+x.y.z` (with space for a million internal nodes), and `192.168.x.y` (with space for about 65,000 internal nodes). These addresses are guaranteed to never be used on the publicly visible Internet, so using those addresses inside a NAT-routed network is guaranteed to not clash with anything outside the NAT. For more information, see [RFC1918].

In our example, the NAT device has address `10.0.0.1` on the inside and address `81.226.155.187` on the outside (with apologies to whoever currently uses that address). The nodes on the inside of the NAT are `10.0.0.2` and `10.0.0.3`, and the sample site we are trying to connect to is `64.125.216.191` (again with suitable apologies to whoever uses that currently). Presumably, the ISP for the user with the NAT box has allocated the `81.x` address, and the `64.x` address has been allocated by the hosting provider for the destination server, and found by the user using DNS.

Putting it all together, when nodes inside the NAT start up, they are assigned addresses out of a private address range, and their gateway is configured to be the NAT router. When they want to communicate with some node on the outside (say, `64.125.216.191:80` for a Web connection), they form their network packets as usual (say, using source address `10.0.0.2:6000`), and forward them to the NAT router. The NAT router then notices that the source address is from within its private network, and substitutes its own, public, address as the source address, so for a device on the outside, it looks like the packet comes from the NAT router.

Unfortunately, more than one internal node may use the same port number for the source port. Thus, the NAT router must substitute a new port number for the original port number, in addition to its own IP address for the private source IP address.

Finally, in turn for returning network packets to make their way back to the right node, the NAT router maintains a table of (source IP, source port, substitute IP, substitute port, destination IP, destination port) tuples to be able to rewrite returning packets. In our example, illustrated in Figure 6.5.2, the tuple for a simple Web request is the first line of the table: (`10.0.0.2,6000, 81.226.155.187,11001, 64.125.216.191,80`). Once the port number 11001 has been allocated on the NAT to be used for the node

10.0.0.2 port 6000, this port number should remain allocated for that address/port pair for as long as the connection is open, or a returning packet addressed to 81.226.155.187:11001 will not make it back to the right place.

Third parties cannot send traffic to the internal node, because the private address of the internal node makes no sense when interpreted in the open Internet; a packet addressed to 10.0.0.2 from the outside would not even make it to the gateway. Similarly, if a packet arrives at the NAT router with a source address or port that the internal node has not recently sent data to, there will be no tuple recorded in the gateway to translate the destination address to an internal address, and the gateway will simply drop the packet. In this way, a NAT router works a lot like a stateful firewall and often provides all the protection a typical home user needs from remote network attacks. It still cannot protect against attacks that rely on user behavior, such as sending Trojans through e-mail or enticing the user to click on malicious Web links, but it is a good first defense.

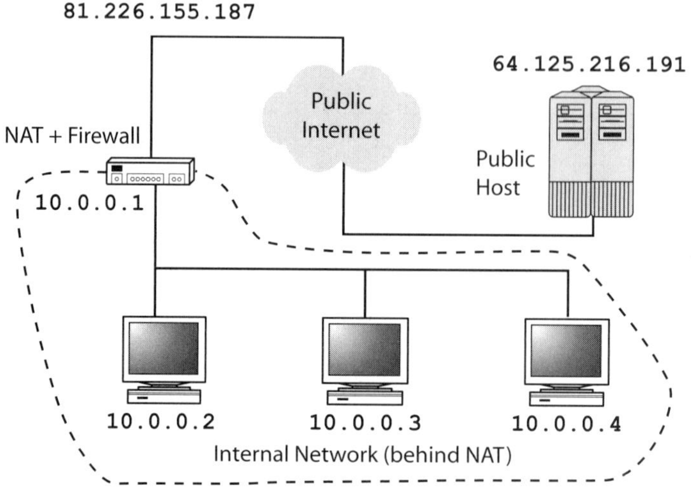

Internal Address	Public Address	Destination
10.0.0.2:6000	81.226.155.187:1101	64.125.216.191:80
10.0.0.2:53	81.226.155.87:53	195.67.199.27:53
10.0.0.2:53	81.226.155.87:53	195.67.199.28:53
10.0.0.4:53	81.226.155.87:11002	195.67.199.27:53

FIGURE 6.5.2 *Example NAT-ed Internet connection.*

How Does NAT Break Client/Server Protocols?

The NAT router substitutes a public source address/port pair for the private address/port pair, remembers the destination address/port, and forwards the packet. For returning packets, it does the reverse translation, and the node on the internal network can communicate flawlessly with the outside world.

Unfortunately, this does not work for all protocols, especially protocols designed before NAT gained widespread acceptance, or without proper understanding of the needs of NAT. One prime example is the File Transfer Protocol (FTP) that is commonly used to download files on the Internet. When FTP was designed, it was designed so that one node could set up a file transfer between two other nodes [RFC959], [RFC1123]. The controlling node C would connect to node A, tell node A to expect a file, node A would start listening on a port, and tell node C what this port is. Node C would then connect node B, and tell node B to connect to node A on that port, sending the file. This also allows the control connection to remain open and issue more commands while data is being transferred on the data connection.

The common case of transferring a file to the controlling node C from the server node B is handled as a special case in the FTP protocol, where the port and address of node C are forwarded to node B, and node B connects back to node C to actually send the data.

The problem is that, because the receiving node listens on a port, rather than actively connecting to the external server, if a NAT router is in the way, the local port and address of node C makes no sense to node B when instructed to connect back. The NAT router translates the source address of the outgoing request to connect back to node C, but it does not have any knowledge of the actual data stream inside the FTP control connection, and thus the internal address and port of the socket waiting for the connection passes through untouched as data on the wire.

An example of how a UDP-based game may make the same mistake as the FTP protocol is found in Listing 6.5.1.

Listing 6.5.1 Embedded Address Code Sample

```
1: Embedded Address Code Sample// An example packet structure for
// connecting to a server.
struct CmdHello {
  char cmd;
  char len;
  unsigned short port;
  unsigned int addr;
};

// Get the local address of a socket; this is not
// something that's generally
// useful on the public internet!
struct sockaddr_in addr;
```

```
socklen_t len;
len = sizeof(addr);
::getsockname( sock, (struct sockaddr *)&addr,
      &len );

// This bad code puts a local address into
// a packet sent to a remote location – do
// NOT do this yourself!
Hello h;
h.cmd = CMD_HELLO;
h.len = sizeof(h);
h.port = addr.sin_port;  // don't do this!
h.addr = addr.sin_addr;  // don't do this!
::sendto( sock, &h, h.len, 0,
      serverAddr, sizeof(*serverAddr) );
```

The Hack

Because FTP is a very common protocol with lots of clients in use, a fix had to be found. Ideally, that fix would not require changing all FTP clients in existence.

The fix that emerged involves adding smarts to the NAT router and having it inspect the data of packets of traffic to certain ports. Most NAT routers today know enough of the FTP control protocol to be able to intercept a control message containing an address and port and rewrite the data of the protocol to contain a public address and port; the router will also add the appropriate tuple in the active NAT session table to allow packets from the serving node to get back in.

While the FTP protocol is so widespread that it enjoys special status in the majority of NAT gateways (but not all), newly designed protocols cannot hope to achieve the same special-case status.

The Fix

The real fix to make a network protocol NAT safe is to structure the protocol so that IP addresses or port numbers do not need to travel within the data stream. The easiest way to make sure that this is sufficient for the protocol needs is to always create a connection from the client to the server, using UDP or TCP, and always have the server reply back to the client using the address visible on the server when the client connects. No forwarding of connection information should occur over back channels between servers. Correct management of peer addresses is illustrated in Listing 6.5.2.

Some very advanced data center equipment exists that is NAT aware. One kind uses *reverse NAT* to load-balance connections, secure clusters against external attackers, or allow freedom in assignment and management of IP address space. Design of a communication system involving reverse NAT in the face of shared authentication has to be done with utmost care and is beyond the scope of this gem.

Listing 6.5.2 Correct Address Management

```
// A proposed packet for acknowledging a
// (corrected) CmdHello packet.
struct CmdHelloAck {
  char cmd;
  char len;
};

// The server uses ::recvfrom() to correctly get the
// address of the peer that connects.
struct sockaddr_in addr;
socklen_t len = sizeof(addr);
union {
   CmdHello hello;
} command;
::recvfrom( sock, &command, sizeof(command), 0,
      (struct sockaddr *)&addr, &len );
// Server registers connected client on a received
// hello packet, and then acknowledges using
// ::sendto() to the received address.
if( command.hello.cmd == CMD_HELLO ) {
   // client_hello() is the function that adds
   // a newly connected client to some internal list
   client_hello( command.hello, addr );
   CmdHelloAck ack;
   ack.cmd = CMD_HELLO_ACK;
   ack.len = sizeof(ack);
   ::sendto( sock, &ack, sizeof(ack), 0,
         (struct sockaddr *)addr, sizeof(addr) );
}
```

Other Problems

A variant of this problem is where a game server cluster uses one server for validating logins, and then passes the information about the player to another server, which attempts to return traffic to the client. Even if the public NAT address of the client is used, the NAT router does not expect to see traffic from the new server, so the return traffic is dropped.

Again, the rule to make a protocol fully NAT safe is to always initiate the connection with each individual server from the client, and to never send IP addresses or port numbers as data, but instead rely on `::accept()`, `::getpeername()`, and `::recvfrom()` (but not `::getsockname()`!) to get the address of the node on the other end.

To support the idea of a central login server that validates username and password for a server cluster, you could use a cryptographic cookie. Share a common secret (frequently, a 128-bit strong random number) between the servers. When the player logs in, the login server creates a hash of user ID, login time, and the shared secret, and returns user ID, time, and hash to the client. The client then submits this same information to each other server; that server need only verify that the hash of user ID, time, and secret (not known to the client) matches the hash supplied by the client, to know that the login server properly validated the name/password that goes with the user ID in question, at the time indicated. The strength of this system is mostly dependent on the strength of the shared secret (which should change every so often) and the strength of the hashing algorithm; on Linux, using 16 bytes from /dev/random works well for shared secret, and MD5 is a commonly used strong hashing function.

If you follow this advice, your client/server service will be NAT safe. However, how does this work when using peer-to-peer networking?

How Does NAT Break Peer-to-Peer Protocols?

Setting up and operating large server clusters is expensive. For a smaller game developer, or a game developer who does not want to charge players $14.95 a month for access after the initial purchase, allowing players to host their own game servers is an attractive option. There are security implications in that you can't really trust an arbitrary server hosted in some hacker's bedroom, but the popularity of peer-to-peer networked games all the way from id Software®'s *Doom*™ through Dice's *Battlefield 1942*™ and on validate the peer-to-peer gaming model.

However, the client/server model we have discussed previously only works when the server has a port and address that is publicly visible on the Internet for clients to connect to. Too often, this means that users behind NAT routers cannot host games, only join them, and if the game is not designed to be NAT safe, a user behind NAT cannot even join a game! With the widespread popularity of NAT in modern networks, this is not really a tenable situation. The diagram in Figure 6.5.3 shows a problem where neither node can actually talk to the other (on port 8960, presumably used by some game), because the NAT routers have no appropriate entry for the second node in their respective session state table. Here is where using the technique in this gem will save your game!

The Hack

Read the README.txt of many games today, and you will probably see mention of port forwarding. Port forwarding means going to the NAT router and telling it to make a special case for packets arriving at a specific port. In effect, port forwarding adds a permanent tuple of (internal IP, port, gateway IP, port, any-remote-IP, any-remote-port) to the session state table of the NAT router.

The effect is that any packet arriving at the designated port is only rewritten in the part of the destination IP address and forwarded to the specific machine set up as the port-forwarding target. Games with half a clue will require you to only forward a single port, and may even let you configure which port to use within the game. Games with less flexibility will require a specific port (such that you cannot ever host

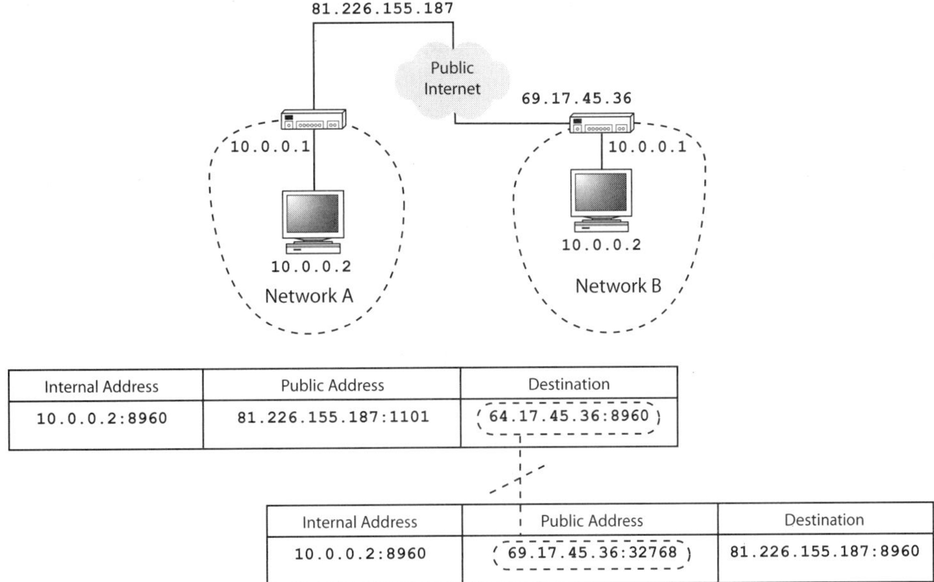

Internal Address	Public Address	Destination
10.0.0.2:8960	81.226.155.187:1101	64.17.45.36:8960

Internal Address	Public Address	Destination
10.0.0.2:8960	69.17.45.36:32768	81.226.155.187:8960

FIGURE 6.5.3 *Neither peer can send packets to the other.*

two games between the same NAT router) or require a whole range of ports to be forwarded. In the latter case, a user may go to the extreme of setting up a De-Militarized Zone (DMZ) host in their NAT router, which negates almost all the security benefits of being behind a NAT gateway, in effect, removing the NAT.

The Fix

Port forwarding is clunky, many consumers have trouble setting it up correctly, and it's often a support hassle for developers and publishers. Luckily, another solution exists, and was first described in [Kegel99] by Dan Kegel, as used in the game *BattleZone*™ published by Activision®.

The core of the problem is that each NAT router is lacking an entry in its session state table for the other peer with whom the internal node wishes to communicate. If we could somehow fool the NAT routers to add such an entry, traffic would flow correctly, and the game could go on!

Remember that when a peer sends a packet out through the NAT router, a tuple is added to the session state table, containing the internal and the external addresses as well as the remote address. As a first approximation, if we assume that a NAT router will preserve the source port of the internal node, assuming that port is not already in use by some other session, we could send packets to the remote node using its public NAT address and the known port. If each node starts sending to the peer in the same way at the same time, and both of them actually get the ports they expect on the NAT router, then the right thing will happen.

The Problem with TCP

This sketch for a solution might work for UDP (assuming we solve the port re-use requirement), but it will not work for TCP. The reason is how TCP connections are allocated: each connection allocates a new port number to uniquely identify the connection. There is no way, in general, to guess which port number will be allocated next, nor how the NAT router will map that port number, so unless you're willing to try 65,536 different port numbers at the same time, you can't really make the three-way handshake work in through a NAT for a TCP connection.

Dan Kaminsky has created an experimental library [Kaminsky03] for punching through NAT routers with TCP connections, but the foundations for this library do not seem solid enough to base production code on. We encourage you to look at the library, because it is educational, but the success rate is low enough that you cannot base a reliable product on it. Unfortunately, that is about as good as it gets regarding TCP and peer-to-peer networking through NAT, so we will return to UDP where the prospects for success are very good.

The End-to-End Solution for Games

There are a few too many "ifs" in the previously sketched-out solution. First, how would the peers know to start communicating to each other at the same time? Second, what if the desired port is already in use on the NAT router, and the router chooses to map the internal port to another external port? Maybe the NAT router implementation always remaps the ports, even, for implementation expediency or extra security.

Bonus Problem

Let us start with the first problem: how do the peers know to start sending at the same time? How do the peers even know what the visible (NAT) address of the other peer is? Ideally, the interface we'd like to present to the players is a roster of available, hosted games, where the player can choose to host a new game or join one of the games already being hosted. Good implementations of this game roster system include Blizzard®'s Battle.net® and the Xbox Live™ service by Microsoft®. *Warcraft III®* on Battle.net uses TCP, and peer-to-peer NAT introduction will not work through TCP, because each connection allocates its own local port. Xbox Live uses UDP, however, and experience is that its game hosting will work through most NAT boxes. So how do you find another player to play against?

Matchmaking

Browsing hosted games is not something you can actually do peer-to-peer, unless you do it using broadcast on a local LAN. You'll have to break down and get at least one server onto the public Internet, where games being hosted can register, and players can go to look up hosted games to join. The upside of this approach is that the traffic and performance requirements for this server are very low; a few hundred bytes per game being hosted, and a kilobyte or two per player connecting and getting the list of all games should do it, even for a game with a lot of active players. Ten-thousand players during a single night, consisting of a peak three hour period, break down to less than a single player per second; with the suggested bandwidth usage, you could host this on a single dial-up modem! Actually, we would recommend getting into at least a minimal hosting facility, because uptime, availability, and dealing with load spikes is important, and well worth the $100/month or so in hosting fees. As a bonus, you can probably run your corporate Web server on the same machine, given that the load is so low. If your game is wildly successful, scaling this solution up can be an almost trivial operation.

In the code file `sample.cpp`, the available games to join are held in the global set `gHosting` in the introducer server, where they are added in response to a `HOST` protocol command, as shown in Listing 6.5.3, and are returned to presumptive clients in response to the `LIST` protocol command, as shown in Listing 6.5.4 (error checking removed).

Listing 6.5.3 Adding a Hosted Game

```
enum {
  MAX_NAME_LEN = 32,
};

// For Request::What::HOST
struct HostRequest {
  unsigned char what;
  char name[ MAX_NAME_LEN ];
};

struct Peer {
  std::string name;
  sockaddr_in addr;
  bool operator==( Peer const & o ) const {
    return name == o.name;
  }
  bool operator<( Peer const & o ) const {
    return name < o.name;
  }
};

std::set< Peer > gHosting;
```

```
// When the introducer gets a HOST packet, handle it.
void introducer_host( char * data, int len, sockaddr_in & sin ) {
  // extract the packet and make sure it's terminated
  HostRequest & hr = *(HostRequest *)data;
  hr.name[ MAX_NAME_LEN-1 ] = 0;
  // Record the fact that there's a new guy hosting
  // (in the real world, we'd also add a timeout-at
  // time, and do some login name/password checking).
  Peer p;
  p.name = hr.name;
  p.addr = sin;
  gHosting.insert( p );
}
```

Listing 6.5.4 Returning Hosted Games

```
struct ListResponse {
  unsigned char what;
  char name[ MAX_NAME_LEN ];
  sockaddr_in addr;
};

// When the introducer gets a LIST packet, handle it.
void introducer_list( char * data, int len, sockaddr_in & sin ) {
  // I just dump all available hosts back - no
  // limiting, no matching, and above all, no re-
  // sending of lost packets.
  ListResponse lr;
  lr.what = Request::LIST_RESPONSE;
  for( std::set< Peer >::iterator ptr =
      gHosting.begin();
      ptr != gHosting.end(); ++ptr ) {
    // Construct a ListResponse packet
    strcpy( lr.name, (*ptr).name.c_str() );
    // I put an address as data, but that's OK, as the
    // address is publicly visible (::recvfrom()).
    lr.addr = (*ptr).addr;
    // Send the packet, ignoring errors (packet may be
    // dropped anywhere, including in the network
    // layer - too bad).
    ::sendto( gSocket, (char const *)&lr, sizeof(lr),
        0, (sockaddr *)&sin, sizeof(sin) );
  }
  // Send a final, empty host name to terminate the
  // list.
  lr.name[0] = 0;
  ::sendto( gSocket, (char const *)&lr, sizeof(lr), 0,
      (sockaddr *)&sin, sizeof(sin) );
}
```

Introduction

Once you have a game browsing server on the public Internet, a client should connect to this server using UDP on a single socket bound to a known port. The publicly visible, NAT-translated address of this socket will be visible to the game browser server when it calls `::recvfrom()` to receive network packets. The browsing server should send this IP address and port to all prospective clients wishing to join the hosted game.

In addition, the browsing server should send the publicly visible IP address and port of clients wishing to joint to the game host. That way, the game host can attempt to proactively send packets to the joining clients. This will have the effect of adding the appropriate tuple to the session state table in the NAT router to allow the packets being sent from the prospective clients to be allowed through to the hosting server.

A server that acts as a repository of publicly visible IP addresses and ports, and furnishes these to other interested peers for purposes of NAT punch-through, is commonly referred to as an "introducer."

Referring to Figure 6.5.4, the difference from the case where we "correctly guessed" the public port numbers, is that the port used by the NAT router to represent the internal node can be arbitrary, because they are made visible to the other peer using the introducer. The wishful thinking that the port would always be untouched is no longer necessary.

Implementation Details

There is one fundamental assumption that makes this introducer-based solution work: when a specific (source IP, source port) address is used for source addressing, the NAT router will translate this to a specific (NAT IP, NAT port), no matter what the destination IP and port is. While we still need to send packets both to the introducer, and to the peer we're being introduced to, to create the full session state tuple in the NAT router session state table, if the NAT chose a different port for different destination addresses, even with the same source port and IP, then the return traffic from the remote peer would not arrive at the expected port, and the technique wouldn't work.

Luckily, there are three good reasons for a NAT router to re-use the same NAT port for the same (source IP, source port) pair.

First, on the public Internet, a client process sending a network packet on a socket bound to a specific address and port expects the sender of that packet to remain fixed, no matter what the destination is. After all, the application bound the socket to a specific port and used that same socket to send packets to different remote nodes. Note that this is only possible with UDP, not TCP, which by design allocates new ports on the client side for each connection.

Second, if the NAT router has several nodes on its inner network, it may be called upon to allocate many ports for a lot of simultaneously active sessions. The number of ports available is not unlimited, so the NAT will conserve port space and be able to

Internal Address	Public Address	Destination
10.0.0.2:8960	81.226.155.187:11002	64.125.216.191:8960

1

Internal Address	Public Address	Destination
10.0.0.2:8960	69.17.45.36:32769	64.125.216.191:8960

Internal Address	Public Address	Destination
10.0.0.2:8960 10.0.0.2.8960	81.226.155.187:11002 81.226.155.187:11002	64.125.216.191:8960 69.17.45.36:32769

2

Internal Address	Public Address	Destination
10.0.0.2:8960	69.17.45.36:32769	64.125.216.191:8960

Internal Address	Public Address	Destination
10.0.0.2:8960 10.0.0.2.8960	81.226.155.187:11002 81.226.155.187:11002	64.125.216.191:8960 69.17.45.36:32769

3

Internal Address	Public Address	Destination
10.0.0.2:8960 10.0.0.2:2960	69.17.45.36:32769 69.17.45.36:32769	64.125.216.191:8960 81.226.155.187:11002

In step 1, each of the peers have a session open to the introducer, which has a public IP and port address. The introducer records the publicly visible IP and port of each participating peer, and makes them available to the others.

In step 2, the first peer has received the public address of the second, and has sent a packet to the second, which causes a session entry to be created in the NAT gateway. At this point, traffic from the second peer to the first peer will make it back through the NAT, but packets sent by the first peer will be dropped at the second gateway.

In step 3, the second peer has otherwise received the public address of the first peer, and such a packet to establish a session. Because the first peer had already sent a packet that established the session, and because the same local port is used to communicate with the introducer as well as the peers, packets can now flow in both directions.

FIGURE 6.5.4 *Peer-to-peer communication setup using an introducer.*

serve more simultaneous clients if it re-uses the same external port for the same internal address, port values.

Third, NAT introduction is quickly becoming a standard technique. A NAT gateway that does not support this technique will be considered faulty by users, and will have higher return rates and support costs than devices that work properly. This behavior is also actively encouraged for all NAT builders since 2001, through the Internet Society document RFC3022 [RFC3022].

In reality, most gateways work well with this technique, because they do proper port matching. There are reportedly a few that do not; the only one we know of for sure that does not conform to RFC3022 is based on the BSD operating system and not very common in home environments. In 1999, some NAT routers would not deal correctly with a packet being sent from the internal network to an external address that refers to another internal address on the same internal network, as would be the case when two peers behind the same NAT router join through an introducer. This bug has since been worked out of most routers, and most devices on the market today should deal properly with this situation. While there is no workaround for the bug where a NAT gateway does not re-use ports, you can work around a gateway that does not allow internal hosts to communicate through the publicly visible NAT address by initially communicating both using the internal and external address of the peer in question, responding to the address from which you actually get a reply, and picking the public address if you get a reply from both addresses, as the public address is guaranteed to be unique.

If you find that your client is behind a NAT gateway that is still broken, you can either throw up your hands and tell the user to fix the gateway, or configure port forwarding, or you can decide to eat the bandwidth cost of serving these users (as they are relatively few), and reflect their packets from your well-connected introducer service. Which option you decide on should depend almost entirely on what trade-off between low support cost and low hosting cost you are willing to make.

Last, there is an implementation flaw in WinSock, the sockets library used on most personal computers connected to the Internet (it is what Microsoft ships with Windows). If you send a UDP datagram to a port that is not listening and receive an ICMP message back saying "port not reachable," WinSock will wedge the socket that sent the initial datagram and return `WSAECONNRESET` when attempting to use the socket. At this point, you have to close and re-open the socket for it to work again. This is highly inconvenient, because you are very likely to receive at least one port not reachable message when setting up the peer-to-peer NAT punch-through, before both gateways have created the appropriate session state records. Luckily, because UDP is connectionless (as opposed to TCP), the NAT gateway will not know that the socket has been closed and re-opened and bound to the same port on the local machine, and everything will proceed as normal. Typical WinSock code will thus look like Listing 6.5.5 to work around this problem (again, some error checking removed).

Listing 6.5.5 Working around WinSock

```
enum {
  GAME_PORT = 8960,
};
#define SOCKET_ERRNO WSAGetLastError()
inline bool SOCKET_WOULDBLOCK_ERROR( int e ) {
  return e == WSAEWOULDBLOCK;
}
inline bool SOCKET_NEED_REOPEN( int e ) {
  return e == WSAECONNRESET;
}
#define INIT_SOCKET_LIBRARY() \
   do { WSADATA wsaData; WSAStartup( \
        MAKEWORD(2,2), &wsaData ); } \
   while(0)

SOCKET gSocket;

// Allocate the single, global socket we'll use in all
// roles.
void allocate_socket() {
  if( gSocket != BAD_SOCKET_FD ) {
    ::closesocket( gSocket );
  }
  else {
    INIT_SOCKET_LIBRARY();
  }
  gSocket = ::socket( PF_INET, SOCK_DGRAM,
      IPPROTO_UDP );
  // Bind to my port on all local interfaces.
  // Because I want to run multiple instances on the
  // same machine, I try a sequence of ports.
  // Once I've bound to a port, I want to re-use that
  // port if I re-allocate the socket, so remember
  // which port was being used using a static variable
  // (this means I can only open a single socket per
  // process using this code).
  static int portUsed = 0;
  for( int port = GAME_PORT; port < GAME_PORT+10;
       ++port ) {
    sockaddr_in addr;
    memset( &addr, 0, sizeof( addr ) );
    addr.sin_family = AF_INET;
    if( portUsed ) {
      //  use the old port if set
      port = portUsed;
    }
    addr.sin_port = htons( port );
    // bind the socket to a specific port
    int r = ::bind( gSocket, (sockaddr *)&addr,
        sizeof(addr) );
    if( r < 0 ) {
      if( portUcod ) [
```

```
          //  if I can't re-use the old port, bail out
          break;
        }
      }
      else {
        portUsed = port;
        break;
      }
    }
  }

// There's a flaw in WinSock where I'll need to re-
// open the socket if I get CONNRESET on a socket.
// This is because it wedges the socket when it
// receives an ICMP for port-not-reachable, which can
// happen during NAT introduction negotiation.
bool maybe_reallocate_socket( int r ) {
  if( r < 0 ) {
    if( SOCKET_NEED_REOPEN( SOCKET_ERRNO ) ) {
      fprintf( stderr,
    "Re-allocating socket because of WinSock.\n" );
      allocate_socket();
    }
    return true;
  }
  return false;
}

    sockaddr_in sin;
    socklen_t slen = sizeof( sin );
    char data[ 512 ];
    //  Wait for an incoming packet
    int r = ::recvfrom( gSocket, data, 512, 0,
        (sockaddr *)&sin, &slen );
    if( maybe_reallocate_socket( r ) ) {
      continue;
}
```

Conclusion

Using the technique presented here in this gem, your games should be one step closer to offering robust multiplayer gaming that works across a variety of networking configurations. As a result, wizards and warriors should be able to go about the business of saving the world, even from the comfort of their local Starbucks.

References

[Man3rresvport] Unix section 3 manual page for the `rresvport()` library call; for example found at *http://www.gsp.com/cgi-bin/man.cgi?section=3&topic=rresvport.*

[RFC793] USC ISI. Request For Comments document 793. TCP Protocol Specification. Available online at *http://www.faqs.org/rfcs/rfc793.html* (September 1981).

[Stevens94] Stevens, W. Richard. *TCP Illustrated*. Addison-Wesley Professional, 1994.

[RFC959] Postel, J. and J Reynolds. Request For Comments document 959. Available online at *http://www.faqs.org/rfcs/rfc959.html* (October 1985).

[RFC1123] Braden, R., editor. Internet Engineering Task Force. Request For Comments document 1123. Available online at *http://www.faqs.org/rfcs/rfc1123.html* (October 1989).

[Kegel99] Kegel, Dan. "NAT and Peer-to-peer Networking." Available online at *http://www.alumni.caltech.edu/~dank/peer-nat.html* (July 1999).

[RFC1918] Rekhter, Y., et al. Request For Comments document 1918. "Address Allocation for Private Internets." Available online at *http://www.faqs.org/rfcs/rfc1918.html* (February 1996).

[Kaminsky03] Kaminsky, Dan. Paketto Keiretsu 1.10: Advanced TCP/IP Toolkit. Available online at *http://www.doxpara.com/read.php/code/paketto.html* (December 2002).

[RFC3022] Srisuresh, P. and K. Egevang. Internet Society. Request For Comments document 3022. Available online at *http://www.faqs.org/rfcs/rfc3022.html* (January 2001).

6.6

A Reliable Messaging Protocol

Martin Brownlow

martinbrownlow@msn.com

This gem describes a simple protocol for implementing reliable, in-order messaging for network communications. The protocol is independent of the transmission medium or network model (client/server or peer-to-peer), so it can be implemented in any situation where reliable networking is needed.

Definition of Terms

Before we begin looking at the details of this gem, we should first take a moment to define the terms used in the rest of this article:

Host/client: For the purposes of this article, we will use the term *host* to signify the sender of a message and *client* as the recipient.

Packet: A packet is the information physically transmitted over the network. It consists of one or more messages. If any of the messages within a packet are set to be reliable, then the packet is said to be reliable.

Message: A message is the smallest form of data that can be sent by the application. Each message can be set to be reliable or unreliable. In each frame, the application creates a series of messages, which are bundled together by the networking library to form a single packet.

System Message: A message sent by the networking library. This is application independent, and the application never needs to know about them. System messages are bundled into packets in exactly the same way as application-specific messages. A good example of a system message is an acknowledgment of packet receipt.

Heartbeat: A heartbeat is a system message that is sent every so often when there are no other messages pending. The purpose of the heartbeat is to signify to the receiver that the sender's application is still running correctly.

Acknowledgment: An acknowledgment is a system message that states that the client has received a given packet from the host.

Message Handler: A function of the application that is called by the network library to process incoming messages.

Why Reliable Messaging?

Reliable messaging is an important part of any networking library. The Internet, although a technological marvel, is not a very safe place for a given packet of data. The nodes that make up the Internet receive unpredictable amounts of traffic at any given time and are under no obligation to let all the traffic pass; if a node becomes overwhelmed, it will start discarding the incoming packets in order to remain operational. Additionally, consecutive packets between two machines are not guaranteed to take the same route across the intervening network. As traffic fluctuates among the Internet's nodes, packets are routed in different ways to try to provide the best pathway.

These characteristics of the Internet provide us with two distinct problems: any given packet of data that we send may fail to arrive at its destination, and any two data packets may arrive at the destination in the opposite order to their original transmission. However, there are some pieces of data that an application must send that absolutely have to arrive at the destination; if this data were to disappear, the application would behave unpredictably and possibly even crash. For this reason, we need to define a way to ensure that a given packet will arrive at the destination in a reasonable amount of time.

Traditional Reliable Messaging

Now that we have defined the terms that we will be using, and have seen why reliable messaging is important, we can look at how a reliable messaging model is traditionally implemented. This will familiarize us with its strengths and weaknesses, allowing us to construct a better model.

In a traditional implementation, when a host sends a reliable packet to a client, it records the time that it was sent, and puts the reliable packet into a list. The reliable packet is removed from this list only when an acknowledgment system message for it is received from the client. If, after a certain amount of time has elapsed, an acknowledgment for the reliable packet has not arrived, the packet is resent and its timer reset.

When a client receives a packet that is marked as reliable, it must construct an acknowledgment system message for transmission back to the host. This message contains an identifier for the packet being acknowledged. If this message is not sent in a timely manner, the host will think that the packet has not been received and will retransmit it.

From this description, we can see that if the acknowledgment for a given packet does not reach the host before that packet's timer runs out, the host will resend the packet, eating up precious bandwidth. This has two important ramifications. The first is that acknowledgments must be sent immediately, even to the point of creating a packet just for them if there are no other messages to be sent. The second is that acknowledgments *must* arrive once they have been sent to avoid the host resending the packet in question unnecessarily. This implies that acknowledgment messages should be set to be reliable, but doing so necessitates having acknowledgments for the acknowledgments, and before you know it, every packet is set to be reliable.

A Simpler Method

From the preceding description of a traditional reliable messaging implementation, we can see some areas that need improvement. The two most important of these are reducing the number of acknowledgments sent, and removing the need for them to be sent reliably.

Reducing the number of acknowledgments sent can be partially accomplished by adding an additional restriction to our reliable messages. If we can guarantee that reliable messages must be processed in the order that they were sent, then receiving an acknowledgment of a given packet automatically implies receipt of every prior packet. This is because, to maintain the in-order restriction, we know that all the previous packets must also have been processed. However, the need to send acknowledgment packets quickly to avoid the host resending packets it thinks have been missed reduces the usefulness of this somewhat.

If we can remove the need to send an acknowledgment quickly, we can reap several rewards. We will not have to send acknowledgments as often, and when we do send one, we can just acknowledge the most recent reliable packet processed. Additionally, there would no longer be a need to send acknowledgments reliably. Unfortunately, while the host is responsible for detecting a missed reliable packet, our hands are tied. This, then, will be our main point of attack.

The simplest way to remove the responsibility for detecting a missed reliable packet from the host is to move it to the client. For this to happen, a client must quickly detect that a reliable packet has been missed. We know that only reliable packets will ever need to be resent, and that ideally two reliable packets will be broken up with one or more unreliable packets. We also know that packets should arrive with a consistent frequency, due to the heartbeat system message.

Using this knowledge, we can formulate a method by which we can quickly detect a missing reliable packet. The easiest way to do this is to allow every incoming packet to contain enough data to infer a missing reliable packet. Since we know that packets are arriving at a consistent frequency (due to the heartbeat system message), we know that we can make such an inference quickly. For example, if 10 packets arrive in a second, we know that we can infer the existence of a missing reliable packet as soon as the next packet arrives, one tenth of a second later.

Packet Identifiers

However, how do we allow an incoming packet to infer the existence of a missing reliable packet? Every reliable packet needs two pieces of data: a flag to say that it is reliable and an identifier, by means of which it can be acknowledged. An unreliable packet, on the other hand, only requires a flag to say that it is not reliable; it does not need an identifier. This means that, should we assign an identifier to an unreliable packet, any number of unreliable packets can have the same identifier without any side effects. By combining the reliable/unreliable flag with the packet identifier, we can create a simple packet numbering system that allows us to infer the existence of a missing reliable packet.

If we use the least-significant bit of the packet identifier to store the reliable/unreliable flag, we can see that, if we choose a bit value of 0 to represent a reliable packet, all reliable packets will have an even-numbered packet identifier and all unreliable packets an odd-numbered one. Then, taking advantage of the fact that any number of unreliable packets can share an identifier, we come up with the following two rules:

- When creating an unreliable packet, the packet identifier should have the reliable/unreliable flag set to 1.
- When creating a reliable packet, the packet identifier should be incremented by 2, and then have the reliable/unreliable flag set to 0.

These simple rules allow a client to detect that a reliable packet has been missed, simply by receiving any type of packet that was sent afterwards. To accomplish this, the client must maintain a record of the identifier of the next expected reliable packet, which we will call `nextReliableID`.

The Incoming Packet Queue

As incoming packets are received, they are placed into a queue, sorted by packet identifier. Each time the network library is updated, it processes this queue, starting with the packet with the lowest identifier. Packets from the queue are processed in order, until the queue is empty or one is found that cannot be processed, according to the following rules:

- If the packet identifier is even (reliable) and equal to `nextReliableID`, we have received the next reliable packet. Process this packet, and then increment `nextReliableID` by 2.
- If the packet identifier is odd (unreliable) and equals `nextReliableID` minus 1, we have received an unreliable packet that should be processed.
- If the packet identifier is less than `nextReliableID`, discard the packet.
- If the packet identifier is greater than `nextReliableID`, we know that we have missed a packet and cannot yet process this new packet or any subsequent packet in the queue.

After processing the incoming packet queue, we know whether a packet has been missed, and the identifier for the missed packet (`nextReliableID`).

One notable exception to these rules is that any system messages in the incoming packets are processed immediately. This happens regardless of whether the packet is queued (care should be taken to only process each system message once). This allows us to quickly fulfill remote system requests such as resends and acknowledgments. If we do not process these system level messages, there is a danger of encountering a deadlock situation. This can happen when two machines both detect missing packets from the other, and their resend requests both get queued behind the missing packet. The resend requests never get processed, thus the machines are deadlocked.

The Resend Timer

If a packet has indeed been missed, a countdown timer, called the resend timer, if not already active, is assigned a small value and started. This small value is called the *out of order delay*. The purpose of this short pause is to allow a short period for the missing packet to arrive in case it is still in transit but out of order. If at any point, the missing packet arrives, the resend timer is stopped.

When the resend timer expires, the client sends a system message to the host requesting a resend of the missing packet (`nextReliableID`). At this point, the resend timer is reset to a larger value, called the *re-request delay* and again started. We continue requesting the missing packet every time the resend timer expires, until the missing packet arrives.

The use of automatically repeated resend requests means that the requests themselves do not have to be sent as reliable messages. Furthermore, the initial delay before requesting a missed packet allows any out of order packets to arrive, and so reduces the chance of a resend request being sent spuriously. A typical value for the out of order delay is around one-tenth of a second, and a typical value for the re-request delay is about one-half of a second.

Acknowledgments

Since the client is now responsible for detecting missed packets and requesting packet resends, there is no longer a requirement that acknowledgments be sent quickly. Additionally, the in-order processing of packets allows us to acknowledge the most recently processed reliable packet. From such an acknowledgment, the host can infer the acknowledgment of every reliable packet sent prior to the acknowledged packet.

The net result of this is that we can send far fewer acknowledgment packets, at a far slower rate. Additionally, acknowledgment packets no longer need to be reliable, since if one is missed, the next one to arrive will imply acknowledgment of all the packets acknowledged by the missed one. Acknowledgments can thus be sent out at a constant rate, regardless of how many reliable messages have arrived in between. A typical value for acknowledgment frequency in such a system is one every two seconds.

The Reliable Packet Queue

The host must keep a record of each reliable packet sent until such a time as it is acknowledged by the client. It does this by means of a reliable packet queue. As each reliable packet is sent, it is placed in the queue. When an acknowledgment arrives from the client, any packet in the queue with an identifier that is less than or equal to that of the acknowledged packet can be deleted.

If a resend request is received from the client, the correct reliable packet is first located in the queue and then resent to the client. A resend request is also an implicit acknowledgment of all prior packets; to detect the missing packet, the client must have processed all packets up to the missing one. Therefore, when a resend request is received, the implicitly acknowledged packets can be deleted from the queue.

Multiple Connections

So far, we have only looked at a single connection, but in reality, we will probably need to allow multiple connections to a single machine. For example, a server application in a client/server system will need one connection per client, and each node in a peer-to-peer system will need a connection to every other node in the network. However, a client application in a client/server system will probably only need a single connection to the server.

When multiple connections are required, each connection will require its own incoming packet queue and reliable packet queue. Additionally, each connection will need to allocate its own packet identifiers, and keep track of the next expected incoming reliable packet, independent of the other connections.

Memory Requirements

In many games, especially those designed to run on consoles, memory can be very tight, even during the single player game. Often, there is only a very small amount of memory available for use by the network library. This has important consequences for reliable messaging, which relies on keeping track of unacknowledged reliable packets so they can be retransmitted. Luckily, memory requirements for this reliable messaging protocol are modest, and with a bit of massaging, we can make some great savings if memory is very tight.

The majority of the memory used by this system resides in the memory used to store elements of the reliable packet and the incoming packet queues. There needs to be enough memory for the reliable packet queue to store all the outgoing reliable packets for a few seconds, long enough for them to be acknowledged. The exact amount of time that we will need to record reliable packets for is unpredictable, and effectively unbounded, however, we can safely assume a value of around two to three times the value of the acknowledgment frequency. This allows us to safely lose an acknowledgment message, without danger of the queue overflowing. If we do ever run out of room in the outgoing reliable packet queue, the game can no longer transmit reliable packets, as there is nowhere to store them so that we can retransmit them if necessary.

Similarly, the incoming packet queue needs enough elements to store all the incoming packets that may arrive while we are waiting for a packet to be resent. However, once the incoming packet queue becomes full, it is safe to start discarding incoming packets that cannot be processed immediately; they can always be re-requested later.

When multiple connections are in use, the amount of memory required rises linearly with the number of connections. However, we can share the memory used by the queues among all the connections; except in extreme network conditions, it is unlikely that all connections will need large amounts of queue space at the same time.

In some cases, though, this will still prove to be too much memory usage. If we need to reduce the memory footprint further, we can choose to reduce the number and size of the packets stored in the queues, although the measures we need to take may seem a little draconian. We know that the arrival of packets and messages not marked as reliable are not critical to the correct execution of our application. Therefore, we can choose not to store these packets and messages in the queues.

The way this works is simple; when we store a reliable packet in the outgoing packet queue, we remove from it all the messages that are not themselves reliable. This ensures that only the most important parts of these packets are queued for possible resend, reducing the memory used. In the incoming packet queue, we can choose not to store unreliable packets that cannot be immediately processed, and we can strip the unreliable elements from reliable packets that do need to be queued.

The effects of such packet and message stripping can be undesirable, causing the times that packets are lost to be more apparent to the user. This can happen because several unreliable packets containing such things as positional updates for visible enemies will be lost each time the client has to wait for a missed packet to be resent. We can ameliorate this effect somewhat by selectively implementing it as the queues become full. When the queues are empty, all messages will be stored, but if a queue surpasses a certain length, the network library should go through and cull unreliable packets and messages from the queue. This reduces the appearance of packet loss, except in the times that it is severe.

Conclusion

We have seen that reliable messaging is an important part of a networking library, and how the traditional method of implementing reliable messaging has several problems. We saw that by moving the responsibility for detecting a missed reliable packet to the client, we could overcome these problems and produce a robust, reliable messaging system. Finally, we examined the memory requirements for this system and looked at ways to reduce memory usage, especially during times of extreme packet loss.

Further Reading

Those interested in learning more about network programming using the TCP and UDP protocols can find information in the following books:

[Donahoo01] Donahoo, Michael J. and Kenneth L. Calvert. *TCP/IP Sockets in C: Practical Guide for Programmers*. Morgan Kaufmann Publishers, 2001.

[Napper97] Napper, Lewis. *Winsock 2.0*. John Wiley & Sons, Inc, 1997.

6.7

Safe Random Number Systems

Shekhar Dhupelia
sdhupelia@gmail.com

There are typically two methods of implementing a networked action game, from a high-level perspective. The first is the synchronous method, or the "lockstep" method, where inputs are passed back and forth and the game is synchronized as much as possible. The second methodology is the asynchronous method. This is where the simulations try to stay in-sync as much as they can, but in between syncs the players are temporarily free to do as they wish, and the program attempts prediction and latency masking to hide the differences between the various machines.

The synchronous model, in particular, is extremely sensitive to any difference between the two machines. While some ancillary items might be different from one machine to the next, anything and everything affecting gameplay must remain *exactly* the same on all machines. A big stumbling block for this methodology is random numbers. Random numbers might be used for a variety of tasks in a game, from artificial intelligence behaviors to selecting sound effects. One of the very first steps when developing a synchronous game should be to implement a random number system that is under application control and is safe for use in networked gameplay.

This gem describes the architecture of a safe random number system, along with steps you can take to save time during later debugging, and even how this type of system could replace an existing instant-replay system.

Random Numbers Affect Online Play

When game code calls the standard C `rand()` and `srand()` functions, the values returned are not truly random. Rather, they are invoking a pseudorandom generation algorithm, a well-defined, standard process.

If two machines are connected for online play, and the networked gameplay is the first thing that both applications are doing since startup, the pseudorandom numbers returned will likely be the same. However, if one application has already been playing a previous, offline session, using the same randomness (in AI, audio commentary, etc.), the connected machines will start getting different results.

Once the machines start getting different random number results than each other, what then happens is called "out-of-sync" or de-synchronization. Essentially, making a random choice on whether a character should move left or right might come back with different decisions, and the games are no longer in the same state. Results can rapidly diverge, and this quickly results in an unplayable game, particularly in a deterministic (lockstep) game, where the game is primarily controlled by player inputs.

What makes this problem easier is the algorithmic nature of random number generation. Since most variations of these algorithms rely on making some sort of calculation based on the previously generated number (the "seed"), this number can then be transferred from one machine to the others. Then, once all the connected machines start gameplay with the same seed value, their random number generators will consistently return the same results to each application, allowing them to keep identical states while remaining independent of one another.

The key to tracking this random number generation, and having direct control over this seed value, is to move the random numbers out of the standard C/C++ libraries and into application-controlled code. Later, a class is discussed that does just that.

A Network Model

When applying this random pools class to a networked game, there is no limit to the number of connected machines that can use this system. In a 32-player game, there still needs to be a decision on what the starting point is for all decision making, and what the seed will be within each pool (which is further described later).

For simplicity's sake, this article only assumes two machines in the networked game. However, whether the application is on 2 or 20 machines, only 1 machine can be designated the session master. This session master is the one whose random seed values will be polled and synchronized across the game at session start. A decision must be made to select a session master within the game/matchmaking logic.

Random Number Pools

While synchronizing random numbers across connected machines may solve many problems with desynchronization, it can actually cause other problems as well. In fact, some of the game subsystems may actually be *adverse* to this system.

An example of this might be an audio commentary system. In a sports title, an event such as a goal might occur that's worthy of playing an audio cue. Further, for greater authenticity, the game might have a selection of audio cues to choose from, all for the same event. Selecting this cue may well be a random event. Now, if the audio clips are all resident in memory, playing the same commentary should be fine, both will start and end at the same time and the synchronized play continues. However, what if the audio cues must be streamed in real time from a physical drive? In this case, one system will likely finish loading the audio clip before the other system, and playback will be different. While this might still be okay, there's also potential for audio clips to start "backing up" over time on the slower hard disk or DVD and eventually cause the games to be out of sync or unplayable with each other.

But looking at this further, the programmers may realize that there is no reason for the audio commentary to stay in sync. As long as the audio is streaming while gameplay continues, never waiting for it to finish, the two connected machines could plausibly play completely different commentary while keeping all essential game systems in a synchronized state.

In this case, the randomness of the AI might need to be synchronized, but the randomness of the audio is either irrelevant or purposefully not synced. To do this, instead of developing a single random number seed and generator, the application can draw from multiple "pools" of random numbers.

Drawing from random number pools is conceptually very similar to drawing from different memory banks in a memory management system. In a partitioned memory bank system, code might be added to debug or log the use of one bank while steering clear of the rest. There might be code to create and destroy some banks during runtime, while other segments are left alone. While each game might have its own requirements, this is an example of a list of pools:

```
enum POOL_TYPE
{
    POOL_DEFAULT            = 0,
    POOL_ENVIRONMENT        = 1,
    POOL_AI                 = 2,
    POOL_COMMENTARY         = 3,
    POOL_MUSIC              = 4,
    POOL_MAX_TYPES
};
```

Now, put simply, a seed is merely the last generated random number. But there has to be a start point, and in standard C/C++, this is performed by calling `srand()`. Typically, this seed value is stored internally as a single 4-byte `int` or `uint` variable. But since we have multiple pools of random numbers for the various game subsystems, our data storage must match:

```
static unsigned int randPools[POOL_MAX_TYPES];
```

Now, if the application ever needs to retrieve the seed for a given pool, it can simply request it based on the pool enumeration:

```
unsigned int getPoolSeed(POOL_TYPE whichPool)
{
    return randPools[whichPool];
}
```

Further, when the session master broadcasts the random seeds to the other connected machines, they in turn can reset their local seed values in a similar fashion:

```
void setPoolSeed(POOL_TYPE whichPool, unsigned int newSeed)
{
   // Make sure the seed is not 0
   if (newSeed != 0)
   {
         randPools[whichPool] = newSeed;
   }
}
```

At this point, the random number generation will act based on this new seed value, throwing away any previous seed.

Random Number Generation

Now, before actually using the random number generators for the first time, this system should require that the application provide an initial seed value for the pools. Further, the system should *not* allow any application code to re-seed the initial values. Rather, the application should be forced to see the `setPoolSeed()` function described earlier after the initial seeding is complete. Here's an example of seeding the pools for the first time and preventing subsequent seeding:

```
static bool seeded = false;
void seedPools(unsigned int seedValue)
{
   // Make sure the seed is not 0
   if (seedValue == 0)
   {
         assert(0);
         return;
   }

   // Make sure we've only seeded the pools once
   if (seeded == true)
   {
         assert(0);
         return;
   }

   // Loop through the random number pools
   for (unsigned short pool = 0;
         pool < POOL_MAX_TYPES;
         pool++)
   {
         // Initialize this random pool
    randPools[pool] = seedValue;
   }

   // Set our seeded flag
   seeded = true;
}
```

Lastly, this system is nothing without an actual random number generator. Many sources on the Internet can be found that provide source code to different algorithms. Some of these are focused on speed, while some are focused more on randomness. Further, some just provide C code implementations of the ANSI C `rand()` function itself. The choice is up to each application, but for this example, a Randomal64 generator is used [Thomas01]. Remember, this will probably be fine for most applications, and if not, the guts of this can easily be replaced.

```
static const unsigned long RDX_RANGE = 0x7FFFFFFF;
static const unsigned long RDX_CONST = 0x00000000000041A7;
static const unsigned long RDX_Q = RDX_RANGE / RDX_CONST;
static const unsigned long RDX_R = RDX_RANGE % RDX_CONST;

unsigned int getRandomNumber(POOL_TYPE whichPool)
{
    // Return random integer32 between 0 & range value
    unsigned long hi =
     randPools[whichPool] /
     RDX_Q;
    unsigned long lo =
     randPools[whichPool] -
     (hi * RDX_Q);
    randPools[whichPool] = (
     (RDX_CONST * lo) -
     (RDX_R * hi)
     );
     if (randPools[whichPool] == 0)
     randPools[whichPool] = RDX_RANGE;

    int rslt = int(randPools[whichPool]);
    if (rslt < 0) rslt = -rslt;
            return rslt;

    return 0;
}
```

Notice that this generator is saving the result of each run back into the pools array, and this value is what's used the next time around.

Overloading Standard `rand()` and `srand()`

Putting together the code up until now gives us a complete random number pool system, ready for use in an application. However, an online programmer will likely find a new problem after this is dropped into an application; many programmers won't know about the new random pool system or simply will forget or not bother to use it. Unfortunately, random numbers might be used anywhere in the game code, in areas the network programmer typically doesn't modify. All it takes is one errant call to `rand()` somewhere in the game to potentially break the online play.

There is an easy solution to this problem. C/C++ allows macros to be defined that overload standard function calls; when resolving the symbols and `#defines` at compile and link time, the compiler will choose the overloaded function calls over the standard library calls.

Overloading standard C calls to `rand()` is as simple as:

```
#define rand() Pools::getRandomNumber(POOL_DEFAULT)
```

Also, a good way of tracking down the engineer responsible for misused `rand()` and `srand()` calls is to trap any calls to standard `srand()` as well:

```
#define srand(x) Pools::seedPools(x)
```

Making sure that the random pools header is available via `#include` high up in the compilation/link hierarchy, or is listed in a precompiled header, is usually all it takes to propagate these macros.

Next Steps: Logging and Debugging

Once the random pool system is in place, it can itself become a powerful debugging tool for online game issues. This is particularly true in deterministic games, where game state must remain completely in lockstep for the duration of the session.

A good method in finding problems between desynchronized machines is by comparing the usage of the random pools on each system. Implementing logging of function calls to `getRandomNumber()` should be fairly trivial (depending on the platform), and comparing the output from each machine should help isolate some of the application code problems leading to "out-of-syncs."

Next Steps: Instant Replay

On top of just providing extra logging and debugging, for some games, the random pools class can actually form the basis for an Instant Replay feature! Instead of recording game state frame-by-frame, simply record the results of calls to `getRandomNumber()` along with controller/keyboard/mouse input. This data should be stored in precise sequential order. These values can then be used to essentially "replay" a frame at any given point, feeding the same inputs back into all the various subsystems at work. While these other systems are oblivious to what's going on, and are essentially re-doing the same work, this data set is very small and economical. This is a benefit even for many offline games.

Conclusion

This gem discussed multiple uses for a random number pool system. Chief among these is the ease in which networked games can be synchronized; this makes sure that a request for a random number comes up with the same result on every machine. In addition, random numbers controlled by the application allows a programmer to replay various subsystems over and over again, either as a debugging tool or as an actual feature of the game.

References

[Isensee01] Isensee, Pete. "Genuine Random Number Generation." *Game Programming Gems 2*. Charles River Media, 2001.

[Thomas01] Thomas, Andy. "Randomal64 Pseudo Random Number Generator." Available online at *http://www.generation5.org/content/2001/ga01.asp*.

6.8

Secure by Design

Adam Martin, Grex Games

gpg@grexengine.com

A system is only as secure as its weakest link, so spending time and money on securing only some aspects of a system is usually a pointless waste. You must check every single link to have any confidence in your security, and yet most project leaders do not even know what links they have, let alone how to evaluate them.

The ability to evaluate security is critical for any multiplayer or online game, yet the modern software engineer seems to fix problems in the completion and a post-release evaluation phases rather than during design phase. We need to design security into our games from the very start.

This gem describes a multistage process that can easily be integrated with your existing development processes. Ideally, you would follow this process from the start of your project, but it is still extremely effective when applied retroactively. The text and examples concentrate on securing servers in particular, but the process itself is equally applicable to client activities.

We work from the basis that an insecure system is formally defined as one where one or more attacks from the actual Threat Model (TM) are not dealt with by the actual Security Policy (SP). If we produce a complete TM and fully adhere to our own SP, we can calculate how secure our system is simply by looking at these two documents. This is the major aim of this gem. This is a simplified view of a concept known formally as a Security Target.

The TM and the SP together fully document the system's weaknesses, its solutions, and enough information to quickly reproduce and re-evaluate the original assumptions and conclusions.

How Important Is Security, Really?

Security flaws tend to be like software bugs in that the cost of fixing them rises exponentially the longer it takes to discover them. However, security flaws tend to rise in cost even faster than normal bugs. For instance, the cost of a flaw that exposes the credit card details of all your subscribers is astronomical compared to the cost of fixing it before going live.

Most people associate security primarily with encryption, passwords, and authentication schemes, but these are merely tools, and do not constitute security themselves. There are currently three main approaches to game security in a wider sense:

- Wait until release, see what breaks, then desperately issue patches as quickly as possible.
- Delegate to someone else (person or company) and hope they are sufficiently afraid of being blamed that they somehow work out how to secure the system.
- Deploy a suite of known tactics in haphazard fashion, hoping you might just manage to make it "a bit more difficult to hack."

In almost all cases, it is extremely expensive—and difficult—to fix security late in the development process. The received wisdom is that security cannot be added retroactively, because it is simply too expensive; it needs to be "designed in from the start." If your development process failed to take proper account of security concerns, you risk being condemned to producing a never-ending stream of security patches, none of which ever completely fix the problems, while "grief players" run amok in your multiplayer game, ruining it for your other players, leading to poor reviews and reducing sales.

On the other hand, perhaps your game is a Massively Multiplayer Online Game (MMOG), and as your game world falls to pieces under the grief-players, subscribers start canceling in large numbers. Worse, one of those holes might expose your per-customer credit-card details, taking the financial and reputation damage to completely new levels. Anything you own or control—data, hardware, bandwidth, even your company's identity—could easily be abused or stolen if your game-server security is inadequate.

Fortunately, the process in this gem is both simple and cheap, and produces benefits right from the start. Every game developer—from professional studios to individual hobbyists—should be able to use this process easily and effectively.

Aims

As [Schneier03] points out, "security" is basically meaningless unless you know from whom and for how long it is secure. Therefore, our first aim is to formalize exactly what we mean; this is a process that needs to be performed separately for each project; there is no single answer for every game.

Assuming we know what we are trying to protect, we also need a way of measuring our success. Developers today are accustomed to using metrics to assess code improvements in the development phases of a project: bug lists, unit tests, playable demos, etc. We need an equivalent for security, that is, we need a precise measure of "secureness."

Then there is the problem of cost: if every game project had infinite time and an infinite budget, it could simply be written very carefully and be penetration-tested extensively. Nevertheless, assuming we have limits on our resources, we need to be able to prioritize where to spend them. We also need to be able to make predictive measures of "secureness" and compare them to each other (e.g., so that we can decide which of two designs to implement). Therefore, another aim is comparability.

Both of the aims also require that results are easily repeatable, not just by the original measurers, but by other people, too. We cannot make the process entirely repeatable, since one aspect of security—the discovery of attacks on a system—is inherently creative rather than methodical, and so there will always be an element of non-determinism. It would be helpful if this non-determinism could be strictly limited in some way.

It is generally too expensive to reassess the entire system for each alternative, and so we need some way of restricting our comparisons. The ideal solution would be some form of encapsulated measurements, so that we only need to remeasure the parts of the system that are changed.

Terminology

Unfortunately, the security industry lags behind software engineering in terms of both formalization and standardization. Until greater formalization is achieved, there continue to be many self-proclaimed experts whose teachings are variable at best and often promote positively dangerous approaches to security; in this environment, it is particularly difficult to know whom to trust as an authority. Until the industry standardizes more widely, most terminology has no single strict definition. This gem attempts to adhere to the most mainstream terminology, but in many cases there is no clear leader.

In particular, many sources define "Security Policy" in wildly differing ways. The version used by this gem is an augmented version of one of the most common definitions. Some sources are passionately contemptuous of that base definition, declaiming, "Policies are not technical manuals." For CIOs running large corporations, there is a document that they describe that has its own value; it is mainly for giving to non-technical staff as a series of daily rules to post next to their workstations, usually just one sheet of A4 that every staff member can memorize. Unfortunately, this document is usually also known as a Security Policy, and has led to some confusion, with a significant number of people coming to believe that this is sufficient to provide security. While it is another one of those useful tools in the over-arching process, it does not provide the core features of repeatability and completeness that our Security Policy does provide.

Threat Model: Measuring Insecurity

[Berg02] states that the first step is to create a method to quantify and evaluate risk. We start with the Threat Model (TM), which models the inherent risks. We then use this to produce a Security Policy (SP), which explains how we deal with them.

The most basic Threat Model is simply a list of things that crackers may attempt to do to subvert the rules of the system. Most of these will share some common elements, but all are written down separately, so that every threat is independent. This ensures that future maintenance is very quick: items can be added or removed without having to rewrite any of the rest of the Threat Model.

Making a system secure is by nature an imprecise task: we really just want to say, "make sure nothing bad can possibly happen, including all the possibly bad things we never thought of," and then do it. If we were to naively apply the concepts of Requirements and Specifications documents to security, our Requirements would be one line long, while the Specifications would be about the same length. Yet we cannot achieve repeatable, credible security without formalizing what we mean, what we intend to do, and how we are doing it.

The Threat Model (TM) is an approximate equivalent to a Requirements document. Instead of saying what the game has to do, it instead says what crackers will attempt to do to the game. This stage is an entirely creative exercise, and it is well worth involving all the members of your team, simply brainstorming any attacks they can think of. No attack should be rejected if it makes sense from the cracker's point of view; whether or not any of these attacks (threats) are dangerous to the system will be dealt with later, but they must be recorded at this stage, thereby demonstrating that later stages have taken them into consideration.

Rejecting attacks at this stage creates two major problems. First, the assumptions that invalidate the attack today may change tomorrow; if the attack is not listed at all in the TM, then simple future reevaluation of the game's security will not notice the activation of this previously inactive threat. If it had been included and discounted in a later stage, it would be easy to discover its activation and to respond appropriately.

Secondly, rejecting attacks loses the fact that they were evaluated at all. If someone else brings up the attack in the future as a possibility, it must be reevaluated, even if some people present remember that it was evaluated and rejected, because they may have mis-remembered.

Threats

Each element in the Threat Model is a description of an attack that a cracker might attempt. Each attack should be concrete rather than abstract; i.e., it should include details of exactly what the attack is and what tools the attacker is using. It is also extremely helpful to record the reasoning—from the cracker's point of view—that motivates the attack, so that future readers can understand why each threat has been included, and in that way, it performs a similar role to source-code documentation. With larger Threat Models, this information is usually best placed in an appendix, to ensure the main document is easily readable and not too verbose.

For instance, good attacks on a subscription-based MMOG might include:

- Attempting to steal another player's character; discovering another user's password and then logging in as that user; changing the password, credit card (CC) details, home address, e-mail address, etc.; permanently taking over the account and making it look as though the cracker is the legitimate user of the account.

- Attacking monsters that are too hard, seeing if you get lucky. If not, removing all the downside by avoiding death: attempt to escape just before actually dying.
- Assuming you cannot escape by in-game means, attempt to disrupt the game so that you are no longer in combat. Attempting to log out of the game. If you are prevented from logging out (or if this will automatically lose the combat), breaking the network connection or reboot your computer. Or, in extremis, attempting to crash the MMOG server so that when it reboots, it will reset your character's location and you will no longer be in danger.

These are necessarily abbreviated and condensed; for a real MMOG, you would expect to go into a lot more detail on some of these issues!

In each of the issues, the motivation of the cracker is included. This is important for three reasons. First, at some point we will want to prioritize which attacks we will defend against, and this information helps us evaluate which attacks are more likely to take place.

Second, understanding the motivation of the cracker leads to the discovery of many more attacks that you would not otherwise think of. This is especially true when you have all your team collectively brainstorming attacks; in practice, the description of the motivation by one person often triggers additional ideas for attacks from other people. The account-stealing attack was originally brainstormed by someone thinking about "things you might do in the game if you could," like stealing someone else's avatar. This led to inventing a variety of different attacks that would all achieve that end.

Third, without understanding this end, the attack described might make no sense at all: why steal someone else's account and change it so that you are being billed for it when you could more easily open a new account? The attack where you steal an account and do not change the CC details is entirely different, motivated by the desire to get a free game, and must not be confused with this other attack. Failing to understand and record this difference may lead to your implementing a "solution" that depends upon the assumption that the original CC details remain correct. In this particular attack, and in many other cases, too, that assumption is completely invalid. Even worse, future readers of the Threat Model may think it a mistake and delete this threat!

Cost

It may sound as though TMs require a large amount of time and effort to put together. In reality, they tend to be extremely quick to produce, mainly because each item is independent of the others, and they can simply be recorded as a plain list. Usually most of the TM can be brainstormed within just a few hours. There is no need to get the whole team in one massive meeting just to generate the TM; each can have separate smaller meetings at convenient times, and then the leaders simply need to meet and merge the results. Since each element is fully independent, merging is usually very straightforward and does not create any conflict.

Structuring Your Threat Model

Even when working on simple games, you can quickly generate a TM with many individual attacks, and it is often necessary to impose some form of structure. Simple categorization rarely helps, mainly because most attacks cross multiple categories and will not easily fit into one rather than the others. Where multiple teams are attempting to merge their individually created TMs, non-deterministic opinionated structure like this can make the merging process extremely difficult and confrontational, without bringing much tangible benefit.

Many people instead like to use Attack Trees [Schneier99] to provide structure to their Threat Model. An Attack Tree is rooted by a specific goal or motivation of the cracker, with each node representing some action they can take to try to achieve that. You quickly end up with a tree, because most actions can be achieved in a variety of different ways, and so you want to show different subactions as children of the main action.

The main advantages of Attack Trees are:

- They are an efficient way of recording the information, cutting down duplication of common elements of multiple attacks.
- They usually preserve most of the independence of each item while still providing structure.
- Decisions on how to organize them are usually noncontentious.

The tree-structure itself also records extra information in the form of the relationships between different attacks. It also makes them easier to read, since you can quickly find a particular group or class of attacks. They also perform a limited form of abstraction of detail; it is possible to read only the highest few levels and get an overview of all the attacks without having to read the full detail of each one.

The main disadvantage is that they encourage constrained thinking, which increases the tendency to leave out some attacks. One common way of alleviating this is to do one or more initial iterations with plain lists, which quickly become unwieldy, and then to convert these to ATs (e.g., at the same time that you merge the TMs generated by different teams). By enduring a brief period of coping with unwieldy lists, you hope to discover very nearly all the threats you possibly could, before quickly bringing things under control.

There is also the significant problem of how to edit a large tree as an electronic document; few teams have good tools for editing trees that even come close to the power of plain document editors such as Microsoft Word. For complex systems, the concrete benefits of structuring a large Threat Model so that humans can easily read it and reason about it typically far outweigh the disadvantages. If the document is difficult or irritating, either to read or to modify, people will be put off doing so, and both usage and update frequency will decline. Ultimately, this leads to a fatal undermining of the whole process, and so it is extremely important to maintain ease-of-use for all the team.

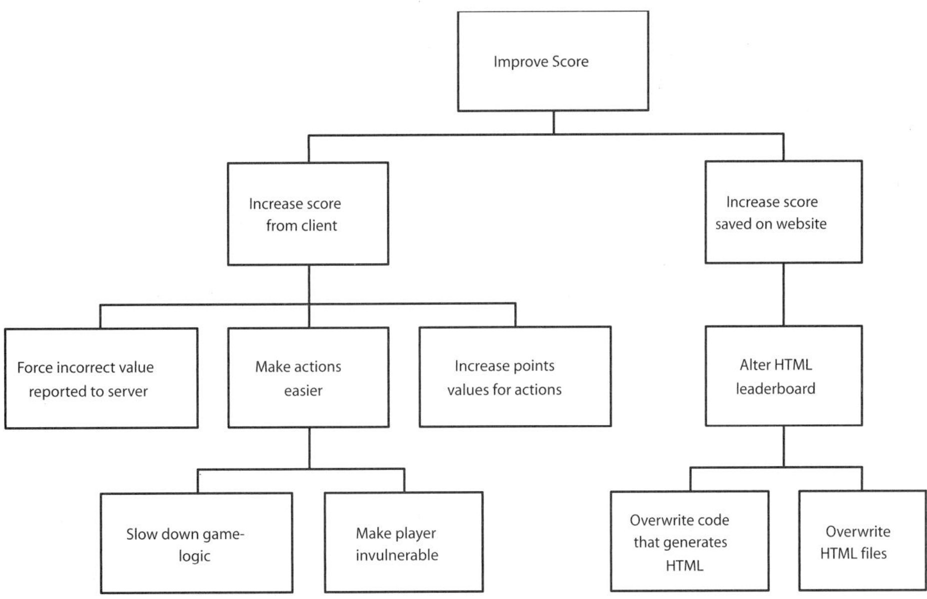

FIGURE 6.8.1 *An example attack tree with 1 root, 3 child nodes, and 1–5 grandchildren.*

Most nontrivial systems usually have multiple independent attack-trees making up the complete Threat Model; there is no need to rigidly constrain yourself to a single tree that contains every attack (this would often require painful coercion of the attack descriptions).

Security Policy: Nullifying Threats

The Security Policy is derived from the Threat Model. It explains how to counteract every potential threat, thereby rendering the system secure. Without a specific Threat Model, a Security Policy is largely useless, since it has become a solution without a precisely defined problem, no longer knowing the answer to: Secure from whom [Schneier03]?

Unlike the TM, the SP's purpose is to specify what the system and its administrators must do. It describes what they do, how they do it, and—where applicable—even why they do it. It must be precise; a vague SP creates ambiguity, which in turn is an opportunity for your team to accidentally create loopholes, or gaps between the secure elements, which will later be discovered and used by attackers.

Without an SP, no one can really take any actions to secure the system since there is no strategy defining what they are doing; all that will happen is that individuals will infer, deduce, or simply invent their own private SPs according to whim. The SP should be seen both as a guiding strategy and the detailed laws laying out how that strategy is to be enacted; the assumption is that all possible side effects were evaluated when the SP was written, and that if the SP says to do something, it's because there is a firm concrete reason for doing so.

Critically, the SP can always be re-created from scratch and should always be the same (or mostly the same) when this happens. This is one of the core advantages we sought: repeatability, and the use of methodical and scientific approaches as opposed to random, haphazard attempts. Security can and should be an engineering discipline, not a hand-waving exercise.

We know that it is repeatable, because the SP was generated methodically from the original TM. The SP should only change when the TM changes. (And it must always change when the TM changes—or at least be reevaluated in light of the TM changes. An SP that is not updated version by version in lock-step with the TM is valueless, since it is no longer a logical step from the TM—it will simply become an interesting historical document.)

The process of creating the SP from the TM is quite simple: you work through each threat and check that your current SP nullifies it. If not, you add to the SP until it does. As you get towards the last of the threats, you will often discover that a threat is already countered by some existing element of the SP and needs no extra procedures.

If a threat is judged too expensive to deal with, or too unlikely to justify worrying about, the SP should explicitly say so and provide reasoning. This is all part of ensuring that the SP is a methodical and logical extension of the TM, and that we retain repeatability and accountability. By explicitly dealing with every element in the TM, we render the SP a standalone instruction manual that fully captures all the information from the TM without needing to reference it; this enables staff to work directly with the SP on its own. Having just one simple proscriptive document to work with increases the chances that the decided upon security policy will faithfully be enacted by all staff.

Ongoing Revision of Both Documents

Most of the value of this process is realized as soon as you complete your first iteration through the steps of generating a Threat Model and a Security Policy. If you then fail to revise them regularly, you will certainly miss some of the advantages, but you will still have gained a lot over more ad hoc approaches. In cases where ongoing revision realistically will not happen, it is still worth starting out in the right way.

In preference, both documents should be rewritten regularly. It is also sensible to revise them in light of any successful attacks. In both cases, the same development process should be repeated, except that you do not have to start from scratch. First, every threat should be reviewed, and any additional threats added (especially true when a new attack has just succeeded!). Then the Security Policy should be examined, at least in light of the new attacks, although preferably in light of all of them. Sometimes the successful attack will prove to be a threat that no one thought of, other times it will demonstrate a flaw in the Security Policy's strategy for a known attack. In either case, both documents should be updated together, and it helps a great deal to have them versioned as a single atomic unit, so that they never get out of sync (assuming you have a document-versioning system).

Additional Benefits to This Technique

The following sections outline some additional benefits.

Introduction to Code-Base

It's a very fast way to introduce new developers to how the game is written or how the code base fits together. By necessity, it is an aspect-oriented view of your code base, and works at the use-case level, since the threat model is a specialized form of "a set of use-cases." For external people or new arrivals to the team, this makes it much easier to comprehend than most documentation.

A Fresh Perspective on Existing Design

A security audit tends to make people look at the system (and their own code) from a new perspective, which can preemptively uncover many non-security-related bugs, in addition to the security holes. It is also a "breath of fresh air," being sufficiently different from the standard process of looking for bugs that it's more mentally stimulating and a nice change from bug hunting.

Benefit from Experience

The threat model and security policy developed for a project may serve as the starting point for other titles. There will certainly be elements that are unique to any given title and design, but giving the team a starting point to serve as a launch pad for their brainstorming can help capitalize on previous work. The opportunity exists to build up a library of threat modes over time, with detailed descriptions of each threat, so that future team members could pick them up and understand them. Such a library would be valuable in much the same way other software libraries are, improvements could be back-propagated to earlier titles, metrics could be defined to measure success, etc.

Further Reading

The industry-standard equivalent of this gem is an evaluative system known as the Common Criteria (CC)–[Cox00, CCEVS04]. The CC was derived from the common elements of the TCSEC and ITSEC programs, from the U.S. and Europe, hence the rather ambiguous name, although it also represents a step forward. The CC is a much larger framework than this gem, designed to provide greater levels of assurance and much more detailed and precise evaluation. As a practical example, you can view a CC evaluation of the Windows 2000 Operating System [Microsoft02]. The CC has three core elements: Protection Profiles, a Target of Evaluation, and a Security Target. This gem uses a Threat Model as a simplified equivalent of the CC Protection Profiles, and an augmented Security Policy instead of a full CC Security Target.

More generally, Bruce Schneier [Schneier00, Schneier03] is considered by many the foremost expert in the security industry, and his books are both approachable and contain practical insights. Ross Anderson [Anderson01] is another highly respected specialist, and maintains a frequently updated Web site [Anderson04] dealing with all matters to do with security, from privacy and data-protection through to cryptography, steganography, and the most esoteric (and interesting) of cryptographic systems.

Conclusion

You now have a methodology for adding security to your games right from the very start of the development process, without increasing your total development time. No specialist knowledge is required, and all members of the team can contribute a great deal to the overall security and can understand how and why it is secured.

This gem has not covered any implementation issues to do with security, which is where the specific understanding of cryptography, etc. comes in to play. Clearly, these issues are still critically important to the "secureness" of your system, but when using this gem, they are encapsulated as late-stage design and implementation details, and can be safely ignored during the main design process.

For instance, where a Security Policy mandates the use of an encrypted stream at a particular point, you will eventually need to decide which cryptographic protocol to use, which is a nontrivial decision. However, the relevant information you need to make this decision will already have been captured by the Threat Model and Security Policy, making such implementation decisions relatively straightforward. For beginners, they start by picking a crypto library, but experts do it almost at the end [Clayton04].

The methodology used in this gem enables you to attack the security problem in a very focused and methodical manner. You gain all the benefits of a disciplined, scientific approach—the approach that Anderson and others term "Security Engineering" (an overt reference to "Software Engineering" and all the good that that discipline has done for software development). It is only a single process, but when applied diligently empowers you to make your entire system secure, and not only that but also to know, empirically, just how secure your system is. No more hand waving; no more finger crossing guesses that it "is probably safe [subtext: I hope!]." You also have a formal specification of your "security design" that you can check against your implementation.

References

[Anderson01] Anderson, Ross. *Security Engineering: A Guide to Building Dependable Distributed Systems.* Wiley, 2001.

[Anderson04] Anderson, Ross. Home page. Available online at *http://www.cl.cam.ac.uk/users/rja14/,* 2004.

[Berg02] Berg, Al. "6 Myths About Security Policies," Available online at *http://infosecuritymag.techtarget.com/2002/oct/securitypolicies.shtml,* October 2002.

[CCEVS04] "Common Criteria Evaluation and Validation Scheme." Available online at *http://niap.nist.gov/cc-scheme/aboutus.html,* 2004.

[Clayton04] Clayton, Richard. Home page. Available online at *http://www.cl.cam.ac.uk/users/rnc1/,* 2004.

[Cox00] Cox, Peter. "Security Evaluation: The Common Criteria Certifications." Available online at *http://www.itsecurity.com/papers/border.htm,* 2000.

[Microsoft02] Microsoft. "Windows 2000 Security Target." Available online at *http://download.microsoft.com/download/win2000srv/CCSecTar/2.0/NT5/EN-US/W2KCCST.pdf,* 2002.

[SANS89] SANS Institute. Available online at *http://www.sans.org*, since 1989.

[Schneier99] Schneier, Bruce. "Attack Trees; Modeling Security Threats." Available online at *http://www.schneier.com/paper-attacktrees-ddj-ft.html,* December 1999.

[Schneier00] Schneier, Bruce. *Secrets and Lies: Digital Security in a Networked World.* John Wiley and Sons, 2000.

[Schneier03] Schneier, Bruce. "A reality checklist for an effective security policy." Available online at *http://searchsecurity.techtarget.com/tip/0,289483,sid14_gci931792,00.html*, 2003.

SECTION 7

AUDIO

Introduction

Mark DeLoura

madsax@satori.org

Audio has come a long way. My first commercial game programming experience was working on a PC-based arcade game, where we used a Gravis Ultrasound card for audio playback. We were pretty excited about it, because the GUS enabled us to download samples into the card and play them back with whatever pan, volume, or pitch we wanted. It was also MIDI compatible. It was so cool! We set up a C++ sound manager layer that ran over the top of the low-level gf1 libraries to automatically handle assigning physical voices, and then we created a pseudo-3D effect by tying sound sources to dynamic objects in the scene and using pan and volume accordingly. We mucked about with sample rates and bit depth, stereo, and mono samples, and did our best to optimize our memory map on the card so that we could fit both the waveforms for the MIDI instruments and the engine sound and environment samples.

I know that for some of you, this reminds you of the days you spent twiddling the speaker on your TRS-80 or Apple II, and how exciting it was when you first coerced your machine to make sounds resembling music. Fortunately for all of us, the state-of-the-art in audio has moved on to the point where we can have composers creating music instead of programmers, and we can simply stream their creations from disc or memory. We can create lush real-time audio environments with the assistance of audio-scripting tools, and they can be played back in high fidelity through 5.1 audio systems with real-time hardware effects processing from built-in DSPs. Our focus now can be more on creating audio environments that enhance the game experience, as opposed to simply getting the machine to make beeps and boops at the appropriate times.

It's with our past firmly in mind that we present these five excellent audio gems. Many thanks to Sean Gugler for his initial work organizing this section. First in this section, you will find a discussion of multithreading and its applicability to audio programming, by James Boer. Matthew Harmon will discuss writing sound APIs that manage groups of sounds easily. Then Sami Hamlaoui will briefly describe a simple technique for making audio appear to emanate from a 3D surface, as opposed to just a simple point source. Christian Schüler digs deeply into the math behind Feedback Delay Networks for environmental reverb. And lastly, with speech recognition gaining increasing prominence in games, Julien Hamaide tackles a way to match incoming speech with a trained dictionary of words.

We hope you find these gems useful, and that you'll be able to apply some of these techniques to your next game!

7.1

Multithreaded Audio Programming Techniques

James Boer

author@boarslair.com

Modern gaming hardware is moving away from a single-threaded execution model, as parallel process execution and even multiprocessor machines are becoming more and more common on users' desktops. Modern CPUs such as Intel®'s Pentium® 4 Xeon™ processors have introduced HyperThreading™ technology to the world, which is essentially a method of simultaneously executing two processes on one chip to take advantage of its built-in parallelism. Additionally, multiprocessor machines are becoming more common on the desktop, and users will expect their games to take full advantage of hardware that they paid good money for. While the sample code in this gem is specifically written for Intel and AMD processors on Windows-based PCs, the concepts of multitasking specific portions of your audio processing code can be applied to different platforms and operating systems, including Macs, Linux, and game consoles.

We'll look at one specific area where we can use multithreaded code for Windows operating systems to take advantage of multiprocessors or HyperThreaded processors: the primary audio decoding and playback loop. Common pitfalls and multithreading mistakes will be examined, and ideas for optimizing various common audio-related algorithms will be discussed. However, the general tips and techniques presented in this gem can be applied to other areas of game development as well.

A (Very) Brief Introduction to Threaded Programming

In a nutshell, threaded programming involves creating two or more code paths that execute simultaneously. These threads are both part of a single process (a single executing program) and share the same address space. In layman's terms, this simply means that any threads spawned from a single process can access the same data. In essence, every single C or C++ program can be considered to have at least one thread (the main thread), which is launched when the program is started. This thread is then responsible for launching other child threads, often for limited or very specific jobs. Figure 7.1.1 shows how this works on a multiprocessor system.

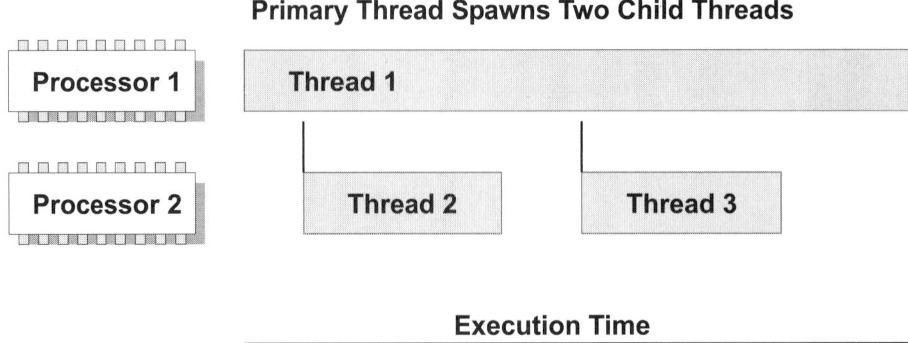

FIGURE 7.1.1 *Main thread spawning other threads on second processor.*

Obviously, a machine with a single processor can't actually execute more than one section of code at a time. The same timeslicing mechanism that allows more than one program or process to execute simultaneously on a multitasking operating system also allows more than one thread to execute simultaneously within a single process. Figure 7.1.2 demonstrates how multitasking is simulated on a single processor machine.

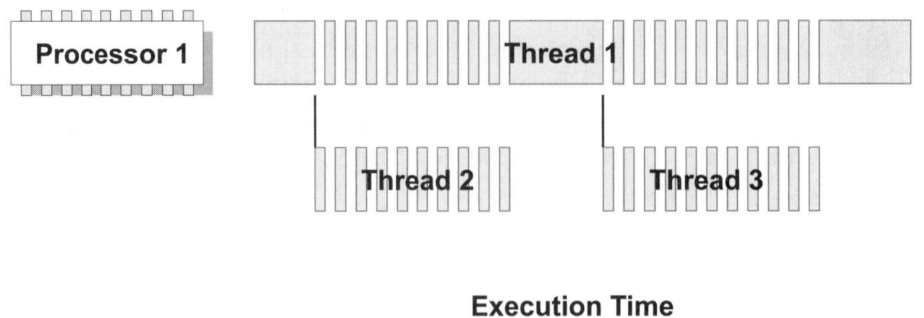

FIGURE 7.1.2 *Multiple threads sharing execution on a single processor.*

Fortunately, it is much more efficient for an operating system to timeslice between multiple threads than multiple processes. Because of this, it is feasible to add some degree of multithreading code to your game to take advantage of those machines with multiple processors (or single processors that can execute multiple threads more efficiently) while imposing very little overhead on machines that must emulate this mechanism with a single processor. However, it would be foolish to create threads for anything but the most obviously suited tasks because of both the overhead for single-processor execution of these threads and the inherent complexity in managing and debugging multithreaded code.

Threading Terminology and Mechanisms

Multithreaded programming not only involves thinking beyond traditional linear programming, it also invokes a complete set of specialized terminology. Many of those terms are described for you here.

Each instance of a program that executes on a machine is considered to be a single *process*. The defining characteristic of a process is that it has its own address space and protected access to disk and other hardware resources. Some operating systems, such as Windows, Mac OS X, or Linux, allow multiple processes to be run at once. Other operating systems, such as those found on game consoles, are optimized to run only a single process. Each process (or program) dispatches one or more concurrently running *threads*. Threads may simply be thought of as paths of execution within a process, all of which have access to the same address space (such as global and static data).

To safely use functions (either your own or library functions) simultaneously from multiple threads, the functions must both be *reentrant* and *thread-safe*. A reentrant function does not hold static data over successive calls or return a pointer to static data. A thread-safe function protects shared resources by use of a lock (such as using a mutex, which we'll describe next). This prevents two threads that may be simultaneously executing the function from corrupting each other's data. The use of global data without locks will make a function non thread-safe.

To *lock* means to prevent access to shared data or resources by more than one thread simultaneously, which prevents data corruption. A common lock is called a *mutex*, a shortening of the term "mutually exclusive." While one thread holds the lock and performs work on the protected code, other threads may be forced to wait or perform other tasks. In order to wait without consuming CPU cycles, a thread may be asked to *sleep* for a specific time or until a specific message or event wakes it.

There are a number of unique error conditions associated exclusively with threads that you must guard against. A *deadlock* occurs when a lock is activated, and, due to specific interactivity with other threads, can never be unlocked. For instance, two threads may end up waiting for each other to become unlocked before proceeding. If there is no external signal that can unlock at least one of the threads, this is a deadlock situation. A *race condition* may occur when two or more threads must operate on the same data location, but the result depends on which order the threads execute it. Typically, locks such as mutexes are used to prevent race conditions.

Additionally, all threads are assigned execution priorities, in much the same way processes are given priorities. This, somewhat obviously, allows the threading dispatcher to better prioritize thread execution. A *priority failure* occurs if a thread fails to complete its assigned task before another thread requires its results. Often, this is a result of assigning incorrect priorities to tasks. A *starvation failure* is similar to a priority failure in that a thread was unable to complete its required tasks in its allotted time.

Identifying Audio Tasks Suitable for Threaded Programming

In general, it is important to clearly identify which programming components are suited to multithreaded programming. Quite frankly, the traditional rule of thumb in game programming has tended to avoid threaded programming altogether, for several reasons. First, most consumer machines did not have more than one processor, as this was not supported on consumer operating systems. Second, since multithreaded programming implied a bit of extra overhead on single-processor machines, it was not deemed worth the price in CPU cycles to provide this simulated functionality.

However, in the past few years, several things have occurred. Today's operating systems such as Windows XP now support multiple processors, and we can expect some gamers to have these systems. Additionally, and perhaps even more importantly, the relative cost of implementing threaded behavior has decreased for single-processor machines for two reasons. First, because the average speed of processors is still rapidly increasing, the relative overhead of threads is lower than ever, since the absolute cost of thread switching has stayed more or less constant. And even beyond this fact, modern processors are being designed to run multiple threads more efficiently than ever. We'll discuss Intel's latest hardware innovations and the ramification of these new chips in the next section.

Audio programming has some obvious ties to threaded programming. The very nature of any audio system is asynchronous behavior—namely, the continuous processing, mixing, and buffering of audio data from its original location on disk or in memory to its final destination in hardware buffers—all of which must happen in real time. Often, we wish to have continuously streaming audio even while other tasks may interrupt the primary thread, such as loading up data resources for a new level. Unlike visual rendering, in which frames can simply be dropped, there is no way to effectively mask starvation of an audio data stream—it will result in audible gaps or popping.

One obvious candidate of threaded programming is that of streaming and decoding high-compression audio data, such as MP3 or Vorbis files. No matter what else is happening, this job requires periodic access to disk resources as well as a percentage of CPU time in order to acquire and decode the audio data from the disk and stuff it into audio buffers, all in real time.

There are also some less obvious uses for threads that execute in the background. 3D audio data, including sound sources and listeners, must stay synchronized with objects in your game world in order to calculate the resultant 3D audio output correctly. However, it may be a waste of processor time to calculate the audio every time the listener or 3D objects move (which may be as often as 60 to 90 times per second). Instead, you may wish to selectively degrade how often the 3D audio data is recalculated. By putting these calculations on a separate thread and by periodically waking the thread at a rate slower than the main update rate, you not only save calculation cycles, but you allow a HyperThreaded or multiprocessor system to operate more efficiently by offloading these calculations to a separate processor. You could also perform data-transfer tasks such as moving audio data into a playing sound buffer on individual threads.

Additionally, you may even wish to access world geometry and perform raycasting and pathfinding for the benefit of your audio system. If these don't sound like audio-related tasks, you might not be aware that most modern audio implementations (like I3DL2 and EAX™) require various tasks such as line-of-sight information and other spatial awareness in order to calculate sound properties such as occlusion and obstruction, in addition to basic reverberation and echo properties. These are wonderful tasks to shunt off to a different thread, because this type of information does not have to update nearly as quickly as visual information. Thus, the thread can be tuned to consume far fewer CPU cycles than might be necessary if it were calculated synchronously with the visual information in the world.

Before we get into the specifics of how we would set up such a multithreaded system, let's examine another recent technology that is making threading more important even on single-processor machines.

Intel's HyperThreading Technology—What Is It?

One of Intel's more recent technological achievements has been dubbed HyperThreading, and it is designed to allow a single processor to appear as two virtual processors to an operating system (and a program). By making more efficient use of the multiple execution units found on the chip (previously used only for out-of-order execution), multiple threads can actually be executed simultaneously, offering much greater efficiency than when executing only a single thread.

As one might expect, it is not quite as efficient as if two true physical processors were executing simultaneously. This is because the separately executing threads will often collide, both requiring the same resources on the processor at once. However, in optimal threading conditions, it is expected to see a nominal performance boost of ~30% on both threads if their workloads are properly balanced. In the best case, users may even utilize two physical processors, each with HyperThreading enabled, giving the system four virtual processors to work on.

However, HyperThreading is not a magic bullet. In fact, it can actually decrease overall performance, if applications are built using only a single thread or the main thread is too heavily loaded compared to secondary threads. The reason for this performance degradation is somewhat logical—if the processor's resources are split between two executing threads, and the game only makes use of one of these threads, the performance will be worse than if the entire chip was dedicated to execution of only the main game thread.

In some sense, this puts game programmers in a bit of an awkward position—should you continue to avoid threads and allow a slight degradation of HyperThreaded systems, or do you take advantage of HyperThreading with extensive use of threads and simply accept the minor performance penalty on single-processor, single-execution chips? There is no one definitive answer, but games (and gamers) have typically pushed forward the technological envelope more than any other type of application, and gamers will be quick to adopt a technology if they see tangible results. Many in both hardware and software development feel that parallel and threaded programming is the wave of the future.

Threaded Programming Techniques and Operations

In certain situations, when creating a background thread in a game, it is not necessary for the thread to be active 100% of the time, because the worker thread is able to perform its task much faster than the primary thread requires. This is the case with decoding MP3 or Vorbis audio data, or with performing most other audio-related tasks.

To decode data at a decelerated rate, we can employ a higher-priority thread that is executed in periodic bursts and sleeps until the timer wakes it up to perform again. This mechanism helps to ensure against thread starvation while also keeping the overall CPU time of the worker threads reasonable.

Perhaps the most important step in designing a threaded system is deciding how and when your worker threads will share their processed information with the primary thread. In essence, this is the only link the two threads will share, and it is critical that the data transfer is done both safely and efficiently. It is important that the multiple threads do not overlap too often, or you will lose efficiency as one thread stalls while another finishes operating within a critical section.

A Threaded Sample Program

We'll now examine a small program designed to evaluate how much computational performance can be gained by splitting decoding tasks into threads. Additionally, it demonstrates how a single program can allow two code paths: multithreaded or single-threaded. This simple threading performance timing application can demonstrate both code techniques as well as performing some useful benchmarks on various systems. We will present the results of the benchmark tests later.

ON THE CD

Listing 7.1.1 shows our multithreaded benchmarking application in its entirety. Please note that it is also included on the CD-ROM.

Listing 7.1.1 Multithreaded Benchmarking Application

```
#include <iostream>
#include <process.h>
#include <windows.h>
#include <conio.h>

using namespace std;

#pragma pack(push,4)

__int64 g_total_val = 0;
int g_num_calculations = 0;
bool g_do_floating_point = false;
CRITICAL_SECTION g_val_update;

// Perform some nonsense calculations to burn up CPU cycles
void DoCalculations()
{
    int val = 0;
    if(g_do_floating_point)
    {
        for(int i = 0; i < g_num_calculations; i++)
        {
            for(int j = 0; j < 1000000; j++)
            {
                val += int((float)i * (float)j *
                    ((float)j - (float)i - 0.25f) /
                    (val + i + j + 1));
            }
        }
        EnterCriticalSection(&g_val_update);
        g_total_val += val;
        LeaveCriticalSection(&g_val_update);
    }
    else
    {
        for(int i = 0; i < g_num_calculations; i++)
        {
            for(int j = 0; j < 1000000; j++)
            {
                val += i * j * (j - i) /
                    (val + i + j + 1);
            }
```

```
        }
        EnterCriticalSection(&g_val_update);
        g_total_val += val;
        LeaveCriticalSection(&g_val_update);
    }
}

// This function is passed to createthread()
void ThreadFunction(LPVOID lpv)
{
    HANDLE hEvent = (HANDLE)lpv;
    DoCalculations();
    SetEvent(hEvent);
}

// Start the threaded timing tests
int main()
{
    char c;
    cout << "Do floating-point calculations (y/n)? ";
    cin >> c;
    if(c == 'y')
        g_do_floating_point = true;

    int threads = 0;
    cout << "How many total threads do you wish" <<
        " to create (including the main thread)? ";
    cin >> threads;


    // Allocate an array of handles if we have
    // more than one thread
    HANDLE* pHandles = 0;
    if(threads > 1)
    {
        pHandles = new HANDLE[threads - 1];
    }

    cout << "How many millions of calculation loops" <<
        " should each thread perform? ";
    cin >> g_num_calculations;
    cout << "Now performing timing calculations...";

    InitializeCriticalSection(&g_val_update);

    // Get the start time
    unsigned int start_time = timeGetTime();

    // Perform all actual calculations -
    // one per thread.
    int i;
    if(threads > 1)
    {
```

```
            for(i = 0; i < threads - 1; i++)
            {
                pHandles[i] = CreateEvent(
                    NULL, FALSE, FALSE, NULL);
                if(_beginthread(&ThreadFunction, 4096,
                    pHandles[i]) == -1)
                    return -1;
            }
            DoCalculations();
            // Wait for all other threads to finish
            // before continuing
            WaitForMultipleObjects(threads - 1,
                pHandles, TRUE, INFINITE);
        }
        else
        {
            // Do a simple set of calculations for the
            // single-threaded path
            DoCalculations();
        }

        // Get the end time
        unsigned int end_time = timeGetTime();

        // We no longer need this critical section
        DeleteCriticalSection(&g_val_update);

        // Close and delete handles used for synchronization
        if(threads > 1)
        {
            for(i = 0; i < threads - 1; i++)
            {
                CloseHandle(pHandles[i]);
            }
            delete[] pHandles;
        }

        cout << " Finished!" << endl;
        cout << "Performed all calculations in "
            << end_time - start_time <<
            " milliseconds" << endl;
        getch();
        return 0;
    }

    #pragma pack(pop,4)
```

Essentially, this is a small thread-based benchmarking program that times mathematical calculations spread over any number of threads. The user is asked what type of algorithm to run (floating point or integer), how many threads to run, and how many million calculation cycles to run per thread.

To simulate data flow from the threads into a common pool, the calculated values are periodically added to a global variable named `g_total_val`. This is the all-important data transfer point we talked about earlier. Because this is a shared access point, it is imperative that access to this variable is protected. However, don't be fooled since we don't do anything with the variable. It's only there to show you how to access common/global data from threads. Let's briefly walk through this code to see how we manage our threads, and discuss how we might approach applying these techniques to an audio system.

The first function you will notice is `DoCalculations()`. This performs a series of calculations in loops incrementing by a million, to perform meaningful timing tests. The results of these calculations are stored in the global variable `g_total_val`. Because this is a global variable and potentially accessible by multiple threads simultaneously, we must first use a mutex to lock access to the global, then unlock it after we've finished accessing it. When writing multithreaded code, it is important to endeavor to minimize the number of locks you must perform. If we, for example, locked and unlocked the global variable on each iteration instead of once every million iterations, the threading performance would be degraded because of an increase in collisions of threads when trying to access the variable, leading to stalled threads.

The `DoCalculations()` function is wrapped in a function called `ThreadFunction()`, which takes a pointer to a void pointer as an argument. This is the entry point to a new thread. When this function exits, the thread terminates itself.

The rest of the program is rather straightforward upon inspection. The program asks the user a few questions, such as what type of calculations to perform and how many calculation threads to create. After getting the information it needs, the program sets a timer, then proceeds to launch either one or multiple threads, each performing a series of calculations inside the `DoCalculations()` function. The "results" of the calculations are all stored in a global variable `g_total_val`.

This sample project demonstrates how to split up a task into a variable number of multiple, concurrently executing tasks. We'll use this program to do some simple timing tests on several different test machines to demonstrate how threading can improve efficiency in an ideal case.

For these tests, the sample program was run on two test machines. Machine One is a dual Xeon Pentium 4 2.4 GHz machine running Windows XP Professional. Tests were conducted both with HyperThreading turned on and off to demonstrate different results. Machine Two is a Pentium 4 1.5 GHz Windows 2000 Professional machine with no HyperThreading capability and only a single processor. For each configuration, we ran tests that demonstrated both integer and mixed integer and floating-point calculations. The number of test cycles (1.2 billion) was chosen so as to obtain a reasonable length of time for execution. Remember, the total times are much less relevant than the relevant execution time of each test within a particular configuration row. We've used a somewhat primitive timing mechanism, so figure that our execution timing error is approximately plus or minus 20 milliseconds overall. Table 7.1.1 provides the results.

Table 7.1.1 Test Results of Sample Program

Configuration	1 thread	2 threads	3 threads	4 threads	5 threads	6 threads
M1, HT, integer	28078ms	16625ms	12172ms	10125ms	10438ms	10516ms
M1, HT, float	68719ms	34843ms	23500ms	19813ms	20672ms	20578ms
M1, no HT, integer	28063ms	14047ms	14062ms	14046ms	14141ms	14078ms
M1, no HT, float	68859ms	34422ms	29797ms	27484ms	26032ms	25125ms
M2, integer	43312ms	43332ms	43492ms	43593ms	44163ms	43442ms
M2, float	147232ms	108246ms	95247ms	90059ms	85943ms	82418ms

Key: M1 = Machine 1, M2 = Machine 2, HT = HyperThreading enabled, no HT = HyperThreading disabled, integer = integer-based calculations performed, float = floating point and integer calculations performed.

You can see how the most significant improvement is achieved switching from one to two executing threads on a dual-processor machine. This is not unexpected, as the two threads can both execute simultaneously on two physical processors. The only loss of efficiency comes in synchronizing the execution and data collection from the two threads. This is why you should theoretically never see a 100% improvement in performance in this situation.

When examining the performance gains from HyperThreading (meaning three or four threads are running on the dual processor machine with HyperThreading enabled), you can see a more modest but still substantial gain of approximately 30%. This corresponds to research done by Intel indicating how much you can expect to gain in optimal cases. One of the more interesting results to take note of is the odd fact that floating-point tests run on both machines continued to show improved performance beyond two threads, even when one might logically expect the opposite results. While the exact cause of these results are not clear, it could be surmised that both the operating system and processor are designed and optimized for execution of multiple threads, and so perform more optimally in this configuration, even on a multiprocessor machine. The fact that these results are primarily achieved with mixed floating-point and integer calculations may also play a part.

Last, it is interesting to note how much overhead (or rather, how little) each thread actually incurs—in our tests, the results are almost negligible. You would have to either greatly increase the number of threads or increase the time the tests are allowed to run to get more accurate measurements. On Machine Two, since it is single processor by nature with no HyperThreaded technology, any thread count above one must be emulated by the operating system.

What can we deduce from these numbers? On modern PCs running Windows operating systems, running multiple tasks on a single processor is very efficient, so long as the number of threads doesn't become too large. However, on systems designed for parallel execution, we can see a substantial performance boost when the number of currently executing and balanced threads equals the number of processors, whether virtual (in the case of HyperThreading) or physical. If any game systems can be robustly designed to take advantage of this parallel execution model, it would seem highly beneficial to do so.

Real-Time Streaming Data Mechanisms

Let's envision we want to set up a threaded system to assist in decoding MP3 or some other type of audio data which requires preprocessing. There are a couple of models for transferring streaming data from one system to another (such as between different threads).

One method of transfer is called a "push" transfer, so called because the system representing the data's source is responsible for notifying the destination system when it is ready to transfer a chunk of data. In this way, the data is "pushed" from the source to the destination. Streaming audio data over a network might operate in this manner. Since music cannot stream faster than the network allows, it makes sense for whoever is sending the music to take control of the transfer rate. If the music is streaming faster than real time, it can simply be buffered until it is needed. Or, the system may use a throttling mechanism to ensure that only a limited amount of data is buffered.

Another method of transfer is called a "pull" transfer, because the destination system is responsible for notifying the source system when it is ready to receive more data. In this way, you can think of the destination system as "pulling" the data out of the source. Typically speaking, this would be the most common model for implementing a threaded MP3 decoder. If you wish to read more about these models and how an interface to a streaming object might look, the COM IStream interface is available on Microsoft's sites, along with descriptions of these two models.

Streams and Threads

Assuming you will create a streaming interface similar to IStream, there is only one more decision to make regarding how the threads in your audio system are implemented. We'll present two options—neither is necessarily right or wrong, but both have advantages and disadvantages to consider.

The essential question now is: How do you create the threading interface? We'll assume for now that you'll be using a pull model. The audio system will periodically need small chunks of audio data. As it is required, this system will request decoded data from the MP3 decoder object.

One option is to create an IStream-based decoding object and to treat is as a threaded black box, allowing it to create an internal thread that is responsible for grabbing data, decoding it, and presenting it through the interface functions whenever asked. The client operates from the main thread and requests data as needed. The IStream decoder object always anticipates the next request and decodes data on the thread. When the amount of decoded data in the decoder object falls below a specific threshold, the thread is kicked into action, and more data is decoded until a specified maximum buffering threshold is reached. In this way, decoded data is always available for the main thread, and the threading problems are entirely contained behind the decoder object's interface. Figure 7.1.3 demonstrates how these objects interact with each other.

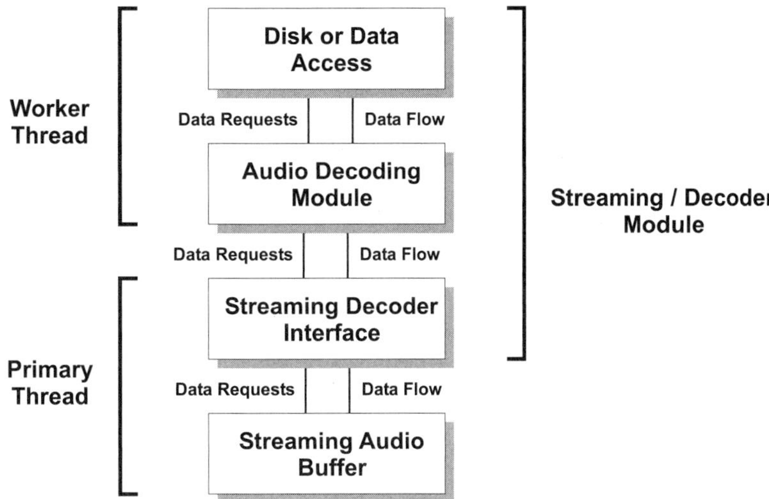

FIGURE 7.1.3 *Threading behind the decoder interface.*

This method is highly attractive for one main reason—because the threading is entirely contained within the decoder object. This keeps the interface between the two threads highly constrained—always a good thing. For those looking for a simple and robust solution, it's hard to beat this one.

As with any simple solution, there are bound to be a few drawbacks as well. For starters, this implies that any new stream will be using its own thread. If you are planning on creating multiple decoding objects, this may or may not be what you had in mind. Based on the rather surprising results of our timing tests, running multiple decoders, each in its own thread, may actually be more efficient than attempting to schedule them all yourself on a single thread, even on a single-processor machine. Unfortunately, there are also some special situations that might not work as well with this mechanism. For instance, when a sound buffer first starts, the buffer is typically filled with initial data to start with. You would need to either keep some prebuffered and decoded data ready to use, or the system would have to be intelligent enough to wait for the initial set of data to be decoded before attempting to play the sound buffer. Either way, it adds unfortunate complexity to an otherwise simple and elegant solution.

An alternative method is to create a thread that encompasses a much larger subsystem. The thread can maintain a list of streaming sound buffers and their respective decoder objects. This thread is then periodically activated, at which point each streaming buffer is filled with as much data as is needed. The thread then sleeps until it is again awakened by a timer, at which point the cycle begins again.

This system has some definite advantages and disadvantages. One advantage is that the problem of prefilling the buffer goes away to a large extent, because this all occurs using the same thread that adds new data to the buffer periodically. The result is that this initial decoding is invisible to the rest of the system. The downside to this system—and it is a considerable one—is that with so much data being managed by a single thread, the interface between this thread and the primary thread will tend to grow much more complex. This is because instead of simply filling a buffer in real time, this thread must block complete access to the sound buffer during the time in which the thread is directly accessing it. In essence, this means that any other member that accesses the sound buffer can potentially be thread-unsafe. It will take a large amount of engineering effort to ensure that this interface is completely bug-free. Figure 7.1.4 shows how these systems would interact with each other.

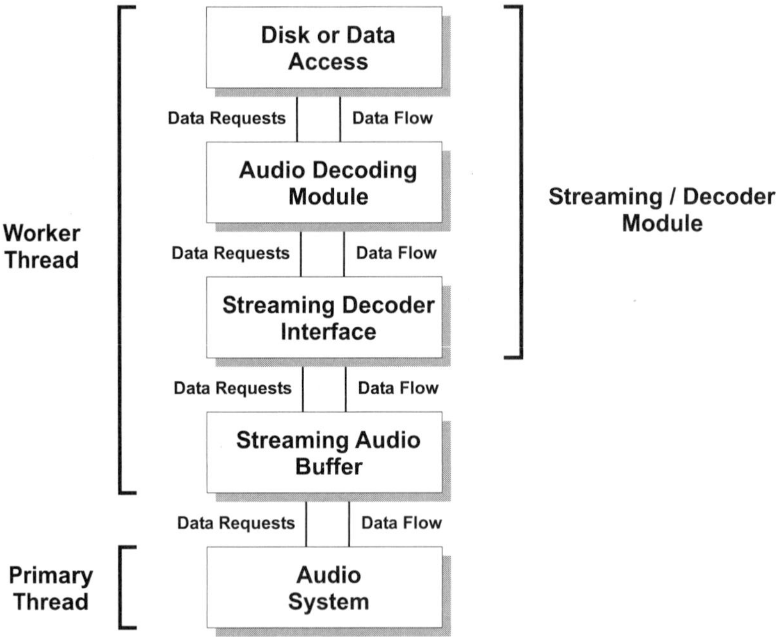

FIGURE 7.1.4 *Threading at the audio system level.*

Conclusion

The decision to enter into the world of threaded programming is not one to be made lightly. While threading can help programs run more efficiently when designed correctly and supported by hardware, it can also make programs more difficult to debug, and introduces an entirely new lexicon into your programming vocabulary—one which, as with anything new, takes time and effort to master.

It seems highly likely that games will, in the future, wish to take advantage of the new multiprocessor or HyperThreaded technologies available in current and next generation PCs and game consoles. After all, a game can never have too many CPU cycles to burn, and game programmers have traditionally been the true push behind the blazing advance of new hardware technology and innovations.

References

[Boer02] Boer. *Game Audio Programming*. Charles River Media, Inc, 2002.

[Intel] Multithreaded and Hyperthreaded documentation. Available online at *www.intel.com*.

[MSDN] Multithreaded documentation. Available online at *msdn.microsoft.com*.

7.2

Sound Management by Group

Matthew Harmon, eV Interactive Corporation

matt@ev-interactive.com

Current sound programming interfaces provide a good amount of control over the playback of individual sounds. Volume, playback rate, pan position, and pause/resume state are some common features provided by today's APIs. Most also provide a master volume control that alters the level of all sounds being played by the system.

There are many cases, however, where programmers need to manage the playback of related sounds as groups. Being able to quickly and easily alter the properties of an entire group of sounds can be very convenient, and integrating this capability into the game's sound API up front can save considerable time and frustration later in a project. These benefits are highlighted by a few simple cases.

- A team is developing an adventure game with both indoor and outdoor areas. As the player walks indoors, all the environment sounds from the outdoor areas—birds chirping, wind blowing, crickets chirping, etc.—should be reduced in volume. Occlusion technologies could be used here, but this is often overkill and not supported on all platforms. Instead, the team just needs the simple ability to dynamically balance the volume between "indoor" and "outdoor" sounds as the player transitions from one area to another.
- Programmers working on an air combat game finally get around to implementing the user preferences menus. The audio screen must provide an interface that allows the player to independently adjust the volume of several categories of sound effects: engine and environment noises, cockpit warnings, radio messages, and background music. The programmers add volume scale factors for each group of sounds but must then track down every place a sound is triggered and apply the correct scaling factor. Worse still, this is only a quick fix, as already active sounds won't be affected as the user slides the volume control back and forth.

- An innovative cartoon-style game gives the player the ability to dynamically accelerate time. To support the whimsical nature of the product, the team wants to scale the playback rates of sound effects but leave music and interface sounds at normal speed.

Dealing with each case becomes trivial if group-based sound management is built directly into the API wrapper at the beginning of a project.

API Wrapper Overview

Most sound playback APIs are quite similar at their core, and this gem assumes that the low-level sound API will be wrapped in a custom interface layer. For the sake of example, let's propose a simple 2D API wrapper in which sounds are managed by a generic handle.

```
handle = SndPlay(sampleBuffer);
SndSetRate(handle, newPlaybackRate);
SndSetVolume(handle, newVolume);
SndPause(handle);
SndResume(handle);
SndStop(handle);
```

To enable group management, we'll add a few simple new functions. First, we need a way to associate a sound with a group.

```
SndSetGroup(handle, group);
```

Alternatively, we can enforce the use of sound groups by requiring a group assignment at the time a sound is triggered.

```
handle = SndPlay(sampleBuffer, group);
```

Next, we add some very simple routines to manipulate playback parameters of entire groups of sounds.

```
SndSetGroupRate(group, newPlaybackRate);
SndSetGroupVolume(group, newVolume);
SndPauseGroup(group);
SndResumeGroup(group);
SndStopGroup(group);
```

This basic pseudocode can be extended to an object-based API as well as a 3D-enabled interface. Control over additional sound parameters can be similarly added.

Capabilities

Theoretically, just about every parameter that controls a playing sound can be managed at the higher "group" level. In practice, however, only a small handful of parameters are typically useful, as shown in the API outline earlier. It is worth examining these properties to see how the group controls are factored in.

Volume

It is not difficult to see that changing the volume of entire groups of sounds at once can be very useful. Adding group-level control to the volume parameters results in each playing sound having the following volume control factors:

$$V_{actual} = V_{sample} * V_{master} * V_{distanceAttenuation} * V_{group}$$

V_{sample} controls the volume of the individual sound being played, V_{master} is the system's overall master volume and, in the case of 3D sounds, $V_{distanceAttenuation}$ would also be applied, possibly by the sound hardware itself. To this we add V_{group}, which scales the playback volume based on the group to which it is assigned.

Pitch

Pitch, or playback rate, is another useful property to place under group control. The factors controlling the pitch of a sample become:

$$P_{final} = P_{normal} * P_{sample} * P_{dopplerEffect} * P_{group}$$

Here, P_{normal} is the sound data's original sampling rate and, as with volume, each sound that is played has its own rate modifier, P_{sample}. $P_{dopplerEffect}$ is the result of 3D processing, applied either in software or by the hardware. Finally, we apply P_{group}, which modifies the rate of all sounds in the group.

Pause and Resume

Pausing and resuming groups of sounds involves a few logic decisions. In most implementations, it is probably wisest to have the group-level control operate at a level above the individual sound states. That is, a sound will play only if both its local and group controls are in a "playing" state. Similarly, the group control calls will never directly affect a sound's local control state; a sound that is in paused mode will not start playing even if its group is commanded to play. The sound's lower-level local control must also be set to play in order to activate the sound.

Stop

Stopping a group of sounds is straightforward enough. In practice, however, many sound systems issue callbacks or otherwise post notifications when sounds are finished playing. When stopping a group of sounds, you must be sure to trigger the notification system so the game correctly understands the state of the grouped sounds.

Defining Groups

In the basic API outlined earlier, sound groups are identified by an undefined type that we simply referred to as `group`. As it turns out, there are several methods of defining groups, each with its own benefits and difficulty of implementation.

Simple Group IDs

The most basic way to categorize sounds is to use a simple integer to identify a group. With just a byte, we can manage 256 different groups and, of course, with a full double-word we can manage many millions of groups. While millions of unique groups may seem like overkill, the example of the adventure game arises again. Each enclosed area in the game could be assigned a different group Id, and the category management system suddenly becomes a gross culling system as well.

Conceptually, management by simple group is straightforward. However, since each group will need to maintain some data, mapping categories to Ids requires an indirection and some additional management. You certainly won't want to preallocate 232 `group` data structures and index them directly.

Group Bitfield

Another option is to use an integer as a category bitfield. With a double-word integer, we have 32 different sound categories. Using bitfields adds the flexibility of being able to control several categories at once by simply OR-ing category flags together. This proves to be quite flexible. In fact, it even provides generic "master" control over all sounds by simply using a fully set bitfield. Bitfield management is also the easiest-to-implement option, as a fixed array of 32 `group` data structures can be allocated ahead of time and indexed directly.

When using bitfield-based categories, playing sounds takes this form:

```
typedef enum
    {
    SNDGRP_MENU    = 0x00000001,
    SNDGRP_VOICE   = 0x00000002,
    SNDGRP_EFFECT  = 0x00000004,
    SNDGRP_MASTER  = 0xFFFFFFFF
    } SNDGROUP;

// fire off a few sounds
hSndBeep     = SndStart(sampleBeep);
hSndHello    = SndStart(sampleHello);
hSndGoodbye  = SndStart(sampleGoodbye);

// assign them to groups
SndSetGroup(hSndBeep,     SNDGRP_MENU);
SndSetGroup(hSndHello,    SNDGRP_VOICE);
SndSetGroup(hSndGoodbye,  SNDGRP_VOICE);

// change the pitch of all voices
SndSetGroupRate(SNDGRP_VOICE, 1.3f);

// change the volume of all in-game sounds
// (effects and voices)
SndSetGroupVolume(SNDGRP_VOICE | SNDGRP_EFFECT,
    0.75f);
```

The category bitfield option inherently limits the number of sound categories available. In many applications, this will not be an issue, and the simple bitfield method becomes the design of choice. However, as in the previous example, there are situations when more categories are needed. Even in this case, a wide-bitfield object such as `std::bitset` or `boost::dynamic_bitset` could be used.

Group Objects

A third option is to manage sound groups via objects. By creating a class that manages sound group data, we allocate only as many group objects as we need.

Managing sound groups with objects may look something like this:

```
// define some groups
SNDGRP  sndGrpMenu;
SNDGRP  sndGrpVoice;
SNDGRP  sndGrpEffects;

// fire off a few sounds - here we assign the group
// when the sound is triggered
SndStart(sampleBeep,    &sndGrpMenu);
SndStart(sampleHello,   &sndGrpVoice);
SndStart(sampleGoodbye, &sndGrpVoice);

// change the pitch of all voices
sndGrpVoice.SetRate(1.3f);

// change the volume of all in-game sounds (effects
// and voices)
sndGrpVoice.SetVolume(0.75f);
sndGrpEffects.SetVolume(0.75f);
```

Group management via objects requires some special handling. For example, what should happen if a group object is deleted before all associated sounds have stopped playing? Will all associated sounds now belong to no category? While situations like this are unlikely to arise, they should at least be accounted for.

It is also possible to structure the system such that the group object acts as a proxy for the sound playback controls, and all sound parameters are manipulated via the group object itself. This design, however, may prove to be overly complex and upset the natural simplicity of most sound APIs.

Implementation Issues

The following sections address some implementation issues.

Tracking Playing Sounds

To dynamically change the properties of a group of sounds, the interface will need to keep track of all sounds that are currently playing (or paused). In many instances, an existing sound interface may only track sounds individually (by handle or object) and not maintain a global list of all active sounds.

To be able to dynamically control the properties of a group, the system will need to update each affected sound's properties when the group's properties are changed. That is, when a call like `SndSetGroupVolume()` is made, the system will need to access and update each currently active sound that is part of the group.

In APIs that manage playing sounds as objects (not necessarily C++ objects but architectural objects), like OpenAL and DirectSound, this commonly involves keeping a list of all active sounds. When group commands are issued, the list is walked and all appropriate sounds are updated.

In "track"-based APIs, like FMod and the Miles Sound System, it is likely that your wrapper API already tracks which sounds are playing on which channels, so group management may be a bit easier to implement.

Simplified, One-Shot Sounds

One-shot sounds are short effects that a game plays and never needs to control. Gunshots and footsteps are good examples. In many cases, wrapper APIs include simplified calls to play back one-shot sounds without exposing dynamic management of the sound. A gunshot, for example, is so short in duration that there is no reasonable need to change its volume or pitch while it is playing. Instead, the system calculates all significant parameters when the sound is triggered, and these stay constant for the duration of the sound. A one-shot sound may be triggered by a call like:

```
SndPlayOneShot(sample, volume, rate, pan, loopCount);
```

When implementing sound group management, you will need to decide if it is important to support dynamic group-based control of one-shot sounds. Likely, the answer will be no, but if the system allows for uncontrolled playback of longer samples, group control may be needed.

Even if dynamic control is not needed after a sound is triggered, one-shot sounds should still be assigned to groups. Thus when the sound's initial parameters are calculated, the group factors will be taken into account. This merely involves adding a group assignment to the sound triggering call:

```
SndPlayOneShot(sample, group, volume, rate, pan,
    loopCount);
```

Portability

As with any interface wrapper you create, it is best to become familiar with all the various sound APIs that you may encounter. This will help structure your group management system to make it flexible enough to be used on a variety of platforms and with a variety of underlying sound systems. As mentioned earlier, different sound systems may take very different approaches to the management of individual playing sounds, and understanding these differences is the key to constructing a truly portable API wrapper.

Conclusion

This simple gem shows how the concept of managing sounds in groups, in addition to at the individual level, can be useful and easy to implement. Adding this feature to a sound API wrapper may take only a few hours, yet the benefits can be far reaching. This is particularly true when the need for group-based management isn't identified early in development. Including these features in the sound API also keeps the game code base clean and allows for easier inclusion of additional features down the road.

7.3

Using 3D Surfaces as Audio Emitters

Sami Hamlaoui

disk_disaster@hotmail.com

In games today, sound sources are represented by a single point, regardless of the type of sound being represented. Gunshots? Points. Laser beams? Two Points. Rain? Lots of points. Although this has sufficed up until now, the level of detail in games is increasing with each generation of hardware, and while technologies like EAX go some way to improving the realism of game audio, all sound still comes from an infinitely small point in 3D space. We don't want sound that comes from a point anymore—we want sound that comes from an entire surface.

This gem will show you how to create sound that appears to do just that, with almost no extra processing time required and with full hardware acceleration. Intrigued? Then read on.

Method

Instead of using a single point as the location of the sound source, you use a standard geometric primitive such as a line, box, or sphere. Then for each frame, you calculate the closest point to the listener on the primitive and send it to the audio API as the sound's position.

This all seems rather underwhelming until you realize that as the listener moves around these emitters, the sound will travel with it. Move parallel to a line and the sound will move along with you, keeping the same distance until you move past the end of the line, at which point the sound will move behind the listener. As you walk around a sphere, the sound will appear to be a point emitter until you walk inside it and the sound comes from all directions at full volume, as if the sound is really being generated from inside the sphere itself. Use a box to represent rain outside a building, only to walk out into the open and find yourself deafened by the sound of the rain.

The best part of it all is that the sound API and the sound card still think they're working with points, meaning that the audio is accelerated on the hardware. The only thing performed in software is a closest-point algorithm, which is so simple for all the emitters that there won't be any kind of performance hit from using it!

In the following sections, four different emitters are covered: the point, line, sphere, and box. Presented alongside each description is a list of components that make up the emitter (the origin, direction, radius, etc.), the closest-point equation with a line-by-line walkthrough, and a couple of suggestions for what the emitter could be used for in a game.

A Word on Volumes

As mentioned earlier, once the listener is inside a volume emitter (an emitter that has a definable "inside," like a sphere or box as opposed to a line or point), the sound will come from all directions at full volume. This is a deliberate part of the technique and can be used for quite a large number of special effects. They aren't listed here, as they can be found with the appropriate emitter. Suffice to say that the few examples given earlier are only the tip of the iceberg.

A Word on the Math

In the list of components for each emitter will be the mathematical representation of the variable in the closest-point equation. However, there are a few values that will be used in each equation, and it seems daft to include them every time, so they are listed in Table 7.3.1.

Table 7.3.1 Standard Variables

Name	Math Notation	Type
Audio Position	$\mathbf{A}$	Vector
Listener	$\mathbf{X}$	Vector

They are defined as follows:

Audio position: This is the vector that is passed to the audio API. It is calculated by the closest-point algorithm. It is represented by **A** (for audio).

Listener: This is usually the camera's position. It is where the sound is currently being heard from. It is represented by **X** (because **L** is used for the line components).

Two temporary variables are used throughout the equations, too, and they also always have the same meaning. They are listed in Table 7.3.2.

Table 7.3.2 Temporary Variables

Name	Math Notation	Type
Direction	$\mathbf{V}$	Vector
Distance	d	Scalar

They are defined as follows:

Direction: This is the direction from something to something else. Unless stated, this value is not normalized and therefore contains distance as well as direction information.

Distance: The distance between something and something else. This is a scalar value and is usually used when projecting points towards the listener.

Points

Table 7.3.3 shows the point components.

Table 7.3.3 Point Components

Name	Math Notation	Type
Origin	$\mathbf{P}_{\text{origin}}$	Vector

The first type of emitter we are going to cover is the point emitter, because although this gem focuses on alternatives, for the vast majority of the cases you need to play a sound, the point emitter will work fine. It is best if you use the other emitters when it suits the effect being created—and *only* then. Otherwise, stick to the point.

Using a point emitter is exactly like using points for sound sources. Just set the audio position to the value of the point. As points have no properties other than their location, the closest point to the point is itself. For completeness sake, Table 7.3.3 lists components, and Equation 7.3.1 shows the nearest point on the point.

$$\mathbf{A} = \mathbf{P}_{\text{origin}} \tag{7.3.1}$$

Set the audio at the same location as the point.

Uses

As mentioned earlier, this is useful for any small sound effect that isn't better suited to the other emitters. So, that'll be the voices, footsteps, gunshots, small explosions, rag dolls hitting things, rocket trails, fire, water dripping, etc.

Lines

Line emitters come in two flavors: infinite lines and line segments. You will probably use the line segments most of the time, but for cases when the line is either very big or infinite, the infinite line emitter will suit you perfectly.

Infinite Lines

Table 7.3.4 shows the infinite line components.

Table 7.3.4 Infinite Line Components

Name	Math Notation	Type
Point on Line	$\mathbf{L}_{point}$	Vector
Direction	$\mathbf{L}_{dir}$	Vector

Infinite lines are just that—lines that go on forever. To store them, you only need to keep track of a single point on the line and the direction the line is going in (Table 7.3.4). To calculate the audio position, you need to orthogonally project the listener's location onto the line. Don't worry if that scares you as it's very simple to do. Just remember that you must use the same point on the line throughout the equation otherwise the audio position will be created in the wrong place!

The closest-point equation for an infinite line is presented in Equation 7.3.2.

$$\begin{aligned} \mathbf{V} &= \mathbf{X} - \mathbf{L}_{point} \\ d &= \mathbf{V} \cdot \mathbf{L}_{dir} \\ \mathbf{A} &= \mathbf{L}_{point} + \mathbf{L}_{dir} d \end{aligned} \tag{7.3.2}$$

It is created by the following steps:

1. Create a vector between the listener and any point on the line.
2. Take the dot product between this vector and the direction of the line. This will tell us how far along the line to create the new point from the test point.
3. Set the new audio location by scaling the direction by the distance and adding it to the point on the line used in step 1.

Line Segments

Table 7.3.5 shows the line segment components.

Table 7.3.5 Line Segment Components

Name	Math Notation	Type
Origin	$\mathbf{L}_{origin}$	Vector
Direction	$\mathbf{L}_{dir}$	Vector
Length	$\mathbf{L}_{length}$	Scalar

Line segments represent a portion of an infinite line. Like the infinite line, they require a point on the line and the direction, but also the length of the segment (Table 7.3.5). The point on the line should be the start of the line segment, and the length is how far away from this point the line ends.

The audio position is calculated exactly the same as in Equation 7.3.2, except you must clamp the distance between the range of zero and the line's length. If you don't, the result will be exactly the same as the infinite line.

The closest-point equation for a line segment is:

$$\mathbf{V} = \mathbf{X} - \mathbf{L}_{\text{origin}}$$
$$d = \text{clamp}\left(\mathbf{V} \cdot \mathbf{L}_{\text{dir}}, 0, L_{\text{length}}\right)$$
$$\mathbf{A} = \mathbf{L}_{\text{origin}} + \mathbf{L}_{\text{dir}} d \tag{7.3.3}$$

It is created with the following steps:

1. Create a vector between the listener and the start of the line.
2. Take the dot product between this vector and the direction of the line and clamp it between the range of 0 (zero) and the length of the line. This will tell us the distance to the new point from the line's origin.
3. Set the new audio location by scaling the direction by the distance and adding it to the line's origin.

Uses

Some possible uses include the following:

Fluorescent Tubes: As the tube flickers on and off, you could have a sound effect that plays along with it. Combine it with a dynamic lighting and shadowing system for a very atmospheric set piece.

Laser Beams: Laser beams shot from futuristic rifles are an obvious choice for the line emitter. Instead of the sound being generated at the gun's location and the impact point, the entire beam will hum with energy.

Spheres

Table 7.3.6 shows sphere components.

Table 7.3.6 Sphere Components

Name	Math Notation	Type
Origin	$\mathbf{S}_{\text{origin}}$	Vector
Radius	$\mathbf{S}_{\text{radius}}$	Scalar

The sphere is the first of the volume emitters we will cover. Unlike lines or boxes, there is pretty much only one way to represent a sphere, and that's with an origin and a radius (Table 7.3.6). As explained in the "Method" section, the volume emitters have a special function that occurs when the listener is inside them—the sound is played at full volume in all directions. There is no special case math required for this, as both the sphere's and the box's closest-point equations take this into account automatically.

Using a sphere for a sound effect like a small explosion will not give you much benefit. In fact, most sphere emitters can be replaced by a point emitter without the player noticing the difference. The spheres become useful only when there is a visual representation of the sound to go with the sphere, and it's one that the player can walk into and out of. Note that the boxes do not suffer from this, as they change the way the sound moves (along a single axis as opposed to spherically, like the points and spheres), and therefore can't be replaced by any other emitter.

The closest-point equation for a sphere is provided in Equation 7.3.4.

$$\begin{aligned} \mathbf{V} &= \mathbf{X} - \mathbf{S}_{\text{origin}} \\ d &= \min\left(\left|\mathbf{V}\right|, S_{\text{radius}}\right) \\ \mathbf{A} &= \mathbf{S}_{\text{origin}} + \hat{\mathbf{V}}d \end{aligned} \tag{7.3.4}$$

It is created with the following steps:

1. Create a vector between the listener and the center of the sphere.
2. Take the smallest value between the magnitude of this vector and the radius of the sphere. This will be how far away from the sphere's origin to place the sound source. If the listener is inside the sphere, the magnitude will be the smallest, otherwise, it'll be the radius.
3. Calculate the source position by scaling the normalized vector by the distance and adding it to the sphere's position. This point will be on the surface of the sphere if the listener is outside, otherwise, it will be at the same place as the listener.

Uses

Some possible uses include the following:

Explosions: Although most small explosions are best represented with a point primitive, if the explosion has an expanding radius, the sphere emitter would be the best option. It would be even better if you could tie in the radius of the emitter with the radius of the shockwave on screen.

Shields: When surrounded by a shield, the noise will appear to surround you. To those outside, it will be generated on the surface. The bigger the shield, the more obvious the effect. If the players can walk into and out of the shield, it is another way of letting them know that they're inside it.

Boxes

Table 7.3.7 shows box components.

Table 7.3.7 Box Components

Name	Math Notation	Type
Origin	$\mathbf{B}_{origin}$	Vector
Min Bounds	$\mathbf{B}_{min}$	Vector
Max Bounds	$\mathbf{B}_{max}$	Vector

Axis-aligned box emitters are probably the most useful to designers after points. As most game entities already have a bounding box defined, having a sound emit from it doesn't require any extra calculations, other than the closest point! Sound on the box travels on two axes at a time (*xy*, *yz*, and *xz*). This means that as you walk parallel to the box, the sound will always appear to be the same distance away from you until you completely walk past it, at which point it will stick in the corner until you walk down another side. Of course, being a volume, as soon as the listener is inside, sound will come from all directions at full volume, but you should know that by now.

There are two ways of storing bounding boxes: offset and absolute. Offset boxes' bounds are relative to the box's origin, while absolute boxes contain real values in 3D space. Remember that unlike the segmented and infinite lines, both offset and absolute boxes will produce *exactly* the same results—they are just two different ways of storing the same information. Table 7.3.7 provides the list of components for both boxes, although the origin is only used for the offset type.

The two closest-point algorithms for a box are presented in Equations 7.3.5 and 7.3.6.

$$\mathbf{A} = \text{clamp}\left(\mathbf{X}, \mathbf{B}_{min}, \mathbf{B}_{max}\right) \tag{7.3.5}$$

$$\mathbf{A} = \text{clamp}\left(\mathbf{X}, \mathbf{B}_{origin} + \mathbf{B}_{min}, \mathbf{B}_{origin} + \mathbf{B}_{max}\right) \tag{7.3.6}$$

This does the following:

1. Clamp the components of the listener to the minimum and maximum bounds of the box (Equation 7.3.5).
2. If the box's bounds are centered around [0,0,0] instead, you must add the box's origin before the clamp takes place (Equation 7.3.6).

Uses

Some possible uses include the following:

Environment Effects: For example, you're standing at the end of a long corridor. At the end is an open door that leads to the outside. You can hear the rain from a distance. As you move closer to the door the rain gets louder and louder until you are outside and the rain is coming from everywhere, deafening you, making you unaware of the masked figure approaching stealthily.

The Block Puzzle: Every time a block is moved into the wrong position, it could flash blue and red and produce a deafening screech at the player.

Summary

This gem, has shown you how to create the illusion of sound coming from an entire surface. However, just because only a few different objects are covered doesn't mean that this is all you can use—polygons, planes, cones, and if you really want a challenge, convex hulls for brush-based levels, will all find their place in a game engine. For games using a full physics SDK, you should ideally provide an emitter for every primitive available (and then some).

If you do decide to implement this technique, don't bury the emitters under a mountain of options and menus that the designers will never find, as it defeats the whole purpose of providing them in the first place (unless of course they implement the block puzzle idea mentioned earlier, in which case, bury them as deep as possible!). Make emitter creation and placement as intuitive as possible, and try to provide a way of binding them to the movement of game entities or exposing them to the scripting language so they can be further tweaked and enhanced.

Finally, if you have any comments/questions/praise/flames about this gem, by all means, please e-mail the author.

On The CD-ROM

ON THE CD

In the audio folder on the accompanying CD-ROM, you will find a small demo that shows off the five (the two boxes count as one) emitters covered in this gem. It uses GLUT for the framework and FMOD for the audio processing [FMOD05]. FMOD is one of the easiest to use and most fully featured audio APIs out there and is free for noncommercial use. Check out the reference at the end of the gem for more details.

The closest-point algorithms are in Primitives.cpp, and the emitter-management code is in Emitters.cpp. Feel free to play around with the source code and add a few more emitter types to it to test out your ideas. There are absolutely no licenses attached to the source code, so any new code you come up with (and the original code) can be used in a commercial engine without fear of lawsuits, bad press, or hissy-fits.

References

[FMOD05] Firelight Technology. "The FMOD Sound System." Available online at *http://www.fmod.org/*.

7.4

Fast Environmental Reverb Based on Feedback Delay Networks

Christian Schüler, Phenomic Game Development

cschueler@gmx.de

A question that appears once in a while on DSP-oriented mailing lists is, "How can I calculate a reverb effect?" The questioner usually wants to know what computation is necessary on a sound signal to make it appear reverberated, like what happens in a real room. Many commercial programs and hardware devices demonstrate that this can be done.

Usually, the common answer to this question is "this is black art," because the theory is age-old, and tinkering with the implementation is everything. Often a hint to some permutation of Schroeder's comb filters ([Schroeder62], [Moorer79]) is given. People who then try to implement their own reverb effect based on published material are soon disappointed.

This gem aims to introduce *Feedback Delay Networks (FDNs)*, which date back to Gerzon [Gerzon76] and Stautner and Puckette [Stautner82]. An excellent review about FDN reverberation can be found online [SmithOnline], although you will not find a single line of code there. FDNs are kind of the granddaddy of delay networks, because it has been demonstrated that other algorithms, including Schroeder's, can be formulated as special cases of an FDN ([Jot91], [Smith96]). An FDN with a specific tone-correction filter has been patented [Jot93].

How to Apply This Material

This gem is focused on a reverb *algorithm*, not on using a specific sound API. As such, the audience that benefits the most from this gem includes people that currently have no ready-made reverb solution at their disposal. All other people are invited to enjoy reinventing the wheel for possible insight and better understanding of existing solutions.

By the end of this gem, you will have a function that can process audio buffers. Such a function may be plugged into anywhere your sound system allows, for manipulation of audio streams. For example, the FMOD sound system [FMOD], which is available for various platforms, has the concept of *custom DSP filters* that can be plugged into the audio stream exactly for this purpose. The same holds for DirectSound, where you could attach a custom effect implemented as a *DirectMediaObject* to any `IDirectSoundBuffer8` via the `SetFX()` function [MSDN].

What would be really nice to have is a form of *audio shading language*, which would allow for a standard way to express user algorithms executed on sound hardware. Without such a mechanism, we are bound to consume CPU power whenever we want our own effects. Luckily, audio data does not demand much in terms of bandwidth, and platforms without dedicated sound hardware would use the CPU anyway, so no loss there.

What Is Reverb?

A smooth reverb is perceived when echoes arrive so densely packed that they become inseparable to the ear. But they must do so randomly, not in a regular pattern. Think of what happens when you snap your fingers in St. Peter's Cathedral. Imagine the sound wave originating from your hand and expanding in all directions. Soon it will hit the first obstacles, and the first reflections will arrive at your ear. Then come the reflections of the reflections. Then come the second and third indirect reflections, and so on. The average number of echos per second increases with t^2, while the average number of resonant modes per Hz increases with f^2. Figure 7.4.1 shows the first second of the impulse response of an ideal rectangular room.

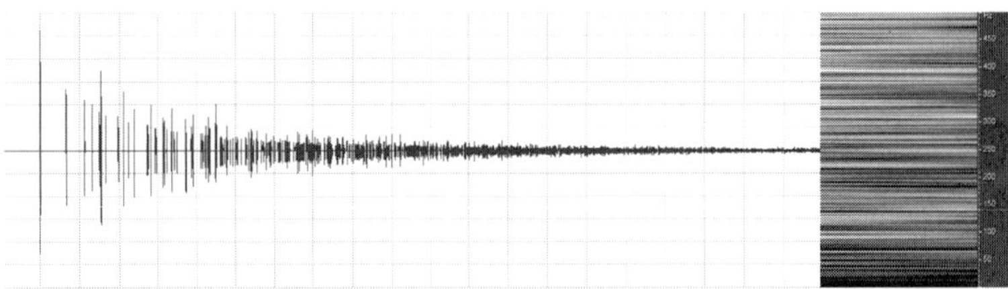

FIGURE 7.4.1 *Time and frequency plot of the impulse response of an ideal rectangular room.*

A real-time reverberator that aims to mimic this process is plagued with multiple problems. First, for a real-time application, you stand no chance but to model the process statistically, since the brute force approach—integration over the simulated volume, a 3D simulation—is prohibitively expensive even for the simplest of rooms.

The FDN is sort of a vectorized 1D-simulation that can develop an increasing echo density over time but not an increasing mode density over frequency, which results in artifacts like ringing tones.

The Feedback Delay Network

See Figure 7.4.2 for a circuit diagram of an FDN with four channels.

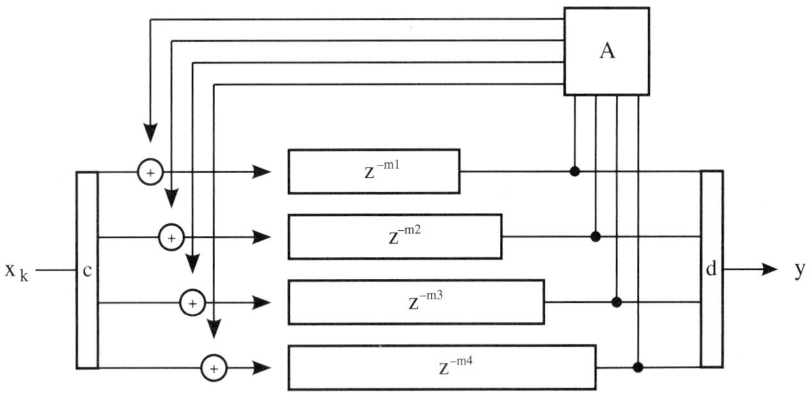

FIGURE 7.4.2 *Circuit diagram of a Feedback Delay Network.*

The heart of an FDN is a feedback loop with the n delay lines z and a square $n \times n$ feedback matrix **A**. In case you are unfamiliar with the z-transform: multiplication with z raised to the power $-m$ stands equivalent to a delay of m samples, a notation common in digital audio. The elements a_{ij} of the feedback matrix control how much signal from line i is taken back to line j. The input signal, x_k, is multiplexed prior to entering the feedback loop by the *input matrix* **c**. Likewise, the output signal, y_k, is formed as a weighted sum over all channels by the output matrix **d**. Alternatively, you could directly access the four output channels to have four uncorrelated signals to place into the listener's 3D space.

The key feature of an FDN is the signal traffic between the delay lines. An echo from the output of one delay line enters all other delay lines, being echoed by all of them, then each echo again enters all other delay lines, etc. Figure 7.4.3 shows the first second of the impulse response of a four-channel FDN. As you can see, the build-up of echo density is quite similar to that found in the rectangular room. The spectrum plot however reveals that the resonant modes are distributed uniformly over the frequency range and not packed as densely. This is the tribute to pay for the computational effectiveness.

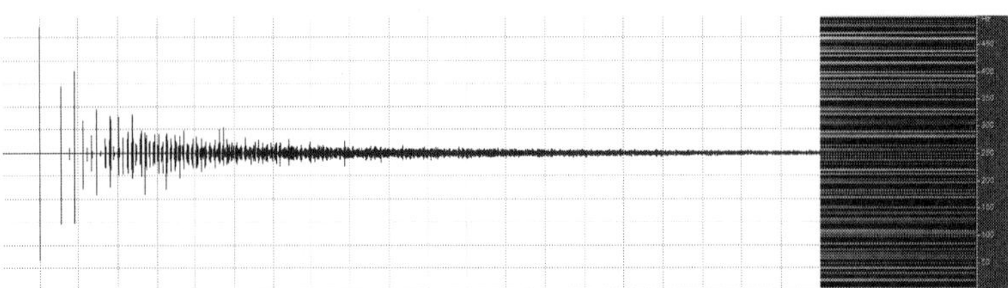

FIGURE 7.4.3 *Time and frequency plot of the impulse response of an FDN.*

Let's talk some code. We choose to build an FDN with four delay lines, which are implemented as simple, ring-buffered FIFOs. We also assume that all samples are floats. The state needed so far:

```
class FDN4{
    float *line[4];         // memory for 4 delay lines
    unsigned size[4];       // the size of the delay lines (always
                            // power-of-2)
    unsigned mask[4];       // size – 1, replaces modulo operation
    unsigned read[4];       // read cursors for FIFO
    unsigned write[4];      // write cursors for FIFO
    float A[4][4];          // feedback matrix
    float c[4];             // input matrix
    float d[4];             // output matrix

    /// ...
};
```

The workhorse of the FDN is a `process()` function, which implements the machinery as depicted in the circuit diagram. In this function, almost all statements are 4-tuples of the same operation, which is why they are abbreviated here with `// etc` ... to save space.

```
void FDN4::process( float *output, const float *input, unsigned n )
{
    for( unsigned k = 0; k < n; k++ )
    {
        // step 1: read signal from the delay lines
        float r[4];
        r[0] = line[0][ read[0] ];
        // etc ...
        // step 2: apply output matrix and output
        output[k] = r[0] * d[0] + r[1] * d[1] + r[2] * d[2] +
                    r[3] * d[3];

        // step 3: apply feedback matrix
        float w[4];
        w[0] = r[0] * A[0][0] + r[1] * A[1][0] + r[2] * A[2][0] +
               r[3] * A[3][0];
        // etc ...
```

```
            // step 4: apply input matrix and add
            w[0] += input[k] * c[0];
            // etc ...
            // step 5: inserted later

            // step 6: write signal into delay lines
            line[0][ write[0] ] = w[0];
            // etc ...

            // step 7: bump cursors
            read[0] = ( read[0] + 1 ) & mask[0];
            write[0] = ( write[0] + 1 ) & mask[0];
            // etc ...
        }
    }
```

Choosing the Right Feedback Matrices

This section gets a little bit mathematical. In Smith's insightful online book [SmithOnline], he discusses special classes of feedback matrices, which are *unitary* ($\mathbf{A}^{\mathrm{T}} = \mathbf{A}^{-1}$), or more generally, *lossless.* A lossless feedback matrix does not change signal energy as it circulates through the feedback loop. An FDN with such a matrix is either called a *lossless prototype* [Smith96] or a *reference filter* [Jot91]. One advantage of lossless matrices is that with some of them, a matrix-vector multiply can be optimized to $O(n)$ time, instead of the usual $O(n^2)$.

An $n \times n$ feedback matrix $\mathbf{A}_{\mathrm{N}}$ is lossless, if and only if it has N linearly independent eigenvectors and its eigenvalues are of unit magnitude. All orthogonal rotation matrices, with and without reflection, can be used as lossless feedback matrices. The "density" of the matrix, which is how many nonzero elements it contains, determines the richness of the cross-coupling and therefore the speed of echo build-up.

A particularly attractive class of matrices is the *Householder reflection*, which is orthogonal and contains no zero elements. Assume $\mathbf{U}_n$ is an $n \times n$ matrix with each element set to one, and $\mathbf{I}_n$ is an $n \times n$ identity matrix, then

$$\mathbf{A}_n = \mathbf{I}_n - \mathbf{U}_n.$$

A Householder reflection is especially nice in the 4×4 case, because all elements are of the same magnitude. A matrix-vector multiply can be implemented as one swizzled vector addition and three swizzled vector subtractions:

$$A_4 = \frac{1}{2}\begin{bmatrix} 1 & -1 & -1 & -1 \\ -1 & 1 & -1 & -1 \\ -1 & -1 & 1 & -1 \\ -1 & -1 & -1 & 1 \end{bmatrix}$$

A variety of other matrices can be tried. See the source code included on the CD-ROM that implements a wealth of other possible feedback matrices, all of which are unitary. The choice of the feedback matrix can make a difference! While ultimately the sum of all delay lengths determines the number of resonant modes (the order of the system), the feedback matrix controls the locus of them.

Choosing the Right Delay Lengths

The time of arrival of the first echoes is the most important clue to the human ear of the size of the environment. This means that the lengths of our delay lines directly reflect the dimensions of the simulated room. For example, at 44.1 kHz sampling frequency, sound travels about 3/4 of a centimeter per sample. A 6 by 10 meter room would thus be modeled by setting the lengths of the shortest delay lines between 800 and 1,200 samples. The other delay lines should be chosen with an eye to increasing the order of the system, because we are in dire need of every resonant mode we can get.

Next, a classic suggestion demands that delay lengths be *incommensurate* [Schroeder62]. A minimum requirement states that the delay lengths are *mutually prime*, but a good "incommensuracy" is most easily done with some graphic help.

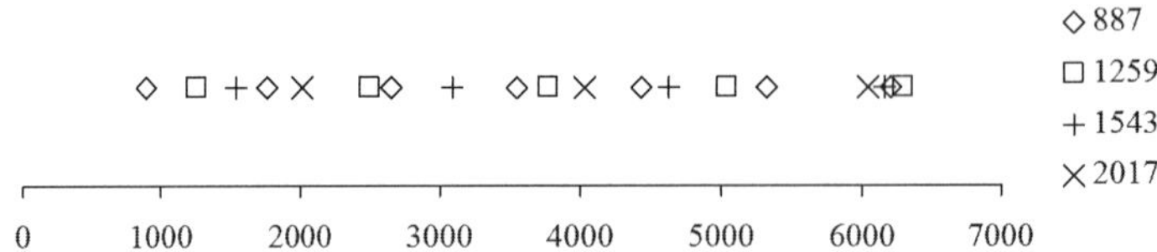

FIGURE 7.4.4 *Echo taps of four delay lines.*

Figure 7.4.4 shows the echo taps of four different delays on a common time line. As you can see, care has been taken that no integer multiple of one delay length overlaps an integer multiple of another. When faced to trade early coincidence for late coincidence, the priority should be to eliminate early coincidence.

If you want the room size to be adjustable in real time, you need an algorithm to set delay lengths upon request. An acceptable solution is to scale a series that is known to be incommensurate to the requested room size, possibly rounding the result to the nearest prime number. Two of such series for a four-channel FDN are presented here, their main difference being the third delay line placed before or after the second tap of the first delay line.

Series A: 1.0000, 1.5811, 2.2177, 2.7207.
Series B: 1.0000, 1.4194, 1.6223, 2.2401.

The CD-ROM includes a spreadsheet that generates diagrams similar to that shown in Figure 7.4.2.

Controlling Reverberation Time

So far, our system is a unitary FDN, where the accumulated signal is circulating forever inside the feedback loop, so we need to add energy loss. Since most rooms have more or less high-frequency damping, we want to allow low frequencies to live longer than high frequencies, so we need the energy loss to be frequency dependent. We are going to insert a *scalar gain*, g_i, with $|g_i| < 1$ in front of each delay line i. Additionally, we insert a *first order filter* with a single coefficient α_i which affects only the higher frequencies ([Moorer79], [Jot91]). The product of both the scalar gain and the filter gives an overall frequency dependent gain $g_i(f)$.

Insert the following code as step 5 of the `FDN::process()` function:

```
// step 5: run the signal through a scalar gain and filter
// before entering the delay line
w[0] = g[0] * ( filter[0] += alpha[0] * ( w[0] - filter[0] ) );
// etc ...
```

Also, augment the FDN class with this new state:

```
float filter[4];    // state variables of the attenuation filter
float alpha[4];     // filter alphas
float g[4];         // scalar feedback gains
```

What follows is presumably the most mathematical part of the whole gem, because we are going to derive g_i and α_i for arbitrary reverb lengths. Let's express our control parameters as *half life* (no pun intended), $\lambda(f)$, which we define as the time it takes for a sinusoid of frequency f to decay to half of its amplitude. We define $\lambda_L = \lambda(0)$, the desired half life at the low end of the spectrum at $f = 0$ (DC), and $\lambda_H = \lambda(f_s)$ the desired half life at the high end of the spectrum at half the sampling frequency f_s (Nyquist limit). Since the signal is not attenuated continuously but rather in intervals of the delay length m_i, the logarithm of $g_i(f)$ must be proportional to that interval. Specifically,

$$g_i(f) = 2,$$

where m_i is the length of delay line i, expressed in the same units as $\lambda(f)$.

So far, so good. The filter as shown in the previous code may be familiar to you as *decaying average*, or as something with another name. It's really the common construct that blends the last output with the current input, and it satisfies the recurrence relation:

$$y_k = \alpha\, x_k + (1 - \alpha)\, y_{k-1},$$

where y_k is the filter output, x_k is the filter input, and α is the filter alpha. Using the *z*-transform [Mathworld] we can obtain the system transfer function $H(z)$ of this filter. The *z*-transform replaces time shift with a multiplication by z, so we can factor out x_k and y_k:

$$y_k = \alpha x_k + (1-\alpha) y_k z^{-1},$$

$$H(z) = \frac{y_k}{x_k} = \frac{\alpha}{1-(1-\alpha)z^{-1}}$$

By plugging in $z = \exp(j2\pi f/f_s)$ to represent sinusoidal signals of frequency f, we can calculate the frequency response $|H(f)|$ for any filter parameter α. In the previous expression, j is the unit imaginary, so complex math is going on here. We are interested in the special cases $f = 0$ and $f = \frac{1}{2} f_s$, which correspond to λ_L and λ_H, respectively. These can be shown to reduce to:

$$f = 0 \rightarrow z = 1 \quad \rightarrow H(1) = 1, \text{and}$$

$$f = \frac{1}{2} f_s \rightarrow z = -1 \rightarrow H(-1) = \frac{\alpha}{2-\alpha}.$$

The result $H(1) = 1$ shows that the filter indeed leaves the low frequencies unaffected, so the scalar gain g_i can be directly calculated from λ_L. For the high end of the spectrum, the filter alpha α_i is set such that $H(-1)$ corresponds to the attenuation not accounted for by g_i:

$$g_i = 2^{-m_i/\lambda_L},$$

$$\alpha_i = \frac{2\beta_i}{1+\beta_i}, \text{ with } \beta_i = \frac{2^{-m_i/\lambda_H}}{g_i}.$$

In case you are lost in all these formulae, just recap that we calculated g_i and α_i to get a controlled energy loss according to λ_L and λ_H.

Sweeping and the Problem of Fractional Delay

We want to make the delay lengths of our FDN time variant, which is also known as *sweeping*. The benefit of sweeping is a reduction of annoying stationary waves that would otherwise build up in a static FDN. Sweeping has been shown to increase the quality of the output, or reduce the number of necessary delay lines [Frenette00]. A sufficient effect is archived by varying the delay lengths a few percent at a slow rate (0.5–2 Hz). If you overdo the effect, you get pitch shift.

As we smoothly vary the delay lengths over time, the read cursors of our delay lines need to point "in between" samples. This is known as *fractional delay*, a problem similar to texture filtering. Rest assured however that audio is an order of magnitude more sensitive to aliasing noise than graphics, so nearest-point sampling is not an option. Next, the problem with linear interpolation is *blurring*, and you can see in Figure 7.4.5 (middle) how this kills us. Here, one second of repeatedly going through linear interpolation sufficed to have eaten all frequency content above 8 kHz.

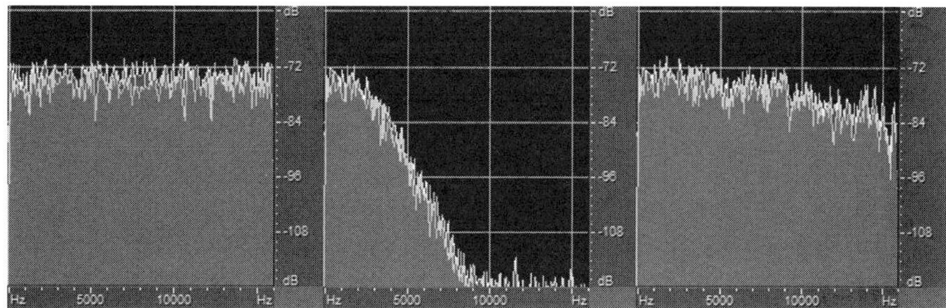

FIGURE 7.4.5 *Cross-section frequency plot of an FDN impulse response at t = 1s. No sweeping (left), sweeping with linear interpolation (middle), and sweeping with linear interpolation and compensation (right).*

There exist a number of sophisticated fractional delay algorithms [Välimäki00], and as an example, Frenette uses all-pass filters for his FDN. Here you'll see how it is possible to stay with linear interpolation, and instead adjust our filters for an extra high-frequency boost that compensates for the *average* loss due to blurring. See in Figure 7.4.5 (right) how this actually works out.

First, we introduce new state to our FDN class to accommodate fractional read cursors.

```
float p[4];         // partial read cursors position
                    // (always stays inside 0..1)
float dp[4];        // sweeping velocities
```

Replace step 1 as follows. Step 1a will just integrate the sweeping velocities over time and bump the integer cursor on occasion:

```
// step 1a: add sweeping velocities to the read cursors
p[0] += dp[0];
// etc ...
read[0] = ( read[0] + int( floor( p[0] ) ) ) & mask[0];
// etc ...
p[0] = p[0] - floor( p[0] );
// etc ...
```

Then in step 1b, we linearly interpolate between the two samples neighboring the read cursor. We also change the code to do the regular advance of the read cursor in the midst of the linear interpolation (so step 7 is left as the advance of the write cursor only):

```
// step 1b: linearly interpolate between the
// samples next to the read cursor, and advance integer cursor here
float r[4];
r[0] = line[0][ read[0] ];
// etc ...
read[0] = ( read[0] + 1 ) & mask[0];
// etc ...
r[0] += p[0] * ( line[0][ read[0] ] - r[0] );
// etc ...
```

What is not shown here is the code that slowly modulates the sweeping velocities, which is a simple sine table lookup or other modulation waveform, and can be done sparsely, like every 16–64 samples.

Let's fight the blurring. Linear interpolation is in effect a first-order finite impulse response filter, which may be cancelled with a first-order infinite impulse response filter, just like the one that is already in place in our feedback loops. We want to calculate which adjustment must be made to the filter alphas α_i to compensate the blurring.

The transfer function of linear interpolation would be written as follows:

$$y_k = (1-p)x_k + px_{k+1},$$

$$H(z) = \frac{y_k}{x_k} = 1 - p + pz.$$

Here, p is the current partial position of a read cursor. If $p = 0$, we are sampling integer positions and no blurring is introduced, while with $p = 1/2$, the blurring is at maximum. Let's assume that p is moving so fast that we get the net effect of a random p. For this case, we can calculate the integral of the absolute value $|H(z)|$ and come up with

$$\int_0^1 |1 - p + pz|\, dp = \int_0^1 \sqrt{\gamma p^2 - \gamma p + 1}\, dp, \text{ with } \gamma = 2 - 2\cos(2\pi f / f_s).$$

The interesting result is at the upper end of the spectrum, at $f = f_s$, where the integral simply evaluates to 1/2. Therefore, we could try and adjust all our filter alphas as to increase by a factor of 2, and have a compensation for average blurring.

But not so fast here; this works as long as p is in effect random, but when it is not, the system may eventually blow up. Imagine a partial read cursor being stationary at or close to zero for long enough; the high frequencies would be amplified into infinity. In practice, the compensation factor must be less than 2 and needs to take into account the sweeping velocity *dp*, where the full compensation only kicks in if *dp* is sufficiently high. To achieve this, the example program on the CD-ROM uses a smooth saturation curve, which saturates at 1.7 and falls with dp^2 if *dp* is below 10^{-5}. Specifically, the program calculates:

$$\beta_i' = \beta_i\left(1 + \frac{0.7dp^2}{10^{-9} + dp^2}\right),$$

and recalculates the filter alphas βi from $\beta i'$ every time *dp* changes.

Conclusion and Possible Improvements

So far, the general concept of FDN reverberation has been introduced, and the most important parameters—feedback matrices, delay lengths and reverberation times—have been discussed. More infrastructure would be needed to get the sound to the FDN and from the FDN to the listener. An example of how this can be done is shown in the example program, which is included on the CD-ROM. This program lets you play stereo wave files through the discussed four-channel FDN and experiment with different reverberation settings. To give you a quick start, the CD-ROM also includes two sample wave files, which are dry (unreverberated) excerpts of a game music remix.

ON THE CD

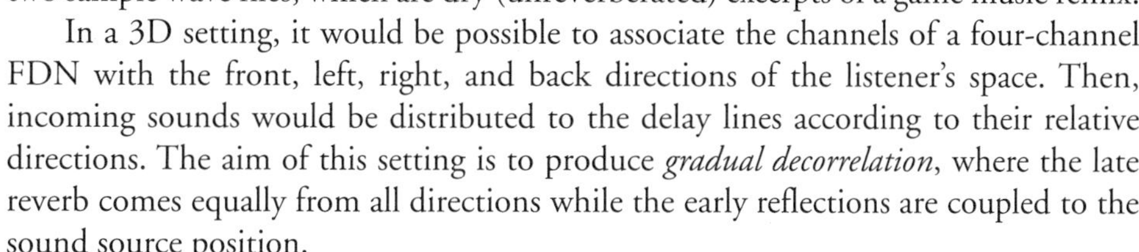

In a 3D setting, it would be possible to associate the channels of a four-channel FDN with the front, left, right, and back directions of the listener's space. Then, incoming sounds would be distributed to the delay lines according to their relative directions. The aim of this setting is to produce *gradual decorrelation*, where the late reverb comes equally from all directions while the early reflections are coupled to the sound source position.

Multiple rooms with different parameters would need to be simulated with multiple FDNs, and the results weighted. A transition of parameters of a single FDN generally does not produce meaningful results but can nevertheless be used for interesting special effects.

Acknowledgments

Special thanks go to Pex "Mahoney" Tufvesson for providing the wave files included on the CD-ROM. Thanks to Peter Ohlmann for tips about the gritty details of MFC.

References

[FMOD] "fmod" music and effects sound system. Available online at *http://www.fmod.org/*.

[Frenette00] Frenette, Jasmin. "Reducing Artificial Reverberation Algorithm Requirements using Time-Variant Feedback Delay Networks." Masters Thesis. University of Miami, December 2000.

[Gerzon76] Gerzon M. A. "Unitary (energy preserving) multichannel networks with feedback." In *Electronic Letters*, vol. 12, no. 11, pp. 278–279, 1976.

[Jot91] Jot, Jean Marc and Antoine Chaigne. "Digital delay networks for designing artificial reverberators." In *Proc. 90th Conv. Audio Eng. Soc.,* Feb. 1991, preprint 3030.

[Jot93] Jot, Jean Marc and Antoine Chaigne. "Method and system for artificial spatialisation of digital audio signals." United States Patent 5,491,754., Feb 1993.

[Mathworld] Erich Weisstein's world of mathematics. Available online at *http://www.mathworld.com.*

[MSDN] Microsoft Developer Network. Available online at *http://msdn.microsoft.com/default.aspx.*

[Moorer79] Moorer, J. A. "About this reverberation business." In *Computer Music Journal*, vol. 3, no. 2, 1979.

[Schroeder62] Schroeder, J. M. "Natural sounding artificial reverberation." J Audio Eng Soc, vol. 10, no. 3, 1962.

[Smith96] Smith, Julius O. and Davide Rochesso. "Circulant and Elliptic Feedback Delay Networks for Artificial Reverberation." In *IEEE Transactions on Spech and Audio*, vol. 5, no. 1, pp. 51–60, Jan. 1996.

[SmithOnline] Smith, Julius O. "Physical Audio Signal Processing: Digital Waveguide Modeling of Musical Instruments and Audio Effects." Available online at *http://www-ccrma.stanford.edu/~jos/waveguide/pasp.html.*

[Stautner82] Stautner, John and Miller Puckette. "Designing Multi-Channel Reverberators." In *Computer Music Journal*, vol. 6, no. 1, pp. 52–65, Spring 1982.

[Välimäki00] Välimäki, V. and T. I. Laakso. "Principles of Fractional Delay Filters." *IEEE Int. Conf. on Acoustics, Speech and Signal Processing,* June 2000.

7.5

Introduction to Single-Speaker Speech Recognition

Julien Hamaide

julien_hamaide@hotmail.com

In the past years, much effort has been made in the fields of 3D and artificial intelligence but not in the area of human-computer interfaces. In a majority of games, our interactions are still limited to traditional peripherals: keyboard, mouse, joystick, or joypad. This gem presents a technique that will introduce a new dimension to these interfaces: the voice. With the recent apparition of recording systems on consoles, this new type of interaction makes sense. Moreover, it can be the basis for a new type of gameplay.

This gem introduces a single-locutor recognition technique based on examples. This technique is easy to implement, does not ask for much processing power, and is easily integrated in existing software. It does not try to understand the meaning of entire sentences, but rather tries to recognize isolated words. Demo software is provided on the CD-ROM, so you may evaluate the system.

ON THE CD

Introduction

Speech is a pretty complex signal. Its human origin, made of imprecision, makes it difficult to analyze. In this section, the structure of a speech signal will be briefly introduced. In addition, the acoustic properties that make its recognition more difficult will be pointed out.

Voice is a signal produced by our body and our brain. The latter corrects it and adapts it continuously, thanks to the feedback received through the ears. The production of voice results from the circulation of the air through the vocal cords of the larynx. As the air passes through the vocal cords, it makes them vibrate, which results in the production of sounds.

A speech production model can be seen in Figure 7.5.1.

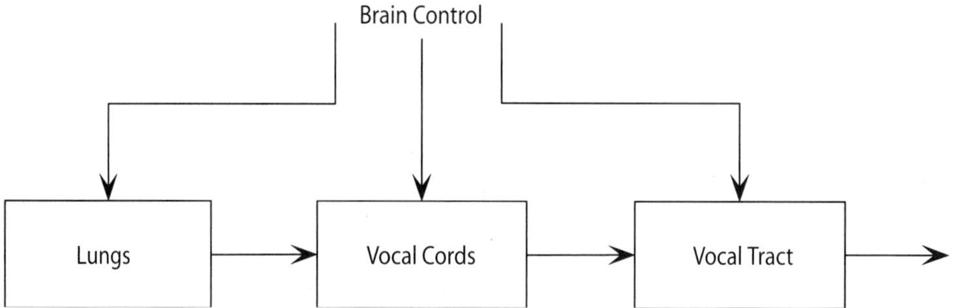

FIGURE 7.5.1 *Speech production model.*

Our languages use two different types of sound: the voiced sound, produced by the vibration of the vocal cords (for example, vowels); and the unvoiced sound, which does not use the vocal cords (such as consonants *t*, *v*, and *s*). Figure 7.5.2 shows a comparison between voiced and unvoiced sounds. The phoneme *u* is a voiced sound, whereas *t* is an unvoiced sound.

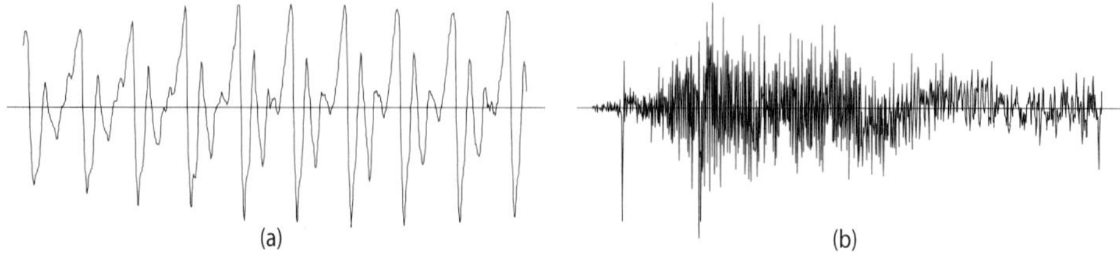

FIGURE 7.5.2 *Comparison between (a) voiced sound and (b) unvoiced sound.*

The major problem when dealing with speech is the great instability of the produced signal. Actually, the production of speech is dependent on the brain's control of different organs: the lungs, the vocal cords, the tongue, and others. As our ear is insensitive to these weak variations, these are not controlled consciously. For a computer system, it is necessary to extract features as independently as possible from these variations.

An important parameter of a speech signal is its fundamental frequency, also called pitch. The fundamental frequency of a speech signal is the frequency at which the vocal cords vibrate. For a man, it varies from 70 to 250 Hz, while for a woman or a child, it varies from 200 to 600 Hz. Due to the high variability of the pitch, features independent from it need to be extracted.

The other important parameter to take into account is the useful bandwidth. It is common to fix the limit of this bandwidth at 3400 Hz in speech processing. According to Shannon's theorem, the sampling frequency has to be around 8 kHz. Most of the time, we only have access to a 44.1 kHz sampled sound. For speed and simplicity reasons, an 8820 Hz sampling rate is used, i.e., 1/5 of initial frequency. The conversion procedure is available on the CD-ROM.

Recognition System

The recognition chain is composed of two distinct blocks, as shown in Figure 7.5.3. The first one discretizes the whole signal into a discrete set of numeric values. This set is then presented to the input of the second block. A distance measure between the references contained in the database and the signal is performed. The nearest reference is then chosen as the matching one, and its identifier is returned. In the following, the implementation of the system and its limitations will be discussed, and a solution for each limit will be proposed.

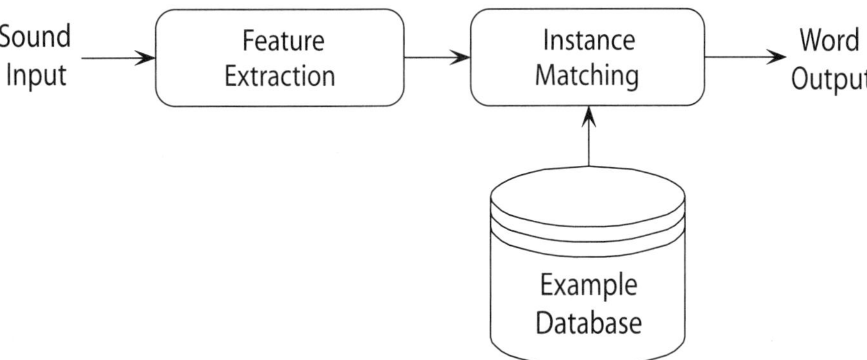

FIGURE 7.5.3 *Speech recognition chain.*

The technique described here has to be able to detect the presence or absence of a speech signal. In order to not waste computing power, a "push the button when I speak" system can be used. The player pushes the button during the pronunciation of the command. This allows some simplification of the recognition system.

Feature Extraction

Feature extraction is an important step in the speech recognition process. The techniques that give the most accurate results are presented here, but a more general overview can be found in [Schalkwyk]. Actually, feature extraction allows the discretization of a signal slice into a fixed set of numeric values. The length of this slice has to be fixed. The signal within the slice is supposed to be pseudostationary. Experts have decided to take a 20–30 ms slice every 10 ms. A feature vector is produced every 10 ms. The words are then represented as sequences of vectors. Before performing any processing on a slice, a pre-emphasis filter is applied in order to spectrally flatten the signal (Equation 7.5.1). A Hamming's window is then applied to get rid of the border effect.

$$y(n) = x(n) - 0.9 * x(n-1) \tag{7.5.1}$$

Figure 7.5.4 shows the original slice (a), the Hamming's window (b), and the resulting slice. We will now introduce the different feature extractions from this 30 ms of signal.

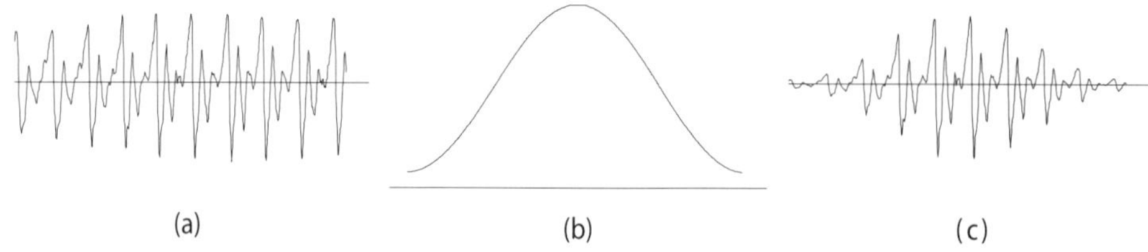

FIGURE 7.5.4 *(a) Slice of signal, (b) Hamming's window, (c) result of Hamming's window on the slice.*

LPC

The LPC (Linear Prediction Coding) analysis, used in [Edwards02], attempts to model the speech production using a linear system. The method tries to find the linear combination that estimates the best sample $x(n)$ from the t last samples, t being chosen to get the desired precision degree. Equation 7.5.2 shows the estimation function. The interesting coefficients are a_i, which represent weights obtained from the linear prediction.

$$x(n) = e(n) + \sum_{i=1}^{t} = a_i x(n-i), \text{ with } e(n) \text{ being the residual error.} \tag{7.5.2}$$

One can show that the frequency response of the linear filter from Equation 7.5.3 is the envelope of the spectrum of the studied signal.

$$\tilde{x}(n) = \sum_{i=1}^{t} -a_i x(n-i) \tag{7.5.3}$$

Figure 7.5.5 depicts this phenomenon. This representation has the advantage of being independent from the fundamental frequency of the signal. The order of the method represents the number of samples used for prediction. The number of coefficients a_i is equal to the order of the method. For the recognition process, an analysis with an order equal to the sampling frequency in kHz plus 4 is performed. In this case, an order of 13 will be used. Higher order coefficients are not interesting, because they do not carry enough information.

ON THE CD

The computation details have been treated in [Edwards02], so we will not linger on this problem, as the code is also available on the CD-ROM.

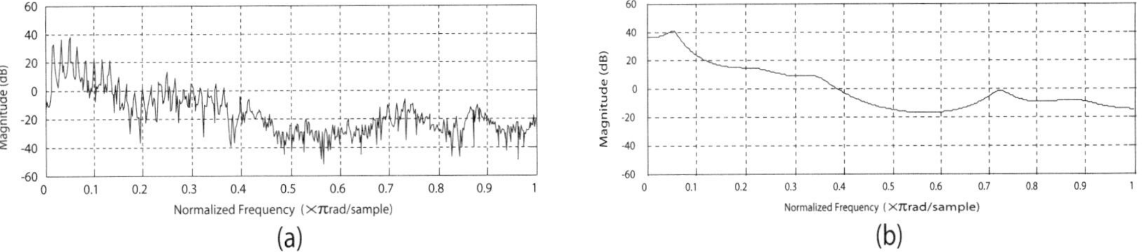

FIGURE 7.5.5 *(a) Signal spectrum, (b) frequency response of the LPC filter.*

Unfortunately, these coefficients are unstable, and they change significantly for small signal changes. Therefore, they will be transformed into cepstral coefficients *c(i)* with Equation 7.5.4. *p* is the order of the LPC analysis. This recurrence allows us to find more stable coefficients suitable for the recognition process.

$$c(i) = a_i + \sum_{k=1}^{i-1}\left(\left(1-\frac{k}{i}\right) * a_k * c_{i-k}\right); 1 < i < p \qquad (7.5.4)$$

These coefficients, although giving good results, do not take into account the nature of human hearing. Another technique, a little more computationally expensive, can be used. This technique is called Perceptual Linear Prediction (PLP).

PLP

This technique is another type of LPC analysis adapted to human hearing. The concept lies on two properties of the human ear:

- The spectral resolution of hearing decreases when the frequency increases.
- The ear is more sensitive to medium frequencies.

This technique will not be explained in detail, given its mathematical complexity. The interested reader can refer to [Boite00] and [Costache02] for more information.

ON THE CD

The code related to this technique is also available on the CD-ROM.

Signal Energy

The last introduced parameter is the variance of the signal σ_x^2, an image of the energy of the slice. This parameter allows us to distinguish marked parts of the word (tonic accent, more energetic phonemes, etc.) from others. Equation 7.5.5 shows the evaluation formula for variance.

$$\alpha_x^2 = \frac{1}{N-1}\sum_i^N (x(i) - \bar{X})^2$$
$$\bar{X} = \frac{1}{N}\sum_i^N (x(i)) \qquad (7.5.5)$$

Even if the energy is an important parameter, it is not usable in its current form. Actually, if the player speaks louder, the energy increases and moves away from the reference value. Therefore, we will use the relative variation of energy (Equation 7.5.6) instead of its absolute value.

$$\Delta\sigma_x^2(n) = \frac{\sigma_x^2(n) - \sigma_x^2(n-1)}{\sigma_x^2(n)} \qquad (7.5.6)$$

Conclusions

To perform speech recognition in video games, two methods can be used: the LPC analysis, which is computationally inexpensive, and the PLP analysis, which demands more processing power but also gives better results. They both produce 13 coefficients. The choice must be made considering the available computing power and the desired precision.

Whatever method is chosen, the vector contains 14 coefficients (13 coming from the LPC or the PLP, 1 from the variance) that will compose the identity of the slice. It will be denoted as the acoustic vector in the following sections.

Instance Matching

The set of feature vectors is now available. We will use them to retrieve, among the references, the closest one from the presented word. To measure the distance between two words, called distortion, we have to define a distance between two acoustic vectors. We choose the Euclidian distance (Equation 7.5.7) for simplicity reasons. Other distances, such as city block distance, can be used.

$$d(x,y) = \| x - y \|^2 = \sqrt{\sum_{n=1}^{N} (x_n - y_n)^2} \quad (7.5.7)$$

The first approach is to compare vector to vector for each 10 ms slice and to sum the distances between each vector's couples. Unfortunately, a word is rarely pronounced at exactly the same speed as we expect. The signal is subject to temporal compression and dilation. Therefore, a technique that automatically adapts the rhythm of the route of the acoustic vector will be used. This technique is called Dynamic Time Warping (DTW).

The goal of DTW is to find the best path in the sequence of acoustic vectors of both words, i.e., the path with the lowest accumulated distance.

The word to recognize will be referenced as X, the words from the database will be referenced as Y_k. Figure 7.5.6 represents the type of awaited path. Each axis represents one of both words to compare. Each point represents a couple of acoustic vectors.

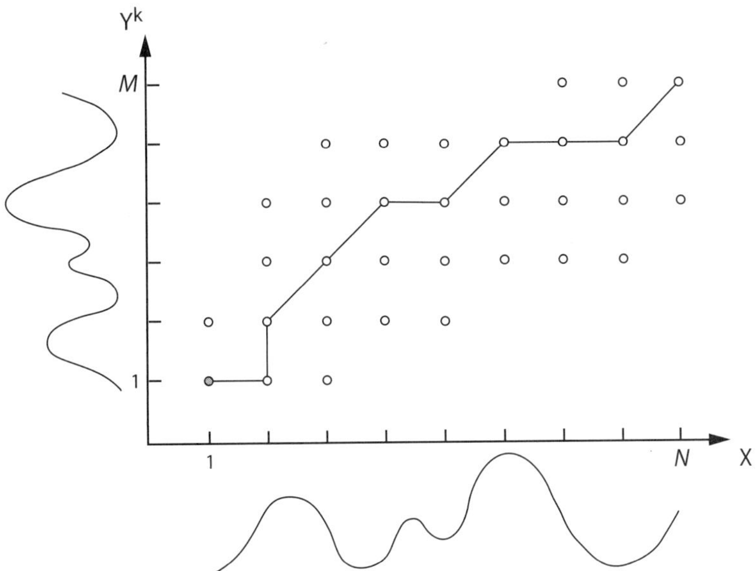

FIGURE 7.5.6 *Example of the DTW algorithm path.*

To respect the constraints of speech production, the progression of the system has to be limited. Constraints have been chosen to respect the nature of speech. The three main constraints are:

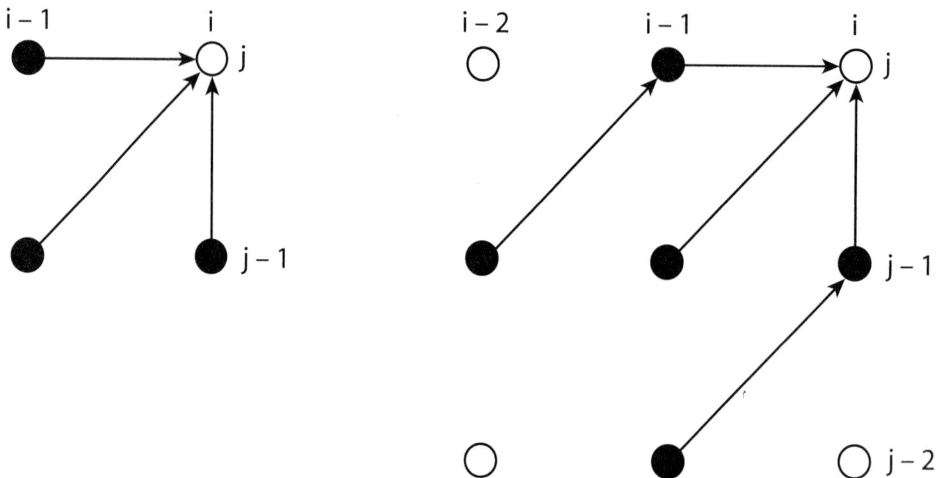

FIGURE 7.5.7 *Progression constraints. Black dot = starting point.*

The monotonic evolution: Seen acoustic vectors represent a temporal notion, no return is allowed.

The border conditions: The path begins at (0,0) and finishes at (N,M), N and M are respectively the size of the sequence of the reference and the size of the word to recognize.

The progression constraints: One can find in Figure 7.5.7 some examples of constraints. Only displayed arrows are authorized displacements. The first constraint lets the system be totally free. The second one requires a diagonal progression just before a vertical or a horizontal progression.

Route Algorithm

To compute the minimal distance, we use the property exposed by Equation 7.5.8. The couple (i,j) represents a feature vector couple, i represents the temporal index of the vector to test, and j represents the temporal index of the reference vector, $D(i,j)$ being the minimal distance to access the point (i,j). $p(i,j)$ represents the possible predecessors of (i,j) (depending on the progression constraints shown in Figure 7.5.7).

$$\begin{aligned} D(i,j) &= d(i,j) + \min_{p(i,f)}\{D(p(i,j))\} \\ d(i,j) &= \| X_i - Y_j^k \|^2 \end{aligned} \tag{7.5.8}$$

We have to successively compute the accumulated distance for each (i,j) couple gradually. We do not have to exactly know the traversed path, only the final score is of interest.

Once each reference from the database has been compared to the words to evaluate, the one having the smallest distortion is chosen as the solution. A maximum distortion threshold has to be fixed, to avoid the execution of a command when the user pronounces a word that is not in the reference database.

ON THE CD

More information about the DTW algorithm and implementation can be found in [Keogh03]. The DTW code can also be found on the CD-ROM.

Training

Before being able to recognize words, a database must be constituted. Therefore, the user is asked to pronounce the words to recognize a fixed number of times. The sequences of acoustic vectors are then extracted from the recordings. These vectors will be saved for two reasons. First, we do not have to perform feature extraction again on references, and second, the space needed to save these vectors is smaller than storing samples of the signal. If the recording conditions are good, or if the vocabulary is limited, two or three recordings will be enough. In a noisy environment, or with a bigger dictionary, it could be necessary to record about 10 examples of each word.

Limitations

This very simple system, in adapted conditions of use (using a microphone of sufficient quality, in a quiet environment) gives results near 100%. Unfortunately, it has many limitations.

First, the system is sensitive to environmental noise. Therefore, its use should be limited to a quiet room. Some signal-processing techniques can be applied to remove this environmental noise. If the background noise comes from the game, it is straightforward to subtract it from the signal.

Second, the recognition process is locutor dependent. Other techniques independent from the locutor also exist but need more computation and are greedy for resources.

Third, the complexity of the system depends on the number of words in the database. As the size of the database increases, the number of references the input word will have to be compared to will also increase. The only way to solve this problem is to try to extract phonemes from the signal, rather than comparing the word to examples.

The bigger constraint is the constitution of the example database. The user is asked to record examples of command words. In most cases, three recordings should normally be sufficient.

The solution to the limitations described is the use of more complex systems, based on probabilistic models, neural networks, or Hidden Markov models. These systems are out of the scope of this gem. More information on these systems can be found in [Boite00].

Conclusion

This gem introduces the basics of speech recognition theory and systems. Even if the described system is rudimentary, feature extraction is common to all these systems. The presented technique is simple, quick, and easy to implement. It gives good enough results to be used in videogames. In ideal conditions, the method approaches 100% efficiency. The technique has its limitations, but it provides a simple way to introduce speech recognition in an application. For integration in more complex systems, it will surely be necessary to use third-party software, as the problem is far from being trivial. With the apparition of sound-recording systems on most recent consoles, speech recognition might play an important role in the near future.

References

[Boite00] Boite R., H. Bourlard, T. Dutoit, J. Hancq, and H. Leich. "Traitement de la Parole." *Presses Polytechniques et Universitaires Romandes,* 2000.

[Costache02] Costache, Gavat, Raileanu. "Voice Command System." In *International Workshop Trends and Recent Achievements in Information Technology.* Cluj Napoca, Romania, May 2002.

[Edwards02] Edwards E. "Linear Predictive Coding for Voice Compression and Effects." In *Game Programming Gems 3,* 613–621. Charles River Media, Inc., 2002.

[Keogh03] Keogh, E., and J. Pazzani. "Derivative Dynamic Time Warping." In *Learned Representations in AI.* Division of Computer and Information Sciences, Rutgers University of New Jersey, 2003.

[Schalkwyk] Schalkwyk, J. "Feature Extraction." Available online at *http://www.cslu.ogi.edu/toolkit/old/old/version2.0a/documentation/csluc/node5.html.* November 27, 1996.

About the CD-ROM

About the Game Programming Gems 5 CD-ROM

This CD contains source code and demos that demonstrate the techniques described in the book. Every attempt has been made to ensure that the source code is bug-free and will compile. Please refer to the Web site *http://www.gameprogramminggems.com/* for errata and updates.

Contents

Code: The source code and demos contained on this CD are contained in a hierarchy of subdirectories based on section name and Gem title and author. Source code and listings from the book are included. At each author's discretion a complete demo is sometimes included. Windows demos were compiled using either Microsoft Visual C++ 6.0 (projects with a .dsw file) or Microsoft Visual C++ 7.0 (projects with a .sln file).

GLUT: In this directory you will find the GLUT v3.7.6 distribution for Windows. For Windows-specific information, please visit Nate Robins' website at *http://www.xmission.com/~nate/glut.html.*

J2SE: Sun's Java 2 Platform, Standard Edition (J2SE), version 1.4.2, for those code samples written in Java. Both the Windows and Linux versions are included as self-extracting archives.

DirectX: If you're running on Windows, you're very likely using the DirectX API. For your convenience this directory holds version 9.0 of the DirectX SDK.

System Requirements

Windows

Intel® Pentium®-series, AMD Athlon or newer processor recommended. Windows XP (64MB RAM) or Windows 2000 (128MB RAM) or later required. 3D graphics card required for some of the sample applications. DirectX 9 and GLUT 3.7 or newer are also required.

Linux

Intel® Pentium®-series, AMD Athlon or newer processor recommended. Linux kernel 2.4.x or later required. 64MB RAM recommended. 3D graphics card required for some of the sample applications. XFree86 4.0, GLUT 3.7, OpenGL driver, glibc 2.1 or newer are also required. Mesa can be used in place of 3D hardware support.

INDEX

Numbers with "GPG" proceeding refer to previous editions of the Game Programming Gems Series. Numbers without this notation refer to the current volume.

F

P

Q

R

S

T

X

Y

Z